STRUGGLE FOR THE UNION

Connecting the Causes and Conflicts of the American Civil War

SANDRA ZINK

HUGO HOUSE PUBLISHERS, LTD.

© 2023. Sandra Rose Zink. All rights reserved.

No part of this book may be reproduced or transmitted in any form or by any means, electronic or mechanical, including photocopying, recording, or by an information storage and retrieval system without written permission of the publisher.

All photographs are courtesy of the U.S. Library of Congress.

ISBN: 978-1-948261-71-5

Library of Congress Control Number: 2023914786

Cover Design & Interior Layout: Ronda Taylor, www.heartworkcreative.com

Hugo House Publishers, Ltd.
Austin, TX • Denver, CO
www.HugoHousePublishers.com

About the Cover:

The cover images illustrate the separation of North from South during the Civil War. Southern states that seceded from the Union to form the Confederate States of America are shown south of the so-called Mason-Dixon line, a demarcation that roughly identified slave states in the South versus free in the North. Border States included Missouri, Kentucky, Maryland and Delaware which did not secede but still supported slavery and contributed troops to both the Union and the Confederate armies. Although Oklahoma was still Indian Territory during the Civil War, American Indians fought in the war, for both North and South.

The photographs by Matthew Brady (1822-1896), who became famous for his photography and portraits during the American Civil War, show President Abraham Lincoln and Gener-al Ulysses S. Grant in the North for the Union. The dead soldiers after the Battle of Antietam at Sharpsburg, Maryland, in 1862 were photographed by Alexander Gardner, who worked as an assistant to Brady. The Dunker Church is shown in the background.

Below the Mason-Dixon Line is a photograph of seven Blacks, dressed in Union uniforms, working as wagon teamsters for the Union Army at Bermuda Hundred, Virginia. After the Emancipation Proclamation January 1, 1863, Blacks could enlist in the Union Army. The portrait photograph of Confederate General Robert E. Lee in full uniform was taken in 1827 by Julian Vannerson and published about 1864. The final major battles of the Civil War in 1865 pitted General Grant against Lee in the horrific battles of the Overland Campaign, which led to the surrender of Lee at Appomattox and the end of the war.

PRAISE FOR *Struggle for the Union: Connecting the Causes and Conflicts of the American Civil War*

From **Nicholas Taylor**, a graduate student from Colorado State University (CSU), Fort Collins, Colorado, who is pursuing a master's degree focused on public history and 19th-century American history. He earned his bachelor's degree in history from West Virginia University in 2020. Taylor has worked as a research assistant, collecting data on Union sailors who served in the Mississippi Squadron. He has also worked as a seasonal park ranger for the National Park Service.

"Sandra Zink's manuscript is primarily a military history book, though it does not fall into the category of 'old-style military history,' meaning that the manuscript does not glorify Civil War generals on both sides. It instead points out their successes and failures to lead effectively (for example, George B. McClellan was a great organizer, but was overly cautious in sending his troops to pursue Lee during the Antietam campaign). I particularly liked the press and the public's reaction to these events at the end of each chapter, from both the North and the South.

"The manuscript does well in addressing what happened in each of the battles/campaigns and the causes and effects behind them. Sandra Zink also brings up the harsh conditions of soldiers during the war, particularly on the treatment of Union POWs in Andersonville, Georgia.

"The biggest strength, in my opinion, is the way Zink organizes the sections in this manuscript. Each of the chapters on the Civil War battles (from Chapter 3-8), has one section on the Eastern Theater and another one on the Western Theater, as well as several campaigns and battles under each theater. This makes it easier for the reader to follow. During my seasonal employment at Vicksburg National Military Park in the summer of 2022, the manuscript helped in introducing me to the Vicksburg Campaign."

"Having read several other books about the Civil War, I found the organization of this book made the facts and flow of the war much easier to understand. In addition, the Appendices dedicated to the military generals was very useful and is not easily found in other books about the Civil War."

—Ida Jeppesen, Austin, Texas

DEDICATION

Dedicated to my sons
Wade Moody
and
Allen Moody

CONTENTS

LIST OF MAPS xi

PREFACE xv

I. INTRODUCTION and OVERVIEW 1
- FOUNDING THE NEW AMERICA 2
- SEVEN DECADES OF CONFLICT AND COMPROMISE 3
- SOUTH SECEDES AFTER ELECTION OF LINCOLN 4
- DEADLY COST TO THE NEW COUNTRY 4
- THE STRUGGLE FOR EQUALITY FOR THE BLACKS 5

II. CAUSES OF THE CIVIL WAR 7
- SLAVERY VIOLATED PRINCIPLES OF FREEDOM 7
- SLAVERY CORNERSTONE OF SOUTHERN ECONOMY 9
- THE ABOLITIONIST MOVEMENT 11
- KING COTTON DEMANDS MORE SLAVES 13
- EQUAL BALANCE OF FREE VS SLAVE STATES 15
- AMERICA GAINS NEW LANDS: SLAVE OR FREE? 16
- COMPROMISE OF 1850 19
- KANSAS-NEBRASKA ACT OF 1854 20
- "BLEEDING KANSAS" 22
- PRESIDENTIAL ELECTION OF 1856 26
- SUPREME COURT ENDORSES SLAVERY (1857) 29
- LINCOLN-DOUGLAS DEBATES OF 1858 29
- LINCOLN ELECTED PRESIDENT IN 1860; SOUTH SECEDES 30
- ELEVEN STATES SECEDE TO FORM THE CONFEDERACY 32

III. WAR BEGINS, APRIL 1861 37
- SOUTH CAROLINA SEIZES CHARLESTON HARBOR 37

CONFEDERACY FIRES ON FORT SUMTER 38
NORTH & SOUTH PREPARE FOR WAR 40
ORGANIZATION OF THE MILITARY UNITS 44
UNION AND CONFEDERATE NATIONAL FLAGS 46
STRENGTHS AND WEAKNESSES: NORTH VS SOUTH. 47
VIEWS FROM THE PUBLIC AS WAR BEGINS 50

IV. THE FIRST YEAR: 1861 57

BATTLES IN THE EASTERN THEATER. 58
MEDICAL SUPPORT FOR THE WOUNDED 64
BATTLES IN WESTERN & TRANS-MISSISSIPPI THEATERS 66
LINCOLN REORGANIZES UNION ARMIES. 74
VIEWS FROM THE PUBLIC FOR THE YEAR 1861 76

V. THE SECOND YEAR: 1862 83

PASSAGE OF THREE IMPORTANT ACTS 83
LINCOLN'S GENERAL ORDER NO. 1 84
BATTLES IN WESTERN & TRANS-MISSISSIPPI THEATERS 84
BATTLES IN THE EASTERN THEATER. 102
PENINSULA CAMPAIGN, VIRGINIA. 107
BATTLES IN VIRGINIA AND MARYLAND 116
BATTLES IN THE WESTERN THEATER 127
SOUTH'S HEARTLAND OFFENSIVE (KENTUCKY CAMPAIGN) 128
CONFEDERATES ABANDON HEARTLAND OFFENSIVE. 140
UNION LAUNCHES VICKSBURG CAMPAIGN 143
VIEWS FROM THE PUBLIC FOR THE YEAR 1862 151

VI. THE THIRD YEAR: 1863 161

BATTLES IN THE EASTERN THEATER. 162
LEE INVADES THE NORTH 169
BATTLES IN THE WESTERN THEATER 179
THE VICKSBURG CAMPAIGN 181
TWO UNION DIVERSIONARY FEINTS 188
BATTLES IN EAST TENNESSEE 197
CHICKAMAUGA & SIEGE OF CHATTANOOGA 198

    BATTLES IN THE DEEP SOUTH & GULF COAST 212

    VIEWS FROM THE PUBLIC FOR THE YEAR 1863. 214

VII. THE FOURTH YEAR: 1864 225

    LINCOLN CHOOSES GRANT AS NEW GENERAL-IN-CHIEF. 227

    UNION WAR PLANS FOR 1864 228

    BATTLES IN THE EASTERN THEATER 229

    THE OVERLAND CAMPAIGN, VIRGINIA 231

    DEADLY COST OF THE OVERLAND CAMPAIGN 246

    SHENENDOAH VALLEY CAMPAIGNS, MAY-JULY 1864 247

    SIEGE AND BATTLES OF PETERSBURG, VIRGINIA 1864 252

    UNION OPERATIONS AT PETERSBURG & RICHMOND 256

    SHENANDOAH VALLEY CAMPAIGNS, FALL 1864 260

    BATTLES IN TRANS-MISSISSIPPI THEATER 265

    BATTLES IN THE WESTERN THEATER 274

    THE ATLANTA CAMPAIGN, GEORGIA 277

    RIVER LINE AT THE CHATTAHOOCHEE 284

    CONFEDERATE ARMY GETS NEW COMMANDER 286

    SHERMAN'S "MARCH TO THE SEA" 300

    BATTLES FOR TENNESSEE 313

    BATTLES FOR CONFEDERATE SEAPORTS. 319

    VIEWS FROM THE PUBLIC FOR THE YEAR 1864. 324

VIII. THE FINAL BATTLES AND SURRENDER, 1865 337

    BATTLES IN THE WESTERN THEATER 338

    THE CAROLINAS CAMPAIGN 341

    NEW COMMANDER FOR CONFEDERATE ARMY 346

    BATTLES IN THE EASTERN THEATER. 348

    APPOMATTOX CAMPAIGN, VIRGINIA 354

    ASSASSINATION OF PRESIDENT LINCOLN 369

    CONFEDERATE ARMIES SURRENDER 372

    FINAL REVIEW OF UNION ARMIES WASHINGTON, D.C., MAY 23-24, 1865. . . . 378

    VIEWS FROM THE PUBLIC FOR THE YEAR 1865. 379

IX. THE FREED BLACKS 389

APPENDIX A—COMMANDERS FOR THE UNION. 397

APPENDIX B—COMMANDERS FOR THE CONFEDERACY. 443

ACKNOWLEDGEMENTS. 479

SOURCES OF INFORMATION. 481

GENERAL INDEX 487

INDEX OF COMMANDERS DURING THE CIVIL WAR 491

INDEX OF BATTLES 513

INDEX OF HIGHLIGHTED BOXES (BY TITLE). 517

ABOUT THE AUTHOR 521

LIST OF MAPS

Fig. 1. Configuration of United States in 1803 5
Fig. 2. Missouri Compromise of 1820 16
Fig. 3. Compromise of 1850 19
Fig. 4. Kansas-Nebraska Act of 1854 21
Fig. 5. Battle of Fort Sumter 41
Fig. 6. Graph of North/South Populations 1860 48
Fig. 7. Battle of First Bull Run (First Manassas) 62
Fig. 8. Map of Missouri Battle Locations 68
Fig. 9. Configuration of Rivers at Cairo, Illinois 69
Fig. 10. Grant Attacks Belmont, Kentucky 73
Fig. 11. Western Theater Overview Map 88
Fig. 12. Battle of Pea Ridge 91
Fig. 13. Overview Prior to Battle of Shiloh 95
Fig. 14. Battle of Shiloh 97
Fig. 15. Battle Locations in Shenandoah Valley 105
Fig. 16. Siege of Yorktown, Peninsula Campaign 108
Fig. 17. Seven Pines Battle, Peninsula Campaign 111
Fig. 18. Seven Days Battles, Peninsula Campaign 114
Fig. 19. Battle of Fredericksburg, Virginia 124
Fig. 20. Overview of Confederate Kentucky Campaign 129
Fig. 21. Battle of Iuka, Mississippi 133
Fig. 22. Second Battle of Corinth, Mississippi 135
Fig. 23. Confederate Raid on Holly Springs 144
Fig. 24. Battle of Chickasaw Bayou 148
Fig. 25. Battle of Chancellorsville 166
Fig. 26. Battle of Gettysburg 172

LIST OF MAPS

Fig. 27. Battle of Arkansas Post, Arkansas 180
Fig. 28. Mississippi Delta, Vicksburg Campaign 184
Fig. 29. Union Canals on Mississippi River. 186
Fig. 30. Union Cavalry Raid through Mississippi 189
Fig. 31. Union Troops Cross Mississippi River 191
Fig. 32. Union Army Captures Jackson, Mississippi 195
Fig. 33. Map of Cracker Line, Chattanooga, Tennessee 204
Fig. 34. Grand Union Charge at Chattanooga 210
Fig. 35. Howlett Line at Bermuda Hundred Peninsula 229
Fig. 36. Union Launches the Overland Campaign .230
Fig. 37. Battle of the Wilderness, Overland Campaign 233
Fig. 38. Battle of Spotsylvania 234
Fig. 39. Union Cavalry Raids Yellow Tavern 236
Fig. 40. Bloody Angle of the Mule Shoe 237
Fig. 41. Battle of North Anna 239
Fig. 42. Battle of Cold Harbor. 240
Fig. 43. Union Army Crosses James River 244
Fig. 44. Field of Lost Shoes, Shenandoah Valley 248
Fig. 45. Confederates Nearly Raid Washington 250
Fig. 46. Battle of Old Men and Young Boys 253
Fig. 47. Shenandoah Valley, Sheridan's Ride 264
Fig. 48. Overview of Red River Campaign, Louisiana 266
Fig. 49. Navy Fleet Advances on Red River 268
Fig. 50. Failed Camden Expedition from Arkansas. 271
Fig. 51. Battle of Dalton, Atlanta Campaign 278
Fig. 52. Union Crosses Lay's Ferry near Resaca 280
Fig. 53. Battles of Marietta, Georgia, May-June. 282
Fig. 54. Union Reaches Atlanta Entrenchments 284
Fig. 55. Union Fails to Capture Railroads Supplying Atlanta 291
Fig. 56. Confederates Leave Georgia 297
Fig. 57. Gen. Sherman Launches March to the Sea 305
Fig. 58. Union Army Reaches Milledgeville, Georgia 307
Fig. 59. March to the Sea Reaches Savannah 310

LIST OF MAPS

Fig. 60. Confederates Invade Tennessee. 314

Fig. 61. Battle of Franklin, Tennessee. 315

Fig. 62. Battle of Nashville, Tennessee 317

Fig. 63. Battle of Mobile Bay, Alabama. 320

Fig. 64. Mobile Bay Battle Configurations. 321

Fig. 65. Battle of Fort Fisher, North Carolina 323

Fig. 66. Assault on Fort Fisher, North Carolina 339

Fig. 67. Union Army Commences Carolinas Campaign 343

Fig. 68. Battle of Fort Stedman, Petersburg, Virginia 350

Fig. 69. Battle of Five Forks, Virginia 352

Fig. 70. Confederates Defend Fort Gregg 353

Fig. 71. Confederates Abandon Petersburg. 360

Fig. 72. Grant Pursues Lee to Appomattox 362

PREFACE

After I retired from a career in science, I became interested in writing a book about the American Civil War. I wanted to create an easy-to-read reference book that could be used by the high school or college student or the adult reader interested in American history. This book is not a historical document. It is a story about the Civil War. The young country, founded on the principle of a government by the people, quickly had to deal with the concept of a divided nation in which one side is free of slaves, the other is dependent on slavery for its way of life. After several decades of compromise and concessions on both sides, the two opposing opinions from the North and the South reached a breaking point of irreconcilable differences that would only be resolved by bloody conflict. Civil War between North and South would become a violent struggle, full of death and suffering, that would take the lives of three-quarters of a million soldiers, most of them young men. The North won and we have a "United States" today, one country, free of slavery, but left with a continuing struggle to create a society where all citizens are treated as equals.

The style of the book reflects my writing background as a young woman working in a weekly newspaper office. The narrative flows through a pattern of headlines, with highlighted boxes to call attention to interesting facts or features. This facilitates the casual reader who wants to simply flip through the book to focus on a topic of interest without having to search through the entire volume. With this in mind, each section may include repetitive information that briefly reviews and repeats the names or events from a previous account to provide the basic background.

The battles were important to me. Famous names of battles had come to my attention over the years: Shiloh, Antietam, Gettysburg, Vicksburg, Atlanta, Cold Harbor, the Wilderness. These were all important deadly battles, but how did they fit together during the four years of the Civil War? By following the facts, the battles are presented in chronological order, separated by the three major theaters of the war: Eastern, Western and Trans-Mississippi, which included the states west of the Mississippi River. This organization allows the reader to follow the progression of the various battles and place them in context of the overall picture. Descriptions of the battles, often illustrated with a relevant map, are necessarily brief and provide only a basic framework to understand the battle. More complete versions are easily attainable by searches on the internet or from individual books written by experts and historical professionals.

As we review America's history and follow the conflicts active in our society today, the similarities are striking. Today, some political parties in power have implemented laws that make it difficult for Black populations to vote. Losers of elections have demanded endless recounts of votes, hoping to sway the results in their favor. Accuracy of voting machines has been challenged without any evidence that errors exist. An insurrectional mob invaded the Capitol on January 6, 2021, planning to alter the electoral votes and change the outcome of the Presidential election. All of these events in today's society have close counter-parts in the Civil War.

Democracy is a struggle; it requires accepting another's opinion when it does not conform to your own. The founders and writers of our Constitution in 1787 did not reach consensus easily. A representative group of the thirteen states argued, discussed, compromised and negotiated for more than three months to create America's Constitution. Benjamin Franklin, very aware of the challenges the new country faced, made the motion to adopt the Constitution on September 17, 1787, with these words. "I agree to this Constitution with all its faults … I doubt, too, whether any other Constitution we can obtain, may be able to make a better Constitution. For when you assemble a number of men to have the advantage of their joint wisdom, you inevitably assemble with those men all their prejudices, their passions, their errors of opinion, their local interests and their selfish views. From such an assembly can a perfect production be expected? It therefore astonishes me, Sir, to find this system approaching so near to perfection as it does." Thirty-nine delegates of the fifty-five delegates present signed the document and it was presented to the states for ratification, which occurred on June 21, 1788, making it the law of the land. As Franklin left Independence Hall, a voice shouted from the crowd, "Doctor, what have we got? A republic, or a monarchy?" To which Franklin responded, "A republic, if you can keep it." As we contemplate these wise words, we must continue the struggle of creating a more perfect union and use the knowledge of our country's history to guide us as we refine our most unusual democracy in the world.

I. INTRODUCTION AND OVERVIEW

Two brothers faced each other across a battlefield in Virginia on May 25, 1862. One fought for the Union Army to preserve the "United States." The other had joined the army of the "Confederate States of America," a collection of states that seceded from the Union to preserve slavery. Both brothers survived the battle, but one was taken as a prisoner-of-war by the other. The Civil War would devour hundreds of thousands of soldiers and consume four years of the young country's history. In the end, the Union prevailed.

INTRODUCTION

The American Civil War (1861-65) was fought over a national conflict about slavery that began with formation of the new nation following its Declaration of Independence written in 1776. When the Constitutional Convention assembled in Philadelphia in 1787 to replace the Articles of Confederation and form the basis for a representational government, slavery became a major issue among the fifty-five delegates. Southern slave-holding states, dependent on slaves for their economic base, would not tolerate any declarations in the new Constitution that threatened their economy. The North, on the other hand, did not require slaves to maintain its society and objected to slavery on moral grounds.

Compromises were made to create a working government for the new country, but the next seven decades would produce a series of national conflicts about the extension of slavery into new states. The South was determined to expand slavery into new territories because its agriculturally-based economy and way of life depended on slave labor. But the industrial North wanted to contain slavery where it already existed and eventually eliminate it. The struggle to dominate reached a breaking point in 1861. The Civil War would determine the outcome. It would last four years and take the lives of more than three-quarters of a million Americans.

OVERVIEW

FOUNDING THE NEW AMERICA

Slavery was well established in North America when the country declared its independence from Great Britain in 1776. A Spanish expedition brought African Black slaves to Charles Town, South Carolina, in 1526. The arrival of "20 and odd Africans" was documented in 1619 at Port Comfort, Virginia, the location of Fort Monroe today. The first U.S. Census in 1790 showed about seven hundred thousand slaves out of approximately four million people, or about eighteen percent of the population. In the South, slaves accounted for roughly one-third of the population in 1790, about eighty percent of them working in agriculture producing rice, tobacco and cotton

Despite wide acceptance of slavery in the colonies in 1776, there was nevertheless strong opposition to its continuation in the new country. America's proclamations of "*freedom and equality for all men*" in its Declaration of Independence directly conflicted with the institution of slavery. As delegates convened at the Constitutional Convention between May and September 1787 to write a new Constitution for the United States, slavery became a dominating issue. The South resisted any attempts that would threaten its slavery-based economy. But antislavery advocates, mostly in the North, wanted to contain slavery where it existed and create a policy of gradual and compensated emancipation to eliminate it altogether.

Two important compromises regarding slavery were made to avoid some Southern delegates from abandoning the Convention. The proposed foundation for the government required that the number of delegates from each state in the House of Representatives be based on each state's population, which would also dictate how much each state would pay in taxes. Southern states demanded that slave populations be counted in determining their number of delegates, but the Northern states objected because slaves were not citizens, did not vote and were considered property. A compromise was finally reached that slaves would be counted as three-fifths of a person, for both representation and taxation.

The second concession regarding slavery for the new Constitution was the abolishment of the international slave trade into the country, a requirement that Northern delegates fiercely defended. When some of the Southern delegates threated to leave the Convention if it was placed in the Constitution, a compromise was made that the importation of new slaves would continue for another twenty years, but cease after January 1, 1808.

I. INTRODUCTION AND OVERVIEW

SEVEN DECADES OF CONFLICT AND COMPROMISE

Northwest Territory was created by the Continental Congress in July 1787 at the same time that the Constitutional Convention was taking place in Philadelphia. The Northwest Ordinance adopted the principal features outlined by Thomas Jefferson in 1784, mainly to define a mechanism for the creation of new states and a process by which lands would be surveyed and sold. Significantly, slavery was prohibited in the territory, establishing the principle that all states north of the Ohio River and east of the upper Mississippi would be free.

As states were added over the next decades to the original thirteen colonies, Congress maintained an even number of free states versus slave so that the balance of power in the government remained equally divided. But when Missouri was granted statehood as a slave state in 1820 (Maine admitted as free), an amendment was added that excluded slavery north of latitude 36°30' (Missouri's southern boundary) in any area within Louisiana Territory (except Missouri itself), which had been purchased from France in 1803. The amendment became known as the Missouri Compromise of 1820 and remained in force for more than three decades until the Kansas-Nebraska Act of 1854.

As states were admitted over the next thirty years, the balance of free states versus slave remained equal. Arkansas, a slave state, was admitted in 1836, followed by Michigan (free) in 1837. Both Florida and Texas were admitted as slave states in 1845, followed by Iowa (1846) and Wisconsin (1848). But Mexico challenged the admission of Texas to the United States in 1845, as it did not agree with the boundaries that Texas claimed after its war of independence from Mexico in 1835-36; Mexico declared war.

The Mexican-American War (1846-48) ended with the defeat of Mexico, which was forced to cede California and New Mexico and Utah Territories to the United States, an addition of more than 500,000 square miles of new land. The uneasy compromise that had maintained a balance of free states versus slave was now shattered with the addition of vast new territory acquired from Mexico. The South eagerly anticipated expanding its economic system of cotton and slavery into Texas and the new territories, which together now totaled 850,000 square miles. Tensions mounted as the North vigorously opposed the addition of slave states in the new lands.

Congress responded with the Compromise of 1850, which admitted California as a free state, but New Mexico and Utah Territories would be able to determine their status about slavery by popular vote. An unsettled calm lasted across the country until 1854, when Congress passed the Kansas-Nebraska Act, creating two new territories that could determine their own status of slave versus free by popular vote. But the Act nullified the Missouri Compromise of 1820 that prohibited any new states from Louisiana Territory being admitted as slave. The country responded with a firestorm of violence in Kansas as pro- and antislavery factions rushed into the territory.

SOUTH SECEDES AFTER ELECTION OF LINCOLN

The Presidential elections of 1856 and 1860 brought the issue of slavery in the new territories squarely in front of the national awareness. The proslavery Democratic candidate James Buchanan won the 1856 election, which prompted Abraham Lincoln to find his political voice. Through his debates with Stephen Douglas in 1858, Lincoln became well known from his writings and speeches and was nominated as the Republican Presidential candidate for 1860. Lincoln's moderate approach during his campaign won him the election, a policy that slavery could continue where it already existed, but could not expand beyond its current boundaries, and in time, would eventually be eliminated by gradual emancipation.

Although momentum for secession from the Union by the Southern states had been steadily mounting for decades, the election of Abraham Lincoln to the Presidency in November 1860 lit the final spark. When Lincoln's election was confirmed, the South perceived it as their imminent destruction. South Carolina seceded from the Union on December 20, 1860, and was joined shortly by six more southern states, including Mississippi, Florida, Alabama, Georgia, Louisiana and Texas. The Confederate States of America was declared on February 7, 1861, and soon joined by Virginia, Arkansas, Tennessee and North Carolina.

Through the previous decades, political power had been used by both North and South to prevail over the other regarding the issue of slavery, but the increasing tensions and intransigeance had now reached a boiling point. The deep and strongly held beliefs on both sides were no longer willing to compromise on the issue of whether the country would exist as one "United States," in a representational democracy, or as a collection of sovereign states, each determining its own government and policies and making decisions about slavery within its own borders. In the end, it required a bloody Civil War to resolve the conflict.

DEADLY COST TO THE NEW COUNTRY

The first shots fired by the Confederate States of America on a Union fort in Charleston Harbor, South Carolina, occurred April 12, 1861, initiating the American Civil War. It would require four years of costly battles until the Confederacy surrendered in 1865. The trauma of war to the country in its loss of men's lives and destruction of infrastructure, mostly in the South, left enduring scars. Battles fought in Southern states left lasting damage to major cities, factories, railroads, farms and plantations.

The economic cost of the war left little capital in the South to rebuild its damaged environment. Rural farms languished during the war and in the post-war environment. Women in the South were especially vulnerable after the war. The loss of able-bodied men, pressed into military service or killed in battle, left the women alone, often

I. INTRODUCTION AND OVERVIEW

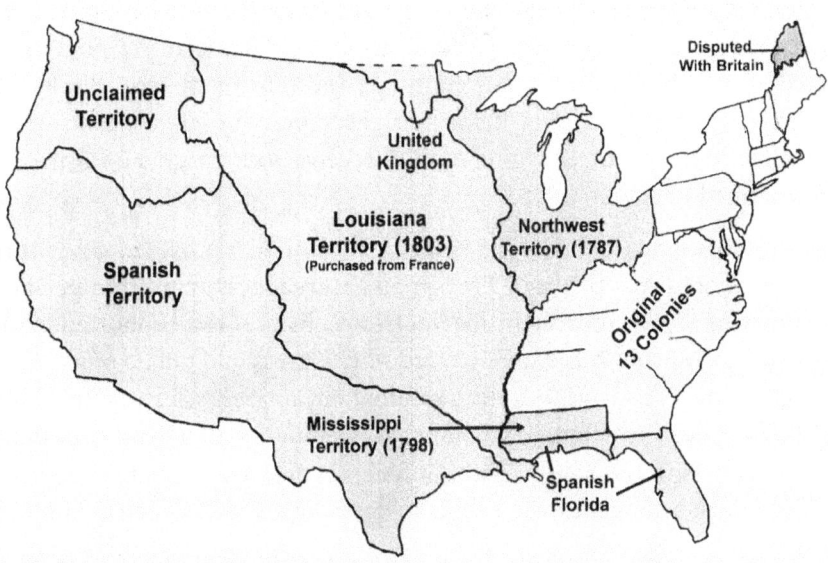

Fig. 1: Map illustrating the approximate distribution of land in the United States about 1803 after the Louisiana Purchase from France, which added about 828,000 square miles to the country, doubling its territory.

without adequate food or shelter, with little support from the government to manage the homesteads, the farms and the children. The emotional scars of anger and hatred against the North would last for generations.

The agricultural economy of the South, based on cotton as its major crop, now had to be rebuilt. Land owners needed to rely on former slaves for their workforce but many Blacks had abandoned the South to seek new lives in the North. For those who remained, a new system of share-cropping and tenant farming was created in which newly freed Blacks rented land from landowners and paid with a portion of the crop.

Some estimates place the cost of the Civil War at about six billion dollars, or about twenty times that amount in today's dollars. When the loss of human capital is included, the loss represented a staggering sum for the young country. The Northern economy, with a diverse industrial and economic base, that had largely been stimulated by the war, was soon able to recover. The Southern economy was forced to shift from a dominant agrarian society to a more balanced one, with a greater focus on industrial growth and would require years to accomplish.

THE STRUGGLE FOR EQUALITY FOR THE BLACKS

With the end of the Civil War, the 13th Amendment to the Constitution abolishing slavery was ratified in December 1865, making it the law of the land. The 14th

Amendment, ratified in 1868, provided Blacks with citizenship and voting rights, and equal protection under the laws. But many Southern states implemented practices at the polls that were designed to prevent Blacks from voting. "Black codes," policies that discriminated against Blacks and unfair contracts and mistreatment of Blacks were common. The 15th Amendment clarified the right to vote for eligible Black males, although women, both Black and white, did not receive voting rights until the 19th Amendment, ratified in August 1920.

A period of Reconstruction after the end of the Civil War provided government assistance to former slaves through Freedmen's Bureaus. During this period of Reconstruction, which was enforced by federal troops, Blacks were supported in their transition to citizenship and some were elected to Congress and public office. But in 1876, challenges to the Presidential election resulted in Congress selecting Republican Rutherford B. Hayes as President, in exchange for removing all federal funding for Reconstruction efforts in the South. Without federal constraints, white supremacist racist attitudes flourished against the Blacks in the South and Reconstruction came to an end.

The Civil Rights Act of 1964, vigorously opposed by the Southern bloc in the Senate, eventually passed and was signed into law by President Lyndon B. Johnson in July 1964. Its provisions did much to overcome and prohibit discrimination on a variety of issues, that included race, color, religion, sex, or national origin. But, even into the 21st Century, the United States still faces the challenge of creating a country that lives up to its national promise of freedom for all and that *"all men are created equal."*

II. CAUSES OF THE CIVIL WAR

SLAVERY VIOLATED PRINCIPLES OF FREEDOM

The Constitution of the United States

THE ARTICLES OF CONFEDERATION, WRITTEN IN 1777, CREATED A COALITION OF STATES that governed the country through its War of Independence from Great Britain. When the Treaty of Paris was signed in 1783, Great Britain recognized the independence of the United States and the country turned its attention to forming a new government. While the Articles of Confederation had created a foundation for a Constitution, it had provided no powers of enforcement or controls over disputes between the states over territory, taxation or trade.

The Declaration of Independence of 1776 proudly stated, *"We hold these truths to be self-evident, that all men are created equal, that they are endowed with certain unalienable rights, that among these are life, liberty and the pursuit of happiness."* And yet, all thirteen colonies supported legalized slavery. Antislavery advocates resisted the dogma, as it violated the principles of freedom and equality for all men. Proslavery supporters argued it was their right to own slaves as property who would perform work for them. Three of the founding fathers, George Washington, Thomas Jefferson and James Madison, were slave owners and remained so all of their lives. Benjamin Franklin, a prominent leader and one of the principal founding fathers, had owned slaves, but had freed them all by 1781 and founded the Pennsylvania Abolition Society.

A new Constitutional Convention with fifty-five delegates assembled in Philadelphia in May 1787 and over three months of vigorous debate through the summer, created America's Constitution that defines the laws and rights of citizens in a representational government, a Republic, in which the supreme power of the government is held by the people through their elected representatives. The new government, *" ... for the people,"* created a foundation that separated the three basic functions of government: executive, legislative and judicial. Executive power would be exercised by a single President, judicial power by a Supreme Court, and a representative Congress would create the laws. Congress would consist of a Senate and a representational House of Representatives. Equal representation in the Senate would be defined as two Senators from each state that would be named by the state legislatures. Senators would not be elected by popular vote until adoption of the 17th Amendment to the Constitution in 1913.

Delegates to the House of Representatives and the Electoral College would be elected by popular vote and the number of delegates would be apportioned to each state according to its population. Southern delegates demanded that slave populations be counted in the determination of their representation in the House. Northern delegates refused, given that slaves were not citizens, did not vote and were considered property. But delegates from slave-holding states threatened to leave the proceedings if demands to recognize their slave populations were not met. The compromise that was agreed to by both sides counted each slave as three-fifths of a person. This concession increased the number of Southern delegates in the House of Representatives and their electoral votes by at least a dozen. The enhanced political power enabled the proslavery South to control legislation for decades, and increased their influence on the presidency, the Supreme Court and other positions of power. Eight of the first twelve presidents owned slaves while in office, through the presidency of Zachary Taylor in 1848.

A second important issue regarding slavery that required compromise was the abolishment of the importation of new slaves into the country. Ten states had already outlawed the practice of international slave trade, but Georgia and North and South Carolina threatened to leave the Convention if it was banned. A high priority for the North, a compromise was finally reached to allow the practice for twenty years until January 1, 1808. The Constitution, signed September 17, 1787, was ratified by June 1788. The first ten Amendments, the Bill of Rights, which defined the fundamental rights of citizens, were ratified in December 1791 and became part of the Constitution.

Northwest Territory Prohibits Slavery

The Northwest Ordinance, adopted by the Confederation Congress on July 13, 1787, created Northwest Territory, land that had been acquired from Great Britain after its defeat in the American Revolution. Its primary purpose was to define the process for the admission of new states and how land would be surveyed and sold. The Territory included all the land west of Pennsylvania to the upper Mississippi River and on the south to the Ohio River. The northern boundary was the country's border with Great Britain. The Ordinance prohibited slavery within the territory, making the Ohio River on the south and upper Mississippi River to the west as demarcation lines between slavery states and free states.

Adoption of the Northwest Ordinance occurred at the same time that the Constitutional Convention was taking place and its features would be adopted, with slight modifications, by the U.S. Constitution two years later in August 1789. A significant feature of the Ordinance was the definition of the various legal and property rights of citizens within the Territory. These "natural rights" would become the first ten amendments to the Constitution, known as the "Bill of Rights," defining the most fundamental principles of freedom and culture for the nation. The first two would play significant roles as the country's new democracy was put into practice, namely: (1) freedom of speech, a free press, freedom of religion, freedom to assemble peacefully and the right to petition the government; and (2) a well-regulated militia, being necessary to the security of a free State, the right of the people to keep and bear Arms, shall not be infringed. These two fundamental rights continue to be challenged and tested in the country today.

SLAVERY CORNERSTONE OF SOUTHERN ECONOMY

Labor Intensive Agriculture

The South's economy was mostly rural and primarily devoted to agricultural production, with few cities and little industrial development. The Northern economy, on the other hand, relied mostly on factories that manufactured goods to be marketed for its economic base. According to the 1860 U.S. Census, the country's total population included four million slaves, but only two percent were in the Northern states. In the South and Border States, slaves constituted about thirty-two percent of the total population and nearly half the families of Mississippi and South Carolina were slave-owners.

A planter was loosely defined as a person owning land and twenty or more slaves. But the larger plantations owned one hundred or more slaves. Belonging to the "planter class" was a sign of wealth and prestige. The "planter aristocracy" of the South enjoyed a "refined life" of affluence and elegance and wielded great power in their communities, local and state governments and in the United States Congress. Although this "Southern way of life" applied to a relatively small minority, less than five percent of the population, the preservation of this "peculiar institution" with its dependence on slavery was a major factor in secessionist thinking.

Abuses to Slaves by Owners

Slaves had no rights, no individual freedom to lead an independent life and no recourse or defense against abusive treatment. Slave owners could use cruel brutality and humiliation to invoke fear among the slaves to enforce dominance of the owner. A belief among whites that they were racially superior fostered the attitude that Blacks were incapable of taking care of themselves, that slavery was good for them. Reality, however, was anything but paternal.

- Numerous accounts described cruel whippings, beatings, imprisonment, branding, mutilations and even murder as punishment for slaves.

- Slave women were subject to rape and their offspring from a man of any race became the property of the owner, to be worked as a slave or sold.
- Working conditions could be harsh and inhumane. Field hands worked dawn to dusk, a long, arduous day of fifteen to eighteen hours in the hot and humid southern climate. Life expectancies were short when compared to the same aged whites.
- Medical treatment was limited or nonexistent.
- Attempts on the part of slaves to learn to read or become educated were promptly discouraged or outlawed out of fear that knowledge would foster rebellion and insurrection.
- By order of the U.S. Constitution, importation of slaves was prohibited in 1808 which then created an active domestic slave trade. The most prominent center was Washington, D.C., the nation's capital. The daily spectacle of shackled humans placed on auction blocks to be sold to the highest bidder became more and more offensive to the city's inhabitants.

The Fugitive Slave Act, passed by Congress in 1793, and a much stronger version in 1850, became federal laws that enforced the return of captured runaway slaves to their owners.

Southern Fears of Rebellion

The possibility of slave revolts and rebellions invoked white Southern fears of being overcome by their slaves. The planter elite feared the loss of its power that could change their "peculiar institution" into the urban, industrial growth of the North. A few isolated events added fuel to their apprehension.

The slave insurrection of Haiti in the 1790s defeated French colonial rule and founded the sovereign state of Haiti in 1804. French slave owners demanded reparations for their lost property, forcing Haiti to be saddled with enormous debt until it was paid off in 1947.

- The largest slave revolt in American history occurred in 1811 near New Orleans when a group of rebelling slaves captured and plundered several sugar plantations. The U.S. Army and local militia defeated the rebels and over one hundred slaves, guilty or innocent, were executed.
- Denmark Vesey, a free Black pastor for the large African Methodist Episcopal Church in Charleston, South Carolina, was accused and convicted of organizing a major slave revolt in the summer of 1822. The alleged plot would have killed local slaveholders and thousands of freed slaves would sail to Haiti. Vesey was hanged July 2, 1822.

II. CAUSES OF THE CIVIL WAR

- Nat Turner, a Black minister, led a slave rebellion in Southampton County, Virginia, in 1831. Local militias with U.S. military support mounted a frenzied response which executed or murdered over one hundred Blacks, many of whom were not part of the rebellion. Turner was later captured and hanged. The event was portrayed in the movie *Birth of a Nation (2016)*.

- A leading event just prior to the Civil War was carried out by John Brown, a staunch abolitionist from Massachusetts, who planned to initiate a slave revolt in Virginia. His small band of followers invaded the U.S. arsenal at Harpers Ferry, Virginia, in 1859, planning to capture weapons and distribute them to local slaves who would revolt against their masters. Brown's small group was quickly defeated by U.S. Marines and Brown was later executed December 2, 1859, by hanging.

To defend against real and imagined threats, local Southern militias rapidly organized into protection units and new legislation was passed by the states to prohibit the education, movement and assembly of slaves. The rights of free people of color were also severely limited.

THE ABOLITIONIST MOVEMENT

Active Antislavery Advocates Unite

After the Revolutionary War, the entire institution of slavery, fueled with tales of violence and mistreatment against slaves by their owners, spawned an abolitionist movement in the North that sought an end to all slavery and the full emancipation of former slaves. Small and limited in its 1775 Quaker beginnings in Philadelphia, the movement continued to grow and a number of abolitionist laws were passed in eight northern states by 1804.

Manumission, the process by which slave owners freed their slaves, grew dramatically after the creation of the new American republic. Virginia passed a Manumission Law in 1782 and many thousands of slaves were freed. Between 1790 and 1810, individual slaveholders in the Upper South continued to free their slaves so that by 1810, freed Blacks in that region had grown from one percent in 1790 to ten percent in 1810, with most of the increases in Virginia, Maryland and Delaware.

William Lloyd Garrison of Massachusetts became prominent among the abolitionists during the 1830s. Founder of the American Antislavery Society and editor of *The Liberator*, Garrison repeatedly condemned slavery as a direct contradiction of the principles of freedom and equality in the country's foundations. Proslavery advocates there reacted with murder and violence, destroying printing presses and property. Garrison barely escaped being lynched by a Boston mob.

> ### HEROINE OF THE "UNDERGROUND RAILROAD"
> **Harriet Tubman,** born into slavery in Maryland around 1820, escaped her slave-owners about 1849 and single-handedly walked a distance of some ninety miles into Pennsylvania. Her achievement brought her to the attention of the Underground Railroad, which enabled her to return to the South multiple times to bring out members of her family and many others over a period of ten to eleven years. She maintained strict secrecy about her identify and was never caught, but her exploits caused abolitionist William Lloyd Garrison to name her "Moses" after the Biblical prophet who led Hebrews from Egypt to freedom. She supported the Union during the Civil War as a cook, nurse, armed scout and a spy. She led a Union expedition into Beaufort, South Carolina, that freed seven hundred slaves. The movie "Harriet" (2019) portrays her remarkable story.

Former escaped slave and Black activist, Frederick Douglass, editor of the *North Star* newspaper, wrote two books that documented his experiences as a slave which became bestsellers, aiding the cause of abolition.

Harriet Beecher Stowe, a young wife and mother in Maine, submitted the first installment of her novel *Uncle Tom's Cabin* to the *National Era* in 1851, which portrayed an appalling picture of slavery and the plight of the runaway. When five thousand copies of her book were published in April 1852, it became a best seller, eventually selling three hundred thousand copies in the United States and one million in Great Britain. The book had a profound influence on Northern thought and attitudes about slavery.

The Underground Railroad

Escaping from a slave owner was a perilous undertaking. The "Underground Railroad" came into existence in the early 1800s to assist runaway slaves and became a highly organized collection of abolitionists, Quakers, former slaves, free-born Blacks, American Indians and sympathizers. Being captured could mean severe punishment, such as crippling, maiming or even death for a runaway slave who was returned to the slave owner. The Underground created a network to bring runaways into freedom by providing safe houses, food, water and transportation and a guide to the next stop. A "code" for the fugitives used railroad terminology. "Stations" and "depots" were safe houses. "Station Masters" hid slaves in their homes. "Conductors" were guides for the escapees between stations and "Stockholders" provided money and supplies. Its "Underground" status demanded complete secrecy for its success as the "passengers" moved from one station to the next.

There were a variety of routes that enabled escaped slaves to reach free states or Canada, which had abolished slavery in 1834. But not all free states welcomed the escaped slaves. Indiana, for example, a free state, had an active Underground Railroad, but passed a state constitutional amendment that banned free Blacks from settling in the state. Some escape routes led to Mexico, where slavery had also been abolished and to islands in the Caribbean that were not part of the slave trade. Most runaways, however, traveled to Canada, where an estimated 30,000 slaves settled. After the United States entered into the Civil War, many Black refugees in Canada returned to enlist in the Union Army. When the war ended, a number of former slave refugees returned to the American South, hoping to reconnect with friends and family that had been left behind.

KING COTTON DEMANDS MORE SLAVES

Effect of the Cotton Gin

The expanding cotton industry after 1800 sealed slavery as an essential element of the Southern economy. Prior to the invention of the cotton gin in 1793, tobacco, rice, indigo and sugarcane were the South's main crops, but the market for these crops was growing smaller because of competition from Caribbean plantations. Tobacco depleted the soil and growers were adapting to other crops that did not require slavery as an essential component. It was widely assumed that slavery was on the way out because soon there would be no profit in it. The cotton gin, however, changed all that.

Eli Whitney's invention of the cotton gin increased production of cotton by fifty times. Manual labor required a day to clean one pound of cotton, but the cotton gin could clean fifty pounds a day. With such a dramatic increase in production, Southern agriculture quickly adapted to growing more cotton and it soon became the major export for America.

To take advantage of the expanded production, more cotton needed to be planted and harvested, but that required more slaves to do the work. Ironically, just when growing more cotton created a need for more slaves, their importation from Africa was to be banned on January 1, 1808, by the U.S. Constitution. To compensate, the South imported great numbers of new slaves before the ban took effect. According to the U.S. Census, the slave population increased by 350,000 between 1790 and 1810.

After international slave trade was no longer legal, domestic slave trading became big business and slave values increased dramatically. The dollar value of the four million slaves in 1860 was estimated at about $4 billion. Slaves were encouraged or forced to breed and women slaves were subjected to rape

> **THE BLACK BELT** was a term that originally described the black soils and prairies of Alabama and Mississippi. When thousands of Black slaves were forcefully migrated to the area with the rapid expansion of cotton production, it became more broadly known as a region in the Deep South dominated by plantations and Black slaves.

to produce new slaves and profits. Their children were often sold as slaves to other masters, destroying the slave family's connections, sometimes forever.

As cotton crops depleted the land, southern planters continued to press west for new land. Expansion into new undeveloped areas brought about the creation of four new states in the Deep South: Louisiana (1812), Mississippi (1817), Alabama (1819); and Arkansas (1836). Texas joined them in 1845, and with Georgia, they became known as the Old Southwest.

The Black Belt of Alabama and Mississippi, with fertile soil and access to rivers, provided a perfect environment for growing cotton. About a million slaves were forced to migrate there and by 1860, they represented half the total population in the two states, producing the most cotton in the country.

Cotton Created Great Wealth

At about the same time that America was gearing up its cotton production, an industrial revolution was taking place in Great Britain and France. Several inventions, such as Crompton's spinning wheel, the spinning jenny and the power loom, made it possible to mass produce fabrics. The rising textile industries of France and Britain provided ready markets for America's cotton. At the same time, New England states also created a textile industry and initiated their own industrial revolution in the United States. The demand for cotton created America's first great economic boom.

- U.S. production of cotton in 1790 was about two million pounds; by 1860, it was over two billion pounds and accounted for almost sixty percent of American exports and seventy-five percent of the world's cotton.
- Exports of cotton, easily stored and transported, became the cash crop for the country, creating millionaires in the North as well as the South.
- Financial centers in New Orleans and New York City became dominant in the cotton trade, supplying finance, services and goods to the Southern planters. The cotton trade transformed New Orleans into a thriving city.
- The cotton boom built domestic capital for the country, attracted foreign investment and fueled industrial development in the North. Early textile factories in the North became very profitable.
- Great wealth could be achieved in one generation. The "gold rush" to the slave states attracted thousands, who came to make their fortunes. By 1860, there were more millionaires per capita in the Mississippi Valley than anywhere in the country.
- Slaves were forced into the new territories in massive migrations, the majority to work in the hot and humid climate of the cotton fields. Work days from

II. CAUSES OF THE CIVIL WAR

dawn to dusk took their toll on human life. Less than ten percent of the slaves reached the age of fifty.

- The wealthy planter aristocracy, some owning hundreds of slaves, became even more affluent with the growth of cotton and exerted great political, economic and social control.

As America's economic boom continued with an increased demand for cotton, planters promoted the belief that the great textile industries of Britain and France would need America's cotton for their economic industry. An independent Confederacy could support itself. "King Cotton" became an oft-used slogan to support secession of Southern states from the Union.

EQUAL BALANCE OF FREE VS SLAVE STATES

Missouri Compromise of 1820

The thirteen colonies had all joined the Union by 1790, plus Vermont in 1791 (breaking away from New York) to make a total of fourteen states. A slave state was defined as a state in which slavery was legal; a free state, on the other hand, prohibited it. By 1804, Northern states had either abolished slavery or put measures in place to eliminate it. The Mason-Dixon line, so named for the surveyors who created the boundary in the 1760s, ran along the southern border of Pennsylvania, separating it from Maryland, but when connected to the Ohio River, it became the geographical boundary separating North and South. States north of the Line were "free," where slavery was abolished, and those states south of the Line were slave states.

The South's dependence on slavery for its agriculturally based economy made it vitally important for it to sustain a balance of power in Congress and maintain an equal number of slave states versus free. After the admission of Ohio as a free state in 1803, the next state to be admitted was Louisiana in 1812 as a slave state.

In 1818, the Missouri Territorial legislature applied for statehood as a slave state. At the same time that Missouri's application reached Congress, Maine's application for statehood was on the table. Maine had been applying for decades to break away from the Commonwealth of Massachusetts and had finally succeeded. The admission of Maine as a free state on March 3, 1820, and Missouri as slave on August 10, 1821, maintained the balance of an equal number of free states versus slave in Congress. But an amendment to the admission of Missouri excluded slavery in any part of Louisiana Territory north of Missouri's southern boundary (36°30' latitude), except in Missouri itself. This became the Missouri Compromise of 1820 which would be maintained for more than three decades.

At the same time of Missouri's admission as a state, Arkansas Territory was created on March 2, 1819, between the northern boundary of the state of Louisiana and the southern border of Missouri. By 1836, Arkansas was admitted as a slave state, to be swiftly followed in 1837 by Michigan as free. The balance now stood with Ohio (free) 1803, Louisiana (slave) 1812; Indiana (free) 1816, Mississippi (slave) 1817; Illinois (free) 1818, Alabama (slave) 1819; Maine (free) 1820, Missouri (slave) 1821; Michigan (free) 1837, Arkansas (slave) 1836. No more states were admitted until 1845.

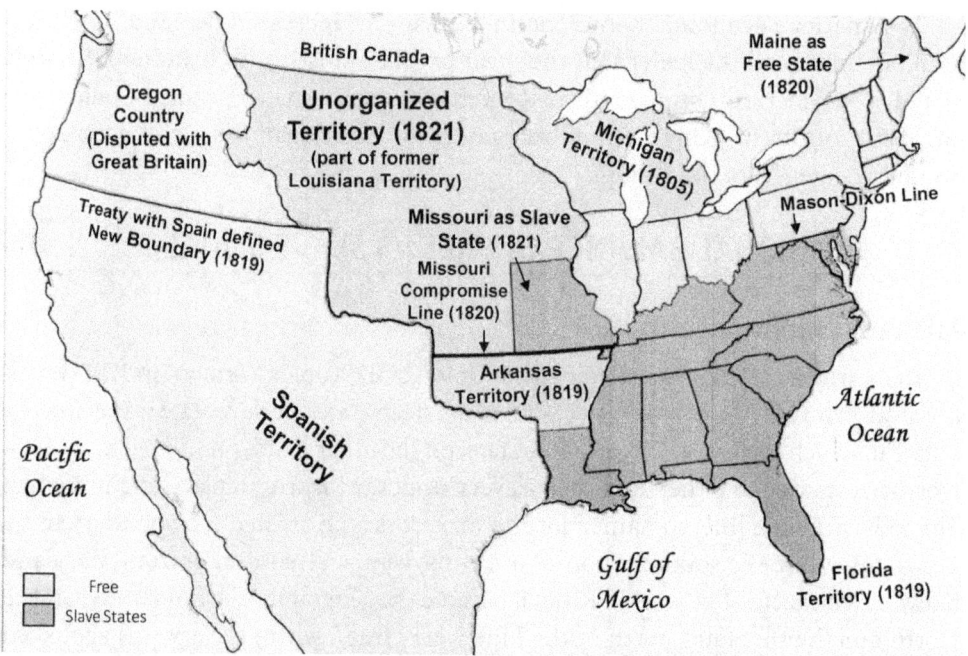

Fig. 2: Approximate configuration of the United States at the time of the Missouri Compromise of 1820, which made it against the law to admit a slave state in Louisiana Territory that was north of the southern border of Missouri, except in Missouri itself.

AMERICA GAINS NEW LANDS: SLAVE OR FREE?

America's Expansionist Destiny

President James K. Polk, who was elected to office in 1844 on a mandate to expand the United States westward, endorsed a policy that was later coined as "Manifest Destiny." The vision included acquisition of the Independent Republic of Texas, disputed by Mexico; Oregon Country, currently held by the British in the Northwest; and the addition of lands in the American Southwest and California, now held by Mexico. A large part of the country shared Polk's vision that it was America's "destiny" to spread across the continent.

Texas had achieved independence from Mexico in 1836 after the Texas Revolution, declaring itself as an independent Republic. But the Treaties of Velasco which granted

Texas its independence had been drawn up while Mexican President Santa Anna was a prisoner, and the Treaties were not recognized by Mexico. Texas had submitted a proposal for United States statehood as early as 1836, but Mexico had threatened war if the U.S. approved it. In addition, antislavery advocates in Congress had resisted admitting another slave state into the unpredictable political climate and Congress had not acted on the proposal from Texas for nine years.

But in mid-1844, before the Presidential elections, U.S. President John Tyler developed a Treaty of Annexation between Texas and the United States that would admit Texas as a state. When Mexico threatened war if the Treaty was approved, the Senate failed to ratify it.

The issue of Texas statehood became a central focus for the 1844 Presidential election and the pro-annexation candidate Polk narrowly won. A few days before Polk took office in March 1845, both the U.S. House and Senate passed the Annexation Treaty and Texas voters quickly approved it. A new Texas constitution, which endorsed slavery, was approved in October and on December 29, 1845, Texas became the 28th state of the Union. Mexico immediately broke diplomatic relations with the United States and the Mexican-American War soon followed.

Mexican-American War Adds California and New Territories

After acquiring Texas as a new state into the Union, the new President James K. Polk proceeded with steps to implement his long-held vision that the United States should expand its territory to the west coast, a goal that would implement the country's "Manifest Destiny." Polk's dream was to obtain the lands that Mexico had won from Spain in 1821, namely California and the Territory of Nuevo Mexico, and enforce the boundaries of Texas that had been established by the Treaties of Velasco. Accordingly, Polk ordered U.S. troops in early 1846 to occupy the contested area of Texas along the Rio Grande River. Mexico claimed its border with the United States was on the Nueces River about one hundred fifty miles north.

Hostilities with Mexico quickly escalated into four major battles in northern Mexico that U.S. Army troops handily won under Gen. Zachary Taylor. Polk then sent the U.S. Army's Commanding General Winfield Scott to the Gulf Coast city of Veracruz, Mexico, in March 1847 for an amphibious attack into the country. Scott crossed inland from the Gulf Coast to Mexico City and after several battles defeated the Mexican Army by October 1847. In the meantime, California had been secured from Mexico by U.S. infantry and naval forces on the West Coast.

The Treaty of Guadalupe Hidalgo, signed February 2, 1848, granted America all of Polk's vision: the state of California and huge territories of land, including what would become New Mexico, Arizona, Nevada, Utah, California and parts of Colorado and Wyoming. The addition of Oregon Territory was also achieved with the Oregon Treaty of 1846 between the United States and Great Britain. The United States now possessed an unbroken expanse of land across the continent.

As Congress addressed how to deal with the vast new lands acquired at the end of the Mexican-American War, slavery was once again on the national stage. Proslavery interests anticipated new regions for cotton expansion, but antislavery forces were prepared to oppose slavery in all new territories. The Compromise of 1820 was still in effect and prohibited slavery in former Louisiana Territory that was north of Missouri's southern border.

The Wilmot Proviso, first introduced in August 1846 by Congressman David Wilmot from Pennsylvania, proposed to ban slavery in any territory attained from Mexico, even though the Mexican-American War was still in its early stages. Although passed by the House of Representatives in 1846 and 1847, it failed in the Senate both times, stimulating bitter debate and sectional antagonism. Reintroduced as an amendment to the Treaty of Guadalupe Hidalgo in 1848, it was again rejected by Southern Democrats.

Elected to the White House in 1848, Mexican War military hero Zachary Taylor, a wealthy slave owner himself, disappointed the southern factions when he opposed slavery in the new territories. He thought slavery in the large regions of the Southwest was impractical because the arid climate would not be suitable for growing cotton. As a political Independent, neither Whig nor Democrat, he would leave the issue of slavery to be determined by the individual states when they applied for statehood.

As the year of 1848 began, the balance of free versus slave states remained even. After defeating the Seminole Indians in a long guerilla war, Florida had been admitted as a slave state March 3, 1845. Texas was admitted as a slave state December 29, 1845, which had launched the Mexican-American War. Admission of Iowa in 1846 and Wisconsin in 1848, both as free, had maintained the balance. With the addition of new states from the western territories, the equilibrium could be overturned. Southern states were prepared to secede from the Union and decide for themselves where they could expand with their slaves and cotton.

California Gold

Discovery of gold in California in early 1848 rapidly produced a massive influx of thousands of people into the territory seeking their fortunes. By early 1849, new residents had written a state constitution and were requesting admission from Congress as a free state. Southern factions threatened secession from the United States if California was admitted as a free state, but President Zachary Taylor said he would lead the U.S. Army himself against any secessionists.

At the same time, New Mexico was blocked from advancing its statehood aspirations because lands east of the Rio Grande were claimed by Texas. Utah attempted to propose an ambitious plan for the State of Deseret (an ancient word for honeybee) from

II. CAUSES OF THE CIVIL WAR

Utah Territory, but encountered strict opposition because of its Mormon practices of polygamy.

COMPROMISE OF 1850

Would California & New Territories Be Free or Slave?

Henry Clay, the venerable 72-year-old statesman from Kentucky, ailing from tuberculosis, rose in the Senate in January 1850 to propose eight compromise resolutions that would relieve the growing momentum for a Civil War over the status of free versus slave in the new territories. Clay led the debate for six months, but when put before Congress in July, the bill failed.

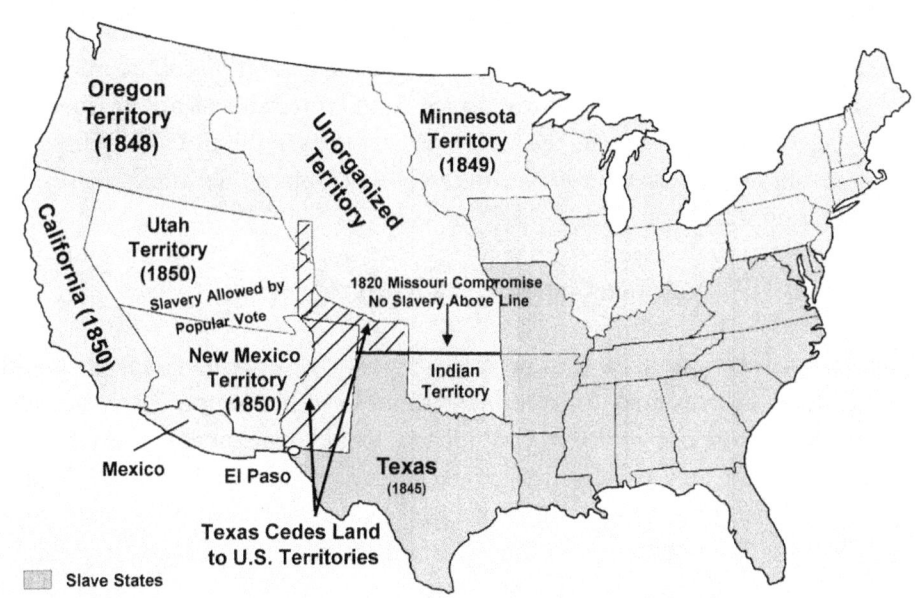

Fig. 3: Map displays the approximate boundaries of the country after passage of the Compromise of 1850. California was admitted as a free state and Texas ceded lands to U.S. territories for $10 million and aligned its northern border to conform to the Missouri Compromise of 1820.

As the disheartened Clay returned home in poor health, Senator Stephen Douglas from Illinois carried the Resolutions forward as five separate bills. President Taylor, who opposed Clay's Resolutions, unexpectedly died of an unknown gastro ailment in early July, and the new President Millard Fillmore came forward in support of the Resolutions. The five separate bills were eventually passed in September 1850 even though each side disliked some of the provisions. As finally approved, the Compromise of 1850, as it came to be known, did the following five things:

- Admitted California as a free state, rejecting a Southern proposal that would have split the state, half slave, half free.
- Texas abandoned its claims to territory in New Mexico and lands north of the Missouri Compromise line (latitude 36°30') in exchange for $10 million and retainment of El Paso where it had established a county government.
- Territorial legislatures of New Mexico and Utah were to determine by popular sovereignty their status as slave states or free.
- A new 1850 Fugitive Slave Act was passed, which outraged Northerners, as it made it much more difficult for sympathizers to assist escaping slaves. The Act continued to deny slaves the right to a trial and many free Blacks were kidnapped and forced into slavery.
- Auction of slaves was banned in Washington, D.C., but not slavery itself. The city had become a major slave depot as slave holders in the declining tobacco regions sold their slaves to the cotton plantations of the Deep South. Long lines of shackled slaves, driven from crowded pens and prisons to the auction blocks, enraged the antislavery activists in the city. The Compromise abolished the slave trade within the District, but it continued to prosper in Virginia and Maryland.

KANSAS-NEBRASKA ACT OF 1854

With approval of the 1850 Compromise, a great sigh of relief swept the country as sectionalism debates died down to make room for other issues. Discussions for a transcontinental railroad rooted in Chicago that would open up new lands for settlement and provide access to California gained increasing support in the U.S. Congress. Democratic Senator Stephen Douglas of Illinois advanced a bill in January 1854 to create Nebraska Territory from the Unorganized Territory of the Louisiana Purchase that would enable the proposed railroad to go west.

Douglas, who had implemented passage of New Mexico and Utah Territories as part of the Compromise of 1850, intended that Nebraska Territory would have the same provisions as the western territories, namely that popular vote would determine the issue of slavery. This approach, however, would violate the Missouri Compromise of 1820 that prohibited slavery north of Missouri's southern border in any lands that were part of the Louisiana Purchase. Acceptance of the Nebraska bill promised stiff political resistance.

Nevertheless, Douglas put forward a revised bill in 1854, the Kansas-Nebraska Act. The bill created two territories, Kansas and Nebraska, responding to objections from Nebraska proponents and Iowa senators that a single territory would geographically

II. CAUSES OF THE CIVIL WAR

be too large for an effective seat of government. The bill allowed the issue of slavery to be determined by popular vote in each of the territories.

Given that slave states had complete power to control slavery within their borders and the federal government was prohibited from interfering with slave trade between the states, the only way to contain slavery was to prohibit its expansion. Both antislavery and proslavery forces understood perfectly that if slavery could expand into the two new territories, there would be no more constraints to prevent its expansion throughout the country.

When brought to the Senate March 4, 1854, the new bill passed 35 to 13, but when introduced two months later in the House of Representatives, furious debate erupted. Armed conflict threatened the proceedings until arrests by the Sergeant of Arms maintained order long enough to tabulate the final vote: 113 in favor to 100 against.

When President Franklin Pierce signed the Kansas-Nebraska Act into law on May 30, 1854, the effect was explosive. By nullifying the Missouri Compromise of 1820, the Act opened all the old wounds inflicted by earlier debates between antislavery and proslavery forces. Kansas and Nebraska could now become slave states. Violence erupted in Kansas.

Fig. 4: The Kansas-Nebraska Act of 1854 allowed each of the two Territories of Kansas and Nebraska to determine slavery by popular vote, which nullified the Missouri Compromise of 1820 and launched a political firestorm.

Kansas submitted the Free State "Topeka Constitution" in 1856 that was approved by the U.S. House of Representatives, but failed in the Senate by two votes. An influx of Missouri proslavery non-residents, who stuffed ballot boxes with illegal votes, drafted the "Lecompton" Constitution and submitted it for statehood in 1857. President James Buchanan, who was a proslavery advocate, accepted the Lecompton version, but the House denied its approval and sent it back to Kansas for a vote where it was defeated in 1858. In the meantime, Kansas Free-Staters achieved a majority in the state legislature and drafted the "Leavenworth" Constitution, which was approved by voters and sent to Washington in January 1859, but Congress failed to take any action. Kansas statehood was on hold. A fourth Constitution, the "Wyandotte Constitution," would not be accepted until 1861 when Congress, diminished by states that had seceded from the Union, approved Kansas as a free state.

"BLEEDING KANSAS"

While there was little concern that Nebraska would attract plantations and slaves with its cooler and northern climate, Kansas, on the other hand, a next-door neighbor of Missouri, was quite plausible as a candidate for slavery and cotton. With passage of the Act, Kansas became a flashpoint for pro- and antislavery forces. The North was swift to react.

New England's antislavery forces organized immigrants to relocate to Kansas and secure a legislature committed to a free state. In response, large bands of armed Southerners, mostly from Missouri and quickly named "Border Ruffians," arrived in Kansas to vote illegally for proslavery delegates. Violence erupted as the antislavery settlers or free-staters, who came to be known as "Jayhawkers," encountered the Border Ruffians. Newspapers described the mounting hostilities as "Bleeding Kansas."

During the Kansas conflicts, bitter debates emerged in Congress as representatives pressed their positions in the struggle to dominate. Massachusetts Senator Charles Sumner, a staunch antislavery advocate, presented a scathing speech, "The Crime Against Kansas," in May 1856 that openly attacked North Carolina Senator Andrew Butler, for taking a mistress that he was totally devoted to—the *"ugly mistress of slavery."* Two days later, Preston Brooks, a South Carolina Democrat, assaulted Sumner in the Senate for insulting the honor of Senator Butler, his cousin. Brooks struck Sumner repeatedly with a heavy walking cane while Sumner was pinned to his chair. Nearly killed in the attack, Sumner required three years of recovery before he could return to his Senate seat.

As Northern antislavery advocates flocked to Kansas to give support to the free-state Kansas voters, one notable abolitionist was among them. John Brown had built a significant following of antislavery supporters in Massachusetts and New York, beginning in 1846. After the Kansas-Nebraska Act passed in 1854, five of Brown's sons moved to

II. CAUSES OF THE CIVIL WAR

Kansas Territory with their families and Brown joined them with another son in 1855. Brown persuaded his followers that armed antislavery advocates and a slave uprising would be needed to throw off the yoke of slavery. Using funding he obtained from prominent abolitionists in Boston, Brown arrived in Kansas with a wagon full of rifles.

As the Border Ruffians from Missouri poured into the state, pro- and antislavery settlers clashed for dominance at the ballot boxes as Kansas applied for statehood. On May 21, 1856, a group of proslavery settlers, led by the sheriff of Lecompton, Kansas, took over the town of Lawrence, populated by free-staters. Two free-state newspapers were attacked and put out of business, one permanently, and the Free-State Hotel was destroyed. At about the same time, Massachusetts Senator Charles Sumner was viciously attacked in the U.S. Congress for his speech, "Crime Against Kansas." John Brown's response to the events was to strike back against proslavery activists without mercy.

> 'JAYHAWKERS' became the nickname for Kansas 'free-staters' as they battled the proslavery 'Border Ruffians' during the state's pursuit of a constitution that would determine its status as free or slave. The free-staters liked the tough image of the nickname which portrayed a combination of the predatory nature of the hawk and the noisy and cantankerous blue jay. The name became widely known and Confederates in Arkansas applied it to any marauder, robber or thief.

Brown and some of his followers retaliated by killing five proslavery supporters at Pottawatomie Creek three days later in a grisly attack that hacked five men to death in front of their families. The Pottawatomie Massacre was well publicized and conflicts in the Territory spread. Two of Brown's sons were kidnapped, but then shortly rescued by their father at Palmyra, Kansas. One month later on August 30, 1856, a band of over three hundred Missouri Ruffians fought Brown and his men at Osawatomie, where Brown's badly outnumbered group was forced to withdraw. Brown and his followers prepared in September to defend Lawrence against a large planned assault by 2,500 proslavery activists but the new territorial governor of Kansas, John W. Geary, engineered a fragile peace, with the help of federal troops.

Taking advantage of the reduced hostilities, Brown returned East to gather support and funding over the next two years from antislavery backers. Brown planned to capture the U.S. federal armory and its weapons at Harpers Ferry, Virginia, about sixty miles from Washington, and create an armed rebellion of slaves from the Maryland and Virginia mountains. His attempts to attract Frederick Douglass, the prominent Black abolitionist, to the cause were rejected as Douglass saw Brown's plan as a flawed "suicidal mission." Brown also met with Harriet Tubman of Underground Railroad fame during this time. She admired Brown and his passion to free slaves, but neither Douglass nor Tubman, who was apparently ill at the time, participated in the subsequent raid at Harpers Ferry.

In May 1858, Brown returned to Kansas to lead a group of twelve fugitive slaves to freedom in Canada, a journey of over fifteen hundred miles, defeating and fighting pursuers along the way. Returning east, Brown solidified his plans to capture the federal armory at Harpers Ferry and traveled there in October 1859 with a small group of twenty-one men.

About three hundred free Blacks and slaves lived in the community of Harpers Ferry that had a population of about three thousand. Surrounding counties housed many thousands of slaves, which Brown believed would rise to the cause of freedom once he seized the Armory's supply of weapons.

Early in the morning on October 17, 1859, at Harpers Ferry, Brown with his small group of men quickly captured several local prominent citizens as hostages. The men then seized the federal arsenal, taking additional hostages as Armory employees arrived for work. Anticipating that local slaves would soon join the uprising, Brown waited for their appearance, but none came. Although Brown's group had cut the telegraph wires, a train was allowed to pass through and news of the raid was swiftly communicated by telegraph at the next stop. Local militias began arriving from nearby towns and President James Buchanan ordered a company of U.S. Marines to the conflict. Leading the Marines, Lt. Col. Robert E. Lee was assisted by his volunteer aide-de-camp J.E.B. ("Jeb") Stuart, both of whom would become famous generals for the Confederacy during the Civil War.

The next morning, October 18, U.S. Marines and about a thousand local militia surrounded the engine house, where Brown and his group had retreated. After offers of surrender were rejected, Marines charged the engine house and survivors were taken prisoner, including Brown, who had miraculously survived a bayonet charge that hit a hard object in his clothing. Ten raiders and one Marine were killed. Brown was tried for murder, slave insurrection and treason against the state of Virginia, found guilty and hanged December 2, 1859. Praised by some, vilified by others, his actions aroused Southern fears of slave revolt and military invasion. An alarmed South enlarged its local militias and prepared for attacks from Black slaves or federal troops. The Kansas events would later be described as a prelude to the Civil War.

Guerilla Warfare in Kansas

Guerilla warfare between pro- and antislavery sympathizers existed in Kansas before and during the Civil War. Although never officially part of the Union Army, a staunchly Kansas abolitionist group, referred to as the Red Legs, served as scouts and spies for the Union Army during the Civil War. They wrapped red cloth around their legs as their uniform, which they would discard as they returned to their homes as farmers and townsmen. One of their commanders, Captain George H. Hoyt, a lawyer from Massachusetts, had defended John Brown at his trial after the Harpers Ferry raid.

II. CAUSES OF THE CIVIL WAR

The band of Red Legs, often referred to as Jayhawkers, numbering as many as one hundred men, were blamed for many vicious attacks on civilians suspected of owning slaves, as they left smoldering ruins of farms and towns during the Civil War. After an attack, the band would disperse and merge back into their farms and villages as normal citizens. The town of Columbus, Missouri, was burned to the ground in 1862 and many of its citizens were hanged by the Red Legs, although some claimed that the worst offenses were done by Red Leg imposters. The group slowly disbanded during 1864 and 1865 as the Civil War came to an end.

Shortly after the onset of the Civil War, William Quantrill, a Kansas proslavery activist, joined a band of slave catchers in Missouri and then formed his own group called Quantrill's Raiders to conduct a number of guerilla attacks against antislavery supporters in Kansas, using Colt revolvers, six-shot, 44-caliber handguns. Quantrill's Raiders numbering about four hundred men, including the outlaws Frank and Jesse James, massacred nearly two hundred men and boys at Lawrence, Kansas, in August 1863, and then sacked and burned the entire town. The massacre attracted the attention of the Union Army with established forces in Missouri and forced Quantrill into Texas where the group broke up. Quantrill continued to lead a few dozen men in various raids during 1864 and 1865 until he was killed in a Union ambush in Kentucky in 1865.

Minnesota, Oregon and Kansas Admitted as Free States

Minnesota Territory, created in 1849, was a large region that extended far west to the Missouri River, into what would become the states of Montana and the Dakotas. The free state of Minnesota was created May 11, 1858, by separating the eastern part of the territory from what would become Dakota Territory in 1861. Acceptance of the Minnesota application for statehood, however, had been linked to the admission of Kansas as a slave state, to maintain an even number of free states versus slave. But the Kansas Lecompton Constitution, granting slavery, had been rejected by Congress because of fraudulent voter ballots. With the admission of Minnesota, there was no longer an even balance of free states versus slave.

By 1858, proslavery factions had been largely driven out of Kansas and a new fourth and last Wyandotte Constitution was submitted in April 1860. It declared Kansas to be a free state, granted voting rights to every white male at least twenty-one years old and adopted a position that Congress could ban slavery in the territories. Women, although not given the right to vote, were granted property rights and could participate in school district elections.

Submitted to Congress, it was passed by the U.S. House in April 1860, but was repeatedly rejected by Southern votes in the Senate. After Lincoln's election in November, South Carolina formally seceded from the Union on December 20, 1860, to be swiftly followed by Mississippi, Florida, Alabama and Georgia. With a greatly diminished

Senate, the bill for Kansas statehood passed and it became a free state to the Union January 29, 1861.

The southern boundary of Kansas was at the 37th parallel, about thirty-four miles north of the 36°30' parallel that defined the Missouri Compromise Line of 1820 (See Fig. 4). The 37th parallel had been determined because of a boundary between the Osage and Cherokee Indian reservations in Indian Territory. The strip of unclaimed land, about one hundred seventy miles long and thirty-four and a half mile tall, was referred to as the "Public Land Strip," but was unorganized, belonged to no territory, and became known as "No Man's Land." Squatters moved onto the land, took up residence and hoped to gain legal possession eventually. "No-Man's Land" would become the panhandle of Oklahoma when it reached statehood in 1907.

Oregon Territory had been created in 1848 after the Oregon Treaty with Great Britain in 1846 ended the disputed boundary between the two countries and placed the international border at the 49th parallel. By 1853, Oregon Territory had been divided into Washington and Oregon Territories, separated by the Columbia River. As more settlers crossed the continent on the Oregon Trail, a Constitution for Oregon as a free state was approved at Salem in September 1857. The Constitution, however, denied free Blacks the right to enter the state and settle. A further provision denied the right to vote to Negroes, Chinamen, or mulattoes. Oregon was admitted as a free state in February 1859 and became the 33rd state for the Union.

In 1854, Mexico agreed to sell land in the Mesilla Valley that bordered the Rio Grande to the United States for $10 million. The land was essential for a proposed U.S. transcontinental railroad that would reach from El Paso, Texas, to San Diego, California. The Gadsden Purchase, so named for the U.S. Ambassador to Mexico at that time, added thirty thousand square miles to New Mexico Territory and defined the southern borders of New Mexico and Arizona as they are today. Actual construction of the railroad was delayed, however, by the onset of the Civil War in 1861.

Two new states were admitted during the period of the Civil War: West Virginia in 1863 and Nevada, 1864. After the conclusion of the war, Nebraska was the next state to be admitted in 1867, followed by Colorado (1876), North and South Dakota (1889), Montana and Washington (1889), Idaho and Wyoming (1890), Utah (1896), Oklahoma (1907) and New Mexico and Arizona (1912). Alaska and Hawaii were admitted in 1959.

PRESIDENTIAL ELECTION OF 1856

Lincoln Challenges Kansas-Nebraska Act

After passage of the Kansas-Nebraska Act in the spring of 1854, Abraham Lincoln from Illinois found an issue for his political ambitions. Illinois Senator Stephen Douglas, who had authored the Act, campaigned throughout the state in September and October, promoting the bill. Lincoln, opposed to the spread of slavery, was appalled by the Act's provision that slavery could be extended into each new territory if approved by the local voters. To counter the arguments for the Act, Lincoln made it a practice to attend Douglas' speeches and follow each performance with a speech of his own.

In Peoria, Illinois, in October 1854 Lincoln challenged the Douglas' doctrine of "popular sovereignty" as a dishonest promise while pretending to support the principles of democracy and self-government. Lincoln pointed out that the Kansas-Nebraska Act, which eliminated the Missouri Compromise of 1820, allowed a few inhabitants in a sparsely populated region to make a decision on slavery that would impact the entire country. Lincoln further contended that the claim of the "right" of some men to "enslave" others was in direct conflict with the country's founding principle that *"all men are created equal."* Lincoln, as quoted in the popular press:

"Nearly eighty years ago we began by declaring that all men are created equal; but now from that beginning we have run down to the other declaration, that for some men to enslave others is a 'sacred right of self-government.' These principles cannot stand together. They are as opposite as God and Mammon; and whoever holds to the one must despise the other."

Lincoln won a seat in the Illinois House of Representatives in the November 1854 election, but declined to accept it when he saw that he had an opportunity to run as a Senator for the U.S. Congress against the incumbent. Senators were appointed by state legislatures until the 17th Amendment to the Constitution in 1913, which made it a law that they were to be elected by the people. But in 1854, the Illinois legislature would determine the state's Senator in the U.S. Congress. The Democratic and Whig factions of Illinois joined forces and named Lincoln's rival, Lyman Trumbull, an "anti-Nebraska" candidate, as the new Senator. Although Lincoln's bid for the Senate seat had been unsuccessful, his words were frequently quoted in newspapers and published in pamphlets. He became well known as a speaker and writer and entered the national stage.

New Republican Party Replaces the Whigs

The Free Soil Party had surfaced in 1848 on a campaign of "Free Soil, Free Speech, Free Labor and Free Men," in response to the threat that territories acquired from the Mexican-American War might become slave states. The Party, staunchly antislavery, called for a Homestead Act that would open up land on free soil to independent farmers and block wealthy plantation owners from seizing large tracts of the best land to expand slavery in the new territories.

At about the same time, the Whig Party, which had arisen in the 1830s to combat Andrew Jackson and the Democrats, was now disintegrating in the face of competing antislavery and proslavery factions. With the passage of the Kansas-Nebraska Act of 1854, which effectively opened up the possibility of new territories becoming slave states if approved by the voters, created the final political clash of wills that merged former Whigs with Free Soilers and the new Republican Party was born in 1856.

Proslavery President Elected in 1856

The first Republican National Convention of 1856 approved an antislavery platform in the new territories that would be under Congressional control. Additional commitments to the platform included the admission of Kansas as a free state, support for a transcontinental railroad, and an end to polygamy in Mormon settlements. They incorporated their candidate, John C. Fremont of California, "Pathfinder of the West," into their new slogan: "Free speech, Free press, Free soil, Free men, Fremont and Victory!"

Lincoln gave a speech promoting Fremont at the national convention and campaigned vigorously for Fremont as President that summer and fall. The platform opposed the entire system of slavery and the so-called Ostend Manifesto of 1854, a proposal developed by proslavery advocates to purchase Cuba from Spain and bring its slaves into the United States.

The Democratic Party, badly split between pro- and antislavery sectional differences, were unhappy with the performance of incumbent President Franklin Pierce and blocked his bid for re-nomination for the 1856 Presidential election. James Buchanan of Pennsylvania had served under Polk as U.S. Secretary of State and was now serving as Minister to Great Britain. An avid supporter of states' rights, popular sovereignty, the Ostend Manifesto, and the proslavery legislature of Kansas, Buchanan was nominated as the Democratic Presidential candidate.

A third party, the Know-Nothings, supported anti-immigration policies that would limit the influence of German and Irish Catholics. Started as a secret society, the standard response to questions about the specifics of their Party was, *"I know nothing,"* which gave rise to its political name. The potato famine in Ireland, which began in 1845, had forced the immigration of large numbers of Catholic Irish refugees to America. By 1854, the Know-Nothing Party, which was well established in Massachusetts, led efforts to prevent immigration of Catholics and end their influence in the country. The Know-Nothings, also known as the American Party, nominated for their presidential candidate former President Millard Fillmore, who had succeeded to the Presidency in 1850 after the untimely death of Zachary Taylor, but Fillmore had not been nominated by the Whigs in the 1852 presidential election.

Democratic candidate James Buchanan and his running mate, John C. Breckinridge of Kentucky, won the election with one hundred seventy-four electoral votes, which included all of the southern states except for Maryland, plus the votes from California, Illinois, Indiana and Pennsylvania. Maryland's eight electoral votes went to Fillmore. Fremont, not even on the ballot in thirteen southern states, garnered one hundred fourteen electoral votes and forty-five percent of the vote in the free states.

II. CAUSES OF THE CIVIL WAR

SUPREME COURT ENDORSES SLAVERY (1857)

The Infamous Case of Dred Scott

A landmark decision by the Supreme Court in 1857, known as the Dred Scott Decision, supported Southern beliefs that Blacks were beings of an inferior race and could never become citizens of the United States. Without citizenship, they had none of the protections of the law, such as the right to a fair trial if arrested for a crime. The Court also declared that the Missouri Compromise of 1820 was unconstitutional and that the country had no power to deny slavery in territories north of latitude 36°.

Dred Scott, born in Virginia about 1799 as a slave, was owned by a U.S. Army surgeon and taken in 1830 from Missouri, a slave state, to the free state of Illinois and in 1836 to Wisconsin Territory, where the Missouri Compromise of 1820 prohibited slavery. The owner eventually left Wisconsin and moved back to Missouri with Dred Scott where he died. Scott, assisted by antislavery advocates, sued for his freedom in 1847 on the grounds that he became a free man when he entered Wisconsin Territory and *"once free, always free."*

In 1857, after a decade of court decisions, appeals and reversals, the U.S. Supreme Court heard his case. In what is perhaps the most infamous case in Supreme Court decisions, Chief Justice Roger B. Taney, a former slave owner from Maryland, wrote the majority decision that all people of African ancestry, slaves or free, were beings of an inferior race, could never become citizens of the United States and therefore had no rights to sue in federal court. Further, the court declared that Congress had no authority to restrict an owner's right to bring slaves into federal territories, and that such previous attempts to restrict slavery's spread through such Acts as the Missouri Compromise of 1820 were unconstitutional.

The decision fell as a lightning bolt on the nation's growing divide about the entire issue of slavery and its continuation in the Union and potential expansion into new western territories. The Mexican-American War of 1846-48 had yielded vast new territories to the United States that would soon bring new states into the Union. The effect of the Supreme Court decision, condemned by the North and embraced by the South, created an even greater chasm between pro- and antislavery forces.

LINCOLN-DOUGLAS DEBATES OF 1858

After the 1856 election, Lincoln continued to make speeches while conducting lawyer business from his Springfield, Illinois, office and became active and well-known in the new Republican Party. In June 1858, the Illinois Republican Convention selected Lincoln as its candidate to run against incumbent Democrat Stephen Douglas for the U.S. Senate.

Lincoln's acceptance speech at the Convention on June 16, 1858, focused on the impossibility of the government to endure if the country was half slave and half free. The Supreme Court's decision in 1857 that denied freedom to the slave Dred Scott had also prevented Congress from excluding slavery in any U.S. territory, including territory north of the Missouri Compromise of 1820. In his speech, Lincoln predicted that either slavery would be arrested and eliminated, or it would exist throughout all States, old and new. Borrowing a Biblical phrase that a *"house divided against itself shall not stand,"* Lincoln incorporated the phrase into his acceptance speech.

> *"In my opinion, it (slavery) will not cease until a crisis shall have been reached and passed. A house divided against itself cannot stand. I believe this government cannot endure, permanently, half slave and half free. I do not expect the Union to be dissolved; I do not expect the house to fall; but I do expect it will cease to be divided. It will become all one thing, or all the other. Either the opponents of slavery will arrest the further spread of it and place it where the public mind shall rest in the belief that it is in the course of ultimate extinction, or its advocates will push it forward till it shall become alike lawful in all the states, old as well as new, North as well as South."*

Each candidate was seeking votes from the Illinois General Assembly in the 1858 election. To enhance publicity for the coming election in November, the two candidates, Douglas and Lincoln, agreed to engage in seven public debates that would be held across the state's congressional districts. Each debate attracted large crowds, ranging in size from five thousand to eighteen thousand people. The largest newspapers in Chicago sent reporter-stenographers who created complete texts of each debate. Thanks to an effective railroad system, the texts were rapidly sent to Chicago where they were incorporated into newspapers and quickly published and distributed throughout the country. Lincoln later edited the texts of all the debates and they were incorporated into a book of four printings and became widely read.

At this stage of American politics, the general public did not elect its senators; legislators had that honor. The Senate seat was awarded to Douglas by the Illinois legislature where Democrats had maintained control. But the campaign and widely publicized debates had brought Lincoln into the national spotlight and his popularity grew as he continued to present his views in invited speeches.

LINCOLN ELECTED PRESIDENT IN 1860; SOUTH SECEDES

Republicans Nominate Lincoln for 1860 Election

As the country anticipated the Presidential Election year of 1860, the Young Men's Republican Union of New York invited promising candidates to present their views in a series of speeches. Lincoln, third in the series, presented his speech at the Cooper

II. CAUSES OF THE CIVIL WAR

Union on February 27, 1860. His principal point was that the South declared they had a Constitutional and moral right to take slaves and own them as property, but Lincoln argued that no such right existed in the Constitution and Free States must continue to assert that slavery is morally wrong and dare to do their duty that "Right Makes Might!" The speech, carried in all the newspapers, electrified the country and propelled Lincoln to be a major contender for the Presidency.

The Republican National Convention met mid-May 1860 in Chicago. Three principal competing contenders included William H. Seward, an antislavery activist and former governor and senator of New York; Salmon P. Chase, a staunch abolitionist from Ohio; and conservative Edward Bates of Missouri, all of whom had individually alienated some faction of the new Republican Party. Lincoln's moderate position on slavery, namely that the government opposed the expansion of slavery into new territories but would not interfere with slavery where it already existed, would appeal to those who recognized the South's need for slavery to support its economic viability. Lincoln's frontier roots in the West (Kentucky and Indiana) promoted his appeal to western states and on the third ballot, he was carried to win the Presidential nomination. The platform of the Republican Party included opposition to slavery in new territories, a Homestead Act, a transcontinental railroad, and a tariff to protect industry.

The Democratic National Convention took place in Charleston, South Carolina, in April 1860 and failed to nominate a candidate. The Convention immediately split into two factions when Southern delegates insisted on a plank favoring a federal slave code for the territories. When the plank was defeated by a small majority, the Alabama representatives led a number of delegates to walk out of the convention. The remaining delegates nominated six candidates with Senator Stephen A. Douglas as the front-runner. But after fifty-seven ballots, Douglas failed to win a majority. Frustrated, the Convention adjourned.

The second Democratic National Convention occurred June 18 in Baltimore, Maryland. This time, one hundred ten Southern delegates walked out because the Convention would not support a policy supporting slavery in territories that did not approve it. The remaining delegates nominated Stephen Douglas as their presidential candidate.

A third Democratic Convention occurred when the delegates who walked out of the second Democratic National Convention formed the "Southern" Democratic Party, which reconvened the same day in a separate building in Baltimore. The Southern Democratic Party's nominee for president was John C. Breckinridge of Kentucky, who was now serving as the United States Vice-President under Buchanan. Breckinridge would represent the slave-holding South,

A fourth candidate was nominated by the former Southern Whigs and Know Nothings, now called the Constitutional Union Party. Avoiding slavery as an issue, the party advocated compromise to save the Union with the slogan, *"The Union as it is and the Constitution as it is."* John Bell of Tennessee was nominated for its presidential candidate.

The 1860 Campaign

The 1860 election offered voters four presidential candidates. Lincoln and Douglas competed in the North and Breckinridge and Bell in the South. Lincoln conducted a traditional type of "front porch campaign," common for the times by not leaving his home town of Springfield, Illinois. He made no formal speeches but met with visitors and distributed his pamphlets and copies of his speeches and former debates with Douglas. Thousands of voters congregated at Lincoln's home in Springfield to read pamphlets of his debates with Douglas and listen to him speak. Promoted at election rallies as "The Railsplitter," Lincoln's work as a young man in Indiana to make rails for fences, appealed to the public's vision of a hard-working frontiersman representing honest labor.

Going against the "front porch" tradition of campaigning that had been in place since the time of George Washington, Douglas campaigned forcefully in person in the Northeastern states, but then also visited Virginia and North Carolina. Warning that some southern states would advocate secession after the election, he campaigned in the swing states of Pennsylvania, Ohio and Indiana, speaking vigorously for maintenance of the Union.

At the November election, voter turnout was eighty-one percent. Douglas received thirty percent of the popular vote but only twelve electoral votes: nine from Missouri and three from New Jersey. Bell won Tennessee, Kentucky and Virginia; Breckinridge took the other slave states except for Missouri. Lincoln won only forty percent of the popular vote, but had a clear majority of one hundred eighty electoral votes, carrying the states of California and Oregon in the Far West and all the states north of the Mason-Dixon Line except for New Jersey. Lincoln did not carry a single slave state, but he had won the election against Douglas.

ELEVEN STATES SECEDE TO FORM THE CONFEDERACY

Lincoln's election made South Carolina's secession from the Union a foregone conclusion. The state had long been waiting for an event that would unite the South against antislavery forces. Once the presidential election returns were certain, a special South Carolina convention adopted on December 20, 1860, an ordinance of secession that declared " ... *the union between this State and the other States of North America is dissolved, and that the State of South Carolina has resumed her position among the nations of the world, as a separate and independent State.*" By early February 1861, six other states, including Mississippi (January 9), Florida (January 10), Alabama (January

II. CAUSES OF THE CIVIL WAR

11), Georgia (January 19), Louisiana (January 26) and Texas (February 2) had adopted ordinances of secession and began seizing federal properties, including buildings, arsenals, garrisons and fortifications.

On February 7, 1861, the seven seceded states adopted a provisional constitution for the Confederate States of America and named Montgomery, Alabama, as its capital. Jefferson Davis of Mississippi, who had resigned from the United States Senate when Mississippi seceded, was soon elected as President of the Confederacy, described as the *"champion of a slave society and embodying the values of the planter class."* Davis had graduated from West Point Military Academy in 1828 and achieved distinction in the Mexican-American War under Gen. Zachary Taylor as Colonel of the Mississippi Rifles. After the war, Davis continued to expand his large cotton plantation in Mississippi and by 1860 owned more than one hundred slaves. Serving in the U.S. Senate 1848-51, he next served as Secretary of War under President Franklin Pierce, and then returned to the Senate in 1856, where he remained until Mississippi seceded from the Union and he resigned from Congress.

The official Constitution of the Confederacy, adopted March 11, 1861, was largely based on the United States Constitution, but declared states' rights to preserve, practice and perpetuate the practice of slavery. The Southern perspective maintained that slavery was not only a required "peculiar institution," it was upheld in Holy Scripture. With its opening preamble that invoked *" … the favor and guidance of Almighty God,"* the new Constitution expressed Southern opinion that the Confederacy was fulfilling God's will.

> **CONFEDERATE MOTTO**
> The national motto of the Confederacy was *Deo Vindice*: "God will avenge."

Abraham Lincoln's inaugural address to Congress and the country on March 4, 1861, was specifically aimed at the secessionists. *"In your hands, my dissatisfied fellow-countrymen, and not in mine, is the momentous issue of civil war. The Government will not assail you. You can have no conflict without being yourselves the aggressors. You have no oath registered in heaven to destroy the Government, while I shall have the most solemn one to "preserve, protect, and defend it."* Declaring the secession as anarchy and "legally void," Lincoln encouraged the Southern states to return to the Union, reiterating his position that slavery would be protected where it already existed. As he closed his remarks, he put forth a plea for peace, stating, *"We are not enemies, but friends … Though passion may have strained, it must not break our bonds of affection. The mystic chords of memory, stretching from every battlefield and patriot grave to every living heart and hearthstone all over this broad land, will yet swell the chorus of the Union, when again touched, as surely they*

> **UNION MOTTO**
> The national motto for the Union: *E Pluribus Unum*: "Out of many, one."

will be, by the better angels of our nature." No foreign government recognized the Confederacy, nor did the United States government.

After the Confederate Army fired shots on Fort Sumter, Charleston Harbor, South Carolina, on April 12, 1861, initiating the American Civil War, four more states seceded from the Union to join the Confederacy: Virginia on April 17; Arkansas, May 6; North Carolina, May 20; and Tennessee, June 8. Virginia, with its long history as the first of the thirteen colonies, a leader in the Revolution against England, and the home of seven United States presidents, represented a significant factor for the Confederacy.

With Virginia included in the Confederacy, the Confederate capital was moved from Montgomery, Alabama, to Richmond, Virginia. States that did not secede from the Union but supported slavery, namely the Border States, included Missouri, Kentucky, Maryland and Delaware. Their sympathies for the South and the Confederate Army remained strong among large segments of their populations. Missouri and Kentucky created secessionist governments in exile and were accepted by the Confederacy in December 1861 as Confederate states. Maryland, bordering the nation's capital, became a focal point for the development of several bitter animosities against Lincoln and the Union, but the state never seceded to join the Confederacy.

WEST VIRGINIA MOTTO
"Mountaineers are Always Free."

When the Virginia legislature voted to secede from the Union, representatives from western Virginia in a separate meeting refused to join Virginia in secession and proceeded to apply to Congress as a separate state. Although West Virginia would not officially achieve statehood until 1863, its Union sympathies identified it as a Border State.

New Mexico Territorial legislature had proposed in 1858 the creation of Arizona Territory along the western half of its existing territory. By March 1861, Congress had still not acted on the proposal, so pro-Southern sympathizers called for a secessionist Confederate Territory of Arizona to be formed along the southern half of the region, dividing the state into two halves, with the boundary at 34 degrees north latitude. The Territory was officially recognized by the Confederacy in August 1861 and Arizona soldiers enlisted in both Union and Confederate armies.

Although remote from most of the Civil War battlefields, several battles and operations still took place in New Mexico Territory given that it was a gateway to pro-Union California. In March 1861, pro-Confederate forces moved north from secessionist Arizona Territory into New Mexico Territory to capture the northern territory to the Confederacy. By-passing the well-fortified Fort Craig, about thirty-five miles south of Socorro, New Mexico, the Southerners proceeded north to occupy Santa Fe. Union forces encountered the secessionists in March 1862 at Glorieta Pass, located on the Santa Fe Trail southeast of Santa Fe. The battle engaged about 2,000 combatants, evenly divided between the two armies. When the Confederates ran out of supplies and ammunition, they were forced to withdraw, giving a decisive victory to the Union. The Arizona secessionist government moved to Texas where it remained for the rest of the Civil War.

The Union reclaimed the provisional Arizona area as New Mexico Territory and in 1863 split the region into two territories by forming U.S. Arizona Territory on the west using a north-south border at the 107th meridian with New Mexico Territory on the east, bordering Texas, along the lines of the states' borders as they are today.

III. WAR BEGINS, APRIL 1861

SOUTH CAROLINA SEIZES CHARLESTON HARBOR

SOUTH CAROLINA, LEADER OF THE SECESSIONISTS, HAD BEEN THE FIRST TO SECEDE from the United States on December 20, 1860. Its Charleston Harbor, a vital seaport for the South, served as an important conduit for exporting cotton and other goods to foreign markets and importing products from Great Britain, France and the Caribbean. Several Union-held military forts in the heart of South Carolina's Charleston harbor presented a stinging symbol of the United States and South Carolina's Governor Francis Pickens demanded the withdrawal of all Union forces from the harbor.

With tensions rising between South Carolina and the Union North, Major Robert Anderson, commander of the Union's Charleston garrison, surreptitiously moved his small command of less than ninety soldiers under cover of darkness on December 26, 1860, from the weakly defended Fort Moultrie to Fort Sumter. Built on an island in the center of the channel, Fort Sumter dominated the harbor entrance and was still undergoing construction that began in 1829 to improve its structural integrity. Ninety percent finished, the fort had been designed to be one of the strongest in the world but was still incomplete and only half of its cannons were in place.

Governor Pickens, responding to the move of Anderson's troops to Fort Sumter, ordered the seizure of all federal property in and around Charleston by State Militia, including those in Charleston harbor. By the end of December, all the forts in the harbor, except Fort Sumter, were in Confederate hands, providing the Southerners with guns and artillery batteries, totaling more than 22,000 weapons.

Although Fort Sumter was in Union hands, its supplies were limited. President James Buchanan, still in office until Lincoln's inauguration, attempted to send a merchant civilian ship, *Star of the West,* to Fort Sumter in January with limited food, supplies and two hundred men to support the Union garrison. The effort failed when

Confederate batteries fired on the ship on January 9, 1861, at the harbor's entrance and it was forced to withdraw. The "Star of the West Battery," located on Morris Island, manned by cadets from the South Carolina Military Academy (now the Citadel), fired the opening shots on what would become the American Civil War.

> **FRIEND AGAINST FRIEND**
>
> Union Major Robert Anderson, commander at Union Fort Sumter, and Gen. P.G.T. Beauregard, commanding Confederate forces in Charleston Harbor, were close colleagues before the war. Anderson had been Beauregard's artillery instructor at West Point and Beauregard became Anderson's assistant after graduation. They now faced each other as combatants in the opening battle of the Civil War.

By February 28, the Confederacy had formed the Confederate States Army (CSA) and granted control and authority of military operations to the new President, Jefferson Davis, now its Commander-in-Chief. On March 1, 1861, Davis appointed Pierre Gustave Toutant (P.G.T.) Beauregard as Brigadier General to command all the Southern forces in the vicinity of Charleston and to take possession of Fort Sumter. Beauregard had graduated second in his class from West Point Military Academy in 1838 and served with distinction in the Mexican-American War under Gen. Winfield Scott. Taking command at Fort Sumter, Gen. Beauregard made several attempts to persuade Major Anderson, his former mentor and teacher at West Point, to surrender the fort, but Anderson refused, obeying orders from the U.S. War Department to hold possession of the forts in the harbor *"to the last extremity."*

CONFEDERACY FIRES ON FORT SUMTER

President Abraham Lincoln, inaugurated March 4, 1861, was soon informed that Fort Sumter's garrison had only six weeks of provisions left. On April 6, Lincoln informed South Carolina Gov. Pickens that an attempt would be made to supply the fort with provisions only, and if the attempt was not resisted, no men, arms or ammunition would be transferred. President Lincoln deliberately avoided communication with Confederate President Davis, because he publicly maintained that the Confederacy was illegal and would not be recognized by the United States government. Pickens passed the communication on to President Davis, who ordered Beauregard to demand the surrender of Fort Sumter before the Union ship could deliver the supplies, and if the Union commander refused, to reduce the fort to rubble.

On April 11, Beauregard issued an ultimatum to Anderson, which was again refused. The first volley, fired from Fort Johnson on Fort Sumter at 4:30 a.m. April 12, 1861, was immediately followed with a general bombardment from four thousand guns and mortars from Forts Moultrie and Johnson, Cummings Point battery and the floating battery (See Fig. 5).

III. WAR BEGINS, APRIL 1861

Fort Sumter, designed to defend against a naval assault from the sea, was ill equipped to fire at the surrounding forts within the harbor. Further, there was little ammunition and Anderson was limited to firing only six guns. Union navy vessels, waiting outside the harbor entrance with small boats, were unable to reach the fort with men, supplies or ammunition because of heavy seas and Confederate artillery.

Outgunned and outmanned, with fires within the fort burning out of control, Anderson was forced to surrender on the afternoon of April 14. During the 100-gun salute to the U.S. flag as it was drawn down, an unfortunate spark ignited a pile of cartridges which killed two privates, the only fatalities of the battle. Under the terms of surrender that allowed the Union soldiers to evacuate, the men were taken by steamer to the U.S. Navy relief ship outside the harbor and returned north. Anderson carried the 33-star flag with him and it became a rallying symbol for supporters of the Union.

With the firing on Fort Sumter and looming armed conflict with the South, United States General-in-Chief Winfield Scott, highest ranking general of Union forces, was tasked to find leaders for the U.S. Army, which at that time numbered only about 16,000 officers and soldiers, distributed across various outposts and garrisons throughout the country. On April 18, Scott invited Lt. Col. Robert E. Lee, who had served under him in the Mexican-American War, and who now held the rank of Colonel of the First Regiment of Cavalry in the Army, to serve in a senior command post as Major General in the Union Army. Scott held the highest esteem for Lee, describing him as " ... *the very best soldier that I ever saw in the field."*

Lee came from a military background, the son of Revolutionary War hero, Henry "Light Horse Harry" Lee. Graduating second in his class from West Point Military Academy in 1829, Robert E. Lee then pursued an engineering career with the U.S. Army for the next several years, mapping, surveying and creating structural river fortifications. With the onset of the Mexican-American War, Lee was selected by Gen. Scott as one of his chief aides prior to the invasion of Mexico and Lee performed brilliantly against the Mexican Army during the march from Veracruz to Mexico City. After the war, Lee was appointed superintendent of West Point in 1852 for three years and then promoted to combat command in West Texas in 1855, a frontier assignment.

In 1857, Lee took a two-year leave of absence from the army to manage his wife's estate, inherited from her father, George Washington Parke Custis. The holdings included about two hundred slaves and several plantations, including Arlington House, near Washington, D.C. Lee considered it a most unpleasant duty and according to several accounts treated the slaves badly. In 1859, back with the U.S. Army, Lieut. Col. Lee led the Marines who captured the abolitionist John Brown who raided Harpers Ferry. Lee's career with the army had been one of success and merit.

When his mentor and commander, Gen. Scott, invited Lee to be a leading general in the Union Army, Lee reluctantly declined the offer. Although Lee opposed secession as an unconstitutional betrayal to the founding fathers of the nation, his native state of

Virginia had seceded from the Union on April 17 and joined the Confederacy. Writing to Scott on the night of April 19, Lee regrettably resigned from the U.S. Army after his thirty-two years of service, stating that he could not "*raise his hand against his native birthplace of Virginia, his relatives, his children, his home.*" The Confederacy named him one of its first five full generals.

After joining the Confederacy in May 1861, Lee predicted the terrible ordeal facing the South if war came. "*They do not know what they say. If it (secession) came to a conflict of arms, the war will last at least four years. Northern politicians will not appreciate the determination and pluck of the South, and Southern politicians do not appreciate the numbers, resources and patient perseverance of the North ... I foresee that our country will pass through a terrible ordeal, a necessary expiation, perhaps, for our national sins.*"

Following the onset of the Civil War, the U.S. Army seized the property of the Arlington Estate that was Lee's wife's inheritance, and used it as a cemetery for burial of Union soldiers as the Washington, D.C., national cemeteries had soon filled with dead soldiers. On June 15, 1864, Arlington was officially designated a national cemetery by order of Secretary of War Edwin Stanton. Its original space of two hundred acres has grown to more than six hundred acres today, where approximately 400,000 veterans from every American war since the Revolutionary War and their eligible dependents are buried.

NORTH & SOUTH PREPARE FOR WAR

Union Volunteers and Draftees

At the time of the firing on Fort Sumter, April 11, 1861, the United States Army numbered about 16,000, mostly posted in small outposts west of the Mississippi River. On April 15, 1861, the day after the Union surrender of Fort Sumter, President Lincoln issued an order for 75,000 volunteers from State militias to serve for ninety days to "*... maintain the honor, the integrity, and the existence of our National Union, and the perpetuity of popular government.*" The call for volunteers was expanded on May 3, for the addition of 18,000 new sailors and 1,000 Marines to the Navy, which increased its size from 7,600 sailors in March to 22,000 by December 1861.

A quota of volunteers was issued for each state to fulfill and the Union's Secretary of War Simon Cameron's message to each governor denoted the number of regiments each state would need to provide. Each regiment should contain 780 men at a minimum. Governors would appoint general officers. Border States that had not seceded were included in the call. California and Oregon were excluded because of the impracticalities of their distant locations. Kansas, as a newly admitted state in January 1861, was also excluded. But all three states still volunteered regiments to the Union Army.

Response from the Northern states was dramatic. Believing that this would be a short war, men who were loyal to the Union did not want to be left out of the excitement, and

III. WAR BEGINS, APRIL 1861

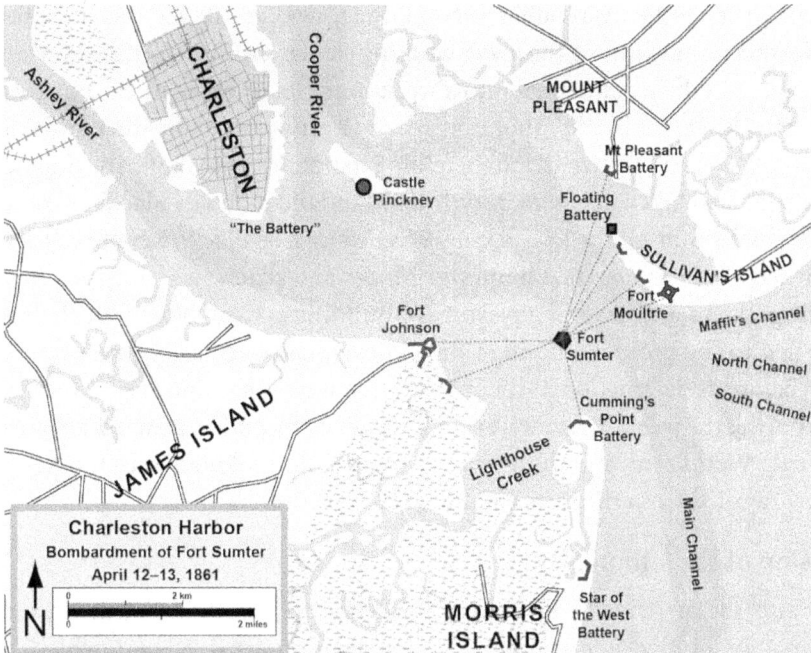

Fig. 5: In April 1861 in Charleston Harbor, South Carolina, all the forts except Fort Sumter were held by the Confederates. Fort Sumter was occupied by eighty-five Union soldiers when it surrendered.
Source: *Creative Commons Attribution 3.0 license. Map by Hal Jespersen, www.cwmaps.com*

eagerly volunteered at parades and barbecues that were held to attract recruits. Several states volunteered more regiments than had been requested. Ohio and Indiana offered almost three times their quotas of volunteers. But after the disastrous loss at the Battle of (First) Bull Run on July 21, 1861, more soldiers were needed. Congress authorized the enlistment of up to 500,000 three-year volunteers on July 22.

When quotas for the Northern armies were not met in July 1862 to meet the call for 300,000 volunteers, Congress enacted the Civil War Military Draft Act in March 1863, requiring all male citizens and immigrants who had filed for citizenship, between the ages of 20 and 45 years, to register for military service. Each state was assigned a quota of recruits to be enlisted, which included both draftees and volunteers. Most states preferred to enlist volunteers, and raised bounties for men to join up. The draft calls were repeated in March, July and December 1864. For the North, more than two million soldiers were enrolled in the Union Army during the four-year war.

A policy was instituted that allowed draftees to hire a substitute for $300, the equivalent of about $6,000 in today's currency, a large sum for most eligible males. The policy caused great resentment among most of the population. Congress abolished the practice in late 1863 after learning that many substitutes deserted soon after enrolling only to then re-enlist under another name to collect the bounty.

When the first lottery was published on July 11, 1863, resistance and anger broke out in the Northern cities among the lower working classes. In New York City's Manhattan district, anger at the draft turned into a week-long riot of white mobs, mostly of Irish descent, attacking free Blacks, abolitionists and antislavery sympathizers, because all people of color were not citizens and therefore exempt from the draft. The Emancipation Proclamation had taken effect January 1, 1863, and the mob saw Blacks as competitors who would take over all the low-paying jobs. Many free Blacks were beaten, tortured and lynched. The mob burned homes of Blacks and Black sympathizers, businesses employing Blacks and several government buildings. The Colored Orphan Asylum was burned to the ground, although the children had been safely moved to another location before its destruction. Over one hundred were killed and at least two thousand injured during the week. The riot was finally quelled by police, New York State militia, cadets from West Point, and the arrival of 4,000 Union soldiers from the Army of the Potomac, recalled from the recent Battle at Gettysburg.

Expansion of the Union Navy

Soon after the surrender of Fort Sumter to the Confederates, President Lincoln issued a Proclamation of Blockade against Southern ports on April 19, 1861, which included Virginia and North Carolina, states nearest the Union capital. The U.S. Navy was able to secure Fort Monroe on the Virginia peninsula and between August and December had established blockades at all but two of the major ports of the South. Wilmington, North Carolina, and Mobile, Alabama, would remain in Confederate hands until the final months of the war.

In April 1861 the U.S. Navy had only about forty ships in commission, but did have a well-established shipbuilding industry. Secretary of War Gideon Welles quickly began an accelerated program to increase its number of ships by converting merchant ships into naval ones, followed by a massive shipbuilding program. By the end of 1861, the Navy's number of blockading vessels had increased to one hundred sixty and fifty-two more warships were under construction. By the end of the war in 1865, the U.S. Navy had more than six hundred warships in active duty, and sixty-five were ironclads.

But the Union faced a massive challenge of patrolling the Confederate shoreline, which consisted of thirty-five hundred miles of shallow shores along the Atlantic Ocean and Gulf of Mexico coastlines, where blockade runners, using boats of shallow draft, successfully avoided capture. To meet the challenge, Secretary Welles reorganized the Navy into blockading squadrons. The North and South Atlantic Squadrons covered ports from Chesapeake Bay in Maryland to Key West, Florida, in the East and West Gulf Squadrons were responsible for ports between Key West to the Rio Grande in Texas. The Mississippi River Squadron was created in 1862 for operations in the Vicksburg Campaign.

III. WAR BEGINS, APRIL 1861

Confederate Volunteers and Draftees

The Battle of Fort Sumter had initiated the first deployment of the new Confederate States Army. Many of its officers had previously been on active duty with the U.S. Army, but resigned their commissions to join the Confederacy. On March 8, the Confederate Congress authorized a call for up to 100,000 volunteers for the Confederate States Army. Eight thousand volunteers were called on March 9 and 20,000 on April 8. After the battle at Fort Sumter, the call for volunteers was increased on April 16, 1861, to 49,000. Anticipating a short war, men eagerly volunteered to fight for the South and enlisted for one-year terms.

But the Battle of First Bull Run (or First Manassas) dispelled hopes of a short war and at the beginning of 1862, about half of the one-year enlistments would soon expire. A Confederate Conscription Act, passed in April 1862, affected all white men ages 18 to 35 for three-year terms and all one-year enlistments were extended to three years. In September, the age range was extended to age 45. Initially, a draftee could hire a substitute, similar to the Union practice, but the policy was heavily criticized and abolished in December 1863. A third Conscription Act in February 1864 changed the age from 17 to 50 years old, with an unlimited period of service, although 17-year-olds and men over forty-six were to only serve in home guards.

The "Twenty Negro Law," enacted in October 1862, allowed an overseer supervising twenty slaves on a plantation, to be exempted from military service. The 1860 Census showed that within those states that would join the Confederacy, nearly one-third of white families owned slaves, but the majority of them owned less than twenty and two-thirds of the population owned no slaves at all. All the overseers for the wealthy plantation planter class would be exempt. The law was resented by many in the South, spawning the cry, *"rich man's war but a poor man's fight."* Nevertheless, the Twenty Negro Law remained in place throughout the war because of fears that enough white overseers were needed to maintain productivity of the crops and to staunch any potential insurrections by Blacks.

The Confederacy had no navy at the beginning of the war and no shipbuilding industry that could create a steam engine large enough to power a ship. Its three naval yards at New Orleans, Louisiana; Pensacola, Florida; and Norfolk, Virginia, were all captured by the Union by 1862. Nevertheless, the South did convert or build over one hundred thirty ships, including thirty-seven ironclads, some with rams, during the war. They also developed "torpedoes," which were underwater mines that destroyed Union ships on contact.

By the end of the war, an estimated one million soldiers served in the Confederate States Army, which constituted a little more than half of all the white males of voting and military age in the Confederacy.

ORGANIZATION OF THE MILITARY UNITS

With the attacks on Fort Sumter, both North and South began accumulating troops, commanders and battle plans in preparation for war. Graduates of West Point and veterans of the Mexican War were highly sought by both sides. Initially, Northern state governors named the officers of the enlisting troops in the volunteers from their states, but with the second call for recruits, President Lincoln revised the organization of command. Companies and regimental officers would still be named by the men or the state's governor, but Lincoln would be in charge of appointing the generals from each state. This chain of command placed Lincoln in control of the generals and troops took orders only from the generals, eliminating governors from engaging in or directing field operations. For the Confederacy, President Davis was commander of all the generals from the beginning, but frequently relied on Gen. Robert E. Lee for advice.

Commanding Officer	Basic Fighting Unit	Category Composition
Colonel or Lieut. Colonel	Regiment: about 1,000 men in the North; 400-800 in the South.	10 Companies A-K, each containing 70-100 men (no company "J" because it could be confused with company "I"). Companies were commanded by a Captain.
Brigadier General	Brigade: average number: about 4,000 men.	2-6 Regiments
Major General	Division: about 12,000 men in the North; more in the South.	3-5 Brigades Confederates usually combined more brigades for a division.
Major General for the North; Lieut. General for the South.	Corps: about 36,000 men.	2-3 Divisions A Corps would include infantry, cavalry and artillery.
General (rank specified by General-in-Chief)	Army sizes varied.	2-3 Corps

General organization of both Union and Confederate armies during the Civil War. The total number of men in each category could vary between North and South.

Organization of the armies differed little between North and South. The United States manual was used as a model for the Confederacy with very few changes. A regiment constituted the primary fighting unit of the Civil War for both sides. Each regiment usually began with about 1,000 men in the Union Army; 400 to 800 in the

Confederacy. Regiments were named by number and state, such as the 1st Texas or 20th Maine. Each regiment began with ten companies, designated by letters of the alphabet, A through K. There was no Company "J" because of potential confusion with Company "I". Volunteers from the same county or region of a state were generally grouped together in companies, commanded by Captains. Regiments were commanded by Colonels, with Lieutenant Colonels as second-in-command. As casualties took their toll, smaller regiments were merged with others.

Brigades, which combined two to six regiments, were commanded by a Brigadier General for both North and South. In the Union Army, brigades were identified by number (the 2nd Brigade), but also by nicknames, such as the Iron Brigade. The Confederates named their brigades for their commander (e.g., the Stonewall Brigade, after "Stonewall" Jackson). Three to five brigades made up a Division in the Union Army; Confederate Divisions tended to include more brigades. Divisions were led by Major Generals. Two to four divisions would be brought together to form a Corps, which would combine units from infantry, cavalry and artillery. Union Corps were commanded by a Major General; a Confederate Corps was led by a Lieutenant-General.

Within Artillery regiments, a company was called a battery. A Union battery generally managed six cannons. Confederate batteries were smaller with only four cannons. Drivers took care of the horses that pulled wagons, cannons and caissons, the two-wheeled carriages that towed ammunition. Gunners repaired and serviced the cannons and carriages; teamsters drove the supply wagons. A typical Union Battery required ninety horses and included a blacksmith. Cavalry was organized into three batteries, each containing four companies.

An Army consisted of two or more corps. Both North and South had more than one army in the field, reporting to the General-in-Chief. Leadership at the corps level was determined by seniority among the major generals or specifically designated by the General-in-Chief. Seniority was based on rank, or if officers were of equal rank, the officer holding the older date of their rank had seniority. At the army level, the general acted with great independence to carry out an objective that had been broadly defined by their Commander-in-Chief or General-in-Chief. The personality and abilities of the commander and character of the region where they operated were primary parameters that determined their success.

The Union Army had four Generals-in-Chief during the course of the war, except for several months in 1862 when President Lincoln himself served in that role. Confederate President Davis served as its General-in-Chief for most of the war, except after January 31, 1865, when the 2nd Confederate States Congress appointed Gen. Robert E. Lee to the position, until his surrender at Appomattox in April 1865.

UNION AND CONFEDERATE NATIONAL FLAGS

The Union flag design remained constant during the Civil War except for changing the number of stars in the top left corner that represented the number of states in the Union. Lincoln refused to remove any stars after Southern states seceded. When the

Union's 35-star flag at end of Civil War

Civil War began, the flag had thirty-three stars, which designated all of the states, including Oregon, which had become a state in 1859. Known as the "Stars and Stripes," it was also referred to as "Old Glory." The 33-star flag flew over Fort Sumter when the first shots were fired in April 1861. Kansas joined the Union early in 1861, adding a 34th star, and West Virginia in 1863 gave the flag its 35th star. Although Nevada became a state in October 1864, the new 36-star flag would not be official until July 4, 1865, after the end of the war.

The first official Confederate flag included thirteen white stars in a circle on a blue square located in the top left corner (the canton) of the flag, against a field of three broad stripes, two red and one white. Known as the "Stars and Bars" flag, it represented the eleven states that seceded from the Union to form the Confederacy, plus two more stars for Missouri and

1st Confederate Flag

Kentucky, which had formed secessionist governments-in-exile. But during battle, the

2nd Confederate Flag

flag was too similar to the Union flag and a new design was developed. The second flag, adopted in 1863 and known as the Stainless Banner, used the Confederate Battle Flag as the canton against a solid field of white. The Battle Flag, designed by Confederate Gen. P.G.T. Beauregard, displayed thirteen stars on two blue lines, outlined in white, crossing diagonally across a red field. But commanders complained that the solid field of white, when hanging limply, could be mistaken as a flag of truce or surrender.

During battles, troops frequently cut off the solid white part of the flag, leaving only the Battle Flag to be visible. Confederates used the Battle Flag almost exclusively as their flag in battle. A third flag design, adopted in March 1865, used the same Battle Flag for its canton against a field of white with a single red vertical stripe on the right edge. The war would end a few months later.

3rd and last Confederate Flag

III. WAR BEGINS, APRIL 1861

Both North and South believed the war would be short-lived. But America's Civil War would endure for more than four years, take the lives of over 750,000 soldiers and an estimated 50,000 civilians, leaving large areas of the South decimated by the ravages of battle.

Southerners would often refer to the war as the War of Northern Aggression, the War for Southern Independence or the War of Secession. Other names, echoed in the North, called it the War Between the States, War of the Rebellion or War for the Union. Most poignantly, it was sometimes called The Brothers' War, as brothers would often face each other from opposite sides on the battlefield.

STRENGTHS AND WEAKNESSES: NORTH VS SOUTH

Both North and South anticipated early victory after the first shots at Fort Sumter. The industrialized North not only possessed abundant facilities for manufacturing ships, arms, ammunition and other supplies, it had a navy and a substantial network of railways for transporting troops, supplies and weapons. The North's twenty thousand miles of railroad track far surpassed the South's nine thousand. Both sides used the seventeen hundred miles of track in the Border States. But the South had a significant disadvantage with their railroad systems, because many states incorporated different gauges for their tracks, creating barriers for interstate troop movements.

The Union possessed over one hundred thousand factories while the Confederacy had less than ten thousand. More than ninety-five percent of the country's firearms and all of the railroad locomotives had been produced in the North. Nevertheless, the South was able to keep ammunition flowing to its guns and melted down bells from churches and town squares to help supply the demand.

Another big advantage for the Union was its long shipbuilding industry in New England and a large merchant marine. The South had virtually no naval resources, which enabled the Union to blockade nearly all the Confederate seaports early in the war. The port of New Orleans, Louisiana, fell to the North in the spring of 1862, the second year of the war. Once Vicksburg and Port Hudson on the Mississippi River surrendered to the Union in July 1863, the North controlled the entire river for the remainder of the war, cutting off Confederate armies in the West from those in the East. The South maintained control of two seaports, Mobile Bay, Alabama, and Wilmington, North Carolina, until nearly the end of the war, enabling blockade runners to support the South. But supplies were limited as their ships were small and built for speed. In addition, importation of items not manufactured in the South were also greatly reduced, which included food, medicine, gunpowder, mechanical parts for machines, and other war supplies.

But the South had its advantages, too. A long coast line with multiple harbors and navigable rivers made it difficult for the Union Navy to prevent Southern blockade runners. Fighting a defensive war in its own territory provided Southerners with a geographical benefit, knowing the lay of the land and the ability to influence local inhabitants. The South had a strong military tradition from wars against the British, Spanish, Mexicans and Indians and provided experienced leaders with military skill and bravery. The South's cavalry consistently out-performed the North's during the first two years of the war.

The 1860 census showed a total population of 31.4 million people in the United States. But the division between North and South showed a distinct advantage for the North. Not counting the Far West or the Border States of Missouri, Kentucky, Maryland and Delaware, the Confederacy's eleven states had a population of 9.0 million people, which included 3.5 million slaves. The North's population totaled 18.9 million with virtually no slaves. The Border States, with a combined total population of about 3.5 million, of which one half million were slaves, contributed soldiers to both sides. The Far West states contributed soldiers, mostly to the North, and included California, Oregon and the Territories of New Mexico, Utah, Washington, Nebraska and Dakota. Kansas became admitted as a free state in February 1861 and enlisted about 20,000 men into the Union Army. During the war, Union armies typically outnumbered their Confederate opponents and towards the end of the war, the South was forced to enlist young boys and old men into local militias to support local defenses.

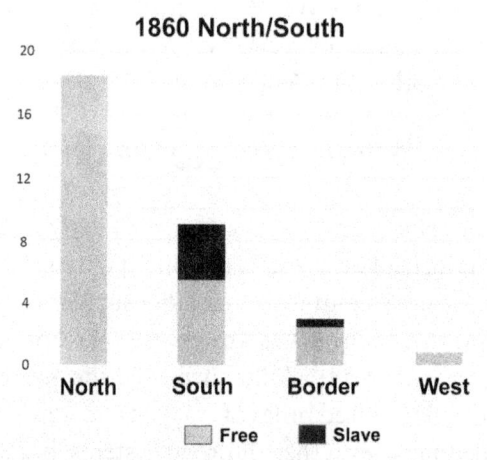

Fig. 6: Graph shows relative populations of North and South at the beginning of the Civil War.

At the early stage of the Confederacy in February 1861, the seven seceded states carried out a self-imposed embargo to stop the sale of cotton from their borders, expecting to generate a world-wide economic crisis that would achieve global recognition for their new nation. Confederate leaders had long believed that European consumers of its cotton, particularly Great Britain's massive textile industry, could support the Confederacy with the purchase of its cotton. Voluntarily implementing an embargo on its cotton exports in the summer of 1861, the Confederacy waited for England to recognize its sovereignty and independence from the Union and give support to its cause. But international recognition did not come.

The textile industries of Britain and France had large cotton stockpiles thanks to bumper American crops the years before the secession. England had already stockpiled about a million bales of cotton and had developed an active trade in other commodities

THE CIVIL WAR SOLDIER

About three million soldiers served in the war, two million in the Union Army and an estimated eight hundred thousand to one million in the Confederacy. The average soldier was about 26 years old and the majority were farmers before the war. Although most were native-born, both sides included large numbers of immigrants from Germany and Ireland. Men fought to preserve the Union, state pride, the chance for adventure and/or steady pay. Toward the end of the war, the Northern soldier fought to end slavery if only to bring the war to an end. The Southern soldier feared a society where Blacks were on an equal footing with whites and fought to preserve their way of life and their homes. Privates were initially paid $11 per month on both sides, but raised to $16 by 1864, slightly more for the Confederates, given their inflated currency. Soldiers expected to be paid every two months, but four-month intervals were common and during the final months of the war, the Southern soldier was not paid at all. After the Emancipation Proclamation, implemented January 1, 1863, Blacks could enlist in the Union military, but were deducted $3 for a clothing allowance.

Uniforms were not well established in the first battles and consisted of a variety of styles and colors representing the different states. For many, the early soldier simply wore what he brought from home. The Union uniform evolved to a dark blue wool coat, blue pants and hat. Shoes came up to their ankles and were called "brogans." Confederate uniforms developed into a uniform of grey, including coat, trousers and hat. Union soldiers were often referred to as the "blues," and "greys" for the South. With wear and tear and constant use, the Confederate uniforms acquired a light brown appearance, producing the nickname "Butternut." Shoes for both sides were frequently unavailable, forcing men to walk barefooted.

More than 800,000 deaths were attributed to the Civil War, including 750,000 soldiers (according to recent estimates) and more than 50,000 civilians. About one in four soldiers who went to war did not return home. Battle deaths accounted for more than 200,000; the rest were from disease and illness, primarily diarrhea and dysentery, typhoid, malaria, smallpox and chickenpox, whooping cough and mumps. All took their toll. About eighteen percent of white males in the South, ages 13 to 45, died in the war; in the North, about six percent of that age group. An estimated 60,000 men lost limbs during the war from amputations. Black troops constituted about 200,000 of the Union forces and about twenty percent of their number lost their lives. An estimated 20,000 American Indians served in the Civil War for both the Union and the Confederacy.

with the United States. Britain was importing many American goods besides cotton, particularly raw materials, and was also marketing its own products to the Americans, particularly in the North. Not interested in a war with the United States, the United Kingdom and France soon declared neutrality from America's Civil War.

The Union's blockade on the South's ports continued to expand through the war as more ships were pressed into service, drastically limiting the Confederacy's export of cotton and the financial resources to support the war. Further, the South was left with millions of bales of cotton from its own embargo that it could not market. News of the reduction of cotton exports from America prompted India, Egypt and Brazil to rapidly increase their cotton production and soon filled in the gap for Britain's textile industry.

VIEWS FROM THE PUBLIC AS WAR BEGINS

About the attack on Senator Sumner ...

The vicious caning of Massachusetts Sen. Charles Sumner in Senate chambers was widely reported in newspapers, both North and South. The Northern public was appalled by the attack on a congressman that occurred in the chambers of the national capital. Rallies and meetings were held to protest the event which had the effect of attracting supporters to the new Republican Party.

In the South, Preston Brooks, the South Carolina Democrat who had beaten Sumner senseless with a heavy walking cane, was declared a hero. Southern men began carrying canes to show their support and multiple newspapers produced cartoons of men with raised canes as they prepared to beat opponents.

About Lincoln's election to the Presidency ...

When Lincoln was nominated to the Presidency at the Republican National Convention in May 1860, his supporters sought a nickname for the coming campaign that would have wide appeal. "Honest Abe" was a favorite but the nickname "Railsplitter" was the name that captured the attention of the press and his appeal to voters. As a young man, Lincoln had split wood for many rail fences while growing up on his father's farm and as a hired hand to nearby farms. At the convention, two rails, decorated with flags, streamers and his name, "Abraham Lincoln, the Rail Candidate," filled the crowd with enthusiasm and the name stuck. Many in the audience shared a similar background and the image strengthened the qualities of hard work and self-reliance.

The election of Abraham Lincoln to the Presidency was greatly supported by free states and generally followed the geographical pattern of states north of the Mason-Dixon Line. Lincoln carried more than fifty percent of the votes in the North and West, but only two percent in the South. His election was proudly proclaimed in the *Chester County Times* in Pennsylvania. "A Clean Sweep! The Country Redeemed" Secession is Rebuked!! Let the Traitors Rave!"

III. WAR BEGINS, APRIL 1861

As news of Lincoln's successful election trickled into the waiting throngs in Springfield, Indiana, Lincoln's home, men began to shout with joy and surrounded the President-Elect with congratulations. Church bells pealed, the entire city shouted from its roof tops and rallies continued until dawn. The Election Day cannon thundered.

The Pony Express, which began operations in April 1860, carried mail on relays of men and horses from St. Joseph on the Missouri River to Sacramento, California, for a period of eighteen months. The first Pony Express rider arrived in California on April 14 having taken only ten days after it left Missouri, a distance of 1,800 miles. News of the presidential election in November reached Sacramento on November 14, just eight days after Election Day in record time. Headlines presented the news of Lincoln's election to wide acclaim in all the California papers, including the *Daily Alta California* of San Francisco. The heroic efforts of the Pony Express were discontinued when the telegraph line between San Francisco and New York was completed in October 1861.

From Kentucky, a Border State, the *New York Times* Correspondent there brought this report: "*Since Mr. LINCOLN's election, the Secessionists here, if there be any, have kept dark and mum. They now scarcely squint at secession. The only point and stand our Breckites* (Breckinridge supporters) *now make is that Kentucky will not let Uncle Sam's troops cross her territory to whip in any of her skittish Southern sisters. They freely admit that Kentucky will not kick up or flash up because Mr. LINCOLN will be President, but will "wait and hope;" and, while not pledged unconditionally to the Union, nor to the surrender of her rights for the sake of peace, still believe there are peaceful remedies within the Union for all impending evils, and will urge upon her sisters moderation and forbearance, and use all her influence to induce them to remain in the Union 'until there is no hope.'*" Lincoln had received less than one percent of the vote in Kentucky.

Blacks were disappointed with Lincoln's position that he would not end slavery in the seceded states. Although Lincoln opposed slavery on principle, he did not believe that the Constitution granted him the authority to end it where it already existed, as the Constitution protected property and slaves were property. Further, he was not convinced in 1860 that Blacks possessed the necessary attributes that qualified them for citizenship. His views on that subject would change over the course of the Civil War and by 1863 he would advocate full citizenship for Blacks and enlist them in the military.

But with his election to the Presidency, the South portrayed Lincoln as a champion for the Black man and presented him in cartoons as planning to prove the superiority of Blacks over the Anglo-Saxon race. The *Charleston Mercury* described him as *a "horrid looking wretch."* He was pictured in cartoons dancing with Black women and forcing the inter-marriage of Blacks with Whites. Some of the Southern coverage described Lincoln as a traitorous Black Republican, including speculation that he must contain "African-American" blood and cartoons showed him as a baboon.

The *Petersburg, Virginia, Express* reported in the *New York Times* on November 10, 1860: "The great national or sectional, battle has been fought, and although the official report of it has not been completed, there can be no manner of doubt that victory has perched upon the Black Republican banner. The issue has been disastrous to the Union cause; for the triumph of sectionalism has laid the foundation for all the mischiefs and ills to the country which were predicted and deprecated by WASHINGTON in his Farewell Address. It is a gloomy exercise of the mind to contemplate the new aspect of things, but the people must look at it and ponder it. It is time now for the wisest hands and most patriotic hearts in the land to enlist in the great work of adjusting matters in such a way as to save the Republic, if possible, from the almost certain perdition which stares it in the face."

The paper also reported that many Virginia officers in the U.S. Army had resigned, concluding that the election of Lincoln was just cause for dissolution from the Union.

About coverage of the War …

Newspaper subscriptions were in high demand in both the North and South during the Civil War, as they were virtually the only source of information for the average citizen about events outside their community. Nearly every town of any size had at least one weekly paper and the larger cities published daily papers. As the war progressed, news of the outcomes of battles, often communicated by telegraph, was vigorously followed and repeated in other newspapers. Daily casualty reports of state regiments were published as newspapers often received the list of killed and wounded before the information was communicated to the next of kin.

Editors exerted great power and influence in forming public opinion in their communities as they digested the news and conveyed their views to subscribers. Northern newspapers were powerful in their reach as the news of their reports and periodicals were copied and reprinted throughout the country, particularly in the South.

Most of the larger newspapers sent reporters to travel with the armies and they reported directly from the battlefield. New York City newspapers were particularly influential. The *New York Herald*, critical of Lincoln, but supportive of the Union, used fifty to sixty staffers to cover news of the war once the Civil War began. The *New York Tribune*, founded by Horace Greeley, became one of the country's most influential newspapers. The *Tribune* and the *Times* each had twenty reporters and illustrators reporting to their offices. Both *Harper's Weekly* and *Illustrated Newspaper* supported artists to provide sketches, drawings and maps of battles. Although newspapers could not yet print photographs, sketch artists that reproduced scenes of battles were called "specials." A sketch of the Battle of Fort Sumter was printed on page one of the *New York Illustrated News* on April 20, 1861. The military, however, on both sides, used censorship to suppress much of the news from the front lines of armies in battle as its content could inform the enemy of troop movements, battle plans and the status of morale.

At the beginning of the war, there were about one hundred forty newspapers and periodicals in Virginia, with nearly every town supporting at least a weekly paper. As the war progressed, however, the Southern press suffered ever increasing handicaps to publish the news. Loss of men to the war effort and a diminishing source of materials, such as paper, ink and machinery, steadily reduced the number of functioning newspapers. Printing became more and more expensive as inflation increased the cost of everything. Transportation and communication services declined as well, increasing the difficulty of getting the news distributed.

About white supremacy ...

Southern editors largely subscribed to the purported "science of the day," expressed in a treatise by R. R. Cobb of Georgia, a leading secessionist lawyer and brother of Howell Cobb, one of the Confederacy's founders. Cobb's treatise postulated that whites were the superior race over the Negro, and slavery was a natural consequence of white supremacy. Alexander Stephens, Vice-President of the Confederacy, declared that *"Our new government is founded ... upon the great truth that the Negro is not equal to the white man ... slavery is his natural condition."*

Northern opinion, on the other hand, generally opposed slavery as an institution, but many tolerated it among their Southern neighbors as a necessary component for the South's economic security. The abolitionist movement, with its beginnings in the North, advocated civil liberties for Blacks and the total elimination of slavery and was supported throughout many of the Northern states. Southerners hated abolitionists, because if Blacks were placed on equal footing with the white man, supremacy of whites and the Southern way of life would be jeopardized.

About avoiding a War, or not ...

The *New York Times* reported on January 3, 1861, about a meeting in Philadelphia that included about one hundred leading citizens. One resolution that was adopted denied the right of the South to secede and recommended that the military establishments of Pennsylvania be placed on a war footing. But a second resolution supported the South for its right to independence and the North should acknowledge it instead of waging an unlawful war. The debate was referred to a committee.

Salem, Indiana, the county seat of Washington County, located only forty miles from the Kentucky border, had many Southern immigrants in its community who had either owned slaves or had relatives who still did. Although Indiana was a free state prohibiting slavery, its Constitution denied the right for Blacks to move into the state and settle there. Public meetings in January and February 1861 urged compromise to prevent war or disunion, as a separation from the South would be fatal to the *"prosperity, glory and wealth of the state."* Meetings continued to be held through the following months, all urging preservation of the Union, but avoiding war with the South.

A moderating opinion from the South was expressed in Raleigh's *North Carolina Standard*: *"As hostile as we may be to Mr. Lincoln, the cause of our country, now in fearful perils, requires that we should be just even towards him. But the Union cannot be maintained by force ... Let both governments scrupulously abstain from any act that may lead to bloodshed. Let things remain as they are, if possible, until ... a Convention of all the States could either reconstruct the Union or permit the seceded States to go in peace. As it is, we appear to be drifting to civil strife against the wish of the people of the United States, and without their having had any opportunity in their primary capacity to remove the evils which threaten all of us, both North and South, with one common ruin."*

Virginia's *Richmond Dispatch* reported April 11 on a resolution from a public meeting in Prince George, Virginia, a neighboring community of Richmond, *" ... that the interest and honor of Virginia require that she should separate from the Northern States of America, now controlled by a hostile party, whose ultimate object is the overthrow of slavery and oppression of the Southern States."*

When the Confederacy's capital was moved to Richmond in late May 1861, the city became the center for Confederate news. Reports from its four dailies, the *Dispatch*, *Whig*, *Examiner* and *Enquirer* were followed and repeated widely throughout the South. With the firing on Fort Sumter, celebration parades in Richmond displayed a large flag of the Confederacy across Main Street. The Richmond *Dispatch* printed, *"We go forth to meet the deadly foe—Let the strife begin. We have no fear of the issue."*

About the Confederate Flag ...

The first flag for the Confederacy was displayed in March in Montgomery, Alabama, the Confederate capital before it was moved to Richmond, and immediately drew criticism from a number of the Southern fronts. Richmond's *Southern Literary Messenger*, a literary magazine, declared that the flag was a *"detested parody"* of the U.S. flag. *"It resembles the Yankee flag and that is enough to make it unutterably detestable."* The *Charleston Mercury* stated *" ... the 'Stars and Bars' will never do for us. They resemble too closely the dishonored 'Flag of Yankee Doodle' ... we imagine that the 'Battle Flag' will become the Southern Flag by popular acclaim."*

A new design was offered from the Savannah *Morning News* that featured the Battle Flag on a white background, accompanied by the statement, *"As a people we are fighting to maintain the Heaven-ordained supremacy of the white man over the inferior or colored race; a white flag would thus be emblematical of our cause."* But its use on the battle field often conveyed surrender or a truce when the flag hung limply and only the white was exposed. Southern commanders frequently cut off the white portion of the flag, so that the battle flag stood alone.

III. WAR BEGINS, APRIL 1861

About the attack on Fort Sumter ...

The *Charleston Mercury* described the opening salvo on Fort Sumter on April 12 as the *"first great scene of a momentous drama that might consist of a single act."* The general feeling among Southerners was that the North was not willing to fight and the "old government" would abandon its hope of forcible control over the Confederate States with the surrender of Fort Sumter. Charleston residents watched with great anticipation as the shells burst over the Fort and flames raged over its barracks. When Fort Sumter flew the white flag of truce, people of Charleston came out in boats to excitedly watch its surrender. Southern cities celebrated by firing cannons and ringing bells. Headlines proclaimed a glorious and bright future for the South as their editors declared the rightness of the Confederate cause as they asserted that God was on their side.

The Northern public reacted to the attack on Fort Sumter with a heated response. Signs proclaiming "Death to Traitors" were hung from lampposts in Pittsburg, Pennsylvania. When the news reached Baltimore, Maryland, people flocked to the newspaper offices and gathered in angry groups to discuss the event for several hours. Throughout the North, flags were raised, parades attracted large crowds, and loyal meetings were held in almost every church and schoolhouse. Crowds of men gathered on sidewalks with only one subject under discussion and that was "War." Business came to a virtual standstill, such as in New York City, where the news had the effect of suspending almost all business and grave uncertainty prevailed through the financial circles.

Some editors deplored the catastrophe as the beginning of a bloody war between brethren who had previously stood shoulder-to-shoulder protecting their common rights. But others demanded a call to action. The *New York Post* printed *"In the name of constitutional liberty; in the name of law and order; in the name of all that is dear to freemen; we shall put down treason and restore the supremacy of the Constitution."* The *New York Tribune* criticized Lincoln for not acting quickly and urged a rapid Union counter-attack on the Confederacy. The paper coined the phrase *"On to Richmond,"* and Editor Greeley urged occupation of Richmond before the Confederate Congress could meet on July 20.

Resolutions were passed at town meetings. Some urged the government to crush the treasonous rebellion and restore the authority and supremacy of the United States and its legal jurisdiction within the seceded States. Others deplored any act that would require them to take arms against their Southern brethren and pleaded for a peaceful reconciliation that would allow the South to maintain its independence and civil rights.

The Salem, Indiana, *Times,* wrote: *"The heart of every true lover of the Union is fired into a blaze of indignation at the attack on Fort Sumter and the insults offered to the star-spangled banner, the pride of the United States, and her true-hearted sons and daughters. Shall this glorious Union be destroyed, broken up, wiped out, by rebels who are rallying under a rattlesnake flag? Is a question that rises in the name of every patriot,*

Shall the American flag be insulted and trailed in the dust? Will Union men look quietly on and see the Capitol fall into the hands of traitors? Never! Never!"

But the Salem *Democrat* wrote an opposing view: *"The battle has begun, and God only knows when it will end. The Abolition party of the land are responsible for the calamity. Abraham Lincoln has done the deed that all good men should regret. He has laid his impious hand upon the best Government man was ever blessed with. By his orders civil war is inaugurated; brother made to fight against brother; and he is but the embodiment of the party he leads. Lincoln, to all appearances an imbecile old ignoramus, is an instrument in the hands of bad men to destroy the Union … Now he imbrues his hands in the blood of his countrymen, and calls for 75,000 Abolition cohorts to help him carry devastation and carnage among our Southern brethren … Men of Washington County, will you do it? Will you imbrue your hands in the blood of your friends? Will you wage war upon your kinsmen? No, you never will!"*

IV. THE FIRST YEAR: 1861

AFTER THE SURRENDER OF FORT SUMTER, PRESIDENT ABRAHAM LINCOLN MADE A call to arms on April 15, 1861, for 75,000 volunteers " ... *to preserve the honor, integrity and existence of our National Union."* His message to Congress on July 4 declared that the attempt by the Confederacy to destroy the "Federal Union" by secession was illegal, unconstitutional and must be defeated. If the Union was to be preserved as a "United States of America," an army would be needed to crush the Confederacy, because the South could succeed by doing nothing.

As Union and Confederate commanders prepared for war, the regions of battle fell into three principal theaters. The Eastern Theater included the area east of the Appalachian Mountains near the two competing capitals of Washington, D.C., and Richmond, Virginia, and the Shenandoah Valley of Virginia. The Western Theater encompassed a broad region west of the Appalachians to the Mississippi River, including Kentucky and Tennessee, but also incorporating the states of Florida, Georgia and the Carolinas. Alabama and most of Mississippi fell into the Western Theater, but were also associated with the Gulf Coast. The Trans-Mississippi Theater included areas west of the Mississippi River, most importantly, Missouri, Arkansas and Louisiana, plus Texas and New Mexico and Indian Territories. The Navy engaged in battles along the coasts and inland waterways to capture blockade runners that were supplying the Confederacy with arms, ammunition and a variety of domestic goods. But the Navy also halted the export of cotton, a major source of currency for the Confederates.

The first battles occurred in the Eastern Theater based on the belief that the Union Army could quickly capture Richmond, the Confederate capital, located only about one hundred miles south of Washington, D.C., and bring the war to a speedy end. Several Union campaigns over the first three years of the war pursued that objective, but they all failed, due to inadequate leadership of the Northern generals, the challenges presented by eastern weather and the superior abilities on the battlefield of Confederate

Gen. Robert E. Lee. Richmond would remain in Confederate control until the final days of the war, the spring of 1865.

In the summer of 1861, after the Battle of Fort Sumter in April, the first battles of the war occurred in western Virginia as both North and South competed to protect their transportation routes through the region. But the first major battle, the Battle of First Bull Run at Manassas, Virginia, occurred in July when two large armies confronted each other at the small river of Bull Run, producing large casualties for both sides. Minor engagements in the Western Theater in the fall occurred near the confluence of the Mississippi and Ohio Rivers as the Union protected its positions on several important rivers.

"FREEDOM FORTRESS"

In May 1861, Union Gen. Benjamin Butler, commanding Fort Monroe at the tip of the Virginia Peninsula, issued his famous decree that declared all slaves behind Union lines would be considered contraband of war and would not be returned to their owners. Butler argued that the Confederacy used slaves to build fortifications and support other activities in its war against the Union and therefore represented a military threat. The federal Fugitive Slave Act of 1850 did not apply because the states had seceded from the Union. The policy was then adopted by the entire Union Army and soon extended to the Union Navy. Fort Monroe became known as "Freedom's Fortress" and thousands of slaves fled to the fort. The army built a large Contraband Camp to house the families.

Names associated with military confrontations soon became familiar to the general population as conflicts were rapidly reported in the popular press. Union names for the battles tended to be designated by rivers or other landscape features near the battlefield, while Confederate designations frequently named the battle for the nearest town. In the battle descriptions that follow, Union designations are given first with the Confederate name often included in parentheses. The progress of the war is described in chronological order within the given Theaters (Eastern, Western, Trans-Mississippi) as the battles occurred. Brief accounts of the most important battles are summarized in highlighted text boxes. Many of the battles are illustrated with maps of the engagement that show the general positions of the combatants.

BATTLES IN THE EASTERN THEATER

Skirmishes, engagements and battles between North and South began almost immediately after the firing on Fort Sumter. The first battle of the war occurred in western Virginia. When Virginia seceded from the Union, western Virginia refused to secede and separated itself from its mother state. Divided by the Allegheny Mountains and rugged landscape, a natural barrier had formed between western Virginia and the rest of the state, creating separate economic, cultural and political philosophies for the two regions. West Virginia would not become a separate state until June 1863, but during 1861-62, it functioned as a Border State, geographically associated with the South, but with Union loyalties.

Battle of Philippi, Western Virginia
June 3, 1861

Northwestern Virginia had few roads and railroads which presented military challenges for the North, because Confederates were able to conceal their operations in the sympathetic and neighboring Shenandoah Valley east of the Allegheny Mountains. But maintaining control of transportation routes for troops and supplies through western Virginia was a major goal for both North and South. In the month of May 1861, Union command received reports that a small Confederate force was burning railroad bridges and threatening the Baltimore & Ohio railroad in northwestern Virginia, a major supply line for the Union.

Responding to the threat, Union Army General-in-Chief Winfield Scott organized the Department of Ohio, which would cover Ohio, Indiana, Illinois, western Pennsylvania and western Virginia and Missouri. A natural choice for a commander in the region was George B. McClellan, who was serving as president of the Ohio & Mississippi Railroad. McClellan had graduated second in his class from West Point in 1846 and was a veteran of the Mexican-American War. Resigning his position with the railroad on May 3, 1861, McClellan was commissioned as a major general and commander of the Department of Ohio and immediately moved troops into western Virginia.

The first battle of the Civil War after the firing on Fort Sumter occurred in the small town of Philippi, located in western Virginia, west of the Allegheny Mountains, about forty-five miles south of the Pennsylvania border and near the B&O Railroad line which ran through Grafton, Virginia. A two-pronged movement of Union troops, converging from different directions on Philippi before dawn on June 3, surprised the Confederate recruits, who rapidly fled thirty miles south to Beverly, near Rich and Cheat Mountains. A precursor to the Battle of First Bull Run (or First Manassas) which would occur on July 21, 1861, the minor engagement at Philippi resulted in only four Union and twenty-six Confederate casualties, but the battle aroused headlines in the Northern press as a major victory for the Union and brought McClellan to overnight prominence.

Battles of Rich Mountain & Cheat Mountain Pass, Western Virginia
July-September 1861

After the Battle of Philippi, Gen. George B. McClellan, commanding the Department of the Ohio with 5,000 troops, pursued the Confederates and found Southern forces near Beverly, Virginia (now West Virginia). Confederates had set up an overlook camp at Rich Mountain, just west of Beverly, to protect the Staunton-Parkersburg Turnpike, an important roadway for the Confederacy that supplied raw materials needed for arms and ammunition. McClellan organized a surprise attack, dividing his forces between himself and his aide-de-camp, Gen. William Rosecrans. With guidance from a local sympathizer, Rosecrans led his half of the army on July 11, 1861, up a mountain path through dense woods in a drenching rain to attack the Confederate camp at its rear. The surprised Southerners, heavily outnumbered, took cover behind rocks and trees, but eventually had to withdraw into the woods where they were pursued by Union troops.

The planned assault was supposed to include a frontal advance from McClellan's half of the army, but it never materialized. The battle, lasting about two hours, resulted in a Union victory and the capture of several hundred prisoners. Although the success was largely due to Rosecrans, McClellan did not share the credit and became the hero of another Union victory. He would soon be called to Washington by Lincoln to command the new Army of the Potomac. With McClellan's departure, Rosecrans was named as commander of the Union forces in western Virginia and would continue to advance and become a leading commander in several important battles in the Western Theater during the Civil War.

After defeating the Confederates at Rich Mountain, Union troops concentrated on defending the Staunton and Parkersburg Turnpike at Cheat Mountain Pass, located between Beverly and Philippi. Col. Nathan Kimball, commanding the 14th Indiana regiment, held the Union fortress on the summit of Cheat Mountain.

Following the Confederate defeat at Philippi, Gen. Robert E. Lee was sent to coordinate Southern troops in northwestern Virginia and regain control of the area. Commanding the Confederate Army of the Northwest, Lee planned an assault on Union troops at the summit of Cheat Mountain for September 12, 1861. A driving rain, thick underbrush and poor communications weakened the initial Southern attack on the mountain. When the exhausted Confederates finally reached the summit, they faced Kimball's three hundred aggressive Union defenders. Believing they were badly outnumbered, the Southerners quickly retreated. Casualties were small as there was little fighting. But the battle revealed the leadership of Col. Kimball, who had left a medical practice to serve in the Mexican-American War where he had distinguished himself in the Battle of Buena Vista. After the war, he returned to his medical practice in Indiana, but then re-enlisted in the U.S. Army at the onset of the Civil War. Kimball would soon play important roles as a leading commander in several important battles in the Eastern Theater.

Gen. Lee withdrew his troops from Cheat Mountain and when his attempts at other offensive operations in the region met with failure, he withdrew to Richmond October 30. The battles at Rich Mountain and Cheat Mountain Pass paved the way for

Union control in northwestern Virginia for the rest of the war, enabling its residents to complete its secession from the mother state of Virginia and form the new free State of West Virginia, which was finally admitted as the 35th state of the Union in June 1863.

Battle of First Bull Run (First Manassas), Virginia
July 21, 1861

At the beginning of hostilities, President Lincoln wanted a quick ending to the war by capturing the Confederate capital of Richmond, Virginia, only one hundred miles south of Washington, D.C. Similarly, the Confederacy wanted a quick victory by capturing the Union capital. Both sides looked at the small town of Manassas, Virginia, about thirty-five miles southwest of Washington, with two major railroad lines that provided access to the Shenandoah Valley and the best overland route between Washington and Richmond. Command of the Union Army of Northeastern Virginia had fallen to Irvin McDowell, a career military man with extensive abilities in logistics and supply, but with no combat experience. When Gen. McDowell protested that his inexperienced 90-day recruits were not ready, Lincoln responded, *"You are green, it is true, but they are green also; you are all green alike."*

On July 16, 1861, Union Gen. McDowell led his 35,000-man army from Washington toward Manassas, Virginia, to meet 22,000 Confederate soldiers under Gen. P.G.T. Beauregard, the Confederacy's "Hero of Fort Sumter," who had established defenses along Bull Run, a small river near the Manassas Railroad Junction. Large crowds of spectators from the Washington capital, including reporters, government officials, members of Congress and wealthy private citizens in fancy carriages, followed the army, some with picnic baskets, expecting to see a splendid show.

When the two inexperienced armies met at Bull Run, there was confusion in the opening battles. Soldiers on both sides wore non-distinctive clothing, mostly what they had brought from home, as neither side had yet had time to create uniforms for their troops. The great similarity between the two flags, the Stars and Stripes (Union), versus the Stars and Bars (Confederate) made it difficult to distinguish the two flags during battle. Initial fierce fire from the Union side pushed the Southerners back. But as the battle progressed, Confederate reinforcements appeared from the Shenandoah Valley under the command of Gen. Joseph E. Johnston to reinforce Beauregard's troops.

Johnston's 12,000 men had made a forced march to reach the Manassas Gap Railroad, eluding Union troops along the way and then traveled by train to enter the battlefield at a critical point. Leading a brigade, Confederate Gen. Thomas Jackson from the Virginia Military Institute held a line on Henry Hill against an intense Union assault when a Confederate officer urged his men, *"There is Jackson, standing like a stone wall. Rally behind the Virginians!"* From that rallying call, Jackson became known as "Stonewall Jackson" for the rest of the war and became one of the Confederacy's most capable

Fig. 7: Battle of First Bull Run, Manassas, Virginia. July 21, 1861. The Union Army under Gen. McDowell was defeated by the Confederates, commanded by Gen. P.G.T. Beauregard. The routed Union Army fled to Washington, losing many wounded soldiers to be captured.

Source: *Creative Commons Attribution 3.0 license. Map by Hal Jespersen, www.cwmaps.com*

generals. His tough, disciplined army would soon defeat Union armies much larger in size, making him a hero for the Confederacy and the Southern public.

With fresh Southern troops entering the battle, a Union brigade was pushed back and Beauregard ordered his entire line forward. Union troops began to panic and soon the Northern army was disintegrating as men ran from the battlefield. The rout became worse as soldiers encountered a massive chaos of tangled wagons, artillery, ambulances and jammed carriages of civilians and observers, who were there to see the spectacle. The frightened young troops stampeded away from the battlefield in complete disarray, discarding weapons, food and canteens along the way, arriving in Washington thirty-six hours later, completely exhausted and devastated. The Secretary of War ordered all the

IV. THE FIRST YEAR: 1861

FIRST MAJOR BATTLE
Battle of First Bull Run (First Manassas), July 21, 1861

On July 16, 1861 Union Gen. Irvin McDowell led the 35,000-man Army of Northeastern Virginia from Washington toward Manassas Junction, Virginia, to meet 22,000 Confederate soldiers under Gen. P.G.T. Beauregard, who had led the Southern victory at Fort Sumter. Hundreds of spectators from the capital, including reporters, government officials and private citizens, which included many of society's elite, followed the army, some with picnic baskets, expecting to see a splendid display of Union superiority over the Confederate forces. The two inexperienced armies converged at a small river, known as Bull Run.

As the battle progressed, Confederate Gen. Joseph E. Johnston arrived with 12,000 men from the Shenandoah Valley, mostly by railroad, to reinforce Beauregard's army. As troops under Confederate Gen. Thomas Jackson from the Virginia Military Institute held the line on Henry Hill against intense Union fire, he became known as "Stonewall Jackson" and would become one of the Confederacy's most famous and capable generals.

When the Northern soldiers faced fresh Southern troops, their lines broke, which quickly became a rout as panic replaced discipline. The shattered Union Army arrived in Washington thirty-six hours later, but there was no pursuit by the Confederates. As news became known of the largest and bloodiest battle that the country had ever experienced, a shocked nation came to realize that the war would not be short and settled by a single conclusive battle. The battle was a wake-up call for Lincoln and his Cabinet as they also concluded that there would be no swift solution to quickly defeat the Confederacy. Congress immediately authorized an enlarged Union army of 500,000 volunteers, to enlist for three years.

militia units to Washington fearing an invasion of Confederate forces in hot pursuit of the defeated Union army. But Southern troops, exhausted and disorganized, did not pursue the routed Union army. New plans for a fortified city of Washington would soon be implemented with a strong defensive ring surrounding the city.

In a battle of about twelve hours, the total dead numbered over 800 men (Union, 460; Confederates, 387) and about 4,000 wounded and missing, most of them on the Union side, captured as prisoners. It was the largest and bloodiest battle that the stunned nation had ever seen. Both sides now realized that, contrary to their original assumptions, this war would not be quickly won with a single battle and it was going to cost many lives.

Gen. McDowell's failure as commander in the battle cost him his command. His replacement, Gen. George B. McClellan, who had received glowing reports from his recent successes in western Virginia, immediately focused on reinforcing the defenses of Washington, D.C., and reorganizing the army into the new Army of the Potomac. Because the 90-day volunteers for the Union were soon to be relieved, the U.S. Congress quickly gave Lincoln authorization on July 22 to enlist up to 500,000 men.

MEDICAL SUPPORT FOR THE WOUNDED

As the walking wounded Union soldiers slowly arrived in Washington, D.C., after the rout of the army at the Battle of First Bull Run, they were on foot because the army had not yet organized an Ambulance Corps. The few ambulances that were present for the battle were driven by contracted civilians who rapidly bolted from the scene when they saw the fleeing soldiers and took their wagons with them. Many wounded soldiers were left in the field for days and many died before help arrived or they were captured by the enemy. The two hospital centers in Washington, D.C., were woefully inadequate for the number of wounded men and improvised centers were set up in abandoned warehouses, churches, schools and other public buildings. Some patients arrived at the U.S. Patent Office where former school teacher Clara Barton worked as a patent clerk, a position she had acquired after being denied the job of principal of a school in Bordentown, New Jersey, that she had founded.

Volunteering to help care for the wounded, she observed first-hand the lack of adequate supplies for the injured soldiers. Barton soon organized relief efforts and spent her time gathering food, clothing and supplies that were then distributed to the centers. She also spent time with the patients, writing letters for them and providing supporting care. Resigning from the Patent Office to work as a volunteer, Barton eventually gained the trust of civil and military authorities and in 1862, the U.S. Surgeon General granted her a general pass to travel with army ambulances. She became a familiar figure at a number of the battlefields, particularly during the Battle of the Wilderness in 1864, and became known as the *Angel of the Battlefield*. Her efforts eventually yielded formal relief organizations to bring medical supplies and help to the battlefronts and she later founded the American Red Cross.

The humanitarian crisis created by the army's inadequate medical preparations for the battlefield prompted rapid change. Before the war, there were 113 doctors in the U.S. Army; by the end of the war there were over 12,000. The Confederate Army increased its doctors in the field also to about 3,000 by the end of the war. General hospitals were established by 1862 in large cities, both North and South, and soldiers were transported to them by wagons, trains or ships. The Union had about four hundred hospitals by the end of the four-year war with 400,000 beds and treated about two million patients. The largest hospital in the South was in Richmond and contained five separate centers.

IV. THE FIRST YEAR: 1861

About 76,000 patients were treated there, while most Confederate patients were treated in private homes and relief organizations.

At the beginning of the Civil War, medicine was still largely practiced using the same medieval methods such as blood-letting with leeches. Most people received health care at home using remedies passed down through generations. But after four years of war, the country had hundreds of hospitals and thousands of field-tested doctors who were well educated in anatomy, anesthesia and surgical practice. Although it would not be until the late 1870s that the knowledge of germs and bacteria spawned a dramatic improvement in the treatment of infection through the simple practice of washing hands, the Civil War soldier did benefit from chloroform and opiates, such as opium pills, morphine and laudanum. Surgeons doled them out widely during and after the war to suffering soldiers.

As the alarming number of wounded soldiers arrived on the doorsteps of Washington after the Battle of First Bull Run, the need for more nurses became abundantly clear. The Sanitary Commission and Relief Societies actively began recruiting women for nursing roles to provide basic care and support for the wounded men. In addition, many women simply volunteered to collect and distribute supplies, prepare food and provide other services for maintaining a healing environment in the hospitals. It is estimated that over 20,000 women served in the Northern medical facilities during the war and although not documented, an equally representative number served in the South. Soon, the gender-related strictures that had prevented women from serving in the field hospitals were broken down and women nurses were providing immediate and decisive services to the doctors and patients.

Before the war, nursing was dominated by men on the assertion that women did not have the mental constitution for the hard work required and they would be too frail for the demanding duties. But in April 1861, Dorothea Dix, an activist reformer who had championed improved conditions for the mentally ill, organized a march of volunteer female nurses in Washington and demanded that the government accept their help to care for the wounded soldiers that would soon arrive from the coming battles. In June she was named as the first Superintendent of Army Nurses for the Union Army and by the end of the war, Dix had appointed 3,000 women nurses to army duties.

Without an Ambulance Corps, men who were wounded during battle had to rely on their individual regiments to rescue them from the field and get them to medical treatment. With no overall plan of evacuation, a muddled system often hired civilians to drive commercial wagons, which resulted in a chaotic response and many wounded were simply abandoned to be captured by the enemy.

The first organized U.S. Army Ambulance Corps was developed by Medical Director Dr. Jonathan Letterman for the Army of the Potomac in August 1862. Non-physician officers commanded the ambulances, which enabled physicians to focus on medical duties. Assignment of vehicles to the Ambulance Corps was controlled by the Medical Director, who established a coordinated system of evacuation back to the army's rear. Trained drivers and stretcher bearers were assigned to the vehicles.

The system first illustrated its effectiveness at the Battle of Antietam in September 1862, where all wounded men within Union lines were rapidly removed from the field. At the Battle of Gettysburg in 1863, the system was put to the test when thousands of casualties were created over the three-day battle. Responding to public pressure, Congress passed the Uniform System of Ambulances Act in March 1864 and the U.S. Army created an Ambulance Corps for all units and theaters of operation, standardizing an ambulance system for all military forces.

BATTLES IN WESTERN & TRANS-MISSISSIPPI THEATERS

EARLY CONFLICTS IN MISSOURI & KENTUCKY

The two border states of Missouri and Kentucky had both Northern and Southern loyalties. About 110,000 men from Missouri volunteered to the Union armies during the Civil War, but about 40,000 served in the Confederate Army. In Kentucky, about 125,000 served in the Union army, with 35,000 volunteering as Confederate soldiers.

Shortly after the formation of the Confederate States of America in February 1861, a special election by the Missouri Constitutional Convention voted overwhelmingly against secession but maintained its proslavery position that had been in place since Missouri applied for statehood and the Missouri Compromise of 1820. The pro-Union legislature designated that the state would maintain a status of neutrality and would support neither Union nor Confederacy efforts. But a pro-secessionist government-in-exile was created and in November, Missouri was accepted into the Confederacy, adding the 12th star to the Confederate flag.

Secessionist supporters in Kentucky created a shadow government in 1861 and designated Bowling Green as the "Capital of the Confederate State of Kentucky," but it never replaced the Union government in Frankfort which had strong Northern support. Nevertheless, the provisional secessionist government was recognized by the Confederacy, which admitted the state to the Confederate States of America in December 1861, adding Kentucky as the 13th star on the Confederate battle flag. Union victories in the state in early 1862, however, drove the secessionist government out of Bowling Green and it traveled with the Confederate Army of Tennessee for the rest of the war.

Camp Jackson Affair, St. Louis, Missouri
May 10, 1861

When President Lincoln called for four regiments from Missouri after the firing on Fort Sumter in April, its pro-secessionist Governor Claiborne Fox Jackson refused

IV. THE FIRST YEAR: 1861

and attracted pro-secession sympathizers to resist Union attempts to take control of the state. Gov. Jackson ordered his supporters to St. Louis, where a U.S. Federal arsenal was located, and set up a so-called drill camp at "Camp Jackson."

But a staunch antislavery U.S. Army officer, Capt. Nathaniel Lyon, who had graduated from West Point Military Academy, served in the Mexican-American War and more recently in the border wars of Bleeding Kansas, was well aware that Jackson's secessionist militia had seized the federal arsenal at Liberty, Missouri, in April. Jackson had also secretly received arms from the Confederate-captured U.S. arsenal in Baton Rouge, Louisiana, which would be restored to Union control a year later. Believing it was Jackson's intent to take control of the federal arsenal at St. Louis, Capt. Lyon led the 2nd U.S. Infantry and pro-Union Missouri volunteer regiments into Camp Jackson on May 10, and captured the entire secessionist troops. When Lyon marched his prisoners through the streets of St. Louis to the federal arsenal, pro-secessionist advocates set off a city-wide riot that resulted in several civilians being killed by Union troops. Outraged by the violence, both pro- and anti-secessionist supporters made preparations for war.

Gov. Jackson, at the capital in Jefferson City, promoted Sterling Price, a former state governor, to Major General of Volunteers for the pro-secession Missouri State Guard. Price, an active politician and life-long proslavery Democrat, had initially opposed secession, but later gave his support to the pro-Confederate Missouri State Guard and was now its commander. Union authorities promoted Capt. Lyon to Brigadier General and placed him in command of the U.S. Army's Department of the West. Lyon and his troops advanced on the capital at Jefferson City and forced Gov. Jackson and his secessionist supporters to flee.

After a minor clash at Boonville where the Guard narrowly escaped being captured, Gen. Lyon pursued Price and the Guard into southwest Missouri with a small force of about 5,500 troops and camped near Springfield, Missouri. With Gen. Price and the Missouri State Guard located about seventy-five miles southwest of there, the stage was set for the Battle of Wilson's Creek (or Battle of Oak's Hills) on August 10.

The Missouri State Legislature reconvened on July 22 and removed Jackson from his office as governor and created a provisional Union government. Jackson and secessionist sympathizers met in Neosho, Missouri, to sign the Ordinance of Secession on October 31, 1861, and Missouri sent delegates to the Confederate Congress. But the former governor and secessionist advocates then took refuge with Price and the Missouri State Guard and moved with the army.

Battle of Wilson's Creek, Missouri
August 10, 1861

The first major battle in the Trans-Mississippi arena took place in southwest Missouri in August 1861. The pro-secessionist government, now under the deposed Gov. Claiborne

Fox Jackson, had taken refuge with the Missouri State Guard, under the command of Gen. Sterling Price, and they were now located in southwest Missouri about seventy-five miles south of Springfield. Union Gen. Nathaniel Lyon had pursued them with about 5,500 troops after a clash at Boonville and was now positioned near the secessionists.

Fig. 8: Map of Missouri, showing approximate locations of first battles August to October 1861.

To support the pro-secessionist efforts in Missouri, Confederate President Jefferson Davis ordered Gen. Benjamin McCulloch in Arkansas to bring reinforcements to Price and the Missouri State Guard and perhaps gain control of Missouri and bring it into the Confederacy. McCulloch, former Texas Ranger and famous for daring exploits in the Mexican-American War, headed the Texas Army of the West, which included troops from Arkansas, Louisiana, Texas and Indian Territory. The united forces of Price and McCulloch numbered about 12,000.

The battle between Union and Confederate forces began at dawn on August 10 at Wilson's Creek (or Battle of Oak Hills), about ten miles southwest of Springfield, Missouri. After a six-hour battle that resulted in the death of Gen. Lyon, the badly outnumbered Union troops withdrew, yielding southern Missouri to the Confederates. Gen. Price wanted to pursue the retreating Union army, but McCulloch refused. He did not trust the Missouri State Guard and had a poor opinion of Price and his generalship. As a result, the two men would maintain a bitter feud that continued until McCulloch was killed in battle less than a year later. McCulloch then led his troops back to Arkansas, leaving Price with the Missouri State Guard to defend their position in the state.

Union Occupies Paducah, Kentucky
September 6, 1861

With the death of Gen. Nathaniel Lyon, Gen. John C. Fremont, "Pathfinder of the West," so named for his five expeditions into the American West, 1842-1853, was given command of the Union Army's Department of the West on July 25, 1861. A primary concern for Fremont was the protection of Cairo, Illinois, situated at the confluence of the Mississippi and Ohio Rivers, with Missouri to the west and Kentucky to the east. Cairo was a critical staging area for movement of Union expeditions along the two rivers into Missouri, Kentucky, Arkansas and Tennessee. In addition, the Tennessee River joined the Ohio River about forty-five miles east of Cairo at Paducah, Kentucky, which became a strategic objective for both North and South because it provided ready access to points south from the two border states of Missouri and Kentucky, both with Southern and Northern loyalties.

As Fremont considered commanders for the Cairo post, he interviewed Ulysses S. Grant, an unobtrusive and recently promoted Brigadier General with headquarters at Ironton, Missouri. Ignoring rumors that Grant had been a drunkard in the Old Army, Fremont passed over other generals and awarded the command to Grant, writing later of the interview, *"I found Grant to be a man of great activity and promptness in obeying orders without question or hesitation. For that reason, I gave General Grant this important command at this critical period. I did not consider him then a great general, for the qualities that led him to success had not had the opportunity for their development. I selected him for qualities I could not then find combined in any other officer, for General Grant was a man of unassuming character, not given to self-elation, of dogged persistence, and of iron will."*

Fig. 9: Cairo, Illinois, with its connection to multiple rivers and states provided a key strategic location for Union movement of troops and supplies.

Grant was made commander of the Union District of Southeast Missouri and established his headquarters on September 4 at Cairo. The day before, Confederate Gen. Leonidas Polk had moved troops into Columbus, Kentucky, located some twenty miles south of Cairo on bluffs overlooking the Mississippi River.

When Grant received word on September 5 that Polk was planning to occupy Paducah, Kentucky, at the strategic intersection of the Ohio and Tennessee Rivers, he immediately moved troops to Paducah (See Figs. 9-10). Although Grant's command was still small at this stage, with only two regiments and one artillery battery, the Union troops entered the city without firing a shot. Confederate forces from Columbus were already underway to occupy Paducah, but when they learned that Union troops now occupied the city, they returned to Columbus.

Grant writes in his *Personal Memoirs* that when his troops entered the city of Paducah, uniform consternation was displayed by all the citizens, who had been expecting Confederates. Grant immediately issued a proclamation, "I have come among you, not as an enemy, but as your friend and fellow-citizen, not to injure or annoy you, but to respect the rights, and to defend and enforce the rights of all loyal citizens ... against an enemy in rebellion against our common Government." The declaration did much to reveal his character and generally relieved the inhabitants. Quickly fortifying the city with troops from Cape Girardeau, his command soon numbered 20,000 men.

Grant had graduated from West Point in 1843, in the middle of his class, where his primary interest had been horses. His expertise in horsemanship was well known to his classmates, as he rode a large and powerful horse named York, a mount generally avoided by the other cadets. *"It was as good as any circus to see Grant ride,"* remarked one cadet. At his graduation ceremonies, cadet Grant was selected to perform a record-breaking high-jump on York, which stood for twenty-five years.

With the outbreak of the Mexican-American War, 1846-48, Grant was assigned to serve under Gen. Zachary Taylor in the battles of northern Mexico and later under General-in-Chief Winfield Scott during the invasion and battles at Mexico City. Initially assigned to duty as quartermaster under Taylor, he then distinguished himself as a daring and competent soldier in several battles. After the war, when he was stationed on the West Coast between 1852 and 1854, he suffered from severe depression while separated from his wife and children and was forced to resign from the army in 1854 for excessive drinking episodes. The reputation of being a drunkard would pursue him through his Civil War years.

After leaving the army, Grant struggled in private life to support his family through unsuccessful years of farming, odd jobs and working in his father's tannery and leather store business in Galena, Illinois. When Lincoln called for 75,000 volunteers after the firing on Fort Sumter at the onset of the Civil War, Grant eagerly volunteered to rejoin the army and led efforts to enlist local recruits. Given his military background, he was placed in charge of the unruly 21st Illinois Volunteer Infantry which he was able to bring into an effective disciplined force. When two more Regiments were placed under his command, he was promoted to Brigadier General, which had placed him in various locations in Missouri, leading to his command at Cairo.

Grant had no sympathy for the South's withdrawal from the Union. *"Secession was illogical as well as impracticable; it was revolution,"* he said. *" ... that cause was, I believe, one of the worst for which a people ever fought."*

Battle of Lexington, Missouri
September 13-20, 1861

After the battle of Wilson's Creek where he had defeated Union forces, Gen. Sterling Price led the Missouri State Guard north toward the Missouri-Kansas border with about 7,000 men to repel forces from a pro-Union Kansas brigade from Fort Scott and then moved farther north to Lexington, Missouri, adding more pro-secession volunteers to his army (See Fig. 8). Many of Lexington's residents were slave owners and slaves constituted more than thirty percent of the city's population.

Gen. John C. Fremont, commanding the Union Department of the West, sent about 3,500 troops to Lexington under the command of Col. James Mulligan, leading the 23rd Illinois "Irish Brigade" and a detachment of the 27th Missouri Mounted Infantry.

Mulligan's orders were to prevent Price and his secessionist supporters from capturing funds from local banks.

Gen. Price, leading his secessionist forces, that now numbered about 15,000, met the Union defenders at Lexington on September 13, who had created strong defenses around the city. Artillery exchanges between the two sides continued for several days before the badly outnumbered Union troops were overwhelmed and forced to surrender on September 20. Price's success was short-lived, however. When Gen. Fremont sent a large Union army to recapture control of this region of the Missouri River Valley, Price was unable to maintain control of the area and had to move his army back to southwest Missouri near Springfield.

Battle of Springfield, Missouri (Zagonyi's Charge)
October 25, 1861

The first Union victory in the West was accomplished by Gen. John C. Fremont in the Battle of Springfield, Missouri, on October 25, 1861. Fremont's immediate goal was to remove Gen. Sterling Price and the Missouri State Guard from the state and possibly carry the war into Arkansas and Louisiana. Leading the 20,000-man Army of the West from St. Louis into southwest Missouri, which included a 5,000-man cavalry, Fremont intended to recover territory lost the previous August in the Battle of Wilson's Creek. The Union army camped out on the Pomme de Terre River, about fifty miles north of Springfield.

Gen. Price, facing Fremont's large Union army, ordered a withdrawal of his troops from the area, but a local Missouri State Guard commander, Col. Julian Frazier, with about 1,500 men and cavalry, had come to Springfield to support Price, only to find the city abandoned. Fremont's personal bodyguard of 300 men, led by Hungarian Major Charles Zagonyi, routinely scouted in front of Fremont's army, and was ambushed by Frazier's men when they tried to enter Springfield. Zagonyi, although outnumbered, successfully led three costly charges against the defenders, routing the Confederates who fled from the battle. Zagonyi freed Union prisoners in Springfield, but abandoned the city before dark, fearing his small force could not defend against a Confederate counter-attack. Fremont's army retook the city two days later and the battle became famous, known as "Zagonyi's Charge."

Fremont's success, however, did not save him from losing his command. Without consulting Lincoln, Fremont had issued on August 30, 1861, an Emancipation Proclamation that all Missouri slaves owned by secessionists would be freed. Fremont's goal was to remove the support that slaves provided to secessionists and eliminate the constant guerilla warfare waged by secession sympathizers. But President Lincoln feared that such an Emancipation Proclamation would undermine the loyalty of Border States to the Union. Fremont's proclamation was revoked and President Lincoln removed him from command October 24, placing Gen. David Hunter in charge.

Lincoln then reorganized the Department of the West in November, 1861, creating new Departments of Missouri, Arkansas, Illinois, and Western Kentucky, and at times, Kansas. After the reorganization, Fremont was reassigned to command the Department of the Mountain District, which included western Virginia, eastern Tennessee and eastern Kentucky. Gen. Hunter was reassigned to the Department of Kansas and ordered to evacuate Union forces from Springfield, which left the area to Confederate Gen. Sterling Price and the Missouri State Guard until January 1862 when Union forces advanced on the Confederates and drove them into Arkansas.

In 1862, Lincoln reorganized the army again and placed Missouri, Kansas, Arkansas and Indian Territory in the Department of Missouri, under the command of Gen. Henry Halleck, with a primary mission to fight Confederate forces in Kansas and Missouri. Halleck, an 1839 graduate of West Point Military Academy, was a recognized expert in military studies and a master of logistics and military politics that kept the army running smoothly.

After serving in mostly administrative duties in California during the Mexican-American War, Halleck had resigned his commission and joined a law firm in San Francisco where he became a wealthy man. When the Civil War began, he rejoined the army and was soon assigned to lead the Department of Missouri. With no combat experience, his cautious approach based on extensive and thorough preparations made him ineffective as a field commander, and earned him the derogatory nickname "Old Brains." Nevertheless, his subordinates, which included Gen. Ulysses S. Grant, achieved several successful victories in the Western Theater early in the war, which eventually earned Halleck a promotion to Washington.

Guerilla warfare continued to exist in Missouri until late in the Civil War with battles and skirmishes occurring at all of its borders.

Battle of Belmont, Missouri
November 7, 1861

By early September 1861, Union armies under Gen. Ulysses S. Grant, District of Southeast Missouri, were located in Cairo, Illinois, and Paducah, Kentucky. Since September 3, Confederate forces under Gen. Leonidas Polk had occupied nearby Columbus, Kentucky, across the Mississippi River from Belmont, Missouri, a small camp and ferry crossing. In early November Grant received orders to create a demonstration on the Mississippi near Columbus so that Gen. Polk would be discouraged from sending Confederate reinforcements to Missouri or Arkansas.

On November 7, Grant led his troops by steamboat from Cairo to disembark at a farm about three miles north of Belmont, out of range of the Confederate batteries at Columbus. Marching toward the Confederate camp, the Union troops, many under fire for the first time, created a battle line in a corn field and faced the Confederate line located on a low ridge. The two sides engaged back and forth through the morning until Union artillery broke through the Southern line. As the Confederates fled, abandoning their flags and artillery, the green Union recruits surged into the camp and became overwhelmed with their victory, partying and cheering. Eventually regaining control, Grant ordered the men with their prisoners back to the riverboats.

As the men were marching back to the steamboats with their captives and two captured guns, they were vigorously attacked and fired on by Confederate reinforcements, who had arrived from Columbus, bringing cannons with them, nearly cutting off the Union retreat. Grant writes in his *Personal Memoirs*, "At first some of the officers seemed to think that to be surrounded was to be placed in a hopeless position, where there was nothing to do but surrender. But when I announced that we had cut our way in and could cut our way out just as well, it seemed a new revelation to officers and soldiers."

Fig. 10: At the Battle of Belmont, Missouri, Ulysses S. Grant led his first battle of the Civil War.
Source: *Creative Commons Attribution 3.0 license. Map by Hal Jespersen, www.cwmaps.com*

As Grant rallied the men to fight their way back to the boats, he became separated from the main group. As he rode his horse back to search for a missing Union regiment, he found only Confederate soldiers and he rapidly returned to the river. When he reached shore, he found himself to be the only man still on land as the boats pulled away. Fortunately, one of the captains whose boat had not yet started its engines, recognized Grant and sent out a gangplank to the sandy shore.

Grant, an expert rider, urged his horse forward to negotiate a virtually perpendicular bank down to the shore below. Grant states in his *Personal Memoirs*, "The horse took in the situation … put his fore feet over the bank without hesitation or urging, and with his hind feet well under him, slid down the bank and trotted aboard the boat, twelve to fifteen feet away, over a single gang plank. I dismounted and went at once to the upper deck."

Once out of range of the pursuing Confederates, Grant found his missing regiment marching upriver and the troops were safely returned to Paducah. Casualties totaled about 600 for each side. Although the battle was viewed as a Southern success, Grant had achieved his objective of eliminating a detachment of Confederate troops headed as reinforcements to Missouri and he had successfully led new recruits into battle. Further, Grant writes, " … … every man felt that Belmont was a great victory and that he had contributed his share to it. The men acquired a confidence in themselves at Belmont that did not desert them through the war."

A significant outcome of the engagement was that Polk's action to occupy Columbus prompted the Kentucky legislature to give up its position of neutrality and voted to accept the support of Federal aid to resist Confederate advances into the state. Kentucky would remain under Union control for the remainder of the war.

LINCOLN REORGANIZES UNION ARMIES

The disastrous defeat of the Union army at the Battle of First Bull Run in July 1861 created a pressing urgency to increase protection for Washington, D.C., the Union capital. Accordingly, Lincoln brought Gen. George B. McClellan, who had achieved national recognition in western Virginia, to Washington and placed him in charge of the Union armies, second only to General-in-Chief Winfield Scott. McClellan's rapid rise was facilitated by a shortage of qualified men available for Union Army command. About a fourth of West Point graduates on active duty in 1861 had resigned to join the Confederate Army.

Prominent among them was Gen. Scott's first choice for Robert E. Lee, whom he had mentored in the Mexican-American War and greatly respected. Although Lee opposed secession as a *"revolution against the founders of this country,"* he declined the offer and instead joined the Confederacy to support his native state of Virginia. Similarly, Albert Sidney Johnston, who headed the U.S. Army's Department of the Pacific in California at the time of the Civil War, resigned from the U.S. Army when his home state of Texas seceded from the Union. Another high-ranking Union officer, Joseph E. Johnston (no relation to Albert S. Johnston), a Virginian, resigned from his post as Quartermaster General of the U.S. Army to join the Confederacy.

New Army of the Potomac

The confident young McClellan took up his new responsibilities in Washington with enthusiasm. Applying his considerable skills as an organizer and administrator, he revamped the command structure and formed the new Army of the Potomac. Officers who had been politically appointed or elected by volunteer militias were removed from their commands and replaced by experienced West Point graduates, many of whom had fought in the Mexican-American War.

McClellan instituted constant drilling with strict discipline and staged impressive troop reviews, the largest numbering some 65,000 infantry. Food for the troops was improved. Admired by his men, he became known as "Little Mac." Defenses for Washington were increased and trained artillery personnel manned nearly fifty forts.

McClellan, however, had a major weakness that would persist through his entire army command. His exaggerated belief that the Confederate armies he faced vastly outnumbered his own hampered his judgment and affected his battlefield tactics. His perception was promoted by inept intelligence from the security services under Allan Pinkerton. McClellan consistently avoided confrontation with the enemy until President Lincoln and political pressures from Congress insisted on action from the reluctant general.

An encounter with the Confederates, known as the Battle of Ball's Bluff, occurred October 21, 1861, on the banks of the Potomac River near Leesburg, Virginia, about forty miles northwest of Washington, D.C. The poorly planned reconnaissance mission became a humiliating and embarrassing defeat for McClellan. More than 500 Union men were captured and over 200 were killed, including a prominent U.S. Senator, Col. Edward Baker from Oregon, who was a personal friend of President Lincoln. The Union defeat, on top of the disastrous loss at the Battle of First Bull Run, prompted Congress to form the Joint Committee on the Conduct of the War, which had the effect of injecting political pressures into Lincoln's role as Commander-in-Chief.

> **THE ANACONDA PLAN**
>
> Gen. Winfield Scott, the aging general from the Mexican-American War, advocated a military strategy to immediately control the Mississippi River, which would enhance the navy blockade of all Southern ports, surrounding the Confederacy and greatly impair its ability to import or manufacture arms and military supplies. His plan, which would envelop the Southern states and slowly squeeze the Confederacy into defeat, was nicknamed "Scott's Great Snake" by the Northern press, and dubbed the "Anaconda Plan." Derided in the press and discarded by Gen. McClellan, its broad outlines were eventually used to bring a successful end to the war.

Confederates Deceive McClellan

After the Union defeat at Bull Run, Confederate Gen. Joseph E. Johnston continued to maintain a Southern army at Centreville, Virginia, about twenty miles west of Washington, D.C. While McClellan was building the Army of the Potomac, Johnston created the appearance of an army twice its actual size of about 40,000 men through the use of so-called "Quaker Guns." Using logs and stove pipes painted black, Southern forces constructed fake cannons that were surrounded by the appearance of extensive rifle pits, which convinced McClellan that he was facing an army of 100,000, greatly outnumbering his own.

Gen. Winfield Scott, Lincoln's General-in-Chief, the aging general and hero of the Mexican-American War, vigorously disputed McClellan's claims of a superior Confederate army and their arguments continued over several weeks, eventually becoming personal. Scott became so disillusioned with McClellan that he offered his resignation, which Lincoln reluctantly accepted, retiring the old general on November 1, 1861, replacing him with Gen. George B. McClellan.

McClellan, as the new General-in-Chief, continued to delay military action and disrespectfully refused to share any war plans with Lincoln. His insubordination and his recent defeat at Ball's Bluff led to intense questioning from the Congressional Joint Committee on the Conduct of the War. After several hours of debate with the Congressional leaders, Lincoln is quoted as saying, *"If General McClellan isn't going to use his army, I'd like to borrow it for a time."*

Called to the White House in early January 1862, McClellan was forced to reveal his war plans for the first time. McClellan's proposal would transport the Army of the Potomac on the Rappahannock River from Urbana, Virginia, and land behind the Confederates only fifty miles from the Richmond capital. But before he could implement his plan, Gen. Johnston, who had secretly learned of McClellan's scheme, quietly pulled his Confederate army away in the night from Centreville in March 1862, and assumed new positions south of the Rappahannock, foiling McClellan's strategy.

When Union troops inspected the abandoned Confederate camp, they discovered that the vast array of defensive cannons were simply fake 'Quaker Guns' that had deceived Union forces as to the strength of the Southern army. McClellan's fabricated claims of his army being badly outnumbered caused him considerable embarrassment and sharp criticism from Congress and the press.

By this time, Lincoln's patience with the reluctant general was at an end and he removed McClellan as General-in-Chief in March, but left him in command of the Army of the Potomac. That spring, Lincoln, newly appointed Secretary of War Edwin Stanton, and a group of officers formed the "War Board" to oversee Union war plans. Gen. McClellan prepared a revised plan to capture Richmond, known as the Peninsula Campaign, which he launched in March 1862.

VIEWS FROM THE PUBLIC FOR THE YEAR 1861

About Northern reaction to the Battle of First Bull Run …

After the Confederate attack on Fort Sumter in April 1861, the Northern press continued to demand action from President Lincoln. The *New York Tribune* published a headline in July 1861, *"Forward to Richmond,"* that urged a quick Union conquest of the Confederate capital that would bring an end to the national conflict. Lincoln, bending under the growing demand to engage the Confederates before the three-month terms of the new Army of Northern Virginia ran out, authorized the army to meet the Southerners in battle at Manassas, Virginia, a mere thirty-five miles south of Washington. The two armies met on Sunday, July 21, 1861, in the Battle of First Bull Run.

IV. THE FIRST YEAR: 1861

Early reports in Northern newspapers erroneously declared a Union victory based on information they had received at the beginning of the battle. In New York City, extras were on the streets by early evening of July 21, declaring a great Union victory. Washington D.C.'s *National Republican* on July 22 reported " ... *the Federals have won the day. The loss on both sides is heavy. But the rout of the rebels is complete."*

Lincoln, receiving positive early reports, was initially buoyed by the news and took his usual carriage ride in the afternoon with his son, accompanied by Attorney General Edward Bates. But then a telegram arrived, stating that the Union army was retreating. *"General McDowell's army in full retreat through Centreville. The day is lost. Save Washington and the remnants of this army."* When the demoralized, exhausted Union soldiers collapsed on the streets and in the doorways of Washington thirty-six hours later, reality soon became crystal clear. Angry crowds assembled at the offices of the *Philadelphia Examiner* as accurate accounts arrived of the Union defeat and the large number of Union casualties.

A correspondent for the *New York World* wrote in the July 21, 1861, issue, *"I saw officers—majors and colonels who had deserted their commands—pass me galloping as if for dear life ... For three miles, hosts of Federal troops ... all mingled in one disorderly rout. Wounded men lying along the banks ... appealed with raised hands to those who rode horses, begging to be lifted behind but few regarded such petitions."*

Although the number of casualties was not large when compared to the battles that would follow, it was the largest number the country had ever experienced and the price had been high. Over 800 men had been killed, the North's total of 460 compared to the South's 387. Over 4,000 were wounded or missing, more than half of them on the Union side, most of whom had been taken prisoner.

A report from a *New York Times* correspondent in its issue on July 24, 1861, described the reality of the battlefield on Sunday, July 21, at Bull Run: "*A Massachusetts Regiment reached here (Washington) Monday evening; the men had been without food since the previous morning at 2 o'clock. They had walked in that time nearly forty miles, besides fighting all day under a hot sun. Their Colonel went to a hotel, and when he was urged to go out and do something for his men, he replied that "his feet were quite sore, and to-morrow would answer quite as well." Many of the sons of the Bay State, that night – particularly the men of his regiment -- slept in the streets, with the rain pouring on them. What does Massachusetts think of this? Did men leave comfortable homes, with a joyous God-speed from earnest patriots, and with fervent prayers from loving women, to be treated thus? Will the actual supporters of the nation in this glorious conflict -- will the men of money in New-York and Boston, unloose their purse-strings and respond liberally to calls for Governmental loans, unless they feel assured that no such stain on our nation is to be inflicted again by incompetent partisans, whose safe care is to line their pockets, even if the nation bleeds at every pore? A leading Senator from New-England told me of the recreant Colonel of his own State, who is here simply because party services demanded he should come, although known to be notoriously incompetent. Similar men in too many regiments helped to bring about the disgraceful rout on Sunday."*

About the failure of the federal government ...

Northern newspapers were quick to blame the administration for the dismal failure of the Union Army at the Battle of First Bull Run. The rush of untrained troops into war with inadequate training, to face determined rebels on their own ground, had resulted in a bloody disaster. Recriminations readily flowed, declaring the incompetence of the army and the entire administration in Washington.

A *New York Times* correspondent reported on July 24 the following: *Gen. SCOTT is almost unmanned by this defeat, and told the President Monday that this fatal and only military error of his long and well-spent life, was brought about by rabid civilians, who goaded on the Cabinet before his plans were fully matured. It seems hardly credible, but it is a fact, that the old hero wished to send over to Gen. MCDOWELL nine additional regiments on Sunday morning (July 21, 1861), but the Commander of Arlington telegraphed 'that he did not want them, they were equal to any emergency.'"*

The *Brooklyn Daily Eagle,* New York City, wrote on July 23, 1861: "*The immediate causes of the reverse are evident enough. The men who have ruled in Washington, since last 4th of March, are as incapable of conducting war as preserving peace. The administration also pushed General Scott into giving the rebels battle on their own terms, on the ground they selected and with every possible advantage in their favor. They were impelled to do this by the abolition wing of the Republican party—a faction the most bloody, cowardly and atrocious that ever disgraced history; a party with the head of an idiot and the heart of a fiend; and its organ, the Tribune, has governed the country since the 4th of last March. The result is before the world, and every American citizen hangs his head and his cheeks burn red to contemplate it."*

On July 27, 1861, a few days after the battle, the *New York Times* published the widely held view that the government and the U.S. Army in particular had done a dismal job of taking care of the wounded soldiers. ""*We are all inexpressibly pained to learn... that very inadequate provisions had been made by the regular authorities, for the proper care of the wounded in that late battle. It seems incredible... that some of our gallant soldiers for sheer want of hospital garments, [are] even yet sweltering in their bloody uniforms, festering with fever and maddened with thirst."*

About Southern reaction to the Battle of First Bull Run ...

The South exulted with its success. The Confederates had won a significant victory in their first real engagement against the Union. President Jefferson Davis telegraphed Richmond from the battlefield: *"We have won a glorious but dear-bought victory. Night closed on the enemy in full flight and closely pursued."* Headlines reported the glorious victory for the South. Dubbed "The Great Skedaddle" by the Southern press, the *Richmond Examiner* wrote, "*We have broken the back bone of invasion and utterly broken the spirit of the North.*" Other reports praised their Southern soldiers as they fought for "*liberty, honor and their homes.*" The Southern press used the success of the battle to press a common refrain that "*… the last man, woman and child would willingly perish before allowing the South to give up its independence.*"

Southern newspapers typically exaggerated the number of soldiers engaged in battle and the report from the *Richmond Dispatch* about the Battle of First Bull Run attributed fifty thousand troops to the Southern army, when the actual number was less than half that when the battle began, although reinforcements did increase the Southern army to about thirty-four thousand. "*It is not ascertained how many of the enemy were actually engaged; though the number could not have been much less than seventy-five thousand. The number actually engaged on our own side was nearly fifty thousand. The skirmishing is said to have begun as early as four o'clock yesterday morning; the heavy fighting between eight and nine o'clock. It continued all day with unabated vigor. Night closed upon the scene with the enemy in full retreat, hotly pursued by our gallant men. The day is ours; but the victory, though glorious, has cost us dearly. … While we rejoice over the public success, we have to mourn the loss of some of the men, gallant spirits and most valuable men of whom the South could boast. The event of today will be looked for with the deepest interest.*"

A later report from the same editor, "*The mortality was immense upon both sides. Upon ours, the returns will show about six hundred killed, and twenty-five hundred wounded. Upon theirs, about fifteen hundred left dead, and forty-five hundred wounded. We could have had as many prisoners as ten thousand, but what good would it have done to take them and feed them? Their return home, with the tale of their fright and discomfiture, will produce far greater benefits in inducing the Northern fanatics to cry—"Hold! Enough." We half-starved "rebels" have actually sent back the great American Eagle squealing to old granny Scott. Let Abraham and his followers beware, for our deeds may be immense when we shall get into a sleek, well-fed condition, consequent upon the recognition of our nationality by the Great Powers of the world. For one, the writer has no desire for a long- continued war, with all its attendant train of horrors; and right earnestly does he hope that the North will now come to its senses and let us alone. If not, then upon their own fertile fields let us hereafter wage the fight, and conquer a peace.*"

About brothers at war on opposite sides…

The August 24, 1861, issue of the *Nebraska City News*, Nebraska Territory, reported an account of two brothers, both local citizens, who had joined opposite sides in the Civil War. Phil K. Reily, severely wounded in the Battle of Bull Run, had been a private in Company E of the 1st Virginia Regiment of the Confederate States of America (CSA). The newspaper account noted that his younger brother, Dr. J.T. Reily, had enlisted as an army surgeon for the 71st Regiment of New York Volunteers.

About the "Freedom Fortress" at Fort Monroe...

The impact of Gen. Benjamin Butler's Freedmen's Bureau on the slaves in North Carolina was reported in the *Boston Traveler* in November 1861. "*The slaves generally in North Carolina sympathize with the North, and improve every opportunity to run away from their masters. A slight insurrection recently occurred near Lexington, in which three negroes were shot. The masters tell their slaves that on reaching Fort Monroe they are either sold to Cubans or have their hands cut off; but the majority disbelieve such fabrications, and 'look away' to BUTLER for deliverance.*"

About the shortage of goods in the South...

By the end of 1861, Southerners were already beginning to feel the effects of the North's blockade on most of the Southern seaports, drastically curtailing imports of items such as shoes, clothing and medicine. A worse effect was the reduced sale of the South's cotton exports that limited the Confederacy's main source of currency.

From the *Boston Traveler*, a semi-weekly newspaper: "*The South has given up all idea of taking Washington; but is ever venting out its spite against the Yankees—calling our Government, the "Rump," and Mr. LINCOLN the "Illinois Baboon," etc. The ladies of North Carolina wear palmetto cockades (a knot of ribbons worn as a symbol of liberty) and are extremely industrious in knitting socks and in preparing clothing for the soldiers; but cloth of every kind, as well as other Northern goods, is very dear. Calicoes are about three times as high as in Boston.*"

About Union soldiers in service....

Reprinted in the *New York Times*, August 15, 1861: "*A letter from our army at Sandy Hook, Maryland, (Gen. BANKS' column) shows us how difficult it must be for a Union soldier to play the agreeable in the midst of a rebel population* (in Charlestown, Virginia). *The ladies, even, forgot the proprieties of life and the decencies of the sex, in insulting officers, who treated them, however, always with marked consideration and politeness. The women would walk far around the flag-staff on which the Stars and Stripes were raised, in order, as they said, not to be dishonored by its shadow. They refused, in most cases, to sell to the troops the commonest necessaries of life; and poisoned two soldiers and attempted it on others. When they sold at all, they asked extortionate prices—twenty-five and fifty cents a loaf for bread... and such price for other edibles as to put them virtually beyond the reach of all but officers, and this too at a time when the soldiers were absolutely suffering from hunger.*" The report went on to describe the hardship placed on the soldiers, who were tempted to forage for food, but orders forbade it. "*The temptation to forage among such a people seemed almost irresistible, particularly when quickened by hunger; but the rule, 'Death without trial,' to anyone detected in 'cribbaging,' was rigidly enforced, and our troops retired from Charlestown without leaving a single mark of their occupation in devastated field or garden, or the destruction of a single dollar's worth of private property. The same regard for the rights of the citizen is observed here.*

IV. THE FIRST YEAR: 1861

Hundreds of acres of corn, and gardens filled with all kinds of vegetables, surround the encampments and are as unmolested as though in the heart of Ohio."

About Union refusal to hand over Blacks to slave-catchers...

A letter to the Editor of the *New York Times*, published on November 30, 1861, reported on an attempt by slave catchers from Maryland to have two Black men in their 20s be delivered to them from the 7th Michigan Volunteers as escaped slaves, but the Blacks could not be found. The Union officer wrote: *"It is doubted whether our superior officers ever heard of the resolution of the last Congress declaring it to be no part of the duty of the army to catch and return fugitive slaves; and certain I am that those persons held to servitude under the laws of Maryland would nowhere have been safer than in the camp of the 7th Michigan immediately after hearing the above document. The field officers of the Seventh were in former times Democrats, and one of them remarked in my hearing that 'he was getting to be too much of an Abolitionist to catch niggers for any man.' He made it a little stronger than this, but the oath was so worthily sworn that it can never be rigidly regarded against him. This, coming as it did from one who in times past has been a Democrat of the sternest sect, but who was ever a high-minded man, is a true exponent of the sentiment everywhere expressed this evening. Nor do I believe that either of the other field officers would be one whit more eager in such a search than the one I have spoken of. The Seventh has never sought to interfere in any way with the 'institution,' nor will it do so. But the slaveowners must catch their own negroes, for we never shall do it for them. At this time, it is ascertained that neither of the aforesaid persons have ever been in our camp, and there is now, if anything, rather a feeling of disappointment that they were not here."*

About America facing a War with itself...

As the first year of the war came to a close, the country watched and waited as neither side engaged in any significant confrontations as they digested the depressing and discouraging results of the Battle of First Bull Run. A shocked public that had expected one quick battle to resolve the nation's conflict, became painfully aware that it was now at war with itself. The large number of casualties dispelled all illusions of a romantic adventure that would yield a quick and easy victory. Both Presidents, Lincoln for the Union and Davis for the Confederacy, authorized the enlistment of vastly more volunteers immediately following the battle. An iron resolve settled on both North and South to remain firm in the righteousness of their cause.

V. THE SECOND YEAR: 1862

NEW DOMESTIC LEGISLATION

WITH SECEDED STATES NO LONGER REPRESENTED IN CONGRESS, LEGISLATIVE POWER shifted from the South to the North after the onset of the Civil War. Since the signing of the Constitution, slaveholding states had dominated Congress for the first seven decades of the country, with twenty-three out of thirty-six Speakers of the House and twenty-four *presidents pro tem* in the Senate. Eight of the first twelve Presidents had been slave-holders while in office and seven had been from Virginia. Twenty of the thirty-five Supreme Court justices appointed before 1860 had been from slave states.

PASSAGE OF THREE IMPORTANT ACTS

But in the spring of 1862, a dramatically reduced Congress considered several new legislative issues that had been blocked by fractious Southern Democrats, who had now withdrawn to the Confederacy. Three important domestic Acts were passed that would have far-reaching effects on the country in spite of the war that had just now begun. The Homestead Act, signed into law May 20, 1862, granted ownership of one hundred sixty acres of land free to any U.S. citizen, 21 years age or head of a family, who had not borne arms against the United States. The land would be theirs if they occupied the land, created a residence and improved it within a five-year period. The Act, which took effect January 1, 1863, attracted hundreds of thousands of settlers, including freed Blacks, naturalized immigrants, single women and all races and eventually distributed over two hundred seventy million acres of land.

A second piece of legislation with a profound impact was passage of the Pacific Railway Act, signed into law July 1, 1862. The Act would aid two railroad companies to construct a railroad and telegraph line that would cross the continent and connect the eastern part of the country with the west. The Union Pacific Railroad would build west from Council Bluffs, Iowa, with connections to Chicago, while Central Pacific would build east from Sacramento, California, and the two would meet in Utah.

Construction began in 1863, but the Civil War slowed progress. Although the telegraph line was completed in the fall of 1861, ending the period of the Pony Express, the two railroad lines would not connect until four years after the end of the Civil War on May 10, 1869, at Promontory Summit, northwest of the Great Salt Lake in Utah Territory. Coast-to-coast transportation of goods and people, plus telegraph communications had a revolutionary impact on the expansion and economy of the country.

The third piece of legislation enacted by the 1862 Congress was the Land-Grant College Act which provided states with land grants to finance the establishment of higher education institutions that supported agriculture and mechanical (A&M) arts. The Act produced a lasting legacy of fifty-seven land-grant institutions, located in every state, U.S. territory and the District of Columbia, forming the backbone of a national system of higher education.

LINCOLN'S GENERAL ORDER NO. 1

With the defeat of the Union Army at Bull Run and with no significant events since then, President Lincoln issued "President's Executive Order – General War Order No. 1," on January 27, 1862, which directed as follows:

"… That the 22d day of February, 1862, (George Washington's birthday) be the day for a general movement of the land and naval forces of the United States against the insurgent forces; that especially the army at and about Fortress Monroe, the Army of the Potomac, the Army of Western Virginia, the army near Munfordville, Ky., the army and flotilla at Cairo, and a naval force in the Gulf of Mexico be ready to move on that day."

The unusual order mostly reflected Lincoln's accumulating frustrations with Gen. George B. McClellan, commanding the Army of the Potomac, who had failed to use the army in any effective way since his appointment the previous year. But Lincoln's Order specifically named the army and naval flotilla at Cairo, Illinois, where Gen. Ulysses S. Grant commanded the District of Cairo in the Western Theater. While Gen. McClellan did not respond to Lincoln's Order until late March, the Order had an immediate effect on Grant, who renewed his proposal to attack Forts Henry and Donelson, Tennessee.

BATTLES IN WESTERN & TRANS-MISSISSIPPI THEATERS

Tennessee, Arkansas, Mississippi

In January 1862, Union military command in the West consisted of three departments: Department of Kansas under Gen. David Hunter; the Department of Ohio under Gen. Don Carlos Buell; and Department of Missouri under Gen. Henry Halleck, who had been promoted to the position following the reorganization of the Department of the West in November 1861. Lincoln's General War Order No. 1, issued January 27, 1862, had specifically named the army at Cairo, Illinois, under the command of

Gen. Ulysses S. Grant who had proposed an advance on Forts Henry and Donelson in Tennessee, in early January but had been ignored by Gen. Halleck, his superior officer. With Lincoln's new Order, Grant renewed his earlier proposition on January 29 which met with greater success. On February 1, he received full instructions to move forward in a collaborative effort with Naval forces under the command of Flag Officer Andrew Foote to advance on Fort Henry on the Tennessee River and nearby Fort Donelson at Dover, Tennessee, both strategically located on the border between Kentucky and Tennessee.

Battle of Fort Henry, Tennessee
February 6, 1862

When Tennessee seceded and joined the Confederacy, it proceeded to take steps to protect its northern boundary with Kentucky, a Border State that did not secede. The ability to move armies and keep them supplied would be critical to victory and would require controlling major transportation routes of rivers and railroads. The Tennessee and Cumberland Rivers were two important rivers that became military and political objectives for both North and South. The Tennessee River empties into the Ohio River only miles upstream of the Mississippi River as it flows through Paducah, Kentucky, on the Kentucky-Tennessee border. The river provides access to parts of Mississippi to the south and points southeast into Alabama. The Cumberland River joins the Ohio only a few miles upstream from Paducah and flows through Nashville, Tennessee, about sixty miles southeast of the Kentucky border. Both rivers protected western Tennessee from attacks.

The Confederacy began construction in May 1861 of two forts on the Tennessee-Kentucky border (See. Fig. 11). Fort Henry was built on the Tennessee River, strategically positioned just south of Kentucky's southern border. Its location on a bend in the river provided direct access for battery guns to fire on enemy ships. But its actual position was poorly located and during periods of high water the fort flooded, making the guns inoperable. Fort Heiman was then built on the opposite bank on high ground to protect it. Fort Donelson was constructed on a high bluff on the Cumberland River near Dover, Tennessee. Its location, about twelve miles east of Fort Henry and a few miles south of Kentucky's border, would protect Nashville from attacks from the river.

Ulysses S. Grant, commanding the Army of the Tennessee in the District of Cairo, moved on February 6 for a land and water attack on Fort Henry. Prior to the attack, he sent an expedition to seize the neighboring defensive Fort Heiman the night before. But when Union troops advanced on Fort Heiman, they found it abandoned. Confederates had already retreated to Fort Henry.

Flag Officer Andrew Foote, commanding the Western Gunboat Flotilla for the U.S. Navy, opened fire on Fort Henry around noon on February 6 with four newly constructed ironclads, backed up by three timberclads, ships with the same design as the ironclads, but without iron armor. All four of the Union ironclads were hit several times by Confederate fire, but much of it was largely ineffective on the gunboats as the shells bounced off the ironclad armor. After less than a two-hour battle, Confederate Gen. Lloyd Tilghman ordered a white sheet raised on the fort's flagpole as the Union fleet moved to within four hundred yards for a close bombardment. Tilghman and about one hundred men were all that was left of the Confederates; the remainder had escaped to Fort Donelson. When the main infantry arrived, the fighting was over. Fort Henry was in Union control.

The Navy Gunboat Flotilla was the predecessor of the Mississippi River Squadron and Flag Officer Foote would soon be promoted to the rank of Rear Admiral.

Surrender of Fort Donelson, Tennessee
February 12-16, 1862

With a small detachment left behind to guard Forts Henry and Heiman, Gen. Ulysses S. Grant's army of 15,000 men marched twelve miles to Fort Donelson in bitter cold on February 12. Simultaneously, Naval Officer Foote took his fleet of gunboats back up the river to the Ohio River to access the Cumberland River and navigate his flotilla to Fort Donelson.

On February 14 all of the navy ironclads proceeded within four hundred yards of the water batteries of Fort Donelson and opened fire. But Officer Foote had under-estimated the impact of Fort Donelson's artillery on his gunboats at close range. Pounding fire from the fort's cannons, positioned on a bluff one hundred feet above the water, devastated the U.S. Navy fleet. In less than two hours, three of the gunboats were disabled and the ships had to withdraw. While the fort's artillery was engaged with the Navy, Grant's land forces surrounded the fort outside. Union infantry, protected from fort artillery and gunfire by the nature of the ground, still suffered greatly from the bitter winter as many of the men had thrown away their blankets and overcoats during the strenuous march from Fort Henry.

Grant anticipated a long siege, but the following day the Confederates launched a surprise attack on the Union's flank, directed by Confederate Generals Gideon Pillow and Simon Bolivar Buckner, subordinates to the Fort's Commander, Gen. John B. Floyd. The Confederates' escape plan to open a route to Nashville for the besieged fort nearly succeeded, but Pillow's decision for troops to leave their trenches and return to the fort to resupply before evacuating, opened a gap in the line that was quickly seized and held by the Union center. The escape route was closed.

As the Confederate commander prepared to surrender the fort, Gen. Floyd feared being tried for treason if captured, as it was alleged that he was guilty of graft and secessionist activities while he still served as Secretary of War under U.S. President Buchanan before joining the Confederacy. Planning to escape before the surrender,

Floyd turned over command of the post to Gen. Pillow, a controversial and disrespected veteran of the Mexican-American War. But Pillow refused and the command passed on to Gen. Buckner, which enabled Pillow to escape by small boat across the Cumberland and then to Nashville. Confederate Col. Nathan Bedford Forrest, commanding his newly formed 1,000-man cavalry, furious with Fort Donelson's commanding leaders and their plans to surrender, led his cavalry away from the fort through icy waters and escaped during the night of February 15. Floyd left the next morning with two Virginia infantry regiments on the only two steamers available and eventually made it safely to Nashville. Confederate President Jefferson Davis soon relieved Floyd of command in March without a court of inquiry.

> **"UNCONDITIONAL SURRENDER"**
>
> The Northern press treated Ulysses S. Grant as a hero after his famous reply to the Confederate commander at Fort Donelson in February 1862. *"No terms except an unconditional and immediate surrender can be accepted. I propose to move immediately upon your works."*

On February 16, Buckner sent a note to Grant requesting a truce and a meeting to discuss terms of armistice and capitulation of Fort Donelson, now under his command. Buckner hoped for sympathetic terms as he and Grant had shared three years at West Point and been friends before the Civil War. But Grant's reply would go down in history, as he said: *"No terms except unconditional and immediate surrender can be accepted."* Although friendly with Buckner, Grant had no sympathy for secessionists who sought dissolution of the Union and had brought the country to war.

When Buckner read Grant's unequivocal terms, his irritated response stated, *"The distribution of the forces under my command, incident to an unexpected change of commanders and the overwhelming force under your command compel me… to accept the ungenerous and unchivalrous terms which you propose."* Grant was courteous to Buckner after the surrender, offering to lend him money through his upcoming imprisonment, but Buckner declined.

Losses for the Confederates at Fort Donelson were large. Over 12,000 soldiers were captured among the total casualties of about 14,000. Total Union casualties were less than 3,000 (about 500 killed). In addition to over seventy pieces of artillery, the Union collected 400,000 rations of rice, 400 barrels of new molasses, twenty large casks of sugar and over 450 rations of beef and pork. Over 7,000 Confederate were sent to prisoner-of-war camps in Chicago and Indianapolis. Buckner was held at Fort Warren in Boston and exchanged in August 1862. Capture of Forts Henry and Donelson were the first significant Union victories of the war. Lincoln promptly promoted Grant from Brigadier General to Major General.

Fig. 11: Overview of Western Theater military events shows Union Generals Grant, Buell and Pope actively engaged in Tennessee and Kentucky in 1861-62. Confederate Gen. Polk joined Beauregard at Corinth, Mississippi, as did Gen. A. S. Johnston, who withdrew from Tennessee. The Battle of Shiloh in April became a significant victory for the Union.

Source: *Creative Commons Attribution 3.0 license. Map by Hal Jespersen, www.cwmaps.com*

Secessionists Leave Kentucky
February-March 1862

The defeat of Forts Henry and Donelson by Union forces under Gen. Ulysses S. Grant had an immediate impact on western Kentucky. Confederate troops under Gen. Albert Sidney Johnston, had occupied Bowling Green, Kentucky, as his headquarters and a pro-Confederate government had existed there in exile, declaring the city as the "Capital of the Confederate State of Kentucky." With the fall of Fort Henry and the threat from Grant on Fort Donelson, Johnston moved his Confederate States Army from Bowling Green to Nashville, Tennessee, on February 11. Union Gen. Don Carlos Buell, who had been assigned to command the newly formed Army of the Ohio the previous November, quickly advanced his army south from Green River, Kentucky, and bombarded Bowling Green across the Big Barren River on February 16. The remaining Confederates, including the exiled secessionist government, fled the area and joined Gen. Johnston and his army at Nashville.

V. THE SECOND YEAR: 1862

With the fall of Fort Donelson, Union Navy gunboats could now move along the Cumberland River unopposed and Nashville was Buell's next target for the Union. Confederates evacuated the city's industrial and transportation center on February 17 and Buell captured the city on February 25, the first Confederate capital to fall. Confederates under Johnston had to withdraw from Nashville to Murfreesboro and then relocated to Corinth, Mississippi, to join the army under Gen. P.G.T. Beauregard. Union forces now controlled middle and west Tennessee and southern Kentucky.

With the defeat of Forts Henry and Donelson, the Union now controlled the Tennessee and Cumberland rivers and could circumvent Confederate defenses at Columbus, Kentucky, that had been in place since September 1861 when Confederate Gen. Leonidas Polk had violated Kentucky's stance of neutrality by moving forces there and building a fort on the high bluffs overlooking the Mississippi River. His act had prompted the Kentucky General Assembly to withdraw its stance of neutrality and declare its allegiance to the Union. Now isolated by the withdrawal of Johnston's forces from Kentucky, Polk left Columbus to head south on March 2 and join the other Confederate armies at Corinth, Mississippi.

After Polk departed Columbus, Union Gen. John Pope was able to capture Island No. 10 near New Madrid from the Confederates between March and April 1862, which opened the Mississippi River for the Union as far south as Fort Pillow, situated about forty miles north of Memphis, Tennessee. A Union Navy flotilla attacked Fort Pillow on April 13, 1862, and forced the withdrawal of Confederate troops from the fort on June 4. Proceeding downriver to Memphis, the Union Navy defeated the Confederacy's naval fleet there on June 6, which gave control of the Mississippi River to the Union all the way down to the fortress at Vicksburg, Mississippi, which would not be defeated until July 1863. Memphis remained in Union control for the rest of the war.

Battle of Pea Ridge, Arkansas
March 7-8, 1862

In the fall of 1861, Union Gen. Henry Halleck, commanding the Union Department of Missouri, directed Gen. Samuel R. Curtis, heading the Union's 12,000-man Army of the Southwest, to drive Confederate forces out of southern Missouri and eliminate their influence in the state. Missouri's Confederate troops, made up of the Missouri State Guard under Gen. Sterling Price, plus secessionist supporters, had been able to maintain a presence in Springfield, Missouri, since defeating Union troops at the Battle of Wilson's Creek in August 1861.

Union Gen. Curtis began his advance to Springfield from Rolla, Missouri, in January 1862 along Telegraph Road, a frontier highway that proceeded southwest from St. Louis across Missouri through Springfield, down to Fort Smith, located at Van Buren, Arkansas, on the border between Arkansas and Indian Territory. Telegraph Road, also known as Old Wire Road, had been built when the telegraph line was created to run between St. Louis and Fort Smith. Armies generally avoided winter campaigns as they tended to be plagued with bitter cold and winter snowstorms, followed by spring thaws which created nearly impassable roads. As the Union army struggled through Missouri in January, intense cold, snow and freezing rain took a terrible toll on the men. One soldier described the march as *"mud without mercy."*

Confederate Gen. Price, surprised to learn that a Union army was approaching his headquarters at Springfield in the middle of winter, made a hasty retreat with his forces and headed south into northwestern Arkansas to connect with Confederate forces under Gen. Benjamin McCulloch, who had troops at various camps near Fayetteville, Arkansas. The two generals still nurtured a bitter rivalry after the Battle at Wilson's Creek, but Price had little choice, as he directed his troops to follow Telegraph Road into Arkansas, crossing the state line February 16. Price reached Bentonville, about ten miles south of the border and continued moving south about twenty miles farther to Cross Hollows, Arkansas, the next day to join the main body of McCulloch's army. The army sacked Fayetteville of all the supplies the men could carry as the combined armies continued about fifty miles farther south to the Boston Mountains, where McCulloch maintained his cavalry.

Union Gen. Curtis, in close pursuit of Price, reached the Arkansas border February 17 to welcoming cheers from Union patriots. He set up his Union headquarters less than five miles south of the Missouri border on Telegraph Road near Elkhorn Tavern, a well-established stagecoach station since 1840 at the base of the highland area known as Pea Ridge. Given the long distance back to his supply line at Rolla, Missouri, Curtis did not penetrate farther into Arkansas. He positioned part of his army on well-defended high bluffs at Little Sugar Creek near Elkhorn Tavern to face any opposing forces from the south and manned several smaller outposts around Bentonville and Cross Hollows to monitor enemy activities.

Half the Union Army under Curtis was composed of German immigrants who spoke little English, many of whom had settled in St. Louis. They were led by Gen. Franz Sigel, a German immigrant himself, who resented not being commander of the operation, but he was tolerated by Union command because of his recruitment of significant numbers of German immigrants to the war effort. The remaining soldiers were largely from northern states bordering the Ohio River.

When Confederate President Jefferson Davis became aware of the invasion of Union forces under Gen. Curtis into Arkansas and the threat to Southern control in the state, he created the District of the Trans-Mississippi, an area that included Missouri, Arkansas, north Louisiana and Indian Territory. Passing over the most capable commander, Gen. McCulloch, because McCulloch had not attended West Point Military Academy, Davis selected Gen. Earl Van Dorn to command the new District, which would include the two armies of McCulloch and Price.

V. THE SECOND YEAR: 1862

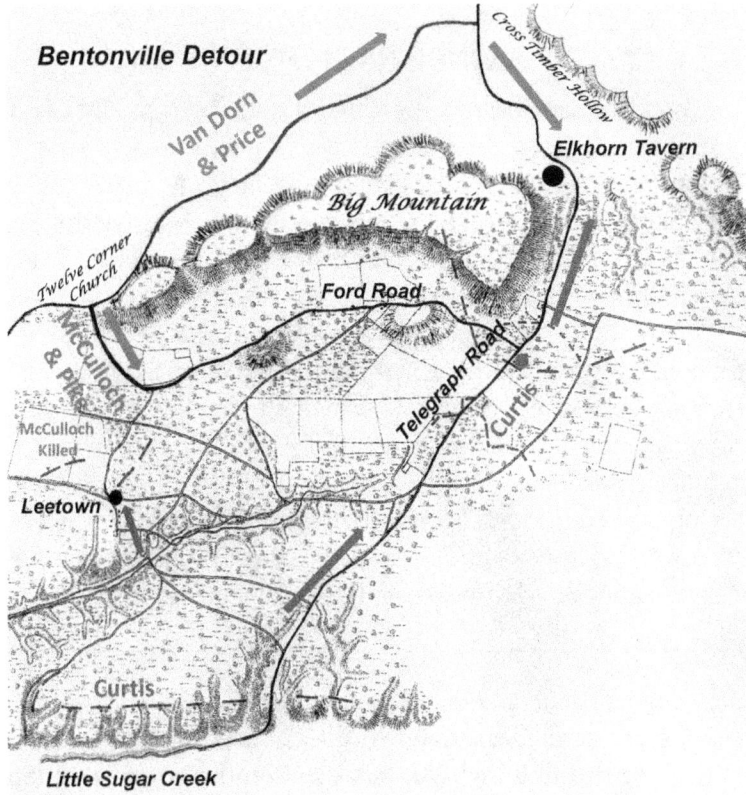

Fig. 12: Confederate Generals Van Dorn, Price and McCulloch attempted a two-pronged attack against Union Gen. Curtis at the Battle of Pea Ridge, Arkansas, in March 1862. The loss of Gen. McCulloch (prematurely killed), bad weather and a lost supply train of ammunition defeated the Confederates.

Source: *This work was modified from a map made by Union soldiers, H.A Ulffers and A. Hoeppner, from a survey conducted by the U.S. Army Corps of Engineers and is in the public domain.*

Van Dorn, a West Point graduate of 1842, had served with distinction in the Mexican-American War and had remained with the U.S. military until the outbreak of the Civil War, when he resigned to join the Confederacy. Taking command of the new District, Van Dorn combined the two armies of Price and McCulloch, renaming it Army of the West, but divided the army into two divisions, to separate the two feuding generals. Van Dorn planned to defeat Curtis and then move north to capture St. Louis, a major industrial and commercial center and gateway to the West. Van Dorn's Army of the West, numbering approximately 15,000, significantly outnumbered the Union forces under Curtis, and would eventually include about 1,000 American Indians, from Indian Territory under the command of Gen. Albert Pike.

The Confederates' three-day 50-mile march north from the Boston Mountains began early on March 4, 1862, in a bitter winter storm. Men were ordered to travel light with forty rounds of ammunition, three days of rations and a blanket. All other

> ## AMERICAN INDIANS IN THE CIVIL WAR
>
> During the American Civil War, an estimated 20,000 American Indians served in both the Union and Confederate armies. Because slavery was legal and practiced in Indian Territory (now Oklahoma), particularly by the Cherokee, many chose to join the Confederacy. Stand Watie, chief of the Cherokee Mounted Rifles, became a general in the Confederate Army. For the Union, Company K of the 1st Michigan Sharpshooters were all American Indians. Many joined, either the Union or the Confederate Armies, hoping that their service would result in better treatment for their tribes, such as an independent nation. But at the end of the war, old hostilities resumed and their lands were even less secure. Participating in battles at Pea Bridge, Second Manassas, Antietam, Spotsylvania, Cold Harbor, Poison Spring and Union assaults at Petersburg, American Indians suffered extraordinarily high death rates in battles. In addition, Indian Territory was often located directly between Union and Confederate combatants, costing lives, livestock and crops. One-third of all the Cherokees and Seminoles died of violence, starvation and war-related illness during the war.

supplies, including tents and additional ammunition, would come along in wagons. A late winter blizzard covered the roads with snow making them nearly impassable and temperatures turned freezing cold. Men slept on the ground with only a single blanket and nearly froze to death. Log fires were lighted to warm the ground, then pulled aside for a place where men would try to sleep. Men fell out of the ranks from cold and exhaustion.

In the meantime, Union Gen. Curtis had consolidated all the elements of his army on the impregnable bluff behind Sugar Creek. As an additional precaution, Curtis had directed engineer Col. Grenville M. Dodge to fell trees on the Bentonville Detour, a road that circled Big Mountain and Pea Ridge to the North, that would slow any Confederates marching along that road. Dodge would become famous later in the Civil War for his ability to rapidly repair and rebuild destroyed railroads, bridges and telegraph lines during the campaigns of Generals Ulysses S. Grant and William T. Sherman.

Van Dorn's forces reached Bentonville late in the afternoon on March 6 with an army of exhausted animals and men that had already depleted their rations. But rather than turning back, Van Dorn split his army. Van Dorn and Price would march through the night around Big Mountain on the Bentonville Detour, intercept Telegraph Road north of the Union position and cut off Curtis' supply line and his retreat back to Missouri. Gen. McCulloch's Division would cut east on Ford Road at Twelve Corner Church, reunite with Van Dorn on Telegraph Road and the combined armies would jointly attack the Union Army where it was entrenched on the bluffs at Little Sugar Creek.

V. THE SECOND YEAR: 1862

The Confederates began their march on the Bentonville Detour the night of March 6 with the addition of about eight hundred Cherokees who had just arrived from Indian Territory under Gen. Albert Pike. Another two hundred Creek, Choctaw and Chickasaw American Indians would arrive the next day. Trudging through knee-deep snow drifts and freezing sleet, the Southerners were delayed as they cleared the felled trees that had been chopped down by Union Col. Dodge to block the route. Van Dorn's lack of an engineering corps and exhaustion of the men added to the delay.

On the morning of March 7, Union Gen. Curtis learned from a local sympathizer that Confederates were moving on the Bentonville Detour, which would bring them to Telegraph Road and access to Elkhorn Tavern, where Curtis had stored hundreds of Union supply wagons. Responding to the potential threat, Curtis deployed about a third of his army to move north and intercept any attacks on the supply wagons, as he still believed the major attack would be at Little Sugar Creek.

When a small Union advance party encountered Confederate McCulloch's full division of about 7,000 men near Leetown, between Little Sugar Creek and Ford Road, both sides opened fire, initiating a vigorous fight involving cavalry and infantry. As Gen. McCulloch rode forward to reconnoiter enemy positions, he was shot in the saddle and instantly killed. His death remained unknown to his men for several hours as the infantry waited for orders to move forward. Belatedly, McCulloch's second-in-command, Gen. James McIntosh, took charge but was also killed in nearly the same place.

The delays, caused by the deaths of McCulloch and McIntosh, provided enough time for Curtis to send Union reinforcements and thwart a third assault led by Confederate Col. Louis Hebert, who was captured in the woods. With no leadership and no food or rest for three days and nights, the exhausted Confederates either moved to join Price's division or returned to Bentonville or the Boston Mountains. McCulloch's Texas Army of the West played no further role in the battle. Although greatly outnumbered, Union forces had prevailed, removing a significant advantage for the Confederates.

Van Dorn, leading Price's division, arrived at Cross Timber Hollow, just north of Elkhorn Tavern, about noon on March 7 with about 5,000 men and prepared to advance up the steep slope to Pea Ridge. To his surprise, he encountered Union troops in front of him as he thought the Union army was still at Sugar Creek. With no sign of McCulloch, Van Dorn decided to attack anyway and slowly pushed the Union troops back through a maze of fences and outbuildings. The Union supply wagons had been safely moved back to Sugar Creek. In fading daylight, Van Dorn tried for another assault, but by this time, Curtis arrived with fresh troops from Sugar Creek and new Union artillery took a devastating toll on the Confederates, halting them in their tracks. Survivors limped back to the woods around the tavern and Curtis abandoned his Sugar Creek fortifications during the night, consolidating his army and artillery to face Van Dorn.

On the morning of March 8, Curtis took the initiative and Union artillery that had been effectively placed for maximum damage by Gen. Sigel unleashed an intense bombardment, wounding and killing hundreds of Confederates. Van Dorn's guns quickly became silent, as the supply train with artillery ammunition had never caught up with the marching men and was now several hours away. After two hours of unremitting artillery bombardment of 3,600 rounds from the Union guns, the Confederate line collapsed. When Curtis passed orders for the army to advance as one unit, the entire 10,000-man Union Army of the Southwest, including infantry, artillery and cavalry, crossed Telegraph Road, and presented a curving blue line that converged on the Confederates from the west and the south.

Van Dorn's forces quickly shrank as thousands of the Missouri Guard troops and the American Indians abandoned the field, leaving the Confederates under Price to their fate. Southern soldiers who escaped to the woods lived on what local inhabitants could provide through the sparse countryside until they could finally reunite with their units at Boston Mountains fifty miles to the south. Elkhorn Tavern, filled with wounded soldiers from both sides, served as a hospital for weeks afterward.

One of the bloodiest battles west of the Mississippi, the Union experienced about 1,400 casualties (200 dead, 1,200 wounded or missing) and the Confederate losses numbered about 2,000. Union Gen. Sigel would receive a promotion for his performance with the artillery on the battlefield. With the Union victory, Southern forces lost the opportunity to dominate Missouri for the rest of the war. Van Dorn took his demoralized army east to join Confederate forces at Corinth, Mississippi, abandoning the South's defense of Arkansas.

Union Gen. Curtis continued southeast to seize Helena, Arkansas, on July 12, which became a vital port for the North on the Mississippi River for the remainder of the war. Located two hundred thirty miles north of Vicksburg, Helena became a target for a Confederate takeover in June-July 1863 at the height of the Union's Vicksburg Campaign. But the Battle of Helena on July 4, 1863, resulted in a resounding Confederate defeat, and put an end to the South's operations in Arkansas, except for isolated guerilla activities. From Helena, Union forces were able to recapture the federal Arkansas installations at Little Rock and Fort Smith in September 1863.

Battle of Shiloh (or Pittsburg Landing), Tennessee
April 6-7, 1862

After securing Forts Henry and Donelson, Gen. Ulysses S. Grant moved his army south along the Tennessee River and established headquarters at Savannah, Tennessee, in March 1862. Grant had been promoted to Major General, commanding the District of West Tennessee, and continued to name his army the Army of the Tennessee. Troops set up camp about ten miles farther downriver at Pittsburg Landing, which would be the staging area for a major Union offensive against Corinth, Mississippi, about twenty miles farther south. Corinth, located on the border between Tennessee and Mississippi, provided the Confederacy with a vital transportation route of railroads for movement of troops and supplies.

A little more than two miles from Pittsburg Landing, the Union Army set up camp near a log house called Shiloh, a Biblical reference to a tranquil and peaceful meeting place. Standing on a ridge between two creeks, Shiloh was in a key position and held by one of Grant's division commanders, Gen. William T. Sherman, who now commanded the District of Cairo after Grant's promotion to the District of West Tennessee.

Gen. Sherman, who had graduated sixth in his class from West Point in 1840 three years before Grant, did not see action in the Mexican-American War, as he had been assigned to administrative duties in captured California. He played an important role in the California gold rush in 1849 when he wrote the first army report that later became public, informing the U.S. government about the discovery of gold. Resigning from the army in 1853 after the California Gold Rush, he pursued private interests in real estate and banking in San Francisco until 1859 when he was named Superintendent of the Louisiana State Seminary of Learning & Military Academy in Baton Rouge, Louisiana.

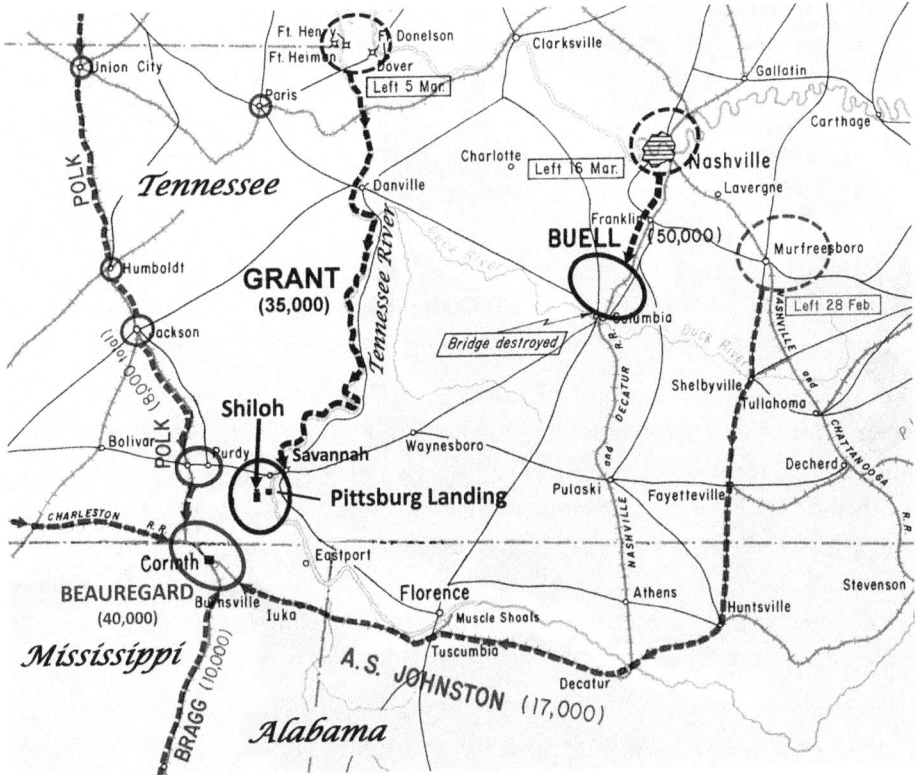

Fig. 13: Prior to the Battle of Shiloh, Confederate armies under Generals A.S. Johnston, Beauregard, Polk and Bragg gathered at Corinth, Mississippi, for a concentrated attack at Shiloh on the Union Army under Gen. Grant, April 1862.

Source: *This map, a work of the U.S. federal government by a U.S. Army soldier, is in the public domain.*

STRUGGLE FOR THE UNION

In December 1860 after the secession of South Carolina from the Union, Sherman spoke passionately in a speech at the Seminary about how secession would destroy the South. *"You people of the South don't know what you're doing. This country will be drenched in blood and God only knows how it will end. War is a terrible thing. The North can make a steam engine, a locomotive, or railway car; hardly a yard of cloth or shoes can you make. Only in your spirit and determination are you prepared for war. In all else, you are totally unprepared... in the end you will surely fail."*

As more Southern states seceded from the Union, an action Sherman vigorously opposed, he declared to the state's governor, *"If Louisiana withdraws from the Federal Union, I prefer to maintain my allegiance to the Constitution as long as a fragment of it survives... I beg you to take immediate steps to relieve me as superintendent, the moment the State determines to secede, for on no earthly account will I do any act or think any thought hostile to or in defiance of the old Government of the United States."*

Sherman resigned from the Louisiana Academy in January 1861 and re-enlisted in the Union Army in May 1861. He earned a promotion for leading a brigade of inexperienced troops at the disastrous Battle of First Bull Run in July, but the impact of command brought on a period of depression and despondency that he admitted *"broke me down."* He was placed on leave for some weeks to recuperate and during this period, he predicted that 200,000 men would soon be needed for the battles to come, prompting the Northern press to claim he was suffering from insanity. When he was ready to return to duty, he was assigned to the District of Cairo to serve under Ulysses S. Grant. Technically, Sherman outranked Grant in seniority, because he had been promoted to Brigadier General, effective May 17, 1861, and Grant's promotion to the same rank did not occur until July 1861. But Sherman did not want the command and quickly assured Grant, *"I have faith in you... Command me in any way."*

Troops under Gen. Sherman's charge at Shiloh were raw recruits who had not yet received any training. Although there had been skirmishes nearby between Union and Confederate patrols, neither Grant nor Sherman believed that a major Confederate force in the vicinity was preparing an offensive. Sherman used the time to train his new recruits and did not prepare strong defenses against an attack. Further, Grant had ordered his commanders not to initiate any major battles until his reinforcements arrived from the Army of the Ohio, now underway from Nashville, under the command of Gen. Don Carlos Buell.

Significant Confederate forces were accumulating, however, at Corinth, Mississippi, under Gen. Albert Sidney Johnston, who had abandoned his secessionist headquarters in Bowling Green Kentucky, when Forts Henry and Donelson fell to Grant in February. Johnston had combined his army with the Army of Mississippi at Corinth under Gen. P.G.T. Beauregard and taken overall command of the two armies, which now totaled about 45,000 men, with Beauregard as second-in-command.

V. THE SECOND YEAR: 1862

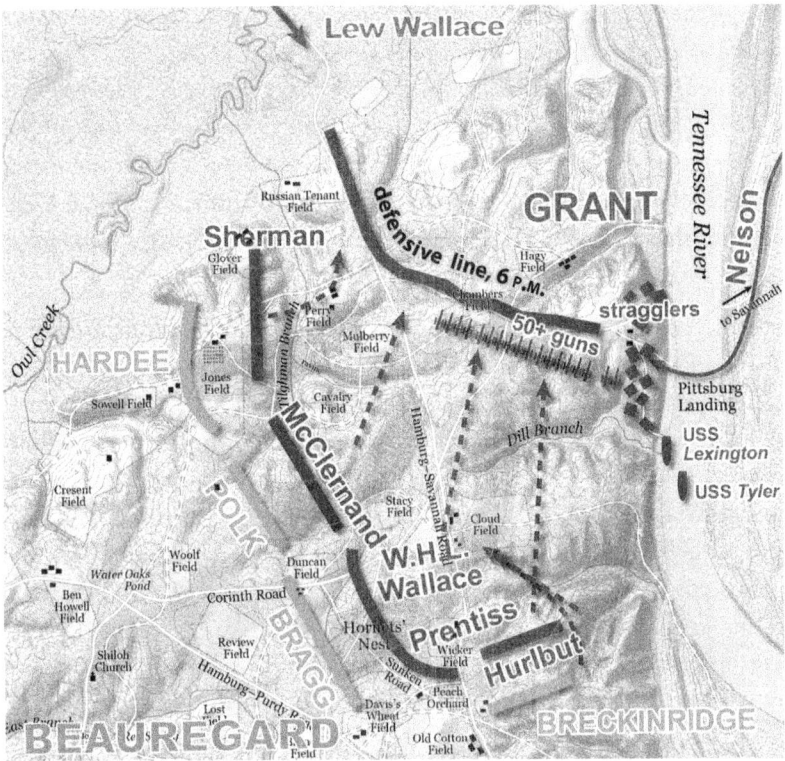

Fig. 14: Battle of Shiloh, Pittsburg Landing, Tennessee, April 6, 1862, at 6 pm, with Confederates winning the battle, but Gen. A. S. Johnston died in battle, placing Beauregard in command of the Confederate Army. Reinforcements under Gen. William Nelson from Ohio arrived in the night to support the Union Army and Gen. Grant won victory the next day.

Source: Creative Commons Attribution 3.0 license. Map by Hal Jespersen, www.cwmaps.com

The Confederates planned a major offensive at Shiloh for April 4, but a heavy rain delayed the assault for forty-eight hours. On the early morning of April 6, Johnston initiated a surprise attack, catching the Union troops off guard as they prepared their breakfast.

The Southerners, advancing through difficult terrain of blackberry bushes uphill, came on *"like a Kansas hurricane,"* in the words of one Union soldier. As the surprised Union men abruptly abandoned their camp, hungry Confederates stopped to grab some of the discarded breakfast until officers could restore discipline. A region of extreme fighting became the "Hornet's Nest" from the noise of zipping bullets. Heavy, intense battles continued to force the Union line back over the next several hours. One of the Union divisions was surrounded by the Confederates and more than 2,000 were captured as prisoners.

Grant, still at Savannah where he expected to meet Buell, heard the sounds of gunfire and immediately proceeded to Pittsburgh Landing. Sherman's division was hit the hardest, but his men rallied as their commander inspired his raw recruits by being everywhere in the battle encouraging the men. Grant wrote in his *Personal Memoirs*: "Although Sherman's troops were then under fire for the first time, and the hardest fighting was in front of them, their commander, by his constant presence with them, inspired a confidence in officers and men that enabled them to render services on that bloody battlefield worthy of the best of veterans." Sherman, shot twice, but not seriously, had three horses killed under him, and was commended by both Grant and Gen. Halleck after the battle. Sherman would become Grant's most trusted and reliable general for the rest of the war.

Confederate Gen. Johnston was shot in the leg during the battle and believing the wound to be relatively minor, bled to death on the field from a severed artery, the highest-ranking officer to be killed in the war. Confederacy's President Jefferson Davis would say later of his death, *"It was the turning point of our fate, for we had no other hand to take up his work in the West."* Command of the Confederates now fell to Gen. Beauregard, who drove the Union troops back to the Tennessee River. Beauregard, who believed that Grant would either be captured or beaten back into his transports on the river the next day, called off the attack at dusk. The exhausted Confederate troops, who had been on short rations, fell into the abandoned Union camps still replete with food and supplies and were protected from a drenching rain that now poured onto the Union soldiers.

Union reserve forces from Crump's Landing under Gen. Lew Wallace belatedly arrived that evening after the fighting was over. A miscommunication had resulted in Wallace's troops taking the wrong road and marching ineffectively for seven hours. Grant's negative report damaged Wallace's military career, which would later be salvaged in 1864 at Monocacy Junction, Maryland. As reinforcements from Gen. Buell's Army of the Ohio arrived during the night, Union forces were increased to nearly 60,000. All through the night, Union gunboats, the *USS Lexington* and *USS Tyler*, dropped shells every fifteen minutes on the Confederate lines.

During the night, Sherman encountered Grant, standing next to a tree, smoking a cigar, still suffering from an injured leg and ankle when his horse fell on him two days earlier. A famous verbal exchange between the two men illustrated Grant's attitude to battle. Sherman said later that his instincts told him not to mention the word, "Retreat." Instead, he asked of his commander, *"Well, Grant, we've had the devil's own day, haven't we?"* "Yep," Grant replied. *"Lick 'em tomorrow, though."* During the night, Grant set up strong Union defenses by mounting a three-mile-long ridge with a massive artillery ring of fifty cannons.

When Grant met Gen. Buell at the river, they found thousands of stragglers who had deserted the front to find a place of safety at the riverbank. Many of the Union men included troops that had been hastily thrown together with little time for drill and discipline and were under fire for the first time. Buell attempted to shame them into returning to their regiments, but to no effect. Grant, observing the exchange, later wrote in his *Personal Memoirs:*

"There were four or five thousand stragglers lying under cover of the river bluff, panic-stricken, most of whom would have been shot where they lay, without resistance, before they would have taken muskets and marched to the front to protect themselves. But, most of these men afterward proved themselves as gallant as any of those who saved the battle from which they had deserted. If Gen. Buell had come in by the front instead of through the stragglers in the rear, he would have thought and felt differently. Could he have come through the Confederate rear, he would have witnessed there a scene similar to our own. The distant rear of an army engaged in battle is not the best place from which to judge correctly what is going on in front."

Grant launched a fierce attack on the Confederate line at dawn the next morning. Beauregard, unaware that he was now badly outnumbered, was surprised by the Union offensive. As the Union attack proceeded, the ground they had lost the day before was regained as the Confederates were driven back. By afternoon, low on ammunition, food and able men, Beauregard organized an orderly withdrawal of the Army of Mississippi to Corinth.

The two-day battle at Shiloh resulted in approximately 13,000 Union and 11,000 Confederate casualties. The shocking carnage of the battle devastated the country and Grant was vilified by the Northern press. Some accounts wrongly accused him of drunkenness during the battle. Grant's officers who were with him denied the allegations and defended him publicly.

THE DEAD AT SHILOH

Grant writes in his *Personal Memoirs* that as he was riding out from Shiloh the day after the battle, *"I saw an open field… so covered with dead that it would have been possible to walk across the clearing, in any direction, stepping on dead bodies, without a foot touching the ground."* On the Union side of the battlefield, the numbers were about equally divided between Union and Confederate, but on the rest of the field, nearly all were Confederates. The force of the battle and the gallant loss of life the Confederates had endured here and at other battles convinced Grant that the war would not be won by any single *"… decisive victory. Union success would be achieved only by complete conquest."*

Col. William R. Rowley, long-time friend of Grant from Galena, Illinois, serving as aide-de-camp to Grant, wrote a public response to comments from the Northern press about Grant, that as a member of Grant's staff, he was in close contact with the general every day. *"I have never seen him take even a glass of liquor more than two or three times in my life and then only a single at a time. And I have never seen him intoxicated or even approximate to it. As to the story that he was intoxicated at the Battle of Pittsburg, I have only to say that the man who fabricated the story is an infamous liar, and you are at liberty to say to him that I say so."*

President Lincoln, inundated with demands for Grant's removal, said of his general, "I can't spare this man, he fights."

Union Navy Captures New Orleans
April 24-25, 1862

When Louisiana seceded to join the Confederacy, the important port of New Orleans at the mouth of the Mississippi River became a chief strategic objective for the Union. Its first step was to institute a blockade at the city to prevent all trade there with the Confederacy. When the Southerners successfully attacked the blockade in October 1861 using the Confederate ironclad *CSS Manassas*, Flag Officer David G. Farragut, commanding the West Gulf Blockading Squadron, made plans to conquer the city. In April 1862, forty-three Union ships entered the lower Mississippi River and bombarded the small Southern fleet which soon surrendered. Forts Jackson and Phillip were captured April 29.

With the fall of the city and the two forts, Farragut moved north to capture the remaining Confederate outposts on the lower Mississippi River. Baton Rouge, seized May 9, was controlled by the Union for the rest of the war. Natchez, Mississippi, also fell to the Union Navy three days later. Port Hudson, a well-fortified fortress seventy miles upriver from Natchez, remained in Confederate hands. When Farragut attempted to capture Vicksburg on May 18, he was beaten back by the great cannons protecting the Vicksburg Fortress and he returned to the Gulf. The Confederacy maintained control of the Mississippi River between Port Hudson and Vicksburg, which allowed the South to continue to share troops, food and military supplies between its Eastern and Western forces until the fall of Vicksburg and Hudson in July 1863.

After the Union Navy's capture of New Orleans, Gen. Benjamin Butler, commander at Fort Monroe on the Virginia Peninsula, formed an expeditionary force of 15,000 troops to occupy the city and entered New Orleans on May 1. But the presence of Union troops in a hostile population resulted in a number of incidents that caused Butler to issue a number of General Orders that offended the public and earned him the label of "Beast Butler." Order No. 28 was issued because of insults against Union soldiers by the females of the city. The Order stated, in part, " *… if any female shall by word, gesture, or movement insult or show contempt for any officer or soldier of the United States she shall be regarded and held liable to be treated as a woman of the town plying her avocation."* The inflammatory order was so controversial that Butler was removed from New Orleans in December and Gen. Nathaniel P. Banks was moved from northern

Virginia and placed in charge of the Army of the Gulf. But the loss of New Orleans was a significant disaster for the Confederacy.

Siege of Corinth, Mississippi
April 29-May 30, 1862

Corinth, located on the Tennessee-Mississippi border about twenty miles south of Shiloh and one hundred miles east of Memphis, was considered an important crossroads for the South. Its strategic location at the junction of two vital railroad lines provided important access to Confederate strongholds on both sides of the Mississippi. The Mobile & Ohio Railroad penetrated south to the Gulf of Mexico and the Deep South; the Memphis & Charleston Railroad ran east-west through the Confederacy, providing a vital link for transporting troops, ammunition and supplies.

Gen. Henry Halleck, who had been advanced to be overall commander of the Western Theater, now commanded the armies of Kansas, Ohio, Tennessee and Mississippi. Halleck, noted for his knowledge of military tactics and nicknamed, "Old Brains," took personal command of the Siege of Corinth, now occupied by the Confederates under Gen. P.G.T. Beauregard. Acting on a long-held dislike of Gen. Ulysses S. Grant, Halleck removed him from commanding the Army of the Tennessee and assigned Grant to serve as his second-in-command, giving him no direct responsibilities for any troops.

Halleck, a masterful and politically adept administrator, had never been in field command and was excessively cautious in his preparations for the Siege of Corinth. As the large Union Army slowly lumbered toward the beleaguered city from Pittsburgh Landing, Halleck stopped it daily to erect elaborate defensive positions. The army took a month to arrive at Corinth only twenty miles away.

Although Beauregard's army had been reinforced in Corinth during the months of April and May, contaminated water had devastated his men and thousands were lost to typhoid and dysentery. The Confederates lost almost as many men to death by disease in Corinth as had been killed in the battle at Shiloh. Outnumbered two to one, Beauregard knew that his troops could not survive an attack from the massive Union army converging on them. False information was passed on to informants to convince Union generals that a Confederate attack would occur May 30. On the night of May 29, welcoming cheers were heard by Northern observers as trains pulled into Corinth. Halleck was persuaded that reinforcements for the Confederates were arriving in anticipation of an attack the next day. But the trains were actually empty when they arrived and loaded with sick and wounded when they left. Dummy Quaker guns and burning campfires added to the deception. Union patrols entered a deserted city on May 30, emptied of all soldiers, including the sick or wounded men, leaving no supplies or ammunition behind.

Gen. Beauregard, quite ill himself, took medical leave without the permission of Confederate President Davis. Learning of Beauregard's absence from the field, a furious Davis removed him from command and placed Gen. Braxton Bragg in charge of the South's Army of Mississippi. Beauregard was then transferred east to organize coastal defenses of South Carolina, Georgia and Florida, replacing Gen. John C. Pemberton, who was sent to defend Vicksburg.

During the long month preceding the Siege of Corinth, Union Gen. Ulysses S. Grant nearly resigned from the Union Army as Gen. Halleck had removed him from leading a command. But a passionate and convincing argument from Gen. Sherman changed Grant's mind. Sherman writes, *"I argued with him that, if he went away, events would go right along, and he would be left out; whereas, if he remained, some happy accident might restore him to favor and his true place."*

Grant's salvation came on July 11 when Lincoln named Halleck as General-in-Chief of all Union armies, a position that had been vacant since Lincoln removed McClellan from the post in March. Shortly afterward, Halleck was moved to Washington and Grant was restored to command the forces at Corinth, the District of West Tennessee, which included his own Army of the Tennessee and the Army of the Mississippi, commanded by Gen. William Rosecrans. Grant set up headquarters at Memphis and organized defenses of the city and the supply lines in western Tennessee and northern Mississippi. Gen. Buell, however, commanding the Army of the Ohio, would report directly to Halleck and was soon ordered to proceed toward Chattanooga.

BATTLES IN THE EASTERN THEATER

SHENANDOAH VALLEY, VIRGINIA

The Shenandoah Valley, named for the river that runs through it, was the rich agricultural region that served as the breadbasket for the Confederacy. Located between the Blue Ridge and Allegheny Mountains, the Valley provided a rich soil, mild climate and multiple agricultural crops that were supported by a slave population that accounted for twenty-five percent of the inhabitants. The main Southside Railroad from Lynchburg reached all the way to Richmond and Petersburg and was used extensively to provide food for the Confederate armies. Southern forces were able to move between the two mountain ranges without detection and threaten Maryland targets. With a population of divided Confederate and Union loyalties, Winchester, Virginia, became a strategic location for several battles throughout the war.

Battle of Kernstown, Virginia
March 23, 1862

In early March 1862, Confederate Gen. Thomas J. "Stonewall" Jackson set up headquarters for his Army of the Valley on Rude's Hill in the southern part of the Shenandoah Valley near Mount Jackson, on the advice of a well-known cartographer,

Jedediah Hotchkiss. Jackson directed Hotchkiss, who had offered his services to the Confederacy, to map the Shenandoah Valley in detail as it had never been done before. Reportedly, Jackson ordered Hotchkiss to show all the points of offense and defense from Harpers Ferry to Lexington, the entire length of the Valley. The large single map, seven feet long by three feet tall, displayed all the geographical features over a terrain one hundred fifty miles long and twenty-five miles wide. The detailed topographical maps were instrumental in Jackson's early successes in the Valley and his subsequent campaigns.

In mid-March 1862, Union Gen. Nathaniel P. Banks commanded the Department of the Shenandoah with headquarters in the Valley at Strasburg, Virginia. On March 21, Jackson received word that Banks was splitting his army so that two divisions could be sent south to support Gen. George McClellan's Peninsula Campaign, an initiative to attack Richmond by landing the Union Army at Fort Monroe at the tip of the Virginia peninsula on Chesapeake Bay and then marching on land to the Confederate Capital. Jackson was to interfere and prevent Union troops from departing the Valley.

Jackson's approach to battle was *"to mystify, mislead and surprise the enemy."* To implement the new orders, he quickly initiated a grueling forced march of twenty-five miles on March 22 and another fifteen miles the next day to reach Kernstown around noon on March 23. Given incorrect information that Union forces at Kernstown comprised only about 1,000 men, Jackson attacked on March 23 with about 3,500 troops against a Union force of nearly 9,000, which quickly repulsed the Confederates. It became one of Jackson's rare defeats. Col. Nathan Kimball, a veteran of the Mexican-American War and a proven leader at the Battle at Cheat Mountain Pass the year before, was acting commander on the battlefield in place of wounded division commander Gen. James Shields. Kimball was later rewarded with a promotion to Brigadier General for the victory over Jackson.

Although a Union victory, the battle had important consequences. Jackson's boldness made Lincoln acutely aware of the very real threat to the Union capital at Washington, D.C., which could fall into Confederate hands. As a result, Banks' entire army would remain in the Shenandoah to protect the capital and defend the arsenal at Harpers Ferry. No troops would be sent to support the Peninsula Campaign.

Battles of Front Royal & Winchester, Virginia
May 25, 1862

After his defeat at Kernstown, Confederate Gen. Stonewall Jackson continued to act on orders to block Union troops being sent from the Shenandoah Valley that would support the Union offensive in the Virginia Peninsula Campaign. In early May, Jackson moved his small army of about 6,500 to meet an advance unit from the Union Army's Mountain Department that had entered the Shenandoah Valley from western Virginia. Gen. John C. Fremont had been removed from his position in Missouri and now commanded the Mountain Department, which covered parts of western Virginia and

> ## BROTHER AGAINST BROTHER
>
> The Battle at Front Royal May 23 was notable as two Maryland regiments, each numbered the 1st Maryland Infantry, one Union and one Confederate, faced each other in battle. Capt. William Goldsborough of the Confederate side captured his brother Charles of the Union 1st and took him prisoner. As the Union prisoners were brought forward, men recognized old friends and acquaintances, greeted them cordially, and shared their rations with each other. Many instances occurred of brothers choosing to fight for opposite sides, which caused life-long friction between them and their families.

eastern Kentucky. At the Battle of McDowell (or Sitlington's Hill) on May 8, Stonewall Jackson forced Fremont's vanguard into a retreat, and then turned his attention north to the Union army under Gen. Nathaniel P. Banks, Department of the Shenandoah, now located at Strasburg.

Confederate President Jefferson Davis, recognizing Stonewall Jackson's limited forces, sent reinforcements under the command of Gen. Richard Ewell and the combined forces increased Jackson's Army of the Valley to more than 16,000 men. On May 21, Jackson force-marched his greatly increased army over Massanutten Mountain and proceeded undetected north along the Luray Valley to Front Royal. The troops marched with such speed, they became known as "Jackson's foot cavalry." An advance unit of the Confederate 1st Maryland Infantry reached Front Royal on May 23 and surprised about 700 soldiers of the Union's 1st Regiment of Maryland Volunteers. Quickly overwhelmed, the smaller Union force surrendered and the soldiers were taken prisoner.

Jackson next moved north to take Winchester and possibly capture the Northern army under Gen. Banks, still located at Strasberg. As Jackson's army advanced, the Union army, numbering about 9,000, rapidly retreated north to Winchester and were nearly trapped when Jackson's troops caught up with them and overran the Union army's position. As the Union troops fled through Winchester and retreated north to cross the Potomac River into Maryland at Williamsport, they left a large supply train behind. The losses included special foodstuffs, one hundred cattle, thousands of pounds of bacon and a huge supply of ammunition, giving Banks a new name from the Confederates as "Commissary Banks." Jackson's pursuit did not capture the Union army because his cavalry was absent from the main army, but his principal objective had been achieved. No Union troops from the Shenandoah would be joining McClellan's Army of the Potomac in the Peninsula Campaign.

Acting as General-in-Chief, Lincoln devised a plan to create a three-pronged attack against Jackson by uniting some of the Union Army at Washington with those of Fremont, now in western Virginia, with the army of Banks, now just across the Virginia

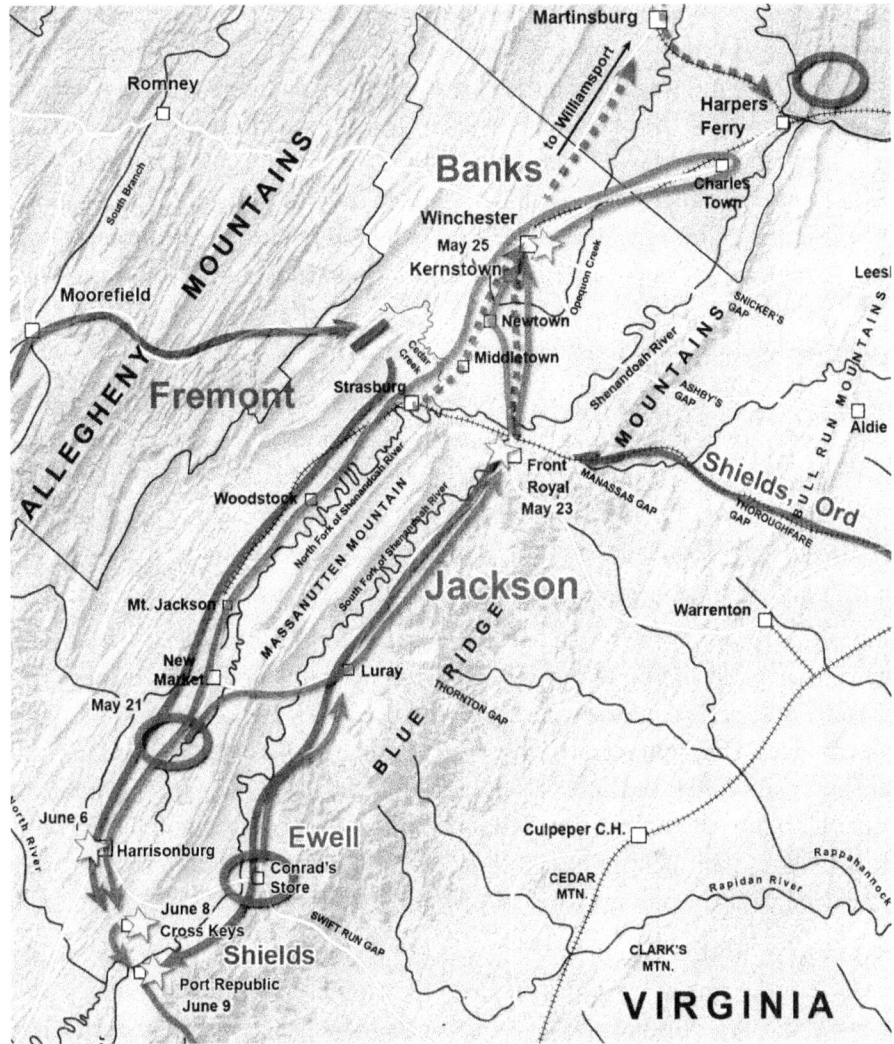

Fig. 15: Confederate Gen. Stonewall Jackson defeated three Union armies under Generals Fremont, Banks and Shields in several encounters during the Shenandoah Valley Campaign of May 1862.

Source: *Creative Commons Attribution 3.0 license. Map by Hal Jespersen, www.cwmaps.com*

border in Maryland. Two divisions of Union troops under Generals James Shields and Edward Ord, were sent to the Shenandoah to join forces with Fremont and Banks.

The plan began to unravel when Banks declared his army would not be able to participate until it had more time to recover from its losses at Winchester. Fremont's forces from western Virginia were on the west side of Massanutten Mountain and Shields' army was on the east. The two armies attempted to corner Jackson without success for eight days, working from opposite sides of the mountain.

As Jackson proceeded south from Winchester to stay ahead of the pursuing Union armies, he saw an opportunity at Cross Keys at the southern end of the Shenandoah Valley, about sixty miles south of Strasburg. By controlling the two bridges that crossed the southern forks of the Shenandoah River, Jackson could prevent the two armies from uniting. At the Battle of Cross Keys on June 8, Jackson confronted Fremont first, while holding Shields at Port Republic. The day did not go well for the Union side and fighting stopped when darkness fell. Fremont did not mount a counter-attack the following day, and Jackson turned his attention to Shields on June 9 at the Battle of Port Republic. Although it was not Jackson's best effort and his army suffered heavy casualties, he was still able to win the battle against Shields.

Neither Fremont nor Shields mounted any further attacks against the Confederates and the two Union armies withdrew from the Shenandoah Valley by the end of June. At that point, Jackson left the Shenandoah and marched his army one hundred twenty miles to the Virginia Peninsula to support Confederate forces defending Richmond against the massive Union effort from Gen. George McClellan that had already begun.

The series of battles in the Shenandoah represented a major victory for Jackson's Valley Campaign and made him a celebrated soldier for the Confederacy. Using a combination of surprise and rapid movement, his army had won five significant victories over armies of superior numbers. Jackson's men had covered six hundred fifty miles in forty-eight days. The Confederate Valley Campaign had disrupted the Union's hold on the Shenandoah Valley and consumed thousands of Union men and resources while eventually driving them from the Valley. Union soldiers were disappointed with the performances of their commanders, Shields and Frémont, and both of their military careers faded after the battles at Cross Keys and Port Republic.

Frustrated with the Union defeats in the Shenandoah Valley, President Lincoln formed the new Army of Virginia in June 1862 that included units of Banks, Frémont, McDowell, and several smaller ones from around Washington and western Virginia. When Fremont learned that his Mountain Department Corps would be merged into the new Army of Virginia and he would be reporting to its new commander, Gen. John Pope, whom Fremont outranked, he refused to serve. Fremont moved to New York City and waited for a new command, but when none came by June 1864, he resigned from the army. Shields received no more combat assignments and resigned from the army in March 1863. The newly formed Army of Virginia would be defeated in the Battle of Second Bull Run in August and then merged into the Army of the Potomac. Pope lost his command and was moved to Minnesota until 1865 when he was given a brief command in Missouri shortly before the end of the war.

V. THE SECOND YEAR: 1862

PENINSULA CAMPAIGN, VIRGINIA

After several months of resisting President Lincoln's pressure to mount a military offensive against the Confederacy, Union Gen. George B. McClellan finally launched in late March 1862 his major campaign to capture the Confederate capital at Richmond, Virginia. But instead of attacking the Confederate capital with a more direct overland approach from Washington, McClellan would advance on Richmond by moving his army to the tip of the Virginia Peninsula at Fort Monroe and then march up the strip of land between the York and James Rivers to Richmond.

The Army of the Potomac left Alexandria on the Potomac River, March 17, 1862, using a fleet of nearly 400 steamers and schooners to move more than 120,000 men, 15,000 horses, 1,150 wagons, 44 artillery batteries and tons of artillery and armaments down the Chesapeake Bay to Fort Monroe at Hampton, Virginia. From this position, a direct route on the peninsula between the York and James Rivers led to Richmond. Fort Monroe, a major base for Northern navy and army operations, had been secured by Union forces shortly after the Confederates fired on Fort Sumter and was the only fort in the Upper South not to fall into Confederate hands.

Naval Battle of Hampton Roads, Norfolk, Virginia
March 8-9, 1862

When the Army of the Potomac arrived at Fort Monroe in late March 1862, anticipated support from the U.S. Navy on the York and James rivers did not materialize. Union Navy ships were busy in Hampton Roads Bay fighting the steam-powered Confederate ironclad *CSS Virginia*. Launched in February, the Confederate gunboat had been constructed by raising the original hull and engines of the scuttled Union steam frigate, the *USS Merrimack,* that was lost to the Confederates when they seized the Naval shipyard in 1861. The *Merrimack* was rebuilt into a Confederate ironclad by placing layers of iron plates over heavy wood backing, sloped so that they would deflect direct hits. The Southerners built the ironclad to combat the Union blockade that had cut off international trade at its industrial centers in Norfolk and Richmond.

A famous battle occurred on March 8-9, 1862, between two ironclads, the Confederate *CSS Virginia* and Union *USS Monitor* in the Battle of Hampton Roads (or Battle of the Ironclads). Although Union ironclads had already been used in the Western Theater, ironclads in the Eastern Theater had never faced each other in battle. The *CSS Virginia* was larger, had ten stationary guns and was fitted with a 1,500-pound battering ram on its bow. The *Monitor,* smaller and shorter in length, had only two rotating guns, but was more maneuverable. On March 8, the Confederate ironclad sank two wooden-hulled Union ships, the *USS Cumberland* and *USS Congress,* and ran another aground, the *USS Minnesota.* The next day, the *USS Monitor* steamed into the bay and the two ironclads battled each other for several hours on March 9 with little effect on either side. The battle ended in a draw when the *CSS Virginia* ran out of ammunition and retired to Norfolk. The two-day battle would remain the U.S. Navy's greatest defeat until World War II.

Battle (or Siege) of Yorktown, Virginia
April 5-May 4, 1862

With no Navy support, the Army of the Potomac left Fort Monroe on April 4 to begin its march up the Virginia peninsula. Within a few miles, the men encountered a blockade along the Warwick River near Yorktown. Confederate Gen. John B. Magruder, commanding a small 11-13,000-man army, had used slaves to build three well-fortified dams along the Warwick River, which created a defense line across the full 12-mile width of the Peninsula, drastically reducing the number of places to cross (See Fig. 16). Magruder, who enjoyed theatrical displays and was known by his men as "Prince John" for his resplendent uniforms, had installed fake "Quaker guns," logs painted black to appear as cannons, along the defensive line and he skillfully marched his troops about to give the impression of a much larger force. Sporadic volleys from his widely spaced artillery added to the theatrics.

After a few unsuccessful Union attempts to break through the Warwick Line, McClellan became convinced that he was facing a much larger force than his own and began the task of installing massive siege artillery batteries all along the front line.

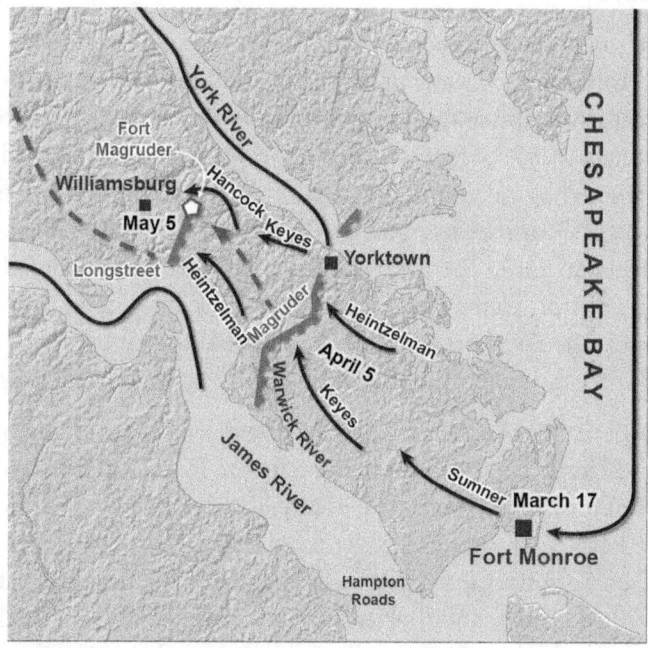

Fig. 16: In the Siege of Yorktown, Virginia, Confederates under Generals Magruder and Longstreet blocked the Union advance led by Gen. George B. McClellan from Fort Monroe for one month as the Northern troops tried to move up the Virginia Peninsula.

Source: *Creative Commons Attribution 3.0 license. Map by Hal Jespersen, www.cwmaps.com*

V. THE SECOND YEAR: 1862

With Union forces stalled at Yorktown, Confederate Gen. Joseph E. Johnston, commanding the newly renamed Army of Northern Virginia, arrived with about 40,000 troops, assembled from scattered winter quarters in eastern Virginia, and took over command of the Southern defenses. Confederate reinforcements continued to arrive over a two-week period and increased the size of Johnston's army over the month of April while McClellan was setting up his siege guns.

Union Balloon Corps Implements New Surveillance Tool

Assisting McClellan at the Yorktown blockade was the Union Army Balloon Corps, established as a civilian operation by President Lincoln in August 1861, under the direction of Professor Thaddeus Lowe, a self-made scientist and veteran balloonist. Lowe arrived at Hampton, Virginia, on March 28 with all his balloon equipment and gas generators on his own flat-topped balloonist carrier that had recently been created by converting the deck of a coal barge, towed by a steam-powered tug. The structure, named the *George Washington Park Custis*, was later described as the Navy's first aircraft carrier. Lowe set up two balloon camps, one at Yorktown and another closer to the James River on the other side of the peninsula. Using silk from India and cotton cording, seven balloons of varying size had been manufactured, coated with varnish to make them leakproof, and then filled with hydrogen gas. Special generators, which accompanied the balloons, were equipped with dilute sulfuric acid and iron filings to generate the hydrogen gas.

Two tethered balloons, the *Intrepid* and the *Constitution*, were deployed at opposite ends of the Union line facing the Confederates. The largest balloon, the *Intrepid*, could hold five men and was equipped with a telegraph transmitter to relay information by wire directly to McClellan. The *Constitution*, the second largest balloon, could support three men in the air. Both balloons carried officers and even reporters aloft to view the fortifications and conduct aerial reconnaissance on Confederate Army movements. The tethered balloons, well behind the front lines, could reach heights of one thousand feet and were only vulnerable to Confederate artillery while ascending before they were soon out of range, or during their descents where they were quickly obscured by forest.

The balloons provided a great weapon for the North, as the Confederate commanders were forced to expend considerable energy to hide their movements from the "Eyes in the Sky." Campfires were blacked out at night and false camps and fake artillery placements were created to deceive the observers. Confederate Gen. James Longstreet noted that, *"The Federals had been using balloons to examine our positions, and we watched with anxious eyes their beautiful observations as they floated out of range of our guns."* Nevertheless, the Confederates successfully camouflaged their actual troop numbers from the balloon observations. The flawed reconnaissance from detective Alan Pinkerton convinced McClellan that a great army was facing him and he continued to install his massive siege artillery.

During this period, McClellan received word that the anticipated reinforcements from Washington, D.C., would not be coming. "Stonewall" Jackson's recent defeats of Union armies in the Shenandoah Valley had convinced Lincoln that the Union capital at Washington was vulnerable to Confederate attack and he needed to maintain sufficient troops nearby to protect the city. McClellan would later claim that the loss of these forces prevented his success in capturing Richmond.

Convinced that he faced a huge Confederate army, McClellan proceeded with plans to conduct a massive artillery bombardment once installation of 103 siege guns was completed. The assault was planned for May 5, but when Confederate Gen. Johnston's informants warned him of the coming attack, he made plans to withdraw. On the morning of May 3, he increased artillery firing on the Balloon Corps that kept them aground most of the day. Early morning observations by the aeronauts the next day revealed that the Confederates had abandoned their fortress and quietly withdrawn in the night.

Union pursuit attempted to cut off the Confederate retreat at the Battle of Williamsburg (also known as the Battle of Fort Magruder) on May 5, but the Southerners successfully escaped. McClellan portrayed the battle as a "brilliant" victory over superior forces.

Union Recaptures Naval Shipyard, Virginia
May 6, 1862

President Lincoln, disappointed with McClellan's lack of progress, personally arrived at Fort Monroe on May 6 and ordered the Navy to bombard Norfolk, a port city located across the Bay from the fort and adjacent to the Union Naval Shipyard at Portsmouth, Virginia. Norfolk quickly surrendered to the Union forces as the Confederates had abandoned the city to support the defense of Richmond. With the Union capture of the Norfolk Naval Shipyard on May 10, the Confederate ironclad *CSS Virginia* lost its home port and the Southerners disabled the gunboat and scuttled it.

With the recapture of Norfolk and elimination of the Confederate gunboat, Union Navy ships immediately steamed up the James River to support McClellan's Peninsula Campaign. The flotilla included four warships, two Navy ironclads, the *USS Monitor* and *Galena,* and a third ironclad *USRC Naugatuck (US Revenue Cutter Service),* loaned to the Navy by the Treasury Department. The Union ships met eight cannons plus naval guns and other artillery at the massive Confederate Fort Darling at Drewry's Bluff which commanded the river for miles in both directions. Underwater obstructions further hampered the Union advance and they were forced to turn back on May 15 even though they were within a short seven miles of Richmond.

V. THE SECOND YEAR: 1862

Battle of Seven Pines (or Fair Oaks), Virginia
May 31, 1862

After the Battle of Williamsburg, the Union Army of the Potomac under Gen. George B. McClellan continued its forward march up the Virginia peninsula. By the end of May, McClellan had reached the outskirts of Richmond and began setting up heavy siege guns within six miles of the Confederate capital. The Richmond and York River Railroad provided transportation to White House Landing, where McClellan established his base of operations. White House was the former home and plantation of W.H.F. "Rooney" Lee, second son of Confederate Gen. Robert E. Lee. The Union Army, numbering about 105,000, spanned the Chickahominy River, a tributary of the James. One-third of the Northern forces were on the south side of the Chickahominy and two-thirds on the north, protecting the railroad and Union supply line.

The Union Army Balloon Corps moved its generators and equipment by boat from Yorktown to White House on its own balloonist barge and established two balloon camps on the outskirts of Richmond north of the Chickahominy River. One camp was placed at Gaines' Mill about ten miles northeast of Richmond and the other at Mechanicsville, seven miles northwest of the city (See Fig. 18).

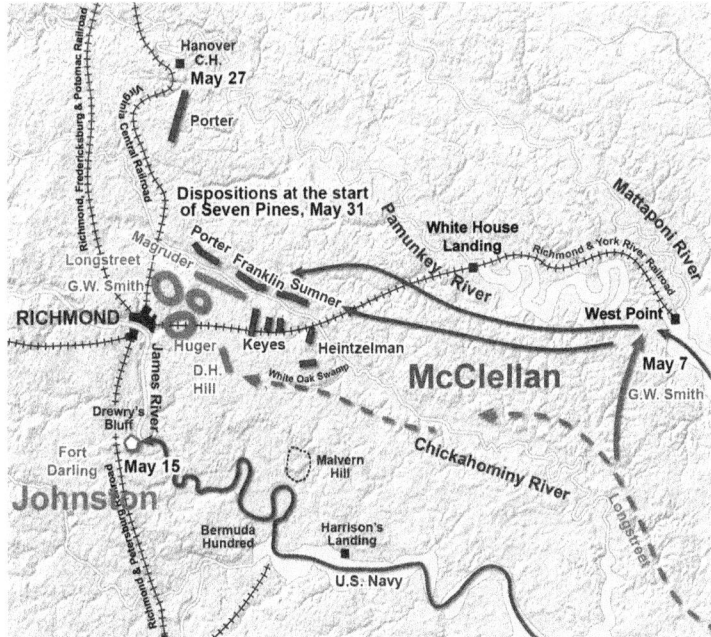

Fig. 17: At the Seven Pines Battle on May 31, Union tethered gas-filled balloons conducted surveillance from the outskirts of Richmond, Virginia, supporting Union forces under Gen. McClellan who pushed back a Confederate assault led by Gen. Joseph E. Johnston at the Chickahominy River.

Source: *Creative Commons Attribution 3.0 license. Map by Hal Jespersen, www.cwmaps.com*

At about the same time, the Confederates launched their own balloonist, Chief of Ordnance Sgt. Edward Porter Alexander, in a tethered gas balloon that was inflated with coal gas from the Richmond Gas Works. By the 1850s, most small to medium-sized towns had centralized plants to generate coal gas, also called illumination gas, that was piped to service street lights and lamps in homes. The gas was generated by heating coal in the absence of air (to avoid combustion) which produced a useful gas for lighting.

The Southerners, unable to obtain the necessary silk material for an observation balloon because of the Union naval blockade, had made one from ladies' dress material acquired from shops in Savannah, Georgia, and Charleston, South Carolina. The multi-colored patchwork cloth was then varnished to create the Confederate "Silk Dress Balloon." Once inflated with coal gas from Richmond, the balloon was attached to a train car that carried it to the battlefield. But coal gas provided only half the lifting power of hydrogen, limiting the Confederate balloon to a height of about five hundred feet, half the distance of the Union balloons. Its air time was also reduced to only three to four hours. Nevertheless, Aeronaut Alexander made several ascents and conveyed information to men on the ground using a "wigwag" system of passing messages with signal flags.

> **ILLUMINATION GAS OR "COAL GAS"**
>
> Gaslighting was in relatively common use for street lights and the wealthier urban homes in America at the time of the Civil War. Gas was produced in centralized plants by distilling the products of burned coal and then piping the gas to lamps. Baltimore, Maryland, was the first American city to use the technology in 1816. "Town gas" was used by the Confederates to man a tethered balloon during the Peninsula Campaign. Union balloons were able to use hydrogen gas made by portable generators and could reach higher altitudes than the coal gas balloons. Improvements in technology for transporting natural gas over long distances slowly replaced the use of coal gas by the mid-20th century.

On May 31, Confederate Gen. Joseph E. Johnston, with a total force of about 60,000, initiated an attack on Union forces located on the south side of the rain-soaked and swampy Chickahominy River in the Battle of Seven Pines (or the Battle of Fair Oaks). Johnston's strategy was to take advantage of McClellan's army being divided by the river and used his Confederate troops to overwhelm one-third of the Union army before troops on the north side could rally. But poor communications and misinformation bungled the attack. As a result of the weak Confederate attack, part of the Union army on the north was able to cross the swollen river on one of its surviving bridges and arrived just in time to reinforce the Northern troops and push Johnston's assault back. McClellan was not on the field, but ill with a resurgence of his chronic malaria attacks.

During the battle, Gen. Johnston was severely injured and fell unconscious from his horse. Confusion in the Confederate command with mixed and contradictory orders resulted in a stalemate between the combatants. By the next day, the opposing sides had withdrawn to their previous positions. But Johnston had brought McClellan's push to Richmond to a halt.

Both sides claimed victory, but casualties were large (Union, more than 5,000; Confederates, over 6,000). Convinced that his army was outnumbered by Southern forces, McClellan did not follow up with an attack on the Confederates and proceeded with his plans for a siege of Richmond. He expected that his superior firepower would eventually defeat the Southerners, so he waited for better weather and reinforcements as he continued installation of his siege guns.

Seven Days Battles, Virginia Peninsula
June 25-July 1, 1862

During the month of June while McClellan was setting up his siege guns around Richmond, the Confederate Army came under the command of Gen. Robert E. Lee, who had been serving as adviser to Confederate President Jefferson Davis. As Gen. Johnston's injuries in the Battle of Seven Pines would keep him out of active service until November, Gen. Lee was brought in to lead Confederate forces protecting Richmond from the advance of the Union Army during the Peninsula Campaign. Lee would then dominate the Confederate defenses in the Eastern Theater for the rest of the war.

When Lee took command of the Confederates, he immediately reorganized the Army of Northern Virginia and planned his offensive campaign against McClellan's Union Army of the Potomac. Beginning on June 25, 1862, Gen. Lee initiated a series of six major battles, the Seven Days Battles (See Fig. 18), which brought an end to McClellan's Peninsula Campaign. Lee's army, which now numbered about 100,000 men, included such generals as Stonewall Jackson, who had recently arrived from the Shenandoah Valley, James Longstreet, Ambrose Powell (A.P.) Hill, and James Ewell Brown (J.E.B., to be known as "Jeb") Stuart, commanding the cavalry. All would play prominent roles in the battles ahead.

Lee launched his first battle to drive Union forces out of positions they occupied near the outskirts of Richmond at the Battle of Beaver Dam Creek (or Mechanicsville) on June 26. The battle did not go well for the Confederates. Poor communications and a lack of adequate maps hampered Lee's battle plan. Further, Stonewall Jackson and his troops were late arriving at the Union rear and missed A.P. Hill's frontal advance. Nevertheless, a concerted Confederate attack at dusk forced the Union army to withdraw through Mechanicsville, but Union forces had blocked a further advance by the Southerners at Beaver Dam Creek.

The appearance of Jackson's army on the field unnerved McClellan, who thought Jackson was still in the Shenandoah. Believing he was facing an army of 200,000,

McClellan decided to withdraw the Army of the Potomac from Richmond to Gaines' Mill, the same battlefield that would become the Battle of Cold Harbor in 1864.

The Battle of Gaines' Mill on June 27 began with a concentrated Confederate attack on the rear and right flank of one-third of the Union Army that was now situated on the north side of the Chickahominy River, protecting the railroad that was the Union supply line. Lee's plan required Stonewall Jackson's men to circle behind the Union's right flank and force them into frontal lines held by the Confederates with the Chickahominy on the Union left. But Jackson's men were late, having taken a wrong turn, and did not arrive at the battlefield until mid-afternoon, delaying the coordinated

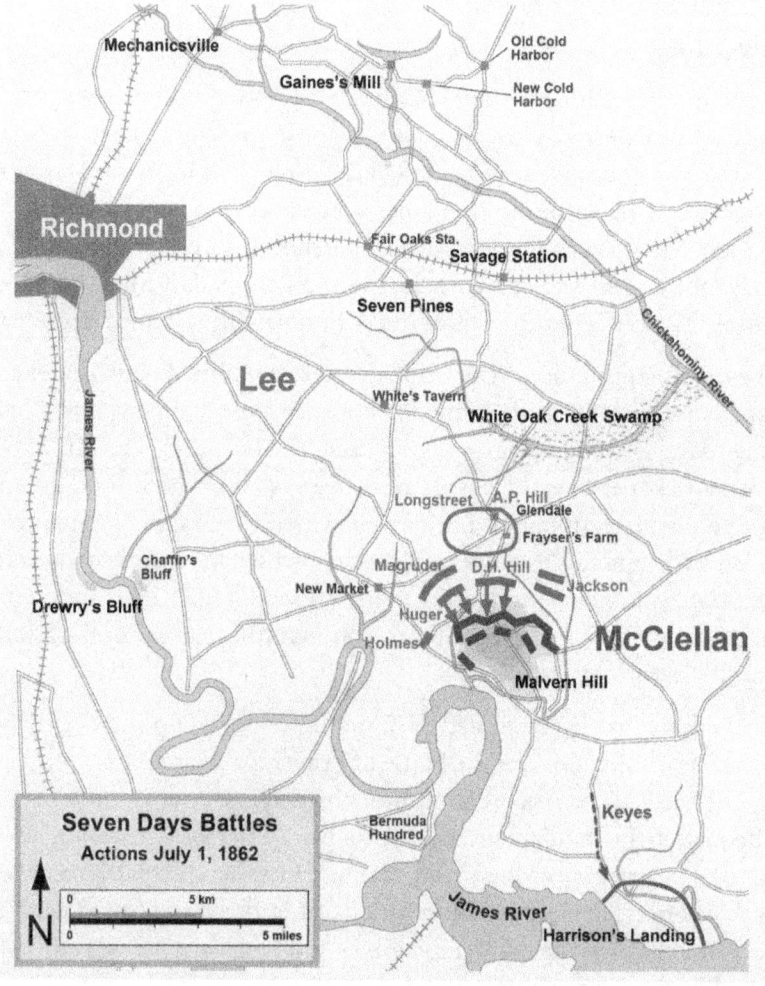

Fig. 18: Confederates battled against Union forces in the Seven Days Battles of the Peninsula Campaign in Virginia. At the Battle of Malvern Hill, Union troops under Gen. McClellan were able to defend against multiple Confederate attacks from Gen. Lee by strategic placements of artillery.

Source: *Creative Commons Attribution 3.0 license. Map by Hal Jespersen, www.cwmaps.com*

Confederate attacks. Nevertheless, the Southerners pushed Northern troops back and they continually lost ground. As the battles continued into the night, Union troops were barely able to withdraw by crossing the Chickahominy at four o'clock in the morning, burning bridges behind them. Casualties were large. The Union lost over 6,000 out of 34,000 engaged; Confederates, about 9,000 out of 57,000, and the loss of four senior commanders.

The Balloon Corps had to move its balloons and equipment quickly from their positions on Gaines' farm, but in their haste, had to leave two of the generators behind, one of which was eventually placed on display in the Richmond town square.

The defeat at Gaines' Mill required McClellan to set up a new supply line and he began to withdrew his army back down the peninsula to the James River where he would set up a new base of operations for his supplies. As the Army of the Potomac retreated, most of its forces concentrated at Savage Station on the Richmond and York River Railroad as they prepared to cross the White Oak Creek Swamp (See Fig. 18).

A disorganized Confederate pursuit failed to take advantage of the Union withdrawal and a brief bloody battle at Savage Station on June 29 ended in a stalemate as darkness fell, with about 1,500 casualties between the two armies. About 2,500 previously wounded Union soldiers were abandoned and left to be captured as prisoners when their field hospital was evacuated. McClellan personally left the field, leaving commanders to protect the army's retreat through the difficult crossing of White Oak Creek Swamp.

Forward elements of McClellan's army set up new defenses on Malvern Hill, a small prominence about one mile north of the James River that gave good visibility and command of the surrounding field. Gen. Fitz John Porter strategically placed Union infantry and heavy artillery on Malvern Hill's western and northern slopes. The final battle of the Peninsula Campaign at Malvern Hill occurred on July 1 when three successive charges by Confederate infantry were repulsed by massive Union artillery barrages. Southern casualties at this battle totaled more than 5,000 compared to the Union's 3,000, prompting one Confederate general to comment, *"It was not war; it was murder."* Gen. McClellan had already withdrawn to Harrison's Landing on the James River.

Darkness ended the fighting and McClellan ordered a retreat of the army to the James during the night. Porter encouraged McClellan to keep Union forces on Malvern Hill and continue the campaign, but the general was done. Convinced that he was under attack from multiple directions by an army greatly outnumbering his own, McClellan abandoned his advance on Richmond and ordered a withdrawal to his secure base at Harrison's Landing even though only a third of the Union army had reached the James as they crossed the swamp. The remaining troops were still marching between White Oak Creek Swamp and Glendale when McClellan boarded the *USS Galena* on the James River at Harrison's Landing and left the field.

Lee's Army of Northern Virginia withdrew to Richmond and waited for a resumption of hostilities, but McClellan was finished and the Peninsula Campaign came to an end. McClellan's failure brought heavy criticism from the Northern press, particularly his departure from the field to the safety of the *USS Galena* while his army battled less than five miles away. Heavy losses were experienced on both sides. Confederate casualties numbered about 20,000 (3,500 killed) from a total of 100,000; Union losses were about 16,000 (1,700 killed) from a total of about 105,000. The North, which had been expecting a major win for the Union, was forced to the realization that the largest army the United States had ever created had been defeated by the Confederates. Gen. Lee, persuaded that McClellan would not return to the battlefield, left the peninsula with the Army of Northern Virginia to pursue new offensives.

Several balloon ascensions were made by Confederate Aeronaut Alexander during the Seven Days Battles from an armed tug boat on the James River until it ran aground on July 4 below Malvern Hill. Although he and the crew escaped, boat and balloon were captured by Union Navy gunboats. The "Silk Dress Balloon" was cut into scraps and given to members of Congress as souvenirs.

Union Aeronaut Lowe, chronically ill with malaria, was placed on leave July 6, but went on to make observations in later battles at Sharpsburg, Vicksburg and Fredericksburg. Political maneuverings, however, between the military and Congress forced the Union Balloon Corps to be disbanded after the Battle of Chancellorsville in May 1863 and Lowe retired shortly afterwards.

BATTLES IN VIRGINIA AND MARYLAND

Battle of Second Bull Run, Manassas, Virginia
August 29-30, 1862

In July, Lincoln promoted Gen. Henry Halleck from commanding the Department of Missouri in the Western Theater to be his new General-in-Chief, a position that had been vacant since March when Lincoln removed Gen. George B. McClellan from the post. Halleck, who would now coordinate all the Union armies, was a superior administrator and master of logistics, but had little to no experience as a field commander. His single command in the field had been the Siege of Corinth, which had been such a slow and ponderous advance of twenty miles that the Confederates had escaped, leaving an empty city to greet the entering Union Army. During his tenure in the Western Theater, however, his subordinates had achieved several important victories and Halleck as their overall commander had reaped the benefits which had brought him to the key position of General-in-Chief.

Gen. McClellan, at Harrison's Landing in Virginia, was still nursing his losses and failure of the Peninsula Campaign when he was ordered to return to Washington in

August. McClellan, who considered himself superior to all the Union commanders, including President Lincoln, resented Halleck as the new General-in-Chief and would frequently challenge his authority. Union Gen. John Pope, who had recently demonstrated success in Missouri at Island No. 10 on the Mississippi River, had been promoted in June to command the newly created Union Army of Virginia.

Confederate Gen. Robert E. Lee, convinced that McClellan no longer presented a danger to Richmond with the end of the Peninsula Campaign, planned his next offensives against the Northern armies. Lee would take advantage of the now widely split Union forces and destroy the northern contingent, currently on hold in Virginia near the capital, while McClellan's Army of the Potomac was still on the Virginia Peninsula.

Planning to destroy Pope's army before McClellan could return from the peninsula, Lee sent Confederate Gen. Stonewall Jackson's army north where he and his men were able to seize the massive Union supply depot at Manassas Junction, Virginia, on August 26. The move was intended to draw Pope's new Army of Virginia away from his well-defended positions at Centreville, Virginia, and place the Union Army on ground best suited for a Confederate defense. The Southerners feasted for two days on the Union's ample supplies at Manassas, collected all the ammunition they could carry, burned the rest, and moved to a defensive position in the woods on Stony Ridge, just northwest of Manassas and near Bull Run, setting the stage for the Battle of Second Bull Run.

> **HEROIC LOSSES AT BULL RUN**
>
> The 5th New York Zouaves, dressed in red and blue uniforms, presented an elite professional, disciplined regiment in the Union Army. At the Battle of Second Bull Run, they suffered over 300 casualties, 120 of them fatal, out of the 525 engaged. As their colorful bodies dotted the hillside, one Confederate officer commented that it looked like Texas wildflowers in bloom.

On August 28, Jackson provoked an attack from Stony Ridge on a Union force marching along the Warrenton Pike to join Gen. Pope's army at Centreville. The action prompted Pope to move his army and launch a series of attacks on Jackson's positions at Stony Ridge the next day. But the Union assaults were all repulsed with heavy casualties on both sides. As the battle continued, Lee brought Gen. James Longstreet's Corps north from Richmond and around noon on August 29, the Confederates arrived to reinforce Jackson. When Pope ordered Gen. Fitz John Porter to make an attack on Jackson, unaware that Longstreet's men had arrived on the field, Porter did not comply with the order because he had received intelligence about the newly arrived Confederate reinforcements in his front.

Union Gen. Pope resumed his attacks the next day and was met with massive Confederate artillery, supported by a 25,000-man counter-attack from Longstreet. Fierce fighting, punctuated by volleys at point-blank range, devastated the Union assaults.

Only heroic defensive actions by the New York Zouaves enabled Pope to withdraw his army to Henry Hill and successfully retreat to Centreville in the dark.

The city of Washington watched in disbelief as the Union Army was once again defeated at its doorstep. The devastating losses at the Battle of Second Bull Run brought severe criticism to Union Gen. Pope for the poor intelligence used in the planning and his confusing and contradictory military orders. Pope accused Porter for the defeat, had him court-martialed for failing to obey orders and Porter was dismissed from the army January 21, 1863. Lincoln relieved Pope of command and dissolved the Army of Virginia, merging the men into the Army of the Potomac. Pope was reassigned to duties in Minnesota and Dakota Territory and in 1865 was transferred to command the Military Division of the Missouri.

Porter worked for the next fifteen years to contradict the findings of the court-martial and restore his reputation. In 1878, a special commission invalidated the conclusions of Porter's court-martial in 1863 and concluded that the Union losses at the Battle of Second Bull Run were the result of Pope's recklessness and uninformed intelligence about the realities on the field. The inquiry further claimed that Porter's perceived disobedience had saved the Union Army from devastating collapse and ruin. In 1886, President Grover Cleveland commuted Porter's conviction and he was restored to the U.S. Army, backdated to May 1861. Vindicated, Porter promptly retired from the army. The same commission of 1878 severely criticized Gen. Irvin McDowell, who had led the disastrous Battle of First Bull Run the year before, for his actions and poor performance in the Battle of Second Bull Run. His reputation suffered, but he remained with the army until his retirement in 1882.

The Union defeat in the Battle of Second Bull Run had resulted in over 14,000 casualties (1,700 killed; over 12,500 wounded or captured) out of 62,000 men. Confederate losses were much smaller, 1,600 killed and 8,000 wounded or missing out of 54,000. With a significant Confederate victory in hand, Lee moved north with an invasion into Maryland.

Battle of Antietam (or Sharpsburg), Maryland
September 17, 1862

After his successes at Manassas, Virginia, and the Battle of Second Bull Run in August, Confederate Gen. Robert E. Lee led his army into Maryland in early September to take the initiative of battle into Union-held territory and possibly capture the capital of Washington, D.C. Weather and invading troops had exhausted food supplies in northern Virginia and Lee hoped to take advantage of the relatively untouched agricultural regions of Maryland and Pennsylvania to relieve shortages of food, forage and other supplies for the Confederate Army.

V. THE SECOND YEAR: 1862

Lee's assault in Maryland would be coordinated with a simultaneous movement on Union strongholds in Kentucky, another Border State, by Gen. Braxton Bragg, now commanding the Confederate Army of Mississippi. If Lee could achieve another victory against Union forces, Northern morale would be crushed and the Peace Democrats would gain momentum to negotiate for an independent South. In addition, the Confederacy would enhance its position for international recognition from Great Britain and France.

Lee entered Maryland east of the Blue Ridge Mountains, crossed the Potomac River near Leesburg, Virginia, and advanced to Frederick, Maryland. Boldly dividing his army, two-thirds were sent under Gen. Stonewall Jackson to capture the garrison and Union arsenal at Harpers Ferry. The rest of the army under Gen. James Longstreet continued its movement into Maryland.

Jackson separated his troops into three contingents and with hard marching converged on Harpers Ferry from three directions, mounting his attack from the high bluffs that surrounded the town. In one of his most brilliant successes in the Civil War, Jackson was able to trap and defeat the Union garrison on September 15, capturing nearly 13,000 Union troops and seizing thousands of arms and seventy-three cannons. Jackson's losses were less than 300, a dramatic victory for the Confederates.

In the meantime, through some unfortunate event for the Confederates, a copy of Lee's Special Orders 191, which described all the operational details of Lee's plans, was found on September 13 by Union men of the 27th Indiana Regiment, wrapped around a few cigars. The stroke of good luck was quickly communicated to Gen. George B. McClellan, now returned from the Virginia Peninsula and underway to intercept Lee with his 85,000-man Army of the Potomac, which had also recently absorbed the Army of Virginia.

In typical fashion, however, McClellan's caution prevailed and by the time he brought his Army of the Potomac into position to meet the Confederates at Sharpsburg, a Southern sympathizer had relayed the information to Lee on September 15 that the Northerners knew his plans. With news from Stonewall Jackson that Harpers Ferry had been captured, Lee made the decision to reunite his army at Antietam Creek near Sharpsburg, and prepare a good defensive position among the high ridges and three bridges that were located about a mile apart over fast-moving water. Leaving Gen. A.P. Hill at Harpers Ferry to parole the Union prisoners, Jackson moved the rest of his army to join Lee at Sharpsburg, less than twenty miles away. Longstreet's troops joined Lee the next day, bringing the Southern army to about 35,000 men. McClellan's army outnumbered them two-to-one.

The two armies met at the Battle of Antietam (or the Battle of Sharpsburg) on September 17, 1862, which became the single bloodiest day of the war. The battle began at dawn as Union troops crept through a field of corn where the stalks were tall enough to hide their movements. Their objective was the Confederate left flank, concealed in the West Woods near Dunker Church, so-called because of the practice of "dunking," total immersion in water during baptism.

Artillery batteries from both sides changed the cornfield into "Artillery Hell." Canister-loaded cannons, transformed into giant shotguns, instantly wreaked horrendous numbers of casualties. As the fight raged on, each side would gain an advantage, only to lose it as the carnage continued. Union Gen. Joseph Hooker wrote of the scene, *"In the time that I am writing, every stalk of corn in the northern and greater part of the field was cut as closely as could have been done with a knife, and the slain lay in rows precisely as they had stood in their ranks a few moments before."* Lee, a brilliant battlefield commander, shifted his men back and forth between battle lines, earning him the nickname "Gray Fox." The morning's casualties for both sides in the battle, that lasted about four hours, totaled nearly 14,000 men, described as the equivalent of one casualty every second.

As the Union side shifted its attack away from the cornfield, men were cut down when they came within range of about 2,000 waiting Confederates, hunkered down in the "Sunken Road," an old country farm lane that had been weathered, through time and use, to a level about five feet below the surrounding ground level. Union casualties mounted from the withering fire until Union Gen. Nathan Kimball was ordered forward with his brigade of four regiments.

Kimball's seasoned veterans became known as "The Gibraltar Brigade" as they withstood the pounding bullets like the Rock of Gibraltar, and gained in-line access to the Sunken Road. As Union artillery brought enfilading fire along the road, the trapped and exposed Confederates were slaughtered.

Casualties became severe in "Bloody Lane," numbering 5,600 (Union, 3,000, Confederate 2,600) men, who lay dead and wounded as they battled for the 800-yard road. The sunken road appeared as a mass burial.

The third and final phase of the day's battles occurred at a stone bridge that crossed Antietam Creek, defended by Confederate sharpshooters from a high bluff. Two unsuccessful attempts to storm the narrow bridge prompted McClellan to order Gen. Ambrose Burnside to take the bridge, "… *if it costs 10,000 men, he must go now.*" The third attempt was successful, but at a critical moment, Confederate Gen. A.P. Hill arrived from Harpers Ferry with 3,000 men after a hard 20-mile march to reinforce the defenders. Hill's troops drove the Union soldiers back, forcing them to give up "Burnside's Bridge," they had worked so hard to capture. McClellan had refused Burnside's request for more men and ammunition even though he had held ample men in reserve throughout the day.

The day's bloody battles resulted in a combined total of nearly 23,000 casualties which included 7,650 soldiers killed in a single day, making Antietam cited as the bloodiest day in all American history. The Union army, nearly 90,000, had outnumbered the

V. THE SECOND YEAR: 1862

> ## BATTLE OF ANTIETAM (OR SHARPSBURG)
> ### Sharpsburg, Maryland, September 17, 1862
>
> After his success at the Battle of Second Bull Run, Confederate Gen. Robert E. Lee lost no time advancing his Army of Northern Virginia into Maryland to carry the Civil War into Northern territory. Taking the bold move of dividing his army, Lee sent Gen. "Stonewall" Jackson to capture Harpers Ferry and its Union arsenal on the Maryland border while his larger force under Gen. James A. Longstreet was deployed to Sharpsburg near Antietam Creek. A copy of Lee's Special Order No. 191 that informed his Confederate generals of operational details about the upcoming campaign became inadvertently lost and was then found by soldiers of the Union's 27th Indiana Regiment, wrapped around cigars. Union Gen. George B. McClellan, commanding the Army of the Potomac, was quickly informed of the vital information of Lee's Order 191, but he did not act on it immediately, which enabled the Southern army to prepare strong defensive positions to use against the Union Army's arrival at Sharpsburg.
>
> When the two armies met on Sept. 17, 1862, it became known as "Artillery Hell." A combined total of five hundred guns fired at soldiers on both sides with devastating effect. The 1st Texas Infantry, known as Lee's "Shock Troops" for their tenacity in battle, lost eighty-two percent of its men that day. The "Cornfield," situated near Dunker Church, became a slaughter field. A sunken road, filled with Confederate sharpshooters, created a hillside of dead and wounded Union soldiers until the brigade of Gen. Nathan Kimball, poured bullets into their ranks, turning it into a "Bloody Lane." As Kimball's Indiana regiments held against withering fire "like the Rock of Gibraltar," the unit became known as the "Gibraltar Brigade." After several costly assaults to cross "Burnside's Bridge," a small stone bridge protected by Confederate sharpshooters, Union troops finally succeeded in reaching the other side, only to be driven off by Confederate reinforcements brought by Gen. A. P. Hill on a merciless hard march from Harpers Ferry. More than 22,000 men lay dead or wounded in the bloodiest single-day battle of the entire Civil War. Although the battle was a draw, McClellan failed to pursue Lee's army, which was able to return back to Virginia. Lincoln declared the battle a Union victory and used the opportunity to announce his Emancipation Proclamation.

Confederates more than two-to-one, but there was no resounding success for either side. Lee remained in place the next day and then withdrew his army that night to safely return to Virginia.

Despite orders to McClellan from both Lincoln and his new General-in-Chief Henry Halleck to immediately pursue Lee after the battle, McClellan delayed, claiming a shortage of supplies and a fear of overextending his men, even though fully one-fourth of his army had been held back as reserves during the battle and not fired a shot. The

Confederates were able to cross the Potomac and return to the Shenandoah Valley. Lincoln's patience with the general had finally reached its limit and in early November McClellan was relieved of command of the Army of the Potomac, to be replaced by Gen. Ambrose Burnside.

Burnside had graduated from West Point in 1843, served in the regular army for about ten years and then resigned to run a private business manufacturing firearms. When his company and business were destroyed by fire, he worked for the Illinois Central Railroad and became friendly with George B. McClellan. At the outbreak of the Civil War, he joined the Union Army leading the Rhode Island Volunteers with two companies armed with his own Burnside Carbines and promoted to brigade command in the Battle of First Bull Run and Antietam. Because of his friendship with McClellan and self-proclaimed recognition of his own general lack of military expertise, Burnside was reluctant at first to take command of the Army of the Potomac. But when he was told that the command would go to Gen. Joseph Hooker, whom he thoroughly disliked, if he did not accept the position, Burnside finally agreed to the promotion.

Battle of Fredericksburg, Virginia
December 11-15, 1862

After the Battle of Antietam, Confederate Gen. Robert E. Lee's Northern Army of Virginia was split in half, separated by Virginia's Blue Ridge Mountains. Gen. Stonewall Jackson had moved back to the Shenandoah Valley at Winchester and the rest of the army was with Lee at the North Anna River near Richmond. Lincoln urged Union Gen. Ambrose Burnside to take advantage of the situation and move at once against Richmond and capture the Confederate capital.

It was unusual for an army to plan an assault in winter because of the increased challenges presented by the terrain in unfavorable weather conditions. With heavy winter rains, roads turned into impassable unyielding mud that swallowed artillery, wheels and caissons and made it difficult for horses and even men to move. Nevertheless, Burnside produced a plan in early November to move against Lee by crossing the Rappahannock River at Fredericksburg with pontoon bridges and then use the Fredericksburg & Potomac Railroad to get the Union army to Richmond before Lee and his army had time to react.

> **"SIDEBURNS"**
>
> The new commander of the Army of the Potomac, Gen. Ambrose Burnside, wore bushy facial hair as distinctive side whiskers that covered his cheeks to join his mustache. His name became so closely associated with his facial hair that the expression transformed later to become a generic term of "sideburns," a description that survives today.

The crossing would take place between Falmouth and Fredericksburg, two cities facing each other on opposite banks of the Rappahannock, about fifty miles south of

PONTOON BRIDGES

River crossings were a constant challenge for combatants in the Civil War. Without a bridge, men, animals and supplies were unable to be placed where commanders needed them. The military solution was to create temporary bridges made from pontoons: wide, wooden, flat-bottomed shallow boats thirty-one feet long with squared ends. Boats were lashed together, side-to-side, twenty feet apart, to form a platform on which planks were laid down, creating a roadway. Each boat was anchored upstream and every other boat anchored downstream. The bridge could be assembled quickly by trained men and made a sturdy road for wagons, horses and men to cross the river. When crossing the bridge, troops needed to march at a walk out of rhythm. If they marched in unison, the walkway would soon heave up and down and become unstable. Engineers were posted along the bridge at intervals to maintain the marching men's out-of-step rhythm. After crossing, the pontoon bridges were disassembled, loaded onto wagons and moved to the next destination.

The cumbersome wood pontoons were heavy and required a substantial infrastructure of men, wagons and animals as part of the army supply train. Each boat required its own wagon. A typical pontoon bridge train contained thirty-four wagons for the pontoons, twenty-two wagons for the planks, plus six other wagons for tools and iron support for anchors and repairs. A minimum team of 368 horses or mules was needed to pull the wagons, plus additional animals to replace those injured or killed. A crew of men, supporting the animals and driving the wagons, plus the trained engineers to assemble the bridge, were all part of the bridge train, which traveled at the end of the army until needed. Lighter pontoons made from floatable cotton canvas were easier to transport, but for long spans, the wooden versions were required.

Washington, half the distance to Richmond. For the plan to work, Burnside would first concentrate most of his army at Warrenton, Virginia, southwest of Washington, hoping to draw Lee there and convince the Confederates that he was moving toward Richmond from that direction. A separate contingent would head directly south to the Rappahannock and set up pontoon bridges for the main army that would make a rapid move from Warrenton and cross the river before the Confederates had time to respond. Rapid response and logistical support to provide the pontoon boats in a timely manner would be essential for the battle plan to succeed.

Burnside reorganized the army into three Grand Divisions, each including infantry, artillery and cavalry. Right Grand Division contained Corps II and IX, headed by Gen. Edwin "Bull" Sumner; the Center Division, Corps III and V, under Gen. Joseph Hooker; and Left Division, Corps I and VI, headed by Gen. William B. Franklin. The Reserve, Corps XI, was under Gen. Franz Sigel.

STRUGGLE FOR THE UNION

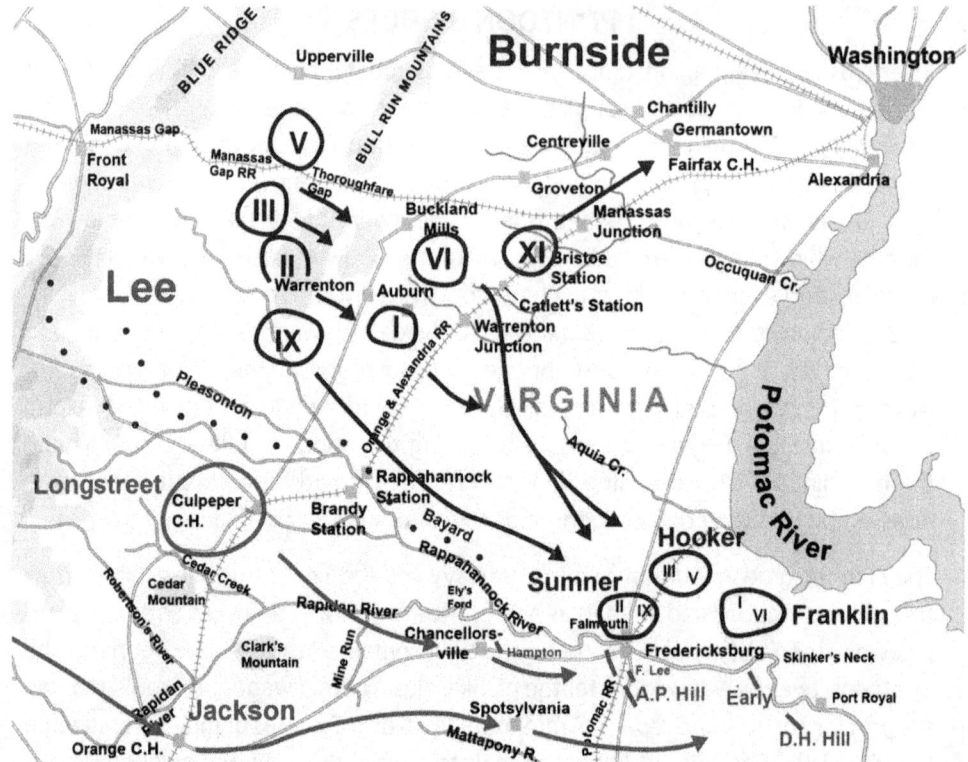

Fig. 19: The Union Army under Gen. Burnside attempted to cross the Rappahannock River with pontoons before the Confederate Army under Gen. Lee could respond at the Battle of Fredericksburg, Virginia, December 1862. But the delay in the arrival of the pontoons resulted in a disastrous Union defeat.

Source: *Creative Commons Attribution 3.0 license. Map by Hal Jespersen, www.cwmaps.com.*

The Northern Army of the Potomac, now numbering about 120,000, began its march November 15, 1862, toward Falmouth with the bulk of it making a visible presence at Warrenton, Virginia, to deceive the Confederates into believing the Union attack would come from that direction. The contingent that would set up the pontoon bridges for the river crossing reached the river two days later.

The planned assault immediately began to go awry. The pontoon bridges needed to be erected quickly so that the rest of the army from Warrenton could rapidly move to the river and cross before the Confederates could respond. But bureaucratic mismanagement delayed the arrival of the pontoon bridges until November 25, when the first boats for a single bridge arrived.

Given the delay in Burnside's movements, Lee soon realized that the Union Army actually planned to approach Richmond by crossing the Rappahannock at Falmouth so Lee sent half his army, under Gen. James Longstreet, to Fredericksburg, directly opposite Falmouth. Longstreet's army arrived November 23 and had already established well-placed defenses on the ridge known as Marye's Heights west of town, prepared to meet an attack when the Union's first pontoon bridge was ready. Confederates were soon reinforced by Stonewall Jackson, who force-marched his troops from Winchester in the Shenandoah Valley to reach Fredericksburg on November 29 and placed his army downriver on high ground east of the town. The rest of Lee's army then joined the battlefield at Fredericksburg directly opposite Falmouth.

When the rest of the pontoons finally arrived, Union engineers began construction on December 11 of six bridges to cross the Rappahannock. Confederate sharpshooters in Fredericksburg picked off Northern engineers as they tried to assemble the bridges. Under fire, a Union landing party, huddled down in boats, eventually crossed the river and secured a bridgehead to take out the sharpshooters. After a full day of fierce urban warfare in the city's streets, Confederates withdrew from town center and repositioned in the Heights. Northern units then successfully created the six pontoon bridges and the entire army crossed the river the following day.

> ### THE ANGEL OF MARYE'S HEIGHTS
> As the cries of the wounded and dying men lay in the fields of Marye's Heights after the day of battle on Dec. 13 at Fredericksburg, a Confederate sergeant, Richard Kirkland, from the South Carolina 2nd Infantry, gathered up canteens to bring water to the casualties, Union and Confederate alike. No one fired on him even though he carried no white flag. This "Angel of Marye's Heights" is immortalized in a monument in front of the stone wall on the Fredericksburg battlefield.

On December 13, wave after wave of Union troops attempted to advance against entrenched Confederate positions on Marye's Heights, but were met with devastating artillery and musket fire. The Heights, rising fifty to sixty feet above open ground, gave the Southerners a superior advantage to repulse the attackers. Confederate Edward Porter Alexander, Chief of Ordnance and Aeronaut for the South's high-rise balloon in the Peninsula Campaign, had been in charge of placing the artillery. When asked of his assessment of the fortifications, he replied, *"A chicken could not live on that field when we open on it."* A line of Confederates, placed behind a four-foot stone wall along a sunken road at the top of Marye's Heights, rose and fired a sheet of flame when Union soldiers came within range. Fourteen individual charges against the Heights cost the Union Army 13,000 casualties; Confederate losses were about 5,400. Confederate Gen. Longstreet later wrote, *"The charges had been desperate and bloody, but utterly hopeless."*

As the cries of the wounded left in the field penetrated into the night, Confederate Sgt. Richard Rowland Kirkland asked permission to carry water to the wounded and dying soldiers. His commander finally granted permission to his request, but said he could not carry a white kerchief. Kirkland responded, *"All right, sir, I'll take my chances."* Kirkland gathered canteens to bring water to the wounded men and was

> ## BATTLE OF FREDERICKSBURG, VIRGINIA
> ### December 11-15, 1862
>
> Gen. Ambrose Burnside, recently named commander of the Union Army of the Potomac, led the bulk of his 120,000-man army in early November 1862 to Warrenton, Virginia, with a plan to deceive Confederate Gen. Robert E. Lee into believing that he was planning to attack Richmond from that direction. But actually, Burnside planned to cross the Rappahannock River at Falmouth, Virginia, directly south of Washington, and then use the Fredericksburg & Richmond Railroad as a direct route to reach Richmond before the Confederate Army of Northern Virginia could react. Burnside's plan required the rapid construction of pontoon bridges to cross the river and success of the mission required swift action and timely arrival of the pontoon boats and equipment. Poor communications and bureaucratic mismanagement delayed the arrival of the pontoons, which gave Lee's army sufficient warning to arrive at Fredericksburg on the opposite bank and prepare strong defensive positions facing the Union troops as they crossed the river.
>
> When the pontoon bridges were finally in place Dec. 11, Confederate sharpshooters strategically positioned in the town of Fredericksburg, picked off Union troops attempting to cross. A landing party eventually rowed across the river by boat and after a day of urban warfare cleared the city, enabling the entire army to cross. When Union forces faced the Confederates, positioned on a ridge line known as Marye's Heights, fifty to sixty feet above open ground, heavy artillery fire and supporting riflemen defeated assault after assault by the Union soldiers who suffered casualty rates of almost fifty percent. By the end of the day on Dec. 13, fourteen Union brigades had been repulsed with the loss of eight battle flags. Total Union casualties for the conflict reached 13,000, more than double the Confederate losses of about 5,000.
>
> The following morning, Burnside's request for a truce was granted and the dead and wounded were removed from the battlefield. The next day, Union forces retreated across the river and withdrew from the field. The astounding loss of Union soldiers in a single battle aroused furious attacks from the Northern press and politicians, who criticized Burnside and the entire Lincoln administration for the disaster.

not fired on by either side, even though he helped Union and Confederate soldiers alike, delivering water, warm clothing and blankets. The "Angel of Marye's Heights" became a legend and a monument remains today at the battlefield, documenting his bravery and compassion.

The high number of Union losses (1,300 killed; 10,000 wounded, 1,800 captured or missing), were more than twice that of the Confederate losses of over 5,200 (600 killed, 4,000 wounded and 650 captured or missing). The Union army lost nine senior officers, three of whom were killed. Lincoln wrote of the battle, *"If there is a worse place than hell, I am in it."*

The armies held their positions on December 14, but in the afternoon, Burnside requested a truce to collect the wounded and dead soldiers and Lee agreed. On December 15, Union troops retreated across the river and the campaign came to an end. The collision of two armies with a combined total of more than 220,000 men, had resulted in another major defeat for the North with the loss of thousands of men. Lee observed, however, that with the victory, *"We had really accomplished nothing; we had not gained a foot of ground… and the enemy could easily replace the men that it had lost."*

BATTLES IN THE WESTERN THEATER

CONFEDERATE INVASION INTO KENTUCKY

Kentucky, a key Border State, had both Confederate and Union sympathizers and became the target for a number of critical battles as opposing sides attempted to gain control of its resources. In 1862, the South was anxious to attract Kentucky into the Confederacy and take advantage of its multiple rivers and railroads for transporting men, ammunition and supplies, vital assets for the Confederate Army. In addition, the Ohio River at its northern border provided valuable access to other navigable rivers, not only the Mississippi, but also the Tennessee and Cumberland Rivers of its border state of Tennessee, now in Union control after the surrender of Fort Donelson.

In July 1862 Confederate President Jefferson Davis designed a plan for an invasion into Kentucky that would capture Louisville and the state capital of Frankfort and secure the state for the Confederacy. Davis was encouraged by the activities of a bold young Confederate Cavalry Officer, Col. John Hunt Morgan, who had become famous as the "Thunderbolt of the Confederacy." Morgan had launched a thousand-mile raid in July 1862 with nine hundred men through Kentucky that matched some of the audacious exploits of other famous Confederate cavalry leaders of the war. During the raid, Morgan recruited three hundred new Kentucky volunteers to his cavalry, destroyed railroad and telegraph lines, acquired several hundred horses, seized supplies, captured hundreds of prisoners, whom he then paroled, and generated national headlines. Morgan's daring feats earned him a promotion to Brigadier General.

During this same period, Union Gen. Don Carlos Buell with the Army of the Ohio had been ordered by the new General-in-Chief Henry Halleck to move east from Corinth to Chattanooga, Tennessee, and capture the main railroad lines that linked eastern Tennessee to the rest of the Confederacy. Buell left Corinth with four divisions, following the Memphis & Charleston Railroad, which ran from Memphis through Corinth to Stevenson, Alabama, where it connected to Chattanooga through the Nashville & Chattanooga Railroad. But Buell's progress was sluggishly slow, averaging barely a mile a day, as he was forced to repair his main supply line, the Nashville & Decatur Railroad that ran north and south and was constantly being torn up by Confederate cavalries headed by Nathan Bedford Forrest or John Hunt Morgan. When Morgan and his raiders burned the Louisville & Nashville Railroad tunnels that connected to the Nashville & Decatur, seriously impacting the Union supply chain, Buell sent his cavalry to pursue Morgan. But the Union cavalry suffered an embarrassing defeat from the raiders, including the capture of its commander, Gen. Richard W. Johnson. Morgan's successes persuaded Confederate President Davis that large numbers of Kentucky sympathizers would join the Southern cause if there was a Confederate invasion into the state.

SOUTH'S HEARTLAND OFFENSIVE (KENTUCKY CAMPAIGN)

August-September 1862

The South's Heartland Offensive, also known as the Kentucky Campaign, was launched in middle August 1862 to attract Kentucky to the Confederacy and draw Union attention away from Vicksburg on the Mississippi River after the Northern victory at Corinth. In addition, Confederate President Davis wanted to eliminate the threat of the large Union force, headed by Gen. Don Carlos Buell, now underway to capture Chattanooga, Tennessee.

After the Siege of Corinth, Davis had replaced Gen. P.G.T. Beauregard with Gen. Braxton Bragg as commander of the Confederate Army of Mississippi, now occupying headquarters at Tupelo, Mississippi, about fifty miles south of Corinth. Bragg, a graduate of West Point Military Academy in 1837, had served with distinction in the Mexican-American War and then resigned from the U.S. Army in 1853 to develop a successful sugar plantation in Louisiana. When Louisiana seceded from the Union in January 1861, Bragg led a group of state militia volunteers to seize the federal arsenal at Baton Rouge and was then commissioned as a Brigadier General into the Confederate States Army. After leading troops in the Battles of First Bull Run and Shiloh, he was promoted to Major General and in June 1862 was given command of the Army of Mississippi.

Bragg's new orders for the South's Heartland Offensive would combine his Army of Mississippi with Gen. E. Kirby Smith's forces in Eastern Tennessee, to seize Union strongholds in Kentucky and bring the state into the Confederacy. The two armies would move as separate invasions into Kentucky, and then converge as they approached Louisville, a major supply center for the Union, located on the Ohio River. Bragg would be overall commander of the two armies. Bragg's first challenge was to move about 30,000 men to eastern Tennessee, a distance of about two hundred fifty miles, so that he could coordinate with the army of Gen. Smith, but still avoid the large Union Army of the Ohio under Gen. Buell, slowly advancing along Tennessee's southern border to Chattanooga.

V. THE SECOND YEAR: 1862

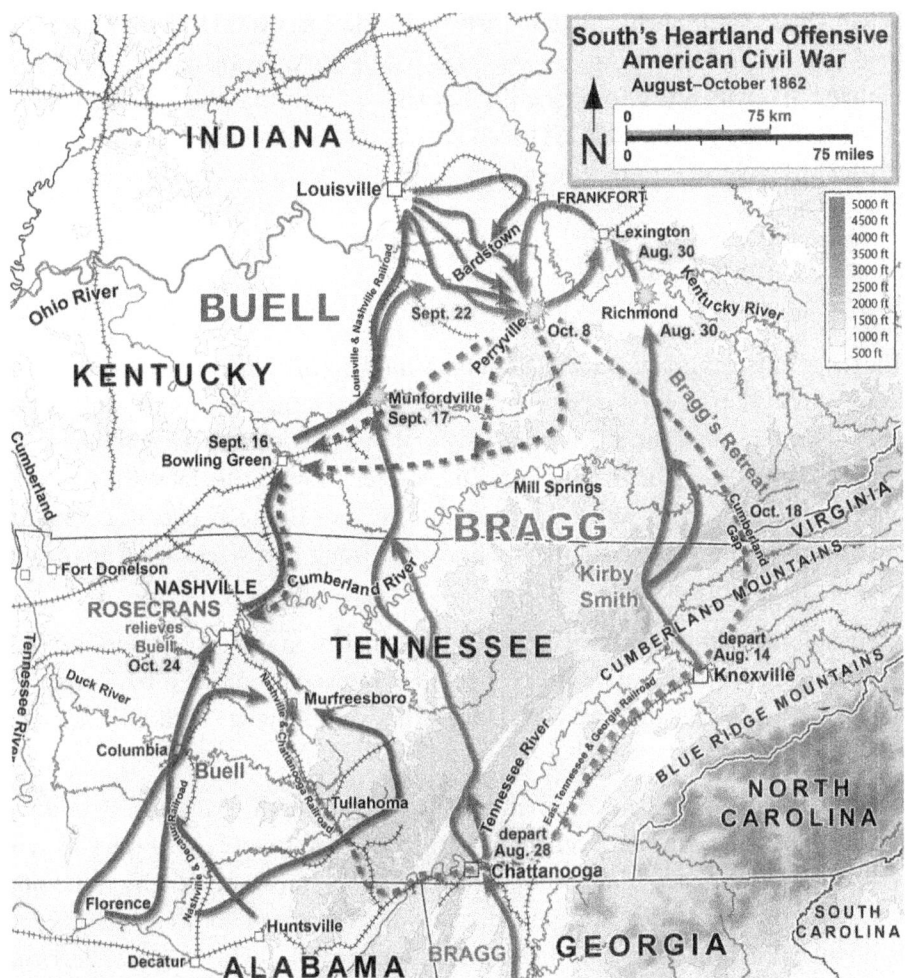

Fig. 20: An overview of the South's Heartland Offensive, or Kentucky Campaign, shows Confederate Gen. E. Kirby Smith moving north from Knoxville, Tennessee, to meet Braxton Bragg from Chattanooga to invade Kentucky in a joint effort to bring the state into the Confederacy. They meet Union forces under Gen. Buell at Richmond and Perryville. Bragg's retreat is shown in dotted lines.

Source: *Creative Commons Attribution 3.0 license. Map by Hal Jespersen, www.cwmaps.com*

Gen. Bragg split his army at Tupelo, Mississippi, leaving 32,000 soldiers there as protection against Gen. Ulysses S. Grant, still located at Corinth. The remaining half of his army was moved by rail from Tupelo to Mobile, Alabama, where they then traveled northward by rail to Montgomery, Alabama, and onward to Atlanta and Dalton, Georgia, and finally to Chattanooga. Bragg's army arrived at Chattanooga ahead of Buell. The roughly 800-mile journey on more than half a dozen different railroads had achieved a remarkable feat of logistics in 1862, efficiently executing rapid troop movements of a sizeable army over large distances. Supply wagons, cavalry and artillery, traveled overland through Rome, Georgia, to complete Bragg's army.

When Union Gen. Buell, still underway on his slow eastward trek to Chattanooga, learned that a Confederate Army now occupied the city, he abandoned his advance and moved his army north to Nashville, Tennessee. News that the Confederates were invading Kentucky prompted Buell to send two brigades of his army north under Gen. William "Bull" Nelson, to defend against a Confederate advance on Louisville and northern Kentucky.

Battle of Richmond, Kentucky
August 29-30, 1862

The two Confederate Generals Braxton Bragg and E. Kirby Smith met in Chattanooga on July 31 to develop their joint plans for the invasion of Kentucky. Smith would operate independently in east central Kentucky, reporting directly to President Davis, while Bragg would proceed through the central and western part of the state. The two armies would consolidate as they approached Louisville with Bragg as overall commander of the Campaign. Smith would depart first and Bragg two weeks later after he had reassembled his army of about 35,000.

A diversionary effort to derail any efforts by the Union to bring in reinforcements from Corinth, would make use of two small armies, commanded by Confederate Generals Sterling Price and Earl Van Dorn, who would engage with Gen. Ulysses S. Grant at Corinth.

Confederate Gen. Smith, commanding the 19,000-man Army of Kentucky, left Knoxville on August 14 and moved into a hot, drought-stricken eastern Kentucky, with his first objective to reach Richmond, Kentucky, about one hundred fifty miles north. The decimated region suffered from a dangerously low supply of water for both men and animals. Pressing north, Smith did not attack the well-fortified Union garrison at Cumberland Gap, but bypassed it by moving through valleys in the mountains west of it. As Confederates began to threaten Union commands in northern Kentucky, 6,500 raw Union recruits were rushed to Louisville from Indiana and Ohio to reinforce a small force under Gen. William "Bull" Nelson, who had deployed two brigades from the Army of the Ohio, which he had renamed the Provisional Army of Kentucky. As the new recruits entered the Union Army with no training or experience, one of the brigade commanders commented, *"It was a sad spectacle for a soldier to look at these raw recruits and contemplate their fate in a trial at arms with experienced troops… (they) could but indifferently execute some of the simplest movements in the manual of arms."*

As Confederate Gen. E. Kirby Smith's army moved north, his advance cavalry met Union cavalry on August 23 at the Battle of Big Hill, about thirty miles south of Richmond, Kentucky. The Union's 7th Kentucky Volunteer Cavalry regiment had just been mustered in August 16, only a week earlier, and had been sent to meet the Confederates at Big Hill. As the new untrained Union recruits faced experienced Confederates, the unequipped and untrained soldiers precipitously fled at the first exchange of fire. Most were either wounded or captured. The Union line was forced to retreat over the next six days as it fell back to Richmond. Gen. Nelson tried to form a defensive line at the Richmond Cemetery, but at sunset on August 30, Gen. Smith's forces broke the Union right flank and the entire line collapsed. As the panic-stricken troops flooded through the streets of Richmond, Confederate cavalry captured nearly the entire command. Of the approximately 6,500 Union troops engaged, nearly 4,500 were captured and another 1,000 were killed or wounded. Nelson, although wounded with two bullets in his thigh, managed to escape with a few others. Total casualties for the Confederates were less than 500.

With the arrival of additional Confederate troops, Smith proceeded to capture nearby Lexington on September 1 and Frankfort, Kentucky, on September 2, 1862, the only Union state capital to fall during the entire war. It was an overwhelming Confederate victory. Gen. Buell, now aware of the impending threat to Louisville abandoned his offensive positions at Nashville on September 7 and raced his army to Louisville. The first troops, exhausted and hungry from the long march, arrived at Louisville unopposed on September 25.

Battle of Munfordville (or Green River), Kentucky
Sept 14-17, 1862

Gen. Braxton Bragg, leading the Confederate Army of Mississippi, left Chattanooga, Tennessee, on August 27. As Bragg and his troops, numbering about 35,000, moved north, they encountered a well-fortified Union garrison about seventy miles due south of Louisville at Munfordville, Kentucky, which refused to surrender. After two days of repulsed attacks, the Confederates, under a flag of truce, met the commander, Col. John T. Wilder, and convinced him to view the size of the Southern forces against him.

When Col. Wilder saw his 4,000 men were surrounded by the large Confederate Army, he surrendered the garrison in the Battle of Munfordville (or Battle of Green River) on September 17, 1862. The Louisville & Nashville Railroad station and the bridge at Green River now came under Southern control. The delay, however, had allowed Union Gen. Buell to get ahead of Bragg in the race to Louisville. Bragg continued moving north and reached Bardstown, about forty miles south of Louisville, on September 22. Col. Wilder, later exchanged from prison camp, would become famous as head of the 17th Indiana "Lightning Brigade."

Battle of Iuka, Mississippi
September 19, 1862

After capturing Corinth, Mississippi, in May 1862, Union forces now held this important railroad center that could support efforts in Tennessee and Kentucky by using the Memphis & Charleston Railroad that connected all the way to Chattanooga, Tennessee. Gen. Ulysses S. Grant, now commanding Union forces around Corinth, had recently responded to calls for reinforcements to be sent to Gen. Don Carlos Buell, Army of the Ohio, for defense of the Union supply center at Louisville, now under threat from Confederate Generals E. Kirby Smith and Braxton Bragg.

To combat the flow of Union reinforcements to Kentucky, Confederate President Jefferson Davis initiated a diversionary effort by sending troops to attack Corinth and discourage any Union efforts to send men to Kentucky. When Grant received information on September 7 that two armies were advancing toward Corinth under Confederate Generals Sterling Price and Earl Van Dorn, he initiated plans to intercept them.

Grant's command, the Department of the Tennessee, included Gen. William S. Rosecrans, commanding the Union Army of the Mississippi, plus Generals William T. Sherman and Edward Ord, both in the Army of the Tennessee, with Grant in overall command of the two armies. Ord and Rosecrans were based at Corinth. When Price occupied Iuka on September 13, about twenty miles southeast of Corinth, he waited for the arrival of Van Dorn, who was bringing a force from Vicksburg. Grant planned to attack Price before Van Dorn arrived, using both Generals Ord and Rosecrans.

Gen. Ord would attack Price from the northwest while Gen. Rosecrans' assault would come from the southwest in Price's rear, in a two-pronged attack that would capture the Confederates. Ord's troops of about 8,000 men were transported on September 18 to Burnsville, about seven miles from Iuka, on the Memphis & Charleston Railroad. Troops would wait there until the attack began on the morning of September 19, when they would march the seven miles to Iuka and join the battle.

Rosecrans, on the other hand, transported his troops of 9,000 men south from Corinth using the Mobile & Ohio Railroad and then marched east using a road that passed through Jacinto, Mississippi. Delayed by woodlands and bad roads, Rosecrans informed Grant by horseback courier that he would not be at Iuka on the morning of September 19 as planned, but would reach it by afternoon. Grant informed Ord of Rosecrans' message and that he should wait for sounds of battle from Rosecrans' army before joining the assault. The message about the change in plan for Ord's attack never reached Rosecrans.

Gen. Rosecrans' troops arrived at Iuka late in the afternoon of September 19 and encountered Price's army about two hours before dusk. A fierce battle raged several hours into the night, but Ord's forces waiting a few miles away never appeared to support the assault. Because of a vigorous wind that cast an acoustic shadow, Ord did not hear any sounds of battle, nor did Grant who was waiting only a few miles farther at headquarters in Burnsville. Price, fully aware of the second Union army under Ord just northwest of Iuka, withdrew his army in the night, knowing he would not be able to defend against both armies. A second road that Rosecrans had not blocked, because it would have divided his forces, enabled Price's army to escape. On the morning of September 20, Gen. Ord entered Iuka to find Rosecrans and his victorious troops and

V. THE SECOND YEAR: 1862

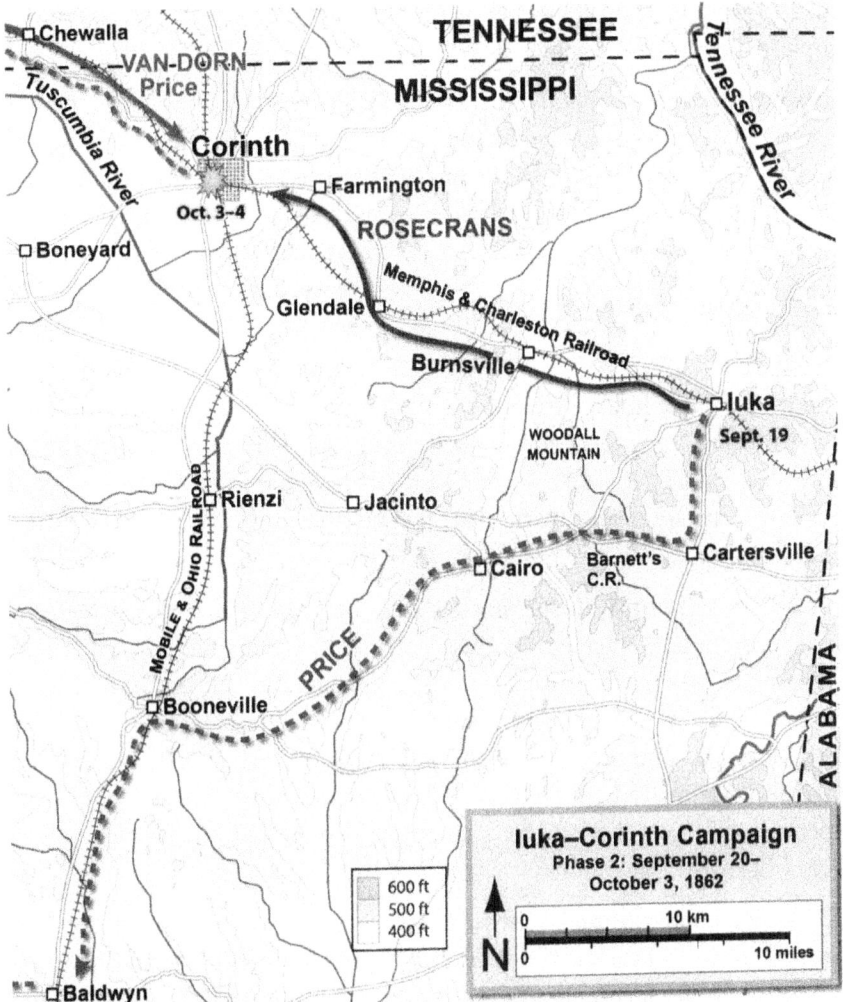

Fig. 21: At the Battle of Iuka, Mississippi, Sept. 19, 1862, Confederate Gen. Price escaped after being defeated by Union Gen. Rosecrans. Price traveled south and then circled back to join Gen. Van Dorn for their combined assault on Corinth, Mississippi, Oct. 7-8.

Source: *Creative Commons Attribution 3.0 license. Map by Hal Jespersen, www.cwmaps.com*

a finished battle. The Confederates had withdrawn in the night. When Grant entered the town shortly afterward, he attempted to organize a pursuit of Price's army, but the chase was soon abandoned because of the Confederates' head start.

Although described as a Union victory, a professional hostility began between Grant and Rosecrans for the perceived failures of each other on why the assault had not captured Price. Grant had ordered Rosecrans to block both roads that would have prevented Price's escape and Rosecrans blamed Grant for failing to get Ord's troops into Iuka to support the battle. The two generals would maintain a contentious relationship for the rest of their lives.

The two Confederate generals, Van Dorn and Price, connected at Ripley, Mississippi, about a week later. Price's army had made a long march that took him south through Baldwyn to join Van Dorn at Ripley on September 28. The combined Confederate armies, renamed the Army of West Tennessee and headed by the more senior Van Dorn, now totaled 22,000 men and moved forward with plans for a second battle on Corinth.

Second Battle of Corinth, Mississippi
October 3-4, 1862

After the Battle of Iuka, the Confederate Army of West Tennessee, under the command of Gen. Earl Van Dorn, moved north from Ripley, Mississippi, with the combined forces of Gen. Sterling Price, to destroy part of the Memphis & Charleston Railroad at Pocahontas, Tennessee. The Southern army then turned southeast to recapture Corinth for the Confederacy.

Union Gen. William S. Rosecrans had returned to Corinth after defeating Price at the Battle of Iuka on September 19. Gen. Ulysses S. Grant, overall commander of the Union forces around Corinth, set up new headquarters at Jackson, Tennessee, for coordination of armies at Corinth and Memphis. On October 2, Grant warned Rosecrans that Van Dorn was planning an attack on Corinth from the north, but Rosecrans was doubtful and committed only half his 23,000-man army to the defense. Troops were positioned in rifle pits that had originally been created by the Confederates prior to the Siege of Corinth.

As Van Dorn's army approached Corinth, they moved into old Confederate rifle pits north and west of the city on the morning of October 3, and successfully pushed Union lines back to a second line of fortifications. By nightfall, Rosecrans' Union army had been pressed into a defensive line only six hundred yards from Confederate rifles. Hand-to-hand fighting at point-blank range was expected the next day.

On October 4, the Confederates opened up a six-gun battery bombardment at 4:30 a.m. on the entrenched Union line, which continued until daylight. The Southern charge, planned for daylight, but then delayed by two hours, initially broke the Union line, capturing artillery and scattering troops. But Northern forces regained their positions when troops that had been held in reserve charged the Confederates. Falling back, the Southerners were placed in a cross-fire of heavy artillery, forcing them into full retreat. Given orders by Grant to pursue Van Dorn's army, Rosecrans failed to do so until the next day, which allowed the Confederate army to escape. The failure to capture Van Dorn's army increased the simmering hostility between Grant and Rosecrans.

Declared a hero by the Northern press, Rosecrans was lauded for his performance at Corinth in the thick of battle. Van Dorn's losses were high (4,200, including 500

V. THE SECOND YEAR: 1862

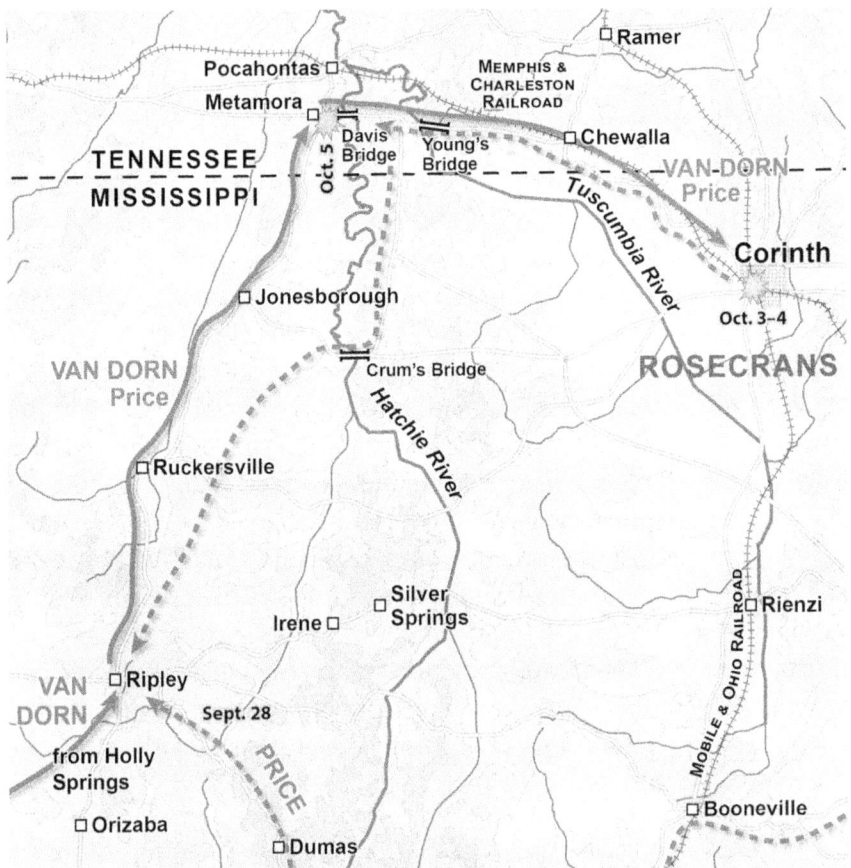

Fig. 22: At the Second Battle of Corinth, Mississippi, Confederate Generals Price and Van Dorn joined forces at Ripley, Mississippi, for a combined assault on Corinth Oct. 3-4, 1862. The assault was defeated by Union Gen. Rosecrans, making him a Northern hero in the war.
Source: *Creative Commons Attribution 3.0 license. Map by Hal Jespersen, www.cwmaps.com*

killed, 2,000 wounded and more than 1,700 captured or missing). Rosecrans lost 2,500 (approximately 350 killed; 1,800 wounded and about 300 captured or missing). Because of his defeat, Van Dorn lost command of his army and it was then merged into the Department of Mississippi and East Louisiana, commanded by Gen. John C. Pemberton at Vicksburg. The feint had backfired for the Confederates. Instead of limiting Union reinforcements to Kentucky, it had lost a significant battle and the victorious Union Gen. Rosecrans would soon be promoted to lead the new Army of the Cumberland east to confront Bragg in Tennessee.

It was during this period of Grant's command along the Mississippi-Tennessee border that he implemented a "Freedmen's Bureau," a haven for fugitive slaves. New army regulations required the care and protection of escaped Blacks, but had not provided any funding for their support. Grant set up a Bureau at Grand Junction, Tennessee, where Blacks harvested crops in the neglected surrounding fields that the government

STRUGGLE FOR THE UNION

> ## GRANT'S FREEDMEN'S BUREAU
> ### Grand Junction, Tennessee
>
> Following the Second Battle of Corinth in October, Grant was placed in command of the Department of Tennessee and set up headquarters at the small railroad town of Grand Junction, Tennessee, about forty-five miles east of Memphis and near the Mississippi border. After Lincoln's preliminary Emancipation Proclamation in September, thousands of fugitive slaves began pouring into Grant's district, needing clothing, food, medical attention, shelter and support. Initially, he sent them north to Cairo for integration into Northern society until political leaders in Illinois complained and Lincoln ended the practice. The army was required to protect Blacks who came in voluntarily, but there were no appropriations for feeding or housing the many thousands of Black men, women and children that were converging on Grand Junction. Without a means to sustain them, the refugees would burden the army. Able-bodied young men could be employed as teamsters, cooks and scouts, but new solutions were needed for the remaining Blacks, particularly the women and children. Grant wrote in his *Personal Memoirs:* "*Humanity forbade allowing them to starve ... But with such an army of them, of all ages and both sexes, as had congregated about Grand Junction, amounting to many thousands, it was impossible to advance.*" It was then that Grant conceived the idea of using liberated slaves as a way of providing for themselves and the army.
>
> All the plantations in this general area of west Tennessee at Mississippi's northern border were deserted, but ripe corn and cotton were waiting to be harvested. To solve the several issues, Grant appointed Chaplain John Eaton of the 27th Ohio Infantry as an organizer to put Blacks to work harvesting the crops. They would be paid 12 ½ cents per pound for picking and ginning cotton and a fair price for corn. Army soldiers would assist Eaton as needed. The harvest was shipped north and sold for the benefit of the government, and the money was then used for the freed people's support. The whole system quickly became self-sustaining. The freedmen also cut wood along the Mississippi River to supply the large number of government steamers, which provided a secondary fund to feed and clothe everyone in the camps and also build comfortable cabins and hospitals for the sick. As Eaton recalled, Grant's vision of making independent laborers from the ex-slaves also paved the way to making them soldiers and citizens.

then sold. The sale of harvested corn and cotton provided funds for food, homes and medical care for the Black refugees. The system became self-sustaining and provided support for thousands of Blacks with their families of women and children as they fled from slavery to freedom.

V. THE SECOND YEAR: 1862

Battle of Perryville (or Chaplin Hills), Kentucky
October 7-8, 1862

Confederate Gen. Braxton Bragg and his army from Chattanooga, Tennessee, finally arrived at Bardstown, Kentucky, about forty miles south of Louisville, on September 22, 1862, after being delayed for two days by a Union commander near Munfordville. Leaving Bardstown, Bragg next moved east towards Perryville on October 4 to join with Gen. E. Kirby Smith, who had reached the area some weeks earlier and already achieved victories over Union forces at Richmond and Frankfort, Kentucky. Bragg, hoping to find supplies and more water for men and horses in the drought-parched countryside, looked to the small town of Perryville, about fifty miles directly south of Frankfort. The town had the strategic value of an excellent network of roads, but more importantly, it was a potential source of water from the rivers and creeks that supplied it. The oppressive drought of the region had exhausted almost all sources of water for men and animals and the armies were now competing for water. Unfortunately, Perryville's water supplies had also been reduced to mere puddles.

Confederate Gen. Smith had captured Frankfort, the capital of Kentucky, September 2 and a fragile secessionist government had been established there. Both Confederate Generals Bragg and Smith attended the inauguration of secessionist Governor Richard Hawes at Frankfort on October 4. But the inauguration was abruptly terminated by the sound of approaching Union cannon fire, causing Hawes and his accompanying supporters to rapidly depart. Union Gen. Don Carlos Buell had dispatched part of his army from Louisville to Frankfort, hoping to prevent the two Confederate armies from joining forces.

On October 7, Union Gen. Buell's cavalry reached Perryville and fought against Confederate Bragg's rearguard. A full attack began again early on October 8 with a Union advance that was weakened by a shortage of men because two of the three Union corps had been deployed separately to search for water. Despite the fact that Union troops greatly outnumbered the Confederates, attacks and counterattacks shifted the course of battle back and forth throughout the day. Buell, not on the battlefield, was confined to an ambulance because of a wounding gash on his leg, caused by a fall from his horse.

The battle raged on into the night until Bragg, running short of supplies and men, fell back to his supply depot at Bardstown. While there, he learned that Generals Price and Van Dorn had been defeated at Corinth in the Western Theater and that Gen. Robert E. Lee had withdrawn from the Battle of Antietam at Sharpsburg, Maryland, and returned to Virginia in the Eastern Theater. Discouraged by these events and the realization that very few Kentuckians had come forward to join his army and the Confederacy during his march north, Bragg gave up on the Kentucky Campaign and ordered a withdrawal the next morning, over Gen. Smith's strenuous objections, into eastern Tennessee and Knoxville by way of the Cumberland Gap.

The Battle of Perryville brought heavy criticism to both Northern and Southern generals from their respective commanders. On the Union side, President Lincoln had become very dissatisfied with Buell's performance in Kentucky. With a force of about 60,000 men, greatly outnumbering the Confederates, the Southerners had still won the Battle of Perryville and when the Confederates withdrew from Kentucky, Buell failed to pursue them, citing that the rough wooded country with few roads would make it too difficult for pursuit. General-in-Chief Halleck telegraphed Buell, *"The president does not understand why we cannot march as the enemy marches, live as he lives, and fight as he fights, unless we admit that there is some inherent defect in our generals and soldiers."* President Lincoln removed Buell from command on October 24, and named Gen. William Rosecrans, recently lauded for his performance at the Second Battle of Corinth, as its new commander, renaming it the Army of the Cumberland. Buell never filled another command post and finally resigned from the army in 1864.

On the Southern side, Confederate officers complained to President Jefferson Davis that Bragg should be removed as head of the Army of Mississippi because of his conduct of the campaign at Perryville. Although the charges were dismissed by Davis, Bragg's relationship with his subordinates deteriorated even more. His prickly and obnoxious command style had offended his senior officers and they now also questioned his leadership.

Casualties and losses at Perryville were high on both sides. The Union's total casualties were over 4,000 and the Confederates, nearly equal to that number. Men killed from wounds in the battle numbered nearly 2,400. The Confederacy's hopes for creating a strong presence in Kentucky were dashed and the North maintained control of the state for the rest of the war.

Union General Murdered
September 29, 1862

Union Gen. William "Bull" Nelson, heading the Provisional Army of Kentucky in its defense against the Confederate forces threatening Louisville, made an imposing figure. At a height of 6'4", weighing three hundred pounds and in his prime, he was physically intimidating, which when coupled with his rude, often offending manner laced with profanity, had earned him the nickname "Bull." Disliked by most of his men and fellow officers for his disparaging and cutting tongue-lashings, he nevertheless enjoyed special status with his superiors because he had been instrumental in maintaining the loyalty of his native state of Kentucky to the Union.

After the Battle of Richmond, where Nelson and his new recruits had been savagely defeated by Confederate forces under Gen. E. Kirby Smith, Gen. Nelson was recuperating at the Galt Hotel in Louisville from a wound in his thigh. With the threat of Confederate armies approaching Louisville, Gen. Horatio Wright, commanding the Department of Ohio, sent Gen. Jefferson C. Davis (no relation to Confederate President

V. THE SECOND YEAR: 1862

Davis) to assist Nelson with improving the defenses of Louisville. Davis had been on convalescent leave at home in Indiana, but had recently reported for duty to Gen. Wright whose headquarters were in Cincinnati.

Two days after his appointment, Davis was called to a meeting at the Galt Hotel with Nelson, who demanded to know what Davis had accomplished in organizing and training local Louisville citizens into a defensive force against invading Confederates. When Davis, who had regarded the assignment as demeaning, reported minimal progress on the project, Nelson rudely relieved him from duty in Louisville and told him to leave and report to general headquarters in Cincinnati, or he would be arrested.

An angry Gen. Davis, greatly offended by the rebuke, returned to Cincinnati, where Gen. Wright informed him that Gen. Buell was now in charge in Louisville and Davis should return there where his leadership was badly needed. Davis had achieved distinction as a young man during the Mexican-American War and had already served as an effective commander in several Civil War battles. Although he had never attended West Point Military Academy, Davis had joined the army as a private and worked his way up the military command to a Brigadier General. Frequently slighted for his lack of military credentials by fellow officers, the slightly built Davis had developed a quick-tempered, feisty and aggressive response to implied insults or attacks on his abilities or character.

Davis returned to Louisville on September 29 and when he encountered Gen. Nelson at the Galt House, he demanded an apology for the insulting way he had been treated at their last meeting. Nelson responded with, *"Go away you damned puppy, I don't want anything to do with you!"* The confrontation prompted Davis to flip a wadded-up paper ball that hit Nelson in the face. The large man then slapped Davis hard on the face with the back of his hand and walked away to return to his room at the hotel. The infuriated Davis quickly obtained a pistol from a fellow Indianan who was present during the confrontation and followed Nelson, shouting, *"General Nelson, take care of yourself!"* As the unarmed Nelson turned to face him, Davis shot him in the chest at point-blank range. The wounded general was still able to climb the stairs to the second floor where he collapsed and was carried to a nearby room. As he lay on the bed, he requested a clergyman, crying out, *"I have been basely murdered!"* He died within the half-hour on September 29, 1862.

Gen. Buell ordered Davis arrested and informed General-in-Chief Halleck that Davis should be tried by court-martial, but that it would have to take place in Washington, because Buell could not spare any officers now on active duty. Halleck deferred the matter to Gen. Wright in Cincinnati. Discussions of a court-martial never materialized as Buell never pressed charges and Wright was satisfied that Davis had acted on the defensive, even though Nelson was unarmed when he was shot. With a compelling need for experienced field commanders who were in short supply, Davis was returned to active duty and never tried for murder.

Davis later served under Gen. William T. Sherman as a corps commander in the Atlanta Campaign and the March to the Sea. But his military legacy was further marred by his actions during the march through Georgia, known as the Ebenezer Massacre. As the Union Army crossed Ebenezer Creek, a tributary of the Savannah River, Davis removed a pontoon bridge before Black slave refugees that were following the army could cross, leaving them at the mercy of pursuing Confederate cavalry. Many drowned or were killed by the Confederates or captured, to be enslaved once more. At the following military inquiry about the incident, Sherman defended the actions of Davis as a military necessity. Davis continued to serve in the army until his retirement, but never received a promotion beyond his final rank at the end of the war.

CONFEDERATES ABANDON HEARTLAND OFFENSIVE

Battle of Stones River (or Murfreesboro), Tennessee
December 31, 1862

After the Battle of Perryville, Kentucky, where the Southerners had achieved a large victory, Gen. Braxton Bragg made the surprising decision to abandon the Confederacy's Kentucky Campaign and withdrew from the state. Recent losses by Confederates at Corinth, Mississippi, and the withdrawal of the army under Gen. Robert E. Lee back to Virginia after the Battle of Antietam (at Sharpsburg, Maryland), had convinced Bragg that his Army of Mississippi would be isolated and at the mercy of Union assaults, which would lead to his capture or bloody withdrawal. In addition, the anticipated high number of recruits that were expected to emerge from Kentucky sympathizers had not materialized.

Gen. E. Kirby Smith, commanding the second army of the Kentucky Campaign, strongly objected to the withdrawal and still wanted to fight, but Bragg, as senior commander, overruled him. Bragg ordered the withdrawal of all the troops to Murfreesboro, Tennessee, where they expected to set up winter quarters and be in good position to attack Union-held Nashville, less than forty miles away. The combined armies of Bragg and Smith contained nearly 40,000 veteran troops who now marched over two hundred miles to Murfreesboro, surviving on little more than parched corn and foul water in the drought-stricken state. Once they arrived in mid-November at the rich agricultural area in Stones River Valley, local residents, sympathetic to the worn and bedraggled army, now renamed the Army of Tennessee, welcomed the emaciated Confederates.

Union forces in Nashville now reported to a new commander, Gen. William Rosecrans, victor in the Second Battle of Corinth, commanding the new Army of the Cumberland. Rosecrans left Nashville on December 26 with half his army, about

V. THE SECOND YEAR: 1862

> ### WOMEN SOLDIERS IN THE WAR
>
> Women were not permitted to enlist as soldiers in either the Union or Confederate military units, but there are many documented cases of women, disguised as men, participating in virtually every major battle on both sides. More than 250 have been accurately documented, but given that the women enlisted secretly, an exact number is unknown. Estimates have placed their actual number at 400 or even more. Discovery of their gender, usually because of a wound when they were transported to the field hospital, prompted immediate dismissal and the women were generally sent home. Many simply reenlisted into a different unit with a different name and returned to the war. Victorian standards at the time meant soldiers slept clothed, bathed separately and avoided public latrines. Loose uniforms hid physical differences and lack of a beard was attributed to youth. Further, physical examinations became rare as more and more soldiers were needed to resupply the armies.
>
> One example of a woman Union casualty is documented at the Battle of Stones River. Frances Elizabeth Quinn, who enlisted at the age of sixteen as B. Frank Miller, was shot in the shoulder. Her gender was revealed when she was treated for her wound. Discharged from the military five times when discovered to be female, Quinn continued to reenlist in different units under different names and once in the cavalry under Gen. Philip Sheridan, who described her as "coarse and masculine, with large features... easily passed for a man." After the war, she married and the couple had two daughters. She died in 1872.

40,000 troops to attack the encamped Confederates in the Stones River Valley, near Murfreesboro. As the two armies bivouacked less than a half mile from each other on December 30, soldiers on both sides made music for each other. "Yankee Doodle" and "Columbia" from the North competed with "Dixie" and "Bonnie Blue Flag" from the South. At the end, soldiers on both sides sang together to the tunes of the sentimental favorite, "Home Sweet Home."

Both commanding generals planned to attack on December 31, but the Confederates struck first at dawn. Southern officers issued an early ration of whiskey against the frigid cold in place of breakfast to avoid lighting campfires that would reveal their positions. The huge wave of Confederates successfully captured several surprised Union batteries that did not have time to fire a single shot and several cannons fell to the Confederates.

Unlike some of his fellow officers, Union Gen. Philip Sheridan and his cavalry were prepared for an early morning attack. Roused at 4 a.m. by their commander, the men were ready and responded quickly when the Confederates attacked. Sheridan organized a strong defense at the center of the Union line, which became known as the "Slaughter Pen" from all the dead and wounded that soon accumulated, but prevented a total Union collapse.

By mid-morning, Sheridan's troops had suffered severe casualties, including three brigade commanders. Low on men and ammunition, Sheridan's men pulled back, leaving only one Union line to hold, under the command of Col. William Hazen, to battle in the Round Forest, known as "Hell's Half-Acre." Murderous artillery at nearly point-blank range repulsed the Confederates' advance. A soldier from the Southern 32nd Alabama infantry described the scene: *"We charged in fifty yards of them and had not the timely order of retreat been given, none of us would now be left to tell the tale… our regiment carried 280 into action and came out with 58."* At the end of the day, Hazen's brigade had withstood four Confederate attacks and prevented the Union army's destruction. Having driven the Union troops to Stone's River, Bragg was confident that victory was at hand and telegraphed Richmond that *"God has granted us a Happy New Year."* That night, some of Rosecrans' generals urged the army to withdraw before its retreat was cut off, but others agreed with Rosecrans to stay and fight.

> **THE ORPHAN BRIGADE**
>
> Kentucky, a Border State, contributed soldiers to both Union and Confederate armies. In the Battle of Stones River, the "Orphan Brigade," commanded by Confederate Gen. John C. Breckinridge suffered devastating losses, prompting their commander to cry out, "My poor Orphans!" referring to their status as brave soldiers who could not return to Union-occupied Kentucky.

The next morning, New Year's Day, both sides regrouped, nursing their wounds and the day was relatively quiet. But on the afternoon of January 2, Bragg ordered Gen. John C. Breckinridge's 5,000 Confederates, to capture a Union position on a hill that overlooked McFadden's Ford, part of Stone's River. Initially successful, the Confederates pushed the Union line back until the men came within range of fifty-seven Union cannon positioned on the other side of the ford. When the Confederates had to cross an open field, thirty-six percent of Breckinridge's troops, 1,800 men, were cut down. The devastating losses of this disaster and the arrival the next day of a large Union supply train with more troops for Rosecrans forced Bragg into retreat that night, yielding the valuable territory to Union control. Casualties numbered nearly 25,000 (13,000 for the Union, and 12,000 for the Confederates) or thirty percent of the 81,000 engaged.

Lincoln sent Rosecrans a congratulatory note for his *"hard-earned victory which, had there been a defeat instead, the nation could scarcely have lived over (it)." In* the wake of Union failures at Fredericksburg, Virginia, and Perryville, Kentucky, the North welcomed the good news with words of praise. The North now had control of nearly all of Tennessee and Nashville became a major supply base for the North for the rest of the war.

V. THE SECOND YEAR: 1862

UNION LAUNCHES VICKSBURG CAMPAIGN

THE VICKSBURG CAMPAIGN, MISSISSIPPI

Grant's Mississippi Central Advance
November-December 1862

In the fall of 1862, the Union had control of the Mississippi River except for the stretch of water between the Confederate fortress at Vicksburg, Mississippi, and a second stronghold at Port Hudson, about one hundred thirty miles south, and only twenty miles north of Baton Rouge, Louisiana. Between the two strongholds, the Confederates had an open gateway across the river to connect the western Confederacy with the east. Lincoln had pointed out early in the war Vicksburg's importance by noting, *"See what a lot of land these fellows hold, of which Vicksburg is the key! The war can never be brought to a close until that key is in our pocket. We can take all the northern ports of the Confederacy, and they can defy us from Vicksburg."*

Vicksburg presented a daunting barrier to Union attack. The heavily fortified Confederate stronghold, built on 300-foot-high bluffs, commanded the Mississippi River, where a horseshoe bend in the river forced enemy vessels to be under direct fire from one hundred seventy-two Confederate cannons positioned in a line eight miles long on the bluffs above. Named the "Gibraltar of the Confederacy," the fortress city was also protected by the massive Mississippi Delta, a network of rivers, bayous and swamps, nearly impassable by horse or man. A naval bombardment from the Mississippi River in May and June 1862 had been repulsed by fierce resistance from the Confederate cannons and failed to dislodge the Vicksburg fortress.

GRANT'S GENERAL ORDERS NO. 11

During this period of the war, Ulysses S. Grant became fully aware of illegal smuggling and corruption around the cotton trade within his military district. The U.S. Treasury had approved the practice of cotton trading for sales to the Northern textile industry and issued limited trader licenses. But corruption and cotton smuggling were rampant as licenses were abused or ignored. Grant, persuaded that Jewish traders were responsible, issued General Orders No. 11 on Dec. 17, 1862, to expel Jews from his military district, which included large sections of Kentucky, Tennessee and Mississippi. The General Order affected all Jews, which caused twenty-four Jewish families in Paducah, Kentucky, to be forced to leave their homes. When President Lincoln was made aware of the situation, he revoked the order. Grant, greatly embarrassed by the incident later in his career during his Presidential Campaign of 1868, explained that he had issued the order without thinking of the Jews as a race, but simply as persons who had violated the practice of licenses to buy cotton.

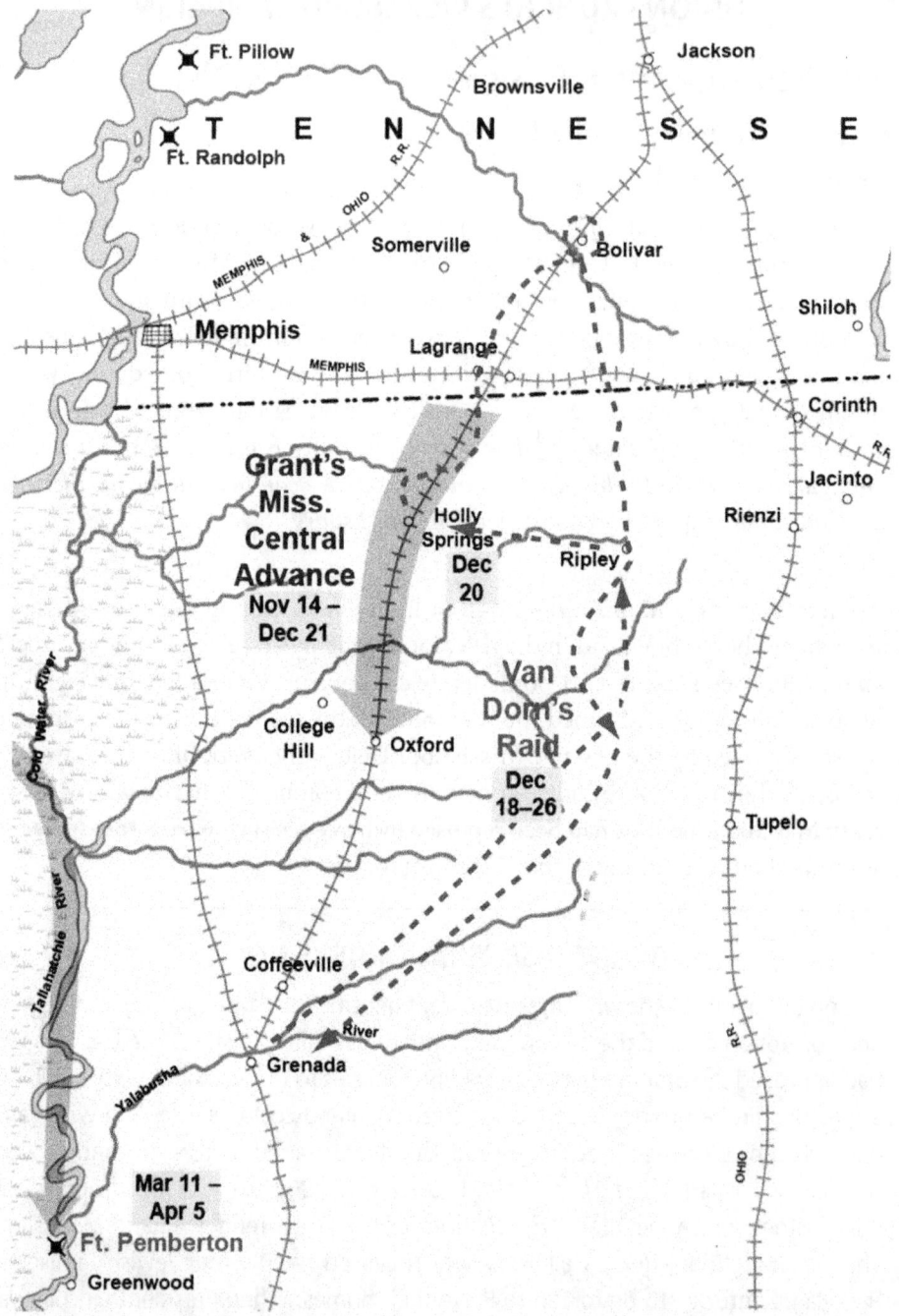

Fig. 23: Confederate Gen. Earl Van Dorn successfully raided Union Gen. Grant's supply depot at Holly Springs, Mississippi, Dec. 20, 1862, foiling Grant's attempt to reach Vicksburg from the east side of the Mississippi River. The loss forced Grant to withdraw and implement a new strategy for how to attack Vicksburg.

Source: *Creative Commons Attribution 3.0 License Map by Hal Jespersen, www.cwmaps.com.*

V. THE SECOND YEAR: 1862

Gen. Ulysses S. Grant, commanding the Department of Tennessee, with forces at Memphis, Tennessee, and Corinth, Mississippi, implemented in early November 1862 the first movements of a two-pronged assault to attack Vicksburg on land from the east. Moving about 30,000 men of his army south from Lagrange, Tennessee, on the Mississippi Central Railroad, Grant's army pushed Confederate forces under Gen. Earl Van Dorn, numbering about 24,000, out of Holly Springs, Mississippi. Van Dorn's army had been transferred to Vicksburg after his loss at the Second Battle of Corinth in October and placed him under the command of Gen. John C. Pemberton.

The second advance of the two-pronged Union assault on Vicksburg would be performed by Gen. William T. Sherman, who departed Memphis, Tennessee, with naval support provided by Rear Admiral David D. Porter, for an expedition down the Mississippi Delta to reach Chickasaw Bayou at Vicksburg on the east side of the Mississippi. Sherman's forces would attack the northern flank of the Vicksburg stronghold at Chickasaw, which would avoid the daunting cannons on the Mississippi River. If successful, Sherman would join Grant on high ground for a land assault on Vicksburg from the northeast.

Grant occupied Holly Springs November 9, set up a new army depot of supplies and munitions and prepared to continue south and engage Confederates at Granada. If successful there, the army would continue another one hundred twenty miles south to Vicksburg where he would join Sherman's forces. Grant called a halt at Oxford thirty miles south of Holly Springs, waiting for supplies to catch up.

The Confederates quickly took advantage of Grant's divided Union army. Pemberton deployed Gen. Earl Van Dorn with a cavalry of 3,500 horsemen to invade Grant's supply depot at Holly Springs on December 20. Although Grant warned the garrison commander at Holly Springs, Col. Robert Murphy, that a Confederate Cavalry was moving toward him, the warning was ignored and Van Dorn's cavalry captured 1,500 Union troops, including Murphy, and plundered warehouses, destroyed all food and forage and confiscated munitions. Grant immediately sent cavalry from his front to drive Van Dorn out of the area, but the Confederates had enough time to move north, almost to Bolivar, Tennessee, wrecking railroad track and bridges. Van Dorn's cavalry successfully evaded Grant's Union pursuit column south of Ripley, Mississippi, and the Confederates were able to return safely to their starting point at Grenada on December 28, after covering five hundred miles in two weeks.

At about the same time, Confederate Gen. Nathan Bedford Forrest, commanding a cavalry of about 2,000, was conducting significant raiding expeditions in western Tennessee. Forrest destroyed large segments of the Mobile & Ohio Railroad and fifty miles of railroad and telegraph lines between Jackson, Tennessee, and Columbus, Kentucky, cutting off Grant's communications for weeks, including those to Sherman, now underway to the Chickasaw Bayou.

Grant, forced to abandon his overland advance, had to rebuild the supply depot lost at Holly Springs and restore communications with his command. With Grant's withdrawal, Confederate Gen. Pemberton was able to move about 13,000 troops from Vicksburg to face the river and block the coming offensive from Sherman at Chickasaw Bayou.

Grant spent the last of December obtaining rations and forage from local civilians to replace what had been destroyed. Grant writes in his *Personal Memoirs*, *"Up to this time it had been regarded as an axiom in war that large bodies of troops must operate from a base of supplies which they always covered and guarded in all forward movements."* Forced to restore food for his men and horses from the surrounding countryside, Grant writes, *"I was amazed at the quantity of supplies the country afforded. This taught me a lesson which was taken advantage of later in the campaign when our army lived twenty days with the issue of only five days' rations by the commissary. Our loss of supplies at Holly Springs was great, but it was more than compensated for by those taken from the country and by the lesson taught."*

Mid-December, Grant learned from General-in-Chief Halleck that his command would be divided into four corps. Gen. John A. McClernand, currently in Springfield, Illinois, would command one of them to operate down the Mississippi as part of the Vicksburg Campaign. Although Halleck assured Grant that he would remain overall commanding general, neither he nor Grant trusted McClernand's experience or qualifications for such an important position. McClernand and President Lincoln had a special relationship as they had been friendly political rivals in Illinois and McClernand had convinced Lincoln that he could recruit a significant army, take Vicksburg and open up the Mississippi River. Lincoln saw an opportunity for gaining new recruits and authorized the plan over the objections of Halleck. MClernand's role in the Vicksburg Campaign would soon present problems for both Generals Grant and Sherman.

Battle of Chickasaw Bayou (or Walnut Hills), Mississippi
December 26, 1862 - January 2, 1863

As Grant coped with his losses at Holly Springs, Gen. William T. Sherman and his troops were already underway with Rear Admiral David D. Porter to reach Milliken's Bend using the Mississippi River (See Fig. 28) and then transport the fleet to Chickasaw Bayou which is on the east side of the Delta, fed by the Yazoo River, which flows through bayous and swamps before it empties into the Mississippi River. Chickasaw Bayou is protected by Walnut Hills, high bluffs next to Vicksburg's northern boundary. If Sherman's troops could gain the high ground and be joined with forces from Grant's infantry from the east, an assault on the Vicksburg fortress could be implemented.

Nine gunboats, including three ironclads, and fifty-nine troop transports departed Memphis on December 20, which included troops sent from Gen. McClernand's recruitment efforts in Indiana and Illinois. The fleet stopped at Helena, Arkansas, to pick up additional soldiers and proceeded on to Milliken's Bend, where the fleet of about 32,000 men disembarked at Johnson's Plantation, opposite Steele's Bayou (See Fig. 24). The troops reached Chickasaw Bayou on December 24 to face Confederate defenders on the well defended Walnut Hills bluffs next to Vicksburg. Sherman planned to defeat Southern forces there, advance to high ground and meet with Grant's troops arriving overland from the east.

With the loss of Grant's communication lines, Sherman was unaware that Grant had been forced to halt his advance and was now back at Holly Springs, restoring his supplies. Grant's retreat had allowed Confederate Gen. Pemberton to redelegate his troops and prepare defenses at Chickasaw Bayou before Sherman's arrival.

On December 26, Sherman's fleet moved slowly through the bayou waters as they encountered natural and man-made defenses from trees and vegetation. Chickasaw Bayou, choked with entangled trees and swampland, was further protected by felled tree barriers the Confederates had placed in chest-deep water in the swamp. Union men were under constant deadly fire from the Walnut Hills bluffs. Sherman writes in his *Memoirs*, "*Our men actually scooped out with their hands (to create) caves in the bank, which sheltered them against the fire of the enemy…firing directly down. So critical was their position, we could not recall the men until after dark, and then one at a time. Our losses were pretty heavy, and we had accomplished nothing… with little loss on our enemy.*"

By December 30, Sherman abandoned plans to resume similar attacks against the bluffs and proposed a joint Army-Navy attack, bombarding nearby Drumgould's Bluff with artillery, using Porter's gunboats to prepare for an infantry landing before the Confederates could respond. But that attack, to begin at daybreak December 31, had to be called off as heavy fog obscured all movements of the boats.

With the element of surprise eliminated, no communication from Grant, and no sounds of battle coming from Grant's army on the bluffs above, plus the steadily increasing number of Confederate reinforcements facing him, Sherman withdrew from his Chickasaw Bayou expedition and moved back to Milliken's Bend on January 2. Battle engagements in the Bayou and at Drumgould's Bluff had cost nearly 1,800 Union casualties out of 30,000 men, compared to only 200 Confederates.

Sending a communication to General-in-Chief Henry Halleck, Sherman wrote: "*I reached Vicksburg at the time appointed, landed, assaulted, and failed.*" Sherman writes in his *Memoirs*, "*… our failure at Chickasaw raised the usual cry from the Northern press 'repulse, failure and bungling.' There was no bungling on my part, for I never worked harder or with more intensity of purpose in my life; and General Grant, long after, in his report of the operations of the siege of Vicksburg, gave us all full credit for the skill of the movement and described the almost impregnable nature of the ground.*"

While he was waiting for further orders with no communications from Grant, Sherman was met at Milliken's Bend by Gen. John A. McClernand, who had arrived

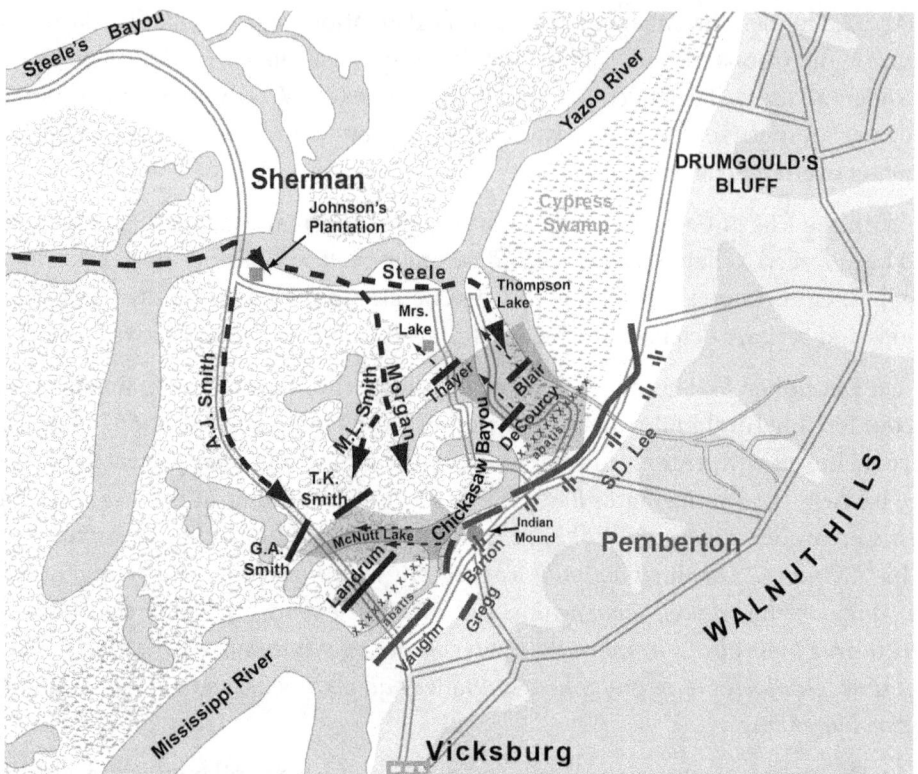

Fig. 24: Confederates under Gen. Pemberton successfully prevented Union attempts led by Gen. Sherman at the Battle of Chickasaw Bayou in the Mississippi Delta to mount an assault on the bluffs near Vicksburg, Mississippi, at the end of the year 1862.

Source: *Creative Commons Attribution 3.0 License Map by Hal Jespersen, www. cwmaps.com.*

by steamer with written orders from General-in-Chief Halleck that McClernand would be taking over Sherman's command for an expedition on Vicksburg. McClernand had been very successful in his recruitment efforts in Indiana and Illinois and six regiments of infantry and a battery had been sent to Memphis, but he had still been in Illinois when the troops left for the Chickasaw Bayou expedition. Halleck had informed Grant that he was overall commander of any troops in the Department of Tennessee, but McClernand did outrank Sherman.

Because communications from Grant were still absent, Sherman learned for the first time from McClerland that Grant's overland operation had been aborted and he was now occupied with restoring his supply base at Holly Springs. McClernand immediately reorganized Sherman's troops and renamed it the Army of Mississippi, hoping that he would soon have a new opportunity to grab headlines that enhanced his political ambitions.

With no specific plan of his own on how to proceed with his new command, McClernand soon adopted Sherman's proposal for an expedition to capture Fort

Hindman at Arkansas Post, a Confederate garrison on the Arkansas River about forty miles inland from its mouth on the Mississippi. Manned by about 5,000 troops, the Confederates frequently captured Union boats as they carried supplies and troops up and down the Mississippi. A recent raid had captured the Union supply steamer *Blue Wing* and the Southerners had taken it to Arkansas Post. U.S. Navy Rear Admiral Porter, who disliked McClernand for his political maneuverings, at first refused to participate in the expedition, but with Sherman's active persuasion, Porter agreed to the new mission. The whole army and navy fleet, loaded on sixty steamboats, convoyed by nine gunboats, left Milliken's Bend for the new expedition on January 5, 1863, to move up the Mississippi more than one hundred miles north of Milliken's Bend to reach the Arkansas River and access to Arkansas Post.

EMANCIPATION PROCLAMATION
September 22, 1862

Lincoln took advantage of Confederate Gen. Robert E. Lee's retreat from the Battle of Antietam in September to declare a Union victory and announced the preliminary Emancipation Proclamation on September 22, 1862, that would be enacted January 1, 1863. Using his war powers as Commander-in-Chief, Lincoln's Executive Order would declare that on that date *all enslaved people in the states currently engaged in rebellion against the Union "shall be then, thenceforward and forever free."* The one hundred days between September 22 and January 1 would allow the public time to adjust to the change in policy.

The Proclamation did not affect slaves in Border States (Kentucky, Maryland, Delaware and Missouri) as the Order was constitutionally supported as war powers. Further, the Union Army was ordered to recognize and maintain the freedom of ex-slaves, with no compensation to slave owners. The Fugitive Slave Act of 1850 that required escaped slaves be returned to their owners was no longer valid.

As escaping slaves made their way to Union lines, Southern war efforts immediately lost the benefits of slave labor. The Emancipation Proclamation also effectively discouraged European support for the Confederacy as both the United Kingdom and France had already abolished slavery in 1834 and 1848, respectively.

Significant opposition to the Emancipation Proclamation came from the so-called "Copperheads," or Peace Democrats, a political faction in the North that opposed the war and advocated an immediate peace settlement that would either meet the Confederacy's demands or allow the Southern states to leave the Union. After the Union's defeat at the Second Battle of Bull Run, Peace Democrats had gained momentum as they challenged Lincoln's management of the war. Most came from states just north of the Ohio River, migrants from slave-holding states or individuals with family members who owned slaves. Some actively opposed freeing the slaves, fearing that Blacks would invade the

North and compete with whites for jobs and opportunities. Blame was placed on the abolitionists for starting the war.

Republicans applied the name "Copperhead" to the Peace Democrats faction, comparing them to the venomous snake because of their poisonous attacks on Lincoln and demands for peace at any price. But the faction embraced the label and cut liberty heads out of copper pennies which they wore as badges to signify their loyalty to a peaceful solution.

CHALLENGE TO LINCOLN FROM THE SENATE
December 1862

The Battle of Fredericksburg, December 11-15, had resulted in a devastating defeat for the Union and unleashed a political fireball in Congress, assisted by new attacks from the Northern press. A group of about thirty Republican senators met with Lincoln, demanding removal of Secretary of State William Seward from the Cabinet. It was widely thought that Seward had orchestrated many of the decisions regarding the war and without Union victories, demands for peace that would grant an independent South to the Confederacy, were gaining momentum.

Seward offered to resign from the Cabinet, but Lincoln responded with a meeting of the other Cabinet members, excluding Seward. At the beginning of his Presidency, Lincoln had appointed his three rivals in the Presidential Election to his Cabinet, who included: Seward as Secretary of State, Salmon P. Chase, Secretary of Treasury and Edward Bates as Attorney General. Each possessed years of experience, offered different points of view and represented all three aspects of the conflict that Lincoln felt he needed to guide the country through the trials ahead: conservative, moderate and radical.

At the end of the vigorously debated Cabinet meeting, Chase offered his resignation, as it was he who had originated much of the original criticism against Seward. Lincoln, with both letters of resignation from Seward and Chase in his pocket, saw his opportunity to refuse both, stating in his letter to both men, "… *the public interest does not admit of it.*" The decision was able to gain support from both sides of the argument and the Senators lost their momentum. Lincoln had successfully commanded the crisis and maintained the cross-section of personalities and political strengths that he needed in his Cabinet for managing the war. His own assessment of his success was later expressed to a Senator, *"Now I can ride. I have a pumpkin in each end of my bag."*

V. THE SECOND YEAR: 1862

VIEWS FROM THE PUBLIC FOR THE YEAR 1862

About financing the War...

Both North and South turned to paper money to finance the war which changed the financial systems of the country that had always backed currency with gold or hard assets. The Confederate State dollar was printed in March 1861 in the form of promissory notes that bore interest and the bearer would be repaid on a specific date printed on the note. The phrase at the top of the bill, for example, stated "... payable twelve months after date (then inscribed)." As time went on and more bills were printed, the date of redemption was changed to later and later dates and in 1864, the phrase read, "... two years after ratification of a peace treaty...". Not surprisingly, as the war continued, the bills became relatively worthless and citizens were forced into bartering for food or dipping into savings of hard assets.

The Union's first federal banknotes were called Demand Notes and circulated in the country in the summer of 1861. In February 1862, Congress passed the Legal Tender Act which decreed that paper money was the universal currency, equal in value to gold and silver, and could be used as payment of all debts. Printed in green ink on only one side, they were called "greenbacks." The Confederate dollar was quickly referred to as "greybacks."

While the value of both kinds of paper money fluctuated with progress of the war, the greybacks steadily lost value as the war went on and the Confederacy continued to print more bills. Initially supported by the South, confidence waned as the war continued and the greybacks became worthless at war's end. Greenbacks were valued at less than 40 cents when first introduced, but by the end of the war were valued at more than 60 cents.

About Southern sacrifices for the War...

In 1862, Southern armies were suffering from a lack of supplies to feed and clothe the men and reports of soldiers walking on bleeding and blistered feet angered the public with the Confederate bureaucracy and the failure of President Jefferson Davis to properly take care of the soldiers. Responding to the need, private citizens organized efforts to gather provisions and other necessities to send to their regiments.

But transportation of whatever supplies of food, clothing and shoes that could be obtained was difficult in the South, as many of the railroads were unable to cross state lines because of different train gauges that had been implemented by the independent states. Further, ammunition and artillery had priority. When the tattered, hungry Confederate soldiers entered the Border State of Maryland, they were surprised when the majority of citizens did not greet them kindly. Local citizens believed that it was the Confederacy that had brought war onto their soil. Farmers had lost crops, livestock and fences and there was very little food available for anyone, especially for an invading army.

Writers and government leaders in the South promoted the need for self-sacrifice and commitment, but Confederate policies, such as the military draft, taxes-in-kind and impressment, a policy that allowed the government to seize supplies from citizens in exchange for the increasingly worthless national currency, depressed morale.

Southern newspapers continued to bolster public morale through 1862 by bragging about the superiority of the Confederate soldier and the morality of the Southern cause. Northern soldiers were described as cold-hearted butchers, guilty of every sin and cruelty imaginable, while the Confederate soldiers were praised for their humanity, courage and bravery. Union casualties were frequently exaggerated while reporting that the Confederacy's armies suffered only minimal losses. As the war continued, newspapers were forced to shrink in size because of increased costs to print, a lack of paper and decreased advertising.

About local inhabitants near Fort Donelson...

The Cincinnati Times (February 20, 1862) Correspondent reported on encounters between Union soldiers and the inhabitants along the road between Forts Henry and Donelson, northwestern Tennessee in early February. *"The settlements in the vicinity of Donelson are very few, but the people seem to be well-supplied with provisions and poultry, and what may be considered in comfortable circumstances. Dover, the capital of Stewart County, a town of some eight or nine hundred inhabitants in ordinary times, is about a mile above the fort, and at this period, I understand, nearly deserted. The entire region is stripped of arms of every kind, and most of the men have either run away, or are in the rebel army. The women were all in a great state of nervous excitement and alarm, and thought their houses would be burned, and their throats cut, but after talking with some of our officers, and being treated with respect and courtesy, they concluded the Federalists were not half so bad as they had been represented. The women and old men complain bitterly of the war, and are at an entire loss to understand the cause of it. They say they were prosperous and happy as they desired before the present troubles, and cannot comprehend what is meant by the 'wrongs of the South.' They ardently desire the restoration of peace on any terms, and declare their hatred of the promoters and leaders of the rebellion. No doubt we shall have a very hard fight, as the fort is much stronger than it was supposed to be."*

About Union victories at Forts Henry and Donelson...

The first major Union victories of the war occurred in February 1862, namely the capture of Forts Henry and Donelson on the Tennessee and Cumberland Rivers in northwestern Tennessee. The news brought out ringing bells and lighted bonfires as Northern cities celebrated. The *Chicago Tribune* reported that the city *"reeled mad with joy,"* on hearing the news about Fort Donelson. When the public learned that "Unconditional Surrender" Grant had won the battle with a cigar clamped between his teeth, he was soon overwhelmed with an excessive supply of cigars. As a result, he became a heavy smoker and by the end of the war, reportedly smoked about twenty cigars a day.

From its Cairo Correspondent, the *New York Times* printed on February 24, 1862, about the battles. *"The intelligence which flashed along the wires that Donelson had fallen—set bells to jubilating and bonfires blazing, that awoke an almost spontaneous cheer from the throats of the twenty millions of the North, that sent the blood pulsating in an almost delirious frenzy of delight through the veins of the nation."* The correspondent continued with a report on 5,000 Confederate prisoners from the Battle of Fort Donelson that had been received at the Indianapolis prison camp. *"They are the hardest looking set of men ever collected together; uniformed in rags of all colors, with carpets for blankets. The privates assert... that they are better treated and fed there* (at the prison camp) *than they have been for the last six months. Most of them are anxious to take the oath* (of loyalty to the Union). *Three of their surgeons have been paroled to their sick which are becoming quite numerous. The officers are not uniformed and don't look much superior to the private prisoners."*

The Cairo Correspondent continued on February 25: *"The Rebel officers seem very generally satisfied with what fighting they have seen, and would be glad to be allowed to go home and stay there. Dozens of them assured me that they would willingly take the oath, and give ample security to keep quiet, if the Government would only allow them to go South. I conversed with a good many privates, who professed the greatest astonishment at the kindly treatment extended them by their captors. They had all along been assured by the South that if taken by the Yankees they would all be hung, and if the Yankees once penetrated the South they would burn all the houses, free all the negroes, hang the men and violate the women. These miserable, outrageous falsehoods they believed, and in view of the supposed fiendish character of Northern men, had been induced to enlist."*

About Southern response to the defeat at Fort Donelson...

The *Richmond Dispatch* wrote the following on February 19: *"If these bloody barbarians, whose hands are now soaked to the elbows in the life-blood of men defending their own homes and firesides, dream that they are now one inch nearer the subjugation of the South than when they started on their infernal mission, they prove themselves to be fools and madmen, as well as savages and murderers... Their success at Fort Donelson, gained only by vast superiority of numbers, will only have the effect of converting the whole population of the South—men, women and children—into an immense army, who will resist them at every step, and everywhere 'welcome them with bloody hands to hospitable graves.' The fortitude of our people is again to be tried, and the metal of which their courage is made once more to be tested, by the last news from Fort Donelson. We have met with heavy disaster there. The wretches who are invading our country were* enabled, by the facilities of river transportation, to bring up reinforcements to their previously whipped troops, and have overwhelmed us with numbers."

About news of the Battle of Shiloh ...

Soon after the Battles of Forts Henry and Donelson, a great battle occurred in early April about one hundred miles south of there on the Tennessee River near Pittsburgh Landing. The Southern Lynchburg *Daily Virginian* reported the Battle of Shiloh two days after the battle as *"a complete (Confederate) victory ... and will probably lead to the liberation of Tennessee."* The *Wilmington Daily Journal* (North Carolina) described Shiloh as *"... a drawn battle. The consequences of this Battle will throw Fort Donelson, Fort Henry and Nashville into the shade."* The Charleston *Daily Courier* published huge headlines to describe the outcome of the battle. On April 7, the headlines ran *"Great Battle Near Corinth! Confederates Triumphant! Great Slaughter of the Enemy! Their Whole Army Engaged."*

The actual situation, however, was that although the Confederates had initially prevailed, the Union Army under Gen. Ulysses S. Grant had forced the Confederates to withdraw and retreat to Corinth, Mississippi, the next day. When it became evident that the Confederates had retreated from Shiloh, the Southern news changed its message to report that the retreat was *"planned and ... the position of things ... remains favorable to our cause."*

But the high number of captured Confederate prisoners at Fort Donelson and the shocking number of killed and wounded at Shiloh produced appallingly long lists of casualties in the newspapers that left many families, both North and South, grieving for the soldier who would never come home. The Battle of Shiloh unleashed a growing dread that something horrible and murderous was going to drench the country in blood.

Despite Gen. Ulysses S. Grant's success in winning the Battle of Shiloh he was accused of drunkenness and had failed to be prepared for the battle. Gen. Sherman writes in his *Memoirs*, *"Probably no single battle of the war gave rise to such wild and damaging reports ... that our army was taken completely by surprise; that the rebels caught us in our tents; bayoneted the men in their beds; that General Grant was drunk; that Buell's opportune arrival saved the Army of the Tennessee from utter annihilation, etc."* Reports in the Northern press continued for some weeks blaming the poor leadership of the Union generals that resulted in the appalling number of casualties. But a few months later, Sherman admitted that in spite of the sudden negative clamor immediately after the battle, subsequent events gave Gen. Grant and others in the Battle of Shiloh their appropriate credit for the victory.

In the same communique, Sherman described how the Lieutenant-Governor of Ohio used the newspaper to further his political career by claiming that all the soldiers from his state had been heroes, but decried the performance of all the others. It was a frequently used method of politicians to gain popular fame by abusing army leaders, an easy and favorite technique to gain notoriety.

About Confederate Victories in the East...

In the Eastern theater, victories were dominated by the Confederates. "Stonewall" Jackson led his small tough army in a series of brilliant maneuvers in the Shenandoah Valley beginning in March 1862 that outwitted and defeated Union armies many times larger in size. With public sentiment in the Valley evenly divided between Unionists and Confederates, Jackson's heroic exploits were widely celebrated by the Confederates and greatly lifted the morale of the South.

The much-vaunted Union advance of a huge army into the Virginia Peninsula was defeated by the aggressive Gen. Robert E. Lee, who drove Gen. George B. McClellan back from Richmond in July. Lists of soldiers killed and wounded in the battles were printed in the newspapers but it required multiple issues of the *Richmond Whig* to report the casualties of Gaines' Mill and Cold Harbor. Several Virginia companies lost more than half their soldiers in the battle.

Northern morale was crushed by the Union Army's failure to take Richmond and Southern optimism skyrocketed with the news. A Confederate soldier from Texas wrote home, saying, *"I think the fight is almost over now; I think the war is nearly over."* Other accounts in diaries and letters in 1862 showed that most soldiers, North and South, thought that only one more battle would now end the war.

A frustrated President Lincoln observed that Grant's successes in the West at Fort Donelson and the Battle of Shiloh did not carry much weight with the public when compared to McClellan's defeats in the Virginia Peninsular Campaign. *"It seems unreasonable that a series of successes, extending through half-a-year, and clearing more than a hundred thousand square miles of country, should help us so little, while a single half-defeat should hurt us so much."*

About the Battle of Second Bull Run...

Northern enthusiasm for the war was further discouraged when the Confederates again soundly defeated the Union Army at the Battle of Second Bull Run in August. Union casualties of killed and wounded were nearly twice those sustained by the South. Northern newspapers heavily criticized President Lincoln for his use of bad generals, such as Irvin McDowell and John Pope. One Union brigade commander commented about the defeat. *"We had plenty of troops to whip them,"* protested Robert Milroy, *"but McDowell is a traitor and Pope is an incompetent egotist... Lincoln is blinded and under bad advisors and things will go from bad to worse. I see no hope. Our govt. is lost and we must bequeath war misery and anarchy to our children."*

The defeated Gen. Pope was removed from command and his Army of Virginia was absorbed into the Army of the Potomac, still under the command of Gen. George

B. McClellan. Southern headlines glorified the Confederate victories and the thrilling defeat of the Union at the Battle of Second Bull Run. The emboldened Lee moved his army north into Maryland.

About the Battle of Antietam (or Sharpsburg)...

The Battle of Antietam (or Sharpsburg), Maryland, in September between Union Gen. George B. McClellan and Confederate Gen. Robert E. Lee resulted in the bloodiest one-day battle of the entire war. The two armies suffered combined losses of nearly 23,000 in only twelve hours of battle, with neither side gaining any significant advantage and both South and North claiming it as a victory.

The *New York Times* reported the battle as follows: *"Gen. McClellan has achieved a glorious victory. A great battle has been fought, and we are victorious. The carnage on both sides was awful."* But McClellan's half-hearted pursuit of Lee after the battle enabled Gen. Lee to safely return with his army to Virginia. At this point, Lincoln finally lost his patience with the uncooperative Gen. McClellan and removed him from command of the Army of the Potomac, replacing him with Gen. Ambrose Burnside.

The Raleigh, North Carolina *Weekly State Journal* wrote, *"The battle of Sharpsburg was one of the most complete victories that has yet immortalized the Confederate arms. It is admitted that the victory was dearly bought, but nothing has since transpired to shake public confidence in the joyous announcement.... We fought the enemy in the ratio of two to five, the close of the battle, with the close of day, leaving the victorious Lee in possession of the field. On the next morning when our army commenced to feel for McClellan on the ground where they had left him at the close of the fight the preceding evening, it was found that he had retreated."*

The *Baltimore American* published a report from their army correspondent who had conversed with captured Southern prisoners from the battle. *"And here let me say that we (interviewed) their captured wounded that were in our possession, and they satisfied us that the rebel army is just now at that stage of discipline, courage, determination, desperation, or call it by any other name, that they cannot be routed."* Southern news generally reported the battle as a rout of the Union army and another glorious triumph for Lee and the Confederates.

But the people of Washington County, Maryland, suffered greatly from the Battle of Antietam, with the county seat of Hagerstown only fourteen miles from the battlefield. Demolished crops, polluted wells, killed livestock and destroyed fences left them with no food and few resources to recover their losses. The war continued to take a toll on the inhabitants and they fervently wished an end to it. Hospitals were set up in homes, barns and churches near the battlefield and filled with wounded soldiers. Clara Barton arrived to set up nursing accommodations at a local farm.

V. THE SECOND YEAR: 1862

When Civil War photographer Matthew Brady displayed images of the dead men killed at Sharpsburg in a New York gallery, the *New York Times* wrote that Brady had *"...done something to bring home to us the terrible reality and earnestness of war. If he has not brought bodies and laid them in our door-yards and along the streets, he has done something very like it."*

About Lincoln's Emancipation Proclamation...

Horace Greeley, editor of the *New York Tribune*, published an open letter on August 20, 1862, to President Lincoln entitled, *"The Prayer of Twenty Millions."* The letter passionately argued for Lincoln to emancipate all slaves in Union territory, stating that it was *"preposterous and futile"* to put down the rebellion without freeing the slaves. *"We must have scouts, guides, spies, cooks, teamsters, diggers and choppers from the Blacks of the South, whether we allow them to fight for us or not, or we shall be baffled and repelled. As one of the millions who would gladly have avoided this struggle at any sacrifice but that of Principle and Honor, but who now feels that the triumph of the Union is dispensable not only to the existence of our country, to the well-being of mankind."*

Lincoln responded that his priority as President was to preserve the Union and that he would free none of the slaves or all of the slaves if that was what it would take. But Lincoln had already prepared his Emancipation Proclamation, which he would soon publish. Declaring the Battle of Antietam at Sharpsburg, Maryland, as a Union victory, Lincoln announced his preliminary Emancipation Proclamation on September 22, which declared that all slaves in states that had seceded from the Union would be freed on January 1, 1863, and freed Blacks could be enlisted into the Union military.

The *New York Times* stated that *"There has been no more far-reaching document ever issued since the foundation of this government."* The public exchange between Lincoln and Greeley had done much to prepare the North for its acceptance of Lincoln's Proclamation and the new policy.

The Proclamation immediately brought forth outrage from Southern newspapers as editors urged the Confederacy to increase its determination to fight the war and preserve slavery and their Southern way of life. Confederate President Davis called the Proclamation the *"...most hateful measure recorded in the history of guilty man."*

Blacks, free or slave, joyfully received the news and welcomed the opportunity for men to join the Union army or navy. Many Northerners embraced the Proclamation as giving the war a higher moral purpose by fighting to free the slave, but some viewed it as an abolitionist plot. The "Copperheads," the Peace Democrats, were apoplectic. Their worst fears had been confirmed, that the "Traitorous Lincoln" would make Blacks equal to the white man.

For the Union soldier, attitudes were divided on the Emancipation Proclamation. Not all soldiers were opposed to slavery, but if freeing slaves helped win the war, they were all for it. But a letter from a Tennessee soldier to his wife revealed a growing attitude among his comrades, namely that they had increased their sympathies for the slaves after seeing the inhumanity with which some had been treated. Most soldiers were relieved that the war policy had changed so that they were no longer obliged to return escaped slaves to their masters, making them into "slave-catchers."

About Brothers Fighting on Opposite Sides...

One of the casualties at the Battle of Perryville was Gen. William Terrill, one of the few Virginia-born U.S. Army officers to remain with the Union after Virginia seceded. A graduate of West Point Military Academy in 1853, he was a career U.S. Army officer at the onset of the Civil War and his loyalties remained with the Union.

But Terrill's angry father, who served in the Confederacy's Virginia militia, threatened to disown him and strike his name from the family. Writing to his son, the elder Terrill is quoted as saying, *"All your brothers, and even your Father whose years would exempt him, will be in the fight and can you be so recreant & so unnatural as to aid in the mad attempt to impose the yoke of tyranny upon your kith & kin. Do so, and your name shall be stricken from the family record, and only remembered in connection with your treachery to the country that gave you birth."* William's letter to his father expressed his loyalty to the Constitutional oath he had given when he joined the U.S. Army, *"The Union cause to which I have devoted my life has nothing but honor to endear it, and it has no terror but that of death which a soldier must always expect. The rebellion, however, offers nothing but dishonor and disgrace and I shall adhere to the flag of the Union and give my life if necessary, in support of the legally constituted Government of the United States."* Leading his green troops into battle at Perryville, Terrill was struck by a piece of shrapnel and died that night. Unable to be buried in his home state of Virginia, he was finally put to rest at West Point.

Two years later in 1864, William's younger brother, James, would be killed in the Overland Campaign during the Battle of Totopotomoy Creek and a third brother, Philip, was killed at the Battle of Cedar Creek near Winchester, Virginia, in November of that year, both fighting for the Confederacy. A fourth brother, Dr. George P. Terrill, survived the war, serving in the Virginia militia.

According to legend, their father erected a stone in honor of his sons, stating *"This monument is erected by their father: God alone knows which was right."*

About the Battle of Fredericksburg...

The Battle of Fredericksburg in December was a disastrous loss for the Union Army of the Potomac, now under Gen. Ambrose Burnside, who had replaced Gen. McClellan as its commander. As Union soldiers were thrown into hopeless assaults against the Confederates on well-placed high ground at Fredericksburg, their casualties accumulated to nearly 13,000, compared to about 5,000 for the Confederates. The Peace

V. THE SECOND YEAR: 1862

Democrats described the battle as *"butchery and slaughter."* Northern support for the war dropped precipitously, as expressed by a Boston attorney who wrote, *"I have lost confidence… things have never looked so black to me at this moment."*

Lincoln was attacked by both politicians and the press. One Senator wrote that *"The President is a weak man, too weak for the occasion, and those fool or traitor generals are wasting time and yet more precious blood in indecisive battles and delays."* Lincoln, shattered by the bloody defeat, said, *"If there is a place worse than hell, I am in it."*

Southern newspapers jeered Burnside as another example of the incompetent Yankee generals, while praising Lee and the Army of Northern Virginia for their outstanding success at Fredericksburg and Sharpsburg and the many victories that had been achieved the previous six months. Jubilant over the great victory at Fredericksburg, the *Richmond Examiner* described it as a *"stunning defeat to the invader, a splendid victory to the defender of the sacred soil."* The *Charleston Mercury* exclaimed that *"Gen. Lee knows his business and the army has yet known no such word as fail."*

Lee, however, although inwardly pleased by his army's performance and victory, said, *"At Fredericksburg we gained a battle, inflicting very severe loss on the enemy in men and material; our people were greatly elated—I was much depressed. We had really accomplished nothing; we had not gained a foot of ground, and I knew the enemy could easily replace the men he had lost, and the loss of material was, if anything, rather beneficial to him, as it gave an opportunity to contractors to make money."*

The *Richmond Dispatch* reported the Battle of Fredericksburg with much praise for the Confederate army and particularly for Gen. Lee. *"This is the tenth pitched battle in which General Lee has commanded, within less than six months, and in all of them he has been victorious."* The Lynchburg *Daily Virginian* wrote, *"The world never saw a better army than that now marshalled under the greatest soldier of the age, Gen. Robert E. Lee."*

As Northern support for the war dwindled in 1862, it was becoming more and more difficult to attract recruits to the Union armies. With the beginning of 1863, the North faced a determined enemy in the Eastern Theater and a growing feeling among the public that the South was winning the war.

VI. THE THIRD YEAR: 1863

On the first day of 1863, President Abraham Lincoln implemented the Emancipation Proclamation that he had announced the previous September which declared that all Blacks in those states that remained in rebellion against the United States of America on January 1, 1863, were now freed from slavery. The Executive Order affected approximately three and a half million slaves in the Confederacy who could gain freedom by escaping to Union lines or be automatically freed as federal troops advanced and took over Confederate territory. But it did not affect slaves in the Border States of Kentucky, Maryland, Delaware and Missouri, which had never seceded from the Union.

The signing was scheduled to take place on New Year's Day after Lincoln had spent several hours meeting the public, diplomats, politicians and others. As he sat down to write his signature on the document, his hand trembled from the strain of three hours of hand-shaking, so he put the pen down and said he would wait. He did not want to give the impression that his signature was tremulous because of uncertainty. When he did sign the Emancipation Proclamation, he said, *"I never in my life felt more certain that I was doing right than I do in signing this paper—if my name ever goes into history, it will be for this act, and my whole soul is in it."*

But because the Proclamation was issued as a war measure by the Commander-in-Chief and not approved by Congress, slaves would remain free only if the Union won the war. The effect was to shift the goals of the Civil War to not only maintain the Union, but to free slaves as well. The 13th Amendment to the U.S. Constitution that freed all slaves, would not be passed by Congress until January 1865.

BATTLES IN THE EASTERN THEATER

Mud March to Richmond, Virginia
January 20, 1863

After the disastrous defeat of the Army of the Potomac at Fredericksburg in December 1862, Union Gen. Ambrose Burnside was anxious to redeem his reputation and reinstate his standing with the army, where morale had sunk to a new low after the tragic losses at Fredericksburg. Burnside developed a new plan to reach Richmond by crossing the Rappahannock River at Bank's Ford about fifteen miles west of the Confederates, now located at Fredericksburg, and then move the army rapidly south in a wide arc that would place him in the rear of Confederate Gen. Robert E. Lee and the Army of Northern Virginia. The plan required rapid movement so that the Union Army could be across the river quickly with the use of pontoon bridges before Lee and his army could respond. Decoy feints at Falmouth, opposite Fredericksburg, would add to the deception.

The offensive was launched on January 20 after several weeks of mild weather and the army made a rapid push west to reach Banks' Ford quickly. Engineers would quickly establish bridges the next morning and two divisions would be across the river in four hours. But that night, a violent storm turned into a torrential downpour that lasted thirty hours without letup. Roads of dirt became virtually impassable as horses, wagons and cannons became buried in thick, unyielding mud. *"The whole country was a river of mud,"* wrote one soldier. Artillery sank until only the muzzles were visible. The 5th New York moved only one and half miles in an entire day as soldiers slipped and fell repeatedly, losing their shoes in the slippery mire.

The delays gave Lee ample time to position his army on the opposite shore of the Rappahannock where he set up his defenses. Confederate soldiers jeered at the Union Army from across the river with shouts and signs, "Burnside's Army Stuck in the Mud." Lee made very little effort to interfere with Union attempts at a crossing, other than sharpshooters who picked off soldiers regularly. Northern troops would be easy enough targets when they crossed the raging river.

Given the conditions of weather and Lee's solid defenses, Burnside was forced to give up the attempt and the army withdrew to return to its winter quarters. A war correspondent traveling with the army wrote, *"The ground had gone from bad to worse... an indescribable chaos of pontoons, vehicles and artillery encumbered all the roads—supply wagons upset by the road-side, guns stalled in the mud, ammunition-trains mired by the way, and hundreds of horses and mules buried in the liquid muck."* The question the army now faced was not how to go forward but how to get back.

Recriminations and accusations from Burnside's officers condemned the "Mud March" and its commander. Burnside's relations with his senior staff went from bad to worse. A furious Burnside offered his resignation, which Lincoln accepted, and transferred him to command the Department of the Ohio in the Western Theater, replacing Gen. Horatio Wright.

With Burnside's resignation, the Army of the Potomac needed a new commander. Gen. Joseph Hooker had served in the Mexican-American War under both Generals Zachary Taylor and Winfield Scott, where he had earned promotions for strong leadership and bravery. With his blue eyes, light hair and ruddy complexion, he made a dashing figure on and off a horse and had acquired a reputation in Mexico as a ladies' man that stayed with him throughout his career. After the Mexican-American War, Hooker resigned from the army in 1853 to make money in California's post "gold-rush economy," but he was largely unsuccessful and reputed to lead a gambling and hard-drinking social life. At the onset of the Civil War, Hooker rejoined the army in August 1861 and soon distinguished himself as a valuable combat commander during the Peninsula Campaign and the Battle of Antietam, where he inspired his men with aggressive leadership against Confederate Gen. Stonewall Jackson. He acquired the nickname "Fighting Joe" from a newspaper headline and it remained with him throughout the war.

> **"FIGHTING JOE" HOOKER**
>
> Gen. Joseph Hooker's nickname as "Fighting Joe" was not achieved by his abilities during battle. Rather, a newspaper editor removed the dash from a headline "Fighting—Joe Hooker" that was intended to describe a Civil War battle. The nickname stuck, much to Hooker's distaste, saying it depicted him as a general without cunning, skill or brains.

Hooker's ambitions to advance, however, frequently offended his fellow commanders as he publicly denounced their performances. Severely criticizing Burnside and the whole army command after the failed Mud March, Hooker suggested that the *"Army and Government needed a dictator to bring success to the Union army."* When Lincoln appointed him as new commander for the Army of the Potomac, he remarked, *"Only those generals who gain successes can set up dictators. What I now ask of you is military success, and I will risk the dictatorship."*

Taking command of the Army of the Potomac, Hooker immediately instituted a number of reforms that raised the low morale of the army. Daily food, medical care and living conditions were improved and new uniforms were issued to replace the "tatty rags" of the soldiers. Hooker lengthened furloughs for the men and ensured that they received several months of back pay. His introduction of a cavalry corps greatly improved the efficiency of the horsemen, who previously had been separately attached to various infantry groups. A major effort by the Army's quartermaster to increase the supply of horses in 1863 also helped improve the quality of the cavalry corps.

Hooker formed a new Bureau of Military Information (BMI) that used infantry and cavalry reconnaissance to take advantage of spies, scouts and signal stations, gathering intelligence data for the military. BMI continued to function throughout the Civil War as the Union's chief intelligence unit. A grand review for Lincoln in early April at Falmouth displayed a greatly improved look and spirit to the 130,000-strong Union Army.

Battle of Chancellorsville, Virginia
April 30-May 6, 1863

In April 1863, Gen. Robert E. Lee's Confederate Army of Northern Virginia at Fredericksburg had nearly exhausted the local supplies of food, forage and firewood. Responding to the shortages, Lee dispatched Gen. James Longstreet with two divisions to southern Virginia near Norfolk on a foraging mission, which reduced Lee's army to about 60,000 men. When Longstreet encountered Union resistance, he became engaged in the Siege of Suffolk until May 4 and did not return until May 9, too late to support Lee in the coming Battle of Chancellorsville. Lee's army at Fredericksburg, across the Rappahannock from the Union Army at Falmouth, was an inviting target for the newly appointed commander of the Union Army of the Potomac, Gen. Joseph "Fighting Joe" Hooker.

By mid-April, Gen. Hooker had produced a plan that would first cut Lee's supply line to Richmond with a 10,000-man cavalry led by Gen. George Stoneman, while at the same time Union troops would trap the Southern army with a double envelopment on its east and west flanks at Fredericksburg. But fate, bad weather, Hooker's own indecisiveness and Lee's aggressive tactics became his enemies.

Stoneman's cavalry departed Falmouth on April 13 for Kelly's Ford, located about twenty-five miles west of Falmouth, to use the bridge there to cross the Rappahannock River and then cross the Rapidan to get behind Lee's Army of Northern Virginia. The mission for the Union cavalry was to move toward Richmond, destroy Lee's supply line and communications and raid the surrounding countryside. But torrential rains flooded the river and roads, forcing Stoneman's cavalry and his artillery to pull back about a dozen miles and wait two weeks before they could finally complete the crossing on April 30. According to Gen. John Buford, heading one of Stoneman's brigades, *"The country at that hour was like a sea... From the time that the brigade struck the river at Rappahannock Bridge on the 15th, up to the crossing of the river on the 29th, it seemed as though the elements were combined against our advance; such rains and roads I had never seen. During the whole expedition the roads were in a worse condition than I could have supposed to be possible, and the command was called upon to endure much severe discomfiture."* Mired roads, sick men and horses delayed Stoneman's progress so much that when he was finally able to reach behind Lee's army, the exhausted men

VI. THE THIRD YEAR: 1863

were falling asleep in the saddle on emaciated horses, and accomplished very little in support of the campaign.

Gen. Hooker, well aware of the muddy conditions left by the rains, did not want a repeat of the Mud March disaster in January and delayed movement of his army until April 27 after the roads had somewhat dried out. Between April 30 and May 1, the main body of Hooker's troops, led by Gen. Henry Slocum, crossed the Rappahannock at Kelly's Ford, using great stealth that prevented the Southern observers from detecting the army's movements. As Confederate spotters watched at the Falmouth front, Union troops at the back of the army, farthest from the front lines, were hidden as they moved west. After crossing the Rappahannock, the army separated into two columns to cross the Rapidan River at Ely's and Germanna Fords, and then turned back east to converge at Chancellorsville, so named for the Chancellor mansion there. About the same time, a second Union contingent of about 40,000 under the leadership of Gen. John Sedgwick crossed below Fredericksburg to be in a position to attack Lee's right flank and remained in place. Hooker next ordered Sickles to bring 13,000 men from the corps at Falmouth across the river to join him, bringing his forces at Chancellorsville to about 70,000.

Once Lee became aware of the Union threat to the west at Chancellorsville, he divided his army and left a small force of 11,000 men under Gen. Jubal Early and fifty-six well-fortified guns in Marye's Heights at Fredericksburg to defend against his front line and the Union contingent threatening his right flank. The rest of the Confederate army, including the troops of Gen. "Stonewall" Jackson, who had been defending on the right, moved west to Chancellorsville on May 1 to meet the Union Army now accumulating.

The two armies met in battle about noon on May 1 at the Orange Turnpike in the midst of the "Wilderness of Spotsylvania," a dense mass of brambles, thickets, vines, and low-lying vegetation that greatly hampered movement of men and the effectiveness of artillery. Two Union corps were initially pushed back, but soon the Confederate advance was halted and Northern troops held strong positions in open ground. A third Union corps under Gen. George Meade was unopposed.

As Confederate Generals Lee and Stonewall Jackson considered the situation, Lee's cavalry commander, Gen. Jeb Stuart, arrived with news that while the Union's left flank facing Lee was solidly anchored on the river, the right flank was "in the air." Taking advantage of the weak point in Hooker's defenses, Lee divided his army again and dispatched Jackson with about 26,000 men to make a hard march of twelve miles on relatively hidden back roads and circle around the main Union Army to reach Hooker's right flank under the command of Gen. Oliver Howard. Confederate Gen. Jeb Stuart's cavalry effectively prevented Union forces from spotting Jackson's march on their right. Although Gen. Hooker warned Howard that a Confederate movement

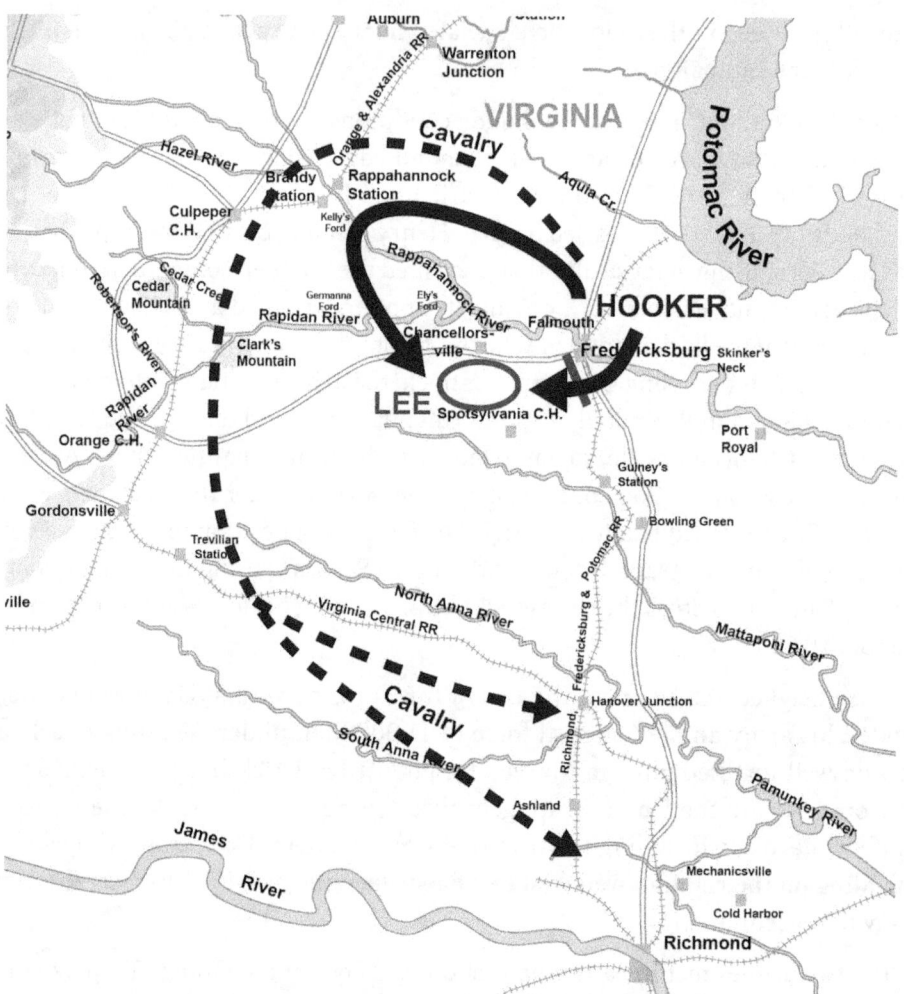

Fig. 25: At the Battle of Chancellorsville, Union Gen. Joseph Hooker planned to capture the Confederate Army of Northern Virginia under Gen. Robert E. Lee with a two-pronged attack at Fredericksburg, supported by cavalry in the Confederate rear. Bad weather, poor decisions and an aggressive response by Lee defeated the Union attempt.

Source: *Creative Commons Attribution 3.0 License Map by Hal Jespersen, www.cwmaps.com.*

had been observed on his right and a few Union patrols detected Jackson's movement on the back roads, their reports were either discarded or ignored by Howard. Even observations by the Union reconnaissance balloon *Eagle* did not get communicated. Meanwhile, Lee kept up an active engagement using his roughly 20,000 troops as a diversion against Hooker's Union center of about 70,000.

Stonewall Jackson was able to arrange his troops in the thick woods by late afternoon on May 2 and ordered an attack on the surprised Union soldiers at supper time, who had unloaded and stacked their rifles. When Jackson's troops broke out of the woods with their terrifying Rebel yell, the Union men had to run for their lives as they were quickly routed. More than 4,000 were captured as prisoners. The rest were able to reach the main army at Fairview Hill near the Chancellor mansion, where a hard core of men and artillery blocked the Confederate advance.

Jackson wanted to take advantage of his position while the Union Army was still disorganized and rode out using the light of a full moon to assess the possibility of cutting off the Union's retreat to the river with a night attack. Traveling beyond his front lines, North Carolina infantry misidentified him and his staff as Union cavalry and fired on them, mortally wounding Jackson who died eight days later.

With Lee's army divided, Hooker had a three-to-one advantage in manpower against the Confederates in front of him but lost the opportunity. With all the strength in Union hands, Hooker ordered all units to pull back on May 3, over the vigorous protests from his commanders, to create a second line of defense north of Chancellorsville. The new positions created a strong defensive line around the Chancellorsville mansion, now Hooker's headquarters, but gave up valuable territory to the Confederates.

When Hooker ordered his artillery to the new positions, the Confederates reaped an immense advantage by capturing a powerful artillery platform with better ammunition on high ground at Hazel Grove that dominated Fairview Hill and all the surrounding area. One Southern officer commented on their fortunate circumstance: *"There has rarely been a more gratuitous gift of a battlefield."* With this gain in their possession, Confederates dominated the fierce fighting that day. Casualties were immense, numbering about 18,000, about equally divided between the two armies.

During the fighting on May 3, Gen. Hooker was leaning against one of the front-porch pillars at the Chancellorsville mansion when a cannon ball struck it, knocking him violently to the ground. Unconscious for some time, incapacitated by the shock and suffering from a concussion, he revived in great pain. Although his second-in-command waited for an order to attack, Hooker did not relinquish command and the army was forced to pull back to positions north of Chancellorsville, which protected its path to cross the Rappahannock.

At the same time, Union Gen. John Sedgwick, commanding the Union contingent below Fredericksburg on the Confederate right, had moved west and broken through their weak defenses on Marye's Heights, and was now occupying Plank Road which could attack the Confederates from the east. But Lee, informed of the advance by Sedgwick divided his army again and leaving half of it to face Hooker, took the other half to block the Union contingent at Salem Church on Plank Road. Sedgwick's men were driven back into a U-shaped defensive line with one flank anchored on Bank's Ford and the other on a well-defended hill.

On May 4, Hooker remained at Chancellorsville, defending against multiple assaults, anxiously waiting for word from Sedgwick. But telegraph communications had failed and Sedgwick, fighting against Gen. Lee with no direction from Hooker, finally retreated

BATTLE OF CHANCELLORSVILLE, VIRGINIA
April 30-May 6, 1863

In mid-April, Gen. "Fighting Joe" Hooker, as new commander of the Union Army of the Potomac, numbering about 130,000, initiated a new plan to capture the Confederate capital at Richmond by using a two-pronged assault that would envelop the Confederate Army of Northern Virginia under Gen. Robert E. Lee facing him at Fredericksburg, Virginia. The plan called for cavalry to initially cross the Rappahannock River, drive behind Lee's rear and disrupt his supply and communication lines. But bad weather and torrential rains delayed the cavalry crossing for two weeks until April 30. Mired roads, sick horses and other delays greatly diminished the cavalry's contribution to the campaign. Union troops were able to cross the Rappahannock undetected upriver April 30-May 1 and converged at Chancellorsville on Lee's left flank while a second Union contingent crossed downriver and secured a bridgehead on Lee's right. A smaller contingent of the Union army remained on the shore at Falmouth, facing Lee's front.

Lee correctly assumed that the major threat was west of him and divided his much smaller army of 60,000, leaving about 11,000 heavily fortified at Fredericksburg and sent Confederate Gen. Stonewall Jackson west on May 2 with about 26,000 troops on a 12-mile roundabout march to make a surprise attack on the Union's weakly defended right flank. Although Jackson's forces successfully hit the Union Army as they settled into their evening meal, they were unable to overwhelm all of the Union troops who then joined the main army at the Chancellorsville mansion. Jackson rode out in darkness to assess positions for a possible night attack when he was mistakenly identified as Union by Confederate North Carolina Infantry and mortally wounded. His death, eight days later, was a major loss for the Confederacy.

With Lee's Confederate army divided, Hooker had the advantage for an attack that could overwhelm the Southerners, but instead ordered his men to new defensive positions, which provided the Confederates with a battlefield advantage that allowed Lee's army to reunite. When Hooker was stunned unconscious for some time by a shell that struck a pillar he was leaning against, the concussion affected his ability to effectively command. Gen. Lee divided his army to block a Union contingent advancing from Fredericksburg and the Northerners retreated across the river during the night. Hooker's resolve for the campaign collapsed and he ordered a withdrawal of the whole army.

across the river during the night of May 4 unmolested. When Hooker received word on May 5 that Sedgwick had withdrawn, he gave up on the campaign, and began his withdrawal that night, which continued through the next day as heavy rains threatened to break the pontoon bridges and block the Union withdrawal. Lee's plans for a two-pronged assault against Union troops at Chancellorsville on May 6 faced an empty battlefield.

The Union cavalry led by Gen. Stoneman had an ineffective week of raiding and failed to achieve very few of Hooker's objectives. The cavalry withdrew into Union lines on the Virginia Peninsula on May 7, still battling swollen rivers and streams, bringing a final end to the campaign. Army historians generally agree that the Battle of Chancellorsville would become Gen. Lee's finest military triumph. But it had come with a terrible cost. The fighting on May 3 in three battles resulted in more than 3,000 men killed, about equally divided between Union and Confederate, second only to the Battle of Antietam as the bloodiest day of the war.

Total casualties for the battle numbered over 16,000 for the Union and nearly 13,000 for the Confederates, more than twenty percent of Lee's army. The Confederates also lost Gen. Stonewall Jackson, Lee's most aggressive field commander, mistakenly shot by friendly fire from North Carolina troops. Perhaps an even more critical aspect of Lee's success, however, was his belief that his army was invincible, a belief he carried with him to Pennsylvania and the Battle of Gettysburg.

LEE INVADES THE NORTH

After Gen. Robert E. Lee's significant victory at Chancellorsville, he persuaded Confederate President Jefferson Davis to authorize another invasion of the North because Southern armies in the Western theater were losing ground against Ulysses S. Grant's campaign against Vicksburg. Except for the Battle of Antietam in Maryland the year before, most of the battles in the Eastern Theater had been in Virginia, straining the South's ability to feed, clothe and supply their armies. By taking the battleground into the Northern cities, Lee hoped to demonstrate that he could threaten the North, gain new support for the Southern cause, and strengthen the peace movement for a separate Confederate States.

As Lee moved into south central Pennsylvania through the Shenandoah Valley with his Army of Northern Virginia in June 1863, an alarmed President Lincoln ordered Union Gen. Joseph Hooker with the Army of the Potomac, now at headquarters in Virginia, to maintain a position between the Confederate army and Washington, D.C. But Hooker wanted to use the opportunity to seize Richmond and regain his self-esteem after his loss at Chancellorsville. Lincoln quickly vetoed the idea, as Hooker's primary mission was to protect the Union capital.

Hooker's communications with Lincoln and General-in-Chief Halleck had been strained after the Battle of Chancellorsville and the conflict had worsened the last weeks of June in a dispute over Union forces at Harpers Ferry. When Hooker offered his resignation, Lincoln promptly accepted it. Gen. George Meade, career army officer, veteran of the Mexican War and Civil War commander, was immediately appointed to lead the Army of the Potomac three days before the onset of the Battle of Gettysburg.

Battle of Gettysburg, Pennsylvania
July 1-3, 1863

As Gen. Robert E. Lee's army of about 75,000 men moved north through Maryland into Pennsylvania, the Confederates concentrated near Cashton, about forty miles southwest of Harrisburg, Pennsylvania's capital, and ten miles west of Gettysburg where ten roads and one railroad intersected. On June 30, a small Confederate unit searching for food and supplies approached the village of Gettysburg, hoping to find shoes for the men. The Union Army of the Potomac, numbering about 90,000, was not far away as it had continued to keep pace with the Confederates in parallel to maintain a position between Lee and the Union capital.

> ### BATTLE FLAGS OF THE CIVIL WAR
> Battle flags played a critical role during a conflict, as signals to the commander about the progress of his troops, and providing guidance to the soldier as to where and what he needed to do in a field where the roar of cannons and rifles made it impossible to hear orders. Carrying the flag was a privilege and an honor, but was also the most dangerous position on the battlefield. No other symbol was as powerful as each regiment's colors, the unique bond that held the men together in battle. During Pickett's charge at the Battle of Gettysburg, thirty-five color bearers were shot down and their flags later captured by the Union victors.

Lee had been out of communication with his chief intelligence scout, Gen. James Ewell Brown, (J.E.B. or "Jeb") Stuart, head of his cavalry, and was unaware of where the Union Army was located. Lee had dispatched Stuart on a scouting and raiding mission on June 23 that would keep him informed about the Union Army's movements and also capture supplies if possible. But Stuart's efforts to maneuver his cavalry around the Union Army that was now on the move had pushed him farther and farther east and Lee had not had any contact with Stuart for the last week. On the opening day of battle at Gettysburg, Stuart was about thirty miles north and east of Gettysburg at Dover, Pennsylvania, with a long wagon train full of fresh supplies that he had captured at Rockville, Maryland. His absence the previous week had left Lee with little intelligence about the strength and position of the Union Army.

VI. THE THIRD YEAR: 1863

THE IRON BRIGADE OF THE WEST
"The Black Hats of Gettysburg"

Composed entirely of regiments from the western states of Wisconsin, Indiana and Michigan, the "Iron Brigade of the West" fought entirely in the Eastern Theater with the Army of the Potomac.

The name came from Union Gen. McClellan's comment after watching them at the Battle of Second Bull Run, "They must be made of iron," he said, and it became the brigade's signature. Legendary for their toughness, the brigade was also known as the "Black Hats" because of the 1858 model Hardee hats issued to the soldiers. Composed of men from the 2nd, 6th, and 7th Wisconsin, 19th Indiana, and then later the 24th Michigan infantry units, they fought in the Battles of Second Bull Run, South Mountain, Antietam, Fredericksburg, Chancellorsville, Gettysburg, Mine Run, Overland, Richmond-Petersburg and Appomattox.

As they held off withering fire from Gen. Stonewall Jackson's forces at the time of the Battle of Second Bull Run, captured Confederates referred to them as the "Black Hat Devils of the Army of the Potomac." At the Battle of Gettysburg, the veteran force arrived on the first day of battle just in time to prevent the Union cavalry from being overwhelmed by the huge Confederate force converging on it. The Iron Brigade advanced so quickly to the front, they loaded their rifles as they ran.

As the 19th Indiana and 24th Michigan pressed the Confederate right flank, the Brigade successfully overwhelmed a Southern unit and captured 200 prisoners. But soon the Iron Brigade was forced back to Cemetery Hill in a battling retreat. Intense fighting continued with heavy losses, including toe-to-toe battles between the 26th North Carolina and 24th Michigan units. The North Carolina 26th Infantry lost eighty-one percent of its men in casualties that day; 24th Michigan, seventy-three percent. At the end of the Battle of Gettysburg, the Iron Brigade had lost 1,150 casualties from a total of about 1,900 men. After these devastating losses at Gettysburg, the Brigade lost its 'all western character' when it was incorporated into the 167th Pennsylvania.

Union cavalry officer, Gen. John Buford, part of a forward scouting patrol for the Army of the Potomac, observed the large Confederate force converging on Gettysburg and realized the importance of holding high ground until supporting infantry could arrive. Union defenses were quickly set up on three ridges west of town. When an advance unit of Confederates attacked the blue-coated soldiers on July 1, expecting small units of Pennsylvania militia, they encountered two brigades of Union cavalry waiting on three ridges, ready for battle.

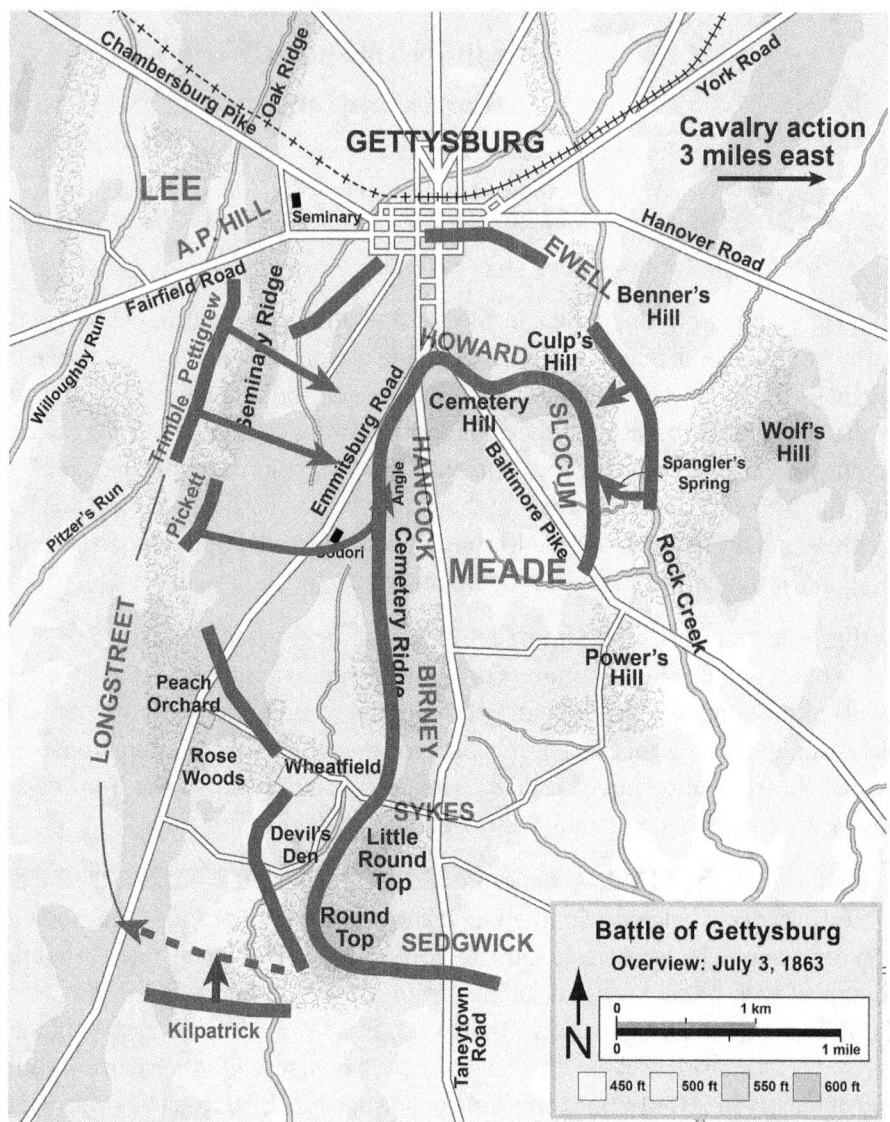

Fig. 26: Union forces under Gen. Meade defend Cemetery Ridge against Confederates under Gen. Lee at the Battle of Gettysburg, Pennsylvania, on July 3, 1863. During "Pickett's Charge," the Confederates suffered disastrous losses which became a turning point of the war.
Source: *Creative Commons Attribution 3.0 License Map by Hal Jespersen, www.cwmaps.com.*

Casualties rapidly became immense as Southern and Northern forces rushed more men into the conflict. The famous Union Iron Brigade of the West, made up of soldiers from Wisconsin, Indiana and Michigan, loaded their rifles as they ran to the battle. The 26th North Carolina regiment, numbering nearly 850, lost all but 212 men as it battled the 24th Michigan in toe-to-toe fighting. Fourteen color bearers of the North Carolina unit were killed in the battle.

VI. THE THIRD YEAR: 1863

When Union positions collapsed north and west of the town, the Northerners retreated to Cemetery Hill and Culp's Hill, south of Gettysburg, where the high ground afforded good defense against the Southern assaults. More Union infantry arrived to strengthen the position. As senior commanders fell in battle, Gen. Winfield S. Hancock took control of the Union defense and held Cemetery Hill through intensive Confederate assaults until conclusion of the day's battles when the more senior Gen. Henry Slocum arrived to take command of the troops.

Gen. George Meade, named commander of the Army of the Potomac only three days previously and unproven in a battle of this magnitude, arrived on the battlefield at midnight July 1 with reinforcements and took overall command of the field. He quickly positioned the Union Army in a nearly two-mile-long defensive line along Cemetery Ridge, which then made a fish-hook shape as it wrapped around Cemetery Hill and Culp's Hill. The second day saw raging battles on the Union's left flank as Confederate Gen. James Longstreet's troops attacked Little Round Top, Devil's Den, Peach Orchard and the Wheatfield. Although the Southerners captured Devil's Den, the Peach Orchard and the Wheatfield, they were unable to dislodge the main Union line on top of the ridge.

At the direction of Gen. Gouverneur K. Warren, the 20th Maine Infantry, under the command of Col. Joshua Chamberlain, held Little Round Top, a small promontory at the far-left flank of the Union line, fighting against a ferocious offense by the 15th Alabama Infantry. If Confederate troops could win Little Round Top, the entire Union line might fall and Chamberlain had been ordered *"This is the left of the Union line. You are to hold this ground at all costs."* When his troops ran out of ammunition, Chamberlain launched a daring bayonet charge that used a "turning movement," in which troops on the left wing of the command wheeled continuously to their right as the center charged frontally down the hill, acting like a door swinging on a hinge, hitting the enemy from the front and the side. The Confederate line collapsed

> **LONGSTREET AT GETTYSBURG**
>
> Speaking of his conversation with Gen. Lee about the battle plan for Pickett's Charge, Longstreet said, *"I asked the strength of the column. He stated fifteen thousand. (My) Opinion was then expressed that the fifteen thousand men who could make a successful assault over that field had never been arrayed for battle; but he was impatient of listening, and tired of talking, and nothing was left but to proceed."* When the charge failed, Longstreet writes, *"General Pickett, finding the battle broken while the enemy was still reinforcing, called the troops off. There was no indication of panic. The broken files marched back in steady step. The effort was nobly made and failed from the blows that could not be fended. It was the saddest day of my life."*
>
> Longstreet, from Manassas to Appomattox: Personal Memoirs of the Civil War in America

> ### UNION CAVALRY COMES INTO ITS OWN
> Cavalry not only opened the battle, but closed it in a decisive showdown on July 3 at the Battle of Gettysburg. A Confederate drive by Gen. Jeb Stuart's Cavalry behind the Union's right flank was defeated by Gen. George A. Custer's Michigan Cavalry. The battle ended the reputation of Union cavalry being an inferior force when compared to the Confederates. At the beginning of the war, horse soldiers from the North were vastly less experienced than their Southern counterparts and suffered in the encounters. But by 1863, Northern cavalries were better equipped with improved horses and significantly improved capabilities and training. Commanders now recognized their valuable contributions for reconnaissance, screening (protecting the movements of Union infantry), and their successful attacks and raids over immediate and distant targets.

as they were attacked from two directions. Little Round Top had held and Chamberlain would receive the Medal of Honor in later years for his actions that day.

On the Union's right flank, Confederate Gen. Richard Ewell attacked at Culp's Hill and reached the crest of Cemetery Ridge, but was unable to hold it against an almost suicidal bayonet charge by the 1st Minnesota Regiment, which held the line long enough for reinforcements to arrive. The Regiment lost 217 killed or wounded out of its total of 282 men. Gen. Meade effectively moved troops back and forth throughout the day to reinforce critical areas and the Confederates were repulsed in the second day of fighting.

Confederate Gen. Jeb Stuart and his cavalry with a large wagon train arrived around noon, ending his extended circuitous route that had denied Lee vital intelligence about the Union Army's movements. Stuart's weary column did not participate in the battles that day.

On the morning of July 3, Union troops launched an artillery bombardment at dawn on Culp's Hill, followed by an aggressive attack, to recapture some of their lost ground from the day before. A furious battle lasted until eleven o'clock that morning when the Southern troops were finally driven from the hill. Having failed to break the Union flanks, Lee decided to attack the center.

Shortly after noon, Gen. Lee launched one of the largest artillery bombardments of the war, with one hundred seventy guns firing at the Union line. Because of heavy smoke and dust from the firing guns, Southern commanders could not observe that most of the Confederate artillery fire fell behind the Union lines, sparing the soldiers. Union artillery responded initially, but then ceased, as Gen. Meade conserved ammunition for the assault he knew was coming. Confederates erroneously believed that the silence meant that Union artillery had been demolished.

Two hours later, a frontal infantry assault of 12,500 Confederate soldiers, nearly a mile long, under Gen. George Pickett, stepped out as one to cross an open field to reach the center of the Union line. When the soldiers were in range, Union artillery opened fire on the exposed Southern infantry. The cannons, armed with cannister that converted them into giant shotguns mowed down the Southern soldiers like ninepins. As they climbed over the two strong and sturdy fences protecting the sunken Emmitsburg Road, men were exposed to withering fire. Only one brigade of the Southern soldiers reached the Union center at the top of the ridge, a small copse of trees, to later be called The Bloody Angle. The event would later be referred to as the High Watermark of the Confederacy. Northern reinforcements rushed in and brutal hand-to-hand combat repulsed the Southern attack. The daring assault had resulted in casualties of nearly sixty percent for the Confederates. Survivors withdrew to their lines, but more than half the men in the attack were dead or wounded on the field.

A diversion from Southern Gen. Jeb Stuart's cavalry in the Union rear was blocked by a successful cavalry charge, led by Union Gen. George Custer's Michigan Cavalry Brigade, which intercepted the Southern horsemen in a surprise attack with the rallying call *"Come on, you Wolverines!"* Although the Confederates greatly outnumbered the Northerners, the unexpected attack from the Union Cavalry, armed with superior Spencer repeating rifles that could deliver seven rounds of bullets in less than one minute, pushed the Southern cavalry out of the battle.

The Army of Northern Virginia had acquired a reputation of being invincible, well documented by Lee's military successes in battles already won. But Lee's unsuccessful assault on the Union center, to be described later as "Pickett's Charge," was an overwhelming blow to the Confederate Army and to Lee himself as he realized his own failure in ordering the attack. *"It's all my fault,"* he said to his men as the survivors limped back to their lines. The next day, July 4, Lee held his army in position in a heavy rain expecting a counter-attack, but it never came. Lee gathered his wounded men and supplies into a 17-mile-long wagon train and started his retreat that evening.

Although Meade finally pursued the Southern army, the effort was slow and halfhearted, which gave Lee sufficient time to cross the swollen Potomac River into safety in late July. Gen. Meade's great triumph in the battle was marred by his failure to capture Lee's army and bring an end to the war in the Eastern Theater. Lee sent a letter of resignation to President Jefferson Davis in August, but Davis refused to accept it.

Burying the Dead at Gettysburg

The three-day Battle of Gettysburg created more than 51,000 casualties, over 7,000 killed in action, the largest number in a single battle in the Civil War. Union casualties numbered about 23,000 (3,000 killed; 15,000 wounded, 5,000 captured or missing). Casualties for the Confederate army were more difficult to estimate, but historians

BATTLE OF GETTYSBURG, PENNSYLVANIA
July 1-3, 1863

The Confederate Army of Northern Virginia under Gen. Robert E. Lee met Union troops in southern Pennsylvania near the village of Gettysburg on July 1 and drove the Northerners to Cemetery Hill south of the village. Arriving that night, Union Gen. George Meade, recently named commander of the Army of the Potomac, extended his forces along the high ground of Cemetery Ridge as reinforcements arrived to meet the Confederates in battle.

On the second day of battle, ferocious fighting occurred as Confederates began their assault on Little Round Top, a small hill at the southern end of Cemetery Ridge, a key position holding the Union's left flank and forces rapidly gathered to protect the small prominence. Col. Joshua Chamberlain, a college professor of modern languages, commanding the 20th Maine, led a successful bayonet charge against the 15th Alabama that defeated the Southern attack. Thirty years later, he was awarded the Congressional Medal of Honor.

Lee's "Old War Horse," Gen. James Longstreet, caused terrible damage to Union troops in the Peach Orchard, the Wheatfield and Devil's Den, but at the end of the day, the Union line at the top of the ridge had held. Lee's cavalry under Gen. Jeb Stuart finally arrived from a long and extended reconnaissance and played no role in the day's battles. On the third day, Lee ordered a prolonged artillery bombardment to weaken the Northerners, but most of the shells fell behind the Union battle line and Meade, anticipating an attack, silenced his artillery early to conserve ammunition. Lee then ordered a massive frontal assault known as "Pickett's Charge" and 12,500 men came forward to cross an open field and then charge up the slope of Cemetery Ridge. Union artillery, held in reserve, opened fire on the Confederate soldiers with devastating results. A few brave Southerners reached the center of the Union line, but were quickly repulsed in hand-to-hand combat. As the survivors struggled back to their own lines, Gen. Lee met his retreating army telling them, "This is my fault; it is I that have lost this fight."

On July 4, Lee waited for a Union counter-attack which never came. At the end of the day, Lee collected his wounded and supplies into an extended wagon train that began the long journey back to Virginia. Lee's army escaped Meade's ineffective pursuit and the war continued.

VI. THE THIRD YEAR: 1863

have placed them at about 28,000 (4,700 killed), more than one-third of Lee's 75,000-man army.

The massive scale of casualties demanded an extraordinary response from the North's medical resources. Every available structure within a ten-mile radius of Gettysburg, including churches, barns, warehouses, public buildings and private homes, were converted into hospitals. A field hospital, Camp Letterman, was created east of Gettysburg near the railroad depot to serve as a central location for incoming medical supplies and outgoing wounded to permanent hospitals in Philadelphia, Baltimore and Washington. The remarkable camp with nurses and doctors provided surgery and care to the wounded with plenty of food and water and cots with clean sheets.

For the residents of the small village of Gettysburg of about 2,400 people, the number of casualties staggers the imagination. With the dead on the battlefield numbering over 7,000 men and 5,000 horses and mules in the sweltering heat of a July summer, the stench of death quickly overwhelmed the entire area and was excruciating until the first frost in October. Bottles of peppermint oil and pennyroyal were carried about as people confronted the grim smell of death on such an unimaginable scale.

Citizens were asked to provide assistance to the Union forces to bury the thousands of fallen soldiers. Families of the killed and volunteers began to arrive to assist in the enormous task. The U.S. Sanitary Commission, created early in the war, provided assistance in aid to the wounded and information to the families. Burial parties created trenches for mass burials, sometimes as many as ninety soldiers in a trench as fears of an epidemic gripped the community. Records were made of their identities and they were later disinterred to be buried in appropriate burial grounds.

Local citizens soon became concerned that a more proper burial ground was needed and funds were collected from every Northern state that had lost men in the engagement. Land was purchased next to the private cemetery to create a new burial ground for the Union dead. The Confederate dead were left buried in the battlefield, but later exhumed in the 1870s and moved to honored plots in Southern cemeteries.

The federal government took possession of the burial grounds and the National Cemetery at Gettysburg was formally consecrated November 19, 1863. A two-hour oration by the brilliant Boston orator, Hon. Edward Everett, was followed by President Lincoln's dedicatory words. The brief remarks by Lincoln became an icon for American democracy as Lincoln memorialized the soldiers, whose lives he dedicated in the Gettysburg Address. Everett wrote to Lincoln the next day, saying *"I should be glad if I could flatter myself that I came as near to the central idea of the occasion in two hours, as you did in two minutes."* The dead Union soldiers were reinterred in the National Cemetery and the work was completed by March 1864.

LINCOLN'S GETTYSBURG ADDRESS

Four score and seven years ago our fathers brought forth on this continent, a new nation, conceived in Liberty, and dedicated to the proposition that all men are created equal.

Now we are engaged in a great civil war, testing whether that nation, or any nation so conceived and so dedicated, can long endure. We are met on a great battle field of that war. We have come to dedicate a portion of that field, as a final resting place for those who here gave their lives that that nation might live. It is altogether fitting and proper that we should do this.

But, in a larger sense, we cannot dedicate—we cannot consecrate—we cannot hallow—this ground. The brave men, living and dead, who struggled here, have consecrated it, far above our poor power to add or detract. The world will little note, nor long remember what we say here, but it can never forget what they did here. It is for us the living, rather, to be dedicated here to the unfinished work which they who fought here have thus far so nobly advanced. It is rather for us to be here dedicated to the great task remaining before us—that from these honored dead we take increased devotion to that cause for which they gave the last full measure of devotion—that we here highly resolve that these dead shall not have died in vain—that this nation, under God, shall have a new birth of freedom—and that government of the people, by the people, for the people, shall not perish from the earth.

Abraham Lincoln, November 19, 1863

VI. THE THIRD YEAR: 1863

Battle of Mine Run, Virginia
November 27-December 2, 1863

Although Lincoln and General-in-Chief Halleck were disappointed that Lee's army had not been vigorously pursued after the Battle of Gettysburg, Lincoln continued to retain Gen. George Meade as commander of the Army of the Potomac. Meade made a final attempt in late November to surprise Gen. Robert E. Lee's Confederates at Mine Run, a small tributary south of the Rapidan River and west of Chancellorsville. After his defeat at Gettysburg, Lee had positioned his army along a 30-mile stretch behind the Rapidan River and set up quarters between Germanna's Ford and Liberty Mills.

The Union Army's surprise attack failed when part of the Army of the Potomac became bogged down fording the river. By the time the army was reassembled, Lee's cavalry had provided sufficient warning so that the Army of Northern Virginia could prepare a strong defensive position. Meade withdrew and both sides settled into winter quarters and waited for spring.

BATTLES IN THE WESTERN THEATER

Battle of Arkansas Post (or Fort Hindman), Arkansas
January 9-11, 1863

In early January 1863, Union Gen. William T. Sherman and his army of 30,000 men and Rear Admiral David D. Porter's fleet of gunboats and steamers had been forced to abandon the failed Battle of Chickasaw Bayou in the Mississippi Delta, December 31, 1862-January 1, 1863, and had set up camp at Milliken's Bend, waiting for further orders. The unsuccessful expedition had been an attempt to capture high ground north of Vicksburg on the east side of the river and join Gen. Ulysses S. Grant who was to meet them with his army on solid land.

But Grant had been out of communication the previous two weeks, so Sherman proposed a joint Army-Navy attack on Fort Hindman, Arkansas Post, on the Arkansas River, which empties into the Mississippi about one hundred twenty miles north of Millikin's Bend. The fort, about forty miles inland on the Arkansas River, was manned by about 5,000 Confederates, mostly cavalry from Texas. Built to protect Little Rock from a Union advance up the Arkansas River, Confederates had used the fort to disrupt shipping on the Mississippi and raid Union ships that were supporting the Vicksburg Campaign. Sherman persuaded Admiral Porter to participate in the offensive and expected to lead the campaign.

But before the expedition could get underway, Gen. John A. McClernand, an influential Illinois politician, unexpectedly arrived on the scene from Memphis with orders from General-in-Chief Halleck that he would take command of Sherman's troops, whom he outranked, and lead an assault on Vicksburg. McClernand had used his close association with President Lincoln to acquire approval to recruit and lead an army that would mount an expedition against Vicksburg. But with no plan of his own when he arrived at Milliken's Bend, he quickly adopted Sherman's proposal and decided to lead the attack himself, hoping that a victory at Arkansas Post would enhance his military and political stature. Although Gen. Ulysses S. Grant was overall commander of McClernand's troops, communications with Grant were still disrupted after the raid on Holly Springs by the Confederates and telegraph lines that had been destroyed were still not repaired, so he was unaware of the Fort Hindman offensive until after its completion.

Fig. 27: The Union Army-Navy expedition captured Fort Hindman at Arkansas Post in early January 1863.

Source: *Creative Commons Attribution 3.0 License Map by Hal Jespersen, www.cwmaps.com.*

The combined Union naval and infantry fleet left Milliken's Bend on January 4, 1863. The nine warships included three ironclads, with the infantry transported on steamers. Using the White River cutoff from the Mississippi River, the Union assault approached the fort from the rear, landing within three miles of the fort on the evening of January 9. The following morning, the entire army of 33,000 men went ashore. As the soldiers advanced through muddy swamps, the Confederate defenders, badly outnumbered, retreated to the fort and its adjacent rifle-pits.

The three Naval ironclads fired at the fort for several hours at close range of four hundred yards until darkness fell. The following day, January 11, navy gunboats were supported by Union artillery and by 4 p.m., the guns of Fort Hindman were silent. Troops on both sides suffered severe losses in a fierce engagement with Confederate defenders in the rifle-pits, but after a half-hour of fighting, white flags appeared along the Confederate lines and the garrison of Fort Hindman surrendered. Confederate casualties numbered 5,500, nearly all by surrender, and accounted for one-fourth of the Confederate forces in Arkansas. Union losses were 1,047 with 134 killed.

McClernand wanted to continue the offensive up the Arkansas River and capture Little Rock and other Confederate targets in Arkansas or neighboring states, basically ignoring any plans to take Vicksburg, the objective that had authorized his position there in the first place. But neither Sherman nor Porter, who both greatly disliked McClernand, had any confidence in McClernand's ability and fitness to continue with the proposed expedition to capture Little Rock.

When telegraph lines had been restored and Sherman was finally able to communicate with Grant on January 10, Grant became aware for the first time that the Army-Navy offense at Chickasaw Bayou had failed and that Sherman's forces were now under McClernand's command. Grant's initial assessment of the Fort Hindman expedition was that it had been an unnecessary side movement with no particular advance for the Vicksburg Campaign. On further reflection, however, he realized that the capture of more than 5,000 prisoners and seventeen guns had removed a potential threat in the Union rear, and eliminated the raiding parties that had been harassing Union ships on the Mississippi. As Sherman informed Grant of McClernand's proposed expedition into Arkansas, Grant immediately rejected the proposal. Vicksburg was the key to the whole campaign and he ordered McClernand to Young's Point near the Vicksburg fortress. McClernand's army was dissolved and Sherman returned to Grant's command.

It was at this point that Grant needed to make a decision whether to approach Vicksburg from the east by capturing Jackson, Mississippi, and retake the route from Holly Springs along the Mississippi Central Railroad to the Yalobusha River, or to capture Vicksburg from the west through the Mississippi Delta. The mid-term elections had occurred and Lincoln's party, the Republicans, now held only a thin majority in Congress. The country had become discouraged with the war, recruits of soldiers were down and another defeat for the Union Army held the risk that the Peace Democrats would gain momentum and negotiate for an independent and separate Confederacy. Grant writes, in his *Personal Memoirs*:

"At this time the North had become very much discouraged. Many strong Union men believed that the war must prove a failure. The elections of 1862 had gone against the party which was for the prosecution of the war to save the Union if it took the last man and the last dollar. Voluntary enlistments had ceased throughout the greater part of the North, and the draft had been resorted to, to fill up our ranks. It was my judgment at the time that to make a backward movement as long as that from Vicksburg to Memphis, would be interpreted ... as a defeat and that the draft would be resisted. There was nothing left to be done but to go forward to a decisive victory. That was in my mind from the moment I took command in person at Young's Point."

Securing the Memphis & Charleston Railroad and giving up the Mississippi Central Railroad on the east side of the Mississippi River, Grant set up new headquarters and supply depot at Young's Point deep in the Mississippi Delta on January 29, 1863, near the base of the Vicksburg bluff and considered options of how to get Union troops in position to strike the daunting fortress.

THE VICKSBURG CAMPAIGN

The major focus for the Union Army in the Western Theater at the beginning of 1863 remained at Vicksburg, the stronghold fortress on the Mississippi River, located about two hundred forty miles north of New Orleans, Louisiana. Union forces controlled the river north of Vicksburg, but Confederates held the river between Vicksburg and Port Hudson, a distance of about one hundred thirty miles. President Lincoln was anxious to open the river's pathway for the Union all the way to the Gulf of Mexico and cut the Confederacy's connections between the west and the east.

Union Gen. Ulysses S. Grant had set up new headquarters at Young's Point on the Mississippi River opposite the Vicksburg fortress so that he could personally oversee operations during the Vicksburg Campaign. The land there presented daunting challenges for the men as it was subject to the rise and fall of waters from the Mississippi Delta, a floodplain of seven thousand square miles, about two hundred miles long and ninety miles wide at its widest point. The bayous and streams were narrow, bending through tortuous courses with overhanging vegetation that would be impossible to navigate for any ships except steamers. It was difficult for troops to find enough land above water where the soldiers could encamp. Out of necessity, troops were spread along many miles of river shore just so they could be above the water line. One camp had to be situated at Lake Providence, about fifty miles to the north (See Fig. 28).

Grant's major challenge now was to find the means to get his army across the Mississippi River where he could establish a secure footing on dry ground for an assault on Vicksburg from the east. The eventual surrender of Vicksburg would require several months, eleven battles and a large number of naval and troop maneuvers until the fort was defeated on July 4, 1863.

The heavy winter rains of 1862-63 from December to April created severe hardships for the men. Tents were scarce because they could not be erected within shooting range of the Confederate cannons at Vicksburg. Deep mud, little shelter and cold weather took their toll. Malaria, measles and smallpox attacked the soldiers. Although hospital tents were set up out of range of the guns and provided good quality medical care for the thousands of sick men, many still died.

McClernand's release to newspapers of false and greatly exaggerated, self-promoting reports of successes at Fort Hindman and Milliken's Bend were a constant source of irritation to Grant. Eventually, McClernand's congratulatory orders to his troops and himself that were subsequently published in public newspapers without army approval were his undoing. Violation of War Department rules provided Grant with the opportunity to remove McClernand from his command. He was transferred to the Army of the Gulf and played a minor role in the Red River Campaign before resigning from the army near the end of 1864.

VI. THE THIRD YEAR: 1863

Yazoo Pass Expedition, Mississippi Delta
February 3-April 10

The Yazoo Pass Expedition was another Union Army-Navy effort to land troops on the Yazoo River on the east side of the Mississippi River where they could mount the bluffs to high ground and place Union troops north of Vicksburg to attack the fortress from dry land. The operation joined the naval forces of the Union Mississippi Squadron with the Army of the Tennessee. The Navy contingent included seven gunboats, five of which were tinclads (thin armor), and a tug. Nine infantry regiments were transported in thirteen steamers.

By breaching a levee on the Mississippi River at Yazoo Pass, located on the northern edge of the Mississippi Delta, additional water would eventually make its way to Coldwater River, and from there to the Tallahatchie River (See Fig. 28). When the Tallahatchie joined the Yalobusha River, their combined waters formed the Yazoo River which continued all the way to Vicksburg. Beginning February 3, Union men worked for twelve days in intensive labor to clear the felled trees that the Confederates had left in Yazoo Pass. By the end of February, the waterways were sufficiently clear for gunboats and steamers for 5,000 men to begin navigating the Coldwater River, but progress was slow, given the narrow, winding channel and the dense overhanging vegetation. Local residents along the way suffered from the influx of high water that inundated their crops and homes.

As the Union fleet of transports and navy ironclads progressed down the Tallahatchie, the path was blocked by felled trees in the streams and rivers. Given the great size of the timber, considerable effort was needed to clear the waterways, which gave the Southerners time to construct "Fort Pemberton," an earthwork structure on a small island of dry ground between the Tallahatchie and Yalobusha Rivers, about one hundred miles north of Vicksburg.

Fort Pemberton, equipped with artillery and manned by about 1,500 men, was in a perfect position for a direct line of fire on the Union gunboats as they made an abrupt turn on the Tallahatchie River. The flooded grounds prevented any land approach by the infantry. After days of pounding between March 13 and 16, the damaged gunboats and the expedition withdrew to steam back up the Tallahatchie. A navy relief flotilla made a second attempt in early April, but multiple artillery fire from the Confederates at Fort Pemberton forced the Union expedition to permanently withdraw.

Canal Efforts, Mississippi Delta
January-March 1863

In late January, work began to enlarge an existing canal effort that had been abandoned in 1862. The canal, to be called Grant's Canal (See Fig. 29), would cut through a plot of land between the ends of the horseshoe bend of the Mississippi that is directly in

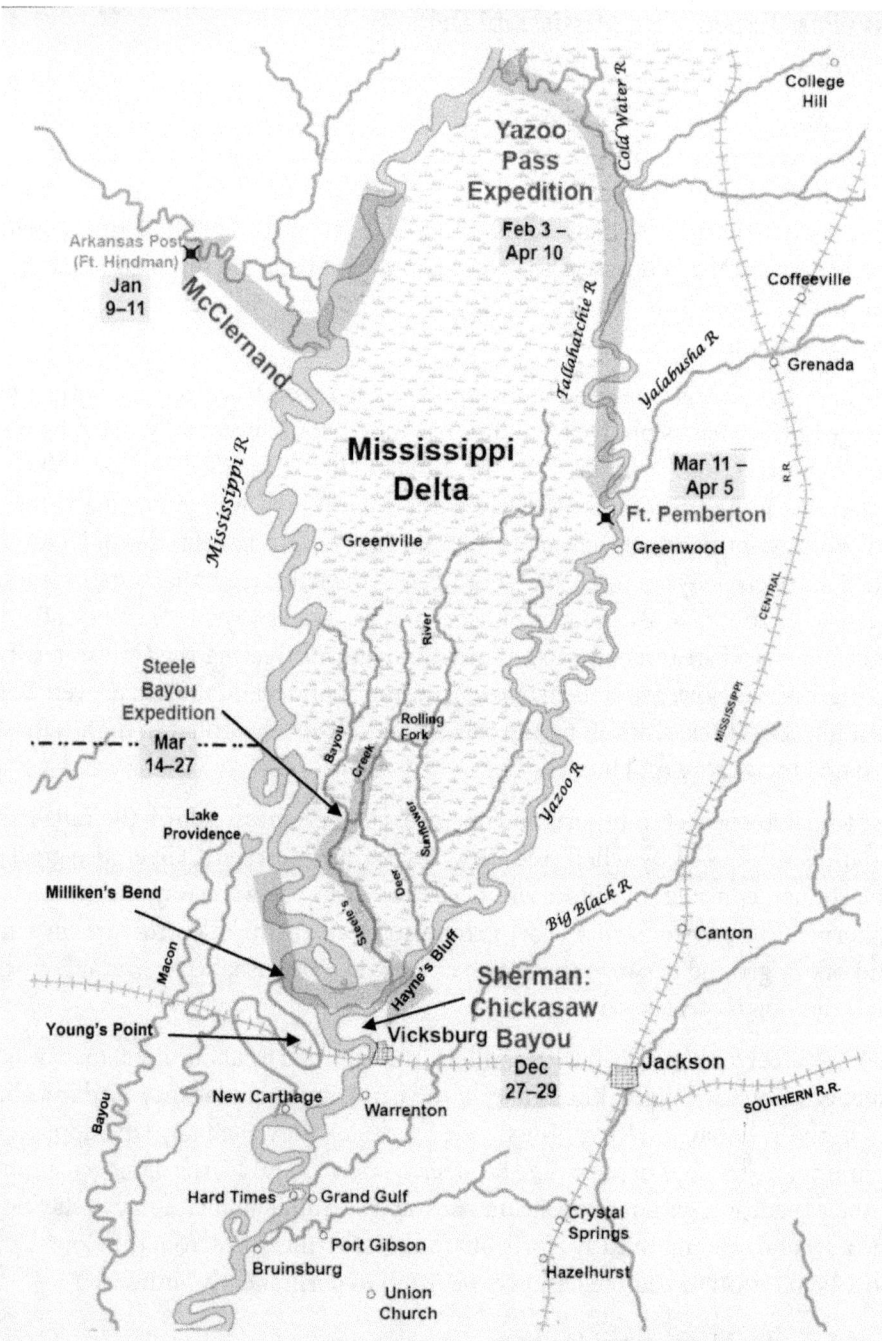

Fig. 28: Mississippi Delta Overview. A floodplain about two hundred miles long and ninety miles wide at its widest point, the Delta presented a formidable challenge to Union Army-Navy expeditions as they attempted to launch attacks on the Vicksburg stronghold from the narrow and tortuous streams and bayous created by the Mississippi River.

Source: *Creative Commons Attribution 3.0 License Map by Hal Jespersen, www.cwmaps.com.*

front of Vicksburg. Gunboats and steamers would be able to pass through and connect with the Mississippi on the other side, mostly avoiding the Vicksburg cannons. But unrelenting rain during the long and dreary winter took a steady toll on the men who suffered from disease, exhaustion and wounds. The dead had to be buried in the same land where the living soldiers were camping. After flooding, the exposed corpses were then moved to higher ground.

Surges of high water occurred at regular intervals, breaking through the dam at the head of the canal, flooding the project and filling it with new sediment and backwater. Steam powered dredges were brought in to speed the progress, but were continuously shelled by the Confederates and became inoperable. By late March, Grant abandoned the plan.

Back at Young's Point, efforts began on March 31 to connect Duckport Landing on the Mississippi with Walnut Bayou by creating a three-mile canal between them (See Fig. 29). From the Bayou side, troops could then reach New Carthage by flatboat. But as work progressed to create a channel seven feet deep and forty feet wide, water levels of the river began to fall and work on the canal came to an end.

Steele Bayou Expedition, Mississippi Delta
March 14-27, 1863

After the failed Chickasaw Bayou expedition, another attempt was made to mount the Mississippi bluff at Vicksburg's north flank with an Army-Navy operation under the command of Gen. William T. Sherman with the Navy's Mississippi River Squadron under Rear Admiral David D. Porter. The Navy led the expedition with five "Pook Turtle" gunboats, as they were called, and four tugs pulling mortar rafts, armed with artillery that fired projectiles in an arc to reach targets behind obstructions. Army troops, carried by steamers, followed the gunboats from the Mississippi River to Steele Bayou and Deer Creek which would get them to the Yazoo just above Vicksburg (See Fig. 29). But the overhanging thick brush presented serious obstacles to the smokestacks and upper structures of the river steamers and they fell behind. As the navy gunboats became separated from the steamers and moved ahead, they soon came under fire by Confederate sharpshooters who were picking off Union men while they cleared the waterway of felled trees.

> **"POOK-TURTLE" GUNBOATS**
>
> Seven Union Navy ironclad warships were the Navy's first gunboats, designed by Samuel M. Pook, a naval architect, to operate on the Mississippi River. Drawing only six feet of water while carrying thirteen guns, the boats had sufficient armor to withstand direct shots. In the water, they looked like mud turtles. Forming the Mississippi River Squadron, the gunboats participated in almost every significant battle on the upper Mississippi and its tributaries.

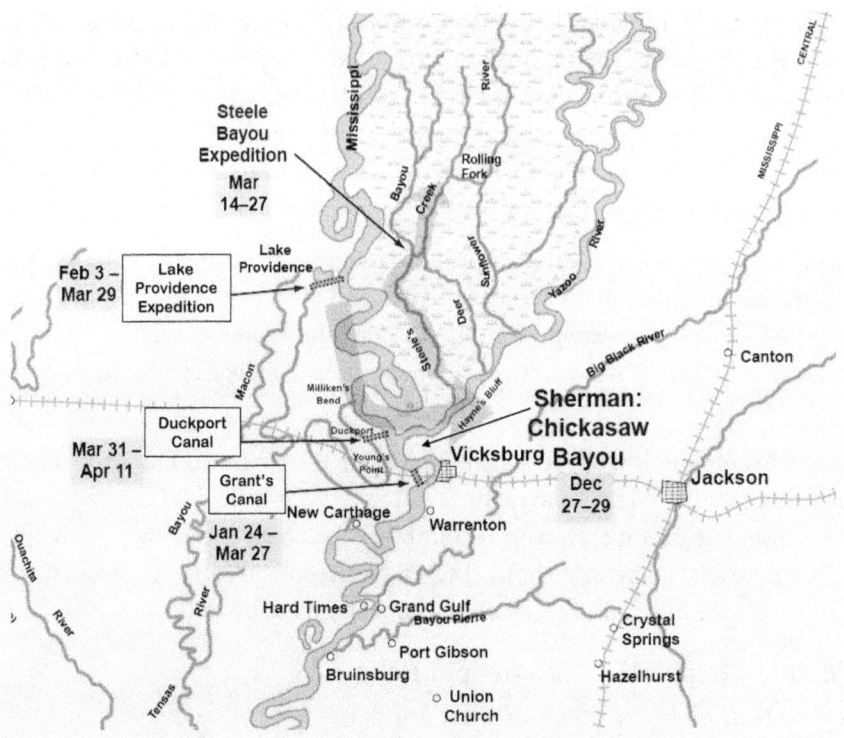

Fig. 29: Various Union efforts were made at Vicksburg during the winter of 1862-63 to create canals that would enable troops to bypass the massive cannons at Vicksburg and reach the crossing at Hard Times below.

Source: *Creative Commons Attribution 3.0 License Map by Hal Jespersen, www. cwmaps.com.*

An urgent request for immediate assistance arrived to Sherman from Admiral Porter, carried by a Black plantation slave who hid the tissue paper message in a piece of tobacco. Sherman sent all the men he had available, about eight hundred, to go immediately to the Admiral's aid while he paddled a canoe down the Bayou and found a steamer with infantry which he immediately engaged for the rescue.

Using a navy tug-boat to tow the steamer, Sherman says, "*We crashed through the trees, carrying away pilot-house, smoke-stacks and everything above deck, but the captain was a brave fellow and realized the necessity.*" When the rescue party was forced to proceed by foot, the night was so dark they lighted their way with hand-held lantern candles for about a mile and a half until they reached open cotton fields on Hill's plantation. At daylight, they resumed their journey on the road next to Deer Creek, marching double-quick as they heard Porter's guns as they got closer to the embattled men. They reached the boats at noon, an arduous twenty-one-mile march, arriving just in time to block the Confederates' plan to cut down trees that would have prevented the navy's escape, bringing cheers from the gunboat sailors. The navy fleet was backed out through the Bayou and returned to the Mississippi River and the expedition was abandoned.

VI. THE THIRD YEAR: 1863

Lake Providence Canal, Mississippi Delta
February-March 1863

Army engineers were challenged to assess all possibilities that would create alternative water routes to transport troops past the Vicksburg fortress. One option that was explored created a channel in a levee that diverted flood waters from the Mississippi into shallow Lake Providence. If the water depth could be sufficiently increased to allow boats to cross the lake, troops could then be transported to Bayou Macon and bypass the Vicksburg bluffs.

On March 17, a canal had been cut into the levee and six days later, water levels were deep enough in Lake Providence for vessels to float through. By that time, however, Grant had developed other means to march the army south by land from Milliken's Bend and the Lake Providence project was abandoned. The flooded waterways provided an unexpected benefit, however, by protecting Grant's marching men from raids by the Confederates from the west and shielded Union camps from floods as water was diverted to Lake Providence.

Navy Runs Past Vicksburg Cannons;
Troops March South, April 16-22

In late March, water levels in the Delta had dropped sufficiently for roads that had been submerged through the winter began to appear. Gen. Grant, headquartered on his command ship *Magnolia* near Young's Point, initiated plans to move his approximately 40,000-man army south of Vicksburg to Hard Times, Louisiana, on roads west of the Mississippi that had finally become passable. Although the roads were of poor quality, full of bayous and swamps, alternate routes were made using pontoon bridges as long as six hundred yards to navigate over water or soil too soggy to support the wagon trains. The bridges were constructed from pontoons and materials found nearby, but were so substantial that no mishaps occurred with the crossing of artillery, cavalry and wagon trains, except for the loss of one siege gun.

Grant now planned to run past the gauntlet of Vicksburg cannons with enough steamers down the Mississippi River to reach Hard Times, where they would be used to transport troops across the river. An assault on Vicksburg could then be made on the east from hard ground. Rear Admiral Porter and his navy ironclads agreed to escort and protect the steamboats and

> **COMPLAINTS ABOUT GRANT**
>
> Impatient with the lack of Union progress to take Vicksburg, a commission of war critics complained to Lincoln that Grant was incompetent and a whiskey drinker and demanded his removal. But after investigating the claims, Lincoln concluded that whatever Grant's drinking habits were, they did not interfere with his ability to plan and win battles. Lincoln responded to the critics, *"If I can find out what brand of whiskey he drinks, I will send a barrel of it to all the other commanders."*

multiple barges carrying supplies of food, forage and coal as the ships passed under the 14-mile-long cannon fire from the high Vicksburg bluffs. Only two steamer captains agreed to run the blockade, so army volunteers were requested, men who had experience navigating western rivers. Volunteer captains, pilots, mates, engineers and deck-hands rapidly emerged, five times more than were needed.

On April 16, seven ironclads and four empty troop transports loaded with stores, each towing barges filled with coal, all painted black, floated past the Vicksburg batteries at night. But Confederates had set up bonfires on the east side to light up the river. Steamboats carried hay and grain with bales of cotton to conceal and protect the boilers. The gunboats hugged the shoreline so that Confederate artillery on the high bluffs could not be aimed at a steep enough angle to get direct hits. Cotton bales and hay protected the gunboats. Although the smoke stacks were damaged, the ironclads suffered little damage through the fourteen miles of artillery attack.

One of the transports was burned and another disabled and abandoned, but no men were killed and few were wounded. A second run, on April 22, ran six steamers and twelve barges, all loaded with hay, corn, freight and rations. Only one of the steamers was sunk and about half the barges got through which provided Grant's army with enough supplies and boats to transport his men across the Mississippi River. By this time, two-thirds of the Union Army had marched nearly sixty miles from Milliken's Bend to Hard Times, Louisiana, and were waiting for transport, directly across the river to Grand Gulf, Mississippi. The march had required a month.

TWO UNION DIVERSIONARY FEINTS

Union Cavalry Raid to Baton Rouge, Louisiana
April 17-May 2, 1863

As the Union Army neared conclusion of its march south to Hard Times, Gen. Ulysses S. Grant ordered two diversionary feints to divert the Confederates while his army crossed the Mississippi River near Grand Gulf. The first diversion was carried out by Col. Benjamin Grierson, a former music teacher, commanding a 1,700-horse cavalry brigade of the 6th and 7th Illinois and 2nd Iowa Cavalry regiments in the Union Army of the Tennessee.

As a strange coincidence, Grierson actually disliked horses, as he had been kicked in the face by one as a young boy and still bore the scars. Nevertheless, he led a cavalry force into unknown and hostile territory to raid the Confederacy. Leaving Lagrange, Tennessee, at dawn April 17, the cavalry rode south with orders to penetrate into the Mississippi heartland and cut Vicksburg's main supply line, the Southern Railroad, which connected the city to Jackson, Mississippi, and the arsenals of Georgia (See Fig. 30).

As the cavalry raid commenced, one hundred seventy-five riders became ill about seventy miles south of Lagrange at Pontotoc and were unable to continue with the raid.

VI. THE THIRD YEAR: 1863

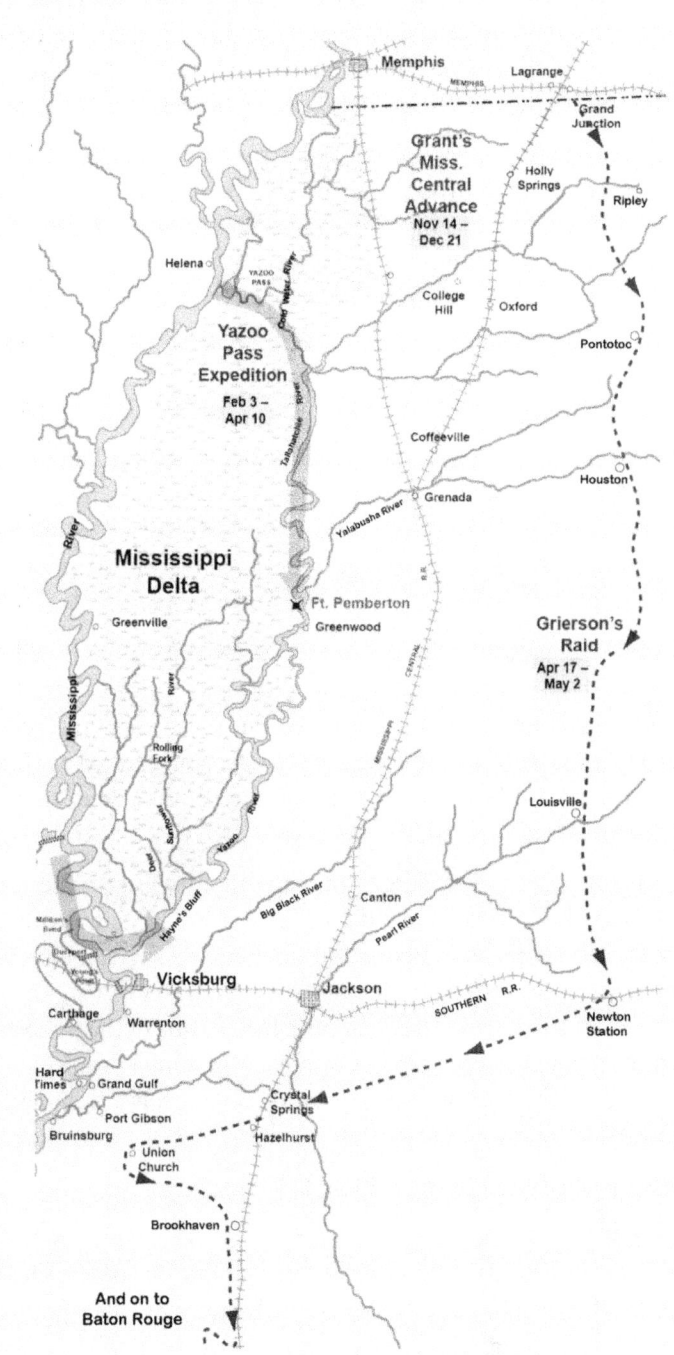

Fig. 30: The Union Cavalry under Grierson made a 600-mile raid through Mississippi all the way to Baton Rouge, Louisiana, eluding Confederates, destroying bridges, railroad equipment, tracks and telegraph lines in their path.

Source: *Creative Commons Attribution 3.0 License Map by Hal Jespersen, www. cwmaps.com.*

They were sent back to Lagrange with instructions to leave tracks that would deceive the Southerners into thinking that the cavalry's main body had returned north. At Houston, Mississippi, one regiment, the 2nd Iowa, was detached and sent east to damage the north/south Mobile and Ohio (M&O) Railroad before returning to Lagrange.

Although the well-guarded M&O was unharmed by the raid, the troops burned several cotton warehouses, captured six hundred horses and freed two hundred slaves, who led the horses back to Lagrange. The five-day raid attracted most of Northern Mississippi's home militia to follow the Union troops north to Lagrange, allowing Grierson's main body to escape south on its primary mission. The 2nd Iowa returned to Lagrange with a loss of only ten men and the first news about Grierson's progress to his superiors.

The remaining one thousand raiders traveled more than six hundred miles with little rest or food, tore up railroads, burned crossties, destroyed locomotives, ripped up bridges and trestles, tore down telegraph lines, burned buildings, freed slaves, and captured arms and horses. Their efforts at Newton Station on the Southern Railroad destroyed track and rails, left a smoldering wreckage of two locomotives and three dozen burning freight cars filled with ordnance and supplies.

Confusing and exaggerated reports in the newspapers convinced Confederate Gen. John C. Pemberton, commander of the Vicksburg garrison, to divert infantry and cavalry from Vicksburg to halt the raiders, but these efforts were unsuccessful. Grierson's men were able to avoid Confederate pursuers and arrived in Union-occupied Baton Rouge, Louisiana, on May 2 with a loss of only 19 casualties, three dead, seven wounded and nine missing.

The Union cavalry was met in Baton Rouge with cheering soldiers and civilians as news of its success had been widely disseminated by the newspapers. Given that Confederate cavalry commanders, such as Nathan Bedford Forrest, John Hunt Morgan and Jeb Stuart had consistently out-performed Union cavalry during the previous two years of the war, Grierson's daring raid was described as one of the most extraordinary and brilliant Union cavalry exploits of the war, earning him a promotion to Brigadier General of volunteers. The 1959 movie, *The Horse Soldiers*, is a fictionally-based representation of Grierson's Raid.

Battle of Snyder's Bluff (or Haynes' Bluff), Vicksburg
April 29-May 1, 1863

The second diversionary feint was Grant's third attempt to attack Vicksburg's right flank at Haynes' Bluff, which became known as the Battle of Snyder's Bluff, on the Yazoo River just north of Vicksburg. The attack was intended to divert Confederate forces north from Vicksburg while Grant's Union Army was landing south at Grand Gulf.

Gen. William T. Sherman led the attack, collecting eight gunboats and all the old boats he could find at Milliken's Bend, including ten transports. After a heavy exchange between the Union gunboats and Confederate batteries, Union troops were put ashore

VI. THE THIRD YEAR: 1863

and battled for control of shore buildings that were firing on the gunboats. But swampy terrain and heavy fire forced the Union troops to return to the transports and disengage after only two days of fighting.

Although little damage was done to either side, the real achievement of the engagement was that a Confederate column headed for Grand Gulf was pulled back to bring support to Snyder's Bluff. Sherman writes of the encounter, *"This detachment of rebel troops must have marched nearly sixty miles without rest, for afterward, on reaching Vicksburg, I heard that the men were perfectly exhausted, and lay along the road in groups, completely fagged out. This diversion, made with so much pomp and display, therefore completely fulfilled its purpose, by leaving Gen. Grant to contend with a minor force on his landing at Bruinsburg."*

Union Troops Cross Mississippi River
April 29, 1863

While Sherman's and Grierson's diversionary exploits progressed, Gen. Ulysses S. Grant was moving the very large Union Army south on roads west of the Mississippi River to Hard Times, Louisiana, where it would meet with Admiral Porter's Navy fleet

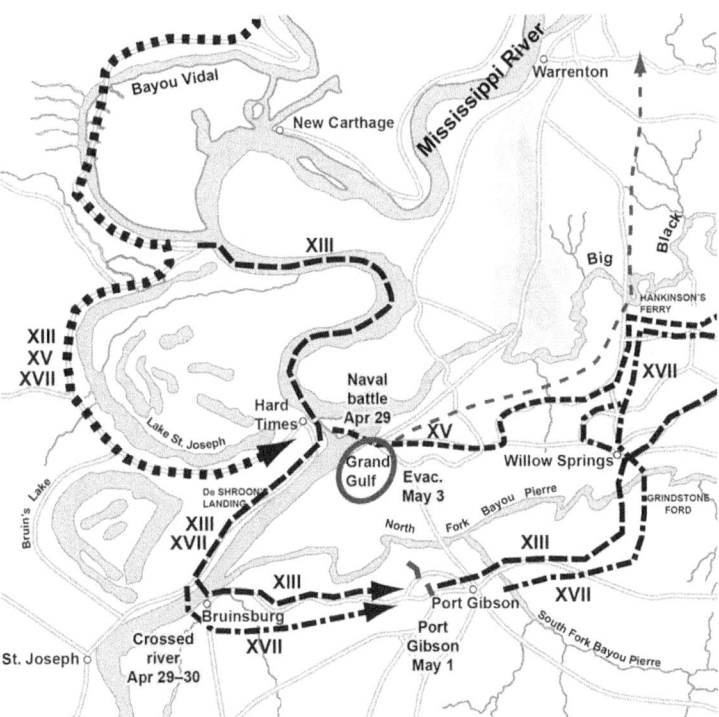

Fig. 31: Union troops under Gen. Grant bypassed the Vicksburg Fortress by marching through swamps and bayous to cross the Mississippi River at Bruinsburg, Mississippi. Confederate forces at Grand Gulf escaped north to join their troops at Vicksburg. Grant's army headed north and east to capture Jackson, Mississippi, and then laid siege to Vicksburg.

Source: *Creative Commons Attribution 3.0 License Map by Hal Jespersen, www. cwmaps.com.*

of ironclads, steamers and barges that had passed through the artillery firestorm from the Vicksburg bluffs.

As soon as the fleet reached Hard Times, Porter attacked the Confederate artillery at Grand Gulf, Mississippi, with gunboats on April 29. The protecting forts of Forts Coburn and Wade blocked the entrance to the Big Black River to the north and the continued flow of the Mississippi to the south. Fort Wade was soon silenced, but Fort Coburn, situated forty feet above the river, continued firing on the Navy gunboats. Although the Union ironclads came within one hundred yards of the Confederate fortifications, they could not defeat the upper batteries. An amphibious assault would be too costly, so troops marched a few miles farther south to reach another landing.

When night fell, the Navy gunboats continued to fire on Grand Gulf to protect the steamboats, transports and barges as they passed the fort's artillery to reach DeShroon's Landing only a few miles farther south. By the evening of April 30, about 17,000 Union soldiers had been transported across the river to Bruinsburg, Mississippi, without opposition. The landing of such a great force would remain the largest American amphibious operation until World War II and the Normandy invasion of France.

Grand Gulf Surrenders to Union Army
May 2, 1863

At Bruinsburg, the men rested in the shade of trees before beginning their march to Port Gibson about ten miles away, where the badly outnumbered Confederates were driven back on May 1. As the Union Army continued to advance north, pockets of Confederates resisted but fell back under the Union onslaught. The Confederates had no cavalry in the area because it had been ordered to pursue Grierson's raiders. Grand Gulf's Confederate commander soon realized that the Union offensive could destroy his retreat to Vicksburg by taking out the bridge at Big Black River. To make their escape, the Confederates destroyed Grand Gulf's heavy artillery, abandoned the fortifications on May 2 and headed to the Vicksburg garrison. Union gunboats then captured Grand Gulf without firing a shot and Grant occupied it on May 3, making it a new supply depot as he moved inland. Grant ordered a wagon train of one hundred twenty wagons with ammunition and provisions of bacon, coffee, sugar and bread from the supply depot at Perkins' Plantation at Milliken's Bend, a journey of about seventy miles. A new supply line would soon be created after Union forces besieged Vicksburg. Grant then rode through the night with his senior staff to Hankinson's Ferry on the Big Black River, arriving there at dawn on May 4 (See Fig. 32). Forage for the animals could be obtained from the countryside. Sherman's XV Corps crossed the river at Grand Gulf and headed north to Hankinson's Ferry, overtaking Grant in person, before the army turned east for Jackson, Mississippi.

After pushing through light Confederate forces at Port Gibson, the main body of the Union Army pressed north and east to reach and destroy the Pittsburg & Jackson

VI. THE THIRD YEAR: 1863

> ### GRANT'S NOTE ON CROSSING THE MISSISSIPPI
>
> *"When this (landing at Bruinsburg April 29, 1863) was affected, I felt a degree of relief scarcely ever equaled since. Vicksburg was not yet taken it is true, nor were its defenders demoralized by any of our previous moves. I was now in the enemy's country, with a vast river and the stronghold of Vicksburg between me and my base of supplies. But I was on dry ground on the same side of the river with the enemy. All the campaigns, labors, hardships and exposures from the month of December previous to this time that had been made and endured were for the accomplishment of this one object."*
>
> Grant's Personal Memoirs, 1885

Railroad that connected Jackson, the state capital, with Vicksburg. Confederate Gen. John C. Pemberton's troops shadowed the Union army from the north side of the Big Black River. Part of the Union Army, numbering about 10,000, met about 4,000 Confederates at Raymond on May 12 (See Fig. 32) and successfully forced the Southerners to withdraw the next day to join Pemberton's forces on the Big Black River. At this point, Grant became aware that Confederate reinforcements were beginning to arrive from other locations in the South to concentrate at Jackson. If Grant turned the Union Army to the west toward Vicksburg, he would have a Confederate army in his rear, so Grant decided to move the army east and reached Jackson on the evening of May 14.

Jackson, Mississippi, Surrenders to Union Army
May 13, 1863

Confederate Gen. Joseph E. Johnston arrived at Jackson on May 13 and took command of the forces there. Aware of a large Union Army rapidly advancing against his small force of only 6,000 Southern defenders, Johnston ordered the city evacuated on May 14 and retreated to the north just hours before the arrival of the Union army.

Grant's army occupied Jackson that night and burned factories, destroyed storehouses, roads and bridges and cut railroad connections to Vicksburg. When a local hotel owner inquired if his hotel was to be burned, Gen. Sherman told him "No, it would not," as there were no orders to burn anything except military assets, but when the troops departed, Sherman noted that the building, named Confederate Hotel, was ablaze.

With the Union Army in pursuit, Pemberton's Confederates began a full retreat west to reach Vicksburg, but on May 16 Union troops caught up with them at Champion Hill. After a brief battle, the Southerners continued their movement west and although the Union captured over 1,700 prisoners and eighteen guns, the Confederates were able to escape over the two bridges at Big Black River, which they then burned. With the bridges burned, Union engineers built three bridges in one day to cross the Big Black. One was a raft bridge; another, using cotton bales as pontoons; and the third, from felled trees on opposite banks of the river, cut so that their tops interlaced in the river. On the morning of May 18, the army crossed the river and soon reached Vicksburg's outskirts. Gen. Sherman, leading his command, moved to Haynes Bluff, finding it abandoned. A Union gunboat, visible on the Yazoo River below, steamed up and the Haynes battery was accepted by the navy.

Grant next ordered all commanders to conduct assaults on Vicksburg on May 19 and 22. When the attacks failed to break the Confederate lines, Grant laid siege to the city. The Union Army had marched for a month through Louisiana to cross the Mississippi and then fought five battles over a stretch of two hundred miles before reaching the Vicksburg outskirts. With Pemberton's forces captive within the city, the Union Army now had access to Hayne's Bluff and with the protection of Admiral Porter's gunboats, Grant had a clear path to the Mississippi River and a new supply line to Memphis. The Union Army could hold siege to Vicksburg as long as necessary.

During the Siege of Vicksburg, a small but significant battle occurred at Milliken's Bend on the other side of the Mississippi River on June 7, 1863. A Confederate brigade of Texans from the Trans-Mississippi Theater attacked the garrison on June 7, mistakenly believing that it was still the main supply for the Union Army. Manned by about 1,000 soldiers of the U.S. Colored Troops, hand-to-hand fighting resulted in seventy percent casualties of Black soldiers on the Union side. But as the Confederates were claiming victory, the *USS Choctaw* gunboat opened fire on them and they were forced to withdraw. The bravery and courage displayed by the Blacks in the battle convinced commanders that former slaves would make good soldiers and many new Black recruits soon joined the Union Army.

Siege and Surrender of Vicksburg, Mississippi
May 22-July 4, 1863

Beginning May 22, Union entrenchments and artillery batteries were constructed on a twelve-mile siege ring around Vicksburg. Two sets of trenches were built. One set faced the fort; the other set faced east toward Jackson, anticipating a counter-attack from Confederate Gen. Joseph E. Johnston. But Johnston needed reinforcements to attack Grant and few were available. Confederate Gen. Braxton Bragg was holding Tullahoma, Tennessee, anticipating an attack from Union forces under Gen. William Rosecrans, which finally commenced in June. At the same time, Gen. Robert E. Lee was advancing his Confederate Army of Northern Virginia into Pennsylvania towards Gettysburg.

Over the next several weeks, the siege of Vicksburg continued as Union trenches slowly advanced toward the city and two underground mines were exploded leaving large craters. Picket lines became so close that soldiers of the two armies exchanged conversations. Confederates addressed the Union men as "Yanks," while Southerners were called "Johnnies." Minor attempts by Confederate forces west of the Mississippi River to come to Vicksburg's aid were repulsed.

VI. THE THIRD YEAR: 1863

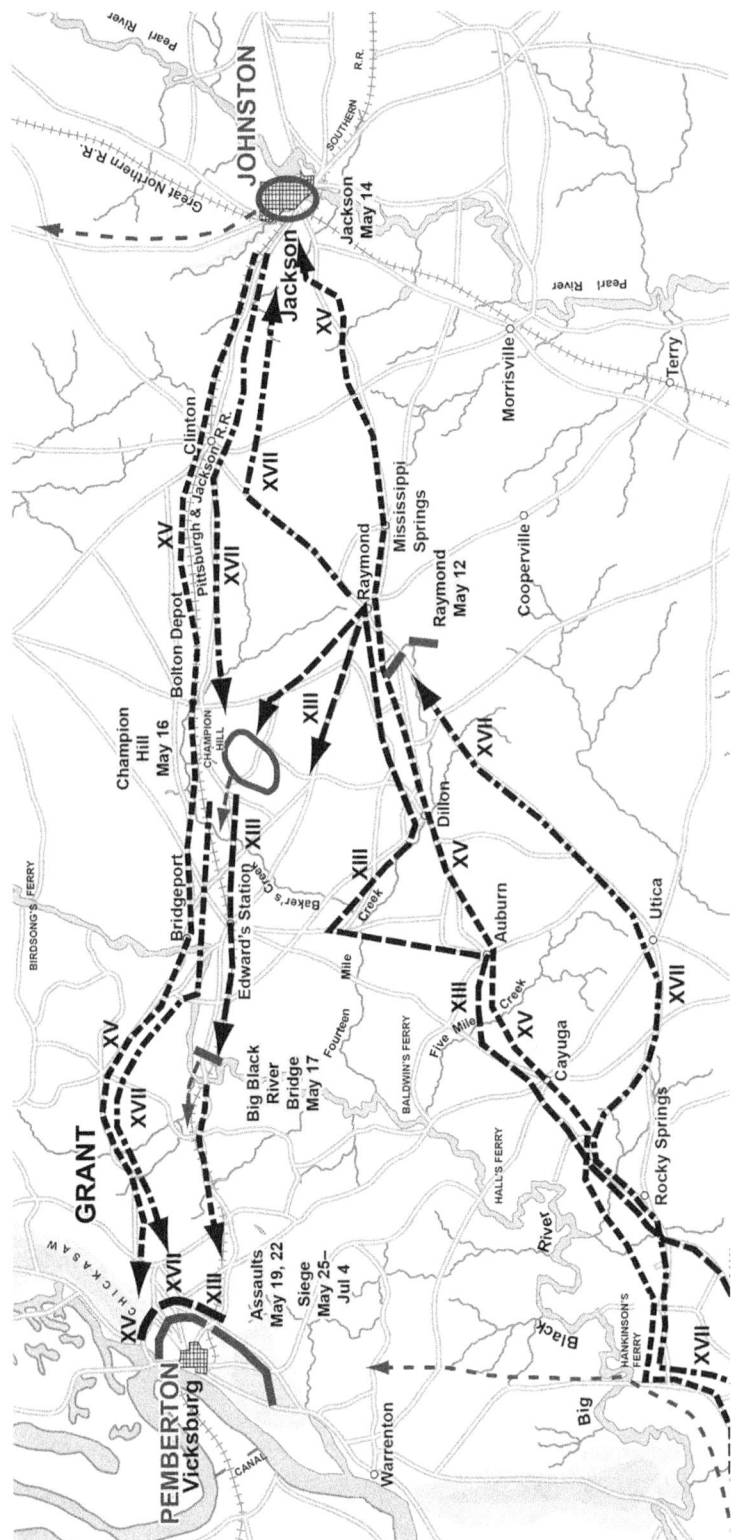

Fig. 32: Grant's Union Army moved into Mississippi to conquer Jackson, the state capital, and then created a siege on the Vicksburg stronghold under Gen. Pemberton, May 1–July 4, 1863

Source: *Creative Commons Attribution 3.0 License Map by Hal Jespersen, www.cwmaps.com.*

During the 47-day siege, Union Army and Navy artillery fired continuous barrages that destroyed much of the city. Over five hundred caves in the hills supported two to three thousand private citizens, who adapted them to use as their homes while the Union Army and Navy fired artillery daily into the city. The wealthier families furnished the caves with rugs, furniture and bedrooms. But as food became severely rationed, horses, mules, dogs and cats were sacrificed and even rats were used to make "squirrel stew." Citizens and troops suffered greatly.

As Gen. Ulysses S. Grant was making preparations for a final assault on July 6, white flags appeared on the Confederate lines on July 3. When Confederate Gen. Pemberton met with Grant, he was hoping that a request for surrender on Independence Day would yield better terms. But Grant's initial demand to Pemberton's request to discuss terms was "unconditional surrender." With more discussion, however, terms were modified when Grant realized that managing and feeding 30,000 starving men and escorting them to prisons would take considerable resources from his army. Grant agreed to parole the Southerners, allowing them to take their horses and personal property, but not slaves. When Union soldiers entered the fort, many of the soldiers shared foodstuffs from their haversacks to feed the suffering Southerners. The city of Vicksburg would not celebrate the 4th of July for several decades.

> **TWO UNION VICTORIES**
>
> The North erupted into wild celebration on July 4th, 1863, the country's 87th anniversary, for the simultaneous victories at Gettysburg and Vicksburg.

The surrender of Vicksburg was formalized on July 4. News of the surrender was transmitted to Washington, arriving with news of the Union success at the Battle of Gettysburg. Five days later, the Confederates surrendered Port Hudson, Louisiana, north of Baton Rouge on the Mississippi River, to Union Gen. Nathaniel P. Banks, Army of the Gulf, at the end of a six-week siege. The Union siege had been supported by several warships from Admiral David G. Farragut during the Army-Navy operation. The last great stronghold of the Mississippi had fallen, completing the Anaconda Plan. Union forces now controlled the great river, an economic lifeblood for the country, from New Orleans to all points north. Southern forces in Arkansas, Louisiana and Texas were now cut off from the rest of the Confederacy for the rest of the war.

Lincoln had long recognized the importance of Vicksburg, noting early in the Civil War its strategic location on a broad map. With news of Grant's victory, Lincoln said, *"The Father of Waters again goes unvexed to the sea."* The combined surrenders of Vicksburg and Port Hudson, when added to the Union success at Gettysburg, raised Northern morale and filled hopes that at last there was a turning point in the war. The Confederacy's hold on the Mississippi River had been broken.

The Siege of Vicksburg cost the Union about 5,000 casualties. Confederate losses were 33,000, of which 29,500 had surrendered. With the end of the Siege of Port Hudson, Gen. Banks paroled nearly 6,000 prisoners. Gen. Pemberton's command at Vicksburg turned over one hundred seventy-two cannons and 60,000 rifles to the Union. Combined casualties for both North and South through the multiple battles over a year and a half, including the siege, totaled over 19,000, one of ten most costly conflicts of the Civil War.

Grant's next move was to send Gen. Sherman east to Jackson with 40,000 troops to drive Confederate Gen. Joseph Johnston's army out of Mississippi. During the Siege of Vicksburg, Johnston had reoccupied Jackson with about 25,000 soldiers. But as Sherman began to surround the city, Gen. Johnston, fearing entrapment, withdrew the army. By July 17, Sherman's army had re-occupied the city, ending Confederate control in Mississippi.

BATTLES IN EAST TENNESSEE

Union Tullahoma Campaign, Tennessee
June 24-July 3, 1863

After defeating Confederate Gen. Braxton Bragg, Army of Tennessee, at the Battle at Stones River, Tennessee, in January 1863, Union Gen. William Rosecrans, commanding the Army of the Cumberland, remained in place at Murfreesboro, Tennessee, through the winter and spring, resupplying and training his troops and building Fort Rosecrans which became a Union supply depot for the rest of the war. During this period, President Lincoln and General-in-Chief Halleck, made multiple requests to Rosecrans to resume the campaign against Confederate Gen. Braxton Bragg, who had wintered his army only fifty miles southeast of Rosecrans at Tullahoma, Tennessee. Finally, Rosecrans was ordered in May to launch his campaign against Bragg to prevent any Confederate forces being sent as reinforcements to the Vicksburg campaign.

Rosecrans left Murfreesboro on June 23 for a nine-day campaign that would go into military history as one of the most brilliant maneuvers of the Civil War. He drove Bragg and the Confederates out of their quarters at Tullahoma with a series of well-rehearsed feints that were perfectly executed during a period of the most extraordinary rains known for that time of year. The Confederate Army, handicapped by continued dissension between Bragg and his senior generals and a lack of supplies, retreated to Chattanooga, Tennessee, near the Georgia border and the Union Army occupied Tullahoma July 3 with minimal losses.

Rosecrans' successful campaign completely removed the Confederate Army from middle Tennessee, an agriculturally productive region. The military success, however, came at the same time as news of two major Union victories at Gettysburg and Vicksburg. Rosecrans resented the lack of acclaim that he felt he deserved, complaining to the Secretary of War, *"I beg in behalf of this army that the War Department may not overlook so great an event because it is not written in letters of blood."* Rosecrans did not pursue the Confederates into Chattanooga, however, which enabled Bragg to restore his minimal losses and overcome his setbacks and he would soon defeat Rosecrans at the Battle of Chickamauga in September.

Union Knoxville Campaign, East Tennessee
August-September 1863

In the fall of 1863, East Tennessee, with a population that strongly supported the Union cause, was still under Confederate control and Lincoln saw an opportunity to secure Knoxville and its Confederate railroad center that linked Chattanooga to Virginia and vital supplies. Gen. Ambrose Burnside, who had been relieved from the Army of the Potomac after his disastrous defeat at Fredericksburg and the failed Mud March in January, was now commanding the Union Department of Ohio. His orders were to move to Knoxville and take control of the city.

Burnside led the army from Cincinnati in August, bypassing the well defended Cumberland Gap in a flanking maneuver which allowed him and his main force to occupy Knoxville on September 2, nearly unopposed. He then accomplished the surrender of the Confederates at Cumberland Gap, capturing 2,300 prisoners.

As Burnside settled into Knoxville in eastern Tennessee, Union Gen. William Rosecrans, headquartered in middle Tennessee at Tullahoma, planned his pursuit of Gen. Braxton Bragg and the Confederates who occupied Chattanooga about eighty miles to the southeast. Rosecrans attacked in early September, implementing a well-executed plan that deceived Bragg into thinking that the main Union force was northeast of the city when it had actually crossed the Tennessee River west and south of him. When Bragg realized that the Union Army was behind him, he abandoned Chattanooga and his army withdrew to the Chickamauga Mountains in northwestern Georgia, about twenty miles south of Chattanooga. Rosecrans informed Lincoln on September 9, *"Chattanooga is ours without a struggle and East Tennessee is free."*

CHICKAMAUGA & SIEGE OF CHATTANOOGA

Battle of Chickamauga, Georgia
September 18-21, 1863

After capturing Chattanooga from Confederate Gen. Braxton Bragg on September 9, 1863, Union Gen. William Rosecrans continued to pursue the Confederate Army into the Chickamauga Mountains, a few miles south of the Tennessee border into Georgia. Rosecrans, persuaded that the demoralized Southerners would continue moving deeper into Georgia, split his 60,000-man army into three columns, widely separated, planning to attack Bragg's army from three directions.

VI. THE THIRD YEAR: 1863

When Bragg discovered the Union Army was split into three smaller units, he planned to attack Rosecrans' spread-out army in separate assaults and nearly succeeded. Misinformation about the Confederate army's movements was encouraged by some of Bragg's soldiers who posed as deserters and passed it on to Union interrogators. At a close encounter September 9-10 at McLemore's Cove, a dead-end valley lying between Lookout and Pigeon Mountains a few miles from Chickamauga, Bragg nearly captured a division of 5,000 Union men. When Rosecrans became aware of his mistake, he took immediate steps to consolidate his army near Chickamauga Creek.

> **THE ROCK OF CHICKAMAUGA**
>
> James Garfield, future president of the United States in 1880, served with distinction during the Civil War at the Battles of Shiloh and Corinth and was Chief-of-staff for Gen. Rosecrans during the Battle of Chickamauga. As Gen. George H. Thomas held his position that protected the Union retreat to Chattanooga, Garfield sent Rosecrans a message stating "Thomas is standing like a rock." The nickname "Rock of Chickamauga" became part of the legacy of Gen. Thomas.

On the morning of September 18, Bragg's cavalry tried to cross Alexander Bridge over West Chickamauga Creek, a narrow and deep creek with steep banks, one of the few bridges that crossed the dangerous waters. But they were blocked by an intensive defense from the Union "Lightning Brigade" facing them on the other side. Lieut. Col. John T. Wilder of the 17th Indiana Regiment had created a mounted infantry, which included elements of Illinois cavalry that could move with the speed of cavalry but fight dismounted as infantry. Equipped with newly introduced Spencer repeating rifles, the men could fire seven or more rounds per minute, compared to three shots per minute from muzzle loaders. Their intense barrage of fire power had earned them the name "Lightning Brigade."

As the day progressed, skirmishing became a full battle as more Confederates were brought in to face the defenders of the bridge. Wilder had less than 1,000 men, but they were able to hold off 8,000 Confederates for five hours. With nightfall, the outnumbered Lightning Brigade was in danger of being captured as more and more Southern units began to find places in the Creek where they could cross. When dusk fell, the Union troops were able to slip away in the dark, leaving campfires burning over a large area, to deceive the Confederates about the size of their army. The successful delay had prevented the Confederates from making a sweeping advance down the Union's flank and cutting off its retreat to Chattanooga. Historians generally agree that the delay at Chickamauga Creek allowed Union Gen. Rosecrans to consolidate his men and develop a defense line that prevented the Union Army's capture.

The Battle of Chickamauga began in earnest the next morning as Confederates swarmed over the creek, but despite aggressive Southern attacks throughout the day, the

BATTLE OF CHICKAMAUGA, GEORGIA
September 19-21, 1863

The largest battle fought in the Civil War Western Theater took place at Chickamauga Creek on the northern border of Georgia about twenty miles south of Chattanooga, Tennessee. Second only to the Battle of Gettysburg, losses numbered more than 34,000 casualties for the two armies. Union Gen. William Rosecrans pursued Confederate Gen. Braxton Bragg's 52,000-man army through Tennessee during the summer of 1863 and successfully removed the Southerners from their headquarters at Tullahoma. A second advance in September drove the Confederates out of Chattanooga into the mountains near Chickamauga, Georgia.

Wrongly assuming that Bragg was demoralized by his defeats and was retreating farther into Georgia, Rosecrans divided his army into three widely separated columns, too far apart to support each other as they pursued the Southern army. Bragg cleverly convinced Rosecrans that the Confederate Army would continue to withdraw deeper into Georgia while he made plans to attack each isolated portion of the Union Army individually. When Rosecrans realized his error, he concentrated his 60,000-man army near Chickamauga Creek.

The two armies met on the morning of Sept. 18 as Confederate cavalry attempted to cross the creek at Alexander Bridge but were repulsed for most of the day by the Lightning Brigade.

Confederates were reinforced in the night by Gen. James Longstreet with troops from the Army of Northern Virginia, which brought Bragg's army to 65,000. While under attack, Union Gen. Rosecrans received an erroneous message mid-day that a gap existed in the Union line. In fact, Union troops were there but partially hidden by heavy forest. Rosecrans ordered a shift of men to close the non-existent gap, which created an actual hole that was quickly exploited by Longstreet and thousands of Southern troops poured through, forcing a frantic Union withdrawal to Chattanooga. The Northern retreat was protected by troops under Gen. George Thomas, who held the strong defense position that enabled the army to escape. He would then become known as "The Rock of Chickamauga," for holding the line. The next day the Union Army was trapped within Chattanooga in a siege that would not be relieved until November by Union Gen. Ulysses S. Grant, recently promoted as overall commander of the army.

Union line held. Southern reinforcements from the Army of Northern Virginia arrived that night under Gen. James A. Longstreet, increasing the Confederate Army to about 65,000. Mid-morning on September 20 in the heavily wooded battlefield, Rosecrans was incorrectly informed of a gap in the Union line. When he ordered a shift of troops to cover it, an actual gap opened and Longstreet's troops poured through, devastating the Union center and right flank.

One third of the Union Army, including Rosecrans himself, fled the field and began its retreat to Chattanooga. Gen. George H. Thomas on the Union left wing created a defensive position on Snodgrass Hill that protected the Union retreat that was also supported by the Lightning Brigade of Col. Wilder. Although Confederates pressed to within a few feet of the Union defense line, the Northerners held, earning Thomas the nickname "The Rock of Chickamauga," saving the army from total destruction.

Rosecrans' army reached Chattanooga after darkness fell and formed a three-mile-long defensive line around the city, taking advantage of Confederate works still in place. Bragg soon occupied the surrounding heights around the city and positioned troops on the Tennessee River that flowed north, placing the Union Army under siege, unable to leave Chattanooga. Its major supply line was now blocked. The army would remain trapped until November when relief forces under the new command of Gen. Ulysses S. Grant freed it.

The Battle of Chickamauga created the largest number of casualties in the Western Theater and second largest of the entire Civil War, reaching nearly 35,000, second only to Gettysburg. The Union Army suffered more than 16,000 in losses (over 1,600 killed; 10,000 wounded and 4,700 captured or missing); the Confederates' losses exceeded 18,500 (2,300 killed; 15,000 wounded and 1,500 captured or missing), and ten of the senior generals of Bragg's Army of Tennessee were killed or wounded. One of the Confederate generals, John Bell Hood, lost one of his legs to amputation, but would still become a leading general in the Atlanta Campaign.

Siege of Chattanooga, Tennessee
September 20-October 29, 1863

After the Battle of Chickamauga, Union Gen. Williams Rosecrans and his Army of the Cumberland were trapped inside Chattanooga on September 20, 1863, after being defeated by the Confederates under Gen. Braxton Bragg at Chickamauga. As the Union Army retreated into the city, Bragg occupied the heights above the city on Lookout Mountain and Missionary Ridge and placed cavalry on the Tennessee River that flowed north. Chattanooga and the Union Army of the Cumberland were now under siege, cut off from the supply line of food, ammunition and provisions for the soldiers.

As news of the disaster reached President Lincoln, Secretary of War Edwin Stanton lost no time in generating a response to the crisis. Reinforcements would immediately be sent from Washington to Bridgeport, Alabama, thirty miles west of Chattanooga. Additional reinforcements would soon arrive from the Union Army of the Tennessee, now at Vicksburg.

Stanton personally took charge of making arrangements to transfer more than 20,000 troops from the Army of the Potomac by rail and steamboat from Washington.

Enlisting the support of railroad executives, a route was selected that ensured every available train needed to complete the mission was in place and of the proper gauge. The 1200-mile route took the army west to Columbus, Ohio, and Indianapolis, Indiana; then south to Louisville, Kentucky, and Nashville, Tennessee; and from there, to reach Bridgeport, Alabama. On September 25, the first train with a contingent of 23,000 men and one thousand horses left Washington under the command of Gen. Joseph "Fighting Joe" Hooker. The first arrival of troops was achieved in twelve days.

In the meantime, ongoing communications with Rosecrans convinced Lincoln that he needed a new commander for the besieged army. He commented privately to his secretary John Hay that Rosecrans seemed "... *confused and acting like a duck hit on the head, ever since Chickamauga."*

On October 3, Gen. Ulysses S. Grant received orders to travel to Louisville, Kentucky, to be met by someone from the War Department. Grant was currently in New Orleans where he had been conferring with Gen. Nathaniel P. Banks for a planned assault on Mobile, Alabama, but he had received a severe injury when his horse fell on him as it shied away from a locomotive. Although still lame, Grant departed at once, first by boat to Cairo, Missouri, and then by train to Indianapolis.

As his train was leaving Indianapolis for Louisville, it was temporarily halted so that Secretary of War Edwin Stanton could board, the first time he and Grant had ever met. On October 18, Grant was awarded command of the newly created Military Division of the Mississippi, which included the Armies of Ohio, Cumberland and Tennessee. Grant selected Gen. George H. Thomas, the "Rock of Chickamauga," to head the Army of the Cumberland, removing Rosecrans from command.

When Grant telegraphed the newly promoted Thomas that "... *he must hold Chattanooga at all hazards,"* he received an immediate reply from Thomas, *"We will hold the town till we starve; our wagons are hauling rations from Bridgeport."* A Union retreat would result in the annihilation of the army itself, the loss of an important strategic position and all its artillery. Additional reinforcements of 17,000 men were underway from Tennessee under the command of Gen. William T. Sherman, with forward elements departing by train on October 11. Leading forces from the Army of the Potomac under Gen. Hooker were already arriving at Bridgeport.

Grant immediately left Secretary Stanton for Chattanooga that took him by rail to Bridgeport and then by horse on a circuitous route for the final sixty miles, following the original federal supply line to Chattanooga (See Fig. 33). The treacherous rain-soaked mountain road through Jasper and Waldron's Ridge was littered with carcasses of thousands of dead mules and horses. A large wagon train of food, ammunition and medical supplies for the relief of Union troops at Chattanooga had been intercepted and burned by Confederate cavalry on October 1. Hundreds of mules had been slaughtered. Grant, still on crutches from his injury, had to be carried by hand over places too unsafe to cross on horseback. They arrived October 23.

VI. THE THIRD YEAR: 1863

UNION ENGINEER REPLACES VITAL SUPPLY LINE

With the Army of the Cumberland under siege at Chattanooga, Gen. Ulysses S. Grant was named commander of all the armies of Ohio, Cumberland and Tennessee in October 1863. At the same time, 17,000 men of the Army of the Tennessee were underway from Vicksburg, under the command of Gen. William T. Sherman, to join forces with Grant at Chattanooga. When Sherman's army reached Athens, Alabama, intersecting the Decatur & Nashville Railroad, the essential north-south artery that provided supplies for the Union army at Chattanooga, Grant ordered Gen. Grenville M. Dodge to be separated from Sherman's main army with a division of about 8,000 men, to repair the railroad all the way north to Nashville. Gen. Dodge, a civil engineer, had acquired considerable experience working for railroad companies before the war.

As Dodge's command followed a path of previous battles, his troops encountered destroyed railroads, bridges and roads and large trees cut down to slow a pursuing army's progress. The railroad passed over a broken country, cut up with innumerable streams, many of considerable width, with some valleys far below the railroad. Bridges and railroad track had been destroyed; damaged cars and locomotives not carried off had to be repaired.

Dodge's primary resource was his men, using axes, picks and spades and their ability to create the needed tools for their work. Soldiers were assigned to protect the workmen from small groups of hostile Southerners; others collected food, forage and steel from the surrounding country. Millers were detailed from the ranks to create flour mills for making bread. Blacksmiths from the ranks created shops that moved with the army, making the needed tools and repairs from the collected iron and steel. Axe men cut timber for bridges and for fuel as locomotives became operational. Car builders were tasked to repair locomotives and cars that could be salvaged. All aspects of railroad building were going on at once, with all the resources provided by the command itself. One hundred eighty-two bridges were rebuilt, many of them over deep and wide chasms. Repaired track covered one hundred two miles. Gen. Dodge finished the work assigned him within 40 days.

from the Personal Memoirs of Ulysses S. Grant, 1885

With the vital supply line for the Union armies in jeopardy, Grant also made special orders for Gen. Grenville M. Dodge to be separated from Sherman's army to repair the Decatur & Nashville Railroad north of Athens, Alabama, to secure supplies for the army to Bridgeport. Although some supplies for Chattanooga were still slipping through the Confederate siege line, one soldier reported in late October that there was a shortage of hardtack and meat. "*We are now living on sweet potatoes,*" he wrote in his journal.

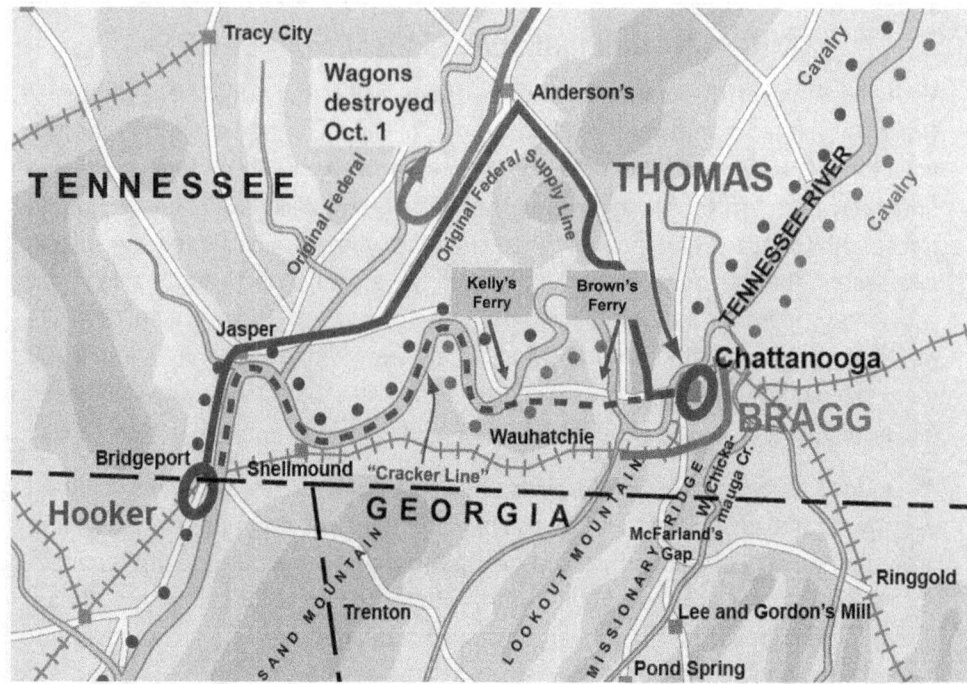

Fig. 33: Creation of the Union "Cracker Line" brought rations and forage to besieged troops under Gen. Thomas at Chattanooga, Tennessee, and eliminated the 60-mile wagon supply line that was frequently attacked by Confederates under Gen. Bragg.

Source: *Creative Commons Attribution 3.0 License Map by Hal Jespersen, www. cwmaps.com.*

"Cracker Line" Breaks the Siege
October 27-29, 1863

The besieged army at Chattanooga was getting short on food by the time Grant arrived with rations now reduced to four crackers of hardtack and four ounces of pork every three days, a fourth of the standard allotment. One Ohio soldier wrote, *"The chief topic of conversation around the diminutive camp fires was concerning something to eat. Every conversation opened and ended about eating. A hungry stomach is a troublesome companion, and acts as a constant reminder that something is wanting."*

Soldiers generally despised the tasteless hardtack, small hard crackers made from flour, yeast, water and salt, which were nearly inedible unless soaked in soup or water or friend in pork fat. Renamed by the soldiers as "tooth-dullers," they were nevertheless a standard part of a soldier's rations. The "Cracker Line" that supplied food for the besieged army, although still operational, had been severely attacked by the Confederates and needed to be strengthened and restore supplies to full rations.

Steamers could transport supplies on the Tennessee River from Bridgeport to Kelly's Ferry, but the river between Kelly's Ferry and Brown's Ferry passed through a narrow gorge that generated rapids and currents too powerful for steamers to negotiate (See Fig. 33). An overland road between Kelly's Ferry and Brown's Ferry would support wagons, but both ferries were still controlled by the Confederates. With reinforcements from the Army of the Potomac that had recently arrived under Gen. Joseph Hooker, animals and wagons would be available to transport supplies on the overland portion once the road was secured from the Confederates.

As soon as Chattanooga had been placed under siege, Gen. Rosecrans, with the support of his Chief Engineer William F. ("Baldy") Smith, had developed a plan for Union forces to capture both ferry stations and open a secure supply line from Bridgeport. When Grant arrived, he immediately supported the plan and placed Smith in command of the operation. Smith had created a sawmill in besieged Chattanooga and accumulated a number of pontoons and enough roadway planks for two bridges using salvaged materials and logs that were rafted in from the river.

At three o'clock in the morning on October 27, about 1,800 men under Union Gen. William B. Hazen left Chattanooga on fifty-two pontoons, to float on a big loop of the Tennessee River in the foggy and moonless pre-dawn hours, drifting unseen past Confederate pickets on Lookout Mountain. Reaching Brown's Ferry crossing, they disembarked and quickly overcame the surprised Southern guards and seized the high ground to hold their position.

A second contingent of about 2,000 men marched along the river out of sight from Lookout Mountain, taking with them all the material needed for laying a pontoon bridge. The two Union forces joined at Brown's Ferry and quickly laid the pontoon bridge hidden from Confederate view by several spurs of hills between them and Lookout Mountain. Brown's Ferry now had a bridge for the Cracker Line.

At the same time, Gen. Hooker from the Army of the Potomac left Bridgeport to advance through Lookout Valley and arrived at Wauhatchie unopposed on the afternoon of October 28. Part of Hooker's forces moved on to meet Hazen at Brown's Ferry and the remaining troops captured the Confederate pickets on the river at Kelly's Ferry. Union forces could now control access for steamers to provide supplies to Kelly's Ferry and open a supply line to Brown's Ferry and Chattanooga. A counterattack at midnight two days later on October 29 by Confederate Gen. James Longstreet in the Battle of Wauhatchie failed to remove the Northerners. The next day, the first steamboats arrived at Kelly's Ferry from Bridgeport with 40,000 rations and tons of animal forage. The Cracker Line was open.

Grant writes about the effect of an operational supply line for the men in his *Personal Memoirs*. *"I had telegraphed back to Nashville for a good supply of vegetables and small rations (coffee, sugar, salt and rice) and within a week, troops were receiving full rations… The men were soon reclothed and also well fed; an abundance of ammunition was brought up, and cheerfulness prevailed not before enjoyed in many weeks."*

> **SOUTHERN SOLDIERS SALUTE GENERAL GRANT**
>
> After the Union supply line was opened, Grant made a personal inspection of the picket sentries along Chattanooga Creek which separated the two armies by only a short distance. The guards of both armies drew their water from the same stream. As Grant came up to the camp, riding alone, the picket guard called out, "Turn out the guard for the commanding general." As Grant writes in his Personal Memoirs, "I said, 'Never mind the guard,' and they were dismissed and went back to their tents. About equally distant from the creek were the guards of the Confederate pickets. The sentinel on their post called out in like manner, 'Turn out the guard for the commanding general,' and, I believe, added, 'General Grant.' Their line in a moment front-faced to the north, facing me, and gave a salute, which I returned." Grant then rode away.
>
> *Personal Memoirs, Ulysses S. Grant, 1885*

With the Union Army no longer besieged and receiving food and supplies, Confederate Gen. Braxton Bragg needed a new strategy. But his poor leadership skills and deteriorating relationship with his senior generals had brought them to the point of sending a petition to President Jefferson Davis demanding Bragg's removal, known as the "Revolt of the Generals."

President Davis had to personally visit the headquarters and conduct a hearing where twelve of Bragg's senior generals complained about their commander, saying he was unfit for command. Longstreet expected Bragg to be removed and that he would be placed in command of the army. But Davis decided to retain Bragg and removed three of his lieutenants. Because Union Gen. Ambrose Burnside and the Army of the Ohio still occupied Knoxville and posed a potential threat if his army joined Grant at Chattanooga, Bragg ordered Longstreet to head north to Knoxville on November 4 with about 11-13,000 troops, including cavalry, which also removed Longstreet from his command, who had frequently quarreled with Bragg.

Although Longstreet did engage with Burnside in three minor battles as the Confederates advanced to Knoxville, the Union Army was able to withdraw safely into fortifications surrounding the city. But with Longstreet now controlling the supply line into Knoxville, President Lincoln was concerned that Burnside's troops were now under siege. But Burnside assured Grant that he had sufficient supplies to hold off the Confederates as long as his ammunition lasted.

VI. THE THIRD YEAR: 1863

> **CIVIL WAR SOLDIER RATIONS**
>
> Basic food rations for a three-day supply for the Civil War soldier included bread (known as hardtack, 12-16 oz.) or cornmeal (20 oz.), fresh or salt beef (20 oz.) or pork or bacon (12 oz.). Supplements to this basic ration included beans or peas, rice or hominy, desiccated vegetables, dried fruit, coffee, tea, sugar, candles, soap, molasses and coffee. Hardtack consisted of baked biscuits or crackers about three inches by three inches in size and a half inch thick, made from a mixture of flour, yeast, water and salt. Four to five crackers of hardtack constituted a soldier's daily ration of hard bread. When aged for several weeks or months, they were hard as a rock, hence the name, "hardtack." Some reports claimed they were "hard enough to stop a bullet." When soaked in coffee, soup or water, or fried in pork or bacon fat, to make "skilly-galee," the crackers could be made edible
>
> For a besieged army, such as at Vicksburg or Chattanooga, the ration would be reduced and reduced again, to as little as one cracker per day. If fresh meat was not available, salt beef or salt pork was substituted. Beans were dried and soaked or even cooked overnight if possible. While the South produced plenty of food at the beginning of the war to feed the Confederate soldiers, the logistics of getting it to the men were often difficult due to blockades and lack of transportation. But as the war continued and food became scarce, the Southern soldiers would descend hungrily on captured Union supplies. Cornmeal was frequently substituted for flour in the South and chicory root for coffee. The peanut, widely available in the Southern climate, was also an important source of food for the Confederate soldier.
>
> Coffee was the most important part of the soldier's diet: it got him up in the morning and held him together during battle. Union Gen. Benjamin Butler planned his attacks around when his men were wired with their coffee and they were ordered to carry it with them in their canteens. Northern soldiers got thirty-six pounds of coffee per year. The Confederates invented a variety of makeshift coffees to make up for their shortages. Southern soldiers traded tobacco for coffee from the Union men if they had the opportunity. One Union soldier wrote in his diary. *"We are reduced to quarter rations and no coffee. Nobody can soldier without coffee."*

Battle of Orchard Knob, Chattanooga, Tennessee
November 23, 1863

Gen. William T. Sherman arrived at Chattanooga at the head of the Army of the Tennessee the night of November 14. More units continued to arrive over the next ten days. Gen. Ulysses S. Grant planned an attack on Confederate Gen. Braxton Bragg's army for November 24. He would use Hooker's forces on the Union right to move onto Lookout Mountain and Bragg's left flank, while Sherman would attack Missionary

Ridge on Bragg's right. Gen. Thomas, heading the Army of the Cumberland, would support Sherman and hold the center.

Gen. Bragg, anticipating that Sherman's Army of the Tennessee was moving toward Knoxville, ordered another 11,000 Confederates to head north on November 23 to aid Longstreet against Burnside, seriously depleting his army. The decision would prove fatal for the Confederates. This move prompted Grant to begin his attack a day early. Thomas would extend the Union defensive perimeter around Chattanooga by taking a small hill about one hundred feet high known as Orchard Knob (See Fig. 34), located about a mile away from the Union entrenchments, halfway between the city and the base of Missionary Ridge.

This area was in full view of the Confederates on Lookout Mountain and Missionary Ridge and provided Thomas with an opportunity to show a display of force. All 14,000 soldiers presented in parade ground alignment, as if in review. With the signal to attack, the Union Army moved out at a double-quick pace directly across the field. The Southern defenders only had time for a single volley before being overwhelmed. A new Union line was established a full mile in advance of the morning's location and Grant quickly set up new headquarters at Orchard Knob. Bragg hastily recalled the units sent to Knoxville that were still within a day's march, but they were unable to return rapidly enough to participate in the coming battles.

Battle Above the Clouds, Chattanooga, Tennessee
November 24, 1863

Lookout Mountain, eighteen hundred feet high, has three sides of nearly vertical rock walls about thirty feet high that protect the summit. It is known for a particular weather phenomenon in which a layer of fog completely surrounds the base and then rises to shroud the entire mountain. Gen. Joseph Hooker launched his 10,000-man force of the Army of the Potomac against the mountain on the left side the morning of November 24. Heavy fog obscured much of the fighting but the sounds of artillery and musketry were clearly audible at Grant's headquarters on Orchard Knob.

Hooker's troops steadily gained ground throughout the day against the badly outnumbered Southerners and by late afternoon the Battle Above the Clouds was over and the Confederates were withdrawing to Missionary Ridge. The next day, Hooker was blocked for several hours by a burned-out bridge over Chickamauga Creek which caused a delay in his planned arrival at Rossville Gap that was to support Gen. Thomas in the center field.

Battle for Missionary Ridge, Chattanooga, Tennessee
November 25, 1863

Gen. Sherman, heading up the Western Army of the Tennessee, launched his attack on Missionary Ridge by successfully crossing the Tennessee River and moving up the slope that he expected would take him to the north end of the Ridge. But the slope was actually a discrete rise known as Billy Goat Hill that was separated from the Ridge by a deep chasm. Crossing the chasm and continuing the next day, Sherman's troops launched several assaults against well entrenched Confederates on Tunnel Hill but could not break the line that was steadily reinforced from Bragg's center and left flanks.

Grant writes in his *Personal Memoirs*, *"From the position I occupied* (on Orchard Knob), *I could see column after column of Bragg's forces moving against Sherman. Every Confederate gun that could be brought to bear upon the Union forces was concentrated upon him."* The expected diversion on Bragg's left flank from Hooker did not occur at the time expected, as he had been delayed at the burned bridge at Chickamauga Creek, which had to be rebuilt before the men and wagons could cross.

Grand Union Charge, Chattanooga, Tennessee
November 25, 1863

To relieve the pressure on Sherman, Grant ordered Thomas to move the Army of the Cumberland forward in center field and seize the first line of the Southern rifle pits and await further orders. But when the assault began, Union troops moved so rapidly forward that they soon merged with Southern forces in the first line of rifle pits.

As the Confederates fled up the steep slopes, Union troops continued to closely pursue them, shouting "Chickamauga! Chickamauga!" Confederate artillery could not fire without hitting their own men. Because Grant had not given the order to proceed up the mountain, he was initially dismayed as the battle proceeded, but as Union forces continued to advance and Confederate lines began to fall, Grant gave orders to go ahead and take the ridge if possible. As the Union charge reached the crest, the Confederates were overwhelmed, precipitating an uncontrolled panic that quickly developed into a rout of the Southern army.

Grant writes, *"The retreat of the enemy along most of his line was precipitate and the panic so great that Bragg and his officers lost all control over their men. Many men were captured and thousands threw away their arms in their flight."*

During the night of November 25, Gen. Braxton Bragg ordered the army to withdraw, first to Chickamauga, and then the next day to Dalton, Georgia, forty miles to the south. Bragg soon resigned as commander of the Confederate Army of Tennessee and was replaced by Gen. Joseph E. Johnston on December 27. Johnston would soon face Gen. William T. Sherman, commanding the Union Army's Atlanta Campaign into Georgia. Bragg was then transferred to serve as advisor to President Davis until October 1864 when he was given command of the Confederate Department of North Carolina and Virginia.

With Chattanooga now securely in Union control, Grant turned his attention to Knoxville and the relief of Burnside. Grant had been receiving daily messages from Lincoln to the effect, *"… Remember Burnside."* With news of the success of defeating

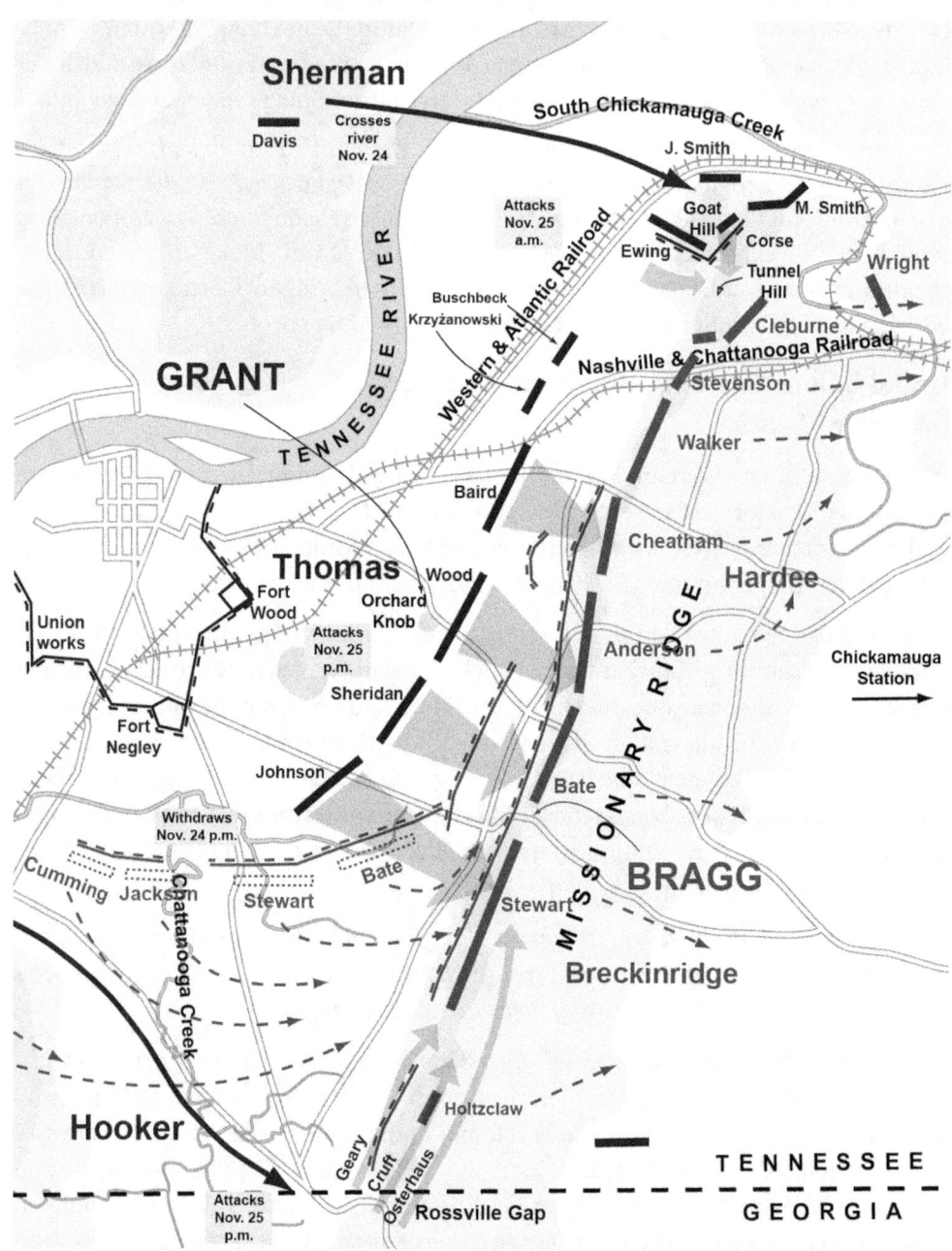

Fig. 34: Union Army under Generals Grant and Thomas made a grand charge up the slopes of Missionary Ridge to attack Confederates under Gen. Bragg during the Battle of Chattanooga on Nov. 25, 1863, which routed the Southerners who fled the battlefield and withdrew to Georgia.

Source: *Creative Commons Attribution 3.0 License Map by Hal Jespersen, www. cwmaps.com.*

Bragg and freeing the Union army from its siege, Lincoln wrote, "*Well done. Many thanks to all. Don't forget Burnside.*" The anxiety about Burnside's situation had placed all in a great state of apprehension, so without delay, Grant sent Sherman with 25,000 men to arrive at Knoxville before Burnside's supplies and ammunition were exhausted.

> **GRANT'S REFLECTIONS ON THE BATTLE OF CHATTANOOGA**
>
> *"The victory at Chattanooga was won against great odds, considering the advantage the enemy had of position, and was accomplished more easily than was expected by reason of Bragg's making several grave mistakes: first, in sending away his ablest corps commander (Longstreet) with over twenty thousand troops; second, in sending away a division of troops on the eve of battle; third, in placing so much of a force on the plain in front of his impregnable position.*
>
> *"I have never been able to see the wisdom of Bragg's move to send Longstreet and his force to Knoxville. His decision to reduce his own force by more than one-third and deprive himself of the ablest general of his command cannot be accounted for....If he should capture Chattanooga, Knoxville would have fallen into his hands...and it would have been a victory for us to have got our army away safely. But it was a manifest greater victory to drive away the besieging army; and a still greater one to defeat that army in his chosen ground and nearly annihilate it."*
>
> from *Grant's Personal Memoirs, 1885*

When Confederate Gen. Longstreet became aware that Bragg had been defeated at the Battle of Chattanooga and that Sherman would soon arrive with a Union Army, Longstreet withdrew from Knoxville on December 4 and moved to northeast Tennessee and after a minor battle at Bean's Station he settled into winter quarters at Russellville, Tennessee. Longstreet's troops would rejoin Lee's Army of Northern Virginia in the spring. After the earlier success of Chickamauga, Confederate enthusiasm had been dashed. Union forces now controlled Tennessee, including Chattanooga, and the base for Sherman's Atlanta Campaign, "Gateway to the Lower South," was firmly established.

Gen. Rosecrans, who lost command of the Army of the Cumberland, left for Cincinnati to await further instructions. Leading the Department of Missouri in 1864, he played a minor role in defeating raids from the Missouri secessionists and remained with the army until his retirement.

BATTLES IN THE DEEP SOUTH & GULF COAST

Battles of Charleston Harbor, South Carolina
April-September, 1863

A Naval attack to recapture Fort Sumter in Charleston Harbor, South Carolina, where the Civil War's first shots were fired, was attempted in April 1863, but the attack failed from a combination of coordinated Confederate artillery, challenging weather conditions and underwater mines. A second assault to capture the harbor occurred over several months between July and September 1863 under the command of Gen. Quincy A. Gillmore.

Fort Wagner (or Cummings Point Battery), located on the northern tip of Morris Island, controlled the entrance to Charleston Harbor and protected Fort Sumter (See Fig. 5). If Union forces could control it and nearby Fort Gregg, the port of Charleston would be closed and deny the Confederacy a vital lifeline. Fort Wagner was a powerful beachhead fortification with earthen parapets thirty feet high and a bombproof roof. The fort could shelter nearly one thousand of the 1,800-man garrison.

On July 10, 1863, Union forces launched a successful amphibious landing on the southern end of Morris Island and routed Confederate troops back to the stronghold of Fort Wagner. Union troops, now controlling the island, made an assault on the fort itself at dawn in thick fog the next day, July 11. The 7th Connecticut Infantry successfully overran the rifle pits, but was then repulsed by the large number of Confederate troops manning the fort.

Bringing in a fleet of heavy siege guns, which included the formidable *USS Ironsides*, one of the heaviest cannonades in the federal fleet, bombardment on the fort began the morning of July 18 which continued for eight hours, but caused little damage to the fort's strong defenses. At dusk, a second frontal infantry assault was led by the 54th Massachusetts Volunteer Infantry of the United States Colored Troops (USCT), a military unit made up of all Blacks, except for its commanding white officers, commanded by Col. Robert Shaw. The 1,000-man Black regiment had been recruited with newspaper advertisements and recruiting posters in both Northern and Southern states to demonstrate the fighting ability of soldiers of Black ancestry.

When the 54th came within range of Confederate cannon and small arms fire, whole ranks fell and Col. Shaw was killed leading the assault. Although some of the men reached the fort's parapet, scaled it and entered the fort, they were beaten back in fierce hand-to-hand combat. Thirty were killed in action and twenty-four died later from their wounds. The assault was called off with fifty percent losses for the regiment. Only 315 of the 600-man assault troops in the 54th were still standing after the battle. Lewis Henry Douglass, son of the famous orator, Frederick Douglass, was wounded in the battle but survived. Sergeant William Harvey Carney was the first Black soldier to receive the Medal of Honor years later on May 9, 1900, for his actions. When the color guard was killed, Carney carried the flag forward to the parapet and when the men had to retreat, he brought the flag back to safety despite being seriously wounded. He was quoted as saying, *"Boys, I only did my duty; the old flag never touched the ground!"*

Although the assault was defeated, the demonstration of courage and bravery by the men of the 54th enhanced respect for the battle worthiness of Black soldiers and their recruitment into the military sharply increased. Their display of courage also helped persuade public opinion to end slavery and free the slaves. The portrayal of the 54th Infantry in the battle was reenacted in the 1989 movie *Glory*.

After the failed infantry assault, Gen. Gillmore turned to siege guns and gunboats to pound the besieged Fort Wagner and the bombardment continued for weeks. A land assault on the fort August 25 captured Confederate infantry and successfully overran the rifle pits, turning them into a new siege line. A new intense bombing on September 5 killed 100 of the defenders and the Confederates abandoned Fort Wagner September 6-7.

When an Army-Navy manned assault on Fort Sumter on September 8-9 miserably failed, the Navy brought in rifled guns to bombard the fort for the next fifteen months without letup. Rifled guns could deliver heavier shot with higher velocity and turned masonry into rubble. Fort Sumter became a ruinous mass. But the fort and the city of Charleston remained in Confederate hands until 1865 when Union Gen. William T. Sherman advanced through South Carolina. Confederates finally abandoned the fort on February 17, 1865, and evacuated the city the next day.

Bayou Teche Campaign, Gulf Coast
October-November 1863

In March and April 1863, Gen. Nathaniel P. Banks, Department of the Gulf, operating in southern Louisiana near New Orleans, sent troops up Bayou Teche, a coastal region west of Baton Rouge near New Iberia and successfully captured Fort Burton at Butte La Rose.

Responding to French efforts to install the Austrian archduke Maximilian as Emperor of Mexico, a second Union Bayou Teche initiative was attempted in October 1863. Union troops moved westward, hoping to reach the Sabine River and establish a land route to Texas. But the effort failed, mostly because of strong Confederate resistance, from the leadership of Gen. Richard Taylor, son of former U.S. President Zachary Taylor.

A separate effort on the Texas Gulf coast was the Union capture in November of Mustang Island near Corpus Christi, Texas, and Fort Esperanza on the eastern shore of Matagorda Island, located north of Corpus. But in the spring of 1864, Union troops withdrew from Matagorda Bay and Fort Esperanza was re-occupied by the Confederates until the end of the war.

VIEWS FROM THE PUBLIC FOR THE YEAR 1863

About shortages in the South...

The Union Navy blockade severely impacted the ability of the South to import goods that were not readily produced in the southern states, such as nails, needles and medicines, which affected the Confederate soldier as much as the private citizen. Southern newspapers were also feeling the pinch as they continued to distribute news of the war to their subscribers. It became more and more challenging to generate a publication with the growing shortages of paper, ink and glue. In addition, chemicals, type and replacement parts for the machinery that had previously been supplied by the North were no longer available. Poor transportation capabilities also limited distribution of the printed page. Journalists relied on telegraphs and railroads to get their stories out, but battles frequently eliminated those means of communication, depriving Southerners of the latest news.

Income supporting the newspapers dwindled as the war went on. Advertising in newspapers was reduced as local businesses either disappeared or could not afford it. In some cases, the number of ads was reduced to provide enough space for news about the war and lists of dead or wounded soldiers. As costs of production climbed and runaway inflation increased the cost of everything, fewer readers could afford to pay for a subscription, which further reduced funds for the publisher. Most shops had to reduce their page size, many only half the size of two years previously, or shut down altogether or merge with other newspapers. After two years into the war, the number of newspapers in Virginia had shrunk from over one hundred in 1861 to less than twenty by the end of 1863.

About food in Richmond...

Food was becoming increasingly difficult to find for the Southerners. In addition to scarcities of salt, sugar and coffee, the loss of manpower had a serious impact on food production in the South. Fewer workers were now available to work the farms due to the enlistment of soldiers in the armies and a steady decrease in the number of slaves as they escaped to Union lines. Additionally, battles in Virginia had destroyed crops, eliminated harvests and affected much of the needed farmland. Loss of value of the Confederate paper currency greatly increased inflation. Food prices skyrocketed from about $7 per month for food in 1861 to $68 in 1863.

Enterprising smugglers exchanged cotton to Northern businesses for food and other supplies, but their impact was limited and black-market prices prevailed. The *Confederate Receipt Book,* the only cookbook printed in the South during the war, contained recipes for artificial oysters, apple pie without apples and substitutes for coffee and cream.

In Richmond, Virginia, a massive shortage of food resulted in a Bread Riot on April 2, 1863. The Union Blockade was effectively preventing food arriving from foreign sources and the Confederate armies had priority on food from local growers. That spring, a massive snowstorm in the local countryside prevented the shipment of homegrown food that normally arrived in Richmond. Facing a food crisis, a group of about one hundred working-class women, armed with axes, knives and other weapons, marched to the state governor's office demanding action. Finding no support there, the women turned to the government food storehouses, shouting *Bread! Bread!*

Soon the crowd swelled to hundreds of rioters who broke into the storehouses and local businesses, grabbing whatever they could find. The riot was only quelled when President Jefferson Davis himself climbed onto a wagon and threatened to have Confederate troops, called out to support the public guard and shoot into the crowd. After a few tense moments, the crowd dispersed. City leaders attempted to keep news of the riot silenced, but the *New York Tribune* published it as a front-page story on April 8.

The Richmond newspapers condemned the Bread Riot as "*… a group of thieves, prostitutes and crones.*" The *Staunton (Virginia) Vindicator* called the event as "*villainous, wholesale robbery.*" Those who complained of sacrifices and shortages during the war were described as dissenters and "croakers," who were "dishonest and unpatriotic" to the Confederate cause. The *Staunton Spectator* alleged that provocateurs from the Noth had organized the hunger protest.

About the Northern economy…

The Northern economy, on the other hand, was minimally affected and many businesses made immense profits. Industries supporting the war effort through government contracts became extremely profitable. Greed encouraged dishonest contractors to resort to cheating and increase their profits. Blankets made from fibers reclaimed from rags fell apart in the rain. Spoiled meat was sold as fresh. Shoes made from heavy brown cardboard dissolved when soldiers marched in water or mud. Uniforms were poorly made from reprocessed "shoddy" wool. One provider produced pants without pockets or buttons. The *New York Herald* commented on the sad state of affairs that reflected the worst aspects of the American character: "*The individual who makes the most money—no matter how—and spends the most—no matter for what—is considered the greatest man… The world has seen its iron age, its silver age, its golden age, and its brazen age. This is the age of shoddy.*"

Soldiers, who could afford it, relied on "sutlers," private peddlers who had licenses to travel with the army, to provide alternatives to inferior clothing or spoiled food that came to the soldiers from government providers. Sutlers not only provided food and clothing items, but also offered tobacco, cigars, snuff and matches. Corruption existed at the highest levels and bribes were often used to obtain approval for a government contract.

About the Emancipation Proclamation...

When Lincoln implemented the Emancipation Proclamation on Jan 1, 1863, it freed slaves in all states that were in rebellion (not in the Border States). *"Men squealed, women fainted, dogs barked, white and colored people shook hands, songs were sung, and by this time cannons began to fire at the navy yard... Great processions of colored and white men marched to and fro and passed in front of the White House... The President came to the window... and thousands told him, if he would come out of that palace, they would hug him to death."* —as quoted in *Voices from the Civil War*. Many Blacks welcomed the opportunity to enlist in the Union Army and carry on the fight to defeat the Confederates. White soldiers in the Union, in general, were neither abolitionists nor fighting to end slavery, but accepted the Proclamation if that was what it would take to maintain the Union and end the war.

But not all Northerners were pleased. Democrats complained that the Emancipation Proclamation would antagonize the South and prolong the war. The Salem, Indiana, *Democrat* vented a bitter and harsh criticism of the President. *"This is the day Abraham Lincoln is to proclaim all the negroes free in the rebellious States. Such an act is a violation of the Constitution, without warrant or force of law. We denounce and condemn the proclamation of the President in taking negroes as soldiers or marines, and allows them to command white soldiers is a damnable act of abolitionism, a disgrace to humanity and age in which we live."*

The *Vermont Journal* observed that not one of the Border States endorsed the President's Proclamation, pointing out that, *"What would slavery be worth in Missouri, Kentucky and Maryland if it is eliminated in the South?"* The editor noted that Missouri was beginning discussions to inaugurate a policy of gradual emancipation of slaves, and ended the column with the observation, *"It is a step wisely taken."*

But the performance of the United States Colored Troops at the Battle of Fort Wagner in Charleston Harbor and at Milliken's Bend during the Vicksburg Campaign had displayed such courage and bravery that it created a turning point in the attitudes of white soldiers and recruitments of Blacks into the Union armies increased.

As predicted, the South reacted to the Proclamation with scorn and denial. Confederate President Jefferson Davis had already denounced it as *"... the most execrable measure recorded in the history of guilty man."* The Confederacy was now determined to defeat the Union and preserve its slave-holding society; it was now a fight to the death.

About the Military Draft...

Facing a shortage of volunteers for the Union military, Congress passed the Enrollment Act in March 1863, also known as the Civil War Military Draft Act, the first national conscription law. The Act immediately affected the lives of any Northern family with men between the ages of 20 and 45, but a draftee could escape being enlisted by paying a $300 commutation fee and finding a substitute to go in his place. The sum represented a figure approximately equal to $6,000 (compared to today's currency) and was out of reach for the vast majority of eligible men and a popular song was rapidly generated with verses as follows:

> "We're coming, ancient Abraham, several hundred strong.
> We hadn't no 300 dollars and so we come along.
> We hadn't no rich parents to pony up the tin,
> So we went unto the provost and there were mustered in."

In some parts of the country, opposition to the draft was so intense it was dangerous for government agents to seek eligible men. Women who harbored deserters or draft dodgers, even if they were husbands, sweethearts or brothers, could also be prosecuted.

French and German immigrants in New York City, however, mostly expressed their support for the Union and its draft. The *New York Times* reported on April 1, 1863, of a large mass meeting of mostly German and French immigrants of about one thousand, who expressed their full support for the Union and their determination to stand by and support the Government in its efforts to maintain it. Many saw the secession by the South as an attempt by "Southern aristocrats" to destroy the American republic.

But a large community of Irish Americans in New York City were already angry about Lincoln's Emancipation Proclamation because they feared free Blacks would take jobs away from them. Feeding this anger, the Military Draft Act exempted free Blacks because they were not citizens. So, when draft officers in New York City called off the names of draftees on July 11, 1863, a race riot erupted over the next few days that smashed government buildings, attacked businesses that employed Blacks and burned homes of Blacks and abolitionists or sympathizers. Many Blacks were killed, some by lynching. The official death toll exceeded one hundred. The riot was finally quelled after five days by the New York State militia and federal troops, numbering several thousand that had been called from the Gettysburg battlefield which had just concluded.

Recruitment for Southern armies had also fallen off and the Confederate Conscription Act of 1863 revised the age of eligible draftees to any white male between the ages of 18 and 45. A Kentucky circular from Monticello, Wayne County, located on the border with Tennessee, was widely distributed.

> "The time has arrived when all able-bodied men between the ages of 18 and 45 must become soldiers. You must now either enter the Northern army, to fight with negroes for corrupt vandals, or the Southern army, to fight for our liberty, our honor, our homes, and all that ennobles man. True Kentuckians will be faithful to the South. Those who still cling to LINCOLN's despotic Administration, and wish to be conscripted to fight with negroes, must leave this county. This atmosphere must not be polluted by their presence."

Underneath the document was written: "*Whoever tears this down and is found out, the penalty is death!*"

About the Battle of Chancellorsville...

In the Eastern Theater, the Army of the Potomac, under its new general, "Fighting Joe" Hooker, suffered another disastrous defeat from Gen. Robert E. Lee in the Battle of Chancellorsville in early May 1863. The drastic Union losses prompted Lincoln to say, "My God! My God! What will the country say?" An Ohio soldier wrote after the battle, "We have fought one of the hardest battles of the war... I think we have been whipped."

The *Springfield (Massachusetts) Republican* carried a report on May 31, 1863, from a local Union officer who had been taken prisoner at Chancellorsville and recently exchanged. "We had men enough, well enough equipped, and well enough posted, to have devoured the ragged, imperfectly armed and equipped host of our enemies ... Their artillery horses are poor, starved frames of beasts, tied on to their carriages and caissons with odds and ends of rope and strips of rawhide. The men are ill-dressed, ill-equipped, and ill-provided, a set of ragamuffins that a man is ashamed to be seen among, even when he is a prisoner and can't help it. And yet they have beaten us fairly, beaten us all to pieces, beaten us so easily that we are objects of contempt even to their commonest private soldiers, with no shirts to hang out of the holes in their pantaloons, and cartridge boxes tied round their waists with strands of ropes. I say they beat us easily, for there hasn't been much of a fight up here on the banks of the Rappahannock... There was an awful noise, for I heard it. There was a tremendous amount of powder exploded, for I saw the smoke of it... but I cannot learn that there was, in any part of the field, very much real fighting. All we have to do is to make up our minds not to run before an equal number of the enemy, to keep cool and save our ammunition... and when the butternuts find we don't run away they will."

Southern opinion was joyful about Lee's success of the battle. A young brigadier general in Lee's army, wrote: "The vandal hordes of the Northern Tyrant are struck down with terror arising from their past experience. They have learned to their sorrow that this army is made up of veterans equal to those of the Old Guard of Napoleon."

Gen. Robert E. Lee, however, had a different opinion about the battle. As Union forces returned to Falmouth to occupy their original positions before the battle, Lee wrote, "At Chancellorsville we gained another victory; our people were wild with delight—I, on the contrary, was more depressed than after Fredericksburg; our loss was severe, and again we had gained not an inch of ground and the enemy could not be pursued."

About the Confederate's loss of Stonewall Jackson...

Southern newspapers, rejoicing about Lee's success in the Battle of Chancellorsville, were nevertheless greatly dismayed by the loss of their heroic Gen. Stonewall Jackson. The Raleigh, North Carolina, *Semi-Weekly Standard* wrote, "He was the foremost fighting man on the continent. In the last great conflict, it was his movement, breaking through and assailing the enemy in the rear, which led to victory. No man deserved in fuller measure... the confidence of the government, the army, and the people."

A similar observation of Stonewall Jackson was carried in the Northern *New York Times*, but noted that it was a heavy blow to the Confederacy. *"In the death of Stonewall Jackson, the rebels have unquestionably lost by far their greatest military leader… The traits of his personal character are nearly as familiar to the public as his military feats. He was a man of narrow mind, but of tremendous will and indomitable purpose; and he flung the great energy of his nature into all that he undertook. He was strictly moral and fanatically religious…. His death is a tremendous and irreparable loss to the secession cause, as no other rebel of like character has been developed during the war. He will figure in history as one of the ablest of modern military leaders…* (but) *it has brought him to an untimely grave."* Gen. Lee expressed the loss of Jackson as *"losing my right arm."*

About the Battle of Gettysburg from the North …

Lee's success at Chancellorsville prompted his invasion into Pennsylvania where his army met Union forces, now under Gen. George Meade, at Gettysburg. Gen. Hooker's political maneuverings and insubordinate behavior had led Lincoln to replace him with Gen. Meade three days before the battle. As the Union army moved north to stay abreast of the Southern invasion by Gen. Lee, people of Maryland and Pennsylvania welcomed Union troops with great enthusiasm. As the cavalry entered Taneytown, Maryland, the whole population turned out to receive them. On the other hand, Confederates were met by local residents with unfriendly scorn and disgust. This terrible war was their fault because of their devotion to slavery.

The Battle of Gettysburg, July 1-3, 1863, yielded a Northern victory at a terrible cost to both armies, with an estimated 23,000 casualties for the Union and 28,000 for the Confederates. The *New York Times* reported on July 4 that *"On the first day's battle, the rebels seem to have gained a temporary advantage—at the terrible battle of Thursday (July 2), our gallant army, in the words of Gen. Meade, repulsed the enemy at all points. And at the engagement of yesterday, after six hours' fighting, had failed to make any impression upon our position. The Army of the Potomac seems to be fighting with the greatest vigor, determination and dash. The rebel army, too, is fighting… It is now really a desperate matter with them, far away as they are from their base, from their homes."*

The *New York Herald's* headline on Independence Day proclaimed *"The Victory Undoubtedly Ours."* Northern reaction, at first exhilarated by the news, was soon disappointed that Lee's Army had escaped back to Virginia and the war would go on. Lincoln complained that *"Our army held the war in the hollow of their hand and they would not close it!"*

About the Battle of Gettysburg from the South …

Southern newspapers had to initially rely on Northern newspaper accounts for their reporting as they had lost contact with Lee's army prior to the Battle of Gettysburg. But versions of Union successes were ignored by the Southern press as they reported that the Union Army had suffered immense losses in the first two days of fighting. The

Richmond *Dispatch* concluded that Lee's army "... *has kept the whole Yankee force at bay two days.*"

It was several days after the end of the battle that news filtered in and the Richmond *Daily Virginian* reported that earlier reports had exaggerated the Union losses on the first two days of the battle. Further, that Lee had been only partially successful on July 3 and was forced to retreat to Hagerstown, Maryland, because of the difficulty in obtaining supplies. The *Dispatch* then printed that Gen. Lee abandoned the battle on July 4 only after Union troops had fled to impregnable positions on high ground behind the town and in a later issue referred to the Gettysburg Battle as a *"triumphant success"* and predicted that Lee would soon *"make a move on Washington."*

With the news that Lee had retreated into Maryland, the Richmond *Daily Whig* wrote, "*... Gen. Lee falls short of the dispatches published yesterday and will prove a grievous disappointment to the high wrought hopes of the public. Superadded to the calamity at Vicksburg, it casts a somber shadow over our affairs.*"

Once the actual outcome of the battle became widely known, prominent Southern newspapers vehemently blamed Gen. Jeb Stuart, Lee's head of his army's Cavalry, for the failure. They claimed that Stuart's long absence from Lee's army on a reconnaissance mission had failed to provide his commander with important intelligence that would have influenced the battle. In actual fact, Stuart had been carrying out Lee's orders that had been given several days earlier and circumstances had created a longer than expected mission before Stuart could reunite with the army. Nevertheless, Lee's officers were nearly all of the opinion that *"The failure to crush the Federal army in Pennsylvania in 1863, in the opinion of almost all of the officers of the Army of Northern Virginia, can be expressed in five words—the absence of the cavalry."* (Confederate Gen. Henry Heth).

About the Dead at Gettysburg...

The *Adams Sentinel*, Gettysburg, wrote on July 7, "*Terrible is the desolation of our homes, our fair farms and friendly firesides, the slaughter of thousands, and the mangling of tens of thousands of our fellow men, our friends, and many of them our own kindred, our fathers, our brothers, our husbands, our lovers, our sons. Terrible in the din, the dread, the dire destruction of war in its most appalling form. The enemy is terribly punished for his reckless villainy in thus attempting to make the North the future battle ground. One feature of this invasion has been peculiarly gratifying to every lover of the Union. Those who have been notorious sympathizers with the enemy, have been required to give tangible and practical evidence of their sympathy. They have been by great odds the heaviest sufferers. Truly there is a God in Heaven.*"

The overwhelming stench of death from dead soldiers and rotting carcasses of horses and mules in the sweltering heat of the July summer forced residents to carry peppermint oil or other aromatics with them as they faced each day and carried out the grim duty of burying the thousands of dead soldiers in their fields. Burial parties worked late into the night using lanterns and placed markers to identify the name of the deceased if the name could be found. In addition to the more than 7,000 dead in the field, an average of 50-100 died in the hospitals each day. In the twelve days following the battle, it was documented that nearly 4,000 Confederates were buried and more than 3,000 Union. But the trenches were shallow and a the Gettysburg National Cemetery was created for a permanent solution.

Over 15,000 spectators arrived to hear Lincoln's Gettysburg Address, delivered on November 19, 1863, to dedicate the cemetery. It would become an American icon of dedication to the sacrifices made by the soldiers who had fallen for the cause to preserve the Union. But public opinion at the time was sharply divided about Lincoln's speech. Lincoln, himself, declared that the speech he delivered in two to three minutes was a failure: *"It is a flat failure and the people are disappointed,"* he said to a companion after seeing the audience's reaction. In contrast, the Philadelphia Evening Bulletin said that those who read the President's few words... *"not many will do it without a moistening of the eye and a swelling of the heart."* But the *Chicago Times* was utterly ruthless: *"The cheeks of every American must tingle with shame as he reads the silly, flat, and dishwatery utterances."*

About the Vicksburg Campaign from the North...

Northern public opinion became impatient with Union efforts to build canals that could circumvent the great batteries of Vicksburg that protected the Mississippi River. Claims began to surface that Grant had succumbed to alcohol abuse and Lincoln received multiple demands that Grant be replaced, but Lincoln stood by him. He realized that Grant had the spirit to fight and even before he heard of the surrender of Vicksburg, Lincoln had said of his western commander: *"He doesn't worry and bother me. He isn't shrieking for reinforcements all the time. And if Grant only does one thing down there—why Grant is my man, and I am his, for the rest of the war."* Grant's persistence in overcoming multiple military and political setbacks to conquer the challenges presented by the Vicksburg fortress and the Mississippi River eventually yielded the surrender of the city.

News of the surrender of Vicksburg arrived in Washington on July 4th just hours after the President had received news of the Union's success at Gettysburg. The two Union victories marked a turning point in the war and brought a major boost in Northern public opinion. With the fall of Vicksburg, the Confederacy lost its connectivity with Louisiana, Arkansas and Texas, and the Mississippi River was free of Confederate interference to Union forces.

From the *New York Times* Vicksburg Correspondent on July 19, 1863, *"... Vicksburg, with its accumulation of forts, traverses, rifle pits and magazines; its guns, large and small; its "whistling dicks" and "whispering jimmys;" its shattered and roofless houses; its skeleton walls and prostrate chimneys; its barricaded streets, dirt, rubbish and filth, its starved and vermin devoured garrison—all are ours... Probably there never were so many hungry men gathered in one place before—and so hungry. Officers and men rushed towards our soldiers, earnestly imploring for food. Our boys immediately emptied their* well-filled haversacks to supply their present wants. The meat and bread thus dispensed were devoured with ravenous appetites, and then they called for more."

About the Vicksburg Campaign from the South...

After the Union Army successfully crossed the Mississippi south of Vicksburg and placed the city under siege, Southern newspapers turned to Confederate Gen. Joseph E. Johnston with his army in Jackson, Mississippi, to save Vicksburg from the Union. From *The Ledger*, Lancasterville, South Carolina, came news on June 3, 1863, of the Siege of Vicksburg. *"The reports from Vicksburg are still meager and somewhat uncertain, but rather more assuring than they were last week. General Johnston's official dispatch is encouraging, and is the latest received. The Yankee accounts differ materially from our own, but as they are some five days older than the date on Gen. Johnston's dispatch, they are not entitled to much credit. The fighting, no doubt, has been desperate and up to the 27th, our men held their own. Johnston is somewhere on this side, in rear of the enemy, and we still have much reason to hope that the General will yet be able to attack Grant in a way that will ensure his utter defeat and capture."*

The *Richmond Dispatch* followed the Siege of Vicksburg with a hopeful view, expressing confidence in Gen. Johnston, even after he had withdrawn in May from Jackson, Mississippi, surrendering the capital to the Union Army. Following the Confederates' defeat at Champion Hill, the *Dispatch* remained confident that *"... the presence of Gen. J. E. Johnston will infuse new confidence in our soldiers... and there is no danger of the fall, immediate or remote, of Vicksburg."* When news of the surrender of Vicksburg became known, the *Richmond Examiner* wrote, "It is the most unexpected announcement which has been made in this war... Vicksburg was impregnable by assault."

The *Richmond Daily Journal* bitterly wrote, "*Vicksburg fell on the 4th—and Joseph E. Johnston is a great General—to do nothing. The immediate pressure of public censure bears down upon General Johnston, who made no effort to relieve Vicksburg... He was getting ready to perform his favorite strategic movement, a masterly retreat.*"

About the Suffering in Vicksburg...

The siege of forty-seven days exacted a terrible toll on Vicksburg's citizens who lived in caves in the adjoining hills to protect them from the daily bombardment of shells that pounded the city. As food became increasingly scarce, mules, dogs and cats were consumed for meat. Even rats at the end were captured and cooked as "squirrel stew." Remains of rice, peas, cornmeal and flour were all that was left. Food was even more scarce for the soldiers who were pushed to the brink of starvation and suffered from scurvy.

Mary Ann Loughborough, wife of a Confederate officer, described some of her experience surviving the Siege of Vicksburg. *"I shall never forget my extreme fear during the night, and my utter hopelessness of ever seeing the morning light. Terror stricken,* we remained crouched in the cave, while shell after shell followed each other in quick succession. I endeavored by constant prayer to prepare myself for the sudden death I was almost certain awaited me. My heart stood still as we would hear the reports from the guns, and the rushing and fearful sound of the shell as it came toward us."

The *Daily Citizen,* Vicksburg, published final editions just days before the surrender on the backs of wallpaper, the plain side intended to stick to the wall, the only paper available. Each single sheet contained four columns. The final edition on July 4, 1863, had been altered by the conquering Union soldiers to claim: *"The banner of the Union floats over Vicksburg."*

About the Battles of Chattanooga and Chickamauga...

Union Gen. William Rosecrans successfully chased Confederate Gen. Braxton Bragg from Tullahoma, Tennessee, to Chattanooga in June and then proceeded to force the Confederates to withdraw from there into Chickamauga in early September. When Bragg abandoned Chattanooga, all news of the loss was censored by the military to the Southern newspapers. So, it was several days later that the Richmond *Daily Whig* learned from a Northern paper of the loss and wrote, *"Rosecrans' Army must be destroyed or driven out, else we fight to little purpose."*

The *Wilmington Daily Journal* wrote discouragingly, *"Falling back, which means abandoning the most defensible positions and sacrificing the richest section of the country, is so much the order of the day out West."* The editor then scathingly continued, *"Bragg is evidently no match for Rosecrans in whose hands he is an infant. But then General Bragg is in the good graces of the President... This tendency of the President to continue to sustain those whom he has once sustained, come what may, and at whatever cost, is working deadly harm in the Southwest. It is sacrificing our territory, disgusting our people and jeopardizing our cause."*

Although they both fought for the Confederacy, the opinion of Gen. Joseph E. Johnston about Bragg echoed the previous editor's comments when he wrote, *"I know Mr. Davis thinks he can do a great many things other men would hesitate to attempt. For instance, he tried to do what God failed to do. He tried to make a soldier of Braxton Bragg..."*

When Bragg defeated Rosecrans in the Battle of Chickamauga in September, forcing the Union army into a siege in Chattanooga, he received new praise from the Southern press. The Macon *Daily Telegraph* wrote: *"The encounter was one of the greatest battles of the war and perhaps the most decisive victory of the war."* The editor concluded with the hope that Bragg would follow up by pursuing and destroying Rosecrans' army.

At about the same time, the Union Army of the Ohio under Gen. Ambrose Burnside captured the city of Knoxville, Tennessee, without a fight. The *Chattanooga Rebel* wrote, *"Considerable apprehension was manifested at the reported advance of Burnside, with a column of 30,000 men, upon East Tennessee… We must urge our fellow-citizens of Tennessee, Alabama and Georgia, to be speedy if they would crush the advance of the enemy. We hope to catch Rosecrans. The fight has hardly begun. Before he is done with Bragg, he will have one of the bloodiest battles of the war."*

The besieged city of Chattanooga produced a defeated and demoralized Rosecrans that prompted Lincoln to put Gen. Ulysses S. Grant in charge of breaking the siege that confined the Union army to Chattanooga. Grant later led battles in November that defeated Bragg and the Union reclaimed Chattanooga, "Gateway to the Lower South." The subsequent withdrawal of the Confederates from Knoxville provided the Union with undisputed control of the entire state of Tennessee.

Southern enthusiasm was dashed with the second loss of Chattanooga, which placed the Union Army at Georgia's doorstep. It would become a vital Union supply base for the Atlanta Campaign of 1864 and an invasion of the Deep South that would be led by William T. Sherman.

About Raiders in Indiana…

In Salem, Indiana, an attack by Confederate raiders led by Gen. John Hunt Morgan plundered the town in July 1863, burning the railroad bridges and depot and destroying railroad cars and the telegraph. Morgan's intent was to arouse Confederate sympathies expressed in the "Copperhead" movement, which advocated a peaceful settlement to the war by giving the Confederacy its independence and right to slavery. The demanded ransom from Salem of $14,540 was paid by a number of citizens before the raiders departed to continue their invasion into Ohio and West Virginia.

But Morgan's raids, instead of encouraging Confederate commitment to the Southern cause, galvanized unifying loyalty for the Union. Numerous militias were formed to chase Morgan and encouraged recruitment into the Union Army. In early July, thirteen regiments and one battalion were organized within Indiana. One full company was raised at nearby Campbellsburg, Indiana, and mustered in as Company C of the 112th Regiment. In July and August, Washington County met the Union call for six months' men, who became Company G of the 117th Regiment.

VII. THE FOURTH YEAR: 1864

LINCOLN PROMOTED AND THEN DEMOTED NUMEROUS GENERALS DURING THE FIRST two and a half years of the war as he searched for military commanders that would carry the Civil War conflict to a Union conclusion. It was said that he changed his generals about as often as he changed his shirts.

Gen. Irvin McDowell was demoted after the Battle of the First Bull Run in 1861 and placed in a lesser position under George B. McClellan who created the well-trained, superbly equipped, and well-organized Army of the Potomac. McClellan soon replaced the aging Gen. Winfield Scott as General-in-Chief, but lacked the skills to be successful on the battlefields. Demoted as General-in-Chief in March 1862, McClellan remained as commander of the Army of the Potomac, but the post of General-in-Chief was vacant until July 1862.

John C. Fremont, Pathfinder of the West, named to command the Department of the West in July 1861, was soon removed from command for exceeding his authority regarding the emancipation of slaves in Missouri. He then led the Mountain Department, responsible for parts of Virginia, Kentucky and Tennessee until June 1862 when his command was absorbed into the Army of Virginia. Fremont refused to serve under its new commander, John Pope, whom he out-ranked and when he was given no more commands, Fremont resigned from the army in 1864.

Lincoln had directed the Union armies as General-in-Chief from March to July with advice from his two principal Cabinet members, Secretary of War Stanton and Secretary of State Seward. On July 23, 1862, he brought in Henry Halleck from the West and appointed him as the new General-in-Chief. An excellent administrator with strengths in logistics and military politics, he was known as "Old Brains" for his cautious and thorough preparations. But Halleck was weak and ineffective as a field commander, which was on full display when he took command of the army during the Siege of Corinth and took the entire month of May to advance twenty miles. Acting on a personal dislike of Gen. Ulysses S. Grant, Halleck had removed him from actively commanding the Army of the Tennessee during the army's march to Corinth. But when Halleck was moved to Washington, Grant was restored to command the Army of the Tennessee and he immediately began making plans for the Union assault on Vicksburg.

McClellan, leading the Army of the Potomac through several battles in the Union Peninsula Campaign was defeated by Confederate Gen. Robert E. Lee in July 1862. Returning to Washington in August, McClellan met Gen. Lee again at the Battle of Antietam in September. Although the battle was a draw, McClellan's failure to pursue Lee as the Confederates safely retreated to Virginia cost McClellan his command of the army. He was ordered to await further orders, but none came. In October 1863, he entered the political arena as a Democratic candidate and was nominated to run against Lincoln in the 1864 Presidential election.

Lincoln next appointed Gen. Ambrose Burnside to command the Army of the Potomac. Burnside's tenure, however, would be short lived. After his disastrous losses at Fredericksburg in December 1862 and the failed Mud March in January 1863, he was replaced by Gen. Joseph Hooker, an aggressive commander who had constantly criticized the administration and government for its lack of decisiveness. But when Hooker lost his nerve in the Battle of Chancellorsville against Confederate Gen. Robert E. Lee in May 1863, it added another defeat to the Army of the Potomac. After the failed battle, Hooker often quarreled with General-in-Chief Halleck and Lincoln and when he offered his resignation in June 1863, Lincoln promptly accepted it. Gen. George Meade was placed in charge of the Army of the Potomac just three days before the first day of the Battle of Gettysburg. Hooker remained with the army, however, and regained some of his lost prestige in the Battle of Chattanooga in November that same year.

In the Western Theater, Gen. William Rosecrans, after his successes at Iuka and the 2nd Battle of Corinth in Mississippi in 1862, was named to command the Army of the Cumberland, which absorbed the Army of the Ohio, relieving Gen. Don Carlos Buell, who had failed to pursue the Confederates after the Battle of Perryville, Kentucky, in October 1862. Rosecrans went on to defeat Gen. Braxton Bragg at the Battle of Stones River in January 1863 and wintered at Murfreesboro, Tennessee, building Fort Rosecrans. Performing brilliantly in the Tullahoma Campaign in 1863, Rosecrans then chased Bragg out of Tennessee into Georgia and occupied Chattanooga on the Tennessee border. His good fortune failed him, however, when Bragg defeated him at the Battle of Chickamauga in September and the Union Army was besieged in Chattanooga.

With Chattanooga under siege, Lincoln promoted Gen. Ulysses S. Grant as commander of the newly created Military Division of the Mississippi, to include the Departments of Ohio, Cumberland and Tennessee and the territory between the Alleghenies to the Mississippi River, placing him as overall commander of the army at Chattanooga. Grant immediately replaced Rosecrans with Gen. George Thomas, the

VII. THE FOURTH YEAR: 1864

"Rock of Chickamauga," to command the Army of the Cumberland. With the loss of his command, Rosecrans was moved to the Department of Missouri. For the battles at Chattanooga, Grant brought reinforcements from Vicksburg under Gen. William T. Sherman, commanding the Army of the Tennessee. Bragg was defeated a second time and forced to withdraw into Georgia in November.

Grant had achieved wide popularity with his battlefield successes the previous two years, first gaining attention at Fort Donelson, Kentucky, when he demanded "unconditional surrender" from its Confederate commander. The battles of the Vicksburg Campaign had gained for him a reputation of pragmatic toughness and versatility on the battlefield. His most recent successes at Chattanooga and Knoxville had been described in the *New York Times* as *"The Great Week of the War; Grant's Victory at Chattanooga."*

LINCOLN CHOOSES GRANT AS NEW GENERAL-IN-CHIEF

As Gen. Ulysses S. Grant contemplated his moves for 1864 after lifting the siege of Chattanooga, Tennessee, and driving Confederate Gen. Braxton Bragg and his army from the field into Georgia, he was called to Washington to meet with President Lincoln. With the opening of 1864, the third year of the war, Lincoln presented Grant with the commission of Lieutenant General on March 9, a rank awarded only to the country's first President, George Washington, and to Winfield Scott as a brevet rank during the Mexican-American War. Grant's special authorization by Congress placed him as General-in-Chief of all Union armies, replacing Henry Halleck, a post Grant would hold until the end of the war. Gen. Halleck would be retained as overall Chief-of-Staff and manage the administration of all the armies.

When Confederate Gen. James Longstreet, an old friend of Grant's from their days at West Point, learned that Grant was in command of all the Union Armies, he prophetically told his fellow officers, *"He will fight us every day and every hour until the end of the war."*

Grant next promoted Gen. William T. Sherman as head of the Western Armies, who would lead the Union forces to defeat the Confederate Army of Tennessee in Georgia and wreak havoc on the agricultural and industrial resources that were supporting the Confederacy. During this same period, Grant would accompany Gen. George Meade, commander of the Army of the Potomac, to face Confederate Gen. Robert E. Lee and the Army of Northern Virginia in the Eastern Theater. The confrontation of the two great armies would yield some of the most horrific battles of the war, as the Union forces fought to push the Confederates into the Siege of Petersburg, Virginia, where the Southern soldiers would remain besieged from June 1864 to March 1865.

UNION WAR PLANS FOR 1864

With the promotion of Ulysses S. Grant to General-in-Chief of the armies, he and President Lincoln developed war objectives early in 1864 that would implement a strategic direction of "total war." Only complete defeat of the Confederate armies and their economic support would bring an end to the conflict. Grant lost no time in planning his "spring campaigns" which called for Union forces to move simultaneously on May 4 all along the line of Confederate defenses. Separate Union armies acting in concert would move on the Confederate strongholds in the Eastern and Western Theaters and the Southern states on the Mississippi River and Gulf of Mexico. The strategy was not unlike the "Anaconda Plan" that had been proposed by Gen. Winfield Scott at the beginning of the war and ridiculed by Gen. George B. McClellan and the Northern press.

> **GRANT'S PHILOSOPHY OF WAR**
>
> "The art of war is simple enough. Find out where your enemy is. Get at him as soon as you can. Strike at him as hard as you can and as often as you can, and keep moving on." That philosophy would be put to the ultimate test when Grant faced the Confederates' most brilliant general, Robert E. Lee.

Grant would direct all the armies as General-in-Chief but would accompany the Army of the Potomac in the Eastern Theater, commanded by Gen. George Meade, to defeat the Army of Northern Virginia under the command of Gen. Robert E. Lee. Grant's orders to Meade were: *"Lee's army will be your objective point. Wherever Lee goes, there you will go also."*

Also supporting Eastern Theater objectives, the Army of the James, under Gen. Benjamin Butler on the Virginia Peninsula, would operate to attack the supply lines of the Confederate capital of Richmond, and if possible, capture the city itself. At the same time, several Union forces would engage in a series of campaigns in Virginia's Shenandoah Valley to remove the breadbasket and railroads that fed the Confederate troops.

In the Western Theater, Gen. William T. Sherman, now promoted to command the Western Armies, would move south from Chattanooga with his main objective to defeat Gen. Joseph E. Johnston's Confederate Army of Tennessee in Georgia and destroy the important Southern economic and rail center at Atlanta.

Along the Gulf of Mexico, Gen. Nathaniel P. Banks, commanding the Department of the Gulf, was to capture Mobile, Alabama, a vital port city for the Confederacy, which supported blockade runners providing ammunition, guns and supplies to the Southern armies. That effort would be delayed, however, as Banks had already been committed to the Red River Campaign in Louisiana, designed to counter potential threats from Texas.

VII. THE FOURTH YEAR: 1864

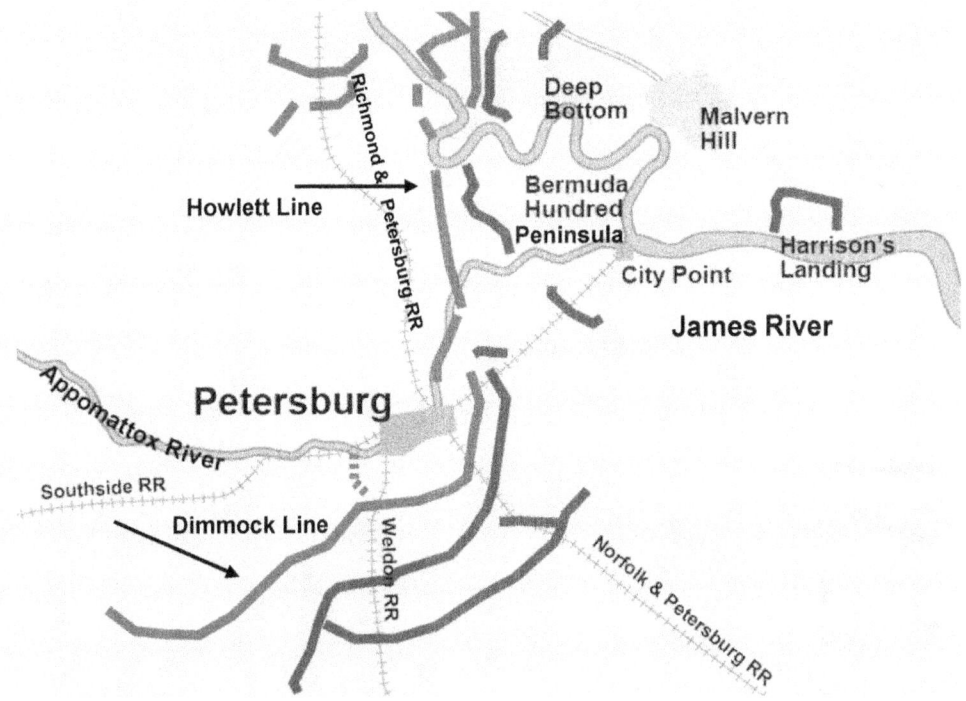

Fig. 35: Confederates created the Howlett Line of defense that boxed in Union forces under Gen. Benjamin Butler at Bermuda Hundred, Virginia, so effectively that his army was "corked" as in a bottle. The Dimmock Line, another Confederate defense line, protected Petersburg and its all-important Southside Railroad, which brought vital supplies.

Source: *Creative Commons Attribution 3.0 License Map by Hal Jespersen, www. cwmaps.com.*

Each Union army would be tasked with the defeat of the opposing armies and destruction of Southern war resources of railroads, factories, arsenals, food supplies and economic bases, leaving a scorched earth in their wake. It would be a conflict of total war.

BATTLES IN THE EASTERN THEATER

Bermuda Hundred Campaign, Virginia Peninsula
May 5-20, 1864

In support of the Union's war operations for 1864, one of its major objectives was to remove principal supply lines that served the Confederate capital of Richmond. The Army of the James, about 35,000 men, would launch its attack from Bermuda Hundred Peninsula, located between Richmond and Petersburg at the confluence of the Appomattox and James Rivers. Gen. Benjamin Butler, a political appointee from Massachusetts would command the operation. He had supported Lincoln for President in 1860 and continued his support in the upcoming election of 1864.

STRUGGLE FOR THE UNION

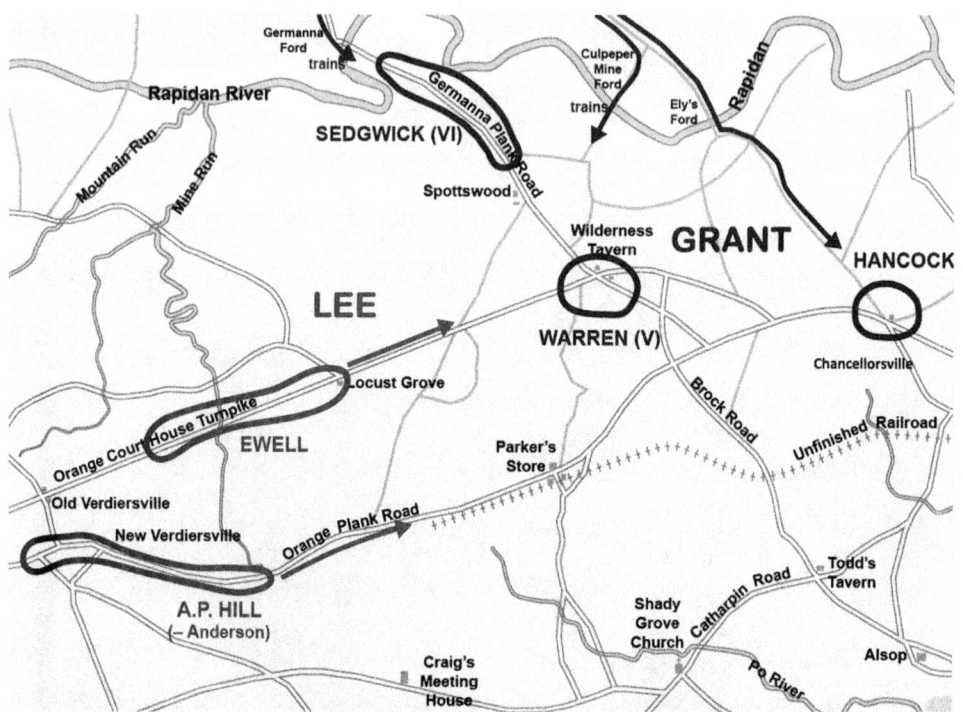

Fig. 36: The Overland Campaign began when the Union Army under Gen. Ulysses S. Grant crossed the Rapidan River into the Wilderness, Virginia, on May 4, 1864, to face Confederate Gen. Robert E. Lee.

Source: *Creative Commons Attribution 3.0 License Map by Hal Jespersen, www.cwmaps.com.*

Butler's army disembarked on May 4 from navy transports at City Point and Bermuda Hundred, a fishing village established in the 1600s, that was named from local tradition as a community that could support one hundred homesteads. The surprise attack planned to cut the Richmond & Petersburg Railroad that transported men, food and supplies to Richmond. But Butler's incompetence as a general became his undoing. Instead of taking advantage of the surprise landing, the troops entrenched in position, which provided sufficient time for the Confederates to bring in reinforcements supporting the command of Gen. P.G.T. Beauregard.

At the Battle of Ware Bottom Church on May 20, Confederate forces under Gen. Beauregard pushed Butler's line back into the Bermuda Hundred Peninsula and the Confederate Army then built a defense line against the Union Army, naming it the Howlett Line, after the Howlett house there (See Fig. 35). The Line consisted of defenses built from earthworks dug across the Bermuda Hundred peninsula between the Appomattox River on the south to the James River on the north (See Fig. 35).

Union entrenchments were secure, but the Confederates had an equally strong line immediately facing the Northern troops. The effect was to hold Butler and his men in place and they ceased to be a threat to the Confederacy. As Grant expressed it, *"(Butler's army) was in a position of great security... (and) as completely shut off from further operations directly against Richmond as if it had been in a bottle strongly corked."* The Dimmock Line, a ten-mile arc of earthworks, built by the Confederates to protect the Southside Railroad, did not come under attack until a month later.

THE OVERLAND CAMPAIGN, VIRGINIA

Battle of the Wilderness, Virginia
May 5-7, 1864

Union General-in-Chief Ulysses S. Grant initiated the 1864 Eastern Theater war campaigns on May 4, 1864, as he accompanied the Army of the Potomac, under the command of Gen. George Meade, into Northern Virginia. The goal was to defeat the Confederate Army of Northern Virginia under Gen. Robert E. Lee and capture the Confederate capital of Richmond. The two armies had fought against each other for three years and although the Confederate Army had defeated the Union Army in most of the battles, neither army had forced the other to surrender. With access to the Union's vast resources of men, ammunition, food and supplies, Grant was confident that he could defeat Lee by driving him to Richmond. But it was going to mean hard fighting through a series of bitter contests.

Grant writes in his *Personal Memoirs*, *"The losses inflicted, and endured, were destined to be severe; but the armies now confronting each other had already been in deadly conflict for a period of three years, with immense losses in killed, by death from sickness, captured and wounded; and neither had made any real progress accomplishing the final end."*

As the Union army, numbering about 120,000, left camp at Culpepper, Virginia, on May 4, 1864, it included four thousand wagons, loaded with ten days rations for the men, plus ammunition and animal forage, accompanied by beef cattle on the hoof. Each soldier carried three days of rations in their haversacks, plus fifty rounds of ammunition. The supply train was seventy miles long.

The army and cavalry crossed the Rapidan River, a tributary of the Rappahannock, at two fords downstream and east of the Confederates, now situated in well-fortified positions along the banks of Mine Run, located about sixty miles south of Washington, D.C. Lee's army had endured a hard winter, with his soldiers rationed to four ounces of meat per day with a pint of cornmeal, hardly enough to sustain them. With a much smaller army and far fewer resources to support it, Lee's objective now was to hold on long enough for the North to give up on the war and settle for a negotiated peace.

The Union army crossed the Rapidan without opposition and planned to move quickly through the Wilderness, seventy square miles of heavy timber, stunted pines and thick underbrush, and continue moving south towards Richmond. The Army of the Potomac had battled the Army of Northern Virginia in the Battle of Chancellorsville about a year earlier in the same woods and been defeated. The Northern troops entered the Wilderness at the head of its long supply train of wagons, which included more than eight hundred ambulances and a herd of beef cattle. Gen. Meade chose to camp overnight near Wilderness Tavern and allow the supply train to catch up (See Fig. 36).

> **STRENGTHS OF THE TWO ARMIES**
>
> Grant points out in his *Personal Memoirs* that the number of combatants listed for the two armies in the Eastern Theater can be somewhat misleading. *"In estimating our strength every enlisted man and every commissioned officer present is included, no matter how employed; in bands, sick in field hospitals, hospital attendants, company cooks and all. In the Confederate Army often only bayonets are taken into account; never, I believe, do they estimate more than (those who) are handling the guns of the artillery and armed with muskets or carbines. In the Northern Armies the estimate is most liberal, taking in all connected with the army and drawing pay."*
>
> Personal Memoirs, Ulysses S. Grant, 1885

Gen. Lee, aware that his army of about 65,000 was greatly outnumbered, knew that he needed to fight the Northern army in the Wilderness, where the superior Union artillery would be at a disadvantage in the thick and nearly impassable underbrush. Moving his troops into position on Orange Turnpike, one of the good east-west roads through the woods, Lee's army was waiting for the Union troops and launched a surprise attack the morning of May 5.

A fierce and heavy battle caused the famous Iron Brigade of the West to break for the first time in its history. As the battle continued throughout the day, Confederate and Union forces crashed into each other through blinding smoke as flames from burst shells ignited the heavy underbrush and overtook wounded men who then burned to death. A second battle about two miles south on Orange Plank Road, another east-west road through the Wilderness, was equally deadly as the terrain made it impossible for commanders to see their own troops or the positions of their opponents. At nightfall, as fighting ceased; neither side had achieved any advantage.

Lee had positioned his "War Horse" Gen. James Longstreet with about 12,000 men at Gordonsville about twenty miles south as his reserve. Lee now ordered Longstreet to join the battle in the Wilderness on Orange Plank Road to arrive the next morning. That day, May 6, Grant ordered an early morning attack on Orange Plank, temporarily overwhelming the Southerners until Longstreet's vanguard of 800 Texans arrived, the strongest brigade of the Army of Northern Virginia. The Union army was soon pushed back and the Confederate line held.

Southern troops took advantage of an unfinished railroad bed that provided easy access to the Union's left flank and a surprise Confederate attack *"rolled up the Union*

VII. THE FOURTH YEAR: 1864

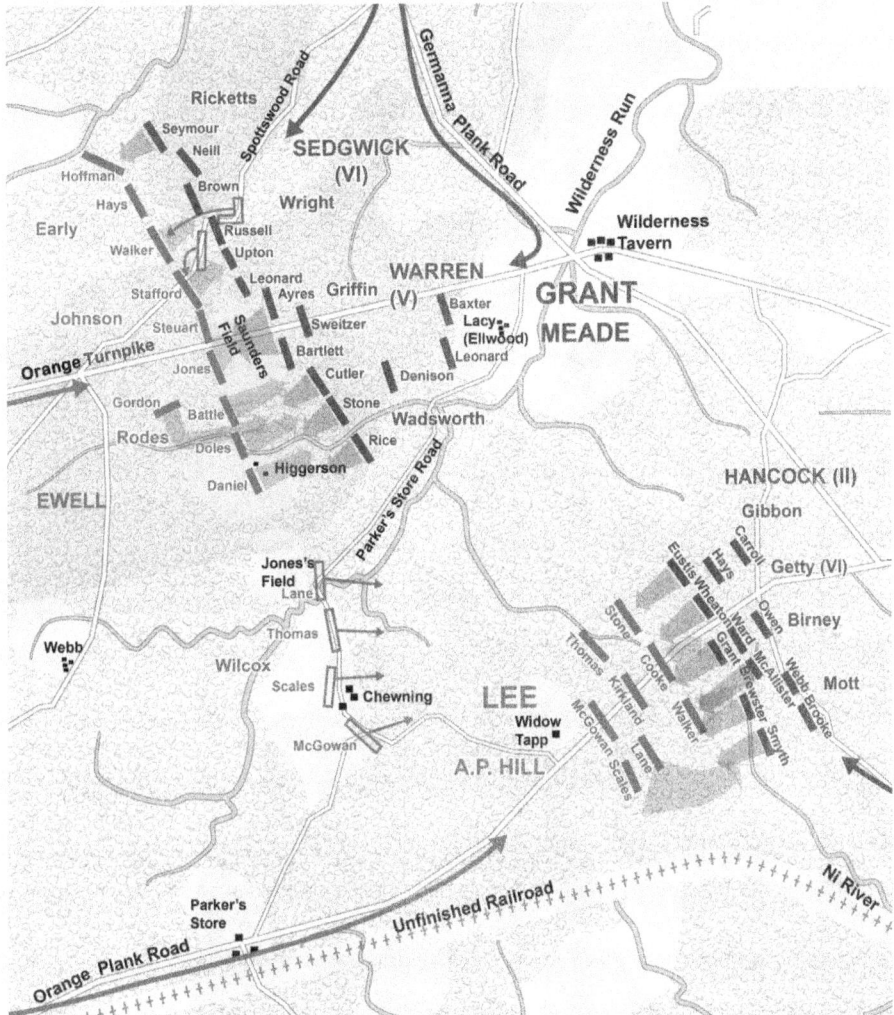

Fig. 37: Union Generals Grant and Meade met Confederate Gen. Lee, for the first time in the Battle of the Wilderness, May 5, 1864. Heavy underbrush, thickets and trees created fires in the raging battle that caused an "inferno from hell."

Source: *Creative Commons Attribution 3.0 License Map by Hal Jespersen, www. cwmaps.com.*

line like a wet blanket." As Longstreet and his senior staff rode forward to review the status, they were fired on by their own men who believed them to be Union troops. Longstreet was seriously wounded and did not return to the Army of Northern Virginia for several months. Fighting continued for most of the day with no benefit achieved for either side. Losses were severe. Union casualties were estimated at about nearly 18,000; Confederates, about 11,000.

Grant writes in his *Personal Memoirs*, "*More desperate fighting has not been witnessed on this continent than that of the 5th and 6th of May.*" Survivors described it as a hell on earth, where "*invisibles fought invisibles,*" as the soldiers were unable to see their

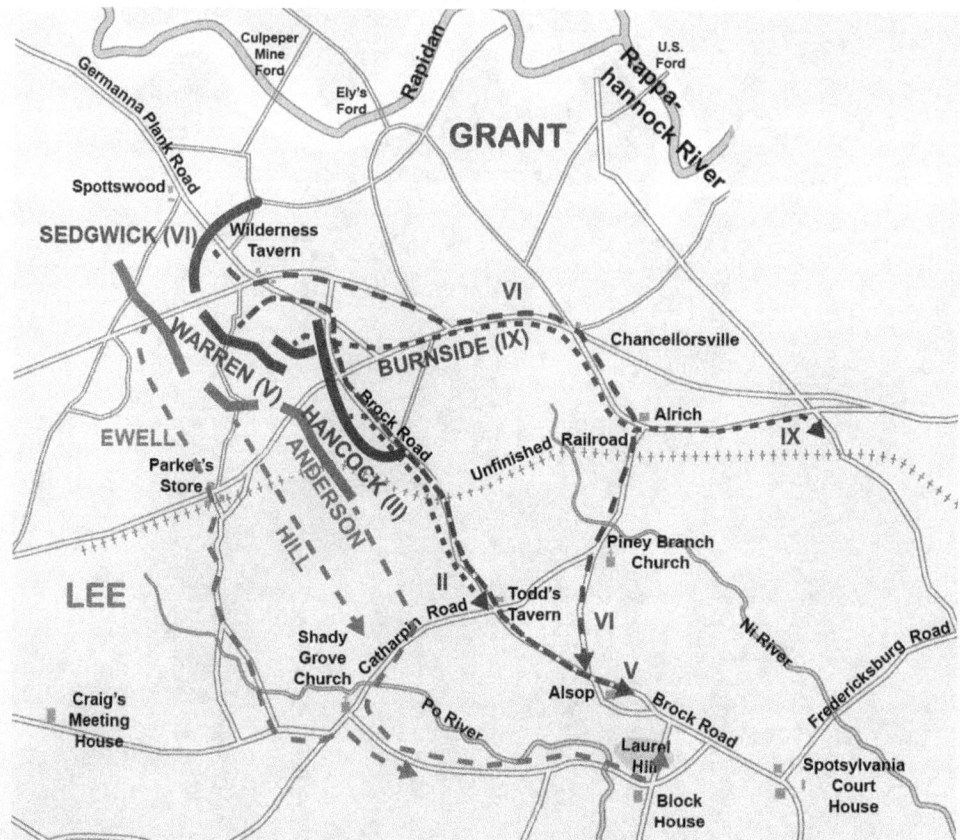

Fig. 38: Gen. Grant attempted to move his Union Army south of the Wilderness to gain better position against the Confederates under Gen. Lee, but the armies collided at Spotsylvania Court House, Virginia.

Source: *Creative Commons Attribution 3.0 License Map by Hal Jespersen, www.cwmaps.com.*

opponents in the smoke-filled inferno. At sunset, Grant called off any further attacks, seeing no advantage to fight Lee in terrain perfectly suited for his army's defense. On May 7, there was no battle during the day, only reconnaissance by each army to locate the positions of its enemy and to collect and care for the dead and wounded.

Battle of Spotsylvania Court House, Virginia
May 7-8, 1864

Grant next focused on moving his army about ten miles south to the crossroads at Spotsylvania Court House. The position would place him between Lee and Richmond and draw the Army of Northern Virginia into more open terrain where Union troops and artillery could be more effectively used. A night march was ordered and Grant and Meade with their supporting staff moved to the head of the column and turned the army south to Richmond. When the men reached the crossroads that would either take them south to Richmond or north to Washington, a rousing cheer rose from the

VII. THE FOURTH YEAR: 1864

marching troops when they turned south. The men realized that, for the first time, the Army of the Potomac was not retreating from Robert E. Lee's Army of Northern Virginia. Its defeats at the hands of Lee had included the Seven Days' Battles, the First and Second Battles of Bull Run, Chancellorsville, Fredericksburg, the Mud March and others. Grant writes about the soldiers' exuberance: *"The greatest enthusiasm was manifested by Hancock's men as we passed by. No doubt it was inspired by the fact that the movement was south. It indicated to them that they had passed through the 'beginning of the end' in the battle just fought. The cheering was so lusty that the enemy must have taken it for a night attack."*

As the Army of the Potomac moved south under cover of darkness to Spotsylvania Court House, Lee was uncertain about Grant's intentions. As protection against a possible advance by the Union army, Lee ordered Gen. Richard H. Anderson, now heading Longstreet's corps, to head to Spotsylvania and hold it. Anderson and his men hacked their way through the brambles of the smoke-filled Wilderness in the middle of the night, arriving at Spotsylvania just ahead of the Union soldiers and quickly erected their defenses. Confederate Gen. James Ewell Brown (J.E.B.), or "Jeb" Stuart and his cavalry made their stand on a ridge called Laurel Hill which was rapidly reinforced with Confederate infantry. After several costly onslaughts, Union troops were unable to break through and the Southerners held the small town of Spotsylvania.

Cavalry Raid and Battle at Yellow Tavern, Virginia
May 9-24, 1864

When Grant was promoted to General-in-Chief to head up the Union armies, he brought Gen. Philip Sheridan from the Western Theater to lead the Cavalry Corps for the Army of the Potomac. Sheridan, a career army officer, had distinguished himself in a number of battles, including the Battles of the Virginia Peninsula, Stones River, Chattanooga and others, and would become famous in the Shenandoah Valley in September. But Sheridan was frustrated with his role in the Battle of Spotsylvania because the dense forest had prevented his cavalry from providing an effective role in the battles, reduced to reconnaissance and screening of the infantry.

When his cavalry failed to clear the way at Todd's Tavern along the road to Spotsylvania, giving the Confederates time to entrench, Gen. Meade lost his patience with Sheridan and a quarrel between the two men required Grant to intervene. Over Meade's objections, Sheridan was sent south to conduct a raid that would threaten Richmond, disrupt Lee's supply lines and allow Sheridan to pursue his often-claimed boast that he could defeat the Confederate Gen. Jeb Stuart and his cavalry, who had long been the nemesis of the Union army. Stuart, a flamboyant and colorful figure, was the darling of the Southern press and one of Gen. Lee's most valuable men. His daring raids and exploits around the Union army had provided valuable and often critical information to the Confederate leaders about Northern movements all through the war.

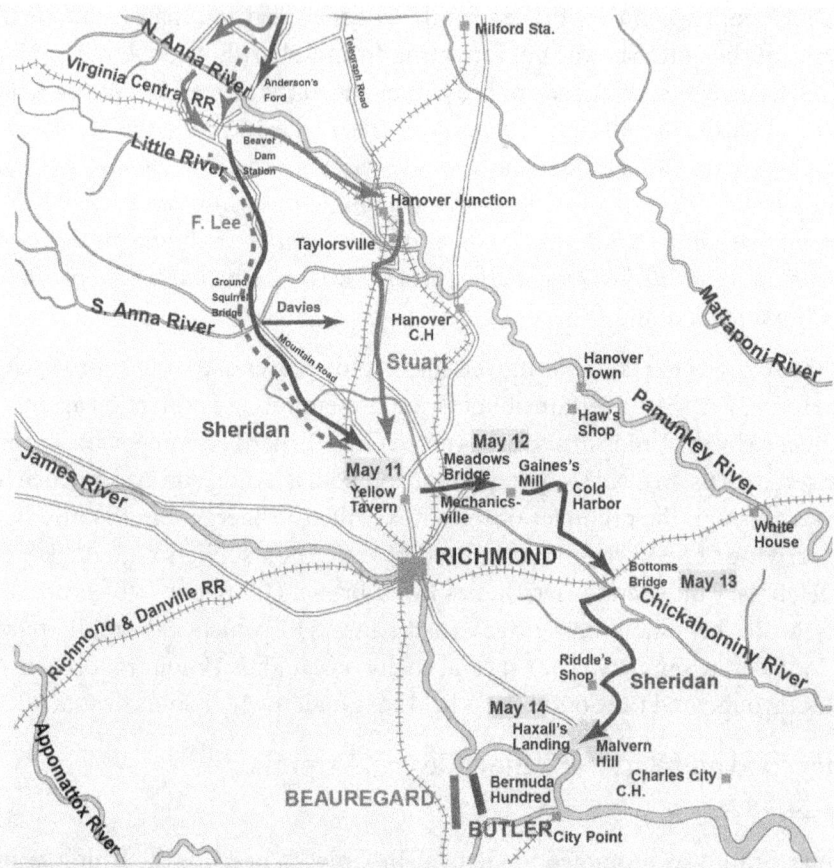

Fig. 39: Union Cavalry under Gen. Philip Sheridan conducted a raid on Confederate Cavalry under Gen. Jeb Stuart at the Battle of Yellow Tavern on May 11, 1863, where Stuart was killed, a major loss for the South.

Source: *Creative Commons Attribution 3.0 License Map by Hal Jespersen, www.cwmaps.com.*

On May 9, Sheridan's cavalry of over 10,000 troopers and thirty-two artillery pieces left Meade's headquarters and moved south to Richmond as the largest cavalry force ever assembled in the Eastern Theater. That night, the unit overwhelmed a Confederate supply base at Beaver Dam Station. Several railroad cars and locomotives and telegraph wires were destroyed and 400 Union prisoners were rescued. Continuing on south, the cavalry met up with Gen. Stuart and the Confederate cavalry at Yellow Tavern on May 11 about six miles north of Richmond. The badly outnumbered Southerners (4,500 troopers) resisted for three hours but were finally forced to withdraw. Stuart, the leader and star of the Confederate cavalry, was shot in the stomach and back during the retreat and died the next day.

By this time, the Union cavalry needed to find food and forage for the men and animals. Sheridan continued south, bypassing Richmond to his right, and met determined Confederate forces on May 12 at Meadows Bridge on the Chickahominy River.

VII. THE FOURTH YEAR: 1864

One of the Union brigades was led by Gen. George A. Custer and the 5th Michigan Division successfully held off Confederate fire that allowed the Union cavalry to cross the river and link up with Union Gen. Benjamin Butler's forces on the James River at Bermuda Hundred.

After resupplying men and horses, Sheridan headed north to rejoin Grant at Chesterfield Station on May 24. Although a tactical success, given the death of Stuart, Sheridan's absence had cost the Army of the Potomac valuable reconnaissance during the costly battles of Spotsylvania. Sheridan's casualties numbered about 625 men for the entire raid

Mule Shoe and the Bloody Angle, Spotsylvania, Virginia
May 10-12, 1864

Northern and Southern troops continued to clash along Brock Road between Wilderness Tavern and Todd's Tavern the next two days. Soon infantry from both sides erected earthworks reinforced by lumber and artillery during the nights of May 8-9. Confederates built an unusual configuration, known as the "Mule Shoe," so named because of its shape that was similar to the shoe of a giant horse or mule, with its prominent apex at the Southern line. The Union side built its own entrenchments and numerous engagements occurred between the two opposing armies over the next two weeks.

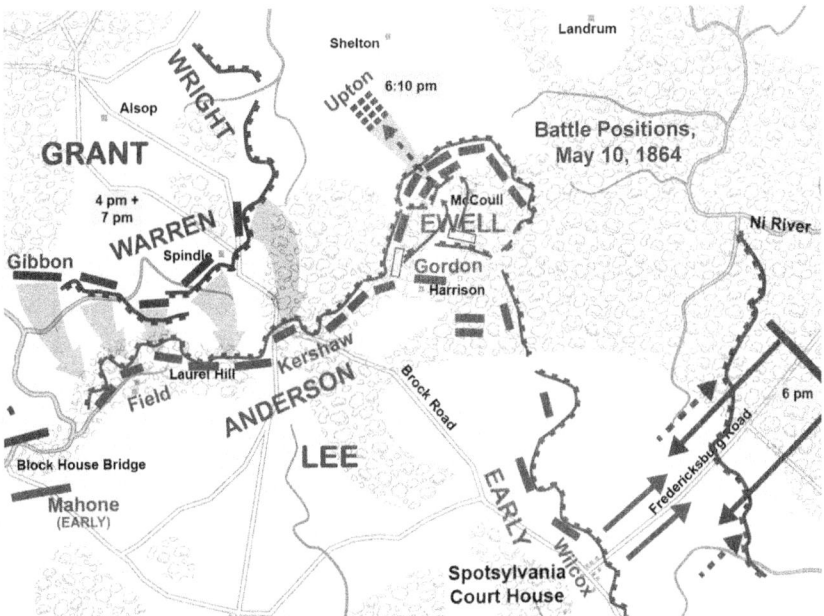

Fig. 40: Union forces under Gen. Grant attacked Confederates at the Mule Shoe at Spotsylvania, Virginia, held by Generals Lee and Ewell. The "Bloody Angle of the Mule Shoe," became a bloody hand-to-hand combat that lasted for twenty hours with no conclusive win for either army.

Source: *Creative Commons Attribution 3.0 License Map by Hal Jespersen, www. cwmaps.com.*

As part of a planned Union assault on the Mule Shoe May 10, young Union West Point Colonel Emory Upton led a new tactic of fighting that would foreshadow methods of trench warfare in World War I. Upton's new approach was a departure from standard infantry assaults of the Napoleonic wars which generally used a wide battle line moving forward. Upton's 5,000 men were condensed into four tight columns that quickly advanced to the apex of the Mule Shoe like a battering ram, moving two hundred yards in heavy fog, not slowing to fire their weapons. The rapid advance achieved a breakthrough in the Confederate defenses and the Union men took about twenty guns and captured nearly 3,000 Georgian prisoners. Upton would receive a promotion to Brigadier General for his efforts.

Rapid Confederate counterattacks, however, soon halted the Union advance which lost its cohesion when Union supporting units did not arrive and Upton had to withdraw. Two days later, a swift dawn attack by Union forces captured most of the Mule Shoe prominence again, only to stimulate vigorous counter attacks from the Confederates that pushed the Union advance back and restored most of the Confederate defensive line to its positions of the morning.

Attacks by Gen. Horatio Wright on the western edge of the Mule Shoe on May 12 at a slight bend in the line became known as the Bloody Angle. Desperate hand-to-hand fighting dominated the battle for over twenty hours. Fighting was extreme and bodies of the dead and wounded were buried in pools of blood and deep water from the driving rainstorm that inundated the battle. *"Nothing can describe the confusion, the savage, blood-curdling yells, the murderous faces, the awful curses, and the grisly horror of the melee,"* wrote one survivor. The battle finally ended when Confederates were able to withdraw after midnight to a new line farther south.

On May 13-16, Ulysses S. Grant reoriented the Union lines to the east of Spotsylvania, crossing the Fredericksburg Road and occupying Myers Hill, which overlooked most of the Confederate lines. A repeat attack on the Mule Shoe was quickly repulsed by Confederate defenses. A quick dispatch to Lincoln from Grant stated, *""We have now ended the sixth day of very heavy fighting. The result to this time is much in our favor. But our losses have been heavy as well as those of the enemy… I propose to fight it out on this line if it takes all summer."* Grant tried to tempt Lee into pursuing a small component of the Union Army so that he could then trap him with a larger force, but Lee did not take the bait. Grant abandoned the battlefield for better terrain and turned the army south on May 20 to go around Lee's right flank. The two armies would soon meet again at the Battle of North Anna.

Casualties at Spotsylvania were almost 30,000, one of the five most costly battles of the war. Union losses were 18,000 men, 2,700 of them killed. Ending enlistments took another 20,000 out of the army so that on May 19, Grant's troops were down to about 60,000 men. Lee's losses were more severe as he lost 10-12,000 men, about twenty

VII. THE FOURTH YEAR: 1864

percent of his army, but with reinforcements, Lee's army was soon restored to about 53,000. Grant was able to restore supplies and men by taking advantage of his proximity to rivers and the coast and not be forced to rely on a long wagon supply chain. With reinforcements, his army was soon restored to more than 100,000.

Battle of North Anna, Virginia
May 23-26, 1864

Faced with another battlefield stalemate at Spotsylvania, Gen. Ulysses S. Grant turned the Army of the Potomac south to the North Anna River and site of an important railroad junction. Lee's army arrived there first and created a strong defensive position at Ox Ford, a large bend on the south side of the river. Southern forces were positioned such that they formed an upside-down V with its apex facing north.

The strength of Lee's defense was apparent when Grant's initial attacks on May 23-24 at the apex and its right wing were quickly repulsed. *"Lee could reinforce any part of his line from all points of it in a very short march, or could concentrate the whole of it wherever he might choose to assault,"* Grant writes in his *Personal Memoirs*. The Union

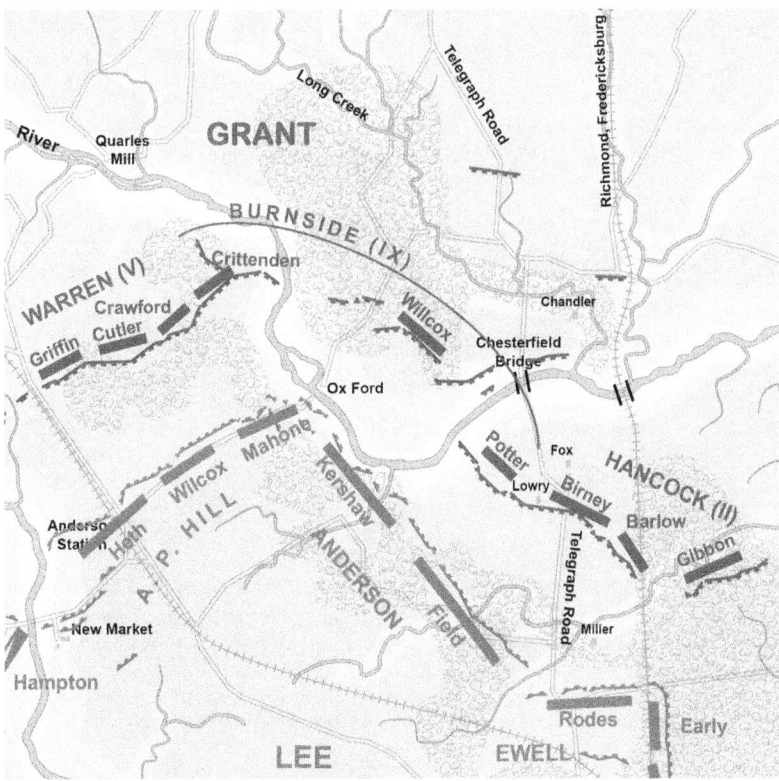

Fig. 41: At the North Anna River, about twenty miles south of Spotsylvania, the Confederates created such an effective V-shaped defense that Union Gen. Grant soon withdrew before Gen. Lee could take advantage and defeat the Union Army.

Source: *Creative Commons Attribution 3.0 License Map by Hal Jespersen, www.cwmaps.com.*

army, on the other hand, would have to cross the river twice to get from one side of the V to the other. The Southern Army's powerful defense made Grant realize that Lee could effectively divide the Army of the Potomac and quickly gain the upper hand. Grant turned his army south again and marched east to cross the Pamunkey River at Hanover Junction.

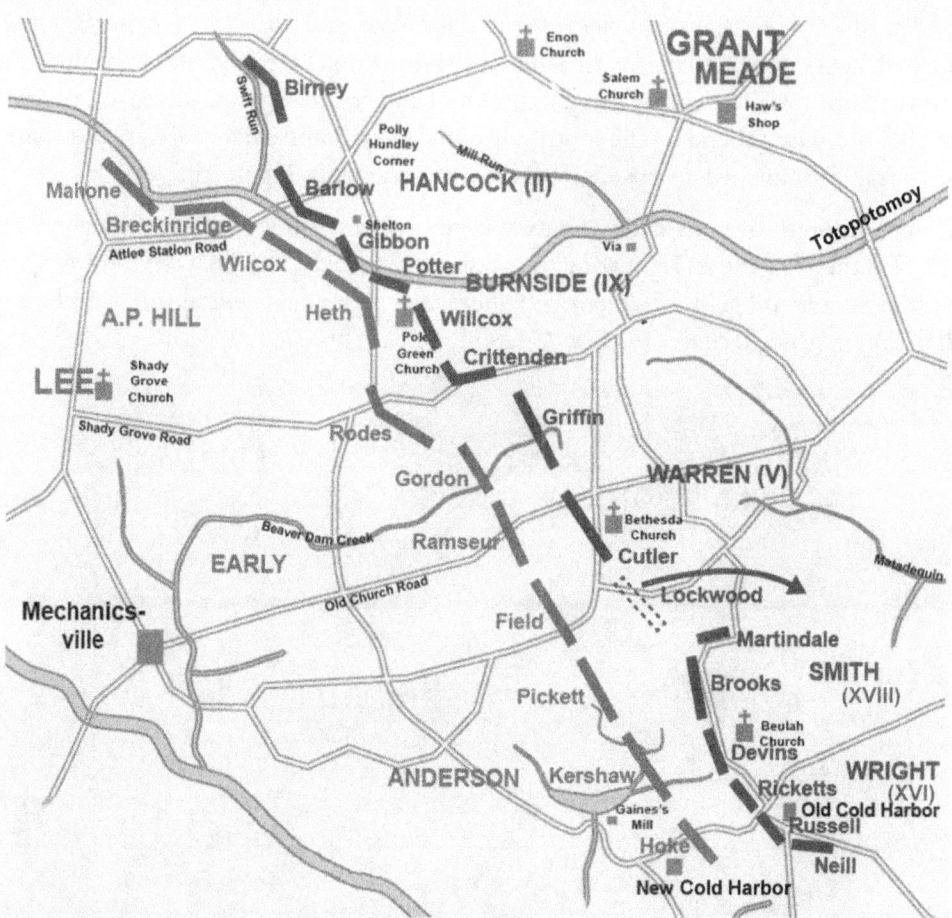

Fig. 42: Positions of the Union and Confederate armies at the Battle of Cold Harbor about twenty miles northeast of Richmond, Virginia. The Confederate defenses under Lee forced the soldiers under Generals Grant and Meade into deadly killing fields that caused 7,000 Union soldiers to fall in the first hour.

Source: *Creative Commons Attribution 3.0 License Map by Hal Jespersen, www. cwmaps.com.*

Lee, bedridden in his tent from an intestinal infection and severe diarrhea, was unable to capitalize on the situation and without his leading commanders, his opportunity was lost. Gen. James Longstreet, absent because of his severe wound at the Battle of the Wilderness, would not rejoin the Army of Northern Virginia until October. Gen.

VII. THE FOURTH YEAR: 1864

Stonewall Jackson had died after the Battle of Chancellorsville the previous year and Cavalry leader Gen. Jeb Stuart had been killed less than two weeks earlier.

Battle of Cold Harbor, Virginia
May 27-June 12, 1864

The Union Army made a wide swing around Lee's right flank at night on May 27 heading east from its location on the North Anna River to reach Hanover Town by crossing the Pamunkey River. Lee and his army followed up quickly, leaving part of his force to protect against a flanking attack on Richmond. The cavalries of the two armies met at the Battle of Haw's Shop on May 28. The seven-hour costly battle was inconclusive, both sides claiming victory.

> **SLAUGHTER AT COLD HARBOR**
>
> Prior to the battle they knew was coming, Union soldiers wrote their names on papers that they pinned inside their uniforms so that their bodies could be identified. One Union soldier's blood-spotted diary had a final entry: *"June 3. Cold Harbor. I was killed."*

Lee's army attacked an advancing Union infantry on May 28 as it marched to Cold Harbor, but the Southern army was forced back in a fierce battle. At the same time, Gen. Philip Sheridan and his cavalry encountered Southern infantry and cavalry at the Cold Harbor crossing and after a hard fight took control of the location. Grant, realizing the importance of Cold Harbor, ordered Sheridan *"… to hold the place at all hazards,"* until reinforcements could arrive.

Cold Harbor, about ten miles northeast of Richmond, was neither cold nor on a harbor. Its name reflected its function as a tavern and shelter or a "harbor" where only cold meals were served. Two taverns (Old and New) stood near the battlefield crossroads. The location was on the same ground where Gen. Robert E. Lee had defeated Gen. George B. McClellan's Army of the Potomac at the Battle of Gaines' Mill during the Seven Days Battles of 1862.

Union reinforcements were ordered from Gen. Benjamin Butler's Army of the James at Bermuda Hundred. In response, Gen. William F. "Baldy" Smith sailed down the James River from City Point, then up the York and Pamunkey Rivers to disembark at White House Landing, bringing with him a force of about 10,000 men. The reinforcements finally arrived at Cold Harbor the afternoon of June 1, and were pushed into battle at 4:30 p.m. Smith's infantry still managed to initially sweep over the Confederates, but a strongly executed counterattack drove the Union soldiers back and the two armies ceased fighting as darkness fell.

Gen. Meade ordered another early morning attack from the Army of the Potomac, but he needed Gen. Winfield S. Hancock's men to be on his left flank to reinforce the assault. Hancock's men had to march nearly all night from their position on Totopotomoy Creek to reach Meade's left flank, a distance of about six miles (See Fig. 42). Too exhausted for an immediate attack in the morning, the assault was postponed to take place that afternoon and then postponed again until 4:30 a.m. on June 3.

The delays provided Lee's engineers additional time to construct formidable defenses. Barricades of earth and logs with artillery platforms were posted to create converging fields of fire on every approach. A labyrinth would funnel the attacking forces into a defensive maze of artillery fire that forced the Union men into perfect killing fields.

In the darkness on the morning of June 3, the men of the Army of the Potomac formed a long, almost unbroken line as they faced the Southern entrenchments. When the men moved out, heavy vegetation, fog and swamps quickly broke up the formations, separating the units into targets for devastating Confederate fire.

Men were mowed down "... *like rows of blocks or bricks pushed over by striking against one another,*" wrote one Union officer. An estimated 7,000 men were killed or wounded in less than the first hour of the Union frontal assault, making it the bloodiest hour of the war. Watching the slaughter continue through the morning, Grant himself rode the Union lines and called off Meade's attack. He would later write, "*I have always regretted that the last assault at Cold Harbor was ever made....no advantage whatever was gained to compensate for the heavy loss we sustained.*"

Thousands of wounded men were left between the lines for the next four days until a truce could be arranged to retrieve them. Most died before help came. Between June 4-12 the two armies faced each other in the hot trenches as sharpshooters and artillery continued their deadly work. Union casualties at Cold Harbor numbered about 13,000. Confederate casualties were about 5,000.

With the realization that the battlefield was another stalemate and no advantage could be gained with continued assaults, once again Grant turned the army south, not to take the Confederate capital of Richmond, but to seize Petersburg about twenty miles south of it, a major crossroads and junction for five railroads. By capturing the main supply base and rail depot for the entire region, Richmond would be either starved into submission or Lee's army would be forced to do battle in the open.

As a distraction that would help conceal the Union Army's withdrawal from the battlefield, Grant sent part of Sheridan's cavalry on a mission to destroy the Virginia Central Railroad near Charlottesville, about sixty miles northwest of Richmond, and a vital source of supplies for the Southern army. Confederate and Union cavalries met at the Battle of Trevilian Station on June 11-12, the bloodiest and most costly cavalry battle of the war. Union casualties totaled more than 1,000 (102 killed, 470 wounded, and 435 missing or captured). Confederate losses were estimated at about 800.

VII. THE FOURTH YEAR: 1864

But the distraction had served Grant's strategic objective to conceal the departure of the Union Army from Cold Harbor, by removing important resources from Lee's army while the Union army was withdrawing to the James River. In addition, Union activities in the Shenandoah Valley were also affecting the source of supplies for Lee, which forced him to send Gen. Jubal Early with troops to protect Lynchburg, Virginia, the critical rail station.

Union Army Crosses the James River, Virginia,
June 12-16, 1864

On June 12, shortly after midnight, the Army of the Potomac began a stealthy movement to quietly leave the Cold Harbor battlefield without alerting the Confederate army and pass by its flank, a perilous undertaking for a large army that would make it most vulnerable to an attack. At daylight Union bands played loud music to disguise the sounds and dust of marching feet. The movement of 115,000 men along a ten-mile front remained undetected by the Confederates as Union components were dispersed along different routes to confuse their activities.

Gen. William F. "Baldy" Smith led his army east to White House Landing where boat transports carried them down the Pamunkey and York Rivers to the James River and then back to Bermuda Hundred. Two other groups crossed the Chickahominy River at two fords, using pontoon bridges and then continued their march south to the James. Another division headed by Gen. Gouverneur K. Warren turned west after crossing the Chickahominy on June 13, to create the impression of an attack on Richmond. Lee responded by sending Confederate Gen. A.P. Hill to block the perceived Union thrust at his right flank.

> **CROSSING THE JAMES**
>
> Col. Horace Porter, Grant's aide-de-camp, wrote of the crossing of the James River June 15-16, 1864. *"The great bridge was the scene of a continuous movement of infantry columns, batteries of artillery, and wagon-trains. The approaches to the river on both banks were covered with masses of troops moving briskly to their positions or waiting patiently their turn to cross. The scene was a matchless pageant that could not fail to inspire all beholders with the grandeur of achievement and the majesty of military power."*

Warren and the cavalry continued to guard against all Confederate approaches east, effectively screening movements of the Union Army as it marched to the James. The army would have to cross the James River, 2,000 feet across, by creating the longest pontoon bridge of the war.

The next morning, June 13, Gen. Lee found the Union army had withdrawn but their destination was unknown. Without Gen. Jubal Early, who had just been sent west to defend the Shenandoah Valley, and two of his three cavalry divisions fighting

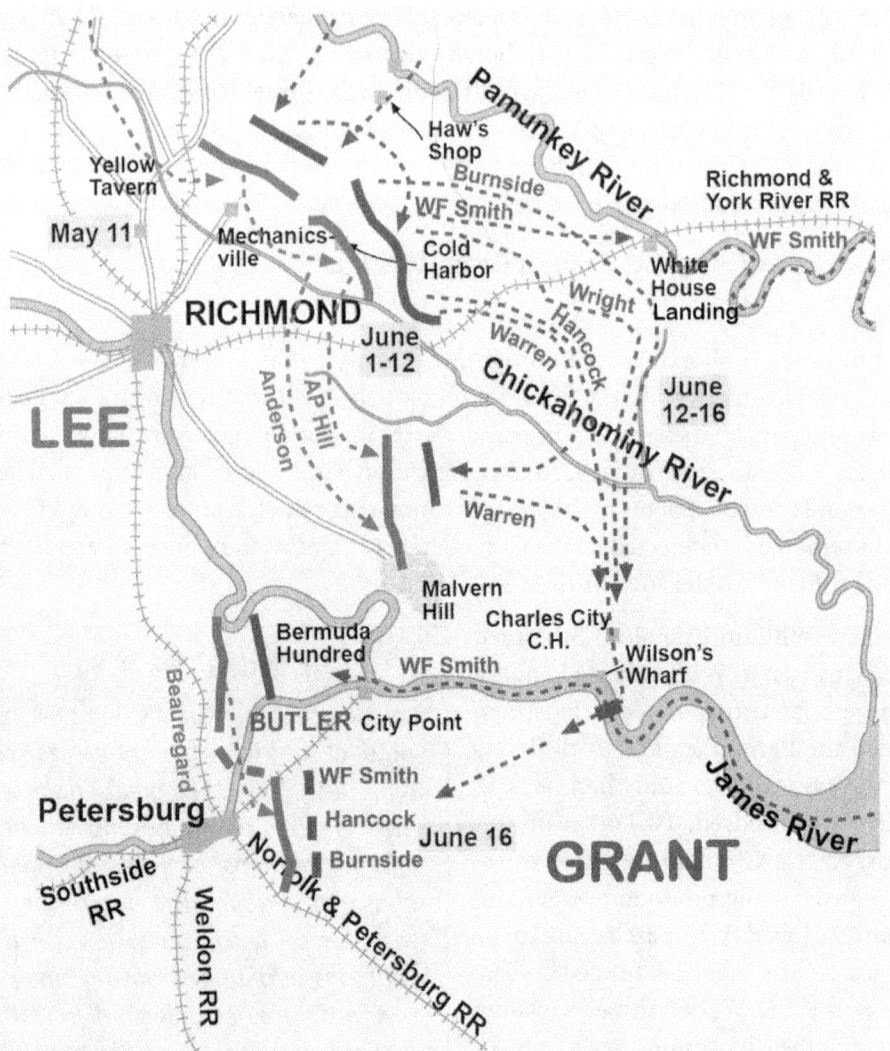

Fig. 43: The 115,000-man Union Army left the Cold Harbor battlefield in the dead of night with such great stealth and collaboration between the units that the army crossed the James River near Petersburg, Virginia, undetected.

Source: *Creative Commons Attribution 3.0 License Map by Hal Jespersen, www. cwmaps.com.*

a desperate battle at Trevilian Station, Lee did not have the resources to determine where the Union army had gone.

Upon reaching the James River, Union Army engineers began their work to build a pontoon bridge that would require 110 pontoons stretching over 2,000 feet to span the river that was nearly one hundred feet deep in the middle and subject to strong tidal currents. Larger pontoons were used in the center of the river to anchor the bridge against fluctuations of three-to-four-foot tides. Beginning late afternoon on June 14, more than four hundred Union engineers working from both banks built the bridge,

VII. THE FOURTH YEAR: 1864

> ### THE CHALLENGE GRANT FACED IN THE OVERLAND CAMPAIGN
> Grant had known at the beginning of the Overland Campaign that confronting the Army of Northern Virginia would be a costly endeavor. As he writes in his *Personal Memoirs*, *"We were operating in a country unknown to us, and without competent guides or maps showing the roads accurately… Lee was on the defensive, and in a country in which every stream, every road, every obstacle to the movement of troops and every natural defense was familiar to him and his army. The citizens were all friendly to him and his cause, and could and did furnish him with accurate reports of our every move. Rear guards were not necessary for him, and having always a railroad at his back, large wagon trains were not required. All circumstances considered we did not have any advantage in numbers."*
>
> *Personal Memoirs, Ulysses S. Grant, 1885*

working into the night, in less than eight hours. Planking, anchored to the equally spaced pontoons, created a roadway eleven feet wide between its guard-rails. The U.S. Navy was coordinated to block any Confederate gunboats from entering the river at its mouth.

Boats ferried most of the troops across the river beginning June 14, and the last of them crossed on the bridge the morning of June 15. Animals, supply wagons and artillery, stretching fifty miles long, began crossing on June 16 and required about thirty hours to get across. More than 100,000 men, 5,000 wagons and ambulances, 56,000 horses and mules and 3,500 head of cattle crossed the river without alerting the Confederates. On June 18, the bridge was dismantled.

As the Union Army approached Petersburg, Confederate Gen. P.G.T. Beauregard frantically called for Gen. Robert E. Lee to send reinforcements to prevent the Northerners from invading the city, but Lee, still unaware of the position of Grant's army was still protecting against an advance on Richmond and ignored Beauregard's requests.

The Union crossing of the James River closed the Overland Campaign. Losses had been immense. Union casualties numbered about 55,000 soldiers over a period of forty days; Confederate losses, about 34,000. As thousands of wounded soldiers arrived in Washington, D.C., Grant was widely criticized in the Northern press as the "fumbling butcher" and Congress urged Lincoln to remove him from command. Lincoln refused, maintaining that Grant's aggressive fighting supported the strategic war objectives that he and Grant had laid out in April. The capture of cities would not achieve success; armies must be defeated. Responding to Grant's message at the crossing of the James, Lincoln's telegram to Grant on June 15, stated, *"I begin to see it. You will succeed. God bless you all."*

DEADLY COST OF THE OVERLAND CAMPAIGN

Union Gen. Ulysses S. Grant's tenacious pursuit of Robert E. Lee and the Confederate Army of Northern Virginia through the Virginia landscape in early 1864 would yield some of the most horrific battles during the Civil War as the two armies confronted each other over the 40-day campaign. The Battle of the Wilderness, May 5-7, took place in an area of thick brush, which not only prevented commanders from seeing their men, the brush was set ablaze by guns and artillery, trapping many of the wounded into fiery deaths. Casualties numbered over 18,000 for the Union, with more than 2,200 killed; Confederate losses reached 11,000, with 1,500 killed. Survivors described it as a *"hell on earth."*

Both armies set up extensive earthworks at the Mule Shoe, Spotsylvania, May 8-21, from which each side battled for dominance. The most ferocious fighting occurred in "the Bloody Angle," where hand-to-hand combat continued without letup for twenty hours as reinforcements were brought in to replace the fallen. Bodies became piled upon each other in layers as the fighting continued through its indescribable horror. Casualties numbered 18,000 for the Union, with 2,700 killed; Confederate casualties reached about 12,000, with 1,500 killed.

At the Battle of North Anna May 23-26, Gen. Robert E. Lee created such a powerful defense at a sharp bend of the river that Grant feared his army could be quickly divided and defeated. Lee, himself bedridden with an infection, and missing three of his essential generals, was unable to capitalize on his advantage and the Union army successfully withdrew. Gen. Jeb Stuart, Lee's cavalry commander had been killed two weeks before, and Gen. Longstreet, Lee's "war horse," was still recovering from a wound received at the Battle of the Wilderness. The formidable Stonewall Jackson had been killed in the Battle of Chancellorsville the year before. Casualties at North Anna numbered 4,000 for the Union, (600 killed); Confederate casualties were estimated at 1,500 (100 killed).

Grant turned his army south again to the Battle of Cold Harbor, May 27-June 12. When a Union assault was ordered into an elaborate Confederate defense system, the Northern soldiers were funneled into killing fields where they were mowed down like grass before a scythe. An estimated 7,000 men were killed or wounded in the first hour. Casualties numbered 13,000 for the Union, with 1,800 killed; Confederate casualties were 5,000, with about 800 killed.

It was after this battle, that Grant accepted the futility of attempting to draw Lee into open battle, where superior Union numbers and artillery would be able to prevail. With an incredible display of stealth and execution, the Union Army of the Potomac with about 115,000 men, wagon trains, horses and cattle, slipped away in the night, crossed the James River, and nearly captured Petersburg before Lee knew where his adversary had gone.

VII. THE FOURTH YEAR: 1864

The total number of casualties for the two armies during the six bloody weeks amounted to about 55,000 (8,000 killed, 38,000 wounded, 9,000 captured/missing) for the Union and about 30,000 total for the Confederacy. The two armies would now face each other in a state of trench warfare for ten months during the Siege of Petersburg before Lee's starving troops would need to finally break through and leave the besieged city.

SHENENDOAH VALLEY CAMPAIGNS, MAY-JULY 1864

Battle of New Market, Virginia
May 15, 1864

In support of Union strategic war objectives that were implemented in the spring of 1864, the Shenandoah Valley Campaigns were launched in May to defeat and destroy the Confederate breadbasket and railroads in the Shenandoah Valley of Virginia. At Lincoln's request, Gen. Franz Sigel was placed in command of the new Department of West Virginia in March 1864 to initiate the offensive. Sigel, a German immigrant, had been a central recruiter of German-speaking antislavery immigrants to the Union armies and had expressed dissatisfaction in not being provided an important command. Given that many of these soldiers spoke little English, Lincoln considered Sigel an important asset and his performance at the Battle of Pea Ridge in 1862 had earned him a promotion to major general. Responding to Sigel's frequent demands for a significant command in the war, Lincoln awarded him the Shenandoah post.

With his new command, Sigel's orders were to cut Confederate supply lines in the Shenandoah Valley and inflict heavy damage at Lynchburg, a critical supply and railroad center for the Confederacy. Three railroads converged at Lynchburg, including the Southside, which had a direct line to Petersburg that supplied Lee's Army of Northern Virginia.

Sigel's army of about 6,300 men soon encountered Confederate troops at the Battle of New Market, Virginia, on May 15 led by Gen. John C. Breckinridge. The Southern army consisted of about 4,800 soldiers that included 261 cadets from the Virginia Military Institute (VMI), located at Lexington. When the battle began, the Confederates successfully held their line against several disorganized infantry attacks from Sigel's men and when a gap opened on the Union side, the Confederates pressed through, forcing the Union Army to retreat across a freshly plowed field thick with heavy mud after several days of rain. Pursuing the Northern troops, several VMI cadets lost their shoes in the battle, which was then renamed the "Field of Lost Shoes." Ten VMI cadets were killed in the battle and forty-five were wounded, but they had defeated Sigel's army.

Sigel's forces retreated north to cross the Shenandoah River at Strasburg, Virginia, burning bridges behind them, but the Union withdrawal allowed local crops to be harvested and Southern railroads and lines of communications were left intact. With

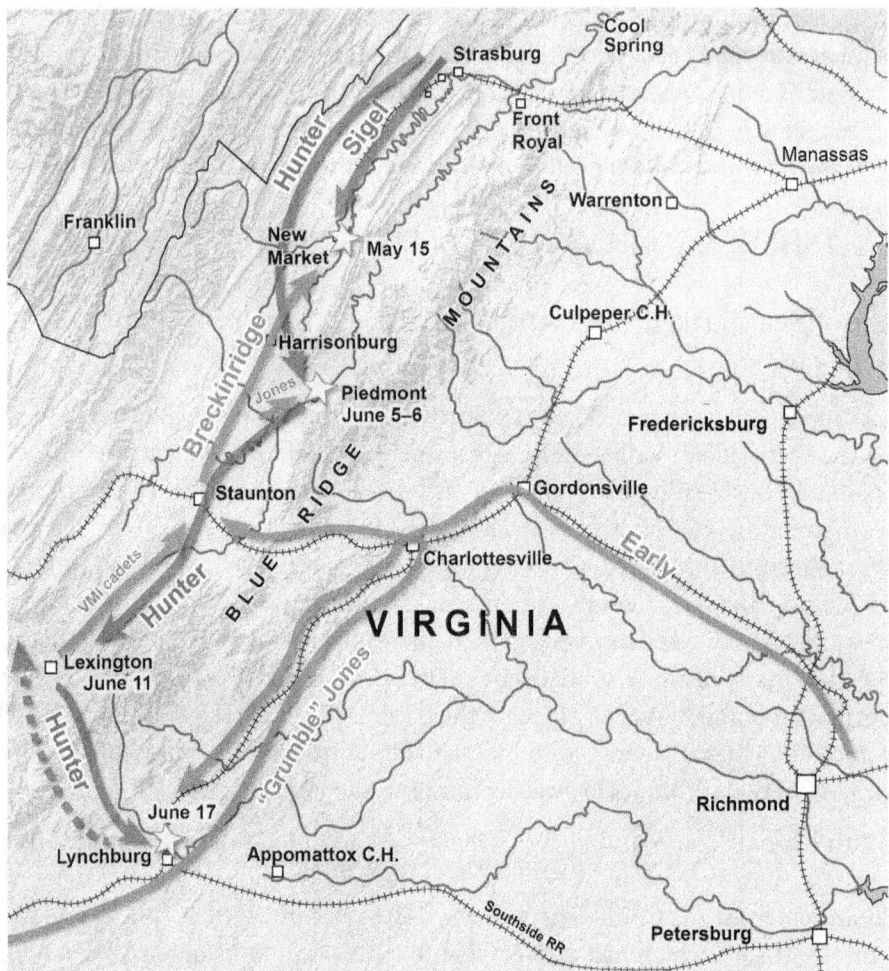

Fig. 44: Losses across the "Field of Lost Shoes" resulted in Union Gen. Sigel being replaced by Gen. David Hunter, who then advanced to Lexington and burned the Virginia Military Institute June 11-12, 1864.

Source: *Creative Commons Attribution 3.0 License Map by Hal Jespersen, www. cwmaps.com.*

the Confederate victory, Breckinridge's forces withdrew south to support Gen. Robert E. Lee and the Army of Northern Virginia now battling against Grant and the Army of the Potomac in the Eastern Theater. Sigel was soon relieved of command and Gen. David Hunter was placed in charge of Union activities in the Shenandoah Valley on May 21 to command the recently recreated Army of the Shenandoah, which had been disbanded in 1861 after the Battle of First Bull Run.

VII. THE FOURTH YEAR: 1864

Battles of Piedmont & Lexington, Virginia
June 1864

Union Gen. David Hunter resumed the offensive in the Shenandoah Valley following the removal of Gen. Franz Sigel. He quickly advanced fifty miles south on May 26 from Strasburg to Harrisonburg, Virginia, encountering little opposition from the limited Confederate troops that were left after Breckinridge's departure. But reinforcements for the Southerners soon arrived from the Confederate Department of Southwest Virginia and East Tennessee under the command of Gen. William E. "Grumble" Jones. During severe fighting between Hunter's forces and Confederates at Piedmont on June 5, Jones was killed while leading a charge and the Northern army prevailed over the Southern troops.

Hunter's army entered Staunton the next day and resumed the offensive. Union cavalry under Gen. William Averell fought against Confederate cavalry headed by Gen. John McCausland, who then withdrew to Buchanan, some sixty miles southwest, to wait for reinforcements. Hunter continued south to Lexington where he shelled and burned the Virginia Military Institute on June 12. He also burned the home of Virginia's former Governor John Letcher, and wreaked havoc on Washington College, earning him the name "Black Dave." Hunter's next objective was to strike the transportation and supply center at Lynchburg, about fifty miles southeast to eliminate its steady support for the Southern armies by cutting the direct railroad line to Petersburg. But as Hunter continued to Lynchburg, he was confronted by Confederate Gen. Breckinridge who had returned from Cold Harbor to meet the threat.

Battle of Lynchburg, Virginia
June 17-18, 1864

Confederate Gen. John C. Breckinridge arrived at Lynchburg on June 16 and was joined by Confederate cavalry under Gen. John McCausland, who had withdrawn from Union forces earlier and waited for Confederate reinforcements. Also arriving on June 17 were Southern troops under the command of Gen. Jubal Early, who moved his army sixty miles from Cold Harbor in three days. Gen. Robert E. Lee, concerned about the Shenandoah and its importance to the Confederacy for critical food and other supplies, had ordered Gen. Early, "... *my bad old man*," to clear out Union forces in the Shenandoah, and if possible, threaten Washington, D.C. The combined forces with Breckinridge now numbered about 14,000 Confederates.

On June 17, Gen. David Hunter now faced a greatly increased Confederate army and his own supplies and ammunition were running dangerously low because of continued attacks on his supply lines by Confederate Col. John S. Mosby and his Rangers. Expected support from Union Cavalry under Gen. Philip Sheridan was not forthcoming as he was actively engaged at the Battle of Trevilian Station, June 11-12, supporting Gen. Ulysses S. Grant's Overland Campaign against Lee.

Without additional cavalry and dwindling ammunition in the face of a reinforced enemy, Hunter withdrew to West Virginia. Breckinridge and Early would now hold the Shenandoah Valley until September, enabling vital support to continue to be provided to Gen. Lee's army and the Confederacy.

Confederates Almost Achieve a Raid on Washington, D.C.
July 11-12, 1864

With the departure of Hunter, Gen. Jubal Early swiftly marched the Confederate army of about 16,000 north, passing through New Market and Winchester, Virginia. When the large army reached Martinsburg, the outnumbered Union troops fled the city, providing the Southerners with some boisterous feasts from captured Union supplies. Turning east, the Confederate cavalry arrived at Frederick, Maryland, on July 7 and skirmished briefly with Union troops from Baltimore.

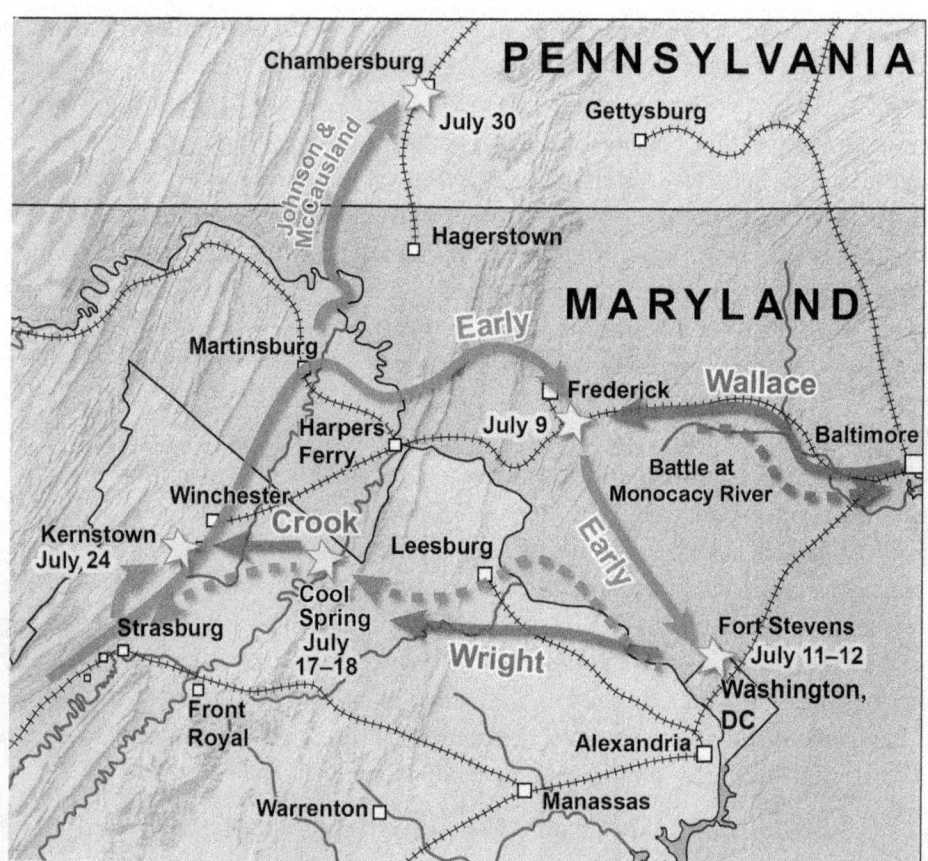

Fig. 45: Confederate attacks in the Shenandoah Valley in July under Gen. Early almost achieved a raid on Washington, D.C., July 11-12, that was barely blocked by Union troops, headed by Gen. Wright who arrived just in time from the Virginia Peninsula.

Source: *Creative Commons Attribution 3.0 License Map by Hal Jespersen, www.cwmaps.com.*

VII. THE FOURTH YEAR: 1864

At this point, the only Union defense between Early's army and Washington, D.C., was a small, mostly inexperienced 2,500-man force garrisoned at Baltimore, commanded by Gen. Lew Wallace, a veteran of the Mexican-American War and a commander in the battles of Fort Donelson, Shiloh and the Siege of Corinth. An author from Indiana, Wallace would become famous in 1880 for writing the historical novel *Ben-Hur*.

The Union men quickly withdrew east from the large Confederate army at Frederick to defend the bridges and railroad at Monocacy Junction, only forty miles from Washington, D.C.

Alarmed by Early's activities in the Shenandoah, Gen. Grant sent about 5,000 men from City Point, Virginia, under Gen. James B. Ricketts to support Union efforts near Harpers Ferry, but they never got that far. Ricketts and his men arrived just in time to support Gen. Wallace on the banks of the Monocacy River. The combined Union forces, now about 6,800 men, were able to mount a fierce resistance on July 9 against five attacks from the Confederates. But when Early's men broke the Union line, the Northerners were forced to retreat to Baltimore.

Gen. Early now set his sights on Washington, D.C., and resumed his plan to attack the Union capital. The Confederates began their march from Monocacy the next day and arrived July 11 at Fort Stevens near Silver Spring, Maryland, on the outskirts of Washington. The troops were exhausted by the long march through one of the worst hot spells in the city's history, which delayed Early's attack until the following day, July 12. The Southerners took advantage that night of the vacant mansion of President Lincoln's Postmaster General Montgomery Blair, who had left Washington with his family to escape the heat.

But the delay achieved at Monocacy Junction had allowed Gen. Grant to reinforce the capital with veteran Union troops by steamboat from City Point to Washington, D.C. As the experienced Union soldiers arrived around noon on July 12 under Gen. Horatio G. Wright, veterans quickly organized the defenses and manned the lines of battle around the city. Confederates commenced skirmishing in the afternoon, but by now

A GRATEFUL GENERAL'S THANKS

Gen. Lew Wallace, with a small force, was able to delay a large Confederate Army marching on Washington in July 1864 long enough for reinforcements to arrive and block the intended raid on the capital. Gen. Grant's comments, in his Personal Memoirs notes the significance of the achievement. "Gen. Wallace's leading (of the defense at Monocacy) might well be considered almost a forlorn hope (given his small and inexperienced troops). If Early had been but one day earlier he might have entered the capital before the arrival of the reinforcements... Gen. Wallace contributed on this occasion... a greater benefit to the cause than often falls to a commander of an equal force to render by means of a victory."

Union defenses were in place, backed by artillery from Fort Stevens. In the face of such a strong opposing force, Early withdrew his army that evening, carrying off supplies they had seized from the Valley, plus several barrels of whiskey and cigars from the Blair household, which was set ablaze as they left.

Union Gen. Wright actively pursued Early and his army from Washington into the Shenandoah Valley, which resulted in several engagements, including Heaton's Crossroads (July 16) and the Battle of Cool Spring (July 17-18). The Confederates withdrew to Strasburg and Wright's command returned to Grant's army, leaving Gen. George Crook in charge of the small Army of West Virginia. With the departure of Wright, Gen. Early defeated Crook on July 24 at the Second Battle of Kernstown and the Union troops were forced to escape through Winchester, crossing the Potomac into Maryland.

Six days later, July 30, Early's cavalry under Gen. McCausland burned the city of Chambersburg, Pennsylvania, when citizens refused their demands for ransom. The retaliation had been ordered by Gen. Early, in response to the damage done by "Black Dave" Hunter in Lexington. More than five hundred structures were destroyed and left two thousand homeless. But as McCausland's troops left Pennsylvania and camped out on the Potomac River in West Virginia, they suffered a major defeat when they were captured by Union cavalry under the command of Gen. William Averell at the Battle of Moorefield, West Virginia, on August 7. About 500 men were taken prisoner and four hundred horses were captured. But the recent sequence of events in the Shenandoah Valley prompted Grant to order Gen. Philip Sheridan in early August to leave Petersburg and command the recently recreated Army of the Shenandoah and take Union control of the Shenandoah Valley.

SIEGE AND BATTLES OF PETERSBURG, VIRGINIA 1864

Petersburg, a city of about 20,000, located twenty miles south of Richmond, was a supply base, major crossroads and rail depot for the entire region. It was a central resource for providing food, men and supplies to the Confederate Army of Northern Virginia under Gen. Robert E. Lee and the city of Richmond itself. Union Gen. Ulysses S. Grant and the Army of the Potomac had battled Lee's army for forty days during the Overland Campaign without defeating it. Grant now focused on a war of attrition by containing Lee and limiting his resources. The larger Union army with a secure base on the Appomattox River and unlimited access to men and supplies that could be conveyed unmolested to him by ship, Grant could defeat Lee's army and the Confederacy; it was only a matter of time.

The Army of the Potomac completed its crossing of the James River on June 16-17 and moved quickly to set up Union headquarters at City Point, located at the junction of the James and Appomattox Rivers, about ten miles from Petersburg. The small city

VII. THE FOURTH YEAR: 1864

(now named Hopewell, Virginia) was quickly transformed into one of the busiest ports in the world as ships delivered soldiers and supplies of food, clothing and ammunition to the Union Army.

First Battle of Petersburg, Virginia
June 9, 1864

While the Union Army of the Potomac faced the Confederate Army of Northern Virginia at Cold Harbor, Union Gen. Benjamin Butler at Bermuda Hundred decided that his opportunity for glory could still be achieved by seizing Petersburg, now weakly defended while the Confederates were occupied at Cold Harbor. Having failed in his initial efforts in May, Gen. Butler was still blocked by the Howlett Line, but

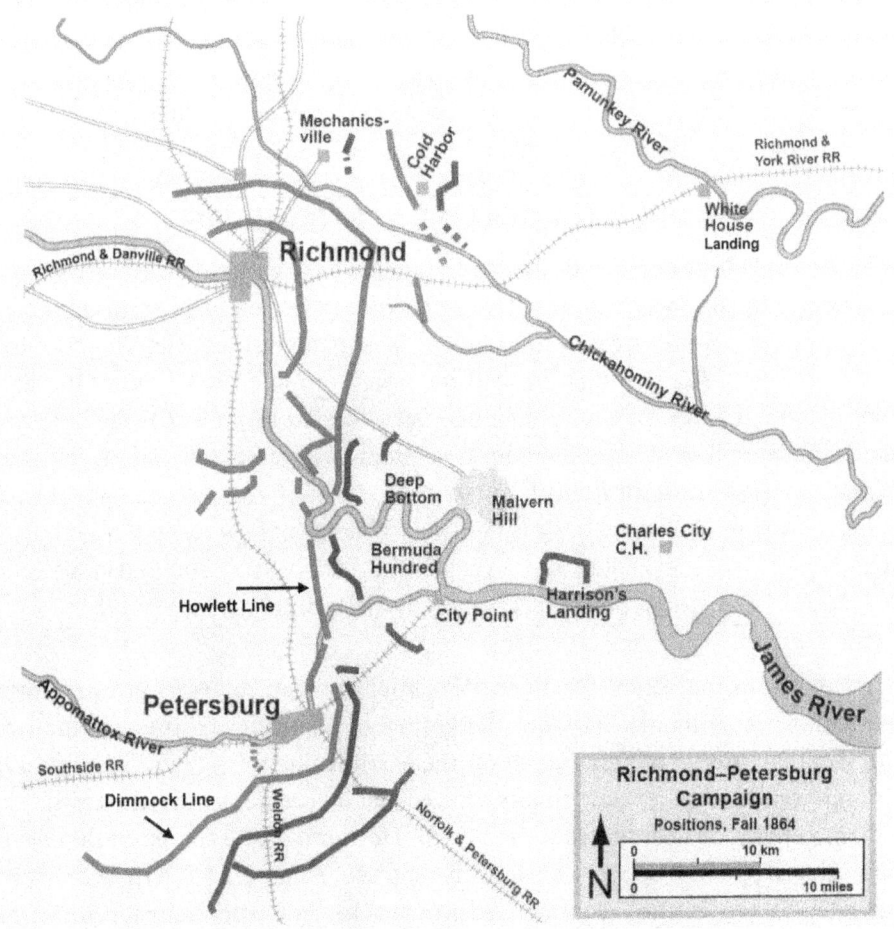

Fig. 46: Union troops failed to overcome a Confederate militia of Home Guard defenders at the Dimmock Line, which became known as the "Battle of Old Men and Young Boys." on June 8-9, 1864.

Source: *Creative Commons Attribution 3.0 License Map by Hal Jespersen, www. cwmaps.com.*

thought his troops could overcome Confederate forces on the Dimmock Line which was poorly defended by only a few hundred troops of the 7th North Carolina Cavalry Regiment. Butler ordered Gen. Quincy A. Gillmore to cross the Appomattox River east of Petersburg on June 9 with about 4,500 men to overcome defenders positioned at the Dimmock Line, a ten-mile arc of earthworks, trenches and fifty-five artillery batteries anchored on the south bank of the Appomattox, built to protect the city and its railroads from attack.

Butler's plan included support from cavalry under Union Gen. August Kautz, who would partially swing around the city and support Gillmore from the south. The troops moved out on the night of June 8. The infantry made slow progress through the night but finally encountered Confederate forces at the Dimmock Line around seven the next morning. Gen. Gillmore, an engineer whose experience had largely been in siege operations against entrenched forts, waited at the Dimmock Line for cavalry support before initiating his attack. But the 1,300-man cavalry under Kautz had been delayed by Confederate Home Guard defenders, a group of teenagers, elderly men and some wounded soldiers, who held a defensive line against Kautz for two hours.

THE DIMMOCK LINE AT PETERSBURG

The city of Petersburg was protected by a ten-mile arc of defenses, consisting of connected infantry earthworks with a series of fifty-five partially enclosed artillery batteries that covered areas east, south and west of Petersburg. The Dimmock Line, built between 1862 and 1864 by soldiers, slaves and free Blacks, under the direction of Capt. Charles Dimmock, had been constructed to protect Petersburg from invasion. More than twelve hundred slaves from Virginia's Eastern shore and North Carolina were impressed from slave owners to work on the project. As labor continued through 1863, slave owners demanded quotas of how many slaves could be conscripted from the plantations to work for the military. Work stopped in the spring of 1864 as Union troops began to move against Petersburg.

In the meantime, Confederate reinforcements began to arrive at the Dimmock Line with supporting artillery, but the Union attack under Gillmore remained on hold. Apprehensive about an assault on the earthworks in his front without cavalry, Gillmore waited. When Kautz finally arrived just before noon with the cavalry at his destination point, he heard no sounds of battle. He improvised a charge on the defending Confederates, but his troopers were quickly repulsed. As more Southern reinforcements continued to arrive, the outnumbered Kautz withdrew and returned to Bermuda Hundred. The Union assault dissolved, but had alerted the defenders of Petersburg's vulnerability. When the large Union army arrived six days later, the Confederates were ready. A furious Gen. Butler had Gillmore arrested for incompetence, but Grant later reassigned him and the incident was dropped.

VII. THE FOURTH YEAR: 1864

The "Battle of Old Men and Young Boys" became memorialized as an annual Confederate celebration after the end of the Civil War. The unit of Virginia reserves, according to the Confederate officer in charge, included a 59-year-old bank officer, three members of the city council and a mill manager who had been guarding prisoners all night, "... *heads silvered over with the frosts of advancing years. And the other men could hardly be called men at all, with no down upon their cheeks.*"

Second Battle of Petersburg, Virginia
June 15-18, 1864

On June 15, the first contingents of the Union Army of the Potomac reached Petersburg from Cold Harbor after crossing the James and were reinforced with troops from Gen. Benjamin Butler's command from Bermuda Hundred. The 16,000-man Union army, now under the command of Gen. William F. ("Baldy") Smith, advanced to Petersburg, surprising Confederates at the outermost trenches of the Dimmock Line and Union troops quickly opened a mile-wide gap in the defenses. Eight artillery batteries were captured, but as darkness fell, Smith inexplicably called off the attack and did not pursue his advantage, deciding to wait until dawn. His failure to capitalize on his surprise attack would extend the war nearly another year.

Confederate Gen. P.G.T. Beauregard, commanding the Department of North Carolina and Southern Virginia at Petersburg, was well aware of the danger he faced defending Petersburg with his weakly assembled 5,000-man force consisting of about 2,500 Confederate soldiers and an equal number of Home Guard militia of teenagers and old men. He had made multiple requests for reinforcements from Gen. Robert E. Lee, but Lee was not aware that Grant had moved the Union Army to Petersburg. Expecting a Union advance on Richmond, Lee had kept his Confederate forces at Cold Harbor.

Beauregard wrote later, "... *at that hour Petersburg was clearly at the mercy of the Federal commander, who had all but captured it.*" During the night Beauregard pulled his forces from the Howlett line at Bermuda Hundred, which had kept Butler's army "corked," and Lee finally responded to Beauregard's frantic requests, sending a division of reinforcements from the Army of Northern Virginia which arrived after darkness fell.

By the morning of June 16, Confederate forces now numbered 14,000. But more Union troops had arrived from Cold Harbor under Gen. Ambrose Burnside, bringing the Northern total to 50,000. A Union attack late in the afternoon achieved breakthroughs in the Confederate defenses, but Beauregard was able to move his trenches back and quickly erect new fortifications. As more Confederates arrived, Beauregard had 20,000 troops by June 18 to defend the city, but Union forces had also been increasing with the arrival of Gen. Gouverneur K. Warren's troops, bringing the total Northern forces to 67,000. Gen. George Meade, commanding the Army of the Potomac, directed a number of assaults for the next four days but made no progress in taking the city.

With Union losses accumulating and casualties now numbering over 11,000, Gen. Grant ordered the assaults to cease and the opportunity to capture Petersburg was lost. Gen. Lee arrived from Cold Harbor and took charge of the Confederate defenses but was unable to prevent the siege of the city. Lee and Grant would now face each other during the long siege that would last ten months until April 1865.

UNION OPERATIONS AT PETERSBURG & RICHMOND

Massive Supply Depot at City Point, Virginia

As both armies braced for a long-term siege, Grant established his headquarters at City Point, ideally situated on the James River, which provided access to Fort Monroe and its port on the Atlantic coast. Gen. Rufus Ingalls, Chief Quartermaster for the Army of the Potomac, was placed in charge of the supply depot for all the Union armies operating against Petersburg and Richmond. Under Ingalls' impressive skills, City Point became the largest port operation in the Western Hemisphere.

Facilities at the small port city were quickly enlarged and enhanced and within thirty days contained eight wharves on eight acres capable of unloading twenty-five ships a day. Over twenty miles of rail track supported a railroad network that provided fresh meat, rations and tons of supplies directly to the fighting men. A massive bakery created 100,000 loaves of fresh bread daily, which were loaded directly onto the train system and delivered to the men.

Over 5,000 wagons were maintained at a giant repair shop. Corrals and handlers managed the 65,000 animals that supported the army, plus 5,000 head of cattle used for beef. Seven hospitals were capable of treating 15,000 wounded patients. Communications systems linked Grant to Washington, D.C., and other Union forces throughout the country. The strength of the logistical support has been cited by historians as *"The tool that gave Grant victory."* Well-supplied and well-fed Union soldiers faced a diminishing and hungry Confederate army as the siege wore on.

Attacks on Confederate Railroads

As the two armies confronted each other across a formidable collection of defensive trenches, artillery and troops, shelling took place daily from both sides. Several Union attempts were made to cut off the supply lines that served the Confederates. The Richmond and Petersburg Railroad to the north, the Southside Railroad to Lynchburg to the east, and the Weldon Railroad which led south to North Carolina and the Confederate port at Wilmington on the Atlantic were all under attack. An effort by Union forces to destroy the Weldon and Southside railroads on June 27 achieved sixty miles of damage but in the face of a large force of Confederate infantry and cavalry, the Union troops had to retreat in "a wild skedaddle" at the cost of 1,500 casualties and the railroads were soon repaired.

VII. THE FOURTH YEAR: 1864

In the first two weeks of July, Grant sent Union reinforcements north to protect Washington, D.C., from an alarming attempt by Confederate Gen. Jubal Early to take advantage of a weakly defended national capital and capture it. After his raid was repulsed, Early withdrew into the Shenandoah Valley, pursued by Union Gen. Horatio Wright, but the Confederate general was able to elude Union efforts to capture and defeat him.

After the long and bitter struggle between Grant's and Lee's armies the previous forty days in the Overland Campaign, operations on the Petersburg front settled into a relatively quiet repose until the end of July.

Battle of the Crater
July 30, 1864

Col. Henry Pleasants of the Pennsylvania Volunteers was a mining engineer in civilian life and commanded a regiment mostly made up of miners. In late June, as the Union Army besieged the Confederates at Petersburg, Col. Pleasants proposed a novel idea to his commander, Gen. Ambrose Burnside, to dig a mining shaft directly below the Confederates. If they placed explosive charges there, they could blow a hole in the ground above it and divide the Confederate army.

The proposed location of the mining shaft would end directly underneath the quarters of South Carolina Confederates, a position known as Elliott's Salient. By creating a hole in the Southern defenses, Union troops could pass around the crater and divide the Confederate army while it was stunned from the blast. Although Gen. George Meade opposed the plan, Gen. Grant gave it cautious approval "... *as a way to keep the men occupied.*" Digging began on June 25 and by July 23, the mine was complete.

A horizontal shaft over five hundred feet long reached the site of the Confederate fort twenty feet above. Southern troops had heard the sound of digging picks and shovels, but were unable to locate the source. Two side tunnels, each seventy-five-feet long, extended in opposite directions from the main shaft and were filled with three hundred twenty kegs (eight thousand pounds) of gunpowder. The main shaft was packed with earth thirty feet back from the entrance to ensure the explosions were projected upward and not out the mouth of the tunnel.

After the explosion, the plan required Union troops to circle around the crater and the debris field and seize Jerusalem Plank Road and the high ground about sixteen hundred feet beyond and split the Confederate army. Gen. Burnside selected the U.S. Colored Troops who were relatively fresh and nearly at full strength to lead the attack and trained them for the mission. The explosion would take place on July 30.

Before giving his approval to explode the mine, Grant arranged an assault at Deep Bottom that would draw some of Lee's army away from the site and provide greater opportunity for Union soldiers to advance after the mine shaft exploded. Deep Bottom, so named for the depth of the river there, is a horseshoe bend of the James River north of the Bermuda Hundred peninsula and eleven miles southeast of Richmond. Using infantry and Sheridan's cavalry, Union troops attacked Confederate fortifications in the First Battle of Deep Bottom, July 27-29 (See Fig. 46), which was an area near the south side of the James River. Although the attack was unable to break through the Southern positions, the effort did succeed in attracting Confederates away from the Crater mine shaft activities.

But the day before the planned explosion, Gen. Meade informed Burnside that he could not use colored troops to lead the assault and ordered Burnside to select a white division for the task. Meade feared political consequences if the attack failed and Black soldiers were needlessly killed. A disgusted Burnside ordered his three other commanders to draw straws as to who would lead the assault. The short straw fell to Gen. James H. Ledlie, who was reportedly drunk in his last two battles and not on good terms with his men. He provided no training to the men for the mission.

On July 30, four tons of explosives were placed in the mine and ignition took place at 4:45 a.m., shooting a tongue of flame two hundred feet in the air, followed by a great heave of red earth, filled with cannon, debris and dead men. The explosion immediately killed between 250 and 350 soldiers of the 18th and 22nd South Carolina units and stunned other troops in the vicinity for about half an hour. Neither Ledlie nor Burnside were on hand to lead the men. Ledlie's troops, with no training or explanation of how the mission should proceed, moved forward awkwardly through their own trenches. When they reached the crater without any leadership, they entered the hole instead of going around it.

The crater, one hundred seventy feet long, sixty feet wide and thirty feet deep, had steep walls covered with slippery red clay, making it almost impossible for the men to climb out of the hole once they were in it. With no leader to direct their movements, more of Ledlie's troops continued to enter the crater. As the Confederates recovered from the blast, the sea of Union men trapped in the crater became a "turkey shoot" for the Southerners and they trained their guns into the pit.

Burnside finally arrived on the scene and ordered the Colored Troops that he had trained to go around the crater according to the original plan. But as they moved around the crater and encountered Confederates who were now recovered from the initial blast and ready to fight, the Black soldiers were met with devastating fire as the Southern men saw former slaves now in uniform. Many captured Blacks were murdered on the spot. After eight hours of fighting, those Union troops who had survived were finally able to leave the crater and withdraw to their own lines, suffering 4,000 casualties.

The colored division suffered the worst with over 1,300 casualties, and of the 450 captured, many were immediately killed after surrendering. Grant described the effort as a *"stupendous failure,"* and said of the event, *"It was the saddest affair I have witnessed in war."* Burnside, censured by a court of inquiry, lost his command and was never again assigned to a command post. Ledlie, censured by the same court for dereliction of duty, was dismissed from service that December on orders from Gen. Grant.

Second Battle of Deep Bottom
August 14-20, 1864

On the same day that the Battle of the Crater explosion occurred, Confederate Gen. Jubal Early's cavalry burned down the town of Chambersburg, Pennsylvania, as he continued to operate against Union forces in the Shenandoah Valley largely unopposed. At this point, Gen. Ulysses S. Grant became resolved to eliminate the continued threats that the Confederate general presented in the Shenandoah.

To discourage Gen. Robert E. Lee from sending any Southern reinforcements that could support Early, Grant initiated the Second Battle of Deep Bottom on August 14. As the Union troops attempted to set up their assault positions in the murderous heat of the hot August summer, several deaths occurred from heat stroke. Skirmishing and some hard fighting over the next several days did not displace the Confederates and Union troops were called off on August 20.

But the battle had occupied Gen. Lee's troops in Petersburg and prevented their support of Gen. Early when Union Gen. Philip H. Sheridan, now commanding the new Army of the Shenandoah, was deployed to the Shenandoah with almost 40,000 men. His mission was to remove the Confederate presence in the Valley and secure it from all Southern control. Success would eliminate threats to the nation's capital and impact Confederate resources by creating shortages of food and supplies that still supported the besieged army in Petersburg.

Battles around Petersburg, Virginia
August-October, 1864

In mid-August, Union troops under Gen. Gouverneur K. Warren were sent to capture the Weldon Railroad, which connected Petersburg with Wilmington, North Carolina, an important link for the Confederates. Grant writes, *"This railroad was very important to the enemy. The limits from which his supplies had been drawn were already very much contracted, and I knew that he must fight desperately to protect it."* Heavy rains and muddy roads hampered the fighting August 18-21 and both sides experienced significant losses. But with strong Union reinforcements, Warren was able to hold several miles of railroad and the Southerners were forced to retreat on August 21. Miles of track and bridges south of there were destroyed. It was the first Union victory of the siege and Northern forces now held control of the railroad until the close of the war. As a result, the Southerners were forced to use wagons on Boydton Plank Road, a distance of over thirty miles, to replace the supplies they had been receiving through the railroad.

> ## BOYDTON PLANK ROAD
>
> Built between 1850 and 1853, the Boydton Plank Road was a hard surfaced all-weather road about seventy miles long that ran between Boydton and Petersburg, Virginia. Built to assist farmers to move their wheat, tobacco and other agricultural products to the city, the toll road was also used for stagecoach traffic between the two cities prior to the Civil War. Pine and oak planks (eight feet long, one foot wide and about four inches thick) were laid across parallel beams all along the road, that were placed at an angle to facilitate drainage. Widely used for almost ten years, the road was condemned in 1860 as being unsafe due to demanding use and poorly suited lumber. It was nevertheless heavily used for troop movements and transportation of supplies for armies during the Civil War. A replacement all-weather road would not occur along the roadbed until the 1930s.

Confederate Gen. Wade Hampton successfully captured three thousand beef cattle from Union troops who were camped at Prince George Court House southeast of Petersburg in the "Beefsteak Raid" September 14-17. For several days, Southern troops feasted on the captured prize as they taunted their enemy across the lines.

North of the James River, an attack at New Market Heights (or Battle of Chaffin's Farm) September 29-30 by Union Gen. Butler's Army of the James resulted in Lee being forced to shift troops from Petersburg to protect Richmond. At about the same time, the Battle of Peebles' Farm September 30-October 2 southwest of Petersburg was a Union attack aimed at the fortifications guarding the Boydton Plank Road, now an important and essential supply line for the Confederates from its railhead at Stony Creek to the south. Although repulsed, the attack did extend the Union left flank which brought it closer to the Plank Road and the lightly defended Fort MacRae was captured.

Actions between the two armies at Richmond and south of Petersburg continued through October with little change in the disposition of the armies. A Union attempt to gain possession of the Confederates' single remaining railroad supply line, the Southside Railroad, on October 24 failed. The Army of the James, under Gen. Butler, made a demonstration on the north side of the James River in late October, but w as soundly repulsed. This effectively closed active operations around Richmond for the winter.

SHENANDOAH VALLEY CAMPAIGNS, FALL 1864

During the last weeks of July, General-in-Chief Ulysses S. Grant's communications to the Shenandoah Valley had been cut off because of a broken cable across the Chesapeake Bay. In early August, Grant soon learned that Confederate Gen. Jubal Early had dominated the Valley after forcing Gen. George Crook and his Army of West Virginia out of the Valley and across the Potomac at the Second Battle of Kernstown on July 24. The supplies of ammunition, food and beef from the Shenandoah Valley continued to be shipped to the Confederates besieged at Petersburg and elsewhere. Grant telegraphed Washington that he was sending Gen. Philip Sheridan with cavalry to the Valley on a special mission. *"... I want Sheridan to be put in command of all the troops in the field, with instructions to put himself south of the enemy and follow him to the death. Wherever the enemy goes let our troops go also."*

President Lincoln responded to Grant's telegram stating his support for the strategy, but pointed out that *"... it will neither be done nor attempted unless you watch it every day, and hour, and force it."* Gen. Halleck and Secretary of War Stanton had continually interfered with Grant's orders in the Shenandoah by keeping Union forces moving right and left so as to maintain protection for the nation's capital. The general effect was that all knowledge of the whereabouts of the enemy was confused and muddled.

Upon receiving the message, Grant left for the Shenandoah immediately and met with Sheridan at Monocacy on August 4 to firmly establish his role in defeating the Confederates in the Shenandoah Valley. Sheridan was warned, however, to proceed cautiously and avoid defeats that would discourage Northern support for the war and negatively impact Lincoln's reelection in the November elections.

Union Clashes with Valley Confederates in Several Battles
August-September (1864)

Gen. Philip Sheridan reached Harpers Ferry August 6 with the Army of the Shenandoah of about 30,000 infantry and 8,000-mounted cavalry. With the garrison at Harpers Ferry, Sheridan commanded nearly 50,000 troops. The army moved south, surprised Confederate columns crossing the Shenandoah River at the Battle of Guard Hill (also known as Front Royal or Cedarville) on August 16, capturing about 300 prisoners. A Confederate retaliation at the Battle of Summit Point August 21 attacked Sheridan with two columns, and Union forces withdrew. Minor conflicts at Smithfield Crossing (August 25-29) and Berryville (September3-4) were inconclusive for either side.

Sheridan launched the Third Battle of Winchester (or Battle of Opequon) on September 19 against Gen. Jubal Early to recapture Winchester while the Confederates were busy raiding the Baltimore & Ohio Railroad at Martinsburg, West Virginia, some twenty miles distant. But Sheridan's arrival at Winchester was delayed by the narrow road from Berryville Pike, which became clogged with wagons and troops, allowing Early to get his men back to Winchester in time to confront the Union attack.

The battle began at noon and resulted in heavy casualties and the loss of officers on both sides. Late in the day, Union reinforcements arrived, which forced the Confederate army into full retreat. One of the Confederate officers to die was Col. George S. Patton, Sr., whose grandson and namesake would become the famous general of World War II. Although a decisive victory for Sheridan, it was the bloodiest battle fought in the

Valley Campaign. Sheridan's casualties of 5,000 out of the 40,000 in battle represented twelve percent of his army. Confederate casualties were fewer, but represented twenty-five per cent of the Southern army. Suffering a significant defeat in the battle, Jubal Early quickly set up a defensive position at Fisher's Hill which Sheridan attacked on September 21-22 and Early was forced to retreat to a point near Waynesboro, Virginia, a few miles southeast of Staunton, where he would be defeated in 1865.

> ### GRAY GHOST OF THE CONFEDERACY
>
> Col. John Mosby, also known by his nickname, the "Gray Ghost," commanded a Confederate cavalry of 'Partisan Rangers' that became famous in the Shenandoah Valley as Mosby's Rangers. After distinguishing himself in the Peninsula Campaign and the Battle of Fredericksburg under cavalry officer Gen. Jeb Stuart, Mosby was permitted by Gen. Robert E. Lee in January 1863 to form his own group of rangers that would operate independently in the Shenandoah Valley. Recognized by the Confederacy as equals to other soldiers, entitled to the same pay and benefits, the partisan rangers were known for lightning-quick raids and their ability to escape and disappear as local farmers and townspeople. Fitted with the Colt 44, a six-shot revolver, each of Mosby's men carried two, and some had spares they carried in their boot-tops. The group eventually grew to the size of two regiments (1,900 men) and became so well known for their disruption of Union supply lines, daring raids, and successful capture of Union officers and couriers, that they demoralized the Northern forces. After the war, Mosby was paroled by Ulysses S. Grant in 1866 and the two became lifelong friends. Mosby later joined the Republican party, supported Grant for the Presidency and then served in a number of government positions for the United States.

While Sheridan's main cavalry battled Gen. Early, a separate division under the command of Union Gen. Wesley Merritt conducted a raiding party in an area of northern central Virginia between September 26 and October 8 to destroy mills, wheat, corn and barns that supported the Confederate armies and had been protected by Mosby's Rangers. The region of destruction became known as "The Burning." Mosby's Rangers were well known for their raids on Union soldiers in the area that Sheridan targeted for the Burning. Rangers routinely captured Union scouts and couriers and destroyed Northern wagon trains, before vanishing into the countryside as farmers and townspeople.

When the war began, the general policy had been to not intentionally destroy civilian property. But as the war went on, Lincoln and Grant had altered war objectives, beginning in 1864, to be one of "total war." Targeting civilian property was allowed if it meant depriving resources for the Confederate armies. A secondary objective was a policy of enforced hardship on the Confederate sympathizers that would break the will power of the Southern people and bring an end to the war, ultimately saving lives. Sheridan energetically supported the policy of obliterating the "Confederate Granary." He wrote, *"There is more mercy in destroying supplies than in killing their young men... If I had a barn full of wheat and a son, I would much sooner lose the barn and wheat than my son."*

After thirteen days of destruction, Union Cavalry Gen. Merritt reported destroying two hundred thirty barns, eight flour mills, 10,000 tons of hay and 25,000 bushels of grain. In addition, thousands of cattle, sheep and horses were driven off and one thousand hogs slaughtered. Twelve of Mosby's Rangers were captured. The Union's destruction of food, animals and crops not only drastically affected the lives of the residents in the area, it had an immediate impact on Confederate Gen. Early's command. He reported to Gen. Lee in besieged Petersburg that his supply line now had to reach to Augusta, Georgia, and supplies there were very limited. Confederate men in the Valley were reduced to picking corn in the countryside in exchange for a farmer's payment in flour.

Sheridan's Famous Ride
October 19, 1864

The Confederates made one last stand against Gen. Philip Sheridan at the Battle of Cedar Creek (or the Battle of Belle Grove) October 19. Gen. Early and his men made a stealthy approach to the Union camp on the banks of Cedar Creek under cover of heavy fog the evening of October 18. The surprise attack about 5 a.m. caught most of the Union troops in their camps off-guard and many fled, half-dressed in panic. The Confederate assault dominated the battle during the morning and numerous Union prisoners and cannons were taken. But the Southern advantage was soon lost as hungry men fell out of their ranks to fill their packs from the abundant Union stores of food and supplies. Sheridan, about twelve miles away at Winchester, returning from a meeting in Washington, was awakened by the sounds of battle.

Mounting his powerful black horse named Rienzi, which stood sixteen hands high at the shoulder, Sheridan made a wild ride to the front and intercepted his men, now fleeing from the battle. The impact of Sheridan's presence had an electrifying effect on the men. One private remembered that when he saw Sheridan ride into sight, *"No more doubt or chance for doubt existed; we were safe and every man knew it."* Forcefully rallying the panic-stricken troops, he stopped their flight and successfully turned them around, shouting, "Turn back, men! Turn back!" and then led a Union counterattack in the afternoon that forced the Southerners to lose everything they had won that morning.

The Confederate Army, nearly annihilated, retired to New Market and then continued all the way south to Staunton, the southern edge of the Shenandoah Valley. The defeat ended their occupation of the Shenandoah and the Confederacy lost its economic support. *"Sheridan's Ride"* became a popular poem that was widely read and

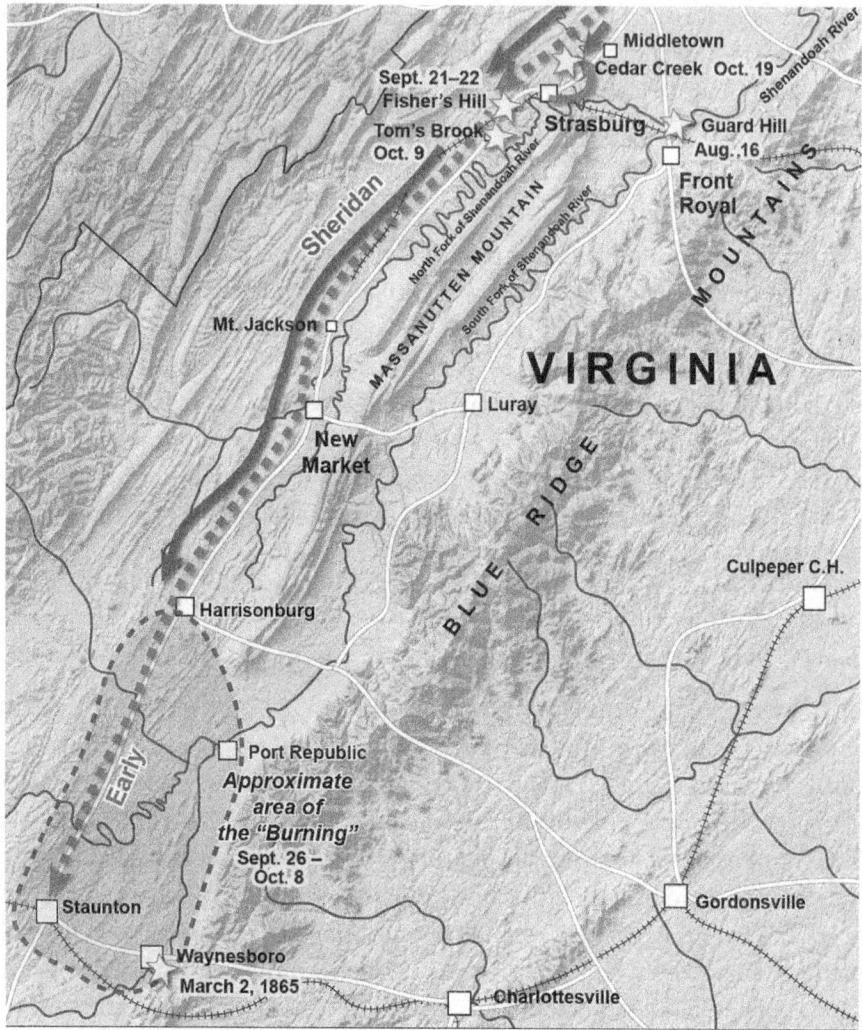

Fig. 47: Union Gen. Philip Sheridan defeated Confederate Gen. Jubal Early in the Shenandoah Valley with a famous ride Oct. 19 on the horse Rienzi forcing Early out of the Valley. Union troops burned local mills, barns, wheat and corn in the "Burning" to eliminate food for the Southern armies.
Source: *Creative Commons Attribution 3.0 License Map by Hal Jespersen, www. cwmaps.com.*

retold over the next few weeks, particularly at election rallies. Sheridan acknowledged that the part of the poem that people liked best was the horse Rienzi, the hero that had delivered Sheridan in the nick of time.

After Sheridan's successful defeat of the Confederates in the Shenandoah, President Lincoln apparently remarked to the Cavalry commander, whose height at five feet, five inches, barely reached Rienzi's shoulder, *"I thought a cavalryman should be at least six feet four inches high (Lincoln's height), but I have changed my mind. Five feet four will do in a pinch."* Public excitement about Sheridan's ride and the news two weeks later about the fall of Atlanta in the Western Theater by Gen. William T. Sherman, helped ensure President Lincoln's reelection that November. With a resounding victory over the Democratic candidate, former Gen. George B. McClellan, Lincoln would remain President until the conclusion of the Civil War.

Grant ordered a 100- gun salute fired in Sheridan's honor at Petersburg and promoted him to Major General. The South was never able to regain its hold on the Shenandoah Valley and the support it provided to the Confederacy was now gone. Left with a small command at Waynesboro, Gen. Early was driven from the Valley permanently by Union Gen. George A. Custer in March 1865. After Early reported to Confederate headquarters in Petersburg, Gen. Lee told Early it was time for him to leave the army and go home. Lee, himself, would surrender to Union troops within weeks.

BATTLES IN TRANS-MISSISSIPPI THEATER

UNION'S FAILED RED RIVER CAMPAIGN
Elaborate Plan for Army-Navy Offensive
March 10-May 22, 1864

An important element of Ulysses S. Grant's overall war strategy in early spring 1864 was that Gen. Nathaniel P. Banks, commanding the Army of the Gulf, would capture Mobile, Alabama, a critical Confederate port city on the Gulf of Mexico, where blockade runners continued to supply the Southerners with guns and ammunition. The effort would be part of a simultaneous advance on all fronts in early May. But Banks had already been committed to the Red River Campaign in Louisiana, a project that had been put in place by then General-in-Chief Henry Halleck and President Lincoln before Grant took command of all armies.

The Red River Campaign objectives were to capture Shreveport, Louisiana, an important Confederate industrial complex, confiscate as much as one hundred thousand bales of cotton from plantations along the Red River and defeat Southern troops in the area. But Confederate Gen. Richard Taylor, commanding the Confederacy's Western District of Louisiana and son of Mexican War hero and former U.S. President Zachary Taylor, had effectively resisted Union efforts in the state the previous three years and would present a serious challenge to any new Union attempt.

Grant objected to the expedition but Halleck invoked White House priority to move forward with the campaign. French imperial troops under Maximillian in Mexico had sufficiently alarmed Lincoln for the need to discourage French interference in supporting the Confederacy. Occupation of Shreveport would provide the opportunity to establish a Union presence in Texas near the Louisiana border. In addition, there was concern that Mexico might try to recapture their lost territory of Texas after the Mexican-American War.

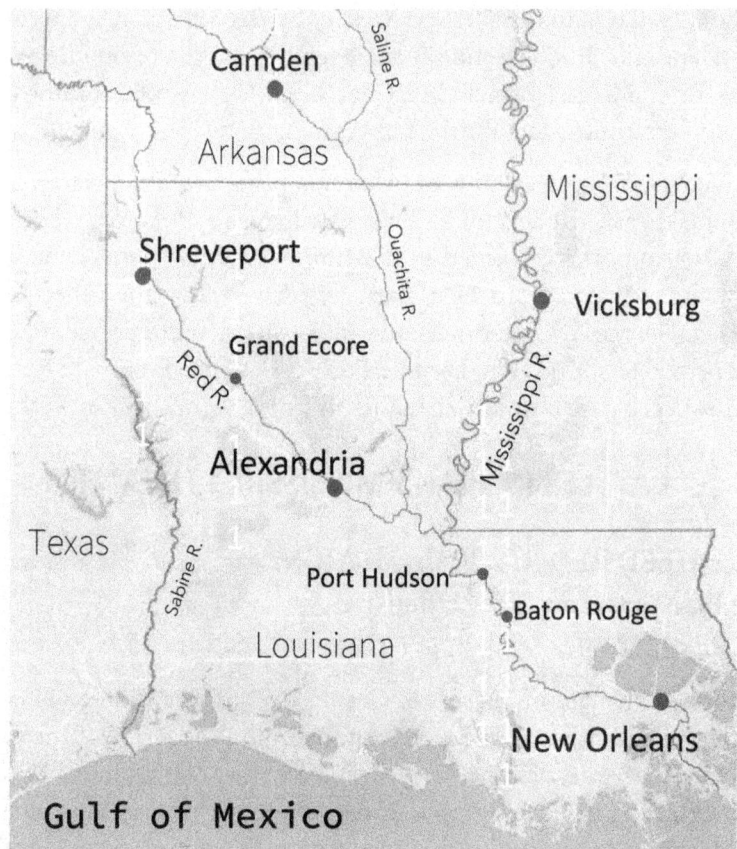

Fig. 48: The Red River Campaign placed Union combined forces of the Army and Navy on the Red River in a campaign to capture Shreveport, Louisiana. The expedition became a disastrous Union defeat.

Another proposed benefit from a successful Red River campaign would be the capture of cotton bales. The Northern textile industry had suffered from the short supply of cotton during the war and only twenty-five percent of the textile facilities were operating. Capture of Southern cotton would benefit the Northern economy and strengthen support for the re-election of Lincoln in the November elections. Banks, an ally of several wealthy New England textile mill owners, hoped to score a major military victory with the campaign that would enhance his political ambitions.

The Red River Campaign combined army forces from the Gulf, Vicksburg and Little Rock, Arkansas, with Union Navy forces under Rear Admiral David D. Porter, commanding the Mississippi River Squadron. The Army of the Gulf with 20,000 men under Gen. Banks would be reinforced by another 10,000, commanded by Gen. Andrew Jackson (A. J.) Smith, seasoned veterans on loan from Gen. William T. Sherman's Army of the Tennessee, now located at Vicksburg. Smith's command was added to protect the Naval fleet in the event the Army of the Gulf withdrew. An additional 8,500 soldiers from the Union Department of Arkansas at Little Rock, under the command of Gen. Frederick Steele, would join the rest of the forces at Shreveport.

Forces under Admiral Porter and Gen. Smith would move up the Red River and meet with Bank's army from the Gulf. The combined Army-Navy contingent would next proceed up the river to capture Shreveport, Louisiana, which would provide a pathway to east Texas. The operation appeared reasonable and practical when generated on paper by Gen. Halleck in Washington. Its execution in the Louisiana woods and on the tortuous, winding Red River would be a disaster.

Combined Army-Navy Expedition
March 10-26, 1864

Union Gen. A. J. Smith, Army of the Tennessee, joined Rear Admiral David D. Porter at Vicksburg on March 10 and the combined Army-Navy fleet traveled down the Mississippi to its junction with Red River. The 210-gun naval fleet under Porter included a paddle-wheel steamer, ironclads, tinclads (lightly armored gunboats), timberclads (which used wood plating), high-speed vessels with rams, barges of light draft, three river monitors (lightly armored gunboats of shallow draft) and troop transports. The entire fleet included ninety boats.

The first vessel to be sent upriver was the heaviest ironclad, the *Eastport*, which immediately became stuck in a sandbar. Once freed, the fleet was able to move upriver for a few miles to the village of Simmesport, which was then used as a supply base. Disembarking from the transports, the Vicksburg veterans made an all-night march and easily overwhelmed Confederate Fort De Russy on March 14, capturing ten guns and 300 prisoners. Confederate command had left the fort with only a skeleton crew and moved most of their troops upriver.

When joined by Porter's fleet, the land and navy components continued thirty miles upriver to arrive on March 20 at Alexandria, which immediately surrendered to the Union forces. While they waited for Gen. Nathaniel P. Banks and his Army of the Gulf to join them, Porter and his men gathered all the cotton they could find and marked it for the U.S. Navy. Under the terms of Naval Prize Law, the proceeds of captured goods would be divided between the navy and the crew and officers of the ship.

Politically appointed Gen. Banks arrived March 26 from New Orleans, more than a week later than the agreed upon rendezvous, on a steamboat filled with Northern cotton businessmen. The boat had been able to travel directly from New Orleans to the mouth of the Red River as the Mississippi River was now in Union control after the fall of Vicksburg and Port Hudson the year before. Troops from the Army of the Gulf, under the command of Gen. William B. Franklin, had arrived by foot the previous day, plastered with mud from rain-drenched roads, as they marched overland from Fort Brashear (today's location is Morgan City), Louisiana.

Admiral Porter, already fuming about the delay of Banks' arrival, did not welcome a boatful of civilian businessmen who would be part of a military mission. Adding to the growing hostility between the army and navy commanders, Banks and the cotton speculators were not happy with the collected cotton bales already bearing the navy's ownership. Sailors had labeled each bale with the letters "C.S.A" (Confederate States of America) that were then crossed out and the initials "U.S.N." (U.S. Navy) placed below, thwarting any plans for Banks to claim them for the army or the cotton dealers to profit from them. At an estimated $500 per bale, seized cotton represented a huge prize.

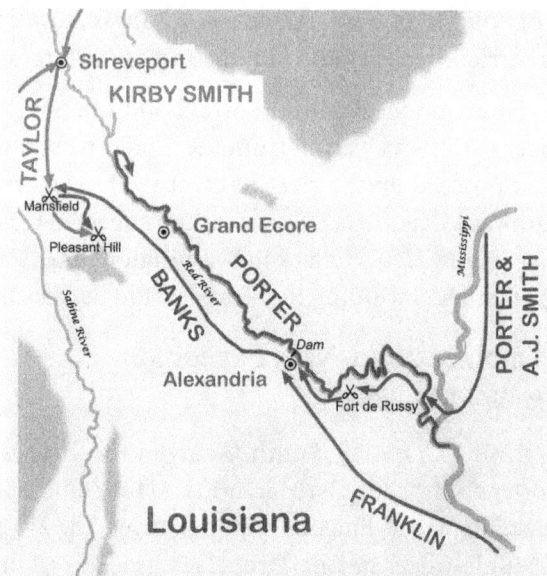

Fig. 49: The Navy fleet under Admiral Porter moved up Red River while the Union Army under Gen. Banks proceeded toward Shreveport against Confederate Gen. Taylor on a separate narrow road to Mansfield.

Source: *This work released into the public domain by its author, Andrei Nacu through the Wikipedia Project.*

An additional hurdle for the mission was the notice from Gen. Grant that the 10,000 men on loan from the Army of Tennessee would need to be returned to Vicksburg and Gen. Sherman by April 15 to participate in the Atlanta Campaign, even if the objective of reaching Shreveport was not met. Banks' leisurely approach to the mission now took on greater urgency.

Red River Challenges

Red River water levels fluctuated with the seasons and its winding tortuous path was fraught with sandbars, snags and stumps. In addition, the Confederates had installed mines and various other defensive measures, such as a sunken steamboat, to thwart passage by the Navy ships. Adding to the obstacles the Navy faced, the river had become dangerously low for the ships to pass over the rapids above Alexandria. Banks, however, intent on a successful mission that would enhance his political reputation, insisted that the expedition continue.

Much to his great reluctance, Porter agreed to continue the effort. With a slight rise in the water level, twelve ironclads and twenty army transports eventually passed through the rapids above Alexandria and proceeded sixty miles upriver to reach Grand Ecore on April 3, with the army marching alongside on the river road. Planters upriver, aware that Union military was confiscating all cotton bales, began to burn their cotton rather than have it fall into Northern hands. The cotton speculators, with no prospects of profit left for them, became bitterly furious with Banks for failing to deliver what they had anticipated, and they were sent back to Alexandria.

At this point, Gen. Banks decided to take most of the army and leave the river and proceed toward Shreveport inland on a road that ran through Pleasant Hill and Mansfield. They would regroup with the naval fleet at Springfield Landing, just below Shreveport. Porter resisted the decision, believing the army should remain with the navy as it proceeded upriver, but Banks thought it would save time and he departed from the river on April 6.

Without useful maps, Banks had mistakenly relied on the advice of a local river pilot, who was determined to lead the army away from the road bordering the river where they would find his fields of cotton and confiscate his crops. Porter's convoy of boats and an infantry of about 2,500 men soon discovered the better road along the river and army troops and navy proceeded together up the river. But Banks' army of about 25,000 men and one thousand well-supplied wagons were already gone and their long wagon train stretched twenty miles on the narrow road with the veteran Vicksburg troops guarding its rear.

Battles of Mansfield (or Battle of Sabine Crossroads) and Pleasant Hill, Louisiana
April 8-9, 1864

Constant skirmishing between Union and Confederate cavalries had occurred since March 21, but on April 8, just three miles from Mansfield, Gen. Banks' army encountered Confederate Gen. Richard Taylor and an army of about 10,000 infantry and cavalry ready for battle. Much of the Union Army was separated and in disarray, stretched out by the long wagon train.

Taylor's men attacked with such fury that the leading Union contingent turned and ran. As the Northerners retreated from the Confederate onslaught, the Southern soldiers paused to loot some of the wagons which gave Union troops time to fall back. Banks was forced to order a retreat and the Battle of Mansfield was over. A second attack by the Confederates the next day at the Battle of Pleasant Hill ran into Gen. A. J. Smith's veteran troops from Vicksburg, who routed the Southerners, which allowed Union troops to rapidly withdraw back to Grand Ecore. Confederate Gen. Taylor requested reinforcements to chase the Union forces, but his superior, Gen. E. Kirby Smith, refused the request. Smith had been transferred to command the Trans-Mississippi Department (comprising Arkansas, Missouri, Texas and western Louisiana) in January 1863, following the failed Heartland Offensive into Kentucky with Gen. Braxton Bragg in September 1862. Concerned about a third Union Army approaching Shreveport from Arkansas, Kirby Smith sent half of Taylor's army north to intercept it.

Navy Fleet Attacked on Red River
April 8-15, 1864

In the meantime, Porter and his convoy were proceeding up a river that was becoming more and more hazardous. River water was getting lower and the passage was twisting and narrow. Sharpshooters and occasional guerrilla fire attacked the boats from both sides. On April 10 at Loggy Bayou, the fleet found a huge river steamer that had been sunk to block passage forward. At the same time, Porter received a message from Banks that he was retreating back to Grand Ecore and the fleet should turn around. The warships, too large to turn, had to steam backwards for several miles to make their turns.

Although half of Confederate Gen. Taylor's army had been ordered north to counter the advance of the Union Army of Arkansas, now underway from Little Rock, the remaining Confederates vigorously pursued the naval fleet as the convoy headed downstream. On April 12, a Confederate four-gun battery pounded the boats, stranding some of them in the river bottom. The next day, the naval convoy continued to face a gauntlet of challenges as boats ran aground and the men struggled to refloat or tow them while under heavy fire. By April 14-15, the fleet miraculously reached Grand Ecore.

Failed Camden Expedition from Arkansas
March 23-May 3 1864

In the meantime, while Porter's fleet was facing increasing difficulties trying to return to Alexandria, Gen. Frederick Steele, commanding the Army of the Department of Arkansas, left Little Rock, Arkansas, on March 23 with an 8,500-man force of infantry, artillery and cavalry to join Union troops under Gen. Nathaniel P. Banks at Shreveport, Louisiana, some two hundred miles to the south. As the army departed with inadequate provisions for the expedition, Steele hoped to resupply rations for his men along the way.

But passing through a thinly populated wilderness that had already been depleted of supplies, Steele found no opportunity to obtain more provisions. Minor Confederate assaults on April 1 and April 3 delayed the army's progress and consumed more of its dwindling rations. Reinforcements from Indian Territory arrived on April 9 in the form of 4,000 men of the Frontier Division while Steele and his men waited at the Little Missouri River. Unfortunately, the frontiersmen brought little food with them and Steele realized that he had no choice but to find food for his now expanded army to be able to continue the expedition. He turned the whole army toward Camden (See Fig. 50).

About this time, Confederate Gen. E. Kirby Smith considered how to meet the threat of three Union armies converging on Shreveport. He took three infantry divisions from Gen. Richard Taylor's army as it was battling Banks and the Union naval fleet on the Red River and combined them with forces from Gen. Sterling Price, who

VII. THE FOURTH YEAR: 1864

had been ordered to bring his small force from southern Arkansas to Shreveport. The Confederates moved north to meet the Union advance from Gen. Steele in Arkansas.

Skirmishes with Confederate cavalry under the command of Gen. Price continued to harass Steele's progress, but he finally arrived at Camden, Arkansas, on April 15. Steele desperately needed to resupply his troops who had been on half rations since leaving Little Rock, but there were no supplies as Confederate forces had drained Camden of its stocks. A Union foraging party found corn and other supplies west of Camden, but lost it in a Confederate ambush at Poison Springs on April 18.

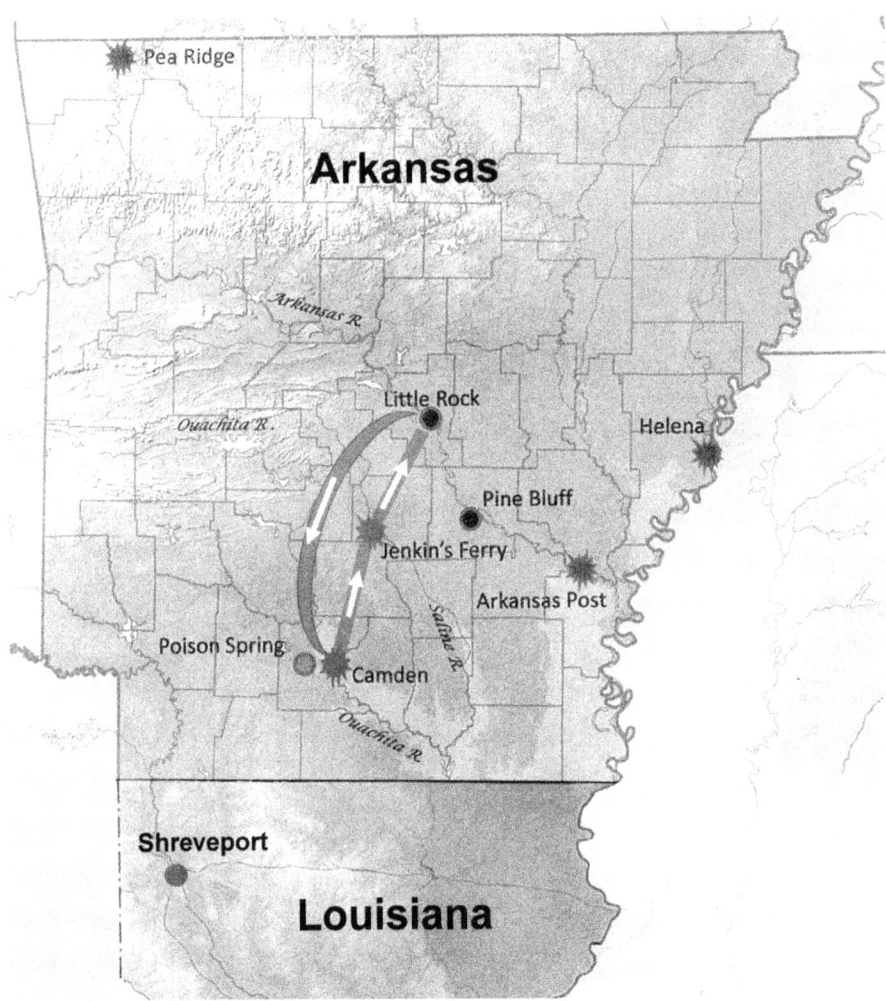

Fig. 50: The Union Army Camden Expedition left Little Rock to support the Red River Campaign at Shreveport, Louisiana, but reduced rations, raids from Confederates and an aborted Union Campaign forced the army to return to Little Rock. The map also shows locations of previous major battles where Union forces prevailed at Pea Ridge, Helena and Arkansas Post in 1862-63.

While Steele waited in Camden for a wagon train of needed supplies that was coming from the Union-supply depot at Pine Bluff on the Arkansas River, he received news of Banks' defeat at Mansfield. At this point, Gen. Steele, now resupplied on April 20, needed to abandon the campaign and return to Little Rock. Although threatened by Confederates on the outskirts of Camden, Steele's army was able to successfully withdraw April 26 under cover of night. Slogging through deep mud, his nearly exhausted men reached Jenkins' Ferry on the Saline River April 29 with the Confederates under Generals Kirby Smith and Price in hot pursuit. Steele's troops struggled to create a pontoon bridge across the swollen river as the Confederates rapidly approached.

The Battle of Jenkin's Ferry commenced in the early morning of April 30 with the Confederates attacking the Union rear guard. Heavy breastworks between a swollen creek on one side and swampy woodlands on the other provided the Union men with good position against the Southern assault. The rest of Steele's army worked to get wagons, animals and troops across the river on the rapidly assembled pontoon bridge. By afternoon, all the Union Army had crossed and the bridge was burned as it would not be needed again. Steele's exhausted army arrived in fortified Little Rock on May 3, bringing an end to the so-called Camden Expedition and any participation in the Red River Campaign.

One of the greatest Union disasters in Arkansas throughout the war, Steele's forces suffered more than 2,500 casualties, the loss of 635 wagons, 2,500 animals and eight artillery pieces. Union forces continued to occupy the fortified locations of Little Rock, Pine Bluff, Arkansas Post and Helena, but Confederates remained free to roam rural Arkansas until the state surrendered.

Navy Trapped on Red River
May 1-May 18, 1864

Back at Grand Ecore, Gen. Banks received an urgent message from Gen. William T. Sherman that the Union troops under Gen. A. J. Smith were to return to Vicksburg at once. A second order was received about the same time from General-in-Chief Grant, ordering Banks to move the Army of the Gulf to New Orleans immediately and prepare to attack Mobile Bay. Admiral Porter's navy fleet had already headed down the river on April 16.

Abandoning his already failed expedition, Banks began his retreat on April 21, pressing his foot-sore troops urgently. After setting Grand Ecore to the torch, the army continued its destruction as farms, plantations and the village of Natchitoches were looted and burned. The lead division of Banks' army reached Alexandria on April 25.

As the navy fleet proceeded to Alexandria, the river became even more treacherous. The heavy gunboat *Eastport* struck a river mine, sinking its keel to river bottom, only a few feet deep, blocking the rest of the flotilla. Six days of effort and two pump boats got it afloat again, only to be irretrievably wedged in a snag pile a few days later. With no more options available, Porter blew up the *Eastport* with a ton of gunpowder on

VII. THE FOURTH YEAR: 1864

April 26 and the rest of the fleet slipped past the destroyed ship. Confederate ambushes shredded the transport boats and severely damaged the warships. Tragic death came to more than one hundred former slaves rescued from plantations when a steamer boiler was pierced with gunfire.

When the flotilla reached the rapids above Alexandria, the mile-long stretch of water that separated the lower and upper rapids, was now less than four feet deep, too shallow for the ships to pass through. The flotilla was trapped. *"I saw nothing before me but the destruction of the best part of the Mississippi Squadron,"* Admiral Porter said. Although river levels normally stayed much higher through the spring, Confederates had blown the dams of two tributary channels upstream, diverting water into bayous just above Grand Ecore.

With no options before him, Porter reluctantly agreed to a proposal from Joseph Bailey, a Lieutenant Colonel in the Army of the Gulf, to build two wing dams on opposite banks that would extend only partway into the river. Bailey, who was not an engineer, but had worked in the rivers of Wisconsin as a lumberman and knew how to create dams that would accumulate sufficient water to carry logs downstream. Given approval to proceed, commanding 3,000 men, Bailey promptly went to work May 1 on the lower falls.

Trees were cut down; wood and bricks were removed from the city of Alexandria and brought to the site. The dam on one of the banks was created by locking large tree branches together with their trunks tied to each other on the upstream with heavy timber. The dam on the opposite side was created with large wooden cribs, anchored in place and filled with sand, mud, stone and bricks. Four sunken high-sided barges, filled with rubble, were anchored between the dams to create a reservoir that would slowly fill. When sufficient water depth was reached, the barges would be shifted and the flotilla could pass as the reservoir slowly drained.

By early dawn on May 8, the water level had risen more than six feet, nearly enough to make a run for passage of the ten boats stranded above the rapids. But just as dawn broke, the two barges shifted from the increased water pressure and water began to rush through the open gap. Watching the water surge through the open hole, Porter ordered one of the lighter-draft boats to enter the wildly churning water. Plunging into the roaring current, the first of four boats, the *Lexington* timberclad, managed to negotiate a rocky passage through the channel to land safely in deep water below the falls to the cheers of thousands of men. Three more boats passed through, including two of the gunboats, before the water levels dropped too low for the remaining ships to make a run.

To solve the problem, Col. Bailey again came to the rescue. He proposed a second wing dam at the upper rapids, which would diminish the weight pressing on a single dam. Using a thousand men, now fully experienced in constructing wing dams, the work was done in three days. On May 11, three more boats successfully passed through the mile-long rapids and over both falls. By May 13, the last of the gunboats had passed through and all the surviving boats were safe.

Although Confederate forces under Gen. Taylor continued their efforts to trap the Union Navy, they were unsuccessful and the convoy safely arrived at the mouth of the Red River on the Mississippi River on May 18. The Red River Campaign, referred to as the Red River Disaster, was a dismal Union failure, which did not achieve one of its objectives. Diversion of Union forces from Grant's strategic war plan to take Mobile Bay, Alabama, may have delayed the end of the war by several months. The delay prevented Union troops under Gen. A. J. Smith from joining the Atlanta Campaign, headed by Gen. William T. Sherman, which commenced on May 4, 1864. Smith's troops were transferred to fight in the Battle of Nashville, Tennessee, under Gen. George Thomas.

The expedition effectively ended Banks' military career and the controversy of using military boats to remove cotton hurt his political aspirations. On arrival at the Mississippi, Banks was removed from command by Gen. Edward Canby, who eventually commanded the troops of the Army of the Gulf, which captured the city of Mobile, Alabama, in 1865.

Porter received significant monetary compensation from the sale of cotton as a prize of war and was named commander of the North Atlantic Blockading Squadron. Bailey was promoted for his extraordinary service in saving the naval fleet from a humiliating defeat in the Red River and a thankful Rear Admiral Porter gave Bailey a $700 gold inlaid sword.

Confederate Gen. Taylor carried a life-long grudge against Gen. E. Kirby Smith who had removed half his army to combat Union Gen. Steele in the Camden Campaign, ruining Taylor's opportunity to capture the Union fleet, as it lay helpless above the falls of Alexandria.

Arkansas remained largely in Confederate hands until the end of the war with isolated Union occupations at Fort Smith, Pine Bluff, Arkansas Post, Helena and Little Rock. Although Confederates did not capture the Union Army or Naval fleet during the Red River Campaign, they had successfully thwarted Union attempts to reach east Texas and prevented any demonstration of strength against a possible Mexican invasion.

The Union Navy lost one hospital boat, five transports, three gunboats, several service boats and twenty-one pieces of artillery. Combined casualties from the Camden Expedition and the Red River campaign exceeded 8,000, plus losses of more than eight hundred wagons. Confederate casualties numbered about 6,000.

BATTLES IN THE WESTERN THEATER

Following the general strategic goals that General-in-Chief Ulysses S. Grant and President Lincoln developed in early 1864, namely that Confederate armies and strongholds in the Eastern and Western theaters must be completely defeated, an all-out offensive was launched May 4, 1864. The Eastern Theater would be directed by Grant himself, as he accompanied Gen. George Meade with the Army of the Potomac. The Western Theater would be consolidated into the Military Division of the Mississippi, commanded by Gen. William T. Sherman. Its primary target would be the Confederate Army of Tennessee, currently located in Georgia.

Grant's instructions to Sherman, *"You, I propose to move against (Gen. Joseph E.) Johnston's army, to break it up, and to get into the interior of the enemy's country as far as you can, inflicting all the damage you can against their war resources."* Sherman's Mississippi command included the newly recreated 2nd Army of the Ohio (14,000 men) under Gen. John M. Schofield; the Cumberland (60,000) under Gen. George H. Thomas; and the Army of the Tennessee (24,000) under Gen. James B. McPherson.

Meridian Campaign, Mississippi-Alabama
February 3-28, 1864

With the capture of Vicksburg and the surrender of Port Hudson in July 1863, Union forces now commanded the Mississippi River all the way to New Orleans. But guerilla attacks along the river, particularly near the Gulf of Mexico, continued to threaten Union movements, making navigation on the river difficult. After Union forces conquered Chattanooga and relieved the siege at Knoxville, Tennessee, in December 1863, Gen. William T. Sherman returned to headquarters at Vicksburg with the Army of the Tennessee and proposed an attack on the Confederate territory in Mississippi east of the river and possibly damage enemy resources at Selma and Mobile, Alabama. Grant approved the proposal, to be coordinated with efforts by the Army of the Gulf, provided that Sherman and his command would be ready for the spring campaigns, targeted to begin May 4.

Meridian, Mississippi, about one hundred fifty miles directly east of Vicksburg on the border between Mississippi and Alabama, was a major hub where three railroads intersected and provided an important center for the distribution of food, weapons and supplies to the eastern Confederacy. Wheat, corn and vegetables, plus beef cattle, were available from the rich agricultural area north of the city and shipped to the Confederate armies on a regular basis. Warehouses, depots, an armory and military hospital made Meridian a tempting target for a Union attack.

Collecting about 20,000 troops from Vicksburg and Memphis, Gen. Sherman departed Vicksburg on February 3, 1864, to move into Mississippi and inflict damage on the railroads and other Confederate resources of war. Accompanying him was a cavalry force of 7,000 men under Gen. William Sooy Smith. Sherman conducted a number of feints along the march which kept Southern forces at Meridian, under the command of Gen. Leonidas Polk, guessing as to where the Union forces were heading. To add to Polk's confusion, Union Gen. Nathaniel P. Banks, Army of the Gulf, arranged for gunboats that appeared to be attacking the port city of Mobile, Alabama. Polk, convinced that Sherman's destination was Mobile, evacuated Meridian hours before Sherman's troops arrived on February 14.

Sherman's infantry entered an undefended city and over a five-day period destroyed warehouses, an arsenal and railroads in every direction. One hundred fifteen miles of track, sixty-one bridges, twenty locomotives, twenty-eight cars and three steam sawmills were destroyed or devastated. The expedition was a preview of Sherman's March to the Sea through Georgia later that year when the Union army would travel through enemy territory, live off the land, inflict heavy damage and then move on.

Gen. Smith and his cavalry never arrived at Meridian, as they got caught in the Battle of Okolona on February 22 against Confederate Gen. Nathan Bedford Forrest. Forced to retreat, Gen. Smith and his cavalry barely escaped capture. Smith and his exhausted men crossed back into Tennessee on February 26, reporting a failed mission.

Fort Pillow Massacre, Tennessee
April 12, 1864

Prior to the onset of Grant's offensives in the Eastern and Western Theaters which would begin the first week in May, a significant event took place at Fort Pillow on April 12, 1864. The fort, some forty miles north of Memphis, Tennessee, on the Mississippi River had been created by the Confedercy to protect Memphis from a river attack by Union forces. Built by Confederate Gen. Gideon Pillow in 1861, the fort was used by the Southerners to block Union ships from using the Mississippi to move supplies and troops. But the fort fell to Union forces in June 1862 and was occupied in 1864 with troops that included Black soldiers from the United States Colored Troops.

Confederate Gen. Nathan Bedford Forrest, an innovative and effective cavalry commander, launched a raid in March 1864 through Tennessee and Kentucky to reinforce his supplies and capture Union prisoners and horses. Forrest communicated on April 4 that Fort Pillow was his next target as it had horses that he needed to resupply his large cavalry.

The fort had been constructed to defend against attacks from the water, but was poorly designed for attacks from land. To defend against approaching raiders, soldiers had to mount to the top of the parapets to fire their guns, which placed them as easy targets for Confederate sharp-shooters, who took a terrible toll on the garrison troops. Forrest's cavalry was soon able to storm the walls of the fort and force the Union commander to surrender.

Among the 600 men stationed there were about 300 Black soldiers. The presence of former slaves that had been elevated to the status of soldiers enraged the Confederates and hundreds were killed outright. Accused of war crimes for not stopping the massacre, Forrest, a former slave-owner who had made millions trading in cotton, land and slaves, was never charged. But his failure to treat captured Black soldiers as legitimate prisoners of war infuriated Gen. Grant and Northern opinion, which, unfortunately, put an end to all prisoner exchanges. All soldiers captured in battle now ended up in prisoner-of-war camps.

Forrest would later become leader of the Ku Klux Klan, a white supremist terrorist group, that brutally assaulted, murdered and lynched Black Americans following the end of the Civil War. Forrest was named the "Grand Wizard" of the organization, taking advantage of his nickname "Wizard of the Saddle." The Ku Klux Klan was largely dissolved in 1869 during Reconstruction, but Forrest was never held accountable and died of natural causes in 1877. Elements of the KKK would re-emerge in later years in the Deep South as white supremacists used the same tactics of terror and intimidation against Blacks.

THE ATLANTA CAMPAIGN, GEORGIA

The city of Atlanta in 1864 had prospered during the war, growing in population from about 9,000 to 20,000. The hub for the Confederacy's war industry, the city was of great importance for its large number of factories, foundries, machine shops and warehouses, all supporting the Southern war effort. Atlanta's factories provided armor plate, pistols and rifles, swords and cannon, plus all manner of railroad equipment and rail tracks, and food and clothing for the Confederates. Multiple roads radiated out from the city in all directions, which connected Atlanta with sources of food from the rich agricultural regions of Georgia and clothes and supplies from neighboring towns and states that were then redistributed to the Confederate armies.

Several railroads converged on Atlanta and trains left hourly with supplies for the Confederacy. In the eastern direction, the Georgia Railroad ran all the way to Augusta, Georgia, and linked with the Confederate Powderworks, a gunpowder facility on the Savannah River. The cities of Macon and Jonesboro to the southeast were connected to Atlanta by the Macon & Western Railroad. The Atlanta & West Point Railroad linked to West Point, Georgia, located on the border between Georgia and Alabama, which then connected to the Western Railway of Alabama. But after the loss of Chattanooga in November 1863 to the Union, the Western & Atlantic Railroad to the north was now under Union control.

Battle of Dalton (or Rocky Face Ridge)
May 7-13, 1864

The three armies which formed the Union Military Division of the Mississippi under Gen. William T. Sherman departed Chattanooga, Tennessee, on Grant's appointed day of May 4, 1864, for the all-out combined offensive on the Confederacy. Sherman's mission was to pursue and defeat Confederate Gen. Joseph E. Johnston, who had been appointed commander of the Confederate Army of Tennessee after the defeat of Gen. Braxton Bragg at the Battle of Chattanooga. Johnston had built extensive defensive protections in Georgia, anticipating a strong Union offensive.

STRUGGLE FOR THE UNION

The Army of the Cumberland under Gen. George H. Thomas, based at Chattanooga, and the Army of the Ohio, headquartered at Cleveland, Ohio, commanded by Gen. John M. Schofield, formed the center and left flank, respectively, of Gen. Sherman's army, as they approached Dalton, Georgia, about forty miles southeast of Chattanooga. The Union Army of the Tennessee, now under the command of Gen. James B. McPherson, formed the right wing of Sherman's forces and focused on the Confederate's left flank in the unoccupied region west of Dalton. The armies of Thomas and Schofield converged at Tunnel Hill, Georgia, about ten miles north of Dalton on May 7, 1864. A small group of Confederates, protecting the railroad at Tunnel Hill, were quickly driven off by the large Union forces. The tunnel had been built by the Western & Atlantic Railroad in the late 1840s and considered an engineering marvel when the first train of cars passed through it in 1850.

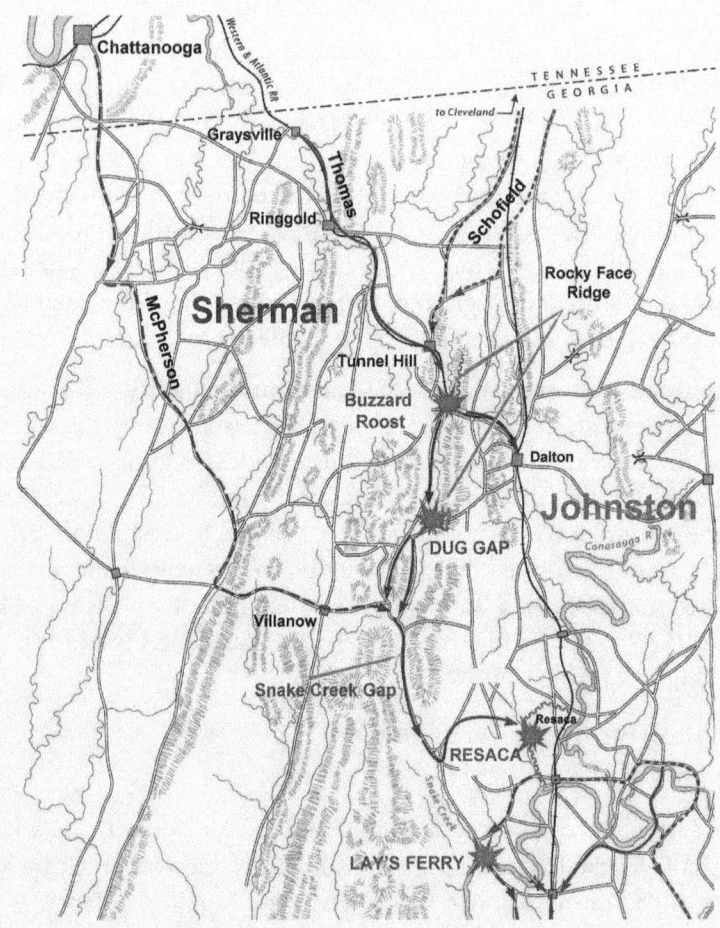

Fig. 51: Union Gen. William T. Sherman advanced into Georgia to face Confederate Gen. Joseph E. Johnston at Buzzard Roost near Dalton in the opening battles of the Union Army's Atlanta Campaign.

Source: *This map is a work of the U.S. federal government by a U.S. Army soldier or employee and is in the public domain.*

VII. THE FOURTH YEAR: 1864

From the tunnel, Sherman looked into the gorge, described as Buzzard Roost, situated between two straight, sharp palisade rock faces that rose seven hundred feet above the valley and ran for ten miles. Known as Rocky Face Ridge, the strong Confederate defenses that Johnston had created over the last several months were clearly visible. Mill Creek, which flowed through a high gap in the gorge had been dammed, flooding the road. In an early encounter in the gorge, Union troops advanced up the steep slopes of Dug Gap but were driven off by the Confederates in hand-to-hand fighting.

In the face of such strong fortifications, Sherman rejected a frontal assault, but pursued a strategy to capture the railroad in Johnston's rear at Resaca and force him to abandon the defenses at Buzzard Roost. While the armies of Thomas and Schofield occupied Johnston's forces at Rocky Ridge, Gen. McPherson's Army of the Tennessee identified a rough wagon road that bypassed Johnston's left flank which was unobserved and unprotected by the Confederates.

Directing his army through the rough country that converged to a single narrow track at Snake Creek Gap, McPherson successfully reached Resaca, coming within a mile and a half of the railroad on May 9. Finding entrenched Confederates, he withdrew to a place of safety three miles back and communicated the news to Sherman. But McPherson's caution lost the opportunity for his army to take Resaca. His troops of 24,000 greatly outnumbered the small number of defenders and an assault at that time would have taken Resaca and placed him firmly in Johnston's rear. Sherman would later write in his *Memoirs*, "*Such an opportunity does not occur twice in a single life, but at this critical moment McPherson seems to have been a little cautious.*"

> **UNION ARMY SLIPS PAST CONFEDERATE DEFENSES**
>
> Gen. Sherman writes, *"The movement of us through Snake-Creek Gap was a total surprise to him (Johnston). My army about doubled his in size, but he had all the advantages of natural positions of artificial forts and roads, and of concentrated action. We were compelled to grope our way through forests, across mountains, with a large army, necessarily more or less dispersed."*
>
> Memoirs, W. T. Sherman, 1875

With the news of McPherson's success, Sherman slowly disengaged his troops from Rocky Face Ridge and all of the Union army passed through the narrow and challenging access of Snake Creek Gap. The entire Union Army had out-flanked the Southerners. When Johnston realized that Sherman was closing on his rear, he quickly abandoned his well-prepared defenses at Dalton and Buzzard Roost and withdrew twelve miles south on the night of May 12 to his well-prepared entrenchments at Resaca.

Battle of Resaca, Georgia
May 14-15

Heavy fighting commenced at Resaca on May 14, with the Confederates blocking any Union advances from a formidable line of entrenchments that covered the whole town. Positioned on high ground, looking down on the Union forces as they attacked, Johnston's troops were able to withstand multiple attacks. Casualties were high, totaling about 6,100 (3,500 Union and 2,600 Confederate). But on May 15, Sherman's army was able to secure a crossing over the Oostanaula River with two pontoon bridges at Lay's Ferry three miles below the town and began its march south to Calhoun (See Fig. 52). Confederate Gen. Johnston, forced to retreat, crossed the Oostanaula during the night, burning the bridge behind him, and withdrew along the Western & Altoona Railroad to Adairsville about ten miles south of Calhoun.

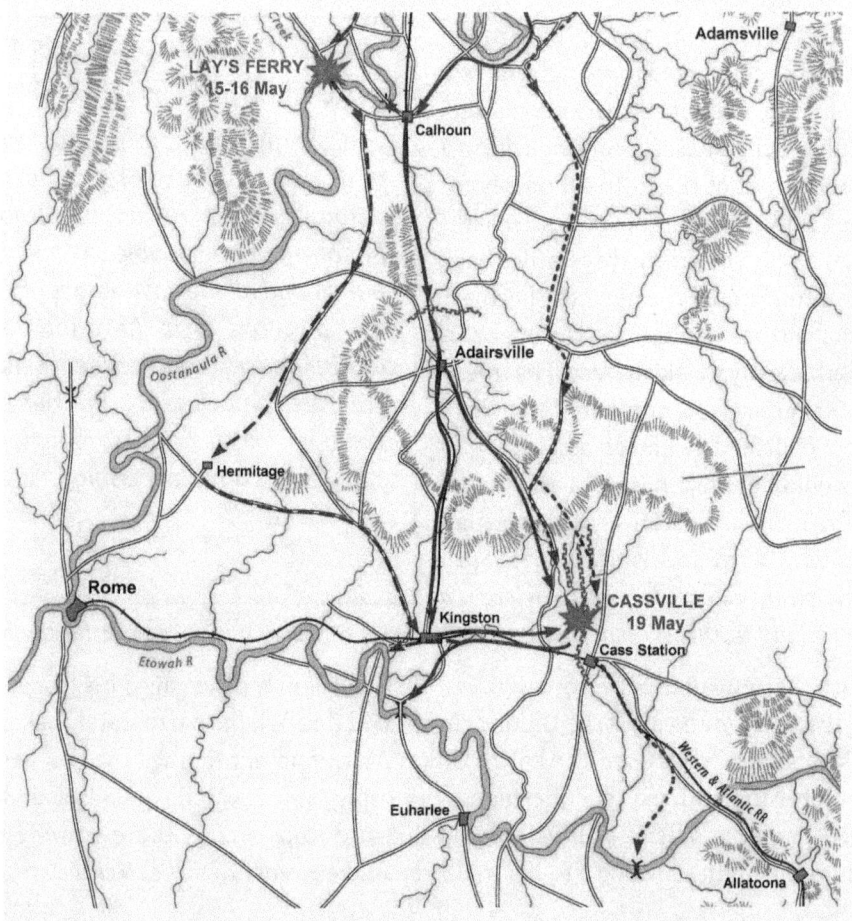

Fig. 52: During the Atlanta Campaign, Union forces crossed the Oostanaula River at Lay's Ferry near Resaca, Georgia, to move south to Cassville. The Confederates retreated to Allatoona Pass.
Source: *This map is a work of the U.S. federal government by a U.S. Army soldier or employee and is in the public domain.*

VII. THE FOURTH YEAR: 1864

Pursuing the Confederates, a Union infantry unit, led by Major Arthur MacArthur, Jr., (father of Douglas MacArthur of World War II fame) suffered heavy losses on May 17 two miles north of Adairsville when they attacked entrenched Confederates and the pursuit was called off. Only nineteen years old at the time, MacArthur had exhibited extraordinary bravery in the Battle of Chattanooga at Missionary Ridge and would later receive the Medal of Honor for his actions. The Union assault continued to press the Confederates, with part of the army moving to Kingston and the rest to Cassville. Failing to find good defenses at Cassville, Johnston retreated again, crossing the Etowah River at night, moving south to Cartersville and Allatoona Pass.

With Johnston positioned south of him, Sherman ordered a rest at Cassville and Kingston to repair damages to the Western & Atlantic Railroad, his only supply line. Col. W. W. Wright, a skillful and industrious railroad-engineer with about two thousand men, repaired the bridge at Resaca in three days and railroad cars loaded with Union supplies and stores arrived at Kingston May 24. Avoiding the well defended Allatoona Pass, the Union Army began its move May 25 toward Dallas, Georgia, thirty miles south.

Battles near Dallas, Georgia
May 25-June 4, 1864

A forward leading cavalry from Kingston led by Union Gen. "Fighting Joe" Hooker from the Army of the Cumberland encountered waiting Confederates on May 25 at New Hope Church, a Methodist meeting house. The battle quickly escalated into a full-scale confrontation as Johnston brought in reinforcements. Prolonged fighting continued into the night and the next day, giving the battle the name of "Hell-Hole." Union Gen. George H. Thomas attempted to send troops to support Hooker at New Hope, but his men were hit hard at the Battle of Pickett's Mill May 27. Gen. James B. McPherson's army arrived at Dallas on May 28 to support Hooker, which quickly drove the Confederates into a full assault on McPherson. The attack was finally driven off on June 1 with large Confederate losses, enabling Union troops to join Hooker at New Hope.

With Johnston's army heavily engaged at Pickett's Mill and New Hope Church, Sherman ordered cavalry to enter Allatoona on June 1 and when they encountered no opposition, the railroad track was repaired back to Kingston. With Allatoona in Union hands, Sherman was able to withdraw troops from Dallas on June 5 and move his army northeast to take possession of the railhead at Big Shanty and the Western & Atlantic Railroad, the Union's vital supply line for supplies.

Sherman reported over 9,000 casualties for the month of May. *"We had steadily driven our antagonists from the strong positions of Dalton, Resaca, Cassville, Allatoona and Dallas; had advanced our lines in strong, compact order from Chattanooga to Big Shanty, nearly a hundred miles of as difficult country as was ever fought over by civilized armies."* Confederate casualties for the month of May were about the same at 8,600.

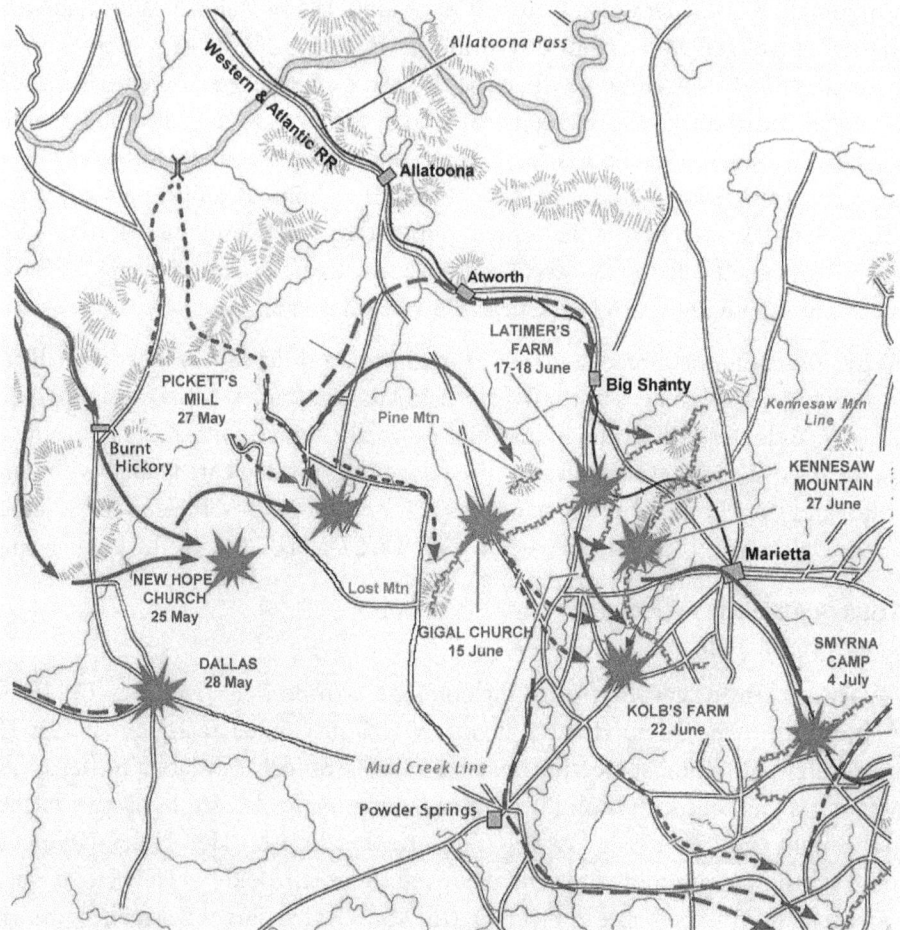

Fig. 53: The Union army engaged in multiple battles around Marietta, Georgia, during the months of May and June 1864 to get past the Confederate defenses as it pressed ever southward to Atlanta.

Source: *This map is a work of the U.S. federal government by a U.S. Army soldier or employee and is in the public domain.*

Battles of Marietta, Georgia
June 9-July 3, 1864

After Sherman moved the Union Army from Dallas to Big Shanty, Confederate Gen. Johnston was forced to quickly establish a defensive position at Marietta and entrenched his troops on Kennesaw, Pine and Lost Mountains about four miles northwest of Marietta. Constant skirmishing occurred between the two armies as Sherman's troops repaired the railroad north from Big Shanty. Col. Wright and his men quickly applied their engineering skills to repair the bridge over the Etowah River at Cartersville which had been destroyed by the Confederates on their retreat.

VII. THE FOURTH YEAR: 1864

On June 11, a loaded train of supplies and ammunition crossed the river and arrived at Big Shanty to welcoming cheers from the Union troops. The railway required protection all the way up the line to Chattanooga to maintain the all-important supplies for the Northerners. Reinforcements, new regiments, and furloughed soldiers returning to duty had successfully brought the Union Army numbers to about 100,000 men. Johnston's Confederate Army now numbered about 65,000.

Heavy rains began on June 1 and continued non-stop, making any movement of troops and artillery difficult and sluggish. On June 14 as the rain slackened, Sherman reviewed the Union's ten-mile-long line, and noted a group of Confederates on top of Pine Mountain. Not knowing that the men on the mountaintop were all Confederate officers, including Gen. Johnston himself, Sherman ordered a nearby Union battery to fire three volleys at the group "... *to keep up the morale of a bold offensive,*" in Sherman's words. The artillery hit its mark and instantly killed Confederate Gen. Leonidas Polk, the "Fighting Bishop," second cousin of President James K. Polk, well liked and popular with his troops who deeply mourned his death. Johnston escaped the volley without injury.

Union Gen. Hooker's troops ran into heavy Confederate fire on June 15 at Gilgal Church, the western flank of a line from there to Lost Mountain. On June 17-18, heavy fighting occurred at the Mud Creek Line of Latimer's Farm. As the Confederates were pushed back, Johnston withdrew his troops to the Kennesaw Mountain Line. Torrents of rain began again June 17-18 preventing any movement of the armies. An attempt to extend the Union right wing on June 22 failed when they ran into Confederate Gen. John Bell Hood at Kolb's Farm. But the Confederates suffered heavy casualties from entrenched Union artillery and swampy terrain.

On June 23, Sherman telegraphed Gen. Halleck in Washington, "*We continue to press forward on the principle of an advance against fortified positions. The whole country is one vast fort, and Johnston must have at least fifty miles of connected trenches, with abatis and finished batteries. We gain ground daily, fighting all the time… As fast as we gain one position the enemy has another one all ready, but I think he will soon have to let go of Kennesaw, which is the key to the whole country.*"

Sherman had avoided direct assaults on Johnston's defenses by using successive flanking maneuvers that had forced Johnston to abandon his well-fortified defenses. But at Kennesaw Mountain, Sherman changed his tactics and ordered a frontal assault on June 27. McPherson commanded the left flank for the Union, Thomas the center, and Schofield on the right. As Union troops attempted to break the Confederate defenses on the well-defended mountain, steep terrain, thick undergrowth and punishing resistance from the defenders above defeated their efforts (See Fig. 53).

After five days of battle at close range, Schofield, with the support of Gen. Stoneman's cavalry, was able to advance against Johnston's left flank on July 2, holding a position within five miles of the Chattahoochee River, the last barrier to Atlanta. Sherman exploited this advantage on July 4 by outflanking Johnston's left position and placed the rest of the Union army with Schofield near the Chattahoochee River. Johnston fell back to Smyrna Campground to take advantage of the powerful defenses on the banks of the river, known as the River Line. Union losses at Kennesaw numbered about 3,000, outnumbering the 1,000 casualties of the Confederates.

RIVER LINE AT THE CHATTAHOOCHEE

"The Shoupade Fortifications"

With Sherman at the Chattahoochee River, Johnston withdrew from Kennesaw and Marietta to fall back on July 4 to new defenses near Smyrna Campground that had been set up in advance along the Chattahoochee. Sherman described the log and earth forts, known as Johnston's River Line, as *"One of the strongest pieces of field fortifications I ever saw."* An escaped slave who had hidden under a log all day to avoid being shot by shells and musket-balls passing over him, finally came forward and

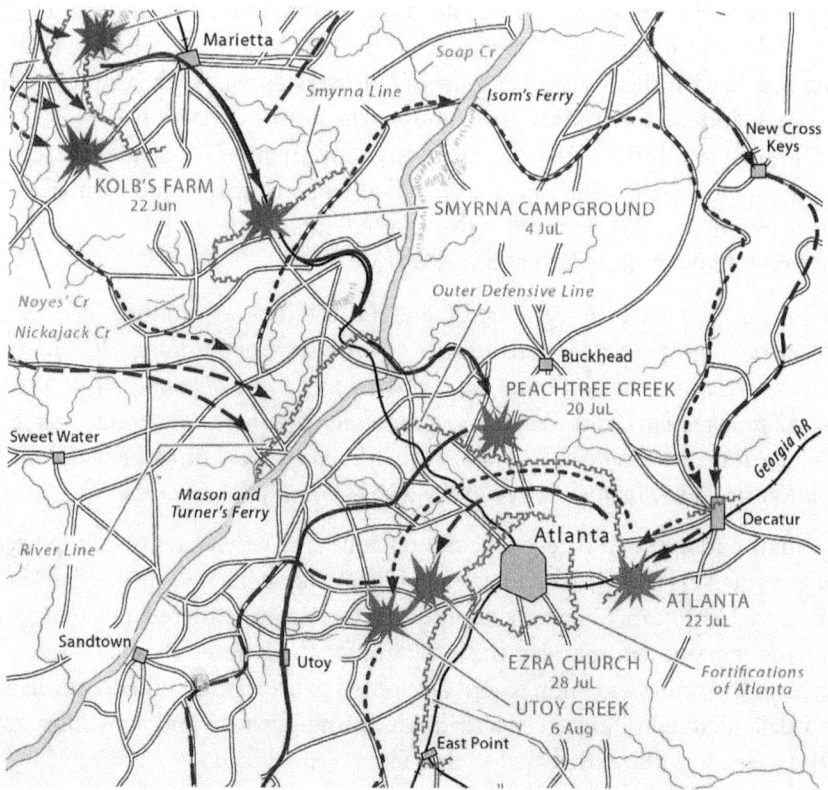

Fig. 54: The Union army bypassed the formidable Shoupade fortifications at Smyrna Campground and engaged the Confederates at Peachtree Creek about ten miles from Atlanta. The Union Army continued with constant fighting to push against the entrenchments surrounding the city of Atlanta.

Source: *This map is a work of the U.S. federal government by a U.S. Army soldier or employee and is in the public domain.*

explained to Sherman that he had been one of a thousand slaves who had worked on the fortifications for a month.

The fortification had been designed by Confederate Gen. Francis Asbury Shoup, a West Point graduate of 1855. A series of triangular-shaped forts with inside walls sixteen feet high, were positioned sixty to one hundred seventy-five yards apart, providing cross-fire support for the adjacent fort, each of which could hold eighty soldiers. Each fort was connected to the next with two artillery pieces at every junction. Capt. Orlando Poe, Sherman's chief engineer, said *"The line… was by far the strongest we had yet encountered… it would cost many lives to carry the position by assault. It was accordingly deemed best to turn it* (go around).*"*

TRENCH WARFARE IN THE CIVIL WAR

The Civil War introduced trench warfare, which was to be used extensively in World War I, little changed from its incarnation fifty years earlier. Infantry assaults of the Napoleonic wars were no longer effective in the face of long-range artillery fire and muskets. Union Gen. Ulysses S. Grant faced one of the most extensive uses of trench warfare when he met Confederate Gen. Robert E. Lee at Petersburg for ten months in 1864-65. Some trenches there were more than thirty miles long.

The basic construction consisted of rifle pits, built behind trees and bushes, that were placed a hundred yards or more in front of the trenches, to create an abatis, a field fortification with sharpened tree tops and branches facing the enemy. Trenches were connected with passageways. Parapets, varying in height from four to six feet, were dirt barriers that rose on the outside of the trench, facing the enemy.

As Union Gen. William T. Sherman described during the Atlanta Campaign in his *Memoirs*, *"The men of both armies became extremely skillful in the construction of these works, because each man realized their value and importance to himself, so that it required no orders for their construction."* As Blacks escaped from slavery to the Union Army before the Emancipation Proclamation, Sherman authorized each division commander to employ them to do the work. The army fed and paid them $10 a month on work details to build parapets. They worked at night, giving soldiers the opportunity to sleep and rest; Blacks then rested during the day.

Sherman's army had about two hundred freed Blacks and the system worked very well. Confederate armies used the same system with slaves doing the work of parapet building. But there, the strategy was for the slaves, well out of the range of the fighting, would strengthen and fortify the Southern Army's rear, at the spot next to be occupied. Sherman writes in his Memoirs, *"During this campaign hundreds if not thousands of miles of similar intrenchments were built by both armies, and, as a rule, whichever party attacked, got the worst of it."*

Rather than storm this heavily fortified position, which extended from the railroad bridge to Turner's Ferry below, a distance of five to six miles, Sherman sought another suitable point along the river for the army to cross. Gen. Schofield found a crossing on July 8 where Soap Creek (now called Sope Creek) flows into the Chattahoochee near Isom's Ferry crossing and the pontoon bridge was completed by nightfall. On July 9 Schofield's army crossed the Chattahoochee and strongly entrenched on high ground. Another Union crossing was achieved by McPherson, which enabled the Union Army to control both banks of the river above Johnston.

That night, Johnston evacuated his army from the "Shoupade" fortifications, crossed the Chattahoochee, burning the bridges and pontoons behind him and the army entrenched south of Peachtree Creek. Gen. Shoup, designer of the Shoupade defenses, was devastated by the abandonment of his novel defensive system, lamenting, *"I took a long look at the works into which my heart had gone to such a degree and felt that the days of the Confederacy were numbered. I made good all I proposed ... the line ... could have been held by three thousand men for any reasonable time against a hundred thousand."*

Advance to Atlanta

The Army of the Cumberland under Gen. George H. Thomas moved south from Marietta and successfully drove away Southern troops from the Chattahoochee River on July 5. When Union pontoons arrived and were set up, the entire Union army crossed the river on July 17-18. Gen. James B. McPherson on the far left flank reached the main Georgia Railroad line to Augusta on July 17 about seven miles east of Decatur where he turned west to Atlanta, breaking up the railroad along the way. Gen. John M. Schofield's army met McPherson's at Decatur and the two armies continued toward Atlanta, now about ten miles west of them, destroying the Confederate's railroad supply line to Augusta. Thomas and his army continued his advance to Peachtree Creek.

CONFEDERATE ARMY GETS NEW COMMANDER

During this movement of the Union Army towards Atlanta, Sherman learned from local newspapers that Confederate President Jefferson Davis had relieved Gen. Johnston as commander of the Southern Army of Tennessee and replaced him with Gen. John Bell Hood on July 18. President Davis had lost patience with Johnston's conservative tactics of prudence and caution and a pattern of retreats during the months of May to July. Hood had graduated from West Point in 1853 and now faced two of his former classmates in battle: James McPherson and John Schofield. With only one leg, having lost the other at Chickamauga, Hood with his unusable prosthetic leg, had to be strapped in the saddle. But even with only one leg and a useless arm from a wound at Gettysburg, Hood was well known to be aggressive, brave, forceful, rash and at times, reckless.

VII. THE FOURTH YEAR: 1864

Battle of Peachtree Creek
July 20, 1864

The Army of the Cumberland crossed Peachtree Creek from the north on July 20 without interference until the newly appointed Confederate Commander Gen. John Bell Hood made a surprise attack on the Union left flank while Gen. Joe Hooker's troops were resting at noon. Hand-to-hand combat in open ground lasted for about two hours until reinforcements from Union Gen. George Thomas pushed the Confederates back into their trenches at Peachtree Line, leaving many of their dead and wounded on the field. The next day Union troops occupied the Peachtree fortifications, which had been abandoned in the night. Confederates withdrew to the entrenchments that encircled the city of Atlanta, with a diameter of two to three miles across. Casualties numbered 2,500 for the Southern troops; 1,700 Northern.

Union Battles Against Atlanta Trenches
July-September 1864

Union Gen. James B. McPherson's Army of the Tennessee had successfully broken up the Georgia Railroad that ran east from the city to Augusta, removing one of the main Confederate supply lines that supported Richmond and Petersburg. But Confederate Gen. John Bell Hood's army, moving within the circle of well-fortified trenches surrounding Atlanta, was able to approach the left and rear of McPherson's army and launch a withering attack on July 22. Supporting cavalry for McPherson had been sent out on other missions which gave Hood the advantage of surprise.

Intense fighting on both sides continued from noon until night as Confederates attacked, boldly and repeatedly at the Union troops near Decatur, who resisted the onslaught with their backs to Atlanta. The Confederates launched another attack around 4 p.m. directly along the railroad line and captured four 24-pound cannons, turning them on the Union troops. Reinforcements from the Army of the Ohio, combined with the forces already in play, eventually drove the Confederates back to their trenches and the four cannons were recovered, although one was now "burst." Two six-pound cannons were lost and taken by the Southerners into Atlanta.

During the battle, as Sherman and McPherson discussed battle plans, shots were heard back toward Decatur and McPherson immediately called for his horse and staff. Riding into the thick woods, he inadvertently moved through a gap in the Union lines which brought him into enemy territory and he was immediately shot from his horse. McPherson's body was soon recovered and brought back to Sherman's headquarters. Highly respected and a great loss to the army, his body was sent to his home town of Clyde, Ohio, with a staff escort, where it was received with great honors.

With the death of Gen. McPherson, Sherman awarded command of the Army of the Tennessee to Gen. Oliver O. Howard, a professional soldier who had graduated fourth in his class from West Point Military Academy in 1854 and performed brilliantly for the

Army of the Potomac during the Seven Pines battles for which he would later receive the Medal of Honor. The promotion of Howard over other generals who out-ranked him, especially Gen. Joe Hooker, provoked simmering conflicts in Sherman's senior staff.

As Sherman proceeded with plans to destroy all railroad supply lines into Atlanta, he now focused his attention on East Point Railroad on the south side of Atlanta, the main railroad line into the city which supported two important railroads bringing supplies from the south. Howard's army moved from the east side of Atlanta to the far west side of the city to gain access to the East Point. Anticipating the move, Confederate Gen. Hood planned a surprise attack during this operation, but forewarned Northern forces were waiting in reinforced trenches with artillery when the Confederates arrived.

At the key crossroads at the Battle of Ezra Church on July 28, the Southerners were pushed back, but they had prevented Howard's troops from reaching the railroad line. Confederates lost about 3,000 in casualties, compared to about 600 for the Union. Southern forces quickly built a fortified defense to protect the East Point Railroad, which continued to sustain Atlanta until late August.

By the end of July, Union infantry controlled a semi-circle north of the city from the Georgia Railroad on the east to Ezra Church on the west, but still faced a well-fortified Confederate line that protected the city. Avoiding a frontal assault on the strong defenses, Gen. Sherman continued to eliminate Atlanta's source of supplies by capturing railroad lines that led into the city. The Union Army now controlled the Georgia Railroad which cut off all Confederate connections east to Augusta and beyond. Union cavalry and infantry continued to maintain control of Sherman's only supply line, the Western & Atlantic Railroad, that went north all the way to Chattanooga, arriving daily with food, ammunition and other needs for the Union Army.

The Confederates were now limited to the single railroad line at East Point, where it joined the Atlanta & West Point Railroad that ran ninety miles southwest to West Point, Georgia, on the Alabama border; and the Macon & Western Railroad, running about the same distance southeast to connect with Jonesboro and Macon, Georgia. Several forays by Union cavalry to capture the two railroads south of Atlanta had ended in failure.

Confederates Capture Two Union Cavalries
July 30-31, 1864

In late July, Sherman sent out two columns of cavalry, one under Gen. Edward M. McCook with about 3,000 troops to sever the Atlanta & West Point Railroad that ran southwest from Atlanta to Fairburn, Palmetto and Newnan. The second column of about 4,000 men under Gen. George Stoneman, would head southeast to destroy the Macon & Western Railroad. After destroying the railroad to the southwest, McCook would join Stoneman at Lovejoy's Station about twenty miles south of Atlanta and the two cavalry commands would tear up Macon & Western Railroad back to Atlanta.

VII. THE FOURTH YEAR: 1864

> ### THE POLITICS OF MANAGING HIS GENERALS
>
> With the death of Gen. James B. McPherson, Gen. William T. Sherman promoted Gen. Oliver O. Howard to be the new commander for the Union Army of the Tennessee. Howard, known as the "Christian General" for his religious piety, had gained recognition as a leader in previous battles. Sherman selected Howard over other qualified candidates, because he sought a professional soldier for the position. *"I wanted to succeed in taking Atlanta, and needed commanders who were purely and technically soldiers, men who would obey orders and execute them promptly and on time, for I knew that we would have to execute some most delicate maneuvers, requiring the utmost skill, nicety and precision."* He rejected politically appointed candidates that would be looking for personal fame and glory for their political ambitions.
>
> Sherman also rejected Gen. "Fighting Joe" Hooker even though he outranked Howard and had commanded the Army of the Potomac until just before the Battle of Gettysburg. But Sherman had not considered him as a viable candidate because of his constant criticisms of other commanders throughout the Atlanta Campaign and his exaggerated claims about his successes in battle and the number of enemy forces in front of him. In one battle, he asserted that his forces had not received the protection that had been promised by Schofield. Sherman quickly established that Hooker's claims were false and forced a face-to-face meeting between the two sparring generals. Schofield angrily denied the charges, pointing out that his dead soldiers, still lying in the field, were in advance of Hooker's. As they left the meeting, Sherman told Hooker *"... that such a thing must not occur again."* Although Sherman considered his reproach to Hooker was mild, considering what had occurred, Hooker *"... from that time began to sulk."* Hooker soon requested to be relieved of his position within the Army of the Cumberland, which his commander, Gen. George Thomas, forwarded to Sherman as *"... approved and 'heartily recommended'."* Although Hooker had performed well in many battles, Sherman was relieved to see him go. *"We were then two hundred fifty miles in advance of our base, dependent on a single line of railroad for our daily food. We had a bold, determined foe in our immediate front, strongly entrenched, with communications open to his rear for supplies and reinforcements, and every soldier realized that we had plenty of hard fighting ahead, and that all honors had to be fairly earned."*

Gen. Stoneman requested permission to alter the mission and proceed another sixty miles south to Macon to free hundreds of Union officers who were imprisoned there. If successful, they would continue another sixty miles farther to seize the Confederate Andersonville Prison Camp and free thousands of prisoners. Sherman agreed to the enlarged plan, but only after the Macon & Western Railroad had been secured and made inoperable.

Obsessed with freeing the prisoners at Macon and possibly even Andersonville, Stoneman disobeyed Sherman's orders and bypassed Lovejoy Station, heading straight for Macon. Confederate Cavalry Gen. Joseph Wheeler soon became aware of the movement of both Union cavalries and sent the bulk of his cavalry after Stoneman and about one-third of it after McCook.

When Stoneman reached Macon on July 30, he found a small militia of citizens and home guards blocking his progress across the river. But with reports of a Confederate cavalry hard on his heels, Stoneman aborted the mission and tried to return to Union lines. When he encountered Wheeler's cavalry of about 3,500 troops at Sunshine Church on July 31, Stoneman sent two of his brigades to break away while he remained to cover their escape. About 700 of Stoneman's men were captured as prisoners, including Stoneman himself, and all were locked up in boxcars to be transferred to the very prison they had hoped to liberate. Stoneman, the highest-ranking Union officer in the war to be imprisoned, was exchanged two months later at Sherman's personal request on October 2.

In the meantime, Union Gen. McCook's cavalry had cut the Atlanta & West Point Railroad at Palmetto, about six miles southwest of Fairburn and then captured and burned over one thousand Confederate supply wagons at Fayetteville on July 28. Continuing east for the planned meeting with Stoneman, McCook reached Lovejoy's Station on July 29 and began wrecking the Macon & Western Railroad. When Stoneman failed to appear, McCook called off the raid and headed back the way he had come, along the Atlanta & West Point Railroad, planning to return to the main Union army.

But by this time, about 1,500 troops from the Confederate cavalry of Gen. Joseph Wheeler was hot on his trail and caught up with McCook at the Battle of Brown's Mill just south of Newnan on July 30, about twenty-five miles southwest of Fairburn. The Confederates were quickly reenforced by another 1,500 soldiers waiting to be transported on the railroad that McCook's men had just torn up at Palmetto.

Knowing he was overwhelmed, McCook gave his commanders orders to break out individually, while he protected their escape. McCook lost 100 men killed and about 1,300 captured, including two brigade commanders, 1,200 horses and two pieces of artillery. McCook was able to cut his way out, and with fragments of his cavalry, slowly made his way back to Union lines. Confederate Wheeler's casualties numbered only about 50. Although Union forces had inflicted great damage to the rail lines and bridges and damaged seventeen locomotives, they did not succeed in destroying the railroad. Confederates rapidly repaired the two railroad lines and some locomotives. Supplies into the city continued.

VII. THE FOURTH YEAR: 1864

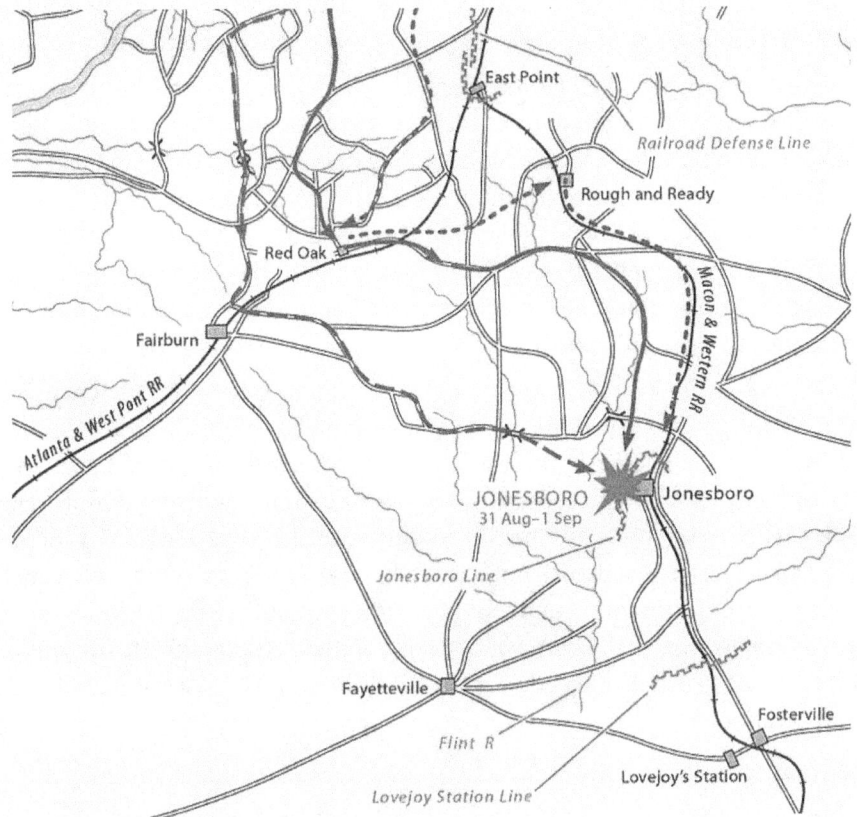

Fig. 55: Two Union cavalries attempted to capture the main railroad lines into Atlanta that supplied the city with food and ammunition. The East Point Station received supplies from the Atlanta & West Point RR to the southwest and the Macon & Western RR to the southeast. Both Union attempts failed and the two cavalries were captured by Confederates.

Source: *This map is a work of the U.S. federal government by a U.S. Army soldier or employee and is in the public domain.*

Union Artillery Bombards Atlanta
July-August

Gen. Sherman, frustrated with his failure to capture Atlanta's supply lines ordered intense Northern artillery barrages into Atlanta that began on July 20 and continued for thirty-six days. More than one thousand shells and shot were fired each day. The barrage reached new heights on August 9 when four heavy naval guns were freighted down from Chattanooga to fire more than 4,500 rounds into the city. Although most of Atlanta's twenty thousand residents had fled, about three thousand civilians remained in the city and as they suffered through the siege, many were killed.

Another attempt by the Union Army to capture East Point railroad station was launched in early August. When Gen. John M. Schofield, commanding the Army of the

Ohio, sent his right flank to make its move to take East Point, they were met with heavy resistance in the Battle of Utoy Creek, August 5-7 and were repulsed with heavy losses.

Confederate Gen. John Bell Hood, attempting to distract Union troops from attacking his railroad supply lines south of the city, sent Confederate Cavalry under Gen. Joseph Wheeler north to raid the Union's supply line at Dalton in the Second Battle of Dalton, August 14-15. Greatly outnumbered by the Confederates, the Union garrison moved to a hill outside of town and held out against the Southerners, fighting into the night. When reinforcements arrived from Chattanooga, the Confederates were driven off on August 15. The track was quickly repaired and trains ran again by August 17, restoring Sherman's supply line.

While Hood's cavalry was occupied north of Atlanta, wrecking the Union supply line, the Western & Atlantic Railroad, Sherman sent Union Cavalry south under Gen. Judson "Kill-Cavalry" Kilpatrick to attack the Macon & Western Railroad that remained successfully held by the Confederates, supplying Atlanta with food and weapons. Kilpatrick reached the railroad lines on August 19 at the Jonesboro supply depot and then tried to destroy the railroad, but it rained so hard the cavalrymen were unable to start fires to burn the ties or bend the rails. Moving on south, Kilpatrick ran into fierce Confederate resistance in the Battle of Lovejoy's Station, August 20. The Union cavalry was forced to flee to avoid being enveloped. The railroad was quickly repaired and soon back in operation.

ENGINEERS KEEP UNION SUPPLY LINE OPEN

The expertise that Union Col. William W. Wright was able to apply to the repairs of the broken railroads became legendary. Gen. William T. Sherman writes in his *Memoirs* about a post-Civil War conversation that he had with his former protagonist, Confederate Gen. Joseph E. Johnston, who expressed much admiration for the Union feats of bridge-building and repairs during the war.

The Confederate general was curious about the identity of the chief railroad-engineer that Sherman had used. Surprised that Col. Wright was a civilian who had been pressed into service, Johnston related an incident during the Battle at Kennesaw. An officer reported to him that his cavalry officer, Gen. Wheeler, had achieved a significant break in the Union railroad which would take at least a fortnight to repair. While they were talking, a train was seen coming down the railroad which had just passed through the very break, and had reached Sherman at Big Shanty as soon as the fleet horseman had reached Gen. Johnston.

VII. THE FOURTH YEAR: 1864

Union Infantry Captures Atlanta's Railroads
August 26-August 31, 1864

The failed efforts of Union cavalry to destroy railroad lines were not isolated incidents. Sherman had been disappointed with cavalry raids before, as he writes in his *Memoirs*: *"I became more than ever convinced that cavalry could not, or would not, work hard enough to disable a railroad properly."* When he saw the trains reentering Atlanta on August 23 a few days after Kilpatrick's raid, on top of the defeats of his two major cavalry commanders the month before, Sherman concluded that he must use his main army to remove Hood's supply lines to the city.

As the shelling on Atlanta continued, Sherman began to move six of his seven infantry corps from the north side of the city to the south. One third of his army would man the city's defenses and continue to protect his telegraph communications and the Western & Atlantic RR, his supply line to Chattanooga. The Army of the Cumberland under Gen. George Thomas pulled out of its positions and moved to Utoy Creek. Units from the cavalry kept their horses out of sight and the Southerners did not detect the shift. Gen. Oliver Howard, Army of the Tennessee, also moved to positions near Utoy Creek on the night of August 26. Gen. John Schofield's Army of the Ohio, remained in position near East Point.

Confederate Gen. Hood, surprised to find the majority of Union entrenchments north of Atlanta empty on August 26, incorrectly interpreted it as a Union retreat and telegraphed the message all over the South: *"The Yankees are gone."* There was great rejoicing in Atlanta and several trains of cars (with ladies) came up from Macon to assist in celebrating the great victory.

But the repositioning now allowed Sherman's army to attack the Atlanta & West Point Railroad with infantry. Howard's troops, Army of the Tennessee, and the Army of the Cumberland, under Thomas, pivoted on Schofield's position at East Point on August 28 and reached undefended Red Oak and Fairburn Railway Stations (See Fig. 55). Union troops spent the entire next day on August 29, breaking up the railroad and turning the rails into "Sherman's Neckties." Sherman writes in his *Memoirs*, *"The track was heaved up in sections the length of a regiment, then separated rail by rail; bonfires were made of the ties and of fence-rails on which the rails were heated, carried to trees or telegraph poles, wrapped around and left to cool. Such rails could not be used again."*

With the Atlanta & West Point Railroad destroyed, the entire Union army began its movement eastward on the morning of August 30 to the Macon & Western Railroad, the last remaining supply line to Atlanta for the Confederates. Howard's army headed straight for Jonesboro. Schofield's troops reached the railroad near Rough and Ready and Thomas landed at two points between Schofield and Jonesboro (See Fig. 55).

When Gen. Hood learned that a large Union infantry force was approaching Jonesboro, he sent two infantry brigades under Generals William Hardee and Stephen D. Lee to move there at once. The Confederates under Hardee, some marching all night, reached Jonesboro at dawn August 31. Gen. Lee's corps arrived shortly after noon.

Finally, around 3 p.m. on August 31, the Confederates began their assault on the Union infantry under Howard and it did not go well for the Southerners. When the Confederates' first lines attacked, they faced an intense rifle and infantry fire that became a one-sided slaughter. Soon the rank-and-file soldiers refused their officers' orders to charge and went to ground. Confederate losses numbered nearly 2,000, while Union troops suffered less than 200. The Confederates has been soundly repulsed. Sherman directed Schofield and Thomas, who were still on the railroad north of Jonesboro to head for Jonesboro, tearing up the railroad as they came.

Hood then ordered forces under Gen. Lee to return to Atlanta that night in preparation for evacuation of the city. The next day, the remaining Southern troops at Jonesboro under Hardee continued to shrink against increasing attacks by Union commanders. Under cover of night, Hardee abandoned his position and was able to slip his army through the woods and escape south to Lovejoy's Station undetected.

Atlanta Falls to the Union Army
September 2-3, 1864

Failure of the Confederates to repulse the Union attack at Jonesboro ensured the loss of the last supply line to Atlanta and Gen. Hood made preparations on September 1 to evacuate the city. The army opened its commissary to civilians to take whatever they wanted and some civilians elected to follow the army as it withdrew to Palmetto, southwest of the city. That night, Hood destroyed all his ammunition depots to prevent them from falling into Union hands, including setting fire to eighty-one freight cars, twenty-eight loaded with ammunition. The resounding explosions and raging firestorm was heard for miles around and carried out into the night. Sherman, twenty miles away, wondered if the explosions represented another battle or if the enemy was engaged in blowing up his own magazines. The raging inferno was dramatically depicted in the movie *Gone with the Wind* (1939).

Union patrols the next day confirmed that the Confederate Army had abandoned Atlanta. Mayor James Calhoun, with a committee of Union-leaning citizens, met with Gen. Henry Slocum on September 2 to surrender the city. Sherman, still at Jonesboro, received a note from Slocum in his own handwriting, confirming that he had entered Atlanta unopposed. When the news was spread to the surrounding troops, they gave out rousing shouts and glorious laughter. The following day on September 3, Sherman sent a telegram to Washington, famously stating: *"Atlanta is ours and fairly won."*

VII. THE FOURTH YEAR: 1864

> ### "WAR IS WAR"
>
> Gen. William T. Sherman's first act when he occupied Atlanta was to issue an order that the city would be appropriated by the military and all citizens and families must leave the city within five days. A further order prohibited hundreds of profit-seeking traders waiting at Nashville and Chattanooga from entering the city. Stating to Washington, *"If the people raise a howl against my barbarity and cruelty, I will answer that war is war, and not popularity-seeking. If they want peace, they and their relatives must stop the war."*
>
> When the city mayor and local citizens vigorously protested the order, Sherman responded: *"War is cruelty and you cannot refine it... The South began war by seizing forts, arsenals, etc... Now that war comes home to you, you feel very different... But you cannot have peace and a division of our country. If the United States submits to division now, it will not stop, but will go on until we repeat the fate of Mexico, which has eternal war."*
>
> Sherman closed his message to Washington with, *"I knew that such a measure would be strongly criticized... but I had seen Memphis, Vicksburg, Natchez and New Orleans, all captured from the enemy, had each (required) an entire full division of troops, if not more... to guard and protect the interests of a hostile population. The people of the South would read two important conclusions (from my orders): one, that we were in earnest; and the other, if they were sincere in their common and popular clamor 'to die in the last ditch,' that the opportunity would soon come."*

Battle casualties for both North and South during the four months of the campaign were surprisingly similar. Union casualties numbered about 35,000 (5,000 killed; 25,000 wounded; and about 5,000 missing). Total casualties for the South were also about 35,000 (3,000 killed; 19,000 wounded; and 13,000 missing). The Union, however, had access to a vast number of replacements; the South did not. Hood left Atlanta with about 30,000 soldiers; Sherman's armies totaled about 80,000.

Sherman demanded that local citizens leave the city because it had been his experience that protecting a city of hostile inhabitants used up Union resources and manpower that he was not willing to expend. He established an agreement with Hood that civilians could gather at the nearby town of Rough and Ready to make their arrangements.

Union Army Occupies Atlanta
September 2-November 15, 1864

By mid-September, Sherman's army had secured the city of Atlanta, repaired the telegraph lines and his supply train arrived regularly with ample provisions. Confederate Gen. John Bell Hood's army had not gone far; they had settled at Palmetto southwest of the city. But Sherman expressed little interest in pursuing Hood and his agile army in the open country where Hood would have ample opportunity to find good defensive ground. Sherman writes, *"It is folly for us to be moving our armies on the reports of scouts and citizens. We must maintain the offensive."* Similarly, simply holding on to Atlanta would achieve no military advantage.

Confederate President Jefferson Davis met with Gen. Hood at Palmetto Station September 25 and their discussions were then relayed to Sherman through Union spies and local newspapers reporting on Davis' speeches. The reports conveyed the news that Gen. Nathan Bedford Forrest, head of the Confederate Army's 7,000-man cavalry, was successfully attacking the Union supply lines in Western Tennessee and Hood would soon be joining him. Sherman writes, *"… he gave us the full key to his future designs. To be forewarned was to be forearmed, and I think we took full advantage of the occasion."*

On September 29, Sherman sent Gen. George H. Thomas, "The Rock of Chickamauga," with the Army of the Cumberland and Gen. John M. Schofield, Army of the Ohio, to proceed to Nashville, Tennessee, to face Hood. Further, General-in-Chief Grant ordered all new recruitments to be directed to Nashville to support Thomas against the anticipated assault from Hood, who was combining his forces with the cavalry under Gen. Forrest.

Confederates Attack Sherman's Supply Line

From his base at Palmetto, Confederate Gen. John Bell Hood initiated several attacks on Union Gen. Sherman's main supply line, the Western & Atlantic Railroad from Chattanooga hoping to bring the Union Army out in the open. Hood launched an all-out attack at Allatoona Pass on October 5, but was repulsed in heavy fighting. As the Confederates withdrew north, they inflicted great damage to the railroad from Big Shanty to Acworth (See Fig. 53) which was later repaired by Col. W.W. Wright, using ten thousand men and a resupply of thirty-five thousand new ties and six miles of iron. The railroad was again ready for business in seven days.

Leaving Acworth, Hood's army continued north to Resaca and on October 12 demanded its surrender, but when refused, moved his army on to Dalton, destroying twenty miles of railroad all the way north to Tunnel Hill (See Fig. 51). Sherman's troops, moving north from Kingston did not reach Resaca until October 13. Hood's army successfully attacked the Union garrison at Dalton, which was short-staffed with only about 750 men, 600 of whom were Black soldiers of the United States Colored Troops (USCT).

Forced to surrender on October 13 to the Confederates, the Black prisoners of the USCT were brutally treated by their Southern captors and six were killed outright. White officers were paroled, but Black captives were forcefully taken west with Hood and cruelly abused on the march that covered several hundred miles all the way to Mississippi. Many died of the ordeal. Survivors of the arduous march were sent to

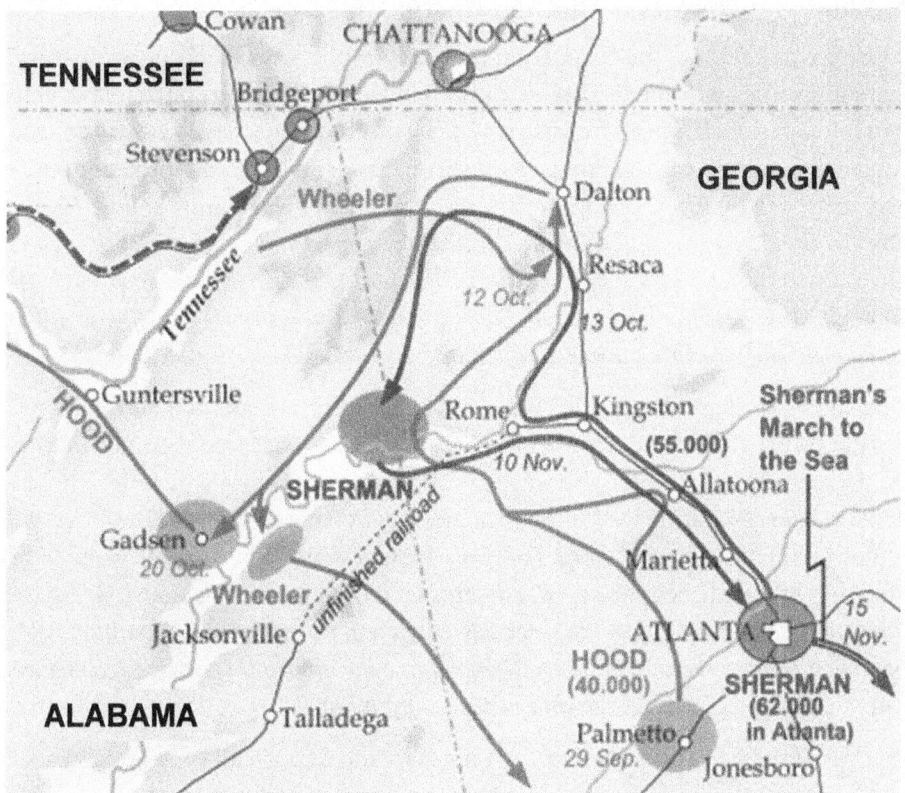

Fig. 56: From his base at Palmetto, Georgia, Confederate Gen. Hood attacked several points of Union Gen. Sherman's supply line on the Western & Atlantic Railroad to Chattanooga before withdrawing to Gadsen, Alabama, where he planned his invasion into Tennessee.

Source: *This work released into the public domain by its author, Andrei Nacu through the Wikipedia Project.*

work rebuilding roads in Mississippi or were returned to their slave-owner masters, or whites claiming to be their masters.

From Resaca, Hood headed west reaching Gadsden, Alabama, on October 20. Sherman followed Hood to within forty miles of Gadsden, but realized he could not catch the light and fast-moving Confederates. Convinced that Hood was headed to Tennessee so that he could join forces with Gen. Forrest's cavalry and threaten Nashville, Sherman returned to Atlanta to prepare for his mission to push into the heart of Georgia and damage the Southern resources supporting the Confederacy.

Leaving Gadsden, Hood moved farther west to Tuscumbia, Alabama, where he met up with Forrest and his cavalry for their advance into Tennessee (See Fig. 60). Gen. Wheeler and his cavalry were sent back to Georgia to combat Sherman on his March to the Sea, which began in mid-November. At Tuscumbia, Hood began collecting the necessary supplies from a beleaguered country in anticipation of his planned invasion of Tennessee and Kentucky.

Sherman Plans His March through Georgia

During this period of the occupation of Atlanta while also defending against attacks on his supply line by Confederate Gen. John Bell Hood, Sherman continued to emphasize to his superiors the need for his army to be on the offensive and not be constantly occupied defending a railroad that was at the mercy of an agile and forceful opponent. Sherman writes, *"With 25,000 infantry and the bold cavalry that he has, Hood can constantly break my railroad. I would infinitely prefer to make a wreck of the road and of the country from Chattanooga to Atlanta, including the latter city; send back all my wounded and unserviceable men (to Chattanooga), and with my effective army move through Georgia, smashing things to the sea."*

Sherman's strategy was at the center of his passion to make the Southern people understand that they could not win the war and their government could not protect them. He particularly wanted the wealthy landowners of Georgia to suffer, those who had insisted on separating the Union to achieve a government for the South that would continue the institution of slavery. For those Confederates, Sherman planned to bring the horrors of war directly to them. He writes, *"Until we can repopulate Georgia, it is useless for us to occupy it, but the utter destruction of its roads, houses, and people will cripple their military resources… I will then make the interior of Georgia feel the weight of war… I can make this march and make Georgia howl!"*

In the meantime, Sherman deployed his forces to destroy all of Atlanta's capabilities as a transportation hub and as a war manufacturing center for the Confederacy. His explicit instructions were to demolish all machine shops, cannon factories, mills, wagon-shops, tanneries, foundries, including all furnace chimneys and their arches, or any facility that could be useful to the enemy. All railroad tracks in the city were to be torn up, heated and twisted so as to be unusable. Supporting infrastructure for the railroads, such as water tanks, depots and railroad car-sheds were to be destroyed as well. Bridges were to be destroyed completely. Churches and hospitals and private dwellings would be spared. Fire was to be avoided to spare the unintentional burning of private homes, court house and other buildings not devoted to war support.

With Hood in Alabama, Sherman finally received cautious approval from Washington to undertake the march across Georgia. The Western & Atlantic Railroad from Chattanooga had suffered severe damage from the Confederates all along the line from Big Shanty to Dalton. But Union expertise with a crew of ten thousand men had been able to repair the lines relatively quickly, re-opening the railroad again between Atlanta and Chattanooga by October 28.

Ensuring that the armies of Thomas and Schofield were adequate to repel Hood in Tennessee, Sherman began operations for his March to the Sea. The repaired railroad from Atlanta to Chattanooga sent the sick and wounded men and surplus stores north. Sherman gave orders to his quartermaster to prepare for twenty days of rations with

VII. THE FOURTH YEAR: 1864

ammunition and guns that would be carried by wagon-train. Soldiers and animals would walk. He writes, "*I propose to abandon Atlanta, and the railroad back to Chattanooga, to sally forth to ruin Georgia and bring up on the seashore.*" He finally received Grant's approval on November 2 for the expedition, but it could not begin until after the presidential election on November 8.

Lincoln Re-elected in November

During the summer of 1864, President Lincoln saw his re-election in November 1864 as highly unlikely. Soldiers were dying by the thousands during the Overland Campaign in the Eastern Theater. The high casualty rates brought the Northern press to label Grant as "the butcher." Lincoln defended Grant, affirming that he was following the strategic objectives laid out at the beginning of the year, but the public was not consoled. Confederate raids from the Shenandoah had reached within a few miles of Washington and the White House, while Sherman was fighting his way south to Atlanta.

Lincoln faced a Democratic candidate who enjoyed wide popularity. Former Gen. George B. McClellan, who had served under Lincoln as General-in-Chief and commander of the Army of the Potomac during the first two years of the war, had been selected as the Democratic Party's candidate for President with the support of the so-called Peace Democrats or "Copperhead" faction. Their peace platform would negotiate an end to the war but embrace two separate governments: an antislavery North and a proslavery South. Lincoln vehemently opposed any negotiated peace with the Southerners. His position was unchanged: the goal of the Union was an undivided nation, without slavery, and would require the unconditional surrender of the Confederacy.

With the fall of Atlanta and defeat of the Confederates in the Shenandoah Valley in September, Northern public sentiment dramatically changed to support the war to its conclusion. Lincoln won in a landslide carrying all but three of the twenty-five Northern states that voted. Only Kentucky, Delaware and New Jersey voted for McClellan. The eleven states that had seceded to form the Confederate States of America did not participate in the election. Lincoln won fifty-five percent of the popular vote and 212 electoral votes, compared to McClellan's forty-five percent of the vote and 21 electoral votes. More than seventy percent of the Union soldiers voted for Lincoln.

Burning of Atlanta
November 12-15, 1864

With President Lincoln's re-election secure, Gen. William T. Sherman made final preparations for his march into Georgia. On November 10, all Union troops that were to accompany Sherman through Georgia were ordered to Atlanta, destroying bridges, railroads and communities as they came. The manufacturing city of Rome was destroyed and burned to the ground, as was the railroad station Marietta.

Within Atlanta itself, considerable destruction had already occurred from the occupation of Hood's army during the defense of Atlanta and Sherman's five-week artillery bombardment that dropped over 100,000 projectiles into the city. As the Confederates evacuated the city September 2, they destroyed a railroad depot that included twenty-eight boxcars of munitions which exploded with such force that every building for a quarter mile around the depot was destroyed.

In early November, Sherman received word from the reinforced Gen. George H. Thomas in Tennessee that he would be able to defend against Confederate Gen. John Bell Hood. With most of Hood's army at Tuscumbia, Alabama, the path through Georgia was now wide open. On November 12, the last of the railroad and telegraph communications were broken; the army now stood on its own. On the evening of November 15, the bulk of the Union forces began their March to the Sea and fire was applied to any remaining debris.

SHERMAN'S "MARCH TO THE SEA"

Union Army Leaves a Burning Atlanta
November 15, 1864

Union Gen. William T. Sherman left Atlanta on November 15 with his refitted army of approximately 62,000, which included 57,000 infantry and artillery, divided into two wings, marching as separate columns that cut a swath sixty miles wide, plus a 5,000-man cavalry, under the command of Gen. Judson "Kill-Cavalry" Kilpatrick. The cavalry commander was unpopular with his men because of his tactics during battle that often showed a disregard for their lives. But Kilpatrick was also known for fearlessly charging enemy encampments and leading daring raids. When Sherman accepted the transfer of the unpopular and notorious cavalry commander, Sherman stated: *"I know that Kilpatrick is a hell of a damned fool, but I wanted just that sort of man to command my cavalry on this expedition."*

The right infantry wing was commanded by Gen. Oliver O. Howard, heading up the Army of the Tennessee. The left-wing commander, Gen. Henry Slocum, for the newly created Army of Georgia, claimed a distinguished career with the Army of the Potomac in the Eastern Theater and then under Grant in the Western Theater.

Each wing of the marching Union army contained two corps. The right wing, under Gen. Howard, contained XV Corps, commanded by Gen. P. J. Osterhaus and XVII Corps, under Gen. Frank Blair, Jr., a Missouri politician who had been instrumental in preventing Missouri from joining the Confederacy. Gen. Slocum's left wing included XIV Corps, commanded by Gen. Jefferson C. Davis (no relation to Confederate President Jefferson Davis), and the XX Corps, under Gen. Alpheus S. Williams. The cavalry, under Gen. Kilpatrick, served both wings.

VII. THE FOURTH YEAR: 1864

> ### SHERMAN'S FINAL LOOK AT ATLANTA
>
> As Sherman and his personal escort made their final departure from Atlanta, they paused to look back. *"Behind us lay Atlanta, smoldering and in ruins, the black smoke rising in the air, and hanging like a pall over the ruined city. I remember the railroad trains going to the rear with a furious speed; the engineers and the few men about the trains waving us an affectionate adieu. It surely was a strange event—two hostile armies marching in opposite directions, each in the full belief that it was achieving a final and conclusive result in a great war; and I was strongly inspired with the feeling that the movement on our part was a direct attack upon the rebel army and the rebel capital at Richmond, though a full thousand miles of hostile country intervened, and that, for better or worse, it would end the war."*
>
> Memoirs, W. T. Sherman, 1875

Sherman's personal escort was the 1st Alabama Cavalry Regiment, the only predominantly white pro-Union regiment from Alabama, which also included a number of men from Tennessee. Their distinguished service had taken a toll on the men. Of the 2,000 who served in the 1st Alabama during the course of the war, only 397 were present at the end. Known casualties for the unit included 345 who were killed or died of disease, 88 captured and 297 desertions. Sherman traveled with Slocum's left wing and kept his plans for the path the army would take through Georgia a tightly held secret. The marching men erroneously believed they were headed for Richmond.

As he worked his way past the men, some called out, *"Uncle Billy, I guess Grant is waiting for us at Richmond!"* The men did not know that the actual objective was the Atlantic coast of Georgia. Although Savannah was Sherman's primary target, he wanted to be flexible and be able to modify his route to another city, such as Charleston, depending on the obstacles and defenses he might encounter along the way.

On the first day out, Howard's army followed the Macon & Western Railroad towards Jonesboro, appearing to threaten Macon, while Slocum's army headed east along the Georgia Railroad towards Decatur and Madison, destroying the railroad between the two towns. Augusta, directly east, appeared to be the army's destination, but Sherman's real objective was Milledgeville, the state capital (until 1867), about one hundred miles southeast, which he expected to reach in seven days. After crossing the Georgia Railroad bridge over the Oconee River, thirteen miles east of Madison, Slocum's left wing burned the bridge and then made a right turn for Milledgeville (See Fig. 57). The cavalry under Kilpatrick followed Howard's army toward Macon and encountered Confederate Gen. Joseph Wheeler and his cavalry the next day at Lovejoy and Bear Creek Stations along the railroad to Macon, but the outnumbered Confederates quickly withdrew. Wheeler had been redeployed to Georgia from the Confederate Army of Gen. John Bell Hood, who was now planning to attack Union forces in Tennessee.

> ### UNION ARMY LEAVES ATLANTA
> Sherman writes in his *Memoirs* as they left Atlanta, *"(The men) marching steadily and rapidly, with a cheery look and swinging pace, made light of the thousand miles that lay between us and Richmond. Indeed, the general sentiment was that we were marching for Richmond, and that there we should end the war, but how and when they seemed to care not. There was a 'devil-may-care' feeling pervading among the officers and men, that made me feel the full load of responsibility ... for success would be accepted as a matter of course, whereas, should we fail, this 'march' would be adjudged the wild adventure of a crazy fool."*
>
> Memoirs, W. T. Sherman, 1875

Sherman's army contained only able-bodied, experienced soldiers, well-armed, well-equipped and provided with ammunition, provisions and animal forage. Great care had been applied to remove the sick, wounded and non-combatants. The wagons, full with supplies needed for the march, could not afford space for sick men; the only place of safety would be the army itself. The command included sixty-five artillery guns, or about one gun for every thousand men. Each soldier carried forty rounds of ammunition, a blanket, a few cooking utensils, and a ration of coffee, sugar, salt and hardtack. The wagon-trains held about two hundred cartridges of ammunition per man plus two hundred rounds for each artillery gun. Six hundred ambulances would care for casualties that occurred in battle.

The four wagon trains, each about twenty-five miles long, contained over a million rations for the troops, or about twenty days' supply. Each corps had its own pontoon-train. Beef cattle were driven along on the hoof. A five-day supply of oats and corn for forage would soon be supplemented by locally-grown corn to be taken on the march. Georgia's state militia had been temporarily withdrawn from Confederate Gen. Hood's army for the specific purpose of gathering in the season's crops for its citizens and the Confederate Army. Sherman's comment on this good fortune, *"I knew that within that time (five days), we would reach a country well stocked with corn, which had been gathered and stored in cribs, seemingly for our use, by Governor Brown's militia."* Corn, molasses, meal, bacon and sweet potatoes were confiscated at Eatonton, as well as several cows and oxen and a large number of mules.

Along the march, railroads were systematically crippled by Union soldiers as the tracks were torn up, melted down and turned into "Sherman Neckties." The destruction of the lifeline that supported the Confederate armies further demoralized the morale of the Southern population.

When opportunity presented itself, Sherman explained to any slaves that he encountered on the march that while Union success would mean their freedom, they must remain where they were for now. They could not follow the army and swell the number of mouths to feed, crippling the army's ability in its mission. Nevertheless, thousands of slaves could not resist following the army and as a result, many died of hunger, disease or exposure.

Foragers Sweep the Countryside

Sherman's Special Field Order No. 120 authorized the army "*... to forage liberally on the country*" during the march, gathering corn, animal forage, meat, vegetables, whatever was needed to maintain a ten-day supply of provisions for the command, plus three days of forage for the animals. Sherman had studied the state's agricultural records and was well informed of the great variety of crops, such as corn, sweet potatoes, sugar cane and cotton that were grown in the fertile Georgian soil. Horses, mules and wagons could be appropriated freely and without limit, with officers authorized to discriminate between the rich, usually hostile, and the poor, generally neutral or friendly. Soldiers were not to enter the dwellings of inhabitants or commit trespass, but could gather turnips, potatoes and any other vegetables during a halt or camp. Foragers were to refrain from abusive or threatening language.

Corps commanders alone were authorized to destroy mills, houses, cotton gins or other buildings. If the army was unmolested, no destruction of property should occur, but should guerillas or bushwhackers attempt to molest the march by burning bridges, obstructing roads, or otherwise manifesting local hostility, then army commanders could enforce a devastation more or less relentless, according to the measure of such hostility.

Foragers served another important military function: they were always sent out on the exposed flanks of each wing of the army, thereby serving as flankers or scouts. Marches began at daybreak and continued until early afternoon when camp was made for the night, and soldiers would create their one full meal of the day. The distance varied between ten to fifteen miles per day, determined by the nature of the roads and the rate of travel of the wagons. Each brigade commander detailed about fifty men at daylight with one or two officers to visit every farm and plantation within five to six miles along their route.

Beginning each morning on foot, the foragers' first acquisitions would be useful animals, such as horses, mules or oxen, plus a horse with wagon or family carriage which they proceeded to fill with bacon, corn, turkeys, chickens, ducks, anything that could be used as food for human or animal. They would then regain the main road in advance of their train, nearly all men mounted on a horse or a mule.

Wagon trains always had the right to the road, but had to maintain their position in line so that there were no gaps. Any wagon or group of wagons that dropped out of place had to go to the rear, which placed them last in camp for the night. To avoid making their wagons last, the foragers would bring their collections ahead of the wagon train and wait. Meanwhile, the loads in the wagons of the marching column would be redistributed so that there might be as many as ten empty wagons, ready for loading. When the wagon train approached the waiting foragers, the empty wagons would be diverted out of the column, hurried forward to be loaded with the new supplies, and then re-inserted into the column line when their group came by so that no gaps occurred. All supplies were accounted for by the quartermaster in charge so that they would be equally distributed.

ANDERSONVILLE PRISON

The Confederate military prison at Andersonville, Georgia, was a death sentence for 13,000 of the 45,000 captured Union prisoners sent there during the last fourteen months of the war. Camp Sumter, its Southern name, was built in February 1864 after prisoner exchanges between the Union Army and the Confederacy collapsed in 1863 because of Southern treatment of Black soldiers captured in battle. The camp, located in the Georgia woods about one hundred twenty miles south of Atlanta, originally sixteen acres, was then enlarged to twenty-six acres in June, surrounded by a fifteen-foot stockade. Overcrowded to many times its capacity, the camp provided little food, an inadequate supply of water and forced men to create their own shelters from scrap material. Although forests were nearby, prisoners were not allowed to possess wood for creating shelters, cooking food or providing heat. Men made shanties from wood scraps and blankets if they could find them.

A creek, polluted with offal and human waste, ran through the camp and frequently flooded. Disease was commonplace and chief causes of death were scurvy, diarrhea and dysentery. During the summer of 1864 when its population reached 33,000 prisoners in a space designed for 10,000, about a third died of dysentery and scurvy. With very little food, men became walking skeletons. News in November of Sherman's march through Georgia prompted most of the prisoners to be transferred to other prison camps. After the war, the Camp commander, Captain Henry Wirz, was tried, convicted and executed in November 1865, the only person to be executed for war crimes during the Civil War.

The infamous Confederate Andersonville Prisoner-of-War Camp was located about eighty miles south of the army's march. When a few escaped prisoners, emaciated and starving, made their way to the Union lines, the shocked and infuriated Northern soldiers felt their retribution against the Southerners fully justified. Some wanted the Union Army to free the prisoners at the camp, but during the time of Sherman's March to the Sea, only a few hundred prisoners remained at Andersonville Prison Camp. After the Union Army conquered Atlanta in September, the Confederacy had quickly moved prisoners from Andersonville to other camps in South Carolina and coastal Georgia.

VII. THE FOURTH YEAR: 1864

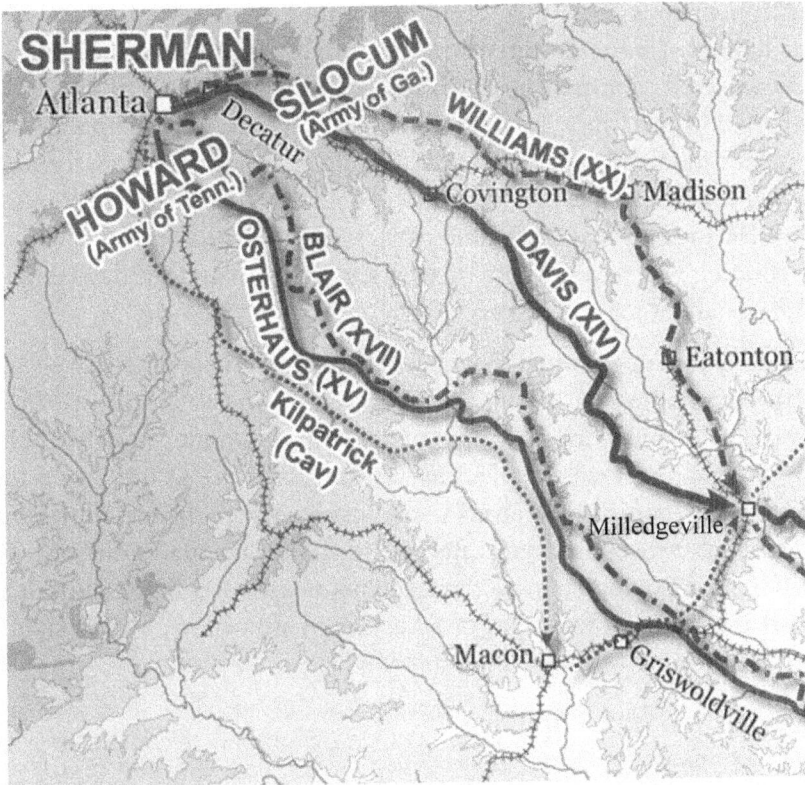

Fig. 57: Gen. William T. Sherman launched the Union Army's March to the Sea on Nov. 15, 1864, leaving a smoldering Atlanta, Georgia. The army numbered about 62,000, which included a 5,000-man cavalry. The two columns covered a swath sixty miles wide.
Source: *Creative Commons Attribution 3.0 License Map by Hal Jespersen, www. cwmaps.com.*

The Shock to Georgia

Soldiers thought it a great privilege to be on a foraging party for the day's collection and would return, mounted on horses, cattle, oxen or mules, bringing along their great prizes with stories to tell around the campfire that night. One story relates how Sherman's men responded to a lady's request to please not take her last chicken. The soldiers were seemingly moved by her appeal, but then one man thoughtfully replied, *"The rebellion must be suppressed if it takes the last chicken in the Confederacy,"* and proceeded to take it. One stop along the march found the plantation of Gen. Howell Cobb, a wealthy and prominent Southerner, who had strenuously advocated for a Confederacy and now served as one of its generals. After carrying off corn, beans, peanuts, sorghum-molasses and other choice provisions, Sherman instructed that nothing should be spared. Large bonfires consumed the house, barns, fences and crops.

Foragers were referred to as "bummers" but not all were part of Sherman's troops. As the Union Army invaded Georgia, citizens became so frantic that convicts were liberated from prisons under their promise that they would serve the army. But there was little danger of being detected and the formerly incarcerated prisoners, which included convicted criminals, took advantage of their situation to loot and exploit the Southern homes in the wake of the Union army's march. They became experts at finding hidden food and valuables. Homes would be vandalized from top to bottom. Silver, jewelry, blankets, meat, food and household items of value were plundered and carried off, leaving households destitute, that were almost all populated with old men, women, children and slaves. A bitter hatred for Sherman and the desecration left by his march would last for generations.

Although Sherman admitted that abuses by the bummers no doubt occurred, he claimed that any such acts by the men in his army were unusual, incidental and not tolerated by the command. Accounts by Georgian civilians, however, revealed the brutality caused by Sherman's march. Small farms were targets as well as the large plantations. Residences, barns, gardens and farms were ransacked; food, horses and wagons were seized. Livestock were either confiscated or killed. Resistance was met with violence. A plantation near Covington lost a thousand pounds of meat in the smokehouse and all the live fowl and pigs were shot or taken. Many women, with their children and slaves, were left without food for the winter and faced starvation.

Milledgeville, the State Capital
November 23, 1864

Arriving at the state capital, Milledgeville, on November 23 (Atlanta would become the state capital in 1867), Sherman's army found citizens at home, but the Governor, State officers and Legislature had fled. Sherman noted with some amusement that the Governor had taken all his garden vegetables, but left some of the State's archives to the invaders. Some Union officers provided an evening of entertainment in the now vacant House of Representatives, as they held a mock legislative session repealing Georgia's ordinance of secession after "a spirited and acrimonious debate."

The local arsenal was destroyed with all its contents as were some of the public buildings. Sherman received Gen. Howard's report that the right wing of the army had reached Gordon, near Macon, tearing up railroad track all along the way. Kilpatrick's cavalry had encountered Confederates at the Battle of Griswoldville on November 22, but support from Howard's infantry had stabilized a defense against the Georgia militia, which retreated with a loss of about 1,000 casualties, including 600 prisoners. Kilpatrick joined the left wing at Louisville on November 29.

Taking an infantry division with him, Kilpatrick fought Confederate Gen. Wheeler on December 4 at the Battle of Waynesboro, where Union forces overran strong defensive barricades and eventually forced Wheeler to withdraw toward Augusta. The right wing of Sherman's army continued to follow the Savannah Railroad, each group damaging railroad along its way.

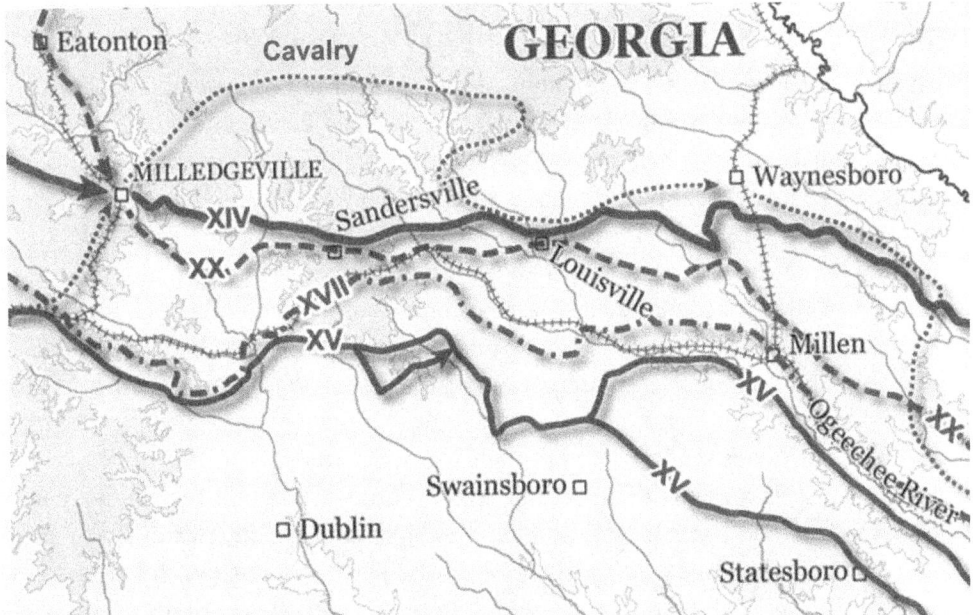

Fig. 58: A primary stop for Sherman's March to the Sea on Nov. 23 was Georgia's state capital at Milledgeville. At the next arrival at Millen on Dec. 3, Union troops found the deserted prisoner-of-war camp, abandoned only ten days earlier.

Source: *Creative Commons Attribution 3.0 License Map by Hal Jespersen, www. cwmaps.com.*

Millen, Prisoner-of-War Camp
December 3, 1864

The next stage of the march reached Camp Lawton at Millen, site of a large Confederate prisoner-of-war camp which had been built by slave labor to absorb the overflow of prisoners from Andersonville. Completed in October 1864, all of its prisoners were removed by November 23 and sent to Savannah as news of the Union march through Georgia reached the camp. Sherman's infantry columns and wagon-trains arrived at Millen unmolested on December 3. As the army examined the recently abandoned prisoner-of-war camp, they found seven hundred unmarked graves. There had been no housing for the 10,000 prisoners interred there. The men had built shelters from brush or burrowed holes into the ground.

After burning down the prison and destroying the railroad depot and other targets in town, the army resumed its march for Savannah, moving parallel to the Ogeechee River. But Confederates under Gen. William Hardee, now commanding the Confederacy's Department of South Carolina, Georgia and Florida, prepared to defend against the advancing Union invaders. After serving under Gen. John Bell Hood in the Atlanta Campaign, Hardee had requested a transfer from the Confederate Army of Tennessee.

> ## PRISON CAMPS DURING THE CIVIL WAR
>
> Soldiers captured in battle were either paroled or sent to prison camps. A paroled soldier pledged that he would not fight until exchanged for a prisoner on the other side of equal stature. A captain was equivalent to six privates, for example, and a brigadier general would be exchanged for twenty privates. But if the paroled prisoner who had not yet been exchanged was captured again on the battlefield, he lost the opportunity to ever be exchanged and would remain in prison for the rest of the war. The Confederacy had several major prisons located in Georgia, Alabama and South Carolina. The Union's largest prison camps were in Indiana, Ohio, Illinois and New York. Although the camp at Andersonville, Georgia, with a death rate of nearly thirty percent, became the most infamous for the inhumane treatment of its captives, both sides treated their prisoners badly. Elmira Prison in New York with a brutal winter environment had a comparably high death rate of twenty-five percent. Overcrowding with a total disregard for limits on capacity, lack of sanitation and contaminated water, malnourishment to the point of starvation, and diseases, such as diarrhea, dysentery and scurvy, led to high death rates in all the camps. Of the nearly 410,000 prisoners during the course of the war, more than 56,000 died in prison camps, or roughly thirteen percent of the captives. Death rates on the battlefield were much lower at about five percent.

About fifty miles from Savannah, the Union Army discovered fresh Confederate defense works that had recently been abandoned. Alarmed Confederates had moved closer to Savannah to frantically create fortifications west of the city that would be strengthened with reinforcements from Georgia and the Carolinas to defend against the approaching massive Union Army.

On December 8, about 14,000 men, which formed the left wing XIV Corps under Gen. Jefferson C. Davis, crossed Ebenezer Creek about twenty miles from Savannah with Confederate cavalry under Gen. Joseph Wheeler in hot pursuit behind. When the last Union soldier had crossed, Davis ordered the pontoon bridge to be cut, leaving 600 escaped freed slaves on the opposite bank at the mercy of the Confederates. Panicked, the abandoned slaves stampeded into the icy river and many drowned or were shot by the Confederates. Those Blacks who remained on shore were either shot and killed outright or captured to be enslaved again. Greatly criticized for the "Ebenezer Massacre" by fellow officers and the Secretary of War for his actions, Davis declared the incident was a military necessity with Sherman's full support. After the war, Gen. Davis remained with the U.S. Army on various assignments, but was never promoted beyond the final rank he held at the end of the Civil War for the remainder of his career. He died at age 51 in 1879.

VII. THE FOURTH YEAR: 1864

Union Army Reaches Savannah, Georgia
December 10, 1864

On December 10, Sherman's army reached the outskirts of Savannah to find Confederate Gen. William Hardee's 10,000 men well entrenched around the city's boundary. The surrounding countryside of rice fields had been flooded leaving only five narrow causeways for entrance. Expecting that a siege would be required to subdue the city, Sherman needed to obtain provisions, artillery and ammunition from the U.S. Navy fleet, now located just off the Georgia coast, about twenty miles southeast of Savannah near Fort McAllister, still held by the Confederates. Both the Savannah and Ogeechee Rivers emptied into the Atlantic at the city's edge, separated by about twenty miles of salt marsh.

Although Union Navy had captured Fort Pulaski at the mouth of the Savannah River in 1862, the river had been blocked by the Confederates with cribs of heavy timber, filled with sand, brick and stone and mines (so-called torpedoes) that would explode on contact. Until cleared, it was impassable by large ships. The Ogeechee River, on the other hand, clear of torpedoes and obstacles, could only support boats with up to 15-foot draft. The river, however, was protected by Fort McAllister, which had resisted several Union naval attempts to capture it. King's Bridge, upstream from the fort, had been burned by the Confederates, but would be needed for Union wagon trains to cross. A division of engineers from Howard's wing repaired the bridge by working all night and it was ready for use on December 13.

Battle of Fort McAllister, Georgia
December 13, 1864

A small Confederate force of about two hundred fifty men occupied Fort McAllister, which had been designed to resist attack from the ocean but not from its rear. The Fort had successfully defeated Union naval attacks between January 27 and March 3, 1863. But the heavy guns, so effective against the Navy, were ineffectual against the 4,000-man division from Gen. Oliver Howard's group, headed by Gen. William B. Hazen, who stormed the fort from behind.

Although Union troops suffered a number of casualties from buried shells that blew up on contact, Hazen's men rapidly overwhelmed the fort which fell in fifteen minutes. Gen. Sherman could see the battle from an observation platform placed on top of an abandoned rice mill and the success was quickly conveyed by signal officer to a navy gunboat making its way up the river. Soon, the heavily laden supply ships had transferred their loads to boats of shallow draft which began to move their supplies upstream to King's Bridge and its newly constructed wharf. The new base delivered siege guns and supplies for the troops, including new provisions and six weeks of mail.

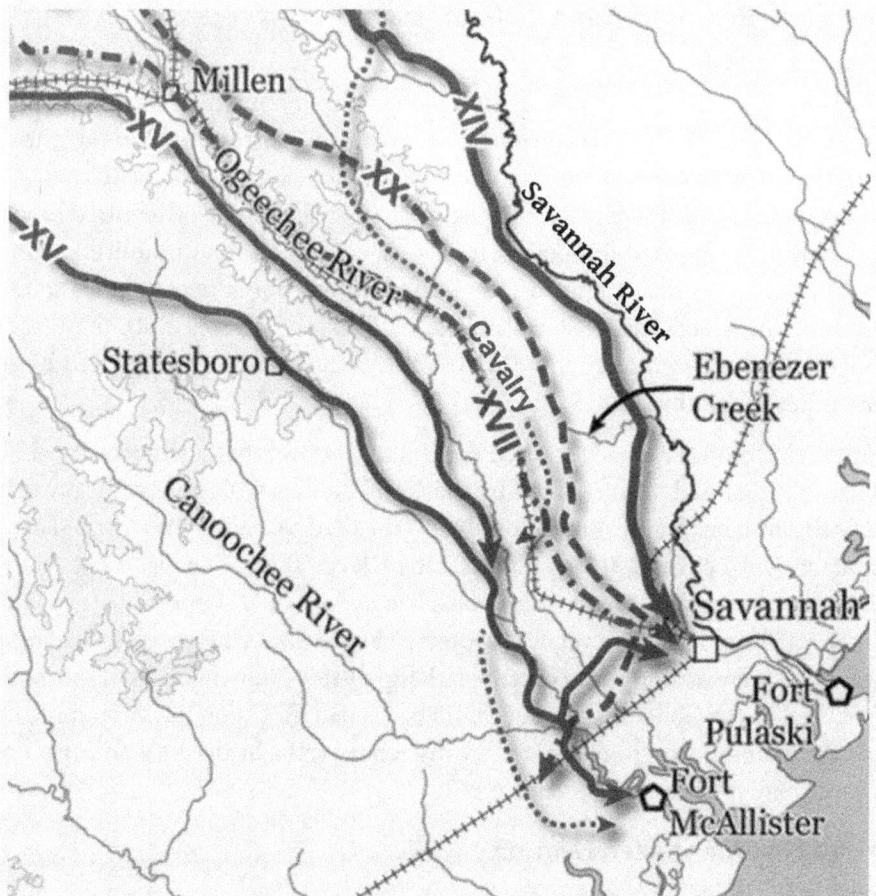

Fig. 59: The Union's 285-mile March to the Sea across Georgia ended with the capture of Savannah on Dec. 21, 1864. The army had ravaged the countryside of Confederate support and its inhabitants all along its path.

Source: *Creative Commons Attribution 3.0 License Map by Hal Jespersen, www.cwmaps.com.*

Savannah Surrenders
December 21, 1864

On December 17, Union Gen. William T. Sherman demanded the surrender of the city by communicating with Confederate Gen. William Hardee, commanding the Confederate forces there. Sherman pointed out that he had guns that could cast heavy and destructive shot on the city and that the avenues for escape were blocked. *"I am prepared to grant liberal terms to the inhabitants and garrison; but should I be forced to resort to assault… I shall resort to the harshest measures, and shall make little effort to restrain my army… to avenge the national wrong which they attach to Savannah and other large cities which have been so prominent in dragging our country into civil war."*

VII. THE FOURTH YEAR: 1864

Hardee's refusal to surrender arrived the next day, but when Union skirmishers probed the Confederate line on December 20, they found the Southern army had secretly withdrawn in the night, crossing the Savannah River using makeshift pontoon bridges. The next morning, the mayor surrendered the city with no resistance and Sherman entered Savannah on December 21.

Sherman wired Lincoln on December 22, stating, "*I beg to present you, as a Christmas gift, the city of Savannah, with one hundred fifty heavy guns and plenty of ammunition, and also about twenty-five thousand bales of cotton.*" President Lincoln quickly responded with "*Many, many thanks for your Christmas gift, the capture of Savannah … and taking the work of Thomas into account* (the defeat of Hood's army in Tennessee) *it is indeed a great success. Please make my grateful acknowledgements to your whole army, officers and men.*"

The 285-mile March to the Sea had captured thousands of draft animals, horses and mules, and a nearly incalculable number of hogs, chickens, turkeys, vegetables and fruit. Some estimates place the number of horses and mules at about ten thousand and more than fifteen thousand head of cattle. In fact, the animals that arrived at Savannah were so well fed and in such prime condition that they were described as the finest in flesh and appearance ever seen with an army.

The March to the Sea had achieved an amazing amount of destruction to Georgia and the Confederacy. By Sherman's estimate, the campaign had inflicted $100 million of damage (about $2 billion in today's dollars) virtually unopposed during the 37-day march. The foraged food consumed by the army had been sufficient to abundantly feed some 60,000 men for nearly forty days. The army destroyed nearly three hundred miles of railroad, plus bridges and telegraph lines, and confiscated about ten million pounds each of corn and animal fodder. Seizure of cotton and destruction of cotton gins and mills robbed the Confederacy of valuable currency for purchasing war materials and weapons. As Sherman described the march " … *we were not only fighting hostile armies, but a hostile people. They needed to feel the hard hand of war.*" His total casualties for the march numbered about 760 and more than 1,300 prisoners had been captured.

> **NEXT STOP: SOUTH CAROLINA**
>
> With Savannah in the grip of the Union army, Sherman writes to Grant, "*With Savannah in our possession … we can punish South Carolina as she deserves, and as thousands of the people in Georgia hoped we would do. I do sincerely believe that the whole United States, North and South, would rejoice to have this army turned loose on South Carolina, to devastate that state in the manner we have done in Georgia.*"
>
> Memoirs, W. T. Sherman, 1875

"40 Acres and a Mule"

About 17,000 Black refugees arrived in Savannah with the army after Sherman's March to the Sea, ex-slaves who escaped from their white masters as the army marched through Georgia. In spite of the army's discouragement, the slaves believed this was their chance for freedom: "... *now or never.*" The Union army had not supported the refugees during the march and survivors were suffering from starvation and disease. With the addition of more than 7,000 freed slaves in Savannah, the Northern government needed to find solutions for the care and future of about 25,000 former Black slaves. Secretary of War Edwin Stanton arrived in Savannah January 11, 1865, to discuss the crisis and met with Sherman, leaders of the Black community and other local officials.

After discussion, the group reached the decision that landownership would be the best way for ex-slaves to establish themselves as freed men. Sherman issued Special Field Order No.15 on January 16, 1865, which confiscated a strip of coastline from Charleston to St. John's River, Florida, as Union property. The Order instructed army officers to settle refugees on the Sea Islands south of Charleston and thirty miles inland on 40-acre plots. The large coastal area, comprising about 400,000 acres of land, was known as the low country and consisted mostly of abandoned rice fields along the rivers that had belonged to slave owners.

Although mules were not mentioned in the Order, Sherman later agreed to loan army mules to the refugees as a necessity for the Blacks to work their farms. After passage of the 13th Amendment on January 31, 1865, which outlawed slavery, Congress debated the issues of social, economic and settlement issues for the freed Blacks and established the Freedmen's Bureau on March 3, 1865. The bill authorized the Bureau to redistribute abandoned or confiscated land in parcels of up to forty acres, with provisions for the occupier to purchase the property from the original owners. At its peak in 1865, the Freedmen's Bureau controlled hundreds of thousands of acres of plantation lands previously belonging to slave owners. Blacks could lease abandoned or confiscated land at six percent of the land's value and have the option to purchase the land at full price after three years.

By June 1865, some 40,000 freed Blacks had settled in the Sea Islands south of Charleston. But when President Andrew Johnson succeeded the Presidency after Lincoln's assassination, he overturned the policy in the fall of 1865 and all the land was returned to the original owners. Thousands of Blacks were forced into sharecropping or tenant contracts to survive.

With the surrender and occupation of Savannah, the Atlanta Campaign came to a close. Commander-in-Chief Gen. Grant wrote of the Atlanta Campaign in his *Personal Memoirs*, "The campaign had lasted four months and was one of the most memorable in history. There was little of anything in the whole campaign, now that it is over, to

VII. THE FOURTH YEAR: 1864

criticize at all, and nothing to criticize severely. It was creditable alike to the general who commanded and the army which executed it."

BATTLES FOR TENNESSEE

Franklin-Nashville Campaign
November-December 1864

As Gen. William T. Sherman departed Atlanta for the March to the Sea on November 15, 1864, the rest of his army was in Tennessee under Gen. George H. Thomas at Nashville, commanding the Army of the Cumberland, and Gen. John M. Schofield, Army of the Ohio, near Pulaski, about eighty miles south of him. Union cavalry under Gen. James H. Wilson, who had served under Kilpatrick in Sherman's Atlanta Campaign, was also deployed to Nashville to support both armies. Schofield had been positioned in Pulaski so that he could respond to any efforts by Confederate Gen. John Bell Hood's Army of Tennessee to interfere with Sherman's March to the Sea through Georgia. If that was not the case, then Schofield would combine his forces with Thomas in Nashville to prevent Hood from moving north to take eastern Tennessee, or possibly even reach into Kentucky. Thomas was overall commander of the two Union armies.

When Confederate Gen. Hood finally received his wagon trains of supplies for his march into Tennessee, he left Tuscumbia, Alabama, crossed the Tennessee River to Florence, and headed north November 21, 1864. Hood's objective was to intercept Schofield before he could reach Nashville and prevent the two Union armies from merging. The Confederate Army was supported by Gen. Nathan Bedford Forrest's cavalry, which had joined Hood at Tuscumbia earlier that month.

Schofield left Pulaski on November 24 once it was clear that Hood was not going to pursue Sherman on his march through Georgia. Hood tried to reach the Duck River at Columbia before Schofield, about thirty miles north of Pulaski and prevent his crossing, but sleet, rain and cold weather made roads difficult for both armies. The Southern army, poorly outfitted, reached Columbia on November 27 just behind Schofield's Union army which had been able to set up a strong defense after successfully crossing Duck River, burning the bridges behind them and setting up camp on the northern side.

Hood, however, took advantage of a ford some miles east of Columbia, and crossed the river with the bulk of his army the next day, undetected by the Union general. Hood left one unit behind to fire artillery across the river, deceiving Schofield that the battle would take place there. As Hood moved north on Schofield's flank, the Northern army was in grave danger of being pinned by Hood against the river with no means of escape.

Union cavalry under Gen. Wilson had been drawn northeast of Schofield by the Confederate cavalry under Gen. Forrest. Constant skirmishing between the two cavalries occurred November 28 and Wilson sent multiple messages back to Schofield that

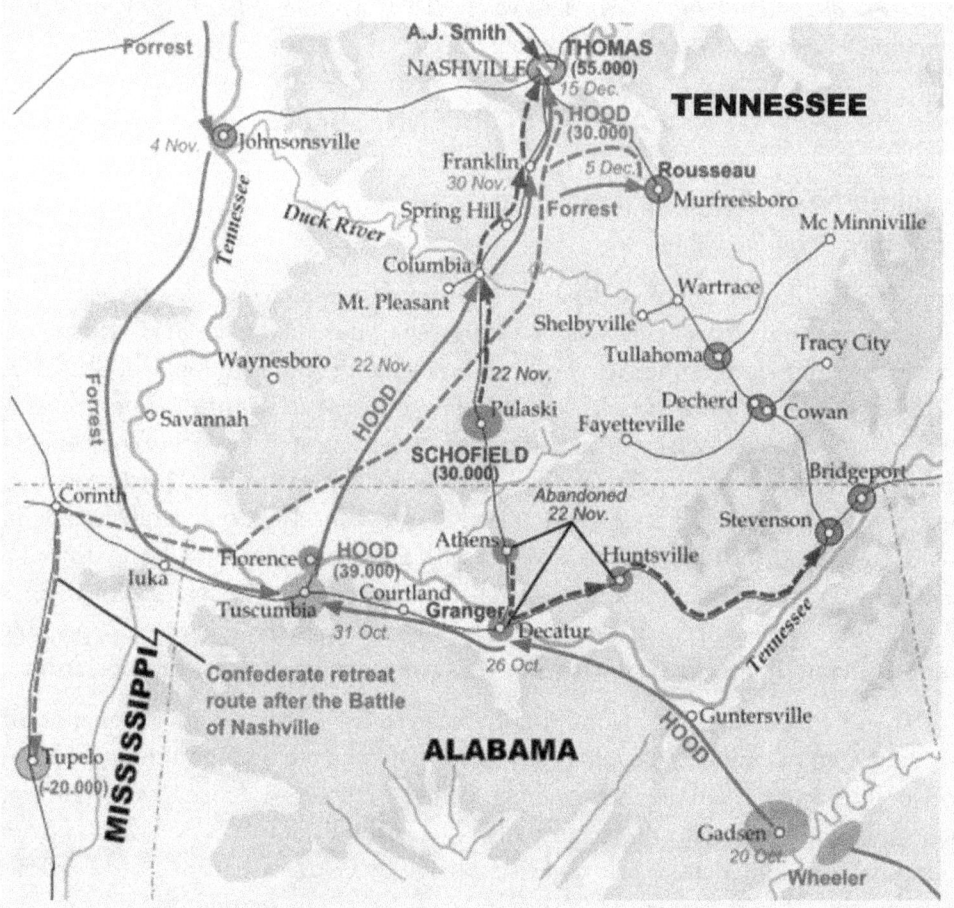

Fig. 60: Confederate Gen. Hood departed Tuscumbia, Alabama, Nov. 21, 1864, for Tennessee, planning to capture Nashville and claim the state for the Confederacy. Hood failed to block Union Gen. Schofield as he left Pulaski to join forces at Nashville and the two armies fought at the Battle of Franklin.

Source: *This work released into the public domain by its author, Andrei Nacu through the Wikipedia Project.*

Hood's infantry was marching north on his flank toward Spring Hill. On November 29 Schofield finally realized the danger and sent part of his army north to protect the 800-strong wagon train already underway and to guard the crossroads at Spring Hill, the army's path north to Franklin. When Hood's lead troops caught up with Schofield's army, a miscommunication in orders led the Southerners to attack at the wrong position, and they were defeated with heavy casualties. With limited visibility at nightfall, the attack was called off, leaving the crossroads and turnpike to Franklin still open. Hood's army bivouacked nearby for the night, some camps only one hundred yards from the road.

VII. THE FOURTH YEAR: 1864

Battle of Franklin, Tennessee
November 30, 1864

While Confederate Gen. John Bell Hood's army settled into camp for the night near the turnpike to Franklin, the last group of Union Gen. John Schofield's army finally got away from Duck River, leaving about 10 p.m. As the lead group approached the turnpike nearest the Confederate camp in the dark, Union scouts reported there were no sentries on the still open road. Using blankets on wooden planks to muffle the sounds of feet and wheels, the 25,000-man Union army quietly slipped by the Confederates in the dark. By sunrise on November 30, the vanguard of the Union army was at Franklin, eight miles north of Spring Hill, and proceeded to create defenses south of the town.

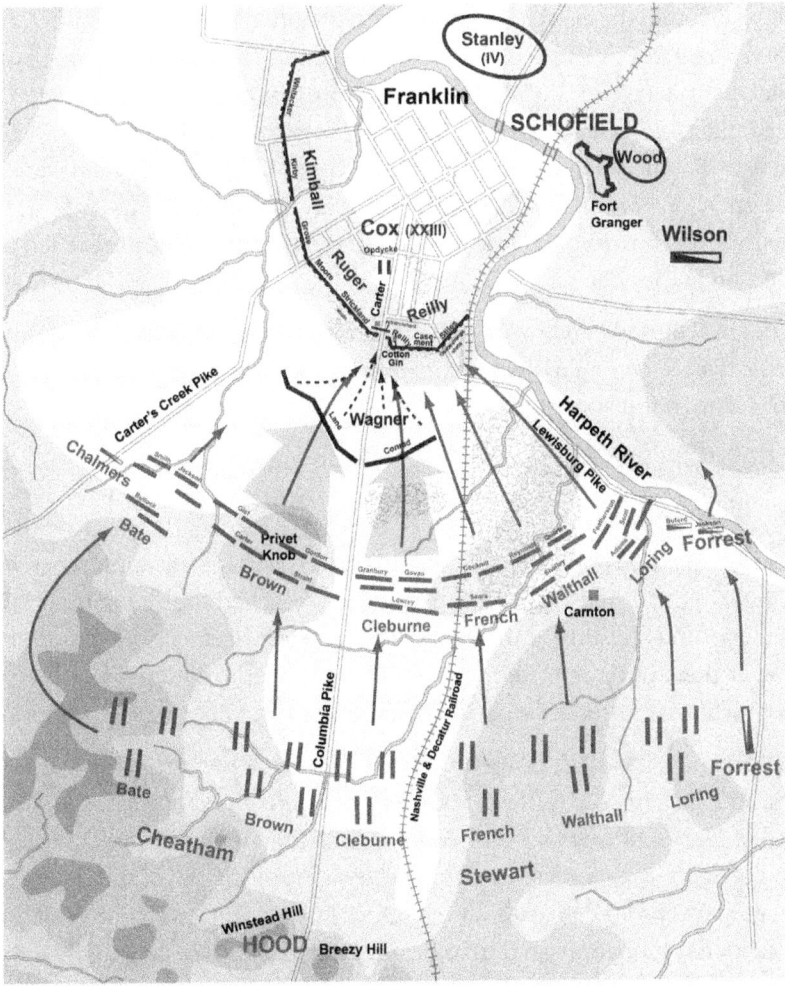

Fig. 61: Confederates under Gen. Hood endured heavy losses from Union forces commanded by Gen. Schofield at the Battle of Franklin, Tennessee, Nov. 30, 1864.

Source: *Creative Commons Attribution 3.0 License Map by Hal Jespersen, www. cwmaps.com.*

When Hood learned that Schofield's army had passed him in the night, he blamed his generals for incompetence and was "... *wrathy as a rattlesnake*," in the words of one subordinate. Catching the Union army in late afternoon, Hood ordered a suicidal frontal assault in late afternoon across an open two-mile long field against the horseshoe-shaped Union defenses just below Franklin. The Confederates broke through the center of the defense, which was a half-mile from the main Union line and poorly defended. Hand-to-hand fighting went on for several hours with murderous effect on the Southern soldiers. Simultaneous attacks on both Union flanks failed and Hood was forced to call off the assault with heavy losses.

The Confederate Army of Tennessee lost fourteen of its generals (six killed, seven wounded and one captured) in the battle and fifty-five regimental commanders killed or wounded. Overall, the army's losses numbered more than 6,000 casualties, including 1,750 killed and 4,000 wounded, in just five hours of fighting, bringing some to call it "The Pickett's Charge of the West." The appalling number of dead affected many of the Confederate soldiers, some of whom never forgave Hood. It was said later that it was the day the Confederate Army of Tennessee itself died. Union losses were less than 200 killed and 1,300 wounded. Around midnight, Schofield and his infantry crossed the Harpeth River, burning the bridges behind them. Union troops reached Nashville about noon on December 1.

Ignoring his council of advisors to withdraw, Hood insisted that the army advance to Nashville, where he established fortified lines south of the city on December 2 and waited for Gen. Thomas to attack.

Battle of Nashville, Tennessee
December 15, 1864

As Gen. George H. Thomas anxiously waited in Nashville for reinforcements, many of his soldiers in the Army of the Cumberland had reached the end of their enlistment and their departures steadily diminished the forces left to defend against the Confederate army now at their doorstep. Reinforcements had been ordered from Missouri but because of torrential rains and early snows, they had still not arrived by November 29.

Good fortune prevailed, however, on November 30 when ships docked on the Cumberland River in Nashville carrying reinforcements from Missouri under the command of Gen. Andrew Jackson (A. J.) Smith. They were followed the next day by the arrival of Schofield's forces from the Battle of Franklin. An additional provisional detachment of troops landed at about the same time under Gen. James Steedman, who had shown remarkable bravery during the Battle of Chickamauga. His detachment included garrison troops and railroad guards from Tennessee and Georgia, and eight regiments of United States Colored Troops. Thomas now had an army of about 50,000 men.

VII. THE FOURTH YEAR: 1864

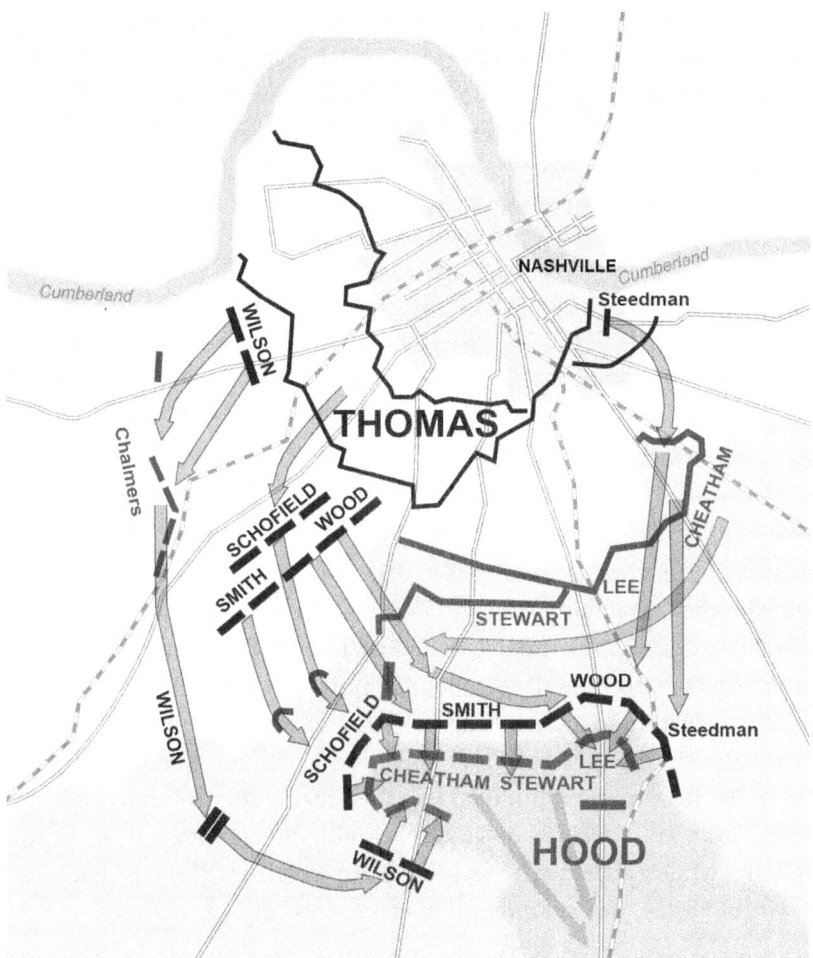

Fig. 62: At the Battle of Nashville, Dec. 15, 1864, Confederate Gen. Hood's badly outnumbered army was unable to defeat the Union forces under Gen. Thomas. Suffering heavy losses, the Confederate Army of Tennessee was forced to retreat to Tupelo, Mississippi, and never recovered.
Source: *This work released into the public domain by its author, Andrei Nacu through the Wikipedia Project.*

With navy gunboats guarding the Cumberland River to his back and strong defensive entrenchments surrounding his front, pressure from Washington urged Thomas to assault Hood immediately. But the "Rock of Chickamauga" was not ready for an attack and constantly disappointed General-in-Chief Grant with delays. But the reality for Thomas was that the large army he now commanded included mostly raw and inexperienced men who needed to be trained to fight effectively with the few veterans who were already there. Furthermore, his cavalry corps under Gen. Wilson, which had greatly increased in size with the influx of new troops, badly needed more horses to be effective against the legendary cavalry of Confederate Gen. Forrest, serving the army under Gen. Hood.

Hood's Confederate Army of Tennessee, numbering about 27,000, now significantly diminished after the Battle of Franklin, had arrived December 2 to settle into fortifications about ten miles southeast of Nashville facing the Union line. The seven-mile semi-circle of Nashville's Union defensive works was too great a span for Hood's army, so they thinly entrenched along four miles of the fortifications and waited to defend against an attack rather than attempt a frontal assault that had been so devastating at Franklin.

Attempting to draw Thomas out of his fortifications, Hood sent Forrest and his cavalry with infantry support to attack the Nashville & Chattanooga Railroad and the garrison at Murfreesboro, Tennessee, about forty miles southeast of Nashville. Although Forrest's cavalry did break the railroad in several places, Union forces drove the Confederates off at the Third Battle of Murfreesboro (also known as the Battle of the Cedars) on December 7. Gen. Thomas did not fall for Hood's trap and kept the bulk of his army at Nashville.

In the meantime, Gen. Grant and Secretary of War Stanton became increasingly impatient with the "slow and plodding" Thomas and his lack of progress for an attack on the Confederate army. The threat of relieving Thomas from command was gathering strength. A bitter ice storm on December 8 removed all possibility of attack as several inches of ice made it impossible for man or beast to move. Sub-freezing weather continued through December 12 as Hood's men, some with no shoes or hats, shivered in holes dug in the frozen earth, huddled together, trying not to freeze to death. Grant, his patience at an end, decided to go to Nashville himself, to relieve Thomas from command. But while underway, he received a dispatch from Thomas that he was ready to move. Grant writes, *"He did move, and was successful from the start."*

A thaw in the weather launched the Battle of Nashville on December 15, with Thomas combining his combat resources—infantry, artillery and cavalry with repeating rifles. A courageous attack by Gen. Steedman's Black troops on Hood's right flank at Peach Orchard Hill convinced Hood that it was the main assault, but the full attack was coming on his left flank. Because Hood's cavalry under Forrest was still at Murfreesboro, Hood was unaware of the threat on his left.

Union troops forced the Confederate left flank into a retreat, shrinking their defense line from four miles to two. As darkness fell, fighting ceased. Thomas initiated an artillery barrage the next morning and by mid-afternoon, Union infantry and cavalry forces had broken the Confederate's left flank, followed by a break in the center. Many of Hood's veterans, psychologically devastated by the losses at Franklin, refused to be sacrificed and fled the field. Fierce fighting by the troops on Hood's right flank during the withdrawal saved what was left of his army.

On the night of December 16, Hood organized a full retreat south along the tarmacked Pike Turnpike to reach Franklin, but was hotly pursued by Union cavalry under Gen.

VII. THE FOURTH YEAR: 1864

Wilson, numbering about 13,000 troopers. Confederate Gen. Stephen D. Lee's hardened veterans defended the retreat of the depleted army, now numbering less than 20,000, with fierce hand-to-hand fighting on December 17 north of Franklin. Confederate cavalry under Gen. Forrest, riding hard from Murfreesboro, caught up with the army on December 18 and created a formidable rear guard as it protected Hood's retreating Army of Tennessee. Union pursuers were delayed at Columbia because the pontoon bridges that were needed had been misdirected to Murfreesboro. Forrest's actions at Pulaski, Anthony's Hill and Sugar Creek delayed the Northern cavalry's pursuit long enough for the Confederates to cross the Duck River on December 19 and then finally cross the Tennessee River near Bainbridge, Alabama, on December 25-28 only hours ahead of the Union pursuers.

Historians describe the agony of the Army of Tennessee during the retreat as one of the most devastating in American history. Rain, sleet, snow, freezing temperatures and sticky mud wreaked havoc on the suffering soldiers. Feet wrapped in blankets left bloody tracks in the snow as the army traveled one hundred twenty miles in ten days to reach the Tennessee River and cross into safety.

Casualties from the Battle of Nashville numbered about 3,000 for the Union (387 killed, 2,600 wounded). Historical estimates place the Confederate losses at about 2,500 killed and wounded and at least 2,000 deserters at Nashville. More than 4,500 Confederates were captured as prisoners during the retreat. Historians rank the Battle of Nashville as one of the most stunning victories for the Union during the war. The formidable Confederate Army of Tennessee, second largest in the Confederacy, had been destroyed as a fighting unit.

Retreating to Tupelo, Mississippi, Hood's army now had only about 15,000 men, less than half its number of 38,000 when Hood entered Tennessee, effectively ending it as an army. Five thousand of its former soldiers were sent to North Carolina to serve in Gen. Joseph E. Johnston's army, now fighting Union Gen. Sherman on his march through the Carolinas. Hood was not given another assignment; his Civil War career was finished. He resigned from the army January 13, 1865.

BATTLES FOR CONFEDERATE SEAPORTS

Battle of Mobile Bay, Alabama
August 5-23, 1864

The Union Navy had established a blockade of nearly all Confederate ports at the beginning of the war which had been very successful in eliminating the importation of most goods for the Confederacy and its export of cotton, a major source of hard currency. Nevertheless, in 1864, the ports of Wilmington, North Carolina, and Mobile, Alabama, still supported blockade runners, the fast, low-slung ships with shallow draft that could either outrun or evade the Union Navy, bringing munitions, food, medicine, brandy and other supplies from the British islands of Bermuda and the Bahamas, or Havana, Cuba. Mobile, the South's fourth largest city and second-largest on the Gulf, was a key center for the export of cotton and source of funding for the Confederacy.

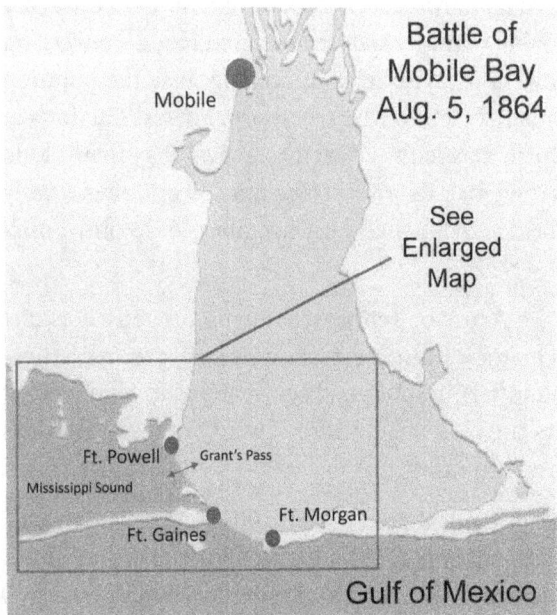

Fig. 63: Mobile Bay, Alabama, protected by three well armored forts, enabled blockade runners to continue to supply the South and its Confederate armies through most of the Civil War.

The capture of Mobile Bay, the last major Confederate port on the Gulf of Mexico, was an important priority for the Union's overall war strategy for 1864. Early May had been designated by General-in-Chief Grant for simultaneous attacks against all Confederate armies. The Overland and Atlanta Campaigns in the Eastern and Western Theaters, respectively, were launched May 4, but the Mobile effort had been delayed by the disastrous Red River Campaign.

But on August 5, the attack on Mobile Bay was finally launched by Rear Admiral David G. Farragut, head of the West Gulf Blockading Squadron, commanding eighteen ships, which included four ironclads. Mobile Bay is a shallow inlet to the Gulf of Mexico, about thirty miles long and twenty-four miles wide at its entrance to the Gulf. The natural harbor is filled by a number of streams and rivers, making it one of the largest estuaries in the United States. The city of Mobile, located at the northern edge of the harbor, was shielded from large vessels by the multiple sandbars that limited passage to all but shallow keel boats.

The entrance to Mobile Bay was guarded by three forts, all facing the sea. Fort Morgan had forty-six guns and Fort Gaines, twenty-six guns, each with a garrison of about six hundred men. A third smaller fort, Fort Powell, with eighteen guns and one hundred forty men, guarded a secondary entrance, named Grant's Pass, on the west side of the Bay. The Pass was dredged by Captain John Grant between 1826 and 1829 to gain access to the Mississippi Sound so that ships could sail between Mobile and New Orleans without entering the Gulf of Mexico.

A torpedo minefield made up of underwater mines blocked the entrance to Mobile Bay, but left a gap on the eastern side nearest Fort Morgan, so that blockade runners and friendly ships could enter safely. Hostile incoming ships, however, would be attacked by the fort's artillery. The minefield was well marked with buoys. The Confederate

VII. THE FOURTH YEAR: 1864

Navy at Mobile included three small sidewheel gunboats and one ironclad, the heavily armored *CSS Tennessee*, which was under the command of the Confederacy's only full admiral, Admiral Franklin Buchanan.

Farragut arranged the four Union ironclad monitors in a column formation, to follow a line between the minefield and the fort. A second column of fourteen armed wooden-hulled ships were lashed together in pairs so that a damaged ship could be towed by its partner. The wooden ships, protected from fort artillery by the Union ironclads, would sail between the ironclads and the minefield.

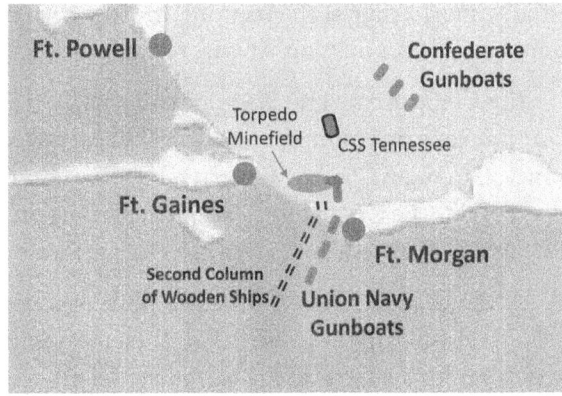

Fig. 64: Enlarged map of the Battle of Mobile Bay, Alabama, on Aug. 4, 1864, illustrates the configuration of the attacking Union fleet against the Confederate gunboats.

One ironclad, the *USS Tecumseh*, mistakenly entered the minefield as it headed toward the *CSS Tennessee*, and was immediately hit by a mine. Nearly all of the crew was lost, including its commander. The lead timberclad ship in the second column stalled, blocking the path for the fleet behind it. As Confederate fire hammered, Farragut moved his ship into the lead, with the order "*Damn the torpedoes. Full speed ahead.*" Following Farragut safely through the edge of the minefield, the fleet quickly overwhelmed three Confederate sidewheel gunboats. One was captured, a second beached and the third fled to the protection of Fort Morgan, the crew escaping to Mobile that night. Left alone, the single Confederate armored ironclad, *CSS Tennessee*, battled against overwhelming odds for three hours, but finally surrendered when its commander, Admiral Buchanan, was severely wounded with a broken leg.

> **"DAMN THE TORPEDOES"**
>
> It was in the Battle of Mobile Bay that Admiral Farragut uttered his famous quote, *"Damn the torpedos! Full speed ahead!"*

Union attention now focused on the forts protecting the harbor. Because the forts' guns were aimed at the Gulf, they had little protection against attacks from the rear. Farragut ordered the Union gunboat *USS Chickasaw* to fire at short range on Fort Powell, whose commander, convinced that resistance was futile, blew up the magazines and the entire garrison waded ashore to make their way to the city of Mobile.

Approximately 1,500 men from the U.S. Army had been loaned to the operation for a siege of Fort Gaines. The men landed about fifteen miles west of the fort on August 3, marched the next day to within a half mile of the fort, where they formed an entrenched skirmish line. With the surrender of the Confederate fleet, Union Navy artillery now fired at short-range at the rear of Fort Gaines with impunity. The commander surrendered after three days on August 8.

The Union Army and Navy next focused on Fort Morgan, which was bombarded continuously by Union monitors at short range and by the rest of the fleet from long range. On August 23 the fort surrendered and the city of Mobile, although not captured, was cut off. The Confederacy's last major port on the Gulf of Mexico had been closed. The city of Mobile would remain in Confederate hands until the last days of the war.

With the successful capture of Mobile Bay, the Confederacy was left with only one seaport at Wilmington, North Carolina. Farragut was promoted to Vice Admiral, the senior ranking officer in the Navy.

Battle for Wilmington, North Carolina, Seaport
First Battle of Fort Fisher, December 23-27, 1864

Wilmington, North Carolina, located about thirty miles inland from the Atlantic Ocean on Cape Fear River, was a major port for the Confederacy throughout most of the Civil War. With the fall of Mobile, Alabama, the preceding August, Wilmington was the South's last remaining open port and an essential source of supplies for the Confederacy. Blockade runners successfully penetrated Union Navy barriers throughout the war and supplied Confederate armies with vital supplies delivered by steamer ships from Bermuda and the Bahamas. Cotton and tobacco were regularly exchanged for munitions, clothing and food. Confederate Gen. Robert E. Lee called Wilmington the lifeblood for his Army of Northern Virginia.

The daunting Fort Fisher, located on one of two inlets to the Cape Fear River, armed with formidable artillery and a long line of bombproofed batteries, protected the river and the city from Union attack. Called the Gibraltar for the Confederacy, the Fort was equipped with twenty-two sea-facing guns and twenty-five land guns, with underground passageways and bomb-proof rooms that were protected by huge earthen mounds.

Union authority for Fort Fisher fell within the area commanded by Gen. Benjamin Butler, Army of the James, now situated on the Virginia Peninsula. A joint Army-Navy operation for an attack on the fort would use naval forces under the leadership of Rear Admiral David Dixon Porter, commanding the North Atlantic Blockading Squadron, with Gen. Butler as overall commander of the operation. Butler conceived the idea of using a steamer loaded with gunpowder to be exploded near the shore to achieve some destruction of the fort and also serve as a distraction. Grant had no confidence in the scheme, but authorities at Washington " ... *seemed desirous to have it tried,*" so he permitted it. Although scheduled to take place in early December, the expedition was delayed by bad weather and the acquisition of necessary munitions and powder for the steamer.

VII. THE FOURTH YEAR: 1864

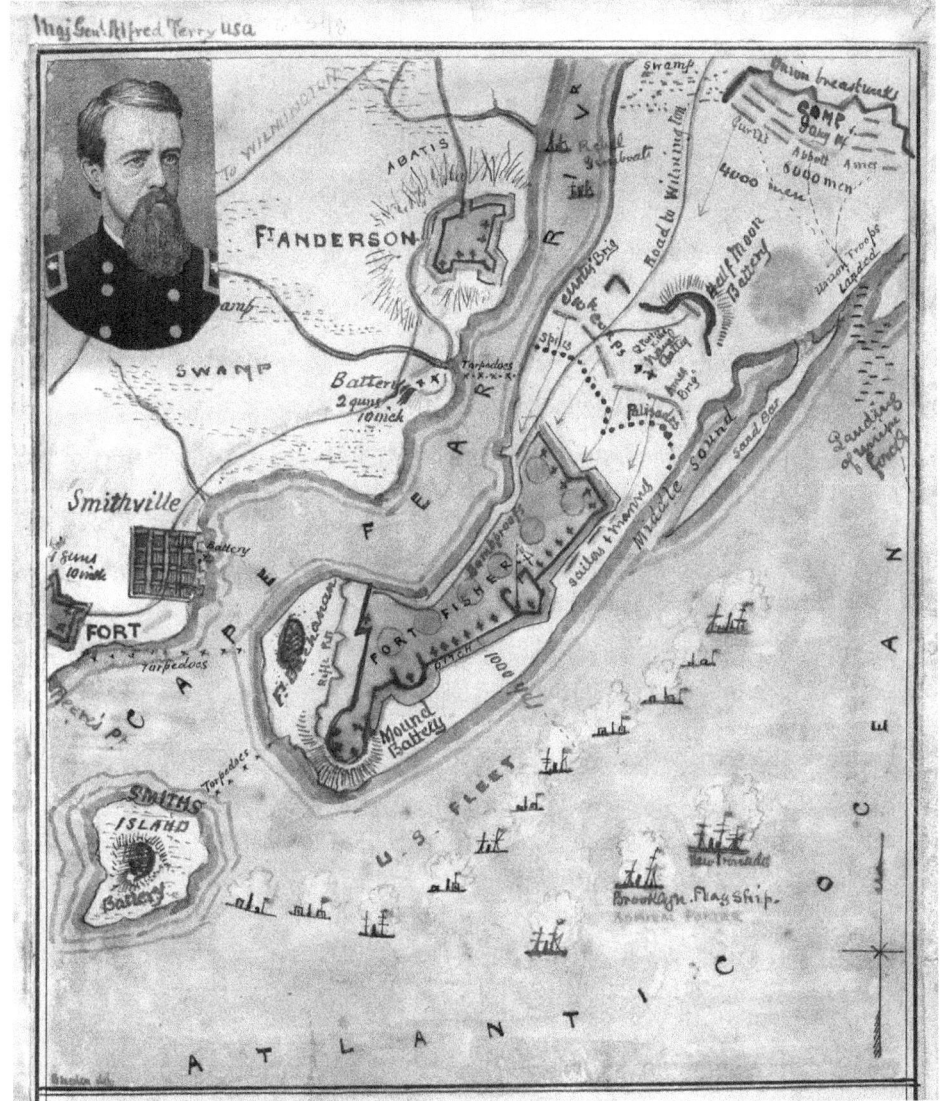

Fig. 65: Fort Fisher at the mouth of Cape Fear River, North Carolina, protected the vital Confederate city at Wilmington for blockade runners who supplied ammunition, clothing and food to the Southern armies.

Source: File is in the public domain, made by a Union soldier in 1865.

On the night of December 23, 1864, the loaded powder-boat was towed in by gunboat near the shore. Grant writes of the event in his *Personal Memoirs*, "When it exploded at 2 o'clock in the morning, it produced no more effect on the fort, or anything else on land, than the bursting of a boiler anywhere on the Atlantic Ocean would have done. Indeed, when the troops in Fort Fisher heard the explosion, they supposed it was the bursting of a boiler in one of the Yankee gunboats." Confederate Col. William Lamb, commander of the Fort Fisher garrison, believed that a Union ship had accidentally run aground and its magazine had exploded.

When the naval offensive began the next morning, Admiral Porter placed his fleet of nearly sixty ships in arcs of concentric circles with heavy iron-clads going in at close range. Between the iron-clads and the outer vessels, Porter was able to fire ten thousand shots that day. But damage was minimal due to the Fort's structure of heavy earth mounds and underground rooms. In addition, Col. Lamb evaluated the bombardment as diffuse and poorly calculated with many of the shells landing in the river and bordering marshes. The garrison suffered only 23 casualties that day; Union losses were 45 due to exploding guns on the ships.

The next day, a Union infantry landing party successfully established a line across the peninsula and captured a small garrison known as the Flag Pond Battery. Reports from captured Confederates revealed that a division of 6,000 men under Gen. Robert F. Hoke, deployed from Lee's Army of Northern Virginia at Richmond, would soon arrive and 1,600 had already landed. Gen. Butler lost his nerve and ordered a retreat of all his men against Porter's strenuous objections.

Three days later, the entire army contingent returned to Fort Monroe at Hampton Roads reporting a failed mission. By ordering the retreat, Butler had ignored Grant's orders which had been explicit: "... *if one* (a landing) *should be affected, the foothold must not be relinquished... on the contrary, a regular siege of the fort must be commenced.*" Butler was summarily relieved of command and a second offensive on Fort Fisher was initiated less than three weeks later on January 13-15, 1865, under Gen. Alfred Terry, heading a provisional corps from the Department of Virginia and North Carolina. Gen. Edward Ord, who had been transferred to the Eastern Theater from the Army of the Gulf during the Siege of Petersburg, was named new commander for the Army of the James, replacing Butler.

VIEWS FROM THE PUBLIC FOR THE YEAR 1864

About the Northern economy and financing the War...

Many industries in the North were able to take advantage of a booming economy that needed to satisfy a seemingly endless demand for uniforms, shoes, firearms, ammunition and food for the Union armies. In 1860, ninety percent of manufactured goods came from the North, including seventy percent of the country's railroad tracks. It produced over three thousand firearms for every one hundred produced in the South. Its factories regularly churned out parts and machinery for the railroads and the Union war machine. The *New York Times* wrote on March 1, 1864, *"In the midst of the most gigantic civil war the world has yet seen, the people of the North were never better fed, better sheltered or better clothed. War, instead of repressing our energies, has only served to expand and quicken them."*

VII. THE FOURTH YEAR: 1864

The Northern agricultural economy had embraced some mechanization of agricultural tools even before the war. In 1860, the increased productivity was yielding half the nation's corn, four-fifths of its wheat and seven-eighths of its oats. With the onset of war, mechanization of agriculture became even more prevalent as many farmers left home to join the Union military and the military draft reduced the number of farm workers. Reapers and threshing machines for harvesting grains could achieve the same results with a tenth of the number of men doing the same task. In 1860, a new harvesting machine was created by McCormick Company that cut manpower requirements for harvesting a crop by a factor of four and it became widely used during the war.

Spencer repeating rifles, invented in 1860, were vastly superior to the standard muzzle loader. Its capacity of seven rounds could be fired in less than one minute. When the inventor demonstrated the rifle to President Lincoln in 1862, his personal secretary John Hay, wrote of the event: *"This evening and yesterday evening an hour was spent by the President in shooting with Spencer's new repeating rifle. A wonderful gun, loading with absolutely contemptible simplicity and ease with seven balls and firing the whole readily and deliberately in less than half a minute. The President made some pretty good shots. Spencer the inventor a quiet little Yankee who sold himself in relentless slavery to his idea for six weary years before it was perfect, did some splendid shooting."* Although the War Department did not immediately pursue a contract to purchase the rifles, the demonstration to Lincoln landed federal contracts for the company and the Union purchased nearly 150,000 rifles by war's end.

Congress had passed the Legal Tender Act in 1862 authorizing the printing of paper money, or "greenbacks," as legal currency and creditors were required to accept them for payment of debts. The greenbacks fluctuated in value depending on Union success in the battlefield, but never fell below about forty cents on the dollar. After the Union success at Gettysburg, for example, a greenback dollar was worth about seventy cents and at war's end, slightly more than sixty cents.

About the Southern economy and financing the War...

The Southern economy, on the other hand, with more than eighty percent of its population working in agriculture that relied on slave labor, could not compete with the North in manufacturing capabilities. The South's economic strength was founded in slave ownership and did not translate well into mobilization of the resources needed for war. The North's advantages in factories, railroads and resources for manufacturing weapons and distributing food to the troops were becoming clearly visible by 1864. Further, the Confederacy's paper money, its "greybacks," not supported by hard assets, such as gold or cotton, continued to lose value as valid currency as the war continued. In addition, the sale of Southern goods, particularly cotton, were unable to generate currency from foreign markets because of Union naval blockades.

From the *Richmond Enquirer* on May 7, 1864, as reported in the *New York Times*, came the following report. "*We publish, today, a number of extracts from rebel papers, which possess no little interest. The Richmond Enquirer, of the 7th inst., feels very downcast over the victories of our armies, particularly in East Tennessee, and strongly censures Vice-President STEPHENS for his criticism of their laws. It also gives the particulars of a very destructive fire in Wilmington, the loss by which is estimated at $4,800,000—of which $900,000 was Government property. Considerable dissatisfaction is expressed at the depreciation of their five-dollar notes and the scarcity of the new issue. The markets are active, but the prices demanded for all goods are fearfully exorbitant.*"

In late 1863, a Texas Senator pointed out that the $11 per month paid to a Confederate soldier amounted to $1 when compared to its buying power at the beginning of the war. A year later in September 1864, the Confederate dollar was the equivalent of three cents of a Union dollar. At the time of Christmas 1864, a turkey sold for $155 in Richmond and a ham for $300. Newspapers became more expensive and fewer pages were printed. In 1864, the *Lynchburg Daily Virginian* paid four dollars for a pound of printer's ink that had cost fourteen cents in 1860. In 1861, the number of newspapers and periodicals in Virginia totaled about one hundred forty. By 1863, there were less than twenty newspapers in the entire state of Virginia and by 1864, less than half a dozen.

About Grant being labeled as the "Butcher"....

The Union Army launched its Overland Campaign into Virginia in May 1864 with the Army of the Potomac, under the overall command of Gen. Ulysses S. Grant, that would confront the Confederate Army of Northern Virginia under Gen. Robert E. Lee. The initial battle about sixty miles south of Washington in the heavy woods and dense undergrowth of the Wilderness, lasted two days and resulted in horrific casualties, particularly for the Union side, at about 18,000 casualties (more than 2,200 killed and nearly 16,000 wounded or captured).

As the sounds and cries of wounded, dying soldiers filled the night, Grant was heard sobbing in his tent and his staff expected an order to retreat the next morning. But the army did not withdraw and instead moved south, bringing forth cheers from the Union troops, as it was the first time the Army of the Potomac had not retreated from the legendary Robert E. Lee, who had proved to be a formidable, dangerous foe. In a letter to his wife, Grant wrote, "*The world has never seen so bloody or so protracted a battle as the one being fought.*"

When one of Grant's commanders expressed his fears about what Lee was going to do next, Grant testily responded, "*I'm tired of hearing about what Lee is going to do. Some of you think he's going to do a double somersault and land in our rear and both flanks ... go back to your command and think about what we're going to do.*"

As the armies moved south from the Wilderness, the Battles of Spotsylvania and Cold Harbor brought an even greater number of casualties for both sides. At Spotsylvania,

VII. THE FOURTH YEAR: 1864

Col. Horace Porter, Grant's personal secretary, wrote: *"It was as though Christian men had turned to fiends, and hell itself had usurped the place of the earth."* At the deadly battle of the "Mule Shoe," bodies piled up in layers and wounded men at the bottom died in a mix of blood and water from the driving rainstorm. *"No Mardi Gras Carnival ever devised such a diabolical looking set of devils as we were,"* recalled a Mississippi soldier. *"It was no imitation of red paint and burnt cork, but genuine human gore and gun powder smoke."* After the battle, Rep. Elihu Washburne, Illinois representative in Congress traveling with the army, asked Grant if he had any message for the President and Secretary of War. Grant replied, *"Tell them I propose to fight it out on this line, if it takes all summer… there will be no turning back,"* a headline that was soon splashed across the Northern press in large letters. Grant's continued pursuit eventually drove Gen. Lee and the Army of Northern Virginia into the Siege of Petersburg, where the Confederates were surrounded for ten months by a tightly held Union Army that could be continually reinforced, supported and well fed.

But the heavy Union losses of 55,000 that had accumulated over the 40-day offensive, compared to Lee's losses of 30,000, provoked the label of "butcher" for Grant, as *"… a commander who had little regard for human life."* Even Mary Lincoln, the President's wife, protested that *"He loses two men to the enemy's one. He has no management, no regard for life."* But Grant was no butcher as later historians were able to point out. His casualties in the Battles of Fort Donelson and the final Battle of Vicksburg in 1862-63 had been achieved with minimal losses. The casualties in the Overland Campaign, although large, had been necessary to achieve the goal of limiting the strength of the Army of Northern Virginia. Robert E. Lee lost half his army during the same Campaign and was now forced into a siege which would eventually defeat the Southerners and bring an end to the war. Grant's strength in continuing the battle against Lee followed his pattern of decisive action as he conducted himself through the battles: *"In war, anything is better than indecision. We must decide. If I am wrong, we shall soon find out and can do the other thing, but not to decide, may ruin everything."* The gruesome six weeks of the Overland Campaign brought Lincoln to pronounce, *"The heavens are hung in black,"* but he kept faith with his new commander because he was steadily destroying Lee's army, a principal objective of the 1864 campaigns. When Union forces dug in around Petersburg, besieging Lee's army, Lincoln sent Grant a telegram, *"I begin to see it. You will succeed. God bless you all."*

About Southern response to the Overland Campaign…

Reports in the Southern press praised the Confederate Army of Northern Virginia under Robert E. Lee against Union Gen. Ulysses S. Grant and the Army of the Potomac in the Battles of the Wilderness and Cold Harbor. Although both Union and Confederate armies were suffering major casualties, Southern newspapers received only sketchy reports about the battles when telegraph lines and railroad connections were cut off by Union assaults. But the *Richmond Dispatch* described the trust which the Confederate public placed in Robert E. Lee on June 1, 1864, by writing, *"The confidence in Lee and his army is not confined to the ranks of that army and to our fellow citizens. It is as extensive as the Confederacy itself. There are few who do not feel it, and bless God when they acknowledge it, for sending us so great a General to lead so brave an army."*

When the Union Army was within a few miles of Richmond in June, the *Richmond Daily Whig*, also confident in the skills of Gen. Lee, wrote, *"Richmond was never safer, nor the Confederate cause on higher or on firmer ground."* But the editor did express concern about the crushing loss of men that was taking place. *"On our part, we are perfectly willing for Grant to cypher away at this sum until he finds and proves it. We think that recent events go to show that it will not be the Confederacy which is first exhausted."*

Another report from the *Richmond Dispatch* on June 9: *"The storm of battle which raged so furiously last week in the immediate vicinity of Richmond has been succeeded by a comparative calm, and matters are now almost as quiet as when the contending armies were seventy miles away. GRANT has evidently become tired of "butting" against the rebel fortifications, and what he failed to effect by brute force he now essays to accomplish by strategy. Consequently, we find him stealthily moving away from our front, and sliding down the south side of the Chickahominy, endeavoring, if possible, to reach the James, with a view of cooperating with BUTLER, who is still pent up between that river and the Appomattox."*

About Andersonville Prison …

Twenty-year-old Union Sgt. Robert H. Kellogg of the 16th Regiment of Connecticut Volunteers, captured by Confederates in April 1864 while stationed at Plymouth, North Carolina, was sent to Andersonville Prison in Georgia and he kept a diary of his experiences that was later published. *"As we entered the place, a spectacle met our eyes that almost froze our blood with horror … before us were forms that had once been active and erect—stalwart men, now nothing but mere walking skeletons, covered with filth and vermin … Many of our men exclaimed with earnestness, 'Can this be hell?' I wonder if they knew at home of our real condition here,"* he wrote. *"If the nation itself knew of it, it seems as if we would be liberated, even if an army had to be raised for this work alone."* Kellogg described Wirz, the camp commander, as *"… a wretch of the first or worst degree; insolent, overbearing, heartless and of course a coward, for no man but a coward would come into camp and draw a revolver upon helpless men as he had done."*

Kellogg's companion, Sgt. Oliver W. Gates, also a prisoner, wrote, *"And if any sight would make a man's heart sink, the middle of this pen would. Twelve thousand men turned into this place just like so many cattle not a tree or shelter of any kind to protect from the sun or rain or cold … it was the hardest trial of my life."* Food consisted of *"… a pint and a half of coarse cornmeal, two ounces of musty bacon and a pinch of salt."* Another prisoner recalled, *"With sunken eyes, blackened countenances from pitch pine smoke, rags, and disease, the men look sickening. The air reeks with nastiness."* Still another recalled, *"Since the day I was born, I never saw such misery."*

About recruitment of soldiers...

Over the four years of war, the South's number of total men eligible for the draft numbered about one million, compared to the North's 3.5 million. By the end of the war, seventy-five percent of the South's eligible males had fought in the war, compared to only about fifty percent in the North. By 1864, the need for soldiers in the Confederate armies prompted President Davis to recommend that newspaper editors could no longer be eligible for immunity from service, which, on top of the increased cost of producing newspapers, further impacted communication about the war to the reading Southern public.

In the fall of 1864, Salem County, Indiana, was behind in its quota of 244 draftees, following the call in July for recruits. By January 1865, the quota had still not been met, so the Washington County Board offered $325 to each volunteer to make up the deficit. Bonds were issued to pay the recruits and money was raised by subscription. The public saw that the Rebellion was tottering and a last effort was needed. Twenty-two men went to Company A of the 144th Regiment; seven to Company B; twenty-six to Company F and about a dozen to other companies.

About the fall of Atlanta...

Shortly after Gen. William T. Sherman's armies advanced into Georgia, a special dispatch was delivered to the *New-York Times* on May 19, 1864: *"The intelligence received here tonight from Gen. SHERMAN is not only very late, but very gratifying. His army had reached the important town of Kingston, Georgia, on the Etowah River, in pursuit of JOHNSTON, which place it thirty-five miles below Resaca, and less than sixty miles from Atlanta, evidently the point now aimed for by both armies. Rome had also been occupied by a portion of SHERMAN's army. This news has caused much jubilation here tonight."*

As Confederate Gen. Joseph E. Johnston continued to retreat toward Atlanta because of the relentless pressure from Sherman's army, Southern newspapers described Johnston's retreats as *"saving his men."* Those who complained of the hardships being suffered by Georgia's defenders were met with disdain as editors described them as *"non-believers in the Southern cause."* But the Georgia press had difficulty portraying the steady losses as successes when Sherman continued to advance. The Union Army's crossing of the Chattahoochee River clearly placed Atlanta in peril.

The *Atlanta Intelligencer* printed June 5, 1864: *"Our army, that now stands like a living wall of destruction between this city and the enemy, will do as they have always done, fight with the herculean blows of giants, and a fearful tale their prowess tells on the foe; but it may occur that Gen. Johnston may find it a wise proceeding to retire even into the very walls of the city... In his hands are placed the trust, we confidently believe, better and more carefully deposited than it could be in the hands of any other man amongst us, and whatever he will do we shall look on and defend as right. But the spirit of the people must be aroused. Let there be no flagging, and if the call for defense comes home to us, let us be ready for the fray. 'To do or die,' in obedience to the mandates of our General, who does all for the best, must be our battle-cry."*

With the fall of Atlanta, Sherman was met with indignant outcry from its surviving citizens when he demanded their exodus from the city. Part of his lengthy reply to the Mayor of Atlanta for its dissemination to his constituency, stated, *"You might as well appeal against the thunder-storm as against these terrible hardships of war. They are inevitable, and the only way the people of Atlanta can hope once more to live in peace and quiet at home, is to stop the war, which can only be done by admitting that it began in error and is perpetuated in pride... Now that war comes home to you; you feel very different. You deprecate its horrors, but did not feel them when you sent car-loads of soldiers and ammunition, and molded shells and shot, to carry war into Kentucky and Tennessee, to desolate the homes of hundreds and thousands of good people who only asked to live in peace in their old homes, and under the Government of their inheritance."* Sherman's order stood and Atlanta would remain under Union control until the Confederacy surrendered the following summer.

The editors of two Richmond newspapers, the *Daily Richmond Examiner* and the *Richmond Daily Whig*, became active voices of opposition to Confederate President Jefferson Davis as he openly quarreled with Gen. Johnston over the continued retreats of the Southern Army against the unrelenting advance of Sherman's troops. When Davis replaced Johnston in the Battle for Atlanta with Gen. John Bell Hood as commander of the Army of the Tennessee, both newspapers described Johnston as *"...a proven battle-tested commander"* and Hood as *"...a commander woefully out of his depth."* When Atlanta fell, they blamed Davis for the loss. Even the troops protested Hood's replacement of Johnston because Hood was known to be aggressive and reckless with the lives of his men. During the battles, his attacks were consistently defeated, losing thousands of men.

A few days after the fall of Atlanta, the *Richmond Whig* attempted to restore public confidence by writing, *"Whenever a manifestly injudicious appointment is made, the exclamation is made, 'Do not destroy confidence in the new commander and in the Government by objections which come too late to do any good.' Whenever the legitimate consequences of an injudicious appointment ensue in the shape of a disaster, such as the fall of Atlanta, the cry is raised, 'Beware how you make bad worse.' At a time like this, when the sky is dark, the plain duty of every patriot is to put on a smiling face, cheer up the people and sustain the government."* But the fall of Atlanta, coupled with the loss of Vicksburg the year before, presented the unthinkable thought: the South might lose the war.

VII. THE FOURTH YEAR: 1864

The Northern press, on the other hand, began to feel a surging hope that the end of the war might be in sight. The Pittsburgh *Evening Chronicle* wrote, "*The fall of Atlanta is the severest blow—considered both in military and political aspects—which the rebels have received since Vicksburg and Gettysburg. Sherman's victory was a sign of God's 'special Providence.'*"

By the end of September, Sherman and his army had advanced through Georgia and now occupied the captured city of Atlanta. At the same time in the Eastern Theater, the Overland Campaign under Grant had successfully placed Robert E. Lee's Army of Northern Virginia under siege at Petersburg. The Northern public became infused with support for the conclusion of the war to its end which helped re-elect President Lincoln.

About Sherman's March to the Sea...

When Sherman's army left the city of Atlanta in November to make its march eastward to the sea, the inhabitants of Georgia began to watch in panic. The Richmond *Sentinel*, November 25, attempted to rally public determination against the Northern forces, by writing, "*The intelligence from Georgia yesterday was very agreeable, and the hope grows more buoyant that SHERMAN will suffer severely for his audacity. Let our troops opposed to SHERMAN adopt sleepless activity for their motto; let them harass him with attacks, harass him by day, and harass him by night. Let them destroy supplies before him and resist his march at every practicable point. All this may be done independently of the heavier operations which we shall doubtless be able to direct against him.*"

From the *Richmond Whig*, November 24, "*There seems to be nothing definite from Georgia. The prevailing opinion, based upon all the information thus far received, is that SHERMAN has passed by Macon, and that he will move toward the coast. Without hazarding an attack upon the defenses of Augusta. He will of course desolate the country through which he passes. Now if SHERMAN has really attempted so wild a mammoth raid, unless we are greatly deficient in forces in that quarter, his expedition will surely come to grief. We look hopefully to Georgia, and confidently expect great results before the close of the present campaign.*"

But the Union Army's march through Georgia was virtually unopposed as the only organized resistance was from a small Confederate cavalry that made a few attempts to halt the army's advance, but its efforts were repulsed and the army moved on. Local citizens felt a growing sense of dread as they watched the columns advance toward them. Newspapers were particular targets as the Northern invaders dismantled and destroyed all printing shops that they encountered. Editors who had proclaimed the invincibility of the South now faced the reality that they were no longer able to print their words for the public.

The *Richmond Dispatch* wrote of their lack of information on November 25. "*We are still without any official information concerning SHERMAN'S movements in Georgia, but we are not without some authentic advices on the subject. It is believed that the enemy has been to Milledgeville, though we are pretty well assured that no official information of this fact has been received at the War Office. There is one fact in the campaign which we think should give much ground for hope—the slow progress made by SHERMAN. He is now in his fifteenth day from Atlanta, and has as yet marched only about 75 miles, and has not reached one point of strategic importance. Perhaps he does not now, as when he started out on his expedition, feel himself positively master of the situation."*

As the massive Union Army moved through Georgia, frightened citizens in its path were appalled that the Confederacy and its armies could not protect them. Although homes were not specifically targeted, livestock, food and forage were confiscated or destroyed. Slaves fled from their owners to follow the army—this was their chance for freedom. Without slaves and the men who had been conscripted to fight in the army, there was no one left to manage the farms, grow food and support the women and children. The demoralized women, left in the middle of winter with no food and no assistance from the government, faced hunger on a massive scale. Desertions increased from the Army of Northern Virginia, besieged at Petersburg, as the men slipped away from the army to go to the aid of their families. The destruction inflicted by Sherman's army brought the reality of war's cruelty to Georgia's average citizens. The hatred of Sherman and a smoldering resentment of the North would persist for generations.

When Sherman reached Savannah and relayed the positive news of his successful March to the Sea, he added, *"We are not only fighting armies, but a hostile people, and must make old and young, rich and poor, feel the hard hand of war, as well as their organized armies. I know that this recent movement of mine through Georgia has had a wonderful effect in this respect. Thousands who had been deceived by their lying papers into the belief that we were being whipped all the time, realized the truth, and have no appetite for a repetition of the same experience."*

Sherman's oft-repeated quote, *"War is hell,"* was not specifically stated as such until years later. But in a speech in 1879 to the graduating class of Michigan's Military Academy, he is quoted as saying, *"There's many a boy here today who looks on war as all glory but it is all hell."* Another quote expressed this opinion more vigorously: *"It is only those who have neither fired a shot nor heard the shrieks and groans of the wounded who cry aloud for blood, more vengeance, more desolation. War is hell."*

About The Burning in the Shenandoah ...

In the summer of 1864, Confederate Gen. Jubal Early had dominated the Shenandoah Valley for some weeks and even reached the outskirts of Washington, D.C., in a daring raid in July that almost reached the Union Government. Early had successfully defeated several Union attempts to dislodge him from the Shenandoah and his successes continued to provide the Confederate armies, particularly Robert E. Lee's army besieged at Petersburg, with supplies and food. In August, Union Gen. Ulysses S. Grant ordered

VII. THE FOURTH YEAR: 1864

Gen. Philip H. Sheridan to the Shenandoah Valley with a large army of 50,000 "... *to put himself south of the enemy and follow him to the death."*

After defeating Early in a number of battles, Sheridan ordered a division of his army to actively destroy crops, livestock and barns, to be called "The Burning," in an area of the Shenandoah that had been protected by Mosby's Rangers and had provided vital support to the Confederacy. No homes were to be destroyed, but fields and farm buildings were to be burned, slaves set free and livestock driven off or destroyed. Many of the Union troops loathed the duty, but it was regarded as a necessary step that would deprive the Confederacy of its resources to continue the war.

"It was a phase of warfare we had not seen before," wrote a Pennsylvania cavalryman, *"and though we admitted its necessity, we could not but sympathize with the sufferers."* Sweeping through the Valley, nothing was left behind them and as one newspaperman wrote, *"The atmosphere, from horizon to horizon, has been black with the smoke of a hundred conflagrations, and at night a gleam brighter and more lurid than sunset has shot from every verge. The completeness of the devastation is awful."*

Charles Humphreys, part of a reserve brigade of the cavalry under the command of Gen. Wesley Merritt during the mission, wrote, *"Some idea of the general destruction may be formed when I relate that in one day two regiments of our brigade burned more than one hundred and fifty barns, a thousand stacks of hay, and six flour mills, besides having driven off fifty horses and three hundred head of cattle. This was the most unpleasant task we were ever compelled to undertake. It was heart-piercing to hear the shrieks of women and children, and to see even men crying and beating their breasts, supplicating for mercy on bended knees, begging that at least one cow—and only support—might be left. But no mercy was allowed."*

The *Richmond Whig* urged retaliation, with its recommendation: *"They chose to substitute the torch for the sword. We may so use their own weapon as to make them repent."* The *Richmond Whig* proposed burning a Northern city in retaliation. *"It is a game at which we can beat them. New York is worth twenty Richmonds."*

About Lincoln's Re-election ...

The Peace Democrats or "Copperheads" had nominated former Gen. George B. McClellan as their candidate for President to run against Abraham Lincoln. The party, racist in its platform, believed that the re-election of Lincoln would bring Blacks into total superiority over the white man. A democratic pamphlet proclaimed the President as *"Abraham Africanus the First"* and declared that the Republican Party's commandment was *"Thou shalt have no other God but the negro."* The Democratic-leaning *Pittsburg Post* applauded the Copperheads' indictment of Lincoln's administration and his policies and predicted that McClellan, affectionately known as "Little Mac" by the men when he led the Army of the Potomac, would win overwhelming support among Union soldiers and their officers.

As political discussions gathered steam in the spring of 1864 for the November elections, the *New York Times* wrote on May 20, 1864: "*These Copperheads may as well open their eyes to the fact that the success of the war is the success of the Administration. Every advance made in crushing the rebellion is an advance in President LINCOLN's popularity, and in the public determination that, so long as the war continues, its guidance shall not be transferred to new and untried hands. Gen. Grant himself desires no other sphere of action than that which he is now engaged in. His highest earthly ambition is to force the rebellion to its last ditch, and there either exterminate it, or obtain its unconditional surrender.*"

By August 1864, prospects for the re-election of Lincoln looked bleak. Even Northern Republicans concluded that "*Lincoln cannot be re-elected, unless great victories can be attained soon, which is next to impossible on account of the worn-out state of the Armies of the Potomac.*" Lincoln himself said, "*I am going to be beaten... and unless some great change takes place, badly beaten.*" With the shocking number of casualties in the Eastern Theater during the Overland Campaign and no Union victories other than Sherman's advances in Georgia, the country was demanding an end to the war, even if it meant a truce with the South, granting the Confederacy its independence.

With the growing probability that he would need to install a new President in March 1865, Lincoln wrote a memorandum, dated August 23, 1864, that it would be his duty to cooperate with the President-elect to save the Union between the election and inauguration day, because "*... he will have secured his election on such ground that he cannot possibly save it afterwards.*" Without revealing its contents, he passed the closed memorandum to the members of his Cabinet and instructed them to sign the outside of it, saying that it was to be opened after the election.

As concern among Lincoln's advisors increased that he would not survive the 1864 election, they suggested that the election be postponed or not held at all. But Lincoln's response was, "*We cannot have free government without elections; and if the rebellion could force us to forego, or postpone a national election, it might fairly claim to have already conquered and ruined us.*" The South was joyful about the despair in the North. "*We will get our independence by Christmas; won't we be a happy and free people.*"

But Gen. Sherman's telegram to Washington on September 3, 1864, changed all that. The message, which stated simply, "*Atlanta is ours and fairly won,*" was picked up and reported in blazing headlines throughout the North which responded with jubilation. From the *New York Times*, September 7, 1864: "*The political skies begin to brighten. The clouds that lowered over the Union cause a month ago are breaking away. The most careless observers cannot fail to notice a marked change in the tone of public sentiment within that time. It was not to be denied, and we did not attempt to conceal, that a profound despondency had taken possession of the public mind.*" The reasons cited included the disastrous casualties of the Overland Campaign; the impending

VII. THE FOURTH YEAR: 1864

draft which bring *"gloom and dread to the public mind;"* the lack of military successes; and the assaults and denunciations of the current Republican administration by the opposing Democratic party. The editor continued, *"Now all this is changed. The public temper is buoyant and hopeful."* The triumph of Sherman by capturing Atlanta and defeating the South's Army of Tennessee, the second largest army of the Confederacy, *"… have revived the national courage and aroused the hope of a speedy close of this great rebellion."*

After the arrival of Sherman's telegram on September 3, Lincoln responded with a grateful thanks. *"The national thanks are rendered by the President to Major-General W. T. Sherman and the gallant officers and soldiers of his command before Atlanta, for the distinguished ability and perseverance displayed in the campaign in Georgia, which, under Divine favor, has resulted in the capture of Atlanta. The marches, battles, sieges, and other military operations, that have signalized the campaign, must render it famous in the annals of war, and have entitled those who have participated therein to the applause and thanks of the nation."*

The successful taking of Atlanta was followed in October by a dramatic Union triumph in the Shenandoah Valley by Gen. Philip H. Sheridan. After engaging in a number of battles with Confederate Gen. Jubal Early between August and October, Sheridan successfully drove the Confederates from the Shenandoah on October 19, eliminating the source of frequent threats and anxious moments for the residents of Washington, D.C.

The victorious battle at Winchester became famous in a popular poem entitled, *"Sheridan's Ride,"* that was widely read at gatherings and election rallies, where Republicans used the poem to full advantage. Rienzi, the powerful horse that had delivered Sheridan to the battlefield in the nick of time, became a national hero. The *New York Tribune* called it *"a magnificent lyric"* and ran all seven stanzas on page one of Election Day, perhaps increasing Lincoln's votes to carry the state by a small margin. Sheridan acknowledged Rienzi's importance, saying about the poem, *"The thing they like best about it is the horse,"* and later renamed Rienzi, "Winchester."

Anticipating a tight election, Lincoln facilitated votes from the military by instituting a liberal leave policy, the first in U.S. history, allowing soldiers to return home to vote in local precincts. Soldiers' Mail-in ballots from the field were also encouraged. Lincoln's slogan for the campaign was *"Don't Change Horses in the Middle of a Stream."* Seventy percent of the army's soldiers voted for Lincoln.

On November 8, Election Day, Lincoln won in a landslide, defeating McClellan by 400,000 popular votes, fifty-five percent, and winning the electoral votes (212 to 24) from twenty-two of the twenty-five states who voted in the North. Response from the South was grim: *"The end has come… We are going to be wiped off the face of the earth."*

VIII. THE FINAL BATTLES AND SURRENDER, 1865

As the year 1865 opened, General-in-Chief Ulysses S. Grant continued the encirclement and Siege of Petersburg and Richmond, Virginia, which contained Gen. Robert E. Lee and the Army of Northern Virginia. Gen. William T. Sherman finalized arrangements for holding Savannah, Georgia, under Union control as he planned his march through the Carolinas, to wreak the same havoc on the secessionists of North and South Carolina as he had done in Georgia.

Union Gen. George H. Thomas held Tennessee and Kentucky after defeating the Confederate Army of Tennessee under Gen. John Bell Hood in December. Gen. Joseph E. Johnston, who had fought against Union Gen. Sherman during the Atlanta Campaign, had been placed in Columbia, South Carolina, in virtual retirement by the frustrated Confederate President Jefferson Davis. Blockade runners at Mobile, Alabama, that had been vital to supporting the Confederate troops under Gen Lee, under siege in Virginia were now halted, although the city of Mobile still remained in Confederate hands. Union forces renewed their attacks on the last remaining Confederate seaport at Wilmington, North Carolina, where blockade runners remained active. But the vise around Southern resistance continued to tighten.

With the beginning of 1865, President Lincoln had a growing belief that the Confederacy would soon be defeated and the Emancipation Proclamation of 1863 that had freed slaves in rebelling states as a war order would no longer be valid when the war ended. An amendment to the Constitution to abolish slavery in all the United States and its territories had been passed by the Republican controlled Senate in April 1864, but Peace Democrats had prevented its passage in the House of Representatives. With an increased number of Republicans sitting in Congress after the 1864 elections, Lincoln pressed for a second vote on the Amendment in January 1865.

The 13th Amendment to the Constitution, which banned slavery in all U.S. states and territories, was finally passed by the U.S. House of Congress on January 31, 1865, with a vote of 119 to 56. The chamber erupted with cheers and a 100-gun salute to broadcast the news to the city. Illinois was the first state to ratify the document on February 1, but the required approval by three-fourths of the states would not occur until after the surrender of the Confederacy. The Amendment became law of the land on December 6, 1865.

With a resounding victory in the 1864 elections, Lincoln addressed the nation with an inspiring speech in his 2nd inaugural address on March 4, 1865. He began by remembering that his first address four years earlier was anxiously directed to an impending Civil War that everyone dreaded and sought to avert. But war had come and inflicted terrible havoc on the country and his words now focused on healing the nation's wounds.

"Fondly, do we hope, fervently do we pray, that this mighty scourge of war may speedily pass away… With malice toward none; with charity for all; with firmness in the right, as God gives us to see the right, let us strive on to finish the work we are in; to bind up the nation's wounds; to care for him who shall have borne the battle, and for his widow, and his orphan—to do all which may achieve and cherish a just and lasting peace, among ourselves, and with all nations."

Lincoln would be assassinated forty days later.

BATTLES IN THE WESTERN THEATER

Defeat of Fort Fisher, Wilmington, North Carolina
January 13-15, 1865

The First Battle of Fort Fisher at Wilmington, North Carolina, on December 23-27, 1864, had been a disastrous failure under Union Gen. Benjamin Butler, who was subsequently relieved of command of the Army of the James. Fort Fisher guarded Wilmington and was now the last Confederate seaport for blockade runners who were providing critical support, including guns, ammunition and other supplies, to the Confederacy. Vital resources were regularly delivered to Gen. Robert E. Lee's Army of Northern Virginia under siege at Petersburg via the Wilmington and Weldon Railroad.

Union General-in-Chief Ulysses S. Grant selected Gen. Alfred Terry to lead a provisional Corps of 9,600 troops from the Department of Virginia and North Carolina to join Rear Admiral David D. Porter, commanding the Navy's North Atlantic Blockading Squadron, for a second joint assault on Fort Fisher in January 1865. Porter's naval forces included fifty-eight ships, manned with 2,300 sailors and Marines. A heavy storm delayed the second joint assault on Fort Fisher until January 13.

VIII. THE FINAL BATTLES AND SURRENDER, 1865

Confederate Gen. Braxton Bragg, who had been removed from commanding the Army of Tennessee after his defeat at Chattanooga, now headed the Confederacy's Department of North Carolina and Virginia and was in charge of Fort Fisher. Because the first Union assault on the fort had failed, Bragg believed it was impregnable and focused on building defenses around the city of Wilmington.

Confederate Gen. Robert Hoke had been transferred to Bragg from the Army of Northern Virginia with 6,000 men. Bragg had positioned them at Fort Anderson, located about halfway between Fort Fisher and Wilmington. Defenders at the fort numbered about 2,000.

On the morning of January 13, Porter ordered the naval fleet of fifty-eight ships to open fire on the ocean-facing guns of Fort Fisher. Unlike the assault in December, this attack was calculated and methodical. Union iron-clads, placed at short range, fired the first rounds at the fort's twenty-two heavy ocean-facing guns so that the larger long-range ships could accurately target the locations of the Confederate artillery. The larger ships, arranged in arcs of concentric circles, then opened fire, maintaining a steady barrage of targeted shells which continued unabated throughout the days and nights of January 13 and 14 until all forty-seven guns of the fort, save one, was silenced by noon on January 15.

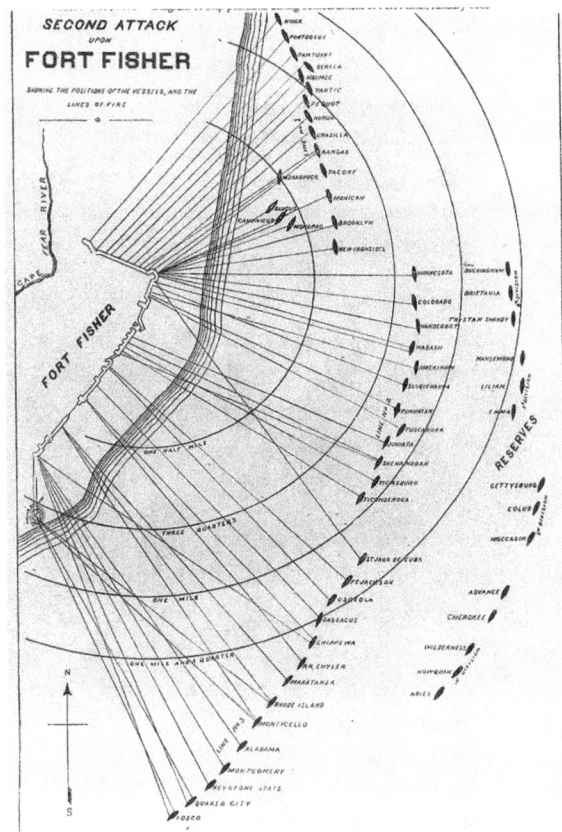

Fig. 66: Configuration of the 58 U.S. Navy ships at the assault of Fort Fisher Jan. 13-15, 1864.

Source: *This map is the work of a sailor or employee of the U.S. Navy made as part of that person's official duties. As a work of the federal government, it is in the public domain. Drawn for the 'SOLDIER IN OUR CIVIL WAR" by WALTER A. LANE, C.E.*

Gen. Terry's Union troops of 3,000 men landed unopposed on the peninsula between Fort Anderson and Fort Fisher on January 13. As Union troops pushed to take the fort's walls from behind, Union naval forces of 1,600 sailors and 400 Marines attacked the sea wall. A grueling battle with desperate hand-to-hand fighting continued throughout the day and into the night. Many of the commanders on both sides were wounded or killed.

Confederate calls to Wilmington for reinforcements continued to be largely ignored by Bragg as he did not want to diminish his defenses of the city. At 10 p.m. that night, a

Union flanking maneuver gained control of the battle and the Confederates surrendered. Union killed and wounded numbered about 1,300; Confederates, over 1,000, with a loss of more than 2,000 prisoners. Fort Fisher was now in Union hands. A major loss for the Confederacy, the military supplies from blockade runners for Robert E. Lee's army under siege at Petersburg were now cut off as there were no other seaports for the South to use. The city of Wilmington remained in Confederate control for another month until its capture in February.

During the assault of Fort Fisher, the disgraced Union Gen. Benjamin Butler, who had lost his command the previous December after the failed first assault of Fort Fisher, used his considerable political influence to insist on a Congressional hearing to defend his performance in the battle. Traveling to Washington in mid-January, he appeared before the Joint Congressional Committee on the Conduct of the War for his actions in the first assault of Fort Fisher.

As his subordinates produced charts, maps and reports to demonstrate that the fort could not be taken by assault, the sound of a newsboy in the hall crying "Extra" could be heard. As written in Gen. Sherman's *Memoirs*, "… the Chairman of the committee, Senator B. F. Wade of Ohio, told me that they called the newsboy in to inquire the news, and he answered 'Fort Fisher done took.' At this point, … all laughed, and none more heartily than Gen. Butler himself."

Navy Captures Wilmington, North Carolina
February 11-22, 1865

With the defeat of Confederate forces at Fort Fisher in January, Wilmington, twenty miles upriver, was now sealed to blockade runners for the Confederacy. Gen. Ulysses S. Grant planned to use the city as a Union base to provide supplies for the Army of the Tennessee under Gen. William T. Sherman as it moved north through the Carolinas, but Confederate Gen. Braxton Bragg still held the city.

Union forces under the command of Gen. John Schofield, Army of the Ohio, arrived at Fort Fisher in early February to take command of the Union forces under Gen. Alfred Terry and Rear Admiral David D. Porter. An Army-Navy joint effort to eliminate the Confederacy at Wilmington began February 11 with an advance on Confederate infantry under the command of Gen. Robert Hoke at Fort Anderson on Cape Fear River, about halfway between Fort Fisher and Wilmington.

While Union navy gunboats pounded the Confederates at Fort Anderson on February 16-17, a wide flanking march by Union infantry threatened to capture the fort from behind, forcing the Confederates to withdraw to Wilmington with Union forces in close pursuit. Alarmed by the advance of the Union Army on Wilmington, Confederate Gen. Braxton Bragg ordered the city to be evacuated, burning large stores of tobacco and cotton as they left. Union troops took control of Wilmington on February 22 and

THE CAROLINAS CAMPAIGN

With Savannah, Georgia, safely in Union control, Gen. William T. Sherman planned the next phase of his campaign which would carry his army north through the Carolinas in a manner similar to his March to the Sea through Georgia. Leaving the city of Savannah under a military governor and a garrison of Union soldiers to guard it, schools, churches, stores and markets were opened and a large warehouse of rice, procured from the North, was distributed gratuitously among the citizens until normal trade and business could be revived.

Gen. Ulysses S. Grant had anticipated moving Sherman's army by boat from Savannah to the James River on the Virginia Peninsula and then merging it with the Army of the Potomac which remained at Petersburg, holding siege against Confederate Gen. Robert E. Lee and the Army of Northern Virginia. But Sherman had other ideas. He proposed marching through North and South Carolina, leaving a scorched earth behind him, similar to the march his troops had just completed in Georgia, destroying railroads and lines of communication, and feeding his army from the land. Sherman's march would break the will of the people to continue the war and limit food and support that were being supplied to Gen. Lee's army in Petersburg. When Grant gave his approval for the march, preparations began in earnest for the next phase.

> ### "SOUTH CAROLINA WILL PAY"
>
> As preparations began for the march north through the Carolinas, Gen. Sherman writes, "... the soldiers and people of the South entertained an undue fear of our Western men, and, like children, they had invented such ghostlike stories of our prowess in Georgia, that they were scared by their own inventions. Still, this was a power, and I intended to utilize it. Somehow, our men had got the idea that South Carolina was the cause of all our troubles; her people were the first to fire on Fort Sumter, had been in a great hurry to precipitate the country into civil war; and therefore, on them should fall the scourge of war in its worst form." The army burned almost everything in its path as it moved north.
>
> *Memoirs, W. T. Sherman, 1875*

Heavy winter rains commenced in early January raising the Savannah River to such levels that the rice fields were flooded and the Union's pontoon bridge was swept away, nearly drowning some of the troops. Sherman maintained an activity level that gave the impression the army was headed to Charleston, South Carolina, northeast of Savannah on the Atlantic coast. Sherman encouraged this delusion, knowing that Confederate forces would be concentrating there instead of in his front. But the actual target was Columbia, South Carolina's capital, about one hundred sixty miles northwest and one hundred miles inland. When rains diminished in late January, the date for departure was set for February 1, 1865.

Union Army Departs Savannah, Georgia
February 1, 1865

Sherman's Army of about 60,000 moved out in two wings very similar to that of the march through Georgia, with the Army of the Tennessee under Gen. Oliver O. Howard on the right wing; and the Army of Georgia under Gen. Henry Slocum on the left. As in Georgia, the cavalry, commanded by Gen. Hugh Judson ("Kill-Cavalry") Kilpatrick, reported directly to Sherman and served both wings. The two columns contained sixty-eight guns, with about two thousand five hundred wagons and six hundred ambulances per column. Each wagon train carried sufficient ammunition for a great battle, animal forage for a week and provisions for twenty days. Fresh meat would depend on beef on the hoof that accompanied the army, supplemented with foraging operations among the many wealthy plantations that populated the region.

The right column moved north, appearing to threaten Charleston, the heart of the secessionist movement, where the first shots had been fired on Fort Sumter in 1861. Passing through the enormous swamps of the Salkehatchie River, Howard's wing bypassed Beaufort, the town closest to Hilton Head and the Sea Islands of South Carolina. The wealthiest secessionists lived there in large mansions, supported by about thirteen thousand slaves, who labored in the huge rice fields, completely isolated from the mainland.

As soldiers moved across the Salkehatchie Swamp, marching through water, quicksand and soggy ground, they had to create corduroyed roads strong enough to support the vast army. Trees were cut down, split and laid down on the wet and soggy surfaces. Whole forests disappeared as the roads emerged to carry wagons, artillery, horses, beef and men through the swamp. Portable pontoons, made of floatable cotton canvas, were assembled to cross the rivers. The Battle of River's Bridge occurred on February 3 as Confederates attempted to block the army's crossing of the Salkehatchie River about eighty miles north of Savannah, but the Confederates caused only a short delay and they then withdrew to a location about thirty miles northeast to Branchville.

The Union Army met little resistance from the scattered Confederate forces on its march north and captured an important railroad junction at Bamberg (near Branchville), South Carolina, on February 7, almost unopposed. As Bamberg's railroad connected Charleston with Augusta, two days were spent twisting the rails and burning railroad ties for fifty miles. Confederate forces had anticipated that Sherman's army would advance on Charleston, but Sherman avoided it, as Charleston had already suffered

VIII. THE FINAL BATTLES AND SURRENDER, 1865

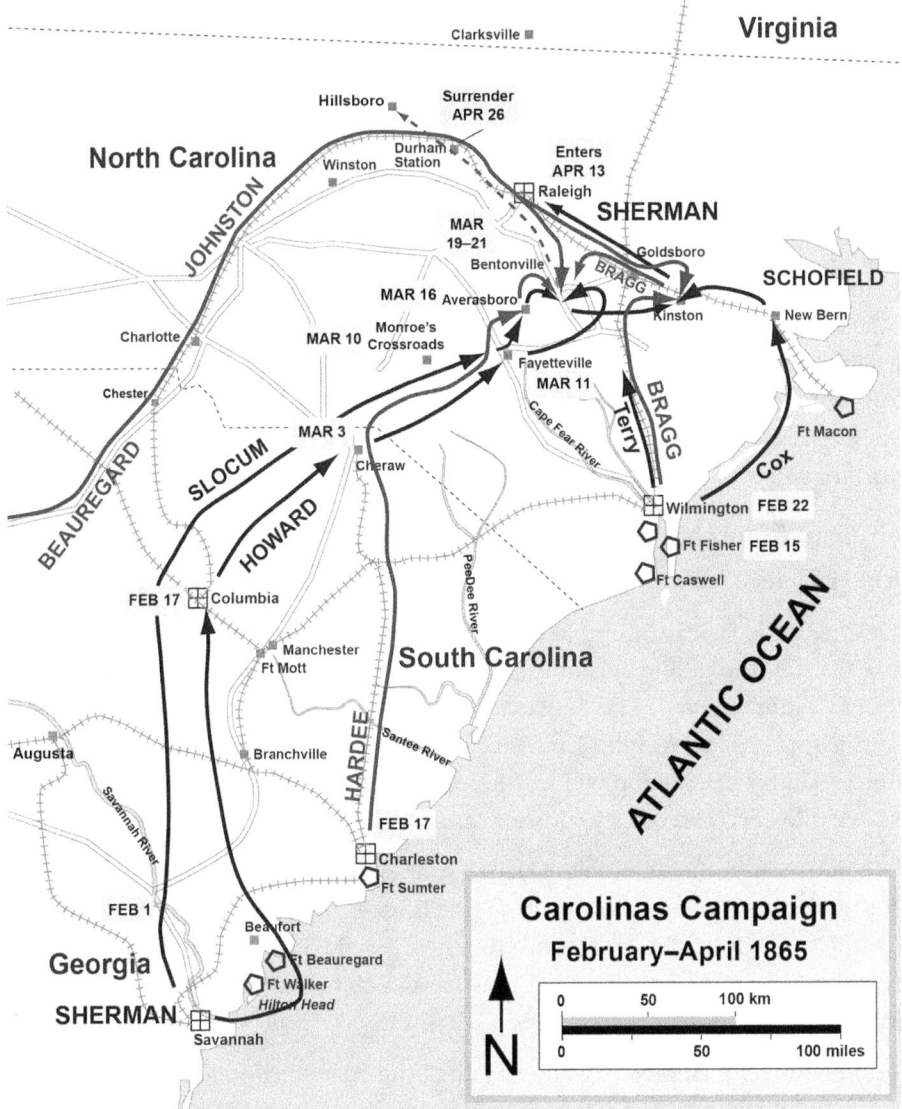

Fig. 67: The Union Army of 60,000 under Gen. William T. Sherman marched north from Savannah for a campaign that would take it through North and South Carolina. The march would replicate the March to the Sea in Georgia, acquiring food and forage for the army along the way, while destroying Confederate war support, leaving a path of destruction.

Source: *Creative Commons Attribution 3.0 License Map by Hal Jespersen, www.cwmaps.com.*

ruinous damage from a great fire in 1861 and bombardment by the Union Navy that began in 1863 and continued for more than a year. Instead, Sherman's destination was the state's capital at Columbia. Confederate Gen. William Hardee, who had fought against Sherman's army at Savannah, before withdrawing to South Carolina, had not anticipated Sherman's move and Hardee had concentrated his troops at Charleston.

The Northerners were unopposed as they headed north to Columbia, leaving a large portion of southern South Carolina in ruins.

Sherman's foragers, known as "Sherman's Bummers," extended the reach of the army forty miles wide as they sacked every farm, home and building within reach for food and supplies. Reports from diaries and letters revealed notorious looting and vandalism by the "bummers." It was against Sherman's orders to take or destroy anything that was not supporting the opposing army. But men from Kilpatrick's cavalry were particularly notorious for leaving total destruction in their wake. They would leave their posts on unsanctioned foraging missions, to take money, watches and other valuables from citizens, including their clothes and boots. One Union soldier from Indiana wrote, *"The march through South Carolina left a track of desolation more than forty miles wide. That state's special guilt in taking the initiative in secession was assumed by officers and men as justification of its devastation. The responsibility does not rest upon us."*

Burning of Columbia, South Carolina
February 17-18, 1865

On the outskirts of Columbia on February 16, Sherman's General Order No. 26 instructed that the public buildings, railroad property, manufacturing and machine shops of Columbia were to be destroyed, but libraries, asylums and private dwellings were to be spared. Confederate Gen. Wade Hampton and his cavalry occupied Columbia, but as the Union Army approached the small cavalry was forced to retreat and set fire to a large pile of cotton bales to prevent their capture.

When Union troops entered the city, they attempted to extinguish the flames, but a high wind pushed the fire into adjoining buildings and the heart of the city was burned out by the next day, including several churches, the old State House and a convent. The State Arsenal, several foundries, railroads and a factory of Confederate money were destroyed by Union troops.

Leaving the city smoldering and in ruins, the army moved north on February 20 towards its next destination, Cheraw, South Carolina. The army was followed by freed Union prisoners and throngs of liberated slaves that grew in number as the march continued. Confederate Gen. P.G.T. Beauregard was now in charge of all Confederate forces in the Carolinas, which included what was left of the old Army of the Tennessee, that had been dissolved after its defeats in Tennessee under Gen. John Bell Hood. Beauregard anticipated the Union Army was headed for Charlotte, North Carolina, due north of Columbia, but Sherman's actual destination was Fayetteville, North Carolina, to the northeast.

With the burning of Columbia, Gen. Beauregard ordered the evacuation of Charleston on February 15 and Confederate troops abandoned Fort Sumter February 17. The mayor surrendered the city the next day to the Union's Southern District of the Department of the South, headquartered on Folly Island, South Carolina. The Union Army formally took control of the fort and the United States Arsenal on February 22 and confiscated the grounds and buildings of the Citadel Military Academy and used them to garrison Union troops for more than seventeen years.

Union Army Reaches Carolina-Virginia Border
March 3, 1865

Leaving a burned-out Columbia, Sherman's Army continued its march northeast, confusing Confederate forces as to its destination, which was actually Fayetteville, North Carolina, more than one hundred seventy miles away, where Sherman would meet Generals Schofield and Terry with troops from Wilmington, North Carolina, after the city had been captured in February. The march involved crossing huge rivers, swollen by rains, and corduroying nearly every foot of road with fence rails and split saplings that would support the large army and all its supporting animals and artillery, plus thousands of former slave refugees.

The Catawba River, about forty miles from Columbia, was so swollen by rains that the pontoon bridge was swept away before all of the army could get across, causing a delay of several days before the crossing could be completed. The army reached Cheraw, South Carolina, on the banks of the Pedee River, March 3, only a few miles from the North Carolina border and halfway between Columbia and Fayetteville. Southerners from the old aristocratic families of Charleston had used Cheraw from the beginning of the war as a storehouse for stockpiling their valuables.

> **MARCHING THROUGH THE SOUTH CAROLINA SWAMPS**
>
> *"When I heard that Sherman's Army was marching through the Salkehatchie Swamps, making its own roads at the rate of a dozen miles a day, and bringing its artillery and wagons with it, I made up my mind that there had been no such army in existence since the days of Julius Caesar."*
>
> from Confederate Gen. Joseph E. Johnston

While headquartered there, Sherman was treated to *"... some of the finest madeira I ever tasted."* The Union Army remained there for three days, leaving most of the city's buildings intact, but carried out the destruction of the city's arsenal, plus twenty-five guns, muskets and 3,600 barrels of gunpowder.

The march of Sherman's Army through the Carolinas required engineering skills that are unmatched even today, given the level of technology available at that time. Achieving an average pace of ten miles a day as it pushed through swamps and mud roads, so saturated with water that nearly every mile had to be corduroyed, the Union troops covered four hundred twenty-five miles in fifty days, as they made roads, built bridges and causeways, while marching, burning and destroying property as they went.

Railroads, factories, arsenals, ammunition, even whole cities were burned to the ground. Plantation homes were left as smoldering ruins. For the Union soldier, South Carolina was at the head of the line for vengeance, with its firing on Fort Sumter, which had initiated the Civil War. One private wrote, *"Nearly every man in Sherman's army say they are ready for destroying everything in South Carolina."* The class of wealthy plantation owners, who wanted to preserve their way of life on the backs of slaves by secession were the cause of the war. Confiscated and destroyed winter stores of food and supplies left families of women and children desolate. Desertions among the Confederate armies increased as soldiers left to go home to protect their families.

NEW COMMANDER FOR CONFEDERATE ARMY

Sherman's army continued to move north into North Carolina relatively unimpeded. Gen. P.G.T. Beauregard, ostensibly the commander of all Confederate forces in the Carolinas, but suffering from poor health, had been ineffective in marshalling defenses against the Union troops. Confederate President Jefferson Davis had removed Gen. Joseph E. Johnston from active duty during the Atlanta Campaign, placing him in semi-retirement in South Carolina. But in the face of the Union Army marching through the Carolinas and Gen. Robert E. Lee and the Army of Northern Virginia in siege at Petersburg, Davis restored Johnston to command in late February 1865.

Johnston's army consisted of the drastically reduced Army of Tennessee, decimated at the Battles of Franklin and Nashville, Tennessee, and now numbered less than 7,000 men. Adding to that army were about 12,000 men under Gen. William Hardee, who had escaped Sherman's advance at Savannah, and Gen. Braxton Bragg's forces of the Department of North Carolina, which had narrowly escaped Union forces as they evacuated Wilmington when Fort Anderson was captured in February. The Confederate Cavalry under Gen. Wade Hampton brought Johnston's combined Army of the South to about 22,000. In contrast, Sherman's army numbered about 60,000 men.

Confederate cavalry under Generals Hampton and Joseph Wheeler surprised Sherman's cavalry under Gen. Hugh Judson Kilpatrick in the Battle of Monroe's Crossroads, March 10, 1865, and nearly captured him. The Southerners attacked a sleeping Union camp at dawn while Kilpatrick was entertaining a lady in a nearby log cabin. The Union general barely escaped in his night-shirt and the battle was soon dubbed "Kilpatrick's Shirttail Skedaddle." Adding insult to his dignity, Kilpatrick lost his four prime personal horses. Regrouping his troops, Kilpatrick soon counter-attacked and with Union reinforcements on the way, the Southerners withdrew. But the battle had enabled the Southerners to cross Cape Fear River unmolested, burning the bridges behind them.

Sherman reached Fayetteville, North Carolina, on the banks of Cape Fear River, March 11, and made his headquarters in the old United States Arsenal which he described as being in fine order. While there, a steamboat arrived from Wilmington with mail and anxious communications from the Union high command at Washington. Sherman wrote to Grant, *"I hope you have not been uneasy about us, and the fruits of this march will be appreciated... The army is in splendid health, condition and spirits, though we have had foul weather, and roads that would have stopped travel to almost any other body of men I ever heard of... We cannot afford to leave detachments, and I shall therefore destroy this valuable arsenal, so the enemy shall not have its use; and the United States should never again confide such valuable property to a people who have betrayed a trust."*

> **GRANT'S EVALUATION OF SHERMAN'S MARCH IN THE SOUTH**
>
> *The march of Sherman's Army from Atlanta to the sea and north to Goldsboro ... had an important bearing ... on closing the war. All the States east of the Mississippi River up to the State of Georgia, had felt the hardships of the war. Georgia, and South Carolina, and almost all of North Carolina, up to this time, had been exempt from invasion by the Northern armies, except upon their immediate sea coasts. Their newspapers had given such an account of Confederate success, that the people who remained at home had been convinced that the Yankees had been whipped from first to last ... .Even during this march, the newspapers in his front were proclaiming daily that his army was nothing better than a mob of men ... hastening to get under the cover of our navy for protection against the Southern people. As the army was seen marching triumphantly, however ... they saw the true state of affairs ... and would have been glad to submit without compromise.*
>
> *Personal Memoirs, Ulysses S. Grant,, 1885*

Sherman also divested himself of 20-30,000 former slave refugees *"... who have clung to our skirts, impeded our movements, and consumed our food."* They were conveyed to Wilmington by steamboats, use of captured horses or marched on foot with an escort. Sherman needed an army *"... in compact form"* to meet Gen. Johnston's army.

Sherman's army left Fayetteville for Goldsboro on March 13-14 (See Fig. 67), leaving a rear-guard to destroy the arsenal. As the left wing under Gen. Slocum proceeded towards Goldsboro, it encountered heavy resistance from an entrenched Confederate Gen. Hardee at the Battle of Averasboro on March 16 which held up the advancing Union wing for two days. As additional Union troops reinforced Slocum, Hardee retreated during the night.

Gen. Johnston, with his Army of the South of about 22,000, surprised Slocum's left column at the Battle of Bentonville on March 19-21 hoping to destroy one wing of Sherman's army before the other could arrive to support it. Johnston's entrenched men routed the lead division, but as reinforcements arrived the next day from the Union's right wing, Johnston's sole line of retreat was nearly cut off. The Confederates withdrew in the night and retreated to Smithfield, about twenty miles due north, which was near the North Carolina Railroad and halfway between Raleigh and Goldsboro. But Sherman did not pursue the Southern army to Smithfield as he was focused on uniting new Union forces now arriving at Goldsboro from Wilmington, North Carolina, to bolster the Union offensive.

Carolinas Campaign Ends March 23, 1865

Reaching Goldsboro on March 23, Sherman and his army were joined by Generals John Schofield and Alfred Terry after the Battles of Fort Fisher and of Wilmington, North Carolina, the previous month. With completion of the long march from Savannah, Georgia, to Goldsboro, North Carolina, Sherman now needed to resupply his expanded army with provisions, equipment, food and clothing, and communicate with his commander, General-in-Chief Ulysses S. Grant, about how to defeat the two remaining principal Confederate armies and ending the war.

Leaving Gen. Schofield in command, Sherman left Goldsboro on March 25 for City Point, Virginia, where he met with Gen. Grant and President Lincoln two days later. Discussions with the President focused on what would be done with the rebel armies when they were defeated. Sherman left the meeting with a deep impression of Lincoln's kindly nature, his desire to end the war without more bloodshed and to return all the men back to their homes, farms, work and shops, to follow their civilian pursuits.

Returning to Goldsboro on March 30, Sherman focused on replenishing his supplies and reorganizing the now expanded Union Army, to be ready to march on April 10, the day agreed upon with Gen. Grant. His orders to his staff on April 5 revealed that the next grand objective would be placement of the army in Virginia to support the capture of Confederate Gen. Robert E. Lee and the Army of Northern Virginia, now under siege at Petersburg. These orders would change four days later with the surrender of Gen. Lee and his army to Gen. Grant at Appomattox, Virginia.

BATTLES IN THE EASTERN THEATER

SIEGE OF PETERSBURG, 1865

As 1865 began, the Confederate Army of Northern Virginia under Gen. Robert E. Lee was locked in place by the Union Army of the Potomac under Union General-in-Chief Ulysses S. Grant and Gen. George Meade. The Northern army surrounded the besieged Southerners as they occupied and defended the cities of Petersburg and Richmond, Virginia, behind a massive array of well-defended trenches. After several unsuccessful attempts to dislodge the Confederates from their nearly impregnable defenses between

VIII. THE FINAL BATTLES AND SURRENDER, 1865

June and December 1864, the Union Army settled into a pattern of short brutal battles and cavalry raids to cut the supply lines that sustained the Southerners.

A successful Union raid in August 1864 still held the Weldon and Petersburg Railroad south of Petersburg. Union Gen. Gouverneur K. Warren had led the battle near Globe Tavern to cut the important railroad line for the Confederates. By September, Gen. Lee had only the Boydton Plank Road to the south and the Southside Railroad that ran to Lynchburg, Virginia, to the west as his last remaining supply routes.

Lee's army suffered miserably through the winter cold with shortages of food, firewood and warm clothing. The army slowly shrank as casualties, illness and desertions brought it to only 55,000 men. The Union Army, on the other hand, numbering more than 125,000, was well taken care of by the huge supply base at City Point ten miles away that supplied food, clothing, ammunition and mail on a regular basis. Ovens at City Point produced one hundred thousand loaves of bread daily for the troops.

A brief Union effort on February 5 at the Battle of Hatcher's Run was an unsuccessful attempt to destroy the Confederate supply wagons on the Boydton Plank Road. The battle did, however, force Lee's army to extend its already thin defensive lines to protect the road. Heavy rains dominated winter conditions, making movement of artillery and teams virtually impossible on the impassable roads. One soldier wrote "... *both my stirrups and the belly of my horse are gripped by mud.*"

Gen. Philip Sheridan, with his 10,000-man cavalry, the Army of the Shenandoah, finally moved out of their winter quarters at Winchester, Virginia, in March and routed the rest of Confederate Gen. Jubal Early's army at Waynesboro on March 1, nearly capturing the entire command. Sheridan then occupied Charlottesville and the University of Virginia, March 3-6, before continuing south, destroying railroads, canal locks, mills and factories. He arrived at City Point March 26 to rejoin the Army of the Potomac at Petersburg. Sheridan wrote later, *"Feeling that the war was nearing its end, I desired my cavalry to be in at the death."*

Battle of Fort Stedman, Petersburg, Virginia
March 24, 1865

On March 24, Confederate Gen. Robert E. Lee launched a surprise attack before dawn on the Union right flank trenches near Fort Stedman. The attack was an attempt to force Union forces to shorten their line that would enable Lee to withdraw from Petersburg with his army and move west where he could obtain food and supplies at Lynchburg, Virginia, or southwest at Danville. From there, he planned to join Confederate Gen. Joseph E. Johnston in North Carolina who was now opposing Gen. William T. Sherman, whose army had completed his campaign through the Carolinas

The Confederate attack, led by Gen. John B. Gordon, was initially successful as the Southerners overwhelmed the Union soldiers roused from sleep in the pre-dawn

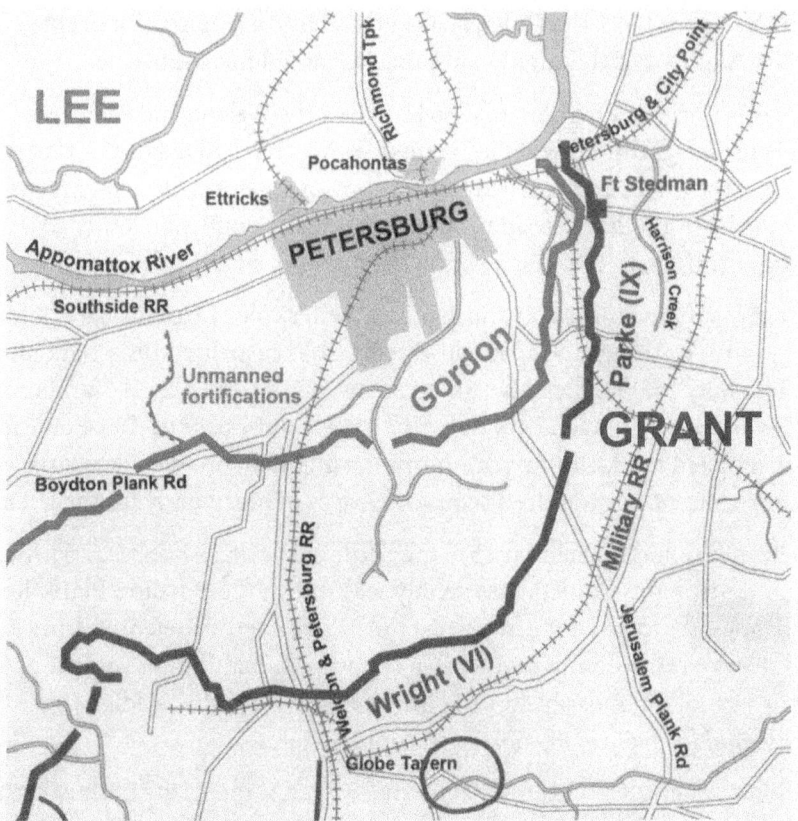

Fig. 68: Confederate forces under Generals Lee and Gordon failed to break through Union defenses under Gen. Grant at the Battle of Fort Stedman, Petersburg, Virginia, on March 24, 1865.
Source: *Creative Commons Attribution 3.0 License Map by Hal Jespersen, www. cwmaps.com.*

darkness. As Gordon continued his attack on nearby Fort Haskell, however, which flanked Fort Stedman, an alert Union sentry noted their approach and heavy artillery fired canister shot into the Southerners as they came within range.

A vigorous Union counter-attack at Fort Stedman prevented the Confederates, under heavy fire, from advancing farther and the fort remained in Union control. As the morning dawned, more Union artillery was brought into play and the Confederates were forced to retreat through a storm of bullets. Confederate losses numbered 4,000, including 600 killed, 2,400 wounded, and about 1,000 captured prisoners.

Battle of Five Forks, Virginia
March 29-April 1, 1865

Near the end of March as the heavy winter rains subsided, Union Gen. Ulysses S. Grant was anxious to move forward with his plans to cut Robert E. Lee's only remaining railroad supply line, the Southside Railroad to Lynchburg, Virginia, and force the Confederates out of their entrenched positions. Grant had already planned an offensive

VIII. THE FINAL BATTLES AND SURRENDER, 1865

before the attack on Fort Stedman and with the arrival of Gen. Philip Sheridan and his cavalry from the Shenandoah Valley, the Union assault was launched on March 29.

Sheridan's cavalry was joined with two corps of the Army of the Potomac to attack Five Forks, Virginia, site of a critical road junction for the Southside Railroad, some twenty miles west of Petersburg. The combined forces of Sheridan included the V Corps under Gen. Gouverneur K. Warren, who would play a critical role in the Battle of Five Forks. The infantry moved west before dawn on March 29. Sheridan and the cavalry took a southerly route to capture the crossroads at Dinwiddie Courthouse, an important junction of the Boydton Plank Road, heavily used by the Confederates for wagon supplies to Petersburg.

Gen. Robert E. Lee realized that the loss of Five Forks would not only eliminate his Southside Railroad supply line but also potentially cut off the main escape route for his army. To counter the Union army's movement west, Lee sent a mobile force of about 11,000 infantry, cavalry and artillery under the commands of Gen. George Pickett and cavalry commander Gen. Fitzhugh Lee (nephew of Robert E. Lee) to protect Dinwiddie and Five Forks.

Heavy rains began on March 30 and continued the next day. Sheridan's cavalry met Pickett's Confederates March 31 at the Battle of Dinwiddie Court House and were forced back into defensive positions that threatened to cut them off from Union infantry. The battle ended with darkness, but Southern troops planned to resume the attack the next morning. As night fell, Union Gen. Warren recognized from the sounds of battle that Sheridan had been pushed back from his position and sent infantry to reinforce him. When Pickett learned that Union reinforcements were underway to Dimwiddie, he withdrew to Five Forks later that night, relieving Sheridan's pinned troops.

The next day, shortly after noon on April 1, Sheridan attacked the Confederates at the Battle of Five Forks from heavily wooded fields with small arms fire that pinned down the front and right flanks of the Confederate line (See Fig. 69). About the same time Confederate Generals Pickett and Fitzhugh Lee were relaxing some two miles away as they enjoyed a late "shad bake" lunch with fellow officers. The rare treat featured shad, a local herring, that was baked on boards surrounding an open fire. Neither Pickett nor Lee believed that Sheridan would organize an attack that late in the day and an acoustic shadow muffled the sound of any battle at Five Forks from the two Confederate generals. Worse, the generals had not informed their lines of command where they had gone or that the ranking officers were temporarily in charge.

As the afternoon battle continued, Sheridan's men were in danger of running low on ammunition and an expected massive blow on the Confederate left flank from Warren's infantry had not materialized. At 4 p.m., Sheridan, who had overall command of the operation, took matters into his own hands and ordered Union infantry to attack. Warren's troops had been held up by a destroyed bridge and were then given

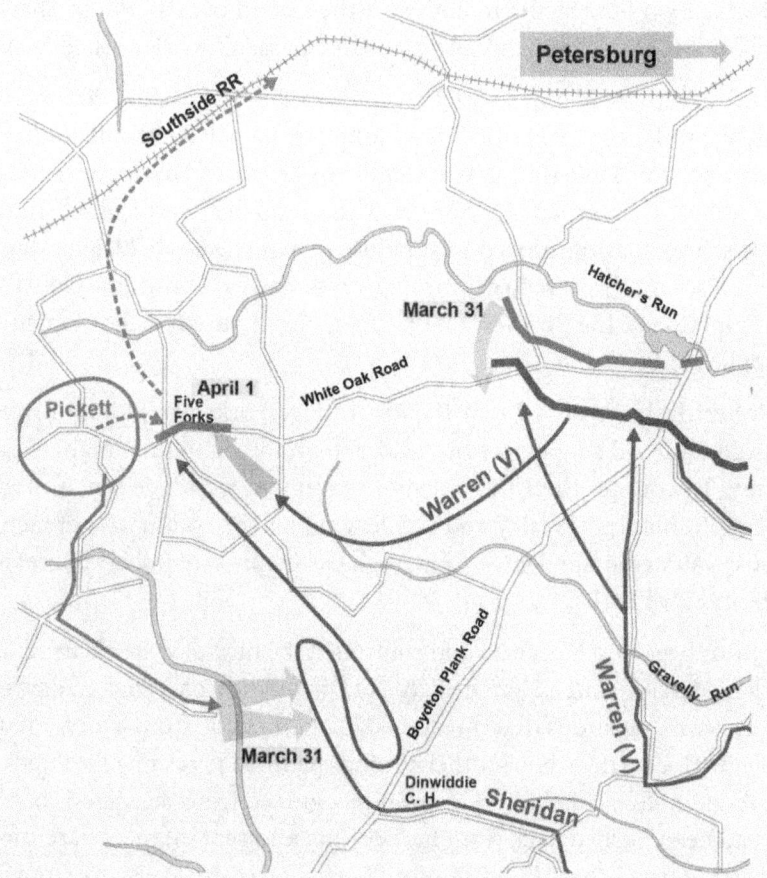

Fig. 69: Union forces under Generals Sheridan and Warren defeated Confederate forces under Gen. Pickett at the Battle of Five Forks, Virginia, on April 1 and captured the important gateway to the Southside Railroad, the last supply line supporting the Confederate Army during the Siege of Petersburg.

Source: *Creative Commons Attribution 3.0 License Map by Hal Jespersen, www.cwmaps.com.*

poor information about the location of the Confederates' left flank in the rough, woody landscape filled with ravines. The actual Confederate line was more than three-quarters of a mile west from its expected position, which resulted in the Union troops missing their target. When Warren found the missing troops, he realized that they were in a favorable position at the rear of the Confederate line.

Reorganizing the men, Gen. Warren led the charge into the rear of the Confederate left flank, losing his horse which was shot from under him. By the time the two Confederate Generals Pickett and Fitzhugh Lee became aware of the unfolding battle and arrived at the scene, their lines had collapsed and most of the Confederate infantry in the front and center became casualties or prisoners. Troops under Gen. Rooney Lee on the far right held their position until dark and were able to withdraw.

VIII. THE FINAL BATTLES AND SURRENDER, 1865

During this pivotal final battle of the day, Union troops rolled up the Southern defense, capturing artillery and prisoners and seized several battle flags. Confederate casualties numbered about 2,500 prisoners and 600 killed or wounded. Union casualties reached a little more than 800. Union forces now held Five Forks and an open gateway to the critical Southside Railroad.

Confederate survivors made their way through the woods and crossed Hatcher's Run to reach Southside Railroad where they could rejoin Lee's army. Union troops pursued them and at the Battle of Sutherland's Station the next day captured another 600 prisoners. The remaining Southern troops who escaped proceeded on the road to Amelia Court House to meet Lee.

After the Battle of Five Forks, Sheridan relieved Warren of command because, *"He had not been at the front!"* and was to report to Gen. Grant. Stunned, Warren objected and asked for a reconsideration, but Sheridan refused and Grant supported

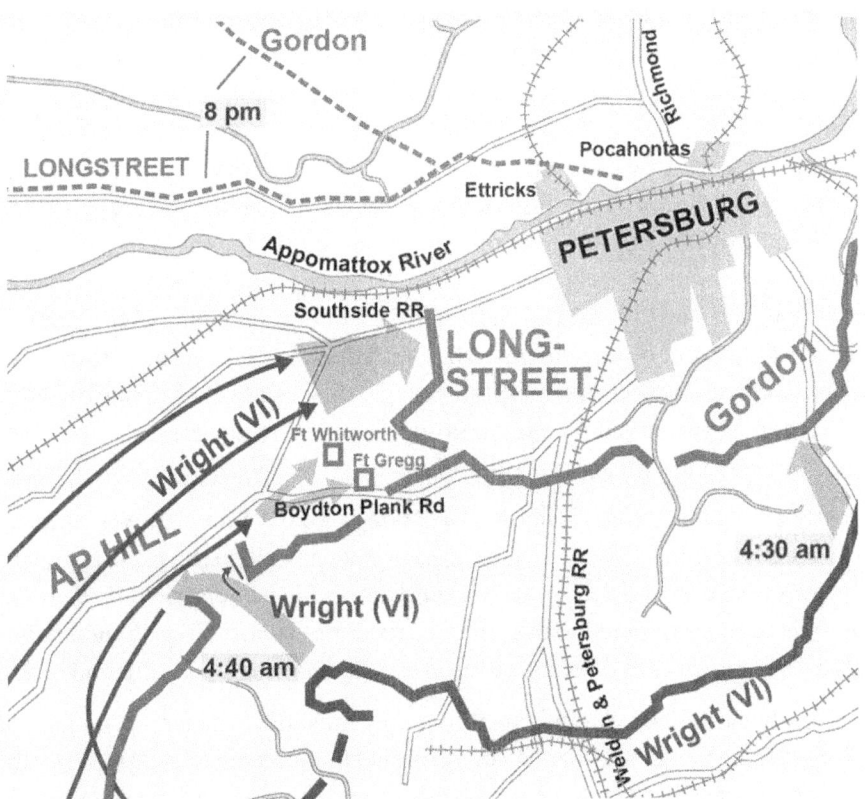

Fig. 70: Only 350 Confederate defenders at Fort Gregg under Gen. Longstreet held off a massive Union assault led by Gen. Wright on April 2, 1865. The defenders provided Gen. Robert E. Lee and his armies under Longstreet and Gordon enough time to escape Petersburg. Called the "Confederate Alamo," less than forty defenders were left standing at the end.

Source: *Creative Commons Attribution 3.0 License Map by Hal Jespersen, www. cwmaps.com.*

the decision, because Sheridan had been given authorization to remove an officer if the situation required it.

Humiliated by the rebuke, Warren urgently requested a Court of Inquiry to exonerate him, but the request was ignored or denied for several years until 1879, nearly fifteen years later, after Rutherford B. Hayes succeeded Grant to the Presidency. Dozens of witnesses testified in 1880 over a period of several months. The Court's conclusions, not published until 1882, that Sheridan's action to remove Gen. Warren from command was unjustified, came three months after Warren's death.

APPOMATTOX CAMPAIGN, VIRGINIA

Breakthrough at Petersburg, Virginia
April 2, 1865

With Five Forks and the Southside Railroad in Union hands, Gen. Ulysses S. Grant issued orders for an all-out assault on April 2 on the Petersburg entrenchments all along the line, the Third Battle of Petersburg. Union artillery opened fire at midnight with a massive bombardment that used every available gun, followed by an attack in the predawn hours shortly after 4:30 a.m. by Army of the Potomac forces led by Gen. Horatio G. Wright's VI Corps. The pickets on Boydton Plank Road line were quickly overwhelmed and Union troops ran over the Confederates before turning to Petersburg. Union Gen. Edward Ord, who was the new commander for the Army of the James, sent one division and two brigades to follow Wright's men. Union forces, numbering about 14,000, faced less than 3,000 defenders in a one-mile stretch of the Confederate line. Heavy fighting continued to push the Confederates back and after thirty minutes the main Confederate line was broken (See Fig. 70). Gen. A. P. Hill, one of Lee's most capable generals, was killed by a small group of Union stragglers as he rode between the lines to the front with a single staff officer.

Shortly after twelve o'clock noon, Forts Gregg and Whitworth were attacked by more than 4,000 Union soldiers. A Georgian private described the scene as, *"The whole country was blue with them as far as we could see and I lost hope right then and there."* Outnumbered more than ten to one, the Confederates at Fort Gregg fought back tenaciously, with two ranks of defenders at each position: one to load a gun and one to fire.

The Southerners had been informed that they must hold the fort "at all hazards" to give Robert E. Lee's Northern Army of Virginia enough time to escape. Described by some historians as "the Confederate Alamo," the battle at Fort Gregg was one of the most desperate fighting of the war. Southern casualties numbered about 300 dead or wounded of the approximately 350 defenders. When forced to surrender, less than forty men were standing. Fort Whitworth fell soon afterward. But their ferocious fighting had given Confederate Gen. James Longstreet enough time to move reinforcements

VIII. THE FINAL BATTLES AND SURRENDER, 1865

from Richmond and protect the bridges over the Appomattox River, which allowed Gen. Lee and his army with Longstreet to escape during the night.

Lee's Army Leaves Petersburg
April 2-3, 1865

Confederate Gen. Robert E. Lee and his army crossed the Appomattox River during the nights of April 2-3 to proceed west where he hoped to find needed food and supplies for his men. From there, Lee would direct his army south to join Gen. Joseph E. Johnston in North Carolina. But Grant, anticipating the move, had already sent additional troops west to strengthen Union forces and block any attempts by the Confederates to move south.

Although Lee's army had a head start on its flight from Petersburg, units of Sheridan's cavalry under Union Gen. George A. Custer were able to pursue the Confederates as they moved west along the Appomattox River and caught up with the rear guard near Namozine Church on April 3 (See Fig. 71). As the Confederates formed their defenses at the church, Gen. Custer's younger brother, Captain Tom Custer, leaped his horse over a hastily erected barricade and captured fourteen prisoners and the battle flag of the 2nd North Carolina Cavalry. He would later receive the Medal of Honor for his actions. Soon after, Confederate infantry arrived to support the cavalry at the Battle of Namozine Church and Custer's troops had to withdraw, but they had captured 350 prisoners, one hundred horses and a cannon.

Union Troops Occupy Empty Petersburg & Richmond
April 3-4, 1865

As Gen. Grant prepared to renew the assault the next morning, he found Petersburg evacuated. With orders for the Union Army to actively pursue Gen. Robert E. Lee and his army that was now moving west, Grant invited President Lincoln, who had been staying at City Point the previous several days on the warship *USS Malvern*, to join him in Petersburg on the morning of April 3. Selecting the piazza of an abandoned house, Grant and his staff waited for Lincoln in the entirely deserted city.

"There was not a soul to be seen, not even an animal in the streets," writes Grant. *"There was absolutely no one there, except my staff officers and a small escort of cavalry."* The level of destruction from ten months of siege and warfare was evident everywhere: shells of buildings surrounded by rubble, cannonballs and canister lying in the streets amid the debris of a fighting army and the remains of homes destroyed by battle.

Lincoln rode by horseback from City Point with 12-year-old son Tad to meet Grant, accompanied by Rear Admiral David D. Porter and William Crook, Lincoln's bodyguard. After receiving Lincoln's warm congratulations on the success of the victory and discussing with the President the further conduct of the war, Grant excused himself after an hour or so with the President, so that he and his officers could catch up with the Union armies now in vigorous pursuit of Lee's army. Lincoln returned to his stateroom on the *USS Malvern* at City Point and continued to follow events as the Union army pursued the Confederates. But Lincoln was anxious to visit Richmond, the Confederate capital that had been the object of so much effort and bloodshed for the last four long years.

Union Gen. Godfrey Weitzel accepted the surrender of Richmond that morning from its mayor amid a city in chaos and mass confusion, still burning in the wake of a retreating army and its Confederate government. Union blue-clad troops, including Black soldiers from the Massachusetts Cavalry, entered the city and quickly raised the Stars and Stripes, now a 36-star flag after Nevada became a state the previous October, to fly over the Capitol building. The Confederate government, including President Jefferson Davis, its employees, and thousands of refugees had fled the city the night before by train, wagons, vehicles and horseback. Fires had been set to destroy documents, ammunition stores, cotton, tobacco and anything that might be of value to the entering Union army. Four gunboats had been set on fire and were still burning. Plundering mobs of civilians added to the chaos. A third of the city was destroyed by fire, called the Great Conflagration of Richmond, including all of its business district.

Union troops managed to extinguish most of the flames and Lincoln was invited to visit the city the next day, April 4, to be escorted by Rear Admiral David D. Porter with a staff of Navy officers and several Marines. Porter attempted to bring the President to Richmond via the James River with an impressive flotilla of boats flying the American flag, but a series of mishaps reduced the flotilla to a single row boat, manned by twelve sailors, which brought the Presidential party to a vacant landing site and no welcoming party.

The streets were empty with no Union soldiers there to meet them and the President was two miles from his destination, Capitol Square. But a group of a dozen Blacks saw the landing party and immediately recognized the President. Soon, Lincoln was surrounded by exuberant former slaves, who crowded around him trying to grab his hand, touch his clothes, laughing and shouting. As the crowd rapidly grew in size, the sailors formed a guard around the President and the group slowly proceeded toward the square. Eventually, a cavalry escort came to rescue the Presidential party, which was now surrounded by a crowd of thousands.

Gen. Weitzel provided an officer's ambulance for Lincoln and his party to tour Richmond. The destruction was evident everywhere, homes burned, shattered buildings, cannon balls among the rubble, but crowds of joyful former slaves followed the group. During the tour, a one-hundred-gun artillery salute was fired at all military posts, arsenals and naval bases, celebrating the capture of the Confederate capital. The tour included a visit to Libby Prison, which now housed Confederate prisoners, its former Union prisoners just released. Weitzel asked Lincoln if he had any orders regarding the

VIII. THE FINAL BATTLES AND SURRENDER, 1865

treatment of defeated Virginians. Lincoln responded that he did not, but added, *"If I were in your place I'd let 'em up easy,"* then repeated the phrase, *"... let 'em up easy."* At the end of the tour, the group was delivered to the *USS Malvern*, which had finally been able to reach the Richmond docks and the Presidential party was returned to City Point.

Lincoln remained at City Point for several days and continued to receive telegrams from Grant, reporting on the progress of the pursuit of Gen. Lee's army. Grant wrote on April 7, *"The country is full of stragglers, the line of retreat marked with artillery, burned or charred wagons, caissons, ambulances, etc."* He ended the telegram by repeating a message he had just received from Gen. Philip Sheridan, who reported on the victory at the Battle of Sailor's Creek where Union troops had captured five rebel generals, including Richard Ewell and Custis Lee, eldest son of Robert E. Lee, plus *"several thousand prisoners, fourteen pieces of artillery with caissons, and a large number of wagons."* Sheridan had added at the end of his report, *"If the thing is pressed, I think Lee will surrender."* Lincoln's immediate response to Grant's message, *"... Let the thing be pressed."* The President left April 8 on the steamboat *River Queen* to return to Washington; Lee would surrender the next day.

Confederate Armies Meet at Amelia Court House
April 4-5, 1865

Lee's first objective was to reach Amelia Court House, about thirty miles west of Petersburg, where all Confederate commands would converge, expecting to find rations for the hungry men. After crossing the Appomattox, Gen. James Longstreet traveled with Lee and his army on the north side of the river, while Lee's cavalry under Generals Richard H. Anderson and Fitzhugh Lee traveled on the south bank; they would meet at Amelia. Gen. Richard Ewell, led troops from Richmond but they were delayed by spring flooding which had eliminated the usual passages across the Appomattox. But by the morning of April 4, most of the Confederate armies had arrived at Amelia.

When Lee's contingent of the Army of Northern Virginia arrived at Amelia, the anticipated supply train for the Confederates contained only ordnance, ammunition and caissons, but no food (See Fig. 71). With his long wagon train delayed by muddy roads, swollen rivers and creeks, Lee sent out foraging parties to look for food and fodder for the animals while he waited for his army to catch up. Unfortunately, the foragers found few provisions, so Lee ordered a new set of two hundred thousand rations to be sent to Danville, about seventy miles directly south of Lynchburg. Lee's army could reach Danville from Amelia, a distance to the southwest of about one hundred miles, by following the Richmond & Danville Railroad.

But the Southern army's delay in resuming its march was costly. Sheridan's cavalry had raced westward from Petersburg and Gen. George Crook, had intercepted Lee's telegram requesting rations be shipped to Danville, Virginia, near the North Carolina border. Anticipating Lee's move to use the railroad line from Amelia Court House,

Crook and his men entrenched within one mile of Jetersville, a small, station on the Richmond & Danville Railroad about twelve miles southwest of Amelia, and reinforcements from the II and V Corps of the Army of the Potomac soon arrived to block the Confederates' move to Danville (See Fig. 71).

On the morning of April 5, a second brigade from Sheridan's cavalry, Gen. Henry E. Davies, scouting north of Amelia Springs, encountered a poorly defended wagon train, containing food, ammunition and headquarters baggage. Davies captured food, horses, mules, artillery pieces and more than 300 prisoners and 300 slaves. Burning about one hundred eighty wagons, Davies proceeded to return to Jetersville with his prisoners, but was intercepted by Confederate Gen. Fitzhugh Lee and his cavalry. A running battle between the two cavalries brought out Union reinforcements from Jetersville and Davies was able to return safely with his command.

Having seen the Union entrenchments across the railroad at Jetersville, Gen. Fitzhugh Lee reported back to Gen. Robert E. Lee that the Richmond & Danville Railroad was blocked. With the weakened Confederate Army stretched out around Amelia, Lee was doubtful that he could mount a strong attack against the Union forces at Jetersville. His alternative was to continue the movement west and have the rations at Danville sent to Farmville on the Appomattox River, now only twenty miles west of him.

Gen. Lee ordered a night march west on April 5 to reach Farmville by morning. As the Southern troops traveled cross-country through the night on small paths and rough roads, some of the famished soldiers, marching without food or rest for three days, fell out of their ranks and simply never returned. Longstreet's command in the vanguard was first to reach Rice's Station on the Southside Railroad the morning of April 6. Rations at Farmville only six miles away would soon be accessible for his troops.

Battle at Sailor's Creek, Virginia
April 6-7, 1865

As the Confederate Army tried to cross Sailor's Creek, a tributary of the Appomattox River, it soon came under attack on April 6 from pursuing Union forces. Broken down bridges slowed progress for the Confederates as wagons became stranded and forces became separated. With the army widely dispersed, three separate battles limited Southern cohesion and Union troops rapidly took advantage of the gaps. The Confederates lost eight generals, including Gen. Ewell, and more than 7,000 prisoners, one of the largest surrenders of an army during the war. George Washington Custis Lee, Gen. Robert E. Lee's eldest son, was one of the prisoners captured. Total casualties for the Confederates numbered nearly 9,000, decimating Lee's already crippled army.

The Confederate survivors of the Sailor's Creek Battles, which included Generals John B. Gordon and William Mahone, pressed forward to High Bridge, a tall (126 ft) bridge, two thousand four hundred feet long, which supported the Southside Railroad crossing the Appomattox River. Two bridges crossed the river, one for the railroad at

VIII. THE FINAL BATTLES AND SURRENDER, 1865

the top and a second one, closer to the river for wagons and stagecoaches. As soon as the Southerners had crossed the river, they set fire to the bridges on April 7, but Union troops were able to extinguish the flames on the lower wagon bridge, which enabled Grant's army to continue its pursuit.

Confederate Gen. James Longstreet's troops left Rice's Station on a night march and arrived at Farmville the morning of April 7. Gen. Robert E. Lee soon joined him, but as he watched from a high bluff as the survivors of his army from Sailor's Creek arrived, he said, *"My God, has the army dissolved?"* Lee's words to Confederate President Jefferson Davis were, *"… a few more Sailor's Creeks, and it will all be over."*

As Longstreet and Lee reached Farmville, some of the 80,000 rations for the men and 40,000 loaves of bread were issued, but with Union forces rapidly approaching, the army was forced to quickly cross the Appomattox on the Farmville bridges and then burn the bridges behind them. The Confederate Commissary General sent the train with the rest of the rations to Pamplin's Station on the Southside Railroad about twenty miles west, but Sheridan's cavalry, alerted to the train, got there first and captured the supplies.

Although Confederates had set the Farmville bridges ablaze after crossing, Union troops were able to find other crossing points or build temporary bridges. Soon, they were in hot pursuit of the Confederates. General-in-Chief Ulysses S. Grant arrived at Farmville from Burkeville, about fifteen miles distant, with his staff in the afternoon, and set up headquarters at Farmville.

Grant sent Lee a message, requesting his surrender:

GENERAL R. E. LEE, April 7, 1865
Commanding C. S. A.

The result of the last week must convince you of the hopelessness of further resistance on the part of the Army of Northern Virginia in this struggle. I feel that it is so, and regard it as my duty to shift from myself the responsibility of any further effusion of blood, by asking of you the surrender of that portion of the Confederate States Army known as the Army of Northern Virginia.

U. S. GRANT, *Lieut.-General.*

Lee replied on the evening of the same day as follows:

LIEUT.-GENERAL U. S. GRANT, April 7, 1865.
Commanding Armies of the U. S.

GENERAL: *I have received your note of this day. Though not entertaining the opinion you express on the hopelessness of further resistance on the part of the Army of Northern Virginia, I reciprocate your desire to avoid useless effusion of blood, and therefore before considering your proposition, ask the terms you will offer on condition of its surrender.*

R. E. LEE, *General.*

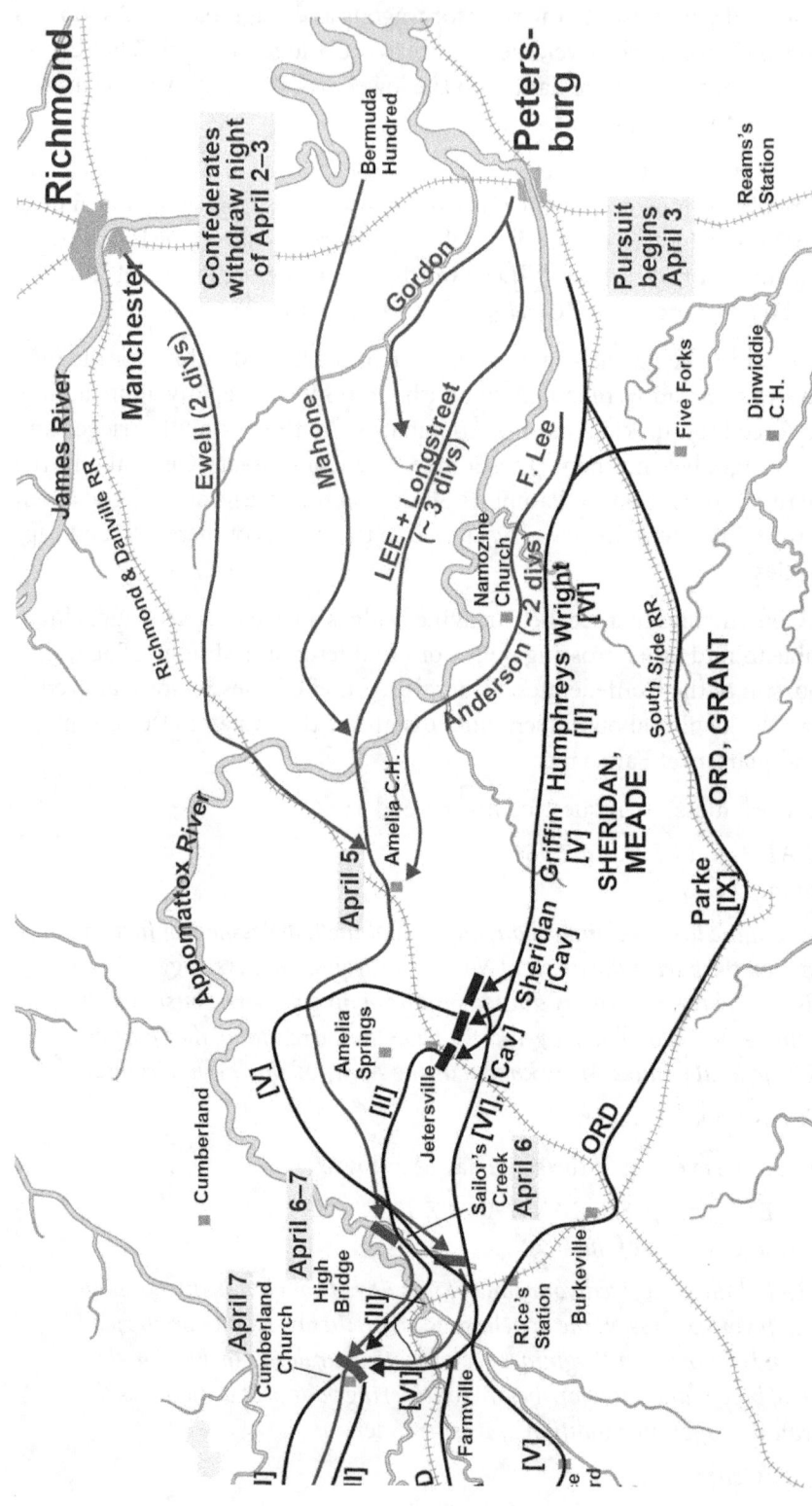

Fig. 71: The Union Armies under Grant, Ord, Sheridan and Meade, pursued the Confederates west after their breakout from the Siege of Petersburg. Confederates under Lee, Longstreet, Ewell, Gordon and Mahone raced westward as the Southerners struggled to reach new supplies for the hungry soldiers who marched without food or rest.

Source: *Creative Commons Attribution 3.0 License Map by Hal Jespersen, www.cwmaps.com.*

VIII. THE FINAL BATTLES AND SURRENDER, 1865

Receiving Lee's message that morning in Farmville, Grant composed a second message:

GENERAL R. E. LEE, April 8, 1865
Commanding C. S. A.

"Your note of last evening in reply of mine of same date, asking the condition on which I will accept the surrender of the Army of Northern Virginia is just received. In reply I would say that, peace being my great desire, there is but one condition I would insist upon, namely: that the men and officers surrendered shall be disqualified for taking up arms again against the Government of the United States until properly exchanged. I will meet you, or will designate officers to meet any officers you may name for the same purpose, at any point agreeable to you, for the purpose of arranging definitely the terms upon which the surrender of the Army of Northern Virginia will be received."

U. S. GRANT, Lieut.-General.

Lee received Grant's message on the morning of April 8. In the meantime, that part of the Confederate Army that had escaped the Battle of Sailor's Creek by crossing High Bridge had set up strong defenses against the Union pursuers at Cumberland Church north of Farmville, now on the north side of the Appomattox River. When fighting ended at dark, Lee ordered another night march to Appomattox Station about twenty-five miles west, where rations from Lynchburg would be waiting for his men (See Fig. 72). It had now become a life and death struggle to get food to his starving army. Mules and horses, also starving, collapsed during the march, and wagons had to be burned when they could not be moved.

Battle at Appomattox Station
April 8, 1865

As Lee and the Army of Northern Virginia moved west towards Appomattox Station, Union Gen. Philip Sheridan learned that seven trains of provisions and forage were waiting at Appomattox and a forced march of about thirty miles would be needed to get there before the Confederates. Grant writes in his *Personal Memoirs*, "Although Sheridan's men had been marching all day, his troops moved with alacrity and without any straggling. They began to see the end of what they had been fighting four years for. Nothing seemed to fatigue them. They were ready to move without rations and travel without rest until the end. Straggling had entirely ceased, and every man was now a rival for the front. The infantry marched about as rapidly as the cavalry could."

Reaching the station ahead of the main Southern army, the leading Union troopers captured four unguarded trains sent from Lynchburg with rations, ordnance and other supplies. Train guards had been alerted that Union troops were about to arrive

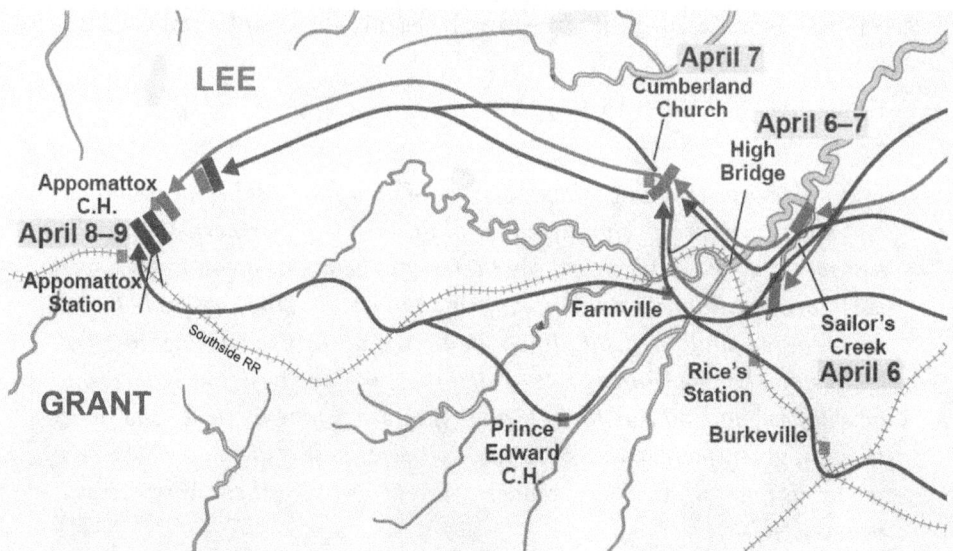

Fig. 72: Confederate Gen. Robert E. Lee surrendered his army to Union Gen. Ulysses S. Grant at Appomattox Court House on April 9, 1865.

Source: *Creative Commons Attribution 3.0 License Map by Hal Jespersen, www.cwmaps.com.*

and were able to run three of them off. A skeleton Confederate force with artillery at the station began shelling the Union cavalry with canister at short range and defeated several charges on April 8. With nightfall and only moonlight to guide them, Union Gen. George A. Custer led a final cavalry charge through woods and brush that broke the artillery defenders, capturing thirty cannon, one hundred fifty to two hundred wagons and nearly 1,000 prisoners.

Grant ordered Gen. Edward Ord to bring up the Army of the James to reinforce Sheridan's forces and close up any gaps that might give the Confederates an escape route. Ord's forces made a forced march at night to reach Appomattox Station at 4 a.m. on April 9.

When the head of Lee's column reached Appomattox Station that morning, their surprise at finding Union cavalry already there prompted a quick fight to retake their trains. Union forces had burned one train and moved the other three back from the battle. The fight continued, but by the time the main force of Lee's army arrived, the Army of the James under Gen. Ord had arrived and was waiting for them. When Confederate Gen. John B. Gordon reached the top of the ridge, he could see nothing but blue-clad Union troops in battle formation ahead of him. With his escape route blocked, and Union forces surrounding his army, Gen. Lee stated. *"Then there is nothing left for me to do but to go and see General Grant, and I would rather die a thousand deaths."*

Lee's officers, including Longstreet, agreed that surrender was the only option left and a fresh white linen dish towel was brought forward as a flag of truce to arrange a meeting between Lee and Grant. Since Grant was on horseback riding with his staff

VIII. THE FINAL BATTLES AND SURRENDER, 1865

to the front to meet with Gen. Sheridan, the only way to communicate with him was by personal messenger.

Lee's message was sent through the Confederate lines with an escorted officer and reached Grant at about 12 o'clock noon.

LIEUTENANT-GENERAL U.S. GRANT, April 9, 1865

Commanding U.S. Armies

GENERAL: I received your note of this morning on the picket-line whither I had come to meet you and ascertain definitely what terms were embraced in your proposal of yesterday with reference to the surrender of this army. I now request an interview in accordance with the offer contained in your letter of yesterday for that purpose.

R.E.LEE, General.

Grant, who had been suffering from a severe migraine for several days, writes in his *Personal Memoirs*, "When the officer reached me, I was still suffering with the sick headache; but the instant I saw the contents of the note I was cured." Grant responded by asking Lee to select the location for their meeting and to provide the information to him while he was underway to Appomattox. Lee received the message within the hour and required his aide, Col. Charles Marshall, to find an appropriate location.

The brick home of Wilmer McLean in the small village of Appomattox Court House was selected and the location was communicated to Grant. In a strange coincidence, McLean had moved to his home in Appomattox after his home at Manassas, Virginia, had been damaged in the Battle of First Bull Run in 1861, while serving as headquarters for the Confederate commander Gen. P.G.T. Beauregard. Now at the end of a four-year struggle, his new home, more than a hundred miles away from his first home, was where terms would be negotiated for the end of the war. Even though it was never confirmed to be his exact words, it was often quoted that he said, "The war began in my front yard and ended in my front parlor."

Both Union and Confederate armies paid a heavy price for the fall of Richmond, the Confederate capital. Estimated casualties during the siege numbered about 42,000 losses for the Union and 28,000 for the Confederates.

Lee's Confederate Army Surrenders
April 9, 1865

After receiving the location of the meeting with Gen. Robert E. Lee to finalize the terms of surrender, Gen. Ulysses S. Grant and his staff reached the McClean House at Appomattox about an hour later, around 1:30 p.m., where Lee had been waiting for some time. Gen. Grant, dressed in clothing he typically wore for field travel, made a sharp contrast to the classical Southern elegance of 58-year-old Robert E. Lee. The 43-year-old Grant wore a soldier's shirt with shoulder straps showing four tarnished gold stars, mud-spattered boots with his trousers inside, a slouch hat and no spurs or sword. With the exception of the shoulder straps, he was dressed much like a private. Gen. Lee, on the other hand, expecting to surrender his sword, was dressed in a new uniform, buttoned at the throat, fine top-boots with handsome spurs, a jeweled sword and full sash. Grant wrote later in his *Personal Memoirs*, "*I must have contrasted very strangely with a man so handsomely dressed, six feet high and of faultless form. But this was not a matter that I thought of until afterwards.*"

Several of Grant's senior staff were invited into the proceedings and stood politely around the room. Lee was accompanied by only one of his staff, his aide-de-camp and military secretary Col. Charles Marshall. Grant, seated at a marble-topped table in the center of the room, faced Lee who sat beside a small oval table next to the window. Grant, as a young lieutenant in the Mexican-American War, had known Lee as one of General-in-Chief Winfield Scott's chief aides. Their difference in age and the great separation in rank would not have brought them into much contact. But as the two commanding generals of the American Civil began to converse, Grant recalled the event in his *Memoirs*.

TERMS OF SURRENDER FOR LEE'S ARMY
SIGNED APRIL 9, 1865

Appomattox C.H., Va., Ap"l 9th, 1865
Gen. R.E. Lee, Comd'g C.S.A.

Gen.: In accordance with the substance of my letter to you of the 8th, I propose to receive the surrender of the Army of N. Va., on the following terms, to wit: Rolls of all the officers and men to be made in duplicate. One copy to be given to an officer designated by me, the other to be retained by such officer or officers as you may designate. The officers to give their individual paroles not to take up arms against the Government of the United States until properly exchanged, and each company or regimental commander sign a like parole for the men of their commands. The arms, artillery and public property to be parked and stacked, and turned over to the officer appointed by me to receive them. This will not embrace the side-arms of the officers, nor their private horses or baggage. This done, each officer and man will be allowed to return to their homes, not to be disturbed by United States authority so long as they observe their paroles and the laws in force where they may reside.

Very respectfully

U. S. GRANT, Lt. Gen.

VIII. THE FINAL BATTLES AND SURRENDER, 1865

"We soon fell into a conversation about old army times. He remarked that he remembered me very well in the old army; and I told him that as a matter of course I remembered him perfectly, but from the difference in our rank, and years (there being about sixteen years' difference in our ages), I had thought it very likely that I had not attracted his attention sufficiently to be remembered by him after such a long interval. Our conversation grew so pleasant that I almost forgot the object of our meeting... and after some time, Gen. Lee called my attention to the object of our meeting." Grant quickly wrote out the terms of surrender in a draft document, which Lee approved with a small correction, remarking that the terms about side arms, and private property would have a happy effect upon his army. When Lee pointed out that the horses of the Confederate cavalry and artillery commands were privately owned and their loss to the men would be a serious blow when they returned to their farms, Grant agreed that the terms of surrender would allow those who owned horses or mules to be able to keep them. The draft document was then made into an ink copy by Grant's military secretary, Col. Ely S. Parker, an American Indian of the Seneca tribe. Parker, later promoted to Brigadier General, would serve as Commissioner of Indian Affairs for President Grant 1869-71. After discovering that Parker was a Seneca Indian, Gen. Lee commented, *""I am glad to see one real American here."* Parker replied, *"Sir, we are all Americans."*

After accepting the terms and drafting his formal reply, both Generals signed the documents, formalizing the act of surrender. It was 3 p.m. Lee then mentioned that his men needed food and Grant promptly issued 30,000 rations for the Southern army. The time of 3 p.m. is commemorated each year at Appomattox Court House National Historical Park with the ringing of bells for four minutes, one for each year of the war. The Army of Northern Virginia had finally been defeated. Grant's generosity at the time of surrender was never forgotten by Lee and he would not tolerate an unkind word about Grant in his presence.

As Gen. Lee and Col. Marshall mounted their horses to leave, Gen. Grant stepped down from the porch and saluted Lee by raising his hat, which was followed by all the officers present. After Grant and Lee separated, the officers of both armies came together in large numbers and enjoyed their meetings with each other as though they had all been fighting battles under the same flag. When Confederate Gen. James Longstreet arrived later at the McLean House, he was happily greeted by Grant, his old friend from West Point days, who offered him a cigar. *"Why do men fight who were born to be brothers?"* Longstreet later asked a reporter. *"His whole greeting and conduct towards us was as though nothing had ever happened to mar our pleasant relations."*

Grant then returned inside the house to write a series of orders that would implement the formal surrender. Once finished, he departed the house for his headquarters, but then realized he had forgotten to convey the message to Washington. Sitting on a large stone, he quickly drafted the following: *"General Lee surrendered the Army of Northern Virginia this afternoon on terms proposed by myself. The accompanying additional correspondence will show the conditions fully."*

> ## ROBERT E. LEE'S FAREWELL ADDRESS TO HIS TROOPS
>
> On April 10, Lee presented his farewell address to the Army of Northern Virginia as General Order No. 9. *"After four years of arduous service marked by unsurpassed courage and fortitude... I need not tell the survivors of so many hard fought battles, who have remained steadfast to the last, that I have consented to the result (surrender) from no distrust of them. But feeling that valour and devotion could accomplish nothing that could compensate for the loss that must have attended the continuance of the contest, I have determined to avoid the useless sacrifice of those whose past services have endeared them to their countrymen. By the terms of the agreement, officers and men can return to their homes and remain until exchanged. You will take with you the satisfaction that proceeds from the consciousness of duty faithfully performed, and I earnestly pray that a Merciful God will extend to you His blessing and protection. With an unceasing admiration of your constancy and devotion to your country, and a grateful remembrance of your kind and generous consideration for myself, I bid you all an affectionate farewell."* Lee returned to Richmond on parole and in October became president of Washington College in Virginia (now known as Washington and Lee University) at Lexington.
>
> Lee would later write about Gen. Grant: *"We all thought Richmond, protected as it was by our splendid fortifications and defended by our army of veterans, could not be taken. Yet Grant turned his face to our Capital, and never turned it away until we had surrendered. Now, I have carefully searched the military records of both ancient and modern history, and have never found Grant's superior as a general. I doubt that his superior can be found in all history."* On another occasion, Lee urged his countrymen, *"Remember, we are all one country now. Dismiss from your mind all sectional feeling and bring them up to be Americans. I believe it to be the duty of everyone to unite in the restoration of the country and the reestablishment of peace and harmony."* Lee remained at Washington and Lee University until his death on October 12, 1870. Lee was not officially pardoned until 1975 when a joint Congressional resolution reinstated it posthumously, effective June 13, 1865.

When the news became public in Washington, a crowd of about 3,000 gathered around the White House on April 10, clamoring for a speech from President Lincoln. Promising a speech the next evening, he requested that the band play Dixie, "... *one of the best tunes I ever heard,"* and one that had been a favorite song for the Confederates. Lincoln then continued to tell the crowd that when he had been challenged by the Southerners that it was their song, he presented the question to the Attorney General, whose opinion was that it had been acquired as a lawful prize. *"That tune is now Federal property,"* he said, *"... and I just want to show the rebels that with us in power, they will be free to hear it again."* The band then played Dixie with particular vigor, followed by Yankee Doodle.

The following evening, April 11, Lincoln presented what would be his final speech to the public from the second-floor balcony of the White House. A single candle was held to light his prepared text. The President spoke of his vision for Reconstruction for the South and used the newly formed Constitution of Louisiana as a model for beginning a process that might be used to restore seceded states into the Union. Louisiana had adopted a new Constitution that pledged loyalty to the Union, abolished slavery, offered free education to all children and presented a path for educating Blacks. During the speech, Lincoln expressed his opinion that voting rights should be granted to educated Blacks and those who served as soldiers in the Union Army. This remark enraged some in the audience, either because it did not go far enough, or that Blacks would be given the same rights as whites, namely citizenship and the right to vote. Confederate sympathizer John Wilkes Booth despised the comment and said to his companion. "*That is the last speech he will ever make."* Lincoln would die from his bullet three days later.

Formal Ceremony for Surrender at Appomattox
April 12, 1865

General-in-Chief Ulysses S. Grant appointed Gen. Joshua Chamberlain, one of his commanders in the V Corps of the Union Army of the Potomac, to organize a formal ceremony at Appomattox Court House for the laying down of arms by the Confederate Army of Northern Virginia. Gen. Chamberlain, a college professor of languages before enlisting in the 20th Maine regiment in 1861, would later receive the Medal of Honor for his *"… daring heroism and great tenacity"* in holding his regiment's position on Little Round Top at the Battle of Gettysburg. Responding to the significance of the historic event that was to take place at Appomattox, Chamberlain writes in his memoir, *The Passing of the Armies,* how he arrived at a procedure that would provide the honor and recognition of bravery and valor that it deserved.

"The momentous meaning of this occasion impressed me deeply. I resolved to mark it by some token of recognition, which could be no other than a salute of arms. The act could be defended, if needful, by the suggestion that such a salute was not to the cause for which the flag of the Confederacy stood, but to its going down before the flag of the Union."

The formal surrender took place on the morning of April 12, 1865. The Union Army of the Potomac and the Confederate Army of Northern Virginia had faced each other in major conflicts for four long years: multiple battles in Virginia and the Shenandoah Valley, the tremendous losses at Antietam and Gettysburg, the horrific battles of the Overland Campaign, and finally, the Siege and Battles of Petersburg, which ended with the Confederate surrender at Appomattox. Union soldiers, drawn up in battle array, were lined up along Stage Road, and faced the Confederate infantry as they marched forward to lay down their arms and battle flags for the last time. Both cavalry and artillery of the Confederate Army had already turned in their weapons on April 10 and 11.

Confederate Gen. John B. Gordon, who had carried the final charge through Union cavalry at Appomattox before the surrender, rode on horseback, leading the procession at the head of the old "Stonewall" Jackson Brigade, as they marched past the Union line to lay down their arms with bayonets fixed to muskets, to be stacked together, with cartridge boxes hung upon the stacks. Beloved torn and tattered battle flags were to be leaned against the stacks or laid down on the ground.

Chamberlain, also on horseback, waited in formation with his men. Writing later, he described the scene. *"Before us in proud humiliation stood… men whom neither toils and sufferings, nor the fact of death, nor disaster, nor hopelessness could bend them from their resolve; standing before us now, thin, worn, and famished, but erect, and with eyes looking level into ours, waking memories that bound us together as no other bond—was not such manhood to be welcomed back into a Union so tested and assured?*

"When the head of each division column came opposite our group, our bugle sounded the signal and instantly our whole line from right to left, regiment by regiment in succession, gave the soldier's salutation, from the 'order arms' (shoulder arms) to the old 'carry'—the marching salute. Gen. Gordon at the head of the column, riding with heavy spirit and downcast face, caught the sound of shifting arms. Gen. Gordon started, looked up, caught in a moment its significance, and instantly assumed the finest attitude of a soldier. He wheeled his horse facing me, touching him gently with the spur so that the animal slightly reared, and as he wheeled, horse and rider made one motion, the horse's head swinging down with a graceful bow and Gen. Gordon dropped his sword point to his toe in salutation… then facing to his own command, gives word for his successive brigades to pass us with the same position of the manual—honor answering honor. At a distance of possibly twelve feet from our line, the Confederates halted and turned face toward us. Their lines were formed with the greatest care, with every officer in his appointed position, and thereupon began the formality of surrender.

"On our part not a sound of trumpet more, nor roll of drum, not a cheer, nor word nor whisper of vain-glorying, nor motion of man standing again at the order, but an awed stillness rather, and breath-holding, as if it were the passing of the dead.

"As each successive division masks our own, it halts, they face inward towards us across the road, twelve feet away; then carefully dress their line, each captain taking pains for the good appearance of his company, worn and half-starved as they were. The field and staff take their positions in the intervals of regiments, generals in rear of their commands. They fix bayonets, stack arms; then hesitatingly, remove cartridge boxes and lay them down. Lastly, reluctantly, with agony of expression, they tenderly fold their flags, battle-worn and torn, blood stained, heart-holding colors, and lay them down, some frenziedly rushing from the ranks, kneeling over them, clinging to them, pressing them to their lips with burning tears. And only the Flag of the Union greets the sky!"

VIII. THE FINAL BATTLES AND SURRENDER, 1865

Confederate Gen. Gordon's words of the same event, *"As my command, in worn-out shoes and ragged uniforms, but with proud mien, moved to the designated point to stack their arms and surrender their cherished battle flags, they challenged the admiration of the brave victors. Chamberlain called his men into line as my men marched in front of them, (and) the veterans in blue gave a soldierly salute to those vanquished heroes, a token of respect from Americans to Americans."* The dignified salute by the Union Army prompted Gen. Gordon to later say of Chamberlain, *"... one of the knightliest soldiers in the Federal army."*

About twenty-eight thousand stands of arms and one hundred battle flags were laid down with unchecked tears and required nearly an entire day. The parole forms needed to complete the final processing of the surrender had been printed on military presses at the nearby Clover Hill Tavern and had taken most of the night. The hungry Confederate soldiers cooked food over camp fires most of the day and for some, at least, the despair of surrender gradually gave way to resignation and acceptance. As one North Carolina soldier expressed it, *"... the question of dispute had been fought to a finish and that was the end of it."* The next day, the remaining Southern men left Appomattox singly, or in squads, and by nightfall on April 13 Union forces were alone.

Some historians have claimed that Chamberlain's writing of the surrender ceremony is not altogether authentic as this account was not published until May 1901 in the *Boston Journal*, one year after Chamberlain's death. Nevertheless, this account has been repeated in numerous books and publications and there is no official account to contradict it. The solemnity of the occasion, as Chamberlain described it, was a fitting end to the four years of blood and sacrifice endured by the two armies.

ASSASSINATION OF PRESIDENT LINCOLN

Lincoln Shot at Ford Theater
April 14, 1865

With the surrender of Robert E. Lee and the capture of Richmond and Petersburg, the city of Washington was jubilant. Responding to crowds around the White House, President Lincoln made a brief speech by candle light from the second-floor balcony on April 11 which reflected his thoughts about "Reconstruction," and the rebuilding of the country after its long and bloody conflict. He expressed support for limited Black suffrage, offending many Northerners who did not agree that the recently freed slaves were ready for voting rights. Among those in the audience was the handsome and talented actor, John Wilkes Booth, a Confederate sympathizer, who had planned with a few conspirators to kidnap the President and deliver him to the Confederacy. With the end of the war now in sight and Lincoln now contemplating citizenship for former slaves, an enraged Booth turned his thoughts to assassinate the President.

President and Mrs. Lincoln made plans to attend Ford's Theater the night of April 14 to see the play, "Our American Cousin." Gen. and Mrs. Grant were also invited to attend, but Mrs. Grant had expressed her desire to see their children and they left the city early for Philadelphia. Booth planned to assassinate the President during the play while two other conspirators would assassinate Secretary of State William H. Seward and Vice President Andrew Johnson at the same time. Seward was at home, still recovering from a carriage fall which had broken one arm and his jaw. Johnson was staying at a local rooming house.

Because of his well-known connections to the theater through his acting roles, Booth had no difficulty gaining access to the Presidential Box where he shot Lincoln in the back of the head during the play's high moment of comedy. As Booth leaped to the stage below, his right boot became entangled in drapery forcing him to land awkwardly on his left foot, seriously injuring his leg. While a stunned and confused audience watched, Booth limped across the stage, exited the theater, and rode away on a horse that was waiting for him. President Lincoln was carried to a boarding house across the street, and laid unconscious on a bed where he died the next morning at 7:22 a.m., at the age of fifty-six. Secretary of War Edwin Stanton is quoted as saying, *"Now he belongs to the ages."* Lincoln, who had fought to preserve the Union through four long years of war, had paid the ultimate price.

Attack on Secretary of State Seward
April 14, 1865

Secretary of State William Seward, recovering from severe injuries when he was thrown from a carriage, lay incapacitated in bed when the assassin Lewis Powell arrived at his house, carrying a large heavy revolver and a Bowie knife. Accompanied by David Herold, a co-conspirator who worked as a pharmacist assistant, Powell gained entrance by claiming to have medication for Secretary Seward. Challenged by Seward's son, Frederick, the Assistant Secretary of State, Powell attempted to shoot Frederick, but the revolver misfired, so Powell bludgeoned his victim into unconsciousness. Powell next charged into Seward's bedroom, knocking Seward's daughter Fanny to the floor, and used his Bowie knife to stab the Secretary of State repeatedly. A soldier nurse in the next room, attending the Secretary, forced Powell back from the attack, but was beaten to the floor. Seward's other son, Augustus, an army officer, alerted by Fanny's screams, also tried to stop Powell, who still managed to escape and ride away. Herold had run away to meet Booth. Powell would be captured by authorities four days later.

Although covered with blood, Seward would recover from Powell's wild stabs to his face and neck, but was left with a permanent scar where the blade had cut his cheek. An extensive metal splint holding his broken jaw had saved his life by deflecting the knife from cutting his jugular vein. Co-conspirator Herold ran from the scene, met Booth outside the city and the two rode away together into the Maryland countryside.

Vice President Johnson was staying at the Kirkwood House Inn and was sleeping when the designated assassin, George Atzerodt, arrived at the bar downstairs around 10:15 p.m. carrying a gun and knife. Atzerodt had agreed to a kidnapping, but was not enthusiastic about committing murder. He remained drinking at the saloon for some time, finally left, and wandered the streets of Washington until around 2 a.m., when he checked into the Pennsylvania House Hotel and went to sleep. Johnson, awakened by a fellow boarder with news about Lincoln being shot, rushed to the President's deathbed, promising, *"They shall suffer for this."* Sworn in as President later that morning, Johnson now faced the challenge of Reconstruction and the end of the Confederacy.

Capture and Execution of Conspirators
April-July 1865

The assassin John Wilkes Booth, joined by David Herold, managed to evade Union soldiers and police after fleeing Washington and reached the home of Samuel Mudd, a doctor with Confederate sympathies, who lived in southern Maryland. Mudd set Booth's broken leg and sent him on his way. When federal troops learned of his assistance to Booth, Mudd was arrested and sentenced to life in prison, but was later paroled by President Andrew Johnson in 1869. From Mudd's house, Booth and Herold crossed the Potomac River and continued into Virginia where Union cavalry caught them hiding in a tobacco barn on April 26. Booth was killed, refusing to be arrested.

Herold, Powell and Atzerodt were brought to trial, along with Mary Surrat, by a military tribunal, ordered by the newly inaugurated President Johnson. Surrat's boarding house had been the location of multiple meetings of the co-conspirators and she had delivered weapons to the conspirators the day of the execution. She was charged with abetting and aiding the co-conspirators and all were convicted and hanged, July 7, 1865. Surrat's son, John Surrat, a Confederate sympathizer, was in Canada at the time of the assassination. Eventually caught and brought to trial, he was not convicted.

Burial of President Lincoln

After Lincoln's death, his body lay in state in the White House for several days and was then opened to the public on April 18 to large crowds, prior to the funeral service the next day. His casket was moved with a formal procession to the Capitol Rotunda where again he lay in state on April 20 for public viewing before being delivered by hearse on April 21 to the nearby Baltimore & Ohio Railroad station. The coffin was carried by an honor guard to the Presidential railroad car now draped in black mourning cloth. The coffin holding the body of his young son Willie, who had died of typhoid three years earlier, traveled on the train with Lincoln. Both would be buried in Oak Ridge Cemetery in Springfield, Illinois.

The funeral train traveled over sixteen hundred miles on a circuitous route to carry it through seven states. Accompanying the burial detail were about three hundred passengers, which included Lincoln's son, Robert Todd Lincoln, for part of the trip, an

Honor Guard, numerous dignitaries and a funeral director who was also an embalmer. Lincoln's widow, Mary Todd Lincoln, was too distraught to travel and their youngest son Thomas (Tad) remained with his mother in Washington.

Stops were made in several principal cities and state capitals where crowds gathered to hear orations and participate in ceremonies dedicated to the late President. Public viewings took place in ten cities along the route to allow mourners to view their leader one last time. Advances in embalming during the Civil War had enabled thousands of families to return the dead soldiers home for burial and Lincoln's embalmer assured the family that there would be no change in his appearance by the end of the tour.

The animosity and anger that had filled so much of the nation the previous four years were no longer visible as thousands of mourners came to pay their respects. Each city arranged for memorial arches, catafalques and elaborate hearses to honor the deceased President. During a 20-hour public viewing in Philadelphia, one hundred fifty thousand people viewed his remains with the casket positioned near Liberty Bell. In New York City, a half-million people watched the massive procession of sixteen horses pulling an elaborate hearse to City Hall and over one hundred thousand passed by his casket for a last viewing of the President. In Chicago, a massive procession accompanied the coffin to Cook County Courthouse, where his body lay in state. Mourners lined up for more than a mile as thousands passed by his casket.

Never exceeding twenty miles per hour, the train was viewed along the route by millions of Americans. People thronged to the railroad tracks for miles to watch the train's passing. Men took off their hats and bowed their heads; others waved flowers or small flags. At night, bonfires were lit alongside the tracks as it moved west and crowds waited even through the darkness of night to watch the train as it passed through. The leader of the country had vowed to save the Union "*for the people*" and had paid with his own life for the cause.

After its 12-day trip from Washington, the train arrived at Springfield on May 3, 1865, to a throng of one hundred thousand mourners. Six horses pulled the funeral hearse to the state Capitol where the Honor Guard carried the coffin to the Representatives' Hall. Public viewing continued for twenty-four hours as 75,000 mourners moved through the hall. Following a lengthy service, attended by Lincoln's son Robert and numerous dignitaries, Lincoln's coffin along with his deceased son Willie were placed in a receiving vault until the Lincoln tomb could be constructed.

CONFEDERATE ARMIES SURRENDER

North Carolina Army of Tennessee Surrenders
April 15-26, 1865

In early April, the Union army of Gen. William T. Sherman was bivouacked in Goldsboro, North Carolina, after pursuing the Confederate Army of Tennessee,

VIII. THE FINAL BATTLES AND SURRENDER, 1865

commanded by Gen. Joseph E. Johnston, for the previous three months. Sherman's Carolinas Campaign had taken its toll on the smaller Confederate army, which was now situated at Greensboro, North Carolina, about one hundred thirty miles away. Sherman had expected to continue north to Petersburg, Virginia, to support Grant and the Army of the Potomac, but with the news of the surrender of Gen. Robert E. Lee at Appomattox on April 9, Sherman's orders were now changed. He would focus on the defeat of Gen. Joseph E. Johnston and the Confederate Army.

Gen Johnston received information on April 11 that Lee had surrendered to Union forces on April 9, dashing any hopes of the two armies joining forces. When Johnston met with Confederate President Jefferson Davis at Greensboro on April 12-13, he told Davis, *"Our people are tired of the war, feel themselves whipped, and will not fight. Our country is overrun, its military resources greatly diminished, while the enemy's military power and resources were never greater and may be increased to any extent desired… My small force is melting away like snow before the sun."* Johnston continued, *" … it would be the greatest of human crimes to continue the war."* Although Davis disagreed with Johnston that the Confederacy was defeated, he agreed to open communications with Gen. Sherman.

The Union Army departed Goldsboro on April 10 and moved to Raleigh, North Carolina, which was about half the distance to Greensboro where Gen. Johnston and the Confederates were located (See Fig. 67). On April 14, Sherman received a note from Gen. Johnston requesting a suspension of hostilities while appropriate arrangements for terminating the war could be determined. Sherman agreed to the meeting, but when Johnston received the reply, President Davis had already departed without informing him. An irritated Johnston arranged a meeting anyway, without Davis, for April 17 near Durham's Station, midway between Raleigh and Greensboro.

As Sherman boarded the train for Durham about thirty miles away on the morning of April 15, the telegraph operator ran to inform him that he should wait for an important message that was just now arriving. After holding the train for half an hour, Sherman received the message from Secretary of War Edwin Stanton that President Lincoln had been assassinated. With the potential danger that such news could have on both armies at this critical moment, Sherman ordered the operator not to convey the news to anyone *"… by word or look until I come back."*

Gen. Hugh Judson Kilpatrick provided cavalry escort for Gen. Sherman and his staff at Durham, where they met Gen. Johnston and his staff, also on horseback. The group traveled together to a farm where Sherman and Johnston were left alone in the small home of James Bennett. Sherman shared the recent dispatch with Johnston, the first person besides himself to learn of Lincoln's assassination.

Johnston was visibly distressed by the news and denounced the act as a *"disgrace to the age."* Assuring each other of their individual beliefs that the Confederate Army

> **FINAL TERMS OF SURRENDER FOR JOHNSTON'S ARMY SIGNED APRIL 26, 1865**
>
> All arms and public property would be deposited to the United States Army at Greensboro; rolls of all the officers and men would be made in duplicate; each officer and man would give his obligation not to take up arms against the Government of the United States; side-arms of officers, and their private horses and baggage would be retained by them; all officers and men would be permitted to return to their homes, not to be disturbed by the United States authorities so long as they observed their obligations and laws in force where they reside.
>
> W. T. Sherman, Major-General, Commanding,
United States Forces in North Carolina
J.E. Johnston, General, Commanding
Confederate States Forces in North Carolina
Approved: U.S. Grant, Lieutenant-General

had nothing to do with the dastardly deed, they discussed the potential effect of the assassination on the country at large and on the armies in particular. Johnston realized that Sherman was in a delicate situation, knowing that a foolish act or situation could madden the Union Army into acts of violence against Raleigh, the capital of North Carolina, that could potentially match the fate that befell Columbia in South Carolina.

Johnston agreed that his army would be unable to defeat the Union forces against him, but rather than surrendering "piecemeal," could they arrange terms that would embrace all the Confederate armies. Alternatively, the Confederates might melt into the hills and conduct guerrilla warfare for years. Each left the meeting with a general commitment to achieve a more encompassing surrender and they would meet again the next day.

Meeting at the same Bennett farmhouse on April 18 to determine specific details of the surrender, Johnston surprised Sherman by bringing along Confederate Secretary of War, Gen. John Breckinridge After lengthy discussions between the three men, Sherman wrote out general terms that he thought expressed the views he had heard from President Lincoln at City Point, but that they would be conditional upon approval from Washington. The armies would remain in status quo until the terms were approved. Copies were made and all parties signed the documents. The group parted company at dark and returned to their posts. Sherman dispatched the papers by fleet-steamer to Washington the morning of April 19. Their arrival set off a political firestorm.

Sherman's terms were far more generous than had been given to Lee upon his surrender, by granting greater civil and political liberties than had been conveyed to the

Army of Northern Virginia. President Johnson and his Cabinet unanimously rejected them and Gen. Ulysses S. Grant was ordered to proceed immediately to North Carolina and take charge of the situation. Grant arrived in Raleigh as quietly as possible and told Sherman "… *to notify Gen. Johnston that the terms which they had conditionally agreed upon had not been approved in Washington, and that he (Sherman) was authorized to offer the same terms Grant had given General Lee.*"

General Johnston Accepts Terms of Surrender
April 26, 1865

When Confederate President Davis learned of the terms of surrender, he ordered Gen. Johnston to disband his army and escape to the hills, but Johnston refused, and met with Sherman at the same Bennett farmhouse near Durham Station on April 26. Gen. Johnston accepted the new terms without hesitation, seventeen days after the surrender of Robert E. Lee at Appomattox. Paroled soldiers could retain their horses and other private property (excluding slaves) and the Union Army would assist them in providing transportation for the men to get to their homes. The surrender was the largest of the entire war, ending hostilities for approximately 90,000 Confederate soldiers in North and South Carolina, Georgia and Florida. Remaining Confederate armies would be surrendered by their commanding generals through the months of May and June.

After the surrender, Sherman issued rations to the hungry Southern soldiers and also ordered cornmeal and flour to be distributed to local civilians. The act of generosity prompted Johnston to write to Sherman in later years: "(This act) *reconciles me to what I have previously regarded as the misfortune of my life, that of having you to encounter in the field.*"

Sherman Attacked in the Press

The firestorm of Sherman's original terms sent to Washington became further inflamed when Secretary of War Stanton released internal documents to the *New York Times* that inferred Sherman had knowingly exceeded his authority in military matters and had paved the way for Confederate President Jefferson Davis to escape the country with loot from Richmond banks.

Upon seeing the published reports, Sherman regarded the bulletin "… *as a personal and official insult, which I afterward publicly resented.*" Writing a long message, which he demanded should also be made public, Sherman denounced Stanton's conduct as an officer of the government and conveyed his great disappointment at the lack of respect and trust for his years of dedicated service. The feud would be life-long. Sherman's letter:

"*I, who for four years have labored day and night, winter and summer, who have brought an army of seventy thousand men in magnificent condition across a country hitherto deemed impassable, and placed it just where it was wanted, on the day appointed, have brought discredit on our Government! I do not wish to boast of this, but I do say that it entitled me to the courtesy of being consulted, before publishing to the world a proposition rightfully submitted (in confidence) to higher authority for adjudication, and then accompanied by statements which invited the dogs of the press to be let loose upon me. It is true that non-combatants, men who sleep in comfort and security while we watch on the distant lines, are better able to judge than we poor soldiers who rarely see a newspaper, hardly hear from our families, or stop long enough to draw our pay. I envy not the task of 'reconstruction,' and am delighted that the Secretary of War has relieved me of it... I will execute my orders to their conclusion and, when done, will with intense satisfaction leave to the civil authorities the execution of the task of which they seem so jealous."*

Confederate President Jefferson Davis met with his Cabinet for the last time on May 4, authorizing belated compensation from funds remaining in the Southern treasury. Reuniting with his wife and children, the family pursued a path through Georgia, planning to escape to a sympathetic foreign nation such as Britain, France or Mexico. But the family was captured by Union cavalry officer Gen. James H. Wilson on May 10 near Irwinville, Georgia, along with Henry Wirz, who had commanded the infamous prisoner-of-war camp at Andersonville. Davis was imprisoned at Fortress Monroe for two years, until he was finally released on bail of $100,000 in May 1867. The government charged Davis with treason, but the trial was delayed until December 1868. When U.S. President Andrew Johnson granted amnesty to all persons involved in the rebellion on Christmas Day 1868, Davis became a free man. Wirz was convicted of war crimes and hanged November 10, 1865.

When Confederate President Jefferson Davis was captured, Sherman pointed out in his *Memoirs* that the contents of his baggage were well documented. *"I suppose the exact amount of treasure which Davis had with him is now known to a cent... at the time of his capture he had a small parcel of gold and silver coin, not to exceed $10,000, which is now retained in the United States Treasury... The 13 millions of treasure, with which Jeff Davis was to corrupt our armies and buy his escape, dwindled down to the contents of a hand-valise."*

Remaining Confederate Armies Surrender

At the same time that Confederate Gen. Robert E. Lee was about to surrender his army to Union Gen. Ulysses S. Grant, the city of Mobile, Alabama, was under attack by Union forces. Although Mobile Bay had been captured in January 1865, the city of Mobile was still defended by two Confederate-held forts: Spanish Fort and Fort Blakely. Union troops under Gen. Edward Canby, Army of West Mississippi, captured both on April 8-9 and the City of Mobile surrendered to Union hands April 12, 1865.

Confederate Gen. Richard Taylor, commanding the Department of Alabama, Mississippi and East Louisiana, and son of former U.S. President Zachary Taylor, surrendered about 10,000 men at Citronelle, Alabama, north of Mobile, to Union Gen. Canby, on May 4, 1865, on the same terms given to Lee at Appomattox and was paroled three days later.

One of the Union's legendary cavalry leaders, Gen. James H. Wilson, who had been detached from Sherman's March to the Sea to support Gen. George H. Thomas at the Battles of Franklin and Nashville in Tennessee, led a successful raid through Alabama and Georgia in March-April 1865. One of Wilson's notable successes was the defeat and destruction of Confederate Gen. Nathan Bedford Forrest and his famous cavalry at the Battle of Selma, Alabama, April 2, 1865, although Forrest escaped. Following the battle at Selma, several all-important Confederate centers of railroads, depots and war manufacturing centers in Alabama, at Tuscaloosa, Montgomery and West Point were also defeated in rapid succession. With news of Lee's surrender on April 9, Forrest surrendered a month later on May 9 at Gainesville, Alabama. In his farewell address to his men, he stated, *"That we are beaten is a self-evident fact, and any further resistance on our part would justly be regarded as the very height of folly and rashness....Obey the laws, preserve your honor, and the Government to which you have surrendered."*

Confederate Col. John Mosby, the "Gray Ghost" of the Shenandoah Valley, who commanded Mosby's Rangers, known for their ability to disappear into local farms and towns, chose not to surrender after Gen. Joseph E. Johnston's surrender in North Carolina. But Mosby did disband the Rangers on April 21, leaving each man to decide his own fate. Most of the officers and several hundred men, numbering about 400 Rangers, soon rode into Winchester, Virginia, to surrender. Mosby, himself, finally surrendered on June 17, 1865.

Confederate Gen. E. Kirby Smith, commander of the Trans-Mississippi Department, operating west of the Mississippi in Texas, Arkansas, Missouri, Louisiana and Indian Territory (now Oklahoma), planned to continue to fight for the Confederacy even though his small 20,000-man force was melting away. Traveling to Houston, Texas, to rally support for his troops in late May, the last of his army departments dissolved and Gen. Simon B. Buckner, acting in Smith's name, surrendered the army on May 26. Gen. Smith, with no army left to command, officially surrendered June 2 in Galveston, Texas.

Texas had accumulated a large number of slaves as the Civil War unfolded because slave owners had migrated there to keep their 'slave property' out of reach of the U.S. Army. Although the surrender of Gen. Robert E. Lee at Appomattox had occurred two months earlier, slavery remained intact in Texas as the state chose to ignore the growing number of Confederate leaders who had surrendered, including the Confederacy's President Jefferson Davis. But after Confederate Gen. E. Kirby Smith surrendered to U.S. forces at Galveston on June 2, 1864, Union Gen. Gordon Granger issued General Order No. 3 at Galveston on June 19, 1864:

> "The people of Texas are informed that in accordance with a proclamation of the Executive of the United States, all slaves are free. This involves an absolute equality of personal rights and rights of property between former masters and slaves, and the connection heretofore existing between them becomes that between employer and hired labor."

The date of June 19 became an annual holiday for Blacks in Texas as it marked for them the official end of slavery in the United States. Texas recognized the date as a state holiday in 1979 and a national movement to proclaim "Juneteenth" as a federal holiday eventually succeeded in 2021 under U.S. President Joseph Biden.

The chief of the Cherokee Nation in Indian Territory, who was also a Confederate General, Stand Watie, was unwilling to accept defeat and kept his troops active even after the surrender of E. Kirby Smith. Finally, on June 23, Watie surrendered at Doaksville, near Fort Towson in Indian Territory, the last Confederate general officer to surrender his command.

The final surrender of the Confederate Navy occurred in Liverpool, England, November 6, 1865, when the Confederate warship *CSS Shenandoah* was relinquished to the British Royal Navy and then turned over to the United States government. The ship was later sold to the Arab Sultan of Zanzibar who renamed it *El Majidi, the Magnificent*.

Thus ended four years of war that took the lives of an estimated 750,000 soldiers. The ten most costly battles of the Civil War, which included Gettysburg, Chickamauga, Spotsylvania, The Wilderness, Chancellorsville, Shiloh, Stones River, Antietam, Second Bull Run and Fredericksburg., totaled more than 280,000 casualties, about one-third of all the battles in the war.

FINAL REVIEW OF UNION ARMIES
WASHINGTON, D.C., MAY 23-24, 1865

Sherman's army began its final march north from Raleigh, North Carolina, to Washington, D.C., on April 30, and camped near Richmond on the James River May 9. With a grand review of the Union armies planned for May 23-24 in Washington, Sherman's army moved to Alexandria, near Washington, May 19-20.

The review began the morning of May 23 with the 80,000-man Army of the Potomac under Gen. George Meade. The march required over six hours to pass the reviewing stand, which included the President, his Cabinet, Gen. Ulysses S. Grant and several other dignitaries. The procession passed by thousands of people, crowds densely lining the sidewalks and streets, celebrating with gaiety and patriotic songs with the soldiers.

Sherman's two armies of 65,000, the Army of the Tennessee and Army of Georgia, began their march at 10 a.m. the next day on May 24 with Gen. Sherman leading, attended by his staff. For many in the crowd, it was their first sight of the Western

VIII. THE FINAL BATTLES AND SURRENDER, 1865

Army, which was accompanied at its end by a large crowd of freed Blacks, adventurers and others who had followed the army from Savannah. Following the marching men, a vast herd of cattle and other livestock that had been taken from the Carolina farms trailed the procession.

Sherman writes, *"The morning of the 24th was extremely beautiful. When I reached the Treasury building, and looked back, the sight was simply magnificent. The column was compact, and the glittering muskets looked like a solid mass of steel, moving with the regularity of a pendulum. All in all, the grand review was a splendid success, and was a fitting conclusion to the campaign and the war."*

Invited to join the dignitaries in the grandstand at the end of the parade, Sherman shook hands with President Andrew Johnson, Gen. Grant, and each member of the Cabinet, but publicly showed his resentment for the unfair treatment that had been inflicted on him by Secretary of War Stanton by refusing to take his extended hand.

President Andrew Johnson signed a Proclamation announcing the end of the American Civil War on August 20, 1866, declaring *"… that the said insurrection is at an end and that Peace, Order, Tranquility, and Civil Authority Now Exists in and Throughout the Whole of the United States of America."* Johnson issued a pardon on Christmas Day, 1868, to all persons who participated in the "rebellion." The Civil War was over.

VIEWS FROM THE PUBLIC FOR THE YEAR 1865

About Sherman's Carolinas Campaign…

During the Carolinas Campaign, foragers were sent out from Gen. William T. Sherman's Union army to collect food and forage for the marching soldiers and to also confiscate cotton and tobacco and burn it. But many of "Sherman's Bummers," took liberties and some wreaked vengeance on local citizens because they had *"caused the war."* When caught by Confederate Cavalry, a few of the bummers were summarily hanged with notes, *"Death to all foragers."* In response, Sherman threatened to shoot a rebel prisoner in his command for every forager the Confederates hanged, *"… a life for a life."* He acknowledged that *"occasions of misbehavior on the part of our men"* had no doubt occurred, but he would not *"consent to the enemy taking the lives of our men on their judgment."* There appears to be an extra space or paragraph separation here.

Sherman reminded his generals that any behavior by the soldiers beyond his original foraging orders was not permitted. *"I will not protect them when they enter dwellings and commit wanton waste, such as woman's apparel, jewelry, and such things as are not needed by our army. They may destroy cotton and tobacco, because these things are assumed by the rebel Government to belong to it, and are used as a valuable source of revenue."* But Sherman was strong in his belief that the determination of the people of the South to hold out against the North and dissolve the Union had forfeited the protections normally afforded civilians during times of war.

Atrocities by Sherman's soldiers did occur, as the following documented account from the diary of North Carolina resident Jane Evans Elliot reveals: *"This day two weeks since, 12 of March was a day of sorrow and confusion never to be forgotten. Sherman's army reached Fayetteville the day before, and at 9 o'clock Sunday morning, a party of raiders rushed in upon our peaceful home. They pillaged and plundered the whole day and quartered upon that night and staid [sic] until 5 o'clock Monday evening. Some part of the time there were at least three different parties. The house was rifled from garret to cellar. Took all our blankets and all [my husband's] clothes, all our silver and knives and forks, all our luxuries, leaving nothing but a little meat and corn. They threatened [my husband's] life repeatedly and one ruffian galloped up to the door and pulled out his matches to fire the house. Oh! it was terrible beyond description. It seems ever present to my mind. One night they strung fire all around us and we took up the children and dressed them and watched all night fearing the fire might consume our dwelling."*

About the Surrender of Richmond...

When Confederate President Jefferson Davis received a message from an orderly while attending Sunday morning church services April 2, 1864, that Gen. Lee could no longer defend Richmond, he immediately set in motion orders for the evacuation of the government. Officials set about destroying documents and ordered the burning of arsenals, powder magazines, cotton and tobacco stores and any other supplies that would be of value to the Northerners.

To prevent Union soldiers from discovering the supplies of whiskey which might lead to the same fate as Columbia, South Carolina, which was ransacked and burned, all the whiskey was to be destroyed. When citizens saw the kegs of whiskey being poured into the streets, they tried to capture it before it disappeared down the city drains, filling their hats and any containers they could find or seizing kegs before they were broken. Word of the evacuation was finally passed on to the residents at four in the afternoon as they saw the retreating army marching through the streets.

When military commanders attempted to burn stores of tobacco, cotton and foodstuffs before the Union could arrive, local residents suddenly became aware of the large reserves of provisions, shoes and clothing that had been hoarded. Speculators had bought up available goods from successful runs by blockaders, planning to make a huge profit when hostilities ceased. Discovery of the hidden supplies enraged the population in a city that had been starving for months, their children going barefoot and wearing rags for clothing. People were observed lugging hams, bags of coffee, flour and sugar from the commissary department. Soon, mobs formed to loot nearby shops and set indiscriminate fires. Even the liquor in the streets caught fire. The skeleton Confederate military was unable to control the mob and law and order vanished; chaos ruled.

VIII. THE FINAL BATTLES AND SURRENDER, 1865

Fires that had been set following government orders got out of control as wind and embers set more buildings on fire, including the Tredegar Iron Works where explosives were stored. Four Confederate ironclads were set on fire and their arsenals exploded with great force, shaking every building to its foundations. Reporter T. Morris Chester for the *Philadelphia Press* wrote, "*A south wind prevailed, and the flames spread with devastating effect. The offices of the newspapers, whose columns have charged with the foulest vituperation against our Government were on fire; two of them have been reduced to ashes, another one injured beyond repair, while the remaining are not much damaged.*" The reporter continued, "*Thousands of persons are gazing hourly with indignation upon the ruins… In short, Secession was burnt out, and the city purified as far as fire could accomplish it.*"

The South saw the fall of Richmond as its death knell. One Richmond resident, Mary Fontaine, wrote of the day the Union soldiers entered the city. "*I saw them unfurl a tiny flag (the Stars and Stripes), and I sank on my knees, and the bitter, bitter tears came in a torrent.*" As the white residents watched, they saw their world turned upside down as the city's former slaves flocked into the streets, dancing and shouting. One observer described the scene as "*… too awful to remember, if it were possible to be erased, but that cannot be.*" Some white citizens, however, who had been against secession, came forward to the Union troops with words of welcome.

Gen. Godfrey Weitzel's telegraph to Secretary of War Stanton, stated: "*We took Richmond at 8:15 this morning. I captured many guns. The enemy left in great haste. The city is on fire in one place. Am making every effort to put it out. The people receive us with enthusiastic expressions of joy.*"

The *New York Herald's* Richmond correspondent George Townsend, wrote, "*This town is the rebellion. It is all that we have directly striven for; quitting it, the Confederate leaders have quitted their sheet-anchor, their roof-tree, their abiding hope. Its history is the epitome of the whole contest, and to us, shivering our thunderbolts against it for more than four years, Richmond is still a mystery.*"

News of Richmond's surrender had been telegraphed across the United States. As the news reached Washington, streets became crowded with people, shouting, laughing, singing. Schools were dismissed, church bells rang, locomotives blew their whistles and army and navy batteries fired nearly continuously for hours. The end of the war was joyous news.

The lead story in the *New York Times* began with "THE GLORIOUS NEWS; *Rejoicings in City and Country; Enthusiasm, Solemnity and Thanksgiving; Business Suspended and Flags Displayed. The Praise of the Army on Every Tongue. Great Mass Meetings in Wall Street and at Union Square. Patriotic Speeches and Patriotic Songs. The Whole City Aglow with Excitement. It has been the boast of any Southern man, that come what might, Richmond was forever theirs; that no power this side of Heaven could take it. For* years this kind of talk has been made by the Southern people, and... our people have felt within them an irrepressible longing for its possession. At length it came, and, too, so suddenly, that the people were quite unprepared for it. It took the city several hours to accept the startling fact, to recognize its magnitude." But as the dispatches continued to flow in, *"The manifestations of exhilaration were boundless; flags were flung to the breeze from innumerable stores and dwellings."* All business stopped, people gathered in the streets, shouting with joy and *"... cheers were given in boundless delight."* But even before the newsboys could distribute the exciting news to the general public, word was out and people began to gather around in groups to share hearty cheers and excited expressions of joy and relief.

Black journalist Thomas Morris Chester, reporting for the *Philadelphia Press*, wrote: *"The people of Richmond, white and black, had been led to believe that when the Yankee army came, its mission was one of plunder. But the orderly manner in which the soldiers have acted has undeceived them. The excitement is great, but nothing could be more orderly and decorous than the united crowds of soldiers and citizens."*

A second entry by Chester continued as he described the need for food for the Richmond people. *"The Capitol building all day yesterday from the moment we took possession was surrounded by a crowd of hungry men and women clamoring for something to eat. The earnestness of their entreaties and looks showed that they were in a destitute condition. It was deemed necessary to station a special guard at the bottom of the steps to keep them from filling the building. These suffering people will probably be attended to in a day or so in that bountiful manner which has marked the advance of the Union armies."*

From Louisville, Kentucky, came the following dispatch on April 6, *"While few doubted the ultimate success of GRANT's combinations, the result was considered as indefinitely remote... the capture of the haughty and defiant capital, if not absolutely impossible, yet as a thing not to be achieved without long months of desperate strife and fearful sacrifice. The tidings 'Richmond is ours,' fell upon such as a bolt from a cloudless sky. But the Union joy was jubilant. It was a day of proud and blissful exhilaration for all staunch, loyal souls who had long been waiting and praying for this grand consummation."*

The Richmond correspondent for the *New York Times* reported that most of the city's newspapers had now disappeared. The *Richmond Dispatch* was completely burned up and its proprietors left the city. The *Enquirer* was also burned up and its owners were gone. The *Examiner* presses and machinery were destroyed and the type removed. No efforts were being made to revive it. The *Whig* building was still standing and would continue as a loyal paper with a new editor that was one of the strongest Union men in the state. The correspondent added, *"This is the present condition of those sheets and their pugnacious editors. The manufacturers of 'last ditch' opinions are (now) defunct institutions."* Noting that one of the former *Examiner* editors was seeking a passport

VIII. THE FINAL BATTLES AND SURRENDER, 1865

to leave the country, the correspondent wrote, *"He will thus do his country the only service of which he is capable."*

About Lincoln's tour of Richmond…

The Union cavalry entered the city on April 3, under the command of Gen. Godfrey Weitzel who accepted the surrender of the city from its mayor. Union troops spent the day putting out fires and were able to save the Capitol building. President Lincoln was invited to tour the city on the following day and would be attended by the Navy under Rear Admiral David D. Porter, who planned to enter Richmond's harbor on the James River with an escort of boats, each flying Union flags at every masthead, in a manner befitting the rank of the President. The flotilla included the warship *USS Malvern*, the President's flagship steamer, the *River Queen*, a small fast gunboat *USS Bat*, a barge and a tug boat that led the ships through a field of obstructions and potential mines in the river. But as the flotilla reached the outskirts of Richmond, a narrow part of the channel at Drewry's Bluff had been blocked by a small steamer that had run aground, preventing the larger ships to pass.

Transferring the Presidential group with sailors to the *USS Malvern's gig*, a twelve-oared rowboat, Porter ordered the tug boat, carrying a complement of Marines, to tow the group toward shore. But when the tug boat ran aground in the shallow waters, the group abandoned the tug boat and sailors paddled the rowboat and the Presidential party the final distance to the nearest landing. The great flotilla had been reduced to a single rowboat paddled by twelve sailors.

With this turn of events, President Lincoln made light of the occasion by telling a story. *"Admiral, this brings to mind a fellow who once came to me to ask for an appointment as minister abroad. Finding he could not get that, he came down to some more modest position. Finally, he asked to be a tide-waiter* (dockside customs inspector). *When he saw he could not get that, he asked me for an old pair of trousers. But 'tis well to be humble."*

Porter wrote, "I had never been to Richmond before by that route and did not know where the landing was…" and neither did any of his crew. Selecting the nearest landing that he could see, Porter put the party ashore at Rockettes Landing, two miles from Capitol Square, and in advance of the expected time of arrival. Describing the scene, Porter later wrote: *"The street along the river-front was as deserted as if this had been a city of the dead… not a soldier to be seen. There was a small house on this landing, and behind it were some twelve negroes digging with spades. The leader of them was an old man sixty years of age. He raised himself to an upright position as we landed and put his hands up to his eyes."* Recognizing the President immediately, he came forward and dropping to his knees, knelt in front of Lincoln, shouting, "Bless the Lord, the great Messiah. Glory, Hallelujah!" An embarrassed Lincoln told him, "Don't kneel to me. That is not right. You must kneel to God only, and thank Him for the liberty you will enjoy hereafter."

As the other Blacks came forward to express their amazement and wonder, soon the group was surrounded by more Blacks, former slaves who were shouting with joy as they crowded around Lincoln, touching him, calling him *"Father Abraham,"* the great emancipator who had freed them from slavery. As word spread, the crowd continued to grow precipitously and as the crowd crushed forward, Porter became anxious for the safety of the President. To force some space around the Presidential party, the twelve sailors acted as a cadre to surround the group, armed with carbines and fixed bayonets, six in front and six behind. Lincoln held up his hand to speak to the crowd, now encompassing hundreds of Blacks who were yelling and shouting with joy. When he started to speak, the crowd fell into total silence.

"You are free," he said, *"...free as air. You can cast off the name of slave and trample upon it... Liberty is your birthright... It is a sin that you have been deprived of it for so many years."* He then went on to say that it was now up to them to use the freedom that was now theirs, to do good works and to learn the laws and obey them. The group then slowly moved through the crowd toward Capitol Square, where they were soon shielded by a Union Cavalry escort that brought them to the Confederate White House and Gen. Weitzel's protection. After the two-mile walk in the dusty, smoke-filled streets, Lincoln gratefully sat down in a chair and asked for a glass of water, while the crowd outside grew to thousands. A Union officer's ambulance provided the Presidential party with a tour of the city, with crowds of Blacks surrounding the group, compelled to see for themselves the great Emancipator. Completing the tour, Gen. Weitzel delivered the group back to the Richmond docks and the waiting *USS Malvern* that had finally been able to pass through the cleared channel. Lincoln was transported back to City Point, where he remained for several days before returning to Washington on the *River Queen*.

About the Surrender of Lee at Appomattox...

When Confederate soldiers heard that the army of Robert E. Lee had surrendered to Ulysses S. Grant on April 9 and the fighting was over, one soldier described their reaction. *"I never expected to see men cry as they did. All the officers cried and most of the privates broke down and wept like little children and oh, Lord! I cried, too."*

The response of Union soldiers was, not surprisingly, one of unrepressed joy. A New Yorker in the 146th Regiment recalled, *"A general jubilee took place. Some of us gave expression to our feelings by running to an orchard nearby and throwing our canteens, haversacks, and coats into the trees, grabbing each other and rolling over and over on the ground; some laughed, some cried, all were overjoyed."*

The new Union editor of the *Richmond Whig* described Lee's surrender in an issue on April 10, as *"...no event of the war has been anticipated with more certainty that the surrender of the 'Army of Northern Virginia'... and the people, North and South, who have Urged for the restoration of Peace may now rejoice at the prospect and early fruition of their heart's desire. The surrender of General Lee and his army is paramount to an end of the Rebellion and the termination of the war."*

Cities throughout the North celebrated with grand processions, cannons firing and bells ringing with illuminations of buildings planned for the evenings. Boston declared the day a holiday. Both houses of the Legislature and the state's Supreme Court adjourned. Presentations were made at meetings in several locations, and a military and a civic procession was accompanied by fire trucks with steam whistles screaming. Chicago's stores, courts and public offices were mostly closed and business activities were entirely suspended as the city celebrated. A parade, over three miles long with fire trucks, promoted rejoicing and glad tidings with firing of two hundred guns during the day. Several public buildings and private homes were brilliantly illuminated that evening.

The *New York Times* wrote on April 10, "*The great struggle is over. Gen. ROBERT E. LEE and the Army of Northern Virginia surrendered yesterday to Lieut. Gen. U.S. GRANT and the Army of the Potomac. The thrilling word PEACE -- the glorious fact of PEACE -- are now once again to be realized by the American people. The history of blood -- the four years of war, are brought to a close. The fratricidal slaughter is all over. The gigantic battles have all been fought. The last man, we trust, has been slain. The last shot has been fired. We have achieved, too, that for which the war was begun -- that for which our soldiers have so long and grandly fought, and that for which so many thousands of brave men have laid down their lives. We have achieved the great triumph, and we get with it the glorious Union. We get with it our country -- a country now and forever rejoicing in Universal Freedom. The national courage and endurance have their full reward.*"

News of Lee's surrender at Appomattox was slow to reach the South with mail and telegraph lines interrupted and the loss of a primary source of information that the now-burned out Richmond newspapers had previously provided. But some newspapers urged their readers to accept defeat gracefully. A Special Dispatch to the *New York Times* on April 12 described the situation in Richmond as follows: "*All is quiet at Richmond. The city is very full of visitors, and presents a lively appearance. The Secessionists admit, without qualification, that they are now completely subjugated, and are already setting to work to let themselves down as gracefully as possible, and to escape, as far as they can, the consequences of their crime.*"

Lee, himself, after the war urged his fellow Southerners to accept defeat and serve the United States as loyal citizens, by saying, "*True patriotism sometimes requires of men to act exactly contrary, at one period, to that which it does at another, and the motive which impels them—the desire to do right—is precisely the same. The circumstances which govern their actions change; and their conduct must conform to the new order of things.*"

About the Assassination of Lincoln...

The assassination of President Lincoln struck the country like a hammer delivering a terrible blow. The Governor of New York spoke to the state assembly on April 15, saying, "*The fearful tragedy at Washington has converted an occasion of rejoicing over national victory into one of national mourning. Such an event is a national calamity, and under the circumstances now attending the bereavement, the nation weeps with heightened anguish. To be deprived of his wisdom, experience and counsel at a time when most important to return to the United States peace, fraternity and prosperity—at a time when the gigantic war which confronted him at the threshold of his Administration is about drawing to a close, and a final deliverance obtained from our civil disturbances for which we have sacrificed so much, is a calamity that will cause the deepest sorrow and gloom to the millions of our land, and to the friends of freedom throughout the world.*"

From the *New York Times*, April 16, 1865: "*The heart of this nation was stirred yesterday as it has never been stirred before. The news of the assassination of ABRAHAM LINCOLN carried with it a sensation of horror and of agony which no other event in our history has ever excited. In this city the demonstrations of grief and consternation were without a parallel. Business was suspended. Crowds of people thronged the streets—great gatherings sprung up spontaneously everywhere seeking to give expression, by speeches, resolutions, &c., &c., to the universal sense of dismay and indignation which pervaded the public mind. His love of his country ardent and all-pervading—swaying every act and prompting every word—his unsuspected uprightness and personal integrity—his plain, simple common sense, conspicuous in everything he did or said, commending itself irresistibly to the judgment and approval of the great body of the people, had won for him a solid and immovable hold upon the regard and confidence even of his political opponents. The whole people mourn his death with profound and sincere appreciation of his character and his worth.*"

The Washington *Morning Chronicle* reported on the search for the co-conspirators of the deadly event. "*The murderer of President LINCOLN was JOHN WILKES BOOTH. His hat was found in the private box, and identified by several persons who had seen him within the last two days, and the spur which he dropped by accident, after he jumped to the stage, was identified as one of those which he had obtained from the stable where he hired his horse. The person who assassinated Secretary SEWARD left behind him a slouched hat and an old rusty navy revolver. The chambers were broken loose from the barrel, as if done by striking. The loads were drawn from the chambers, one being but a rough piece of lead, and the other balls smaller than the chambers, wrapped in paper, as if to keep them from falling out.*"

As pursuit for the perpetrators fanned out through the Virginia countryside, the manhunt was unparalleled with more than a thousand Union soldiers in the search. A bounty of $100,000 was offered for the capture of Booth. Confederate sympathizers assisted Booth and his accomplice David Herold as they attempted to escape, but twelve days after the assassination, they were trapped in a tobacco barn near Port Royal, Virginia. Herold surrendered, but Booth refused and was shot by a Union soldier. Lewis Powell, who had attacked Secretary of State Seward, and George Atzerodt, who had been tasked with assassinating Vice-President Johnson, but who did not make the attempt, were both arrested in Maryland within days of Lincoln's assassination. Herold, Powell and Atzerodt, plus Mary Surrat were tried by a military tribunal and hanged July 7, 1865. Surrat owned the boarding house where the conspirators met and planned the assassination. Her son, John Surrat, a Confederate sympathizer, was in Canada at the time of the assassination. Brought to trial, he was not convicted as part of the assassination.

About Lincoln's Funeral and Burial...

During the pursuit of the perpetrators of Lincoln's assassination, plans proceeded for Lincoln's funeral and burial. Extensive arrangements would fill the country's thoughts and minds for twenty days, beginning with a funeral service in the White House East Room on April 19 and ending with his burial in Springfield, Illinois, on May 3. The funeral train traveled through seven states with viewings in several major cities and state capitals. City buildings were draped with thick black crape and people wore badges framing a small photograph of the president. Thousands lined up at every stop for a final viewing of the late President.

As the train passed through the country, arches were draped in black stretched over the tracks. The train's speed never exceeded twenty miles per hour and millions of people in rural America paid homage to the late President by waiting alongside the tracks. Officials of Richmond, Indiana, estimated the viewers at 15,000, larger than the city's population, as the train passed through at 3:15 a.m. in the morning. It was estimated that over seven million people viewed, visited, or participated in some way the passage of Lincoln to his final resting place. The New York City *Evening Post* summarized the feelings of the country: "*No loss has been comparable to his....Never in human history has there been so universal, so spontaneous, so profound an expression of a nation's bereavement.*"

Describing the loss, Winston A. Goodspeed, Salem, Indiana, Washington County, Indiana, historian wrote, "*News of the evacuation of Richmond, the flight of the Rebel Army and the surrender of Gen. Lee and the surrender of Gen. Johnston, all created in the county intense joy. People were overcome with the glorious news. Then came the dreadful news that President Lincoln had been assassinated. Revulsion by the public of this sickening act. Many a man and woman had learned to love the name of Abraham Lincoln. He had led them through four long years of darkness and death, had been the cloud by day and pillar of fire by night through all the starless gloom of war, and now when the national heart was surging with boundless joy, and every knee was bent and every eye filled in grateful thanksgiving, to have the beloved Lincoln cut down, was indeed bitter and hard to bear. Scores wept as if they had lost their nearest friend.*"

In the Upper South, newspapers such as the *Raleigh North Carolina Standard* and the *Richmond Whig* described Lincoln's assassination as the "*heaviest blow which has fallen on the people of the South."* The *Chattanooga Daily Rebel* was not kind as it declared that, *"Abe has gone to answer before the bar of God for the innocent blood which he has permitted to be shed, and his efforts to enslave a free people."* Confederacy President Jefferson Davis, when informed of the assassination, said, as he quoted Shakespeare: *"If it were to be done, it were better it were well done,"* but added, *"I fear it will be disastrous for our people."*

About the strength of the Church in the South…

The Confederacy had fervently declared that God was on its side, claiming that its search for a separate government was just and righteous. Sermons, orations and editorial opinions published in the Southern press were united in their declarations that they followed a holy cause. As husbands, sons and fathers went off to war, women were left to maintain the homes, care for the children, carry out the work needed to maintain the households and support their men in the Confederate Army. It was the women who filled the pews of their local churches, read their local newspapers and listened to public speeches that championed the Southern cause. The path of destruction left by Gen. Sherman's army through Georgia and the Carolinas strengthened their resolve to resist Northern aggression and left a bitterness in some Southern women that would be fostered and nurtured for generations.

But for the Blacks in the South, the freedom from slavery that had been achieved by the Civil War empowered them. They found in their churches and religion a center where they could focus on their shared sense of purpose in their culture, appreciation of family and their rightful place in American society. After emancipation, Southern churches became a source of inspiration and vision for Blacks about how to achieve the civil and political rights that freedom and citizenship offered. Black churches provided the support that channeled the energies of leaders in their congregations into roles in politics, civil rights and the arts. Churches fostered biracial coalitions and acted as leaders for creating a framework of cooperation between whites and Blacks.

IX. THE FREED BLACKS

With the end of the Civil War, the battles were over. Confederate armies had surrendered and the struggle to save the Union had been victorious. The country would remain one United States and not separate nations and slavery was abolished. But the fight for civil rights for the freed Blacks was just beginning.

Abolition of Slavery, the 13th Amendment, 1865

The 13th Amendment to the Constitution, which abolished slavery and involuntary servitude, except as punishment for a crime, was passed by the United States Senate on April 8, 1864, and by the House of Representatives on January 31, 1865. For the amendment to become law, it needed approval by three-fourths of the states, which was achieved on December 6, 1865, when Georgia approved it as the twenty-seventh state (from a total of thirty-six). By January 1866, five more states ratified the amendment. The last four to ratify were Texas (1870), Kentucky (1876), Delaware (1901) and Mississippi, which did not vote for ratification until March 16, 1995. State officials, however, failed to send formal documentation of the vote to the federal register until February 7, 2013.

Reconstruction and the Changes to Society

The cultural repercussions were profound with passage of the 13th Amendment. Freed Blacks now faced a deeply racist white Southern society that did not recognize Blacks as equals and resented the changes now thrust upon them. Further resistance to bringing Blacks into full citizenship and society came from the newly installed President Andrew Johnson. Southern states found a great ally in Johnson, a former slave holder, who had been inaugurated as President following the assassination of Lincoln. Johnson had been selected by the national convention in the 1864 election as Lincoln's running mate because his reputation as a War Democrat, who supported the Union in spite of belonging to a faction of the Democratic party, would appeal to Democrats as well as Republicans. Lincoln had chosen not to influence the national party's selection for his Vice-President. But Johnson's actions over the next two years following his ascension to the Presidency did much to create the foundations for the subjugation of Blacks in the South that would continue far beyond the end of the war.

Taking advantage of a Congressional recess in 1865 during the first eight months of his term as President, Johnson created his own policies for Reconstruction. He pardoned nearly all Southern whites, restored their political rights and returned their property to them. The Sea Islands south of Charleston, South Carolina, that had been broken up to allow former slaves to purchase forty-acre plots to farm, were returned to the former owners, forcing Blacks to become tenants or engage in contracting arrangements with their former masters.

A series of Johnson's Presidential proclamations implemented his philosophy that Southern states had never really left the Union and they should be allowed to set up their own civil governments with few constraints. Except for the requirement to abolish slavery and repudiate secession, the States were mostly granted a free hand to create their governments as they saw fit.

Before the Civil War, slave states had each developed their own rules about slavery and already had a large body of court decisions regarding how Blacks were to be treated in Southern society. States quickly developed "Black Codes" that dictated where and how former slaves could live and work and how much they would be paid. Laws were passed, for example, limiting the only occupation a Black could hold was farmer or a servant, unless they paid a tax. Mississippi imposed a tax on all Blacks, ages 18-60. If they could not pay it, which was frequently the case, they could be "hired out" to anyone who would pay the tax and the Blacks would be paid nothing for their labor.

Given that the 13th Amendment did permit labor as punishment for a crime, many Southern states enacted laws that defined "crimes," that were targeted at the freed Blacks. Local governments allowed authorities to arrest Blacks for infractions such as 'selling cotton after sunset,' and they could be forced into unpaid labor where they were treated as incarcerated prisoners.

First Civil Rights Act and the 14th Amendment 1866-68

With the end of the Civil War and ratification of the 13th Amendment in 1865, Black Codes had appeared in strength in the South to deny Blacks the same rights enjoyed by whites. Responding to the violations represented by the Black Codes, Congress passed the First Civil Rights Act in early 1866 to ensure that Blacks would receive the full rights of citizenship. But when the Act was presented to President Johnson for signature, he vetoed it on March 27, 1866. Two weeks later, his veto was overturned by a second Congressional vote on April 9, 1866, and the Civil Rights Act of 1866 became the first law to be enacted over a presidential veto.

The Act included several clauses in support of Blacks' rights: Citizenship, Privileges or Immunities, Due Process and Equal Protection. Citizenship specifically declared that all persons born in the United States were citizens "without distinction of race or color, or previous condition of slavery or involuntary servitude." With the new law, Blacks would enjoy the same rights held by all citizens. The law specified that these rights included the making and enforcing of contracts, to sue and give evidence in court, to acquire real and personal property and to benefit from laws that protect the security of person and property enjoyed by white citizens. The Act's broad definition of rights nullified the Dred Scott Decision of 1857 which had denied slaves citizenship and access to the courts and law. Blacks had the right to vote if they were male and twenty-one years of age.

The Due Process and Equal Protection Clauses required states and local governments to provide fair procedures and equal protection under the law when applying its state laws to any individual, including non-citizens. But abuses occurred. Bitterly contested by the Southern states, Black citizens were often denied fair treatment in the courts as Confederate war veterans frequently worked as policemen and judges, which helped to ensure that Blacks were subjected to discrimination and unfair treatment.

The Civil Rights Act of 1866 included authorization of a Freedmen's Bureau, designed to provide practical assistance and support for the freed Blacks during their transition from slavery to freedom. Gen. Oliver O. Howard, who had served under Gen. William T. Sherman during the Atlanta Campaign and the March to the Sea, was placed in charge of the Bureau. Howard, known as the "Christian General" because of his deep evangelical piety, did much to implement systems to protect the Blacks from unfair practices. An important advance established fixed pay scales for freed people working on former plantation lands. The Bureau also built hospitals and gave direct medical assistance to more than a million Blacks and issued more than twenty million rations to the impoverished former slaves.

But Howard's greatest accomplishment was in education. The Bureau built more than one thousand Black schools and established teacher-training institutions. Howard University, founded in 1867 through an act of Congress and named in his honor, was initially conceived as a theological seminary to educate Black ministers. But the enthusiastic interest for a higher-educational institution that welcomed Blacks, prompted an expansion of its mission to provide a curriculum in addition to ministry and Howard University remains a prominent higher-educational institution in downtown Washington, D.C., today.

Although Congress had overturned a presidential veto to enforce the Civil Rights Act into law, many members of Congress believed the Act should be solidified as the 14th Amendment to the Constitution. By June 1866, several legislative proposals, which included the Civil Rights Act, were combined into the 14th Amendment to the Constitution and submitted to the states for ratification. An important section officially nullified the "Three-Fifths Compromise" that had been part of the original Constitution which had allowed Southern Democrats to increase their representation in Congress by counting slaves as three-fifths of a person. With former slaves now counted as full persons, representation in Congress for the Southern states significantly increased. But Southern states vigorously resisted ratifying the Amendment because of the section defining civil rights for Blacks. In response, Congress required ratification of both the 13th and 14th Amendments as a condition for states to maintain their representation in Congress and the 14th Amendment was officially ratified on July 9, 1868.

Reconstruction Acts or Enforcement Acts, established by Congress in 1867, divided the South into five military districts that defined how new governments could be created. Ulysses S. Grant, elected as President in November 1868, supported the Reconstruction Acts and used them as tools to protect Blacks in the South from discrimination. Republicans in the South who supported Reconstruction included former Union soldiers, teachers, Freedmen's Bureau agents and businessmen. Southern Democrats derisively called them "Carpetbaggers," as many had recently arrived from the North, carrying their bags. The locally born white Republicans, non-slaveholders, mostly small farmers from the northern regions of the South that had supported the Union, were described by the Democrats as "Scalawags."

Johnson's conflicts with Congress continued to the end of his term and he was impeached in 1868 for violating the Tenure of Office Act when he fired Secretary of War Edwin Stanton without the consent of the Senate. Johnson was spared the humiliation of being removed from office during his last year of office by one vote in the Senate which required a two-thirds majority for conviction.

Voting Rights for Blacks, the 15th Amendment 1870

Although the 14th Amendment guaranteed Blacks citizenship, which included the right to vote, Southern states were still able to implement policies that prevented Blacks from voting. The 15th Amendment, ratified in March 1870, specifically declared that *voting rights of citizens could not be denied or abridged by the federal government or by any state based on race, color, or previous condition of servitude and granted Congress the power to enforce the amendment.*

Greeted with congratulations and widespread celebration, the Amendment promised a path forward for Blacks to enjoy the rights of full citizenship, which included voting rights. President Grant said that it *"completes the greatest civil change and constitutes the most important event that has occurred since the nation came to life."* For women suffragists, passage of the 15th Amendment was a painful blow as it retained the long-held policy that women, Black or white, could not vote. The right for women to vote would not occur until decades later with passage of the 19th Amendment in August 1920.

Despite the advances that had been achieved with the Amendments to the Constitution that specifically defined civil rights for Blacks, Southern states continued to implement "Jim Crow" laws, named after a Black minstrel show character, that used force, arrest, fines and jail sentences to deny equality and voting rights for the Black citizen. Poll taxes, literacy tests, fraud and intimidation were used to keep Blacks from the ballot box.

Many white Southerners responded to this transformation of their society with violence. The Ku Klux Klan organization, created in 1865 and widely spread by 1870, had as its primary goal the reestablishment of white supremacy through the use of intimidation and violence. Black leaders were targeted for brutal abuse by whites, beatings or even murder by lynching.

Enforcement Acts of 1870, 1871 and the Ku Klux Klan

Two bills, known as the Enforcement Acts, were passed by Congress in 1870 and 1871 and signed into law by President Ulysses S. Grant. They allowed the federal government to intervene with military force to protect the rights of citizens that had been granted in the 14th and 15th Amendments. The main goal of the Acts was to target the Ku Klux Klan (KKK) which advocated white supremacy and used violent methods to prevent Blacks from voting or serving in political office.

The Enforcement Act of 1871, also known as the Ku Klux Klan Act, empowered the President to use the federal army to uphold the rights of Black citizens and to bring charges against offenders who used election fraud, bribery or intimidation of voters to prevent them exercising their constitutional rights and to bring them to trial. Union troops in the Southern states enforced greater conformance to the laws. As a result, hundreds of KKK members were arrested and tried and by 1872, the KKK was all but eradicated. Unfortunately, the KKK would be revived in later decades after the turn of the century, attacking Blacks, Jews, Catholics and immigrants. Its legacy of white supremacy is still supported by small extremist groups today.

Under Grant's Presidency, enforcement of the 15th Amendment did much to overcome the Black Code and Jim Crow laws in the South. Historians have noted that during the Reconstruction Era that lasted until 1877, sixteen Blacks were voted to Congress and more than two thousand Black men were elected to state legislatures and local offices of sheriff and Justices of the Peace across the South.

Civil Rights Act of 1875

Drafted by Sen. Charles Sumner in 1870, who had been a staunch abolitionist, the Civil Rights Act of 1875 was passed and signed into law by President Ulysses S. Grant March 1, 1875, as a memorial to honor Sumner who had just died. The law attempted to provide equal treatment to all citizens in public transportation and accommodations and prohibit exclusion from jury service, but it was not effectively enforced and the Supreme Court struck it down as unconstitutional in 1883. The last major piece of legislation of the Reconstruction Era, elements of the Civil Rights Act of 1875 would be adopted eighty years later in the Civil Rights Acts of 1964 and 1968.

Election of 1876 and the End of Reconstruction

The Presidential election of 1876 brought forth a new administration and the end of Reconstruction for the South. In a disputed election about proper counting of votes, an Electoral Commission was composed to determine which votes would be counted. Through the "Compromise of 1877," an unwritten deal awarded the disputed results to Republican Rutherford B. Hayes in exchange for removing all federal troops from the South. By the time Hayes took office, all federal troops were gone from the South and Reconstruction came to an end. The South now had a free hand to use a variety of barriers to prevent Blacks from voting. With the removal of federal support that had been protecting Blacks from discrimination, Southern white supremacist racist attitudes flourished and white Democrats regained control.

By the 1880-1890s, Jim Crow laws had expanded and were in force throughout the South. The codes affected all aspects of Blacks' lives: how and where they could live or work, how much they would be paid, how they traveled, how they conducted themselves in society. Segregated water fountains, restrooms, building entrances, seating on public transportation, elevators, cemeteries, waiting rooms in bus and train stations are just some examples of how people of color were egregiously treated. Separation of the races was enforced in schools, hospitals, churches, asylums, jails, public parks and facilities, swimming pools, theaters and restaurants. Even children's school books were separated into different texts in some states. Lynching of Blacks became a frequently used technique for powerful whites and local mobs to control and intimidate Blacks to discourage them from voting or holding public office. Recent historical reviews have documented that more than 4,400 lynchings took place between 1877 and 1950, and nearly half were in the period of Reconstruction between 1865 to 1876. By 1905, Blacks had been effectively disenfranchised by Southern state legislatures.

Civil Rights Act of 1964

When President John F. Kennedy assumed the Presidency in 1960, he proposed legislation in June 1963 to address many of the existing Southern laws and policies that continued to discriminate against Blacks, but the proposal was opposed by filibuster in the Senate. After the assassination of President Kennedy in November 1963, Vice-President Lyndon B. Johnson, inaugurated as the new President, made passage of the Civil Rights Act of 1964 his top priority. Signed into law on July 2, 1964, the bill weathered stiff opposition from Southern Democrats, including a filibuster that occupied the Senate for more than sixty days. Sen. Robert Byrd from West Virginia spoke continuously for over fourteen consecutive hours to defeat it.

The Act included eleven sections that prohibit discrimination based on race, color, religion, sex, national origin, and later included sexual orientation and gender identity in the workplace, public accommodations, public facilities and agencies receiving federal funding. It also strengthened prohibitions against racial segregation in schools and discrimination in voter registration and employment. The law, described as the most significant civil rights legislation ever passed in American history, continues to be tested as white supremacist attitudes remain active in some parts of America.

America's Challenge

Lincoln's death created a great chasm for Blacks to achieve equality as racist attitudes strengthened and spread after Reconstruction efforts were withdrawn. The Civil War, fought more than a century and a half ago, debated two issues. The first, can a democracy designed by the country's founders survive; and second, can its founding principle of equality for all its citizens be achieved.

With the conclusion of the Civil War, the concept of a democratic Republic controlled by the people had withstood the test. Before 1861, the country was a collection of states, describing itself as "The United States." After the war, it was a single entity, "United States of America," borne from blood, death, hunger, disease and suffering. But many challenges remained. The country had to rebuild and restore the South, badly damaged by battles and a significant loss of its men. Northern and Southern soldiers alike attempted to regain their spirits and bodies after the ordeals of war. A Southern economy without slave labor had to be reinvented. Political systems needed to be revised that would allow Blacks to enter society as full citizens with jobs, families and self-respect, while they faced racist attitudes of bitterness and violence. The country's Armed Forces remained segregated until Executive Order 9981, signed by Harry S. Truman on July 26, 1948, abolished discrimination in the armed services "on the basis of race, color, religion or national origin."

As for the second question, equality for Blacks remains a challenge to this day. The nation has failed to step forward as a country that lives up to its national promise of freedom for all. Racist attitudes of white supremacy still survive in some areas of the country that intimidate, bully and threaten Blacks. Some states continue to implement laws and policies that make it difficult for people of color to vote. The Civil War preserved the Union, free of slavery, but it is up to its citizens to live up to the promise of equality for all. That legacy is a continual reminder to all Americans that its Declaration of Independence declared to the world that *"all men are created equal."* There still remains much to be done to fulfill America's promise to itself.

APPENDIX A.

COMMANDERS FOR THE UNION
LIST OF UNION GENERALS

Anderson, Robert
Averell, William
Banks, Nathaniel P.
Blair, Francis (Frank)
Buell, Don Carlos
Buford, John
Burnside, Ambrose
Butler, Benjamin
Canby, Edward
Chamberlain, Joshua
Crook, George
Curtis, Samuel R.
Custer, George A.
Davies, Henry E.
Davis, Jefferson C.
Dodge, Grenville M.
Franklin, William B.
Fremont, John C.
Gillmore, Quincy A.
Grant, Ulysses S.
Grierson, Benjamin
Halleck, Henry
Hancock, Winfield S.
Hazen, William B.
Hooker, Joseph
Howard, Oliver O.
Hunter, David
Ingalls, Rufus
Kautz, August
Kilpatrick, Hugh Judson
Kimball, Nathan
Ledlie, James H.
Lyon, Nathaniel
McClellan, George B.
McClernand, John A.
McCook, Edward M.
McDowell, Irvin
McPherson, James B.
Meade, George
Merritt, Wesley

Nelson, William "Bull"
Ord, Edward
Osterhaus, Peter Joseph (P.J.)
Parker, Ely S.
Pope, John
Porter, Fitz John
Ricketts, James B.
Rosecrans, William
Schofield, John M.
Scott, Winfield
Sedgwick, John
Sheridan, Philip
Sherman, William T.
Shields, James
Sigel, Franz
Slocum, Henry W.
Smith, Andrew Jackson (A.J.)
Smith, William F. "Baldy"
Smith, William Sooy
Steedman, James
Steele, Frederick
Stoneman, George
Sumner, Edwin "Bull"
Terrill, William
Terry, Alfred
Thomas, George H.
Wallace, Lew
Warren, Gouverneur K.
Weitzel, Godfrey
Williams, Alpheus S.
Wilson, James H.
Wright, Horatio

NAVAL OFFICERS
Farragut, David G.
Foote, Andrew
Porter, David D.

AERONAUT: Lowe, Thaddeus

COMMANDERS FOR THE UNION
Commander-in-Chief, Abraham Lincoln

Lincoln, Abraham (1809-1865). Born in Kentucky in 1809, his father moved the family of four to southwestern Indiana when he was seven years old, where the family struggled to survive at a poverty level on the edge of the frontier. At age nine, Lincoln's mother died and his father soon brought home a stepmother, Sarah Bush Johnston, a widow who added three children of her own to the family. Greatly encouraged by Sarah to learn how to read, Lincoln managed to teach himself mathematics and to read and write even though he had little schooling and needed to work all through childhood to help support the family. When he was twenty-one, the family moved again to Illinois and as a young man, six feet-four inches tall and physically powerful, Lincoln earned wages working at odd jobs and as a rail-splitter for building fences. He also floated to New Orleans on the Mississippi River working on a flatboat loaded with produce, and then walked back to his home. Studying law, he passed the bar exam in 1836 and moved to Springfield, Illinois, the new state capital, where he built a successful law practice. Marrying Mary Todd in 1842, who came from a distinguished Kentucky family, the couple had four sons, only one of which, the eldest, reached adulthood. Elected to Congress as a Whig in 1847-49 for a single term, he returned to his law practice until passage of the Kansas-Nebraska Act in 1854 which he disputed. He joined the new Republican Party in 1856 and actively engaged in opposing the Act's proposal that allowed territories to determine by popular vote the status of their states as free or slave. His skillfully delivered debates against the Act with Stephen Douglas in 1858 as they competed for the Illinois Senate were widely attended by the public and brought him to the national stage. Lincoln had the debates published as a book and used them in his campaign for the 1860 Presidential election, which he won. When inaugurated as President in March 1861, seven states had already seceded from the Union and formed the Confederate States of America. His first crisis was an attempt to rescue Union soldiers from Fort Sumter, located in the heart of the Deep South in Charleston Harbor, South Carolina, that was being threatened by the seven seceded states. When the Confederacy fired on Fort Sumter in April, the shots initiated the American Civil War. Without military experience of his own, Lincoln relied on his generals, but was constantly disappointed with their results. In frustration, he served as General-in-Chief himself of all Union armies for a period of a few months in 1862 before promoting Henry Halleck to the position. After Ulysses S. Grant captured Vicksburg in 1863, Lincoln had found his man and Grant was named General-in-Chief in March

1864, replacing Halleck. The battles in the Eastern Theater under Grant and the Atlanta Campaign under William T. Sherman, plus the successful raid by Philip Sheridan in the Shenandoah Valley, all in 1864, secured Lincoln's re-election to the Presidency that November. When the famous Confederate commander Robert E. Lee surrendered at Appomattox in April 1865, the Civil War was quickly brought to its final completion. Lincoln's assassination by actor and Confederate sympathizer John Wilkes Booth occurred six days later on April 15, 1865

UNION GENERALS

Generals-in-Chief during the course of the Civil War.

Winfield Scott, July 5, 1841-Nov. 1, 1861

George B. McClelland, Nov. 1, 1861-March 11, 1862

Vacant, March 11, 1862-July 23, 1862

Henry Halleck, July 23, 1862-March 9, 1864

Ulysses S. Grant, March 9, 1864-March 4, 1869

Anderson, Robert (1805-1871). Graduated from West Point Military Academy in 1825 he served in the Mexican-American War during the battles to Mexico City and was severely wounded in the Battle of Molino del Rey. Promoted to Major in 1857, he was commander at Fort Sumter when the first shots of the Civil War were fired by Confederate P.G.T. Beauregard, his former student at West Point. After surrendering Fort Sumter to Beauregard, the Union troops were released to the North and Anderson became a national hero and used the 33-star flag that he carried from the fort as a rallying symbol to conduct a highly effective recruiting tour for the war. He remained with the army in spite of being a former slave owner from his native state of Kentucky and was promoted to brigadier general for his actions at Fort Sumter. He officially retired from the Army in 1863 for health reasons, but after the surrender of Robert E. Lee and the Army of Northern Virginia at Appomattox, Anderson returned to Charleston in uniform to raise the U.S. flag over Fort Sumter on April 14, 1865, only hours before the assassination of President Lincoln. The Confederacy soon surrendered the rest of its armies ending the Civil War.

Averell, William (1832-1900). Graduated from West Point Military Academy in 1855, he was commissioned to the U.S. Army Mounted Rifles that fought in Missouri and New Mexico. At the onset of the Civil War, he participated in the battles of First Bull Run and the Peninsula Campaign and led the Cavalry Brigade at the Battle of Fredericksburg. But he lost his command after the failed cavalry raid at the Battle of Chancellorsville and was moved to the Department of West Virginia. Averell won a major victory in the Shenandoah Valley, capturing Confederate

John McCausland in 1864, who had burned down the village of Chambersburg, Pennsylvania. He then served under Philip Sheridan in the Valley campaigns of 1864. After resigning from the army in 1865, Averell served under Presidents Andrew Johnson and Grover Cleveland and wrote a number of memoirs about the war.

Banks, Nathaniel P. (1816-1894). Raised in Massachusetts, he worked in a textile mill near Boston as a teenager to help support his family. He educated himself by walking to the Boston library and became a successful speaker, well known in political circles. Elected to Congress in 1852 on a Democratic ticket, he eventually joined the Whig Party for its abolitionist positions and he voted against the Kansas-Nebraska Act in 1854. Elected as governor of Massachusetts in 1858, he made a serious attempt to win the Republican Presidential nomination in 1860, but the state delegation rejected his bid. Nevertheless, he received first-ballot votes as a nominee for Vice President, which brought him to the attention of Abraham Lincoln, who considered him for a seat on his Cabinet. With the outbreak of the Civil War, Lincoln selected Banks as one of the first politically appointed generals to have seniority over West Point graduates. An active politician who was adept in Congress and as governor of Massachusetts, Banks was not so successful as an army general. Defeated in the Shenandoah Valley by Stonewall Jackson, Lincoln transferred Banks to command the Army of the Gulf in New Orleans and asked him to organize a recruitment effort in New York and Massachusetts, which he successfully accomplished. Banks and his new large force sailed to New Orleans and Banks replaced Benjamin Butler as commander of the Department of the Gulf. But his poorly managed Siege of Port Hudson was only successful after Ulysses S. Grant took Vicksburg. The disastrous failure of the Red River Campaign in Louisiana brought an end to his military career and he was soon removed as commander of the Army of the Gulf by Edward Canby. But before leaving the army, Banks oversaw the development of Louisiana's new constitution that President Lincoln used as a model for the seceded states returning to the Union after the conclusion of the Civil War. Resigning from the army in 1865 to return to Massachusetts, Banks ran for political office and was elected to the U.S. Congress, serving for several terms between 1865 and 1873.

Blair, Francis (Frank) (1821-1875). Born in Kentucky from a distinguished Scotch Irish background, he joined his brother's law practice in St. Louis in 1842 after he graduated from Princeton University. He became heavily involved in Missouri politics and was elected to Congress in both the House and the Senate. He and his brother, Montgomery Blair, supported Lincoln's presidential campaign in 1860 and Montgomery was named Lincoln's Postmaster-General during the Civil War. Frank remained in Missouri, actively organizing efforts to prevent the state from being absorbed into the Confederacy by equipping a force of several thousand in the Missouri Militia. He was instrumental in appointing Nathaniel Lyon as the new military commander in the Western Theater and assisted Lyon in the transfer of arms from the U.S. Arsenal at St. Louis to Alton, Illinois. Frank Blair was appointed a general in the U.S. Army in 1862 and commanded the XVII Corps under William T. Sherman in the Atlanta Campaign and then in the final campaigns of Georgia and the Carolinas until the surrender of the Confederacy.

Buell, Don Carlos (1818-1898). Graduated from West Point Military Academy in 1841, he served in the Mexican-American War and then as military adjutant in California. At the onset of the Civil War, he supported George McClellan in the formation of the Army of the Potomac and was then posted to command the Army of the Ohio. After the fall of Forts Henry and Donelson, Buell's army captured Nashville and brought reinforcements to Ulysses S. Grant at the Battle of Shiloh. Ordered to move east and capture Chattanooga, his slow progress on the long march to Tennessee was aborted by a Confederate invasion into Kentucky. He was defeated by Confederate Braxton Bragg at Perryville, Kentucky, and Buell lost his command, to be replaced by William Rosecrans. No future assignments were offered to Buell until Grant as the General-in-Chief in 1864 offered him a post under William T. Sherman or George Thomas. Buell refused as he outranked both of them. His refusal prompted Grant to write, *"one of the worst excuses a soldier can make for declining service."* Buell resigned from the army in June 1864.

Buford, John (1826-1863). Graduated from West Point Military Academy in 1848, he was assigned to the 1st U.S. Dragoons. Serving on frontier duty in Texas and Utah, he received news of the firing on Fort Sumter through the Pony Express. Torn by loyalties to his home state of Kentucky and a slave-holding father, he joined the Union Army despite pressure from his relatives fighting for the South, who called him a traitor. He led a cavalry charge in the Battle of Second Bull Run and fought in the Battle of Antietam. Leading the forward cavalry at Gettysburg, he is credited with securing the Union position on high ground just ahead of a large Confederate advance that provided enough of an advantage for Union reinforcements to arrive, an advantage that ultimately gave victory to the North. Falling ill in the months afterward, he died in December 1863.

Burnside, Ambrose (1824-1881). Graduated from West Point Military Academy in 1847 in the middle of his class, he was too late to participate in the battles of the Mexican-American War. But he served in garrison duty around Mexico City after its surrender to the United States. After the war, he was transferred to western duties protecting western mail routes through Nevada to California under the command of Captain Braxton Bragg, who would become a future Confederate general. Transferred to Rhode Island in 1852, Burnside resigned from the regular army in 1853 and in private life invented the Burnside Carbine. The U.S.

Army, under President Buchanan, contracted to purchase a large number of the rifles, but when Burnside's factory was destroyed by fire, the major financial loss forced him to sell his patents. Finding employment west, he worked for the Illinois Central Railroad, where he became friendly with George B. McClellan who would later lead the Army of the Potomac for the Union. Burnside also became friends with the railroad's corporate attorney Abraham Lincoln during this period and their friendship continued through the years of the Civil War. At the onset of the war, Burnside raised the 1st Rhode Island Volunteer Regiment and was appointed its colonel with two companies armed with Burnside Carbines. His 90-day recruits participated in the Battle of First Bull Run and Burnside then commanded the Coast Division of North Carolina's Expeditionary Force. Working with the Navy's North Atlantic Blockading Squadron, the group closed most of North Carolina's seacoast to the Confederates for the rest of the war. Assigned to the Army of the Potomac under McClellan, Burnside led a Corps at the Battle of Antietam, but his poor reconnaissance and leadership contributed to the delay in crossing "Burnside's Bridge," which was ultimately claimed by the Confederates. When Lincoln placed Burnside in command of the Army of the Potomac, after removing McClellan from the post, Burnside led the Army of the Potomac in two disastrous battles at Fredericksburg and the Mud March. When Burnside blamed the disasters on his senior commanders, army morale became so toxic that Lincoln replaced him with Joseph Hooker to lead the army and sent Burnside west to command the Department of the Ohio. Burnside led the Knoxville Campaign in 1863, occupied the city unopposed, and then captured the Cumberland Gap from the Confederates. His occupation of Knoxville helped to defeat Braxton Bragg's army, which was holding Union forces under siege at Chattanooga. Ordered to participate in the Overland Campaign under Generals Ulysses S. Grant and George Meade, Burnside's IX Corps participated in most of the battles, which ended with the Siege of Petersburg. But Burnside's failure to supervise his troops at the explosion of The Crater resulted in massive casualties, including over one thousand Blacks in the U.S. Colored Troops (USCT), many of whom were murdered by Confederates as soon as they surrendered. The fiasco ended Burnside's military career. Removed from command, he was not returned to active duty and soon resigned. Returning to Rhode Island, he served as governor 1866-69 and was then elected to the U.S. Senate 1874-81. He died suddenly while in office in 1881.

Butler, Benjamin (1818-1893). A controversial political figure from Massachusetts, Butler had developed a successful practice as a trial lawyer and served as an officer in the state militia for a number of years, which promoted him to brigadier general in 1855, even though he had no military training. With the onset of the Civil War, he accompanied two regiments from the Massachusetts Militia to Baltimore in April and occupied the Annapolis Naval Academy. The 8th Massachusetts was one of the first regiments to reach Washington, D.C., to protect the capital in case Maryland seceded from the Union. At the same time, two regiments under Butler's command were sent to secure Fort Monroe at the entrance of the James River on the Virginia Peninsula, which was the only federal military installation in the Upper South that was not seized by the Confederates. Lincoln appointed Butler as a major general in the Union Volunteers in May and he was assigned to command the Department of Virginia at Fort Monroe. Butler initiated a policy of treating escaped slaves as contraband and refused to return them to their owners, claiming that the Fugitive Slave Act was no longer valid in the seceded states. The policy was soon adapted by all the Union armies and escaped Black slaves began to flood into Union camps. Butler created "Freedom's Fortress," at Fort Monroe which became a refuge to house escaping Blacks and their families. After the Union captured New Orleans, Butler was named its first governor of occupation. Resenting the presence of Union soldiers, the city's population reacted in a number of hostile and provocative actions that prompted Butler to authorize several controversial and unpopular acts that earned him the name "Beast Butler." Lincoln responded by replacing Butler with Nathaniel P. Banks to head the Army of the Gulf and Butler was sent to Bermuda Hundred as commander of the Army of the James. But Butler's ineffective leadership as a general kept him bottled up at Bermuda Hundred for most of the war. When given command to take Fort Fisher at Wilmington, North Carolina, his mismanagement of the attack ended his military career. He returned to Massachusetts and again became politically active and was elected governor in 1882 after several campaigns. He was a presidential candidate in 1884.

Canby, Edward (1817-1873). Graduated from West Point Military Academy in 1839, he was commissioned into the 2nd U.S. Infantry and served in Florida and the Mexican-American War, earning promotions for the battles that captured Mexico City. After the war, he worked for the army in a variety of posts, which included sorting through the California Archives during the Gold Rush between 1849 and 1851, using his knowledge of Spanish to unravel land titles. Serving in New Mexico Territory at the onset of the Civil War, he commanded Fort Defiance in Navajo Territory in Arizona and later the Department of New Mexico. Successfully convincing the governors of both New Mexico and Colorado Territories to supplement his regular Union troops with forces from their territories, Canby defeated the Confederates at the Battle of Glorieta Pass near Santa Fe in March 1862, which forced the Confederacy to abandon its plans to take over New Mexico Territory. Reassigned to the Eastern Theater, Canby was placed in New York City in July 1863 after the New York Draft riots and then worked in the office of the Secretary of War. Named to suspend Nathaniel P. Banks as head of the Army of the Gulf after the failed Red River Campaign, Canby successfully commanded Union forces to defeat Confederates at Mobile, Alabama, in the spring of 1865. After the surrender of Confederate armies in the Eastern Theater in April, he accepted the surrender of forces under Richard Taylor in the Trans-Mississippi Theater on May 4 and those under E. Kirby Smith on May 26, 1865. A great administrator, he was frequently questioned about army regulations or Constitutional law affecting the military, particularly after the war ended. A colleague described him as a thoughtful man who conducted his work quietly, speaking little and to the point.

Chamberlain, Joshua (1828-1914). Professor of languages at Bowdoin College, Maine, he enlisted in the Union Army in 1862 and was appointed lieutenant colonel of the 20th Maine Regiment in the Army of the Potomac in August. The studious Chamberlain studied *"every military work I could find"* as he prepared for his new role in life, scholar-turned-soldier. His unit fought in the Battle of Fredericksburg, but missed the Battle of Chancellorsville because of a smallpox outbreak. Promoted to colonel in 1863 as commander of the 20th Maine, the Regiment arrived at Gettysburg and was placed at the extreme left of the Union line along Missionary Ridge. Chamberlain achieved lasting fame for extraordinary bravery when the unit saved the Union flank at Little Round Top. After Gettysburg, he was given command of a brigade in the Fifth Corps of the Army of the Potomac, a position he retained until the end of the war. Wounded in 1864 at the Second Battle of Petersburg, he recovered in time to play a pivotal role in the Appomattox Campaign and was given the honor of accepting the surrender of arms of the Confederates at Appomattox Court House, April 12,1865. His memoir of the Appomattox Campaign, *The Passing of the Armies*, was published in 1915, one year after his death.

Crook, George (1828-1890). Graduated from West Point Military Academy in 1852 near the bottom of his class, he was posted to California and Oregon Territory, alternately protecting or fighting against several American Indian tribes. He developed friendships with a number of Indians whose languages he learned, and in the process acquired special wilderness skills that gave him a better understanding of how to select battlefield positions in the Civil War. At the beginning of the war, he was assigned to the 36th Ohio Infantry and led troops in the Battle of Antietam. He then led a cavalry division for the Army of the Cumberland at the Battle of Chickamauga. Given command of the Department of Western Virginia, he led several battles in the Shenandoah Valley, including the Second Battle of Kernstown, Third Winchester, Fisher's Hill and Cedar Creek. It was at Kernstown that the Confederate general Jubal Early drove him out of the Valley, which prompted Ulysses S. Grant to place Philip Sheridan in charge of all Union forces in the Shenandoah and defeat Early's command in the valley. Crook was later assigned a cavalry division in the Army of the Potomac in 1865 during the Appomattox Campaign and played an important role in the final battles that led to Lee's surrender of the Army of Northern Virginia.

APPENDIX A.

Curtis, Samuel R. (1805-1866). After graduating from West Point Military Academy in 1831 near the bottom of his class, he soon resigned his commission in the army and became a lawyer. Rejoining the U.S. Army to serve in the Mexican-American War, Curtis left the army again and became a successful politician in Iowa. Elected to the U.S. House of Representatives between 1858 and 1860, he left Congress to join the Union Army at the onset of the Civil War and was soon commander of the District of Southwest Missouri in December 1861. He led the army to win the battle for the Union at Pea Ridge, Arkansas, in 1862 and then captured Helena, Arkansas, later that year. In 1863, he was reassigned to command the Department of Kansas and Indian Territory. His final major battle occurred in 1864 when he defeated Sterling Price at Westport, Kansas, near Kansas City in October 1864, ending the last major Confederate offensive west of the Mississippi River, establishing Union control of Missouri for the rest of the war.

Custer, George. (1839-1876). Graduated from West Point Military Academy in 1861 at the bottom of his class, he would have been commissioned under normal conditions to an obscure position. But with the onset of the Civil War, the Union Army had a sudden need for junior officers. Assigned to the 2nd U.S. Cavalry Regiment, he was with his regiment at the Battle of First Bull Run and served under George McClellan as aide-de-camp in the Peninsula Campaign. At the Battle of Gettysburg, the new commander of the Army of the Potomac, George Meade, promoted him to brigadier general to lead the Michigan Cavalry Brigade (the "Wolverines"). Custer mounted a cavalry charge that defeated Confederate Jeb Stuart's cavalry in a surprising ending on the final day of the battle. In 1864, Custer served under Philip Sheridan, first in the Shenandoah Valley in the defeat of Jubal Early and then in Virginia as the cavalry pursued Confederates fleeing Petersburg in 1865 in the Appomattox Campaign. Custer's cavalry captured trains at Appomattox containing valuable rations intended for the Confederates and blocked the Army of Northern Virginia's final retreat. After the war, Custer fought in the Indian Wars and met his death at the Battle of Little Bighorn in 1876, which became well known as "Custer's Last Stand," against the Plains American Indians in the Black Hills of South Dakota.

Davies, Henry E. (1836-1894). Son of a New York City judge, he was educated at Harvard, Williams and Columbia Colleges and admitted to the bar in 1857. With the onset of the Civil War, he was named captain of the 5th New York Volunteers and was soon appointed major of the 2nd New York Cavalry Regiment. Promoted to general, he led a cavalry brigade in a number of battles with the Army of the Potomac, including the Battle of Trevilian Station under Philip Sheridan during the Overland Campaign. His troopers captured a Southern supply train and hundreds of prisoners during the Confederate retreat from Petersburg in the Appomattox Campaign, which ended with the surrender of Robert E. Lee's army at Appomattox Court House. One of the few generals who was not professionally trained in the military, Davies' command was described "...as fine a body of cavalry for their size as could be found in the service."

Davis, Jefferson C. (1828-1879) (no relation to Confederate President Davis). Enlisting as a 19-year-old private in 1847 to serve in the U.S. Army during the Mexican-American War, he distinguished himself in several battles and was promoted to second lieutenant in the 1st U.S. Artillery. At the onset of the Civil War, Davis was an officer at Fort Sumter under Robert Anderson when it came under fire from the Confederates. After the Union troops surrendered, they were allowed to return to Union lines and Davis was transferred to northwest Missouri under Samuel Curtis and led a division during the Battle of Pea Ridge in 1862. Granted medical leave in the summer of 1862, he returned to duty in August to provide support in Louisville against the Confederate invasion of Kentucky. Because he was not a graduate of West Point, he was a frequent a target of insults from fellow officers but he was promoted up through the ranks and was well-known for his testy, ready temper if he felt offended. Outraged by a public verbal tongue-lashing from William "Bull" Nelson in Louisville, Davis fired a pistol into Nelson's chest, killing him when Nelson refused to apologize. Although briefly arrested for slaying the unarmed Nelson, he was released and returned to duty. Davis was never brought to trial or suffered any significant confinement. He served under William T. Sherman in the Western Theater during the Atlanta Campaign, heading one of the Army Corps in the March to the Sea and the Carolinas Campaign. His actions at Ebenezer Creek during the March to the Sea clouded his military legacy when he removed a pontoon bridge before former Black slaves could safely cross the creek to the opposite shore. Hundreds were captured or killed by pursuing Confederates or drowned in the creek, but Davis was never charged for the incident. He remained with Sherman until the end of the Civil War and was present for the surrender of Confederate General Joseph E. Johnston in North Carolina, April 26, 1865. After war's end, Davis continued to serve in the army until his death in 1879 but he failed to receive any promotions beyond his last rank in the Civil War, which he attributed to his shooting and killing of Nelson.

Dodge, Grenville M. (1831-1916). Graduated with a degree in civil engineering from Norwich University in Vermont in 1851, he then worked as a surveyor and engineer for several railroad companies. Enlisting in the U.S. Army at the outset of the Civil War, he was appointed colonel of the 4th Iowa Volunteer Regiment and then promoted to brigadier general for his services at the Battle of Pea Ridge. Dodge went on to serve under Ulysses S. Grant and William T. Sherman, particularly during the Atlanta Campaign, repairing railroads, bridges and telegraph lines destroyed by battling armies. Dodge also created an intelligence unit for Grant that was so successful in providing accurate information that it became

APPENDIX A.

a model for the Intelligence Corps for the U.S. Army. After the war, Dodge became a representative to the U.S. House of Representatives from Iowa, serving one term, and helped direct the construction of the Transcontinental Railroad.

Franklin, William B. (1823-1903). Graduated from West Point Military Academy of 1843, first in his class, he served in the Mexican-American War. After the war, he was assigned engineering duties and oversaw construction of several lighthouses on the Atlantic Coast and then supervised the construction of the Capitol Dome in Washington, D.C. With the onset of the Civil War, he was soon assigned to the Army of the Potomac and became a staunch ally of its commander George McClellan. When Ambrose Burnside replaced McClellan, Franklin led complaints about Burnside's lack of leadership at the Battle of Fredericksburg and the Mud March. Further complicating his political life, he refused to serve under Joseph Hooker, who was promoted to replace Burnside. Eventually reassigned to the Department of the Gulf under Nathaniel P. Banks, Franklin led the infantry component of the failed Red River Campaign in Louisiana, where he was wounded at the Battle of Mansfield. His army career was then limited by an on-going disability and he did not serve in any more commands.

Fremont, John C. (1830-1890). Known as "Pathfinder of the West" for his expeditions and well-known reports about the American West for the U.S. Army between 1842 and 1845, he was sent West at the beginning of the Mexican-American War in 1846 and was instrumental in capturing California from Mexico. Retiring from the army, he became the first Senator from the new state of California and was a candidate for President in the 1856 elections. After the onset of the Civil War, he re-enlisted in the army and initially commanded the Department of the West, headquartered in St. Louis. But he was soon removed from command for exceeding his authority by an Emancipation Proclamation that would have freed slaves of secessionists in Missouri. Lincoln rescinded Fremont's order because he was concerned that border states who had not seceded but still supported slavery would be alienated into joining the Confederacy. Fremont was reassigned to command the Mountain Department, which included West Virginia, Tennessee and Kentucky, but when his department was absorbed into the Army of Virginia in 1862, he refused to serve under John Pope, whom Fremont out-ranked. Fremont then moved to New York City and waited for a new command, which never came. He resigned from the army in 1864.

Gillmore, Quincy A. (1825-1888). Graduated from West Point Military Academy in 1849, first in his class, he was appointed to the Corps of Engineers and transferred to construct defense fortifications at Hampton Roads, Virginia. During the Civil War, he became an expert in siege operations using naval gunnery. In April 1862, he advocated the use of rifled guns for the U.S. Navy to defeat Fort Pulaski on the Savannah River in Georgia and close the port to the Confederates. The fort was considered invincible because the Union Navy could not approach close enough to mount an effective assault against the solid walls backed with massive piers of masonry. The rifled guns, however, could throw heavier shot with greater accuracy and higher velocity from greater distance than conventional smooth-bore guns. After thirty hours of bombardment with the new artillery, Fort Pulaski surrendered. The demonstrated power of rifled guns effectively brought an end to the use of large masonry for the construction of forts. In 1863, Gillmore led the assault to retake Charleston Harbor in South Carolina and successfully recaptured Fort Wagner. Using the same technology, he then pounded Fort Sumter with the rifled guns, turning the stone walls into rubble, but the Fort did not surrender until near the end of the war in 1865. Transferred to the Army of the James in 1864, Gillmore, heading the X Corps, took part in the Bermuda Hundred operations and participated in the defense of Washington, D.C., from the threat of Confederates under Jubal Early in July 1864. But Gillmore failed to follow through on a combined army-cavalry assault on the Dimmock Line at Petersburg because of a memorable defense by the Confederates in the Battle of Old Men and Young Boys. His commanding general, Benjamin Butler, blamed Gillmore for the defeat and had him arrested. The feud required their commander, Ulysses S. Grant, to intervene and Gillmore was reassigned to the Department of the South. After the war, Gillmore wrote several books on structural materials.

Grant, Ulysses S. (1822-1885). Graduated from West Point Military Academy in 1843 in the middle of his class. Although he had demonstrated excellence in horsemanship, he was assigned to infantry and not the cavalry. He served in the Mexican-American War 1846-48 with distinction, particularly in the battles for Mexico City. The U.S. Army reinforced its presence on the West Coast after the Gold Rush boom and Grant was posted first to Fort Vancouver in Oregon Territory and then to California in 1852. The long absence from his wife and children brought on a period of depression and excessive drinking and he was forced to resign from the army in 1853, a stigma that followed him through his years as a general in the Civil War. When he returned to Illinois as a civilian, he worked as a farmer and at odd jobs, and in his father's tannery business to support his wife and children. With the onset of the Civil War, he actively recruited volunteers for the Union army and was placed in charge of the unruly 21st Illinois Volunteer Regiment described by the Illinois governor as "a mob of chicken-thieves led by a drunkard." Grant managed to whip the miscreants into shape so efficiently that he was given two more troublesome regiments, which constituted a brigade. Under army regulations, such a command required a brigadier general, and the once-disgraced Grant suddenly found himself wearing the stars of a general officer. John C. Fremont then promoted Grant to command in Cairo, Illinois, which led to successes in the Western Theater over the next three years at Forts Henry and Donelson, the Battle of Shiloh, the Vicksburg Campaign and

APPENDIX A.

Siege of Chattanooga. After Grant's successes in 1863, President Lincoln elevated him to General-in-Chief of all Union armies in the spring of 1864. His pursuit of Confederate General Robert E. Lee in the Overland Campaign eventually yielded Lee's surrender in 1865 and the end of the Civil War. Grant was elected President in 1868 and 1872 and died of throat cancer in 1885 at age 63. His middle initial "S" was the result of an error on his West Point application, but the name U.S. Grant remained with him and his initials prompted his friends to call him "Sam," as in "Uncle Sam."

Grierson, Benjamin (1826-1911). As a young man, he became a music teacher and bandleader in Jacksonville, Illinois. At the onset of the Civil War, he enlisted in the 6th Illinois Cavalry in spite of his dislike of horses because of a vicious kick from one when he was eight years old, that left him with life-long scars. Promoted in 1862 to command the Cavalry Division of the Army of the Tennessee under Ulysses S. Grant, he pursued Confederate Earl Van Dorn after Dorn's raid on Holly Springs, Mississippi, Grant's supply depot. The following year, he led a cavalry raid deep into Mississippi in the spring of 1863, "Grierson's Raid" was described by William T. Shermans as *"the most brilliant expedition of the war."* The Cavalry traveled more than six hundred miles through Mississippi and Louisiana over seventeen days, disabling railroads and military supplies, capturing prisoners and horses, ending the expedition in Baton Rouge to rousing cheers from the Union-held city. The diversionary feint had successfully occupied Confederate cavalry while Grant was landing troops across the Mississippi River south of Vicksburg. Promoted to brigadier general, Grierson then participated in Sherman's Meridian Campaign in Mississippi in 1864. In December 1865, he surprised and captured cavalry under Nathan Bedford Forrest and then captured 500 Confederates on a train near Egypt Station, Mississippi, which earned him another promotion to the rank of major general. His final success in the war was participating in the capture of Mobile, Alabama, in the spring of 1865. After the war, he pursued a career in the Regular Army and organized the 10th U.S. Cavalry in 1866 that was made up of Black enlisted men, nicknamed the Buffalo Soldiers. His faith in the Blacks and their fighting ability, coupled with his lack of West Point credentials, brought criticism from his fellow white officers. Nevertheless, he led a successful Army career in various posts in the western frontier of Texas, New Mexico and Arizona until his retirement in 1890.

Halleck, Henry W. (1815-1872). Graduated from West Point Military Academy in 1839, third in his class, he became so expert in military theory that he was allowed to teach classes on the subject while still a cadet. Serving in California as an administrator during the Mexican-American War, he resigned his commission in 1854 to become a lawyer and enabled California to become a state, being the principal author of its Constitution. Reenlisting in the army at the onset of the

Civil War, he was placed in a senior command post in the Western Theater in the Department of Missouri, where his subordinate commanders, including Ulysses S. Grant, accomplished several successful victories. But after Grant had won the victory at the Battle of Shiloh, forcing the Confederates to withdraw to Corinth, Halleck decided to command the Siege of Corinth himself, making Grant his second-in-command. Halleck, who had nurtured a dislike of Grant, had removed him from the post of commanding general, which almost brought Grant to the point of resigning from the army. But Halleck had never commanded in the field and his overly cautious approach to reach Corinth allowed the Confederates to make a complete secret withdrawal and the Union Army entered an empty city. Halleck, known as "Old Brains" for his knowledge on military theory and practice, was much more competent as an administrator than as a field commander. Shortly after the Siege of Corinth, Lincoln promoted Halleck to General-in-Chief of all armies, moving him to Washington, which restored Grant to command the Army of the Tennessee. In 1864, Lincoln replaced Halleck with Grant as General-in-Chief, but Halleck remained as Grant's Chief-of-Staff until the end of the war and his superior skills in logistics and management of resources were a major factor that brought the Union to victory. After the war, he remained with the army, but was transferred to the Division of the Pacific in August 1865 and then the Military Division of the South in 1869. He became ill in 1872 and died at his post in Louisville at the age of 57.

Hancock, Winfield S. (1824-1886). Graduated from West Point Military Academy in 1844 in the bottom fourth of his class. Initially stationed in Indian Territory, he was transferred to Puebla, Mexico, during the Mexican-American War, and fought in the battles for Mexico City. Duties in Florida and "Bleeding Kansas" occupied him until the onset of the Civil War. He was soon promoted to serve in the Army of the Potomac, fighting in the Peninsula Campaign and the Battle of Antietam under George McClellan, then at Chancellorsville under Joseph Hooker and then at Fredericksburg under Ambrose Burnside. At the Battle of Gettysburg, serving under George Meade, he was briefly in charge of a critical position on Cemetery Hill when the senior commander John F. Reynolds was killed. On the third day, his corps was at the center of the field to face the massive assault of Pickett's Charge. Hancock had commanded the troops with such skill and encouragement against three days of intensive Confederate assaults, that he won high praise and admiration from his men and army colleagues, who called him "Hancock the Superb." He continued to serve in the Army of the Potomac through the Overland Campaign and the Siege of Petersburg, but left field command in November because of lingering effects of his wounds at Gettysburg. Taking lighter duties until the close of the war, he supervised the execution of Lincoln's assassination co-conspirators, a task he did not relish, but he carried out his orders, writing, *"every soldier was bound to act as I did under similar circumstances."*

APPENDIX A.

Hazen, William B. (1830-1887). Graduated from West Point Military Academy in 1855, he was commissioned into the 4th U.S. Infantry, serving in the Pacific Northwest and frontier duty in Texas. His first combat in the Civil War was at the Battle of Shiloh under Don Carlos Buell in the Army of the Ohio. Following Buell's defeat at the Battle of Perryville, Kentucky, Hazen's brigade was reorganized under William Rosecrans and held a defensive line at the Battle of Stones River that saved the Union Army from defeat. Fighting in the Tullahoma Campaign and the Battles of Chattanooga and Chickamauga under Rosecrans, it was during the Siege of Chattanooga that Hazen's troops came under the command of Ulysses S. Grant where they performed a significant role opening up the important "Cracker Supply Line." Promoted to lead a division under William T. Sherman during the Atlanta Campaign, Hazen's troops were part of the March to the Sea and achieved distinction in the capture of Fort McAllister at Savannah, Georgia. At the end of the Civil War, the young 35-year-old Hazen remained with the army until 1885 and led a controversial career filled with criticisms of Presidents, government mismanagement and scandals. The *New York Times*, in its obituary, pointed out that Hazen's "aggressive and disputatious," nature had worked well on the battlefield but resulted in powerful enemies during peace time. He died in 1887 at the age of 57.

Hooker, ("Fighting Joe") Joseph (1814-1879). Graduated from West Point Military Academy in 1837 in the middle of his class, he was commissioned to the 1st U.S. Artillery and initially assigned to fighting in Florida. He received promotions in the Mexican-American War for leadership and gallantry. His reputation as a ladies' man began when local women referred to him as the "Handsome Captain," an army reputation that followed him throughout his military career. After the war, he served in California, but resigned his commission in 1853 to pursue private interests, which reportedly involved mostly liquor, ladies and gambling. Largely unsuccessful in various activities, he returned east with the onset of the Civil War and requested a commission to re-enlist in the army, which was originally denied. But after the Battle of First Bull Run, his letter to Lincoln criticizing the mismanagement of the military received more attention and he was commissioned a brigadier general in the Army of the Potomac to help organize and train the new recruits under George McClellan. During the Peninsula Campaign, he earned a reputation for aggressive leadership and openly criticized McClellan, saying, *"He is not only not a soldier, but he does not know what soldiership is."* After the Battle of Antietam, Lincoln considered Hooker as McClellan's replacement, but instead appointed Ambrose Burnside to the position, who then led the Army of the Potomac into two disastrous battles, Fredericksburg and the Mud March. Lincoln then replaced Burnside with Hooker as the next general to command the Army of the Potomac, but Hooker's failure at the Battle of Chancellorsville and his constant clashes with Lincoln and army headquarters cost him his command. A dispute about the distribution of forces at Harpers Ferry prompted Hooker to offer his resignation in 1863 which Lincoln readily accepted, placing George Meade as commander of the army only three days prior to the Battle of Gettysburg. Hooker continued to serve in the Army of the Potomac in the Eastern and Western Theaters, and acted as a provisional force to support the Army of the Cumberland in Tennessee, which played a significant role in defeating the Confederates and relieving the Siege of Chattanooga. Hooker then led a corps under William T. Sherman during the Atlanta Campaign until he disputed with Sherman about not receiving a promotion that he thought he deserved. Hooker's request for a transfer was readily acknowledged and he was moved to command the Northern Department, headquartered in Cincinnati, and participated in no more battles. He led Lincoln's funeral procession at Springfield, Illinois, in April 1865. After the war, he remained with the army until 1868. He acquired his nickname "Fighting Joe" because of a typographical error in a newspaper headline, a title he resented because he thought it depicted him as a "highwayman or a bandit."

Howard, Oliver O. (1830-1909). Graduated fourth in his class from West Point Military Academy in 1854, he was then posted to Florida for the Seminole Wars. It was there that he was exposed to evangelical Christianity and even considered becoming a minister. For his religious practices, he became known to the men as "the Christian General," generally used with a tone of disdain. Nevertheless, he was an effective commander and later received the Medal of Honor for a brilliant performance in the Battle of Seven Pines in Virginia under George McClellan during the Peninsula Campaign. At the Battle of Chancellorsville, his troops were nearly all captured by Stonewall Jackson's surprise attack, a humiliating setback to his military career. At the Battle of Gettysburg, Howard's Corps successfully carried a defensive line on Cemetery Hill. After the death of James McPherson in the Atlanta Campaign, Howard was promoted to command the Army of the Tennessee under Sherman for the rest of the war, taking part in the March to the Sea and the Carolinas Campaign. After the war, he was appointed commissioner of the Freedmen's Bureau, working for the welfare of the freed slaves. One of his lasting legacies is the founding of Howard University that still functions as a higher-educational institution in Washington, D.C.

Hunter, David (1802-1886). Graduated from West Point Military Academy in 1822, he initially served in the infantry and was then promoted to captain of the 5th U.S. Dragoons in 1833. Soon after the firing on Fort Sumter, he was advanced to colonel of the 6th U.S. Cavalry in 1861 and served under Fremont in the Department of the West and later reassigned to Kansas and the Department of the South. A convincing advocate to arm freed Blacks as soldiers in the U.S. Army, he had a strong influence on Congress and President Lincoln prior to the Emancipation

APPENDIX A.

Proclamation. Hunter led forces into the Shenandoah Valley Campaigns of 1864, doing extensive damage that destroyed military targets and also burned down the Virginia Military Institute. Defeated by Jubal Early, Hunter withdrew into West Virginia which took his army out of the war, bringing forth resounding criticism from army headquarters and he received no further commands. Because of his friendship with Lincoln, which occurred when Hunter was invited to travel with the newly elected President Lincoln in 1861 on the inaugural train to Washington, D.C., Hunter served as part of the honor guard at Lincoln's funeral. He later served as president of the military commission which tried the co-conspirators of Lincoln's assassination.

Ingalls, Rufus (1818-1893). Graduated from West Point Military Academy in 1843 in the same class as Ulysses S. Grant, Ingalls was assigned to the 1st U.S. Dragoons and headed to New Mexico Territory under Stephen Kearny where he served during the Mexican-American War. After the war, he was posted to Fort Vancouver in Oregon Territory during the same period of time that Grant was there. With the onset of the Civil War, he was aide-de-camp for George McClellan and then became Chief Quartermaster for the Army of the Potomac, a role he held for the rest of the war. Under Grant, when the army set up operations during the Siege of Petersburg, Ingalls was promoted to Chief Quartermaster for all Federal Armies and transformed City Point into the largest receiving depot in the western hemisphere. After the war, he served in the army in a variety of quartermaster posts for the next two decades, including the Pacific Division where he retired in 1883.

Kautz, August (1828-1895). A German immigrant, he enlisted in the U.S. Army as a private in the 1st Ohio Infantry to serve in the Mexican-American War, 1846-48. After the war, he entered West Point Military Academy and was graduated in the class of 1852. Commissioned to the infantry, he was stationed in the Pacific Northwest and published a newspaper, *Truth Teller*, that defended American Indians. At the outbreak of the Civil War, he was moved to the Eastern Theater where he served as a captain in the 6th U.S. Cavalry during the Peninsula Campaign in 1862, and then the Western Theater in 1863 with the 2nd Ohio Cavalry. Promoted in 1864, he led cavalry operations for the Army of the James under Benjamin Butler during the Siege of Petersburg. Kautz commanded a cavalry operation designed to capture the weakly defended Petersburg in June 1864, but his attack was unexpectedly delayed by what became known as the Battle of Old Men and Young Boys. Kautz was to rendezvous with Quincy Gillmore for infantry support, but because Kautz was late reaching the destination point, Gillmore never launched the attack and the opportunity was lost. With the surrender of Richmond, Kautz, under the command of Godfrey Weitzel, led a division of Black troops from the U.S. Colored Troops (USCT) into the city, which remained there during Lincoln's visit to the conquered Confederate capital. Kautz continued to participate in the pursuit of Robert E. Lee's army until the surrender at Appomattox Court House. After the war, Kautz served in the army until retirement in 1892.

Kilpatrick, ("Kill-Cavalry") Hugh Judson (1836-1881). Graduated from West Point Military Academy in 1861 just after the onset of the Civil War, he was immediately assigned to the 5th New York Zouave Infantry. Promoted to lead the 2nd New York Cavalry Regiment, he soon acquired the nickname, "Kill-Cavalry," because of his aggressive attacks that alienated his men for the reckless, sometimes suicidal charges, that showed his willingness to exhaust men and horses. His other bad habits of poor discipline in camp, which included frequent visits of prostitutes, did not impress his army superiors. In the Battle of Chancellorsville in 1863, Kilpatrick achieved fame during George Stoneman's raid by swinging deeply behind the army of Confederate Robert E. Lee, reaching the outskirts of Richmond, burning and capturing wagons, destroying railroads and supplies. At Gettysburg, Kilpatrick ordered a charge against Confederate James Longstreet near Little Round Top which suffered significant losses, killing its commanding officer who had objected to the order. On another occasion, his cavalry conducted an unsuccessful raid on Richmond in 1864, but lost contact with the lead contingent commanded by Ulric Dahlgren who was killed. Kilpatrick's cavalry lost over 300 troopers killed and 1,000 captured in the raid. Disgraced by the "Dahlgren Affair," he left the Eastern Theater to be transferred to William T. Sherman in the West, where he played an important role in the March to the Sea and the Carolinas Campaign. Serving as Sherman's escort, he was present at the surrender of Confederate Joseph E. Johnston's army in North Carolina in April, marking the end of the Civil War.

Kimball, Nathan (1822-1898). With a degree in medicine from the University of Louisville in 1844, he established a successful medical practice in two Indiana communities at Salem and Livonia. When the Mexican-American War began, he raised a company from Livonia and displayed impressive leadership in the Battle of Buena Vista as he rallied the men to stand and hold even when the rest of the regiment had fled. He returned to medical practice after the war until the outbreak of the Civil War when he again raised a company of infantry and was named to lead the 14th Indiana Regiment to one of the first battles at Cheat Mountain Pass in the early months of the war. Leading a brigade at the Battle of Kernstown in the Shenandoah Valley when its commander was wounded, Kimball repulsed an attack by Stonewall Jackson, a rare defeat for the capable Jackson. Promoted to brigadier general, Kimball fought at the Battle of Second Bull Run and at the Battle of Antietam, where his brigade held its ground against withering fire at the Sunken Road. His troops acquired the name, "Gibraltar Brigade," later called

APPENDIX A.

the "Gallant Fourteenth," for their demonstrated courage to stand fast even when under intense enemy fire. Kimball served briefly in the Siege of Vicksburg and commanded troops in the Atlanta Campaign under William T. Sherman, who became a close personal friend. He was then transferred to the command of George Thomas to fight in the Battles of Franklin and Nashville, Tennessee. After the end of the war, he returned to his practice in Indiana and was elected State Treasurer and to the Indiana House of Representatives.

Ledlie, James H. (1832-1882). Working as a civil engineer on the Erie Canal and in railroad construction before the onset of the Civil War, he entered the U.S. Army as a major to the 19th New York Infantry, soon renamed the 3rd New York Artillery Regiment, and Ledlie was promoted to colonel with no military experience. He was next promoted to brigadier general to command the Artillery Brigade of the Department of North Carolina and spent most of 1863 on garrison duty for coastal artillery emplacements in North Carolina and Virginia. In 1864, he was transferred to the Army of the Potomac under Ambrose Burnside and was engaged in the Overland Campaign and replaced the commander of the 1st Division of Burnside's IX Corps who was killed. During the Siege of Petersburg, Ledlie was put in charge of troops who were to attack the Confederates after the explosion of "The Crater," a Union offensive tactic designed to disarm enemy troops by blowing up a mine shaft under the Confederates. After the explosion, Union troops were expected to circle the crater's hole and gain access to a strategic road that would divide the Southern army. Reportedly drunk at the time of the explosion, Ledlie provided no training to the troops for the mission nor was he present at the time the Crater exploded. The troops entered the giant hole instead of going around it and were slaughtered when they couldn't exit the steep slick sides of the crater. Ledlie was dismissed from service for dereliction of duty on orders from Ulysses S. Grant. Burnside was also censured and relieved of command for the fiasco and was not returned to command for the rest of the war.

Lyon, Nathaniel (1818-1861). Graduated from West Point Military Academy in 1841, he was assigned to the 2nd U.S. Infantry Regiment. Serving in the Mexican-American War, he was promoted for "conspicuous bravery" in the battles for Mexico City and then became a career army officer. With the onset of the Civil War, he was assigned to Fort Riley, Kansas, in 1861 which brought him to the border wars in "Bleeding Kansas." Staunchly antislavery, he wrote about the secession crisis, *"It is no longer useful to appeal to reason, but to the sword."* Forcing the surrender of the pro-Confederate militia in Missouri, his actions provoked a riot in St. Louis that became known as the Camp Jackson Affair. Promoted to briefly command the Department of the West and block secessionists in Missouri, Lyon was the first Union general to be killed in the Civil War at the Battle of Wilson's Creek near Springfield, Missouri, in August 1861.

McClellan, George B. (1826-1885). Graduated from West Point Military Academy in 1846, second in his class, he was immediately assigned to the Mexican-American War, arriving at his post on the Rio Grande with a double-barreled shotgun, two pistols, a saber, dress sword and a Bowie knife. He was soon struck down with malaria, which plagued him with recurring episodes the rest of his life. He served as an engineering officer for Winfield Scott and after the war, remained with the army and wrote a manual on bayonet tactics that he translated from the original French. In 1855, he was an official observer of European armies in the Crimean Wars but resigned from the army in 1857 to use his engineering expertise in railroads, becoming president of the Ohio and Mississippi Railroad in 1860. With the outbreak of the Civil War, he left civilian life and re-enlisted in the army and soon rose to prominence with battles in western Virginia. The *New York Herald* proclaimed him as "the Napoleon of the Present War." Brought to Washington after the failed Battle of First Bull Run, McClellan created and commanded the new Army of the Potomac for the Eastern Theater. Superior at organization, he produced a superbly trained, well-equipped and disciplined army. But McClellan's weakness to over-estimate the size of the armies against him hampered his battle plans in the field. His first major offensive involved several battles during the Peninsula Campaign, but he was defeated by Robert E. Lee, even though he outnumbered his opponent in men and artillery. At the Battle of Antietam, one of the bloodiest battles of the war, McClellan's reluctance to use reserve troops against Lee resulted in "a draw," with neither side being able to claim victory. McClellan's undisguised rudeness to President Lincoln and failure to pursue Lee after the Battle of Antietam brought him to his downfall. Removed from command, McClellan spent months writing an extensive report about his two major campaigns and how the administration had failed him. On completion of his report in October 1863, he announced his entrance to the political stage as a Democrat and in the following months, the "Peace Democrats" nominated him to run against Lincoln in the 1864 Presidential election. Still on active duty until the day before the election, McClellan's position advocated maintaining the Union, but not the abolishment of slavery. Election results gave a resounding victory to Lincoln. After the war, McClellan worked as an engineer in various projects and as president of the Atlantic and Great Western Railroad. Elected as governor of New Jersey in 1877, he served until 1881. Devoting his final years to traveling and writing, he continued to defend his conduct in the Civil War. Dying unexpectedly of a heart attack at age 58, his memoirs, *McClellan's Own Story*, were published posthumously in 1887. Admired by his men, they called him "Little Mac." Northern newspapers routinely referred to him as the "Young Napoleon."

McClernand, John A. (1812-1900). Using his relationship with Lincoln when they were friendly political rivals in Illinois, he was politically appointed as a general in the Union Army at the outset of the Civil War. Serving under Ulysses S. Grant at the battles of Belmont, Fort Donelson and Shiloh, he soon came into conflict with his commander by making grandiose lectures of victory by his troops, greatly exaggerating his own contributions in the battles. Lincoln continued to support McClernand because of his successful recruiting efforts in Illinois. Greatly disliked by West Point graduates and Navy commanders for his political maneuverings and self-promoting reports to the newspapers, he finally over-stepped war department policy by publishing in the press in 1863 a grossly misleading account that congratulated himself and his troops for carrying the main burden for the Union during the Vicksburg Campaign. Following army procedure that all releases to the press had to be approved by the War Department, Grant relieved McClernand of command. Lincoln gave McClernand a second command in the Department of the Gulf, but illness prevented him from participating in the Red River Campaign and he resigned from the army in November 1864.

McCook, Edward M. (1833-1909). A member of the "Fighting McCooks" of Ohio, his family of brothers and their sons reached national prominence because they all fought for the Union in the Civil War. Edward's four brothers served in various capacities, two of them as chaplains; and ten of his first cousins served as officers, six of them generals. Their father, John McCook, also served as a volunteer surgeon during the war. As a young man, Edward became a lawyer and moved to Central City, Kansas Territory (now in Colorado), in 1859 at the height of the Colorado Gold Rush where he became a prominent resident and served in the Kansas Territorial legislature. At the onset of the Civil War, he traveled to Washington to offer his services and briefly served as a secret agent to gather information for the military. He was soon named to lead the 2nd Indiana Cavalry and commanded a cavalry brigade at the Battle of Perryville, Kentucky, in 1862 and then a division at Chickamauga in 1863. During William T. Sherman's Atlanta Campaign in 1864, he was promoted to head the First Cavalry Division for the Army of the Cumberland, but was defeated by Confederate Cavalry during the Union raid on the Atlanta & West Point Railroad. McCook lost a third of his men and over a thousand horses at the Battle of Brown's Mill near Newnan, Georgia. After the fall of Atlanta, McCook's Cavalry was dispatched to Tennessee to support George Thomas in the battles at Franklin and Nashville, where the cavalry served with distinction. McCook was then assigned to James Wilson's Cavalry for its final sweep through Alabama and Georgia near the end of the war, which resulted in the defeat of Nathan Bedford Forrest and the capture of Selma, Alabama, which contained an arsenal, powder mill and other military resources. McCook also participated with Wilson's Cavalry in the capture of Confederate President Davis and Henry Wirz, commander of Andersonville Prison Camp, on May 10, 1865, as they were trying to flee the country after the surrender of the Confederate armies.

McDowell, Irvin (1818-1885). Graduated from West Point Military Academy in 1838 with classmate P.G.T. Beauregard, who would later join the Confederacy, the two generals would face each other as adversaries in the first major battle of the Civil War. McDowell served in the Mexican-American War in the 1st U.S. Artillery. After the war, he became a career military officer, working as staff officer for higher-ranking generals in the War Department between 1848 and 1861. Named to lead the new Army of Northeastern Virginia in July 1861, filled with 90-day recruits, McDowell's army met the Confederates at the Battle of First Bull Run at Manassas, Virginia, shortly after the firing on Fort Sumter. His green troops, coupled with his own lack of combat experience, led to a disaster that routed the Union army. His former West Point classmate Beauregard became the South's new Confederate hero. The Army of Northeastern Virginia was dissolved, to be replaced by the Army of the Potomac under George McClellan and McDowell was assigned to serve under him. McDowell's military career suffered again at the Battle of Second Bull Run, although he remained with the army, serving in various posts until he reached retirement age in 1882.

McPherson, James B. (1828-1864). Graduating from West Point Military Academy in 1853, first in his class, his classmates included Philip Sheridan and John Schofield who would join the Union Army and John Bell Hood who joined the Confederates. All would become prominent generals in the Civil War. After graduation, he was posted to San Francisco as superintending engineer for the defenses of Alcatraz Island. With the onset of the Civil War, he requested a transfer to the Corps of Engineers and was soon serving under Henry Halleck, then commanding the Department of the West. McPherson next served under Ulysses S. Grant as chief engineer at the battles of Forts Henry and Donelson and after Shiloh he was given command of the XVII Corps in Grant's Army of the Tennessee. When Grant was promoted to General-in-Chief of all the armies, William T. Sherman was advanced to lead the armies in the Western Theater and McPherson was named commander of the Union Army of the Tennessee. McPherson served under Sherman in the Atlanta Campaign through all the initial battles but was killed in the outskirts of Atlanta when he inadvertently passed through a gap in the Union line and was shot by Confederate fire. When the Confederates approached to ask his orderly who the downed officer was, the aide replied. *"Sir, it is General McPherson. You have killed the best man in our army."* His body was soon retrieved and transported by staff to his home town of Clyde, Ohio, where he was buried with military honors. Both Confederate General Hood and Union General Sherman wrote deeply-felt words of McPherson's character and his conduct as a gentleman, not just to his fellow officers, but also to prisoners captured after battle. One of the highest-ranking officers to be killed in action during the war, his death prompted several counties in America to be named in his honor, including the states of Kansas, South Dakota and Nebraska, plus a township in Minnesota.

APPENDIX A.

Meade, George (1815-1872). Graduated nineteenth in a class of fifty-six cadets at West Point Military Academy in 1835, he was then assigned to the 3rd U.S. Artillery to serve in Florida, but then after one year of service, he resigned, to pursue a career in civil engineering. Working for the Alabama, Georgia and Florida Railroad and others, he found it difficult to find steady civilian employment and by 1842, he re-enlisted in the army to support a growing family. Assigned to the Corps of Topographical Engineers, he served in the Mexican-American War and was noted by General Zachary Taylor for superior artillery action under fire at the Battle of Buena Vista. After the war, he was involved in lighthouse construction and coastal surveying in Florida and New Jersey for the army and then surveyed the Great Lakes prior to the Civil War. At the beginning of the war, Meade worked on constructing defenses around Washington, D.C., and was then assigned to the Army of the Potomac under George McClellan. In the Peninsula Campaign, he led a brigade that saw heavy fighting in the Seven Days Battles. At the Battle of Second Bull Run, his troops made a heroic stand protecting the rear of the retreating Union Army. Performing well in the battles of Antietam and Fredericksburg, Meade was promoted to lead the V Corps at the Battle of Chancellorsville under Joseph Hooker. When Hooker ordered the army to pull back from a strong defensive position against the objections of his senior commanders, Meade testily responded, *"If we can't hold the top of the hill, we certainly can't hold the bottom of it!"* Hooker's failure at the Battle of Chancellorsville contributed to his ongoing conflicts with Lincoln and army headquarters and when he offered his resignation in June 1863, Lincoln promptly accepted it. Meade was ordered as Hooker's replacement to command the Army of the Potomac three days before the Battle of Gettysburg, where he achieved a major Union victory. He continued to head the army through the Overland Campaign, with overall leadership under the command of General-in-Chief Ulysses S. Grant who accompanied the army as it faced the formidable Army of Northern Virginia under Robert E. Lee for forty days. At the end of the Overland Campaign, the Union armies kept Lee's army trapped for ten months during the Siege of Petersburg until Lee's forces broke through which led the Union Army to pursue the Confederates to Appomattox, where Lee was forced to surrender. Throughout Meade's military career, the Northern press had not been pleased with his prickly personality and quick temper, which had earned him the nickname "Old Snapping Turtle," and his battlefield successes were frequently downplayed. After the Civil War, Meade served briefly as governor of the 3rd Military District of Atlanta during Reconstruction, and then remained with the U.S. Army as commanding officer of the Military Division of the Atlantic until his death in 1872 at the age of 56.

Merritt, Wesley (1836-1910). Graduated from West Point Military Academy in 1860, he was commissioned to the 2nd U.S. Army Dragoons, serving initially in Utah under John Buford. With the onset of the Civil War, he was soon placed in the

Cavalry Department with the Army of the Potomac and participated in George Stoneman's raid during the Battle of Chancellorsville. He fought in the Battle of Gettysburg and later took over command of the 1st Division of the Cavalry Corps when Buford died of typhoid a few months later and remained in that role for the rest of the war. For most of the Overland Campaign, he was second-in-command to Philip Sheridan and was part of the Battle of Yellow Tavern when Confederate cavalry leader Jeb Stuart was killed. He was also part of Sheridan's successes against Jubal Early in the Shenandoah Valley and led the division that burned mills, wheat, corn and barns in "The Burning." He was promoted to major general for bravery in the Battle of Five Forks in the Appomattox Campaign and participated in the surrender of Robert E. Lee at Appomattox. His final duty in the Civil War was to lead the 1st Division Cavalry from Shreveport, Louisiana, to San Antonio, Texas, as part of the Union occupational forces in Texas. After the war, he remained with the army and continued to serve along the frontier in the cavalry, until he was appointed Superintendent at West Point from 1882-1887. In 1898, he was deployed to the Philippines during the Spanish-American War to serve as its first American governor. He retired from the army in 1900.

Nelson, William "Bull" (1824-1862). Joining the U.S. Navy in 1840 as a 16-year-old midshipman, he achieved distinction as an artillerist in the Siege of Veracruz during the Mexican-American War. At the onset of the Civil War, after serving in the U.S. Navy for over twenty years, he approached new President Lincoln in March 1861 offering to assist the administration in maintaining Union loyalties in his native state of Kentucky, which supported slavery but did not secede. His efforts in Kentucky earned him a command in the Army of the Ohio under Don Carlos Buell and he had leading roles of command in the battles of Shiloh, Siege of Corinth and the Battle of Richmond. His liberal use of profanity and sharp tongue-lashings to his subordinates had earned him a reputation of rudeness and incivility, offending many of his fellow officers. These personal traits, coupled with his 6'3" frame and a 300-pound body earned him the nickname, "Bull." After he publicly insulted fellow officer Jefferson C. Davis in the Galt Hotel in Louisville in 1862, Davis shot him in the chest several days later when Nelson refused to apologize. The death of the unarmed Nelson at age thirty-eight was never investigated and Davis was not brought to trial. Davis continued to serve in the army until his death in 1879.

Ord, Edward (1818-1883). Graduated from West Point Military Academy in 1839 in the middle of his class, he was commissioned to the 3rd U.S. Artillery and first assigned to action in Florida. During the Mexican-American War, he sailed around Cape Horn with Henry Halleck and William T. Sherman to be stationed in the newly acquired territory of California and the three men became life-long friends. His assignment kept him in California through the Gold Rush days and he was

APPENDIX A.

able to earn extra money by surveying and creating an early map of Los Angeles. He served in the Pacific Northwest and then relocated to the East in 1861 at the onset of the Civil War. Assigned to the Army of the Tennessee under Ulysses S. Grant in 1862, Ord's division was to coordinate with William Rosecrans in the Battle of Iuka, Mississippi, but because of communication problems, Ord's troops arrived after the battle was finished. The event created a life-long hostility between Grant and Rosecrans as each blamed the other for the errors of the mission. When Grant relieved John McClernand of command during the Siege of Vicksburg in 1863, Ord was promoted to succeed him, commanding the XIII Corps and in 1865, he was advanced again to lead the Army of the James in Virginia, replacing Benjamin Butler. Prominent in the final battles against Robert E. Lee's Army of Northern Virginia during the Appomattox Campaign in 1865, Ord's troops made a forced night march to Appomattox that was critical to the surrender of Robert E. Lee and the Army of Northern Virginia, which soon brought an end to the four-year Civil War. During Reconstruction, Ord headed the Army of Occupation at Richmond until he was returned to the regular army in 1866 where he served until his retirement in 1880. At his death in 1883, Sherman said of him, *"As his intimate associate since boyhood, the General here bears testimony of him that a more unselfish, manly and patriotic person never lived."*

Osterhaus, Peter Joseph (P.J.) (1823-1917). A German immigrant, who had served for some time as a Prussian Army officer, Osterhaus settled in St. Louis after immigrating to America in 1858. At the onset of the Civil War, he joined the Union 2nd Missouri Volunteer Infantry and participated in the battles of Wilson Creek and Pea Ridge. He fought in the battles of the Vicksburg Campaign under Ulysses S. Grant, including Champion Hill, Big Black River Bridge, the city of Jackson and the Siege of Vicksburg. He was then transferred to fight at Chattanooga and assisted Joe Hooker in the capture of Lookout Mountain. Participating in the Atlanta Campaign under William T. Sherman, Osterhaus commanded the XV Corps in the March to the Sea. In the final weeks of the war, he was appointed chief of staff for the Military Division of West Mississippi under Edward Canby in the Trans-Mississippi Theater and personally accepted the surrender of Confederate E. Kirby Smith at the end of the war. Mustered out of service in 1866, he subsequently returned to Germany where he remained until his death.

Parker, Ely S. (1828-1895). Born on a Seneca Indian Reservation in New York, he was first educated at a Baptist mission school, but then admitted to the Cayuga Academy, an elite school in western New York, where he excelled in language, writing and oratory skills. He used his abilities as translator, interpreter and diplomat for the Seneca leaders in their negotiations with the U.S. government regarding land and treaty rights. He enrolled in the Rensselaer Polytechnic Institute to study civil engineering and pursued several projects upgrading and maintaining the Erie Canal. At the onset of the Civil War, Parker attempted to enter a regiment of Iroquois volunteers to fight for the Union, but was refused because Indians were not considered citizens until the Indian Citizenship Act in 1924. Contacting his friend Ulysses S. Grant, whom he had met years before while supervising a government project in Galena, Illinois, he was admitted as an engineer during the Siege of Vicksburg. When Grant was advanced to head the Military Division of the Mississippi, he named Parker as his adjutant at Chattanooga and he served Grant through the Overland Campaign and the Siege of Petersburg, where he was appointed Grant's military secretary. At the surrender of Robert E. Lee at Appomattox, Parker drafted the surrender documents, where Lee said to him, "*I am glad to see one real American here*," to which Parker responded, "*Sir, we are all Americans.*" After the war, he was appointed Commissioner of Indian Affairs after Grant was elected President in 1868, but resigned in 1871 when Congressional politics stripped the department of most of its power.

Pope, John (1822-1892). Graduated from West Point Military Academy in 1842, near the upper third of his class, he was posted to the Corps of Topographical Engineers, serving in Florida and surveying much of the northeastern border of the United States and Canada. After his service in the Mexican-American War (1846-48), he worked mostly as a surveyor for the army for the Pacific Railroad, a transcontinental railroad that would reach from Council Bluffs, Iowa, to the Pacific coast. At the onset of the Civil War, he was initially assigned to the Western Theater under John Fremont, who successfully pushed secessionist forces under Confederate Sterling Price to southeastern Missouri. After Fremont was removed from the Department of Missouri, Pope was appointed to command the newly created Union Army of the Mississippi and he captured Island No. 10 on the Mississippi River. The success brought him to the Eastern Theater to head the new Army of Virginia, which was formed after George McClellan's Army of the Potomac was defeated in the Union Peninsula Campaign. Meeting the Confederates under Robert E. Lee at the Battle of Second Bull Run in 1862, Pope's army was routed by his poor reconnaissance and contradictory orders. Removed from command, the Army of Virginia was disbanded and troops were merged into the Army of the Potomac, still under McClellan. Pope blamed Fitz John Porter for the loss of the battle and forced a court-martial which found Porter guilty and removed him from the army. But over the next sixteen years, Porter continued efforts to have the verdict reviewed and in 1878, the review board placed the blame squarely on Pope and Porter was exonerated. After losing the Battle of Second Bull Run, Pope was banished to the Department of the Northwest in Minnesota and experienced no more actions in the Civil War, but he did command U.S. forces in the Dakota War of 1862, known as the Sioux Uprising. After the exoneration of Porter, Pope's reputation was damaged but he continued to serve in the U.S. Army until his retirement.

APPENDIX A.

Porter, Fitz John (1822-1901). Graduated from West Point Military Academy in 1845, eighth in his class, he was quickly assigned to fight in the Mexican-American War and noted for bravery in the Battle of Molino del Rey. Returning to West Point as a cavalry and artillery instructor until 1853, his next posting was in the West in Kansas and the Utah Expedition. At the beginning of the Civil War, Porter served in the Army of the Potomac under George McClellan and during the Siege of Yorktown in the Peninsula Campaign, Porter became excited by the Balloon Corps, which used tethered inflated balloons for reconnaissance. He made an aerial observation without the expertise of Aeronaut Thaddeus Lowe and failed to use a backup securing line. When the balloon broke loose and was in danger of being captured by the Confederates and/or killing Porter, a fortunate change of wind allowed him to adjust the gas valves and return the balloon safely to Union lines. He showed a talent for defensive fighting, particularly at Malvern Hill during the Seven Days Battles of the Peninsula Campaign, when his command successfully repulsed multiple Confederate assaults. His military career came to a halt, however, when he was court-martialed after the Battle of Second Bull Run for not obeying an order from John Pope, commanding general for the Army of Virginia, an order which Porter considered suicidal. Convicted by the review for disobedience and misconduct, he was removed from the army in January 1863 and spent the next several years collecting data and information to clear his name. After fifteen years, he was vindicated in 1878 when a board of inquiry determined that he had been unfairly convicted and his actions had actually saved the Union army from total destruction. In 1886 President Grover Cleveland commuted his sentence and he was restored to the army, back-dated to 1861, and he then promptly retired from it.

Ricketts, James B. (1817-1887). Graduated from West Point Military Academy in 1839, he was assigned to the 1st U.S. Artillery. After action in the Mexican-American War, he served in Florida and on frontier duty in Texas. At the outset of the Civil War, he worked on defenses of Washington, D.C., and was then wounded and captured at the Battle of First Bull Run. When his wife, Fanny Ricketts, learned of his capture, she used her husband's friendship with Confederate General Jeb Stuart to obtain a pass that enabled her to go through Confederate lines and find Ricketts in a makeshift hospital, where she nursed him back from near death. When he recovered sufficiently to be sent to Richmond as a prisoner-of-war, she went into captivity with him and remained there nursing James, who was unconscious for several weeks. During her four months in Richmond, Fanny nursed several other Union soldiers who had no one to care for them. Exchanged in December, James fought in the battles of Second Bull Run and at Antietam where he was injured when his horse fell on him. Returning to duty in 1864, he led troops in the Overland Campaign and was recognized for meritorious service at Cold Harbor. In July 1864, he was sent north with his command of about 3,300 men to assist Lew Wallace at Monocacy Junction in the defense of Washington, D.C., against Jubal Early's attempted raid on the capital. During the Shenandoah Valley Campaign under Philip Sheridan, Ricketts suffered a disabling chest wound at Cedar Creek, which affected him the rest of his life, but he remained with the army until he retired from active service in 1867.

Rosecrans, William S. (1819-1898). Graduated from West Point Military Academy in 1842, fifth in his class, he was commissioned into the Corps of Engineers. Although most graduates of his class served in the Mexican-American War, Rosecrans remained with the War Department and was assigned to a number of engineering assignments until 1854. Resigning from the army, he worked in civilian life in a number of capacities, but with the onset of the Civil War, he re-enlisted in the Union Army. Very successful as a military commander in a number of battles, he became a favorite of the Northern press. His successes at the battles of Iuka and Second Corinth, Mississippi, led to his promotion to take over the Army of the Ohio, replacing Don Carlos Buell, which he soon renamed the Army of the Cumberland. He defeated Braxton Bragg at the Battle of Stones River and his brilliant execution of the "Tullahoma Campaign" in Tennessee became textbook material for military history. His rise in the military ended, however, after his failure at the Battle of Chickamauga, Tennessee, that led to the siege of his army at Chattanooga. A great feud between Rosecrans and Ulysses S. Grant had occurred after the Battle of Iuka when a failure in communications left Rosecrans and his army fighting the battle alone, without the support of troops from Edward Ord. The hostility was still in place when Grant was placed in charge of the Siege of Chattanooga. He removed Rosecrans from commanding the Army of the Cumberland, replacing him with George Thomas. Rosecrans was sent to Cincinnati to await further orders, but his role in the major fighting was finished. Nicknamed "Old Rosy" during his cadet years at West Point Military Academy, he was admired for his bravery and personal rallying of his men during battles. After the war, he spent much of his life in California and represented the state in the U.S. House of Representatives between 1881-85. During that period, he voted against a bill to provide a pension for Ulysses S. Grant, who was nearly destitute and dying of throat cancer. In spite of Rosecrans' objections, however, the bill was passed. Rosecrans died of complications of pneumonia in 1898 at the age of 78.

Schofield, John M. (1831-1906). Graduated from West Point Military Academy in 1853, seventh in his class, he spent his first years in artillery in South Carolina and Florida. He returned to West Point in 1855 as an assistant professor until 1860, when he took leave to work as a professor of physics at St. Louis University in Missouri. With the onset of the Civil War, he re-enlisted in the U.S. Army and became chief of staff for Nathaniel Lyon in Missouri, acting with "conspicuous gallantry" at the Battle of Wilson's Creek where Lyon was killed. His battles were mostly confined to Missouri between 1862-63 until January 1864 when he was assigned to command the Army of the Ohio for the Atlanta Campaign under William T. Sherman. After the fall of Atlanta, Schofield's army was detached to join the Army of the Cumberland under George Thomas in Tennessee. With the successful defeat of the Confederates at Nashville in December 1864, Schofield's corps was moved to Fort Fisher, North Carolina, to support Sherman's Carolinas Campaign. After the war, Schofield became Secretary of War under the new President Andrew Johnson.

Scott, Winfield (1786-1866). Served over fifty years in the United States Army and was General-in-Chief for the army at the outset of the Civil War. He served under seven U.S. Presidents and had been the Commanding General of the Army since 1841, leading the army to its successful conclusion of the Mexican-American War, 1846-48. At the onset of the Civil War, the aging General at age 75 and in poor health, was unable to physically oversee Union war efforts and after a quarrelsome few months with George McClellan, Scott retired in October 1861. He was known to his men as "Old Fuss and Feathers," for his unfailing dedication to always appear in full and elaborate uniform when supervising the troops.

Sedgwick, John C. (1813-1864). Graduated from West Point Military Academy in 1837 in the middle of his class. He served in the Mexican-American War and received two promotions for his actions in three major battles at Mexico City. Between 1855 and 1860, he served in the U.S. Cavalry in Kansas, Utah and the Indian Wars. At the onset of the Civil War, he was serving as inspector general in the Department of Washington, D.C., and missed the Battle of First Bull Run. Assigned to the Army of the Potomac, he fought at the Siege of Yorktown and Seven Pines during the Peninsula Campaign, but was wounded in the Battle of Antietam leading his troops against Thomas "Stonewall" Jackson. Sedgwick continued as a commander in the battles of Chancellorsville, Gettysburg and in the Overland Campaign. He was killed by a sharpshooter from a distance of one thousand yards at the Battle of Spotsylvania, as he strode about in the open, criticizing his troops who were ducking to avoid flying bullets. He reportedly had just said, *"What? You men are dodging from single bullets... they couldn't hit an elephant from this distance."* Moments later, he was shot and died in the field, May 9, 1864.

Sheridan, Philip (1831-1888). Suspended from West Point Military Academy in 1852 for getting into a fist-fight with classmate William Terrill after attacking him with a bayonet, Sheridan returned to class a year later and credited his roommate Henry Slocum for helping him pass his examination in mathematics, enabling him to graduate in 1853 near the bottom of his class. His first assignments were to the 1st U.S. Infantry Regiment in Texas and then the Pacific Northwest where he was involved in several Indian disputes and battles. In the fall of 1861, he was transferred to St. Louis where he worked under Henry Halleck as a staff officer and then as quartermaster. During the Siege of Corinth, Sheridan accompanied the army as assistant to Halleck's topographical engineer. Gaining an appointment as colonel of the 2nd Michigan Cavalry, Sheridan led a small brigade at Booneville, Mississippi, and so impressed his superiors that he was promoted to brigadier general. During the Battle of Perryville, Kentucky, in 1862, Sheridan's cavalry successfully defended parched Union troops from Confederate attacks as they gathered water in the scorched landscape. Absorbed into the Army of the Cumberland, now under William Rosecrans, Sheridan's command at the beginning of the Battle of Stones River saved the Union Army from an early defeat which then achieved victory over Confederate forces under Braxton Bragg. When the Army of the Cumberland was later besieged at Chattanooga, Sheridan's command was a principal force in the Union's grand charge up Missionary Ridge that routed the Confederates. His impressive skills as a commander prompted Ulysses S. Grant to bring Sheridan to the Eastern Theater and place him in command of the Cavalry Corps for the Army of the Potomac during the Overland Campaign. Sheridan's troops engaged with Confederate Jeb Stuart's cavalry at Yellow Tavern where the famed Confederate cavalry leader and darling of the South was killed in the battle. Once Confederate Robert E. Lee's army was besieged at Petersburg, Grant sent Sheridan to the Shenandoah Valley to chase Confederate Jubal Early's command "...to the death." Sheridan's powerful black horse would become famous in the battles of the Shenandoah. After a skirmish at Rienzi, Mississippi, in 1862, the 2nd Michigan Cavalry gave Sheridan a powerful black gelding that he named Rienzi after the town. At sixteen hands high, Sheridan's height of five feet, five inches, barely reached the horse's shoulder. But Rienzi delivered Sheridan to his troops just south of Winchester, Virginia, on Oct. 19, 1864, just as they were fleeing an attack from Jubal Early. Sheridan's ability to turn his troops around in the Battle of Cedar Creek and re-take the lost artillery and ground and drive Early's troops away was captured in a poem, "Sheridan's Ride," which ensured lasting fame for both Sheridan and the horse. Rienzi was wounded several times during the course of the war but he survived through forty-five engagements, including nineteen pitched battles. When the old war horse died in 1878, he was mounted and presented to the Military Museum at Governors Island, New York, but was later moved to Washington, D.C., to the National Museum of American History. With the Southerners defeated in the Valley, Sheridan returned to Grant at Petersburg and played a vital role in the pursuit and surrender of Robert E. Lee's army at Appomattox which brought an end to the Civil War. Grant summary of Sheridan's performance in the final days, "*I believe General Sheridan has no superior as a general, either living or dead, and perhaps not an equal.*"

Sherman, William Tecumseh (1820-1891). Entering West Point Military Academy at the age of sixteen, he graduated sixth in his class in 1840. His middle name had been given to him by his father who had great admiration for the famous Shawnee Indian chief who fought for the preservation of Native American lands and died in the War of 1812. After graduation, Sherman was assigned to the 3rd U.S. Artillery and was stationed in Georgia and South Carolina, where, as the foster son of a prominent Whig politician in Charleston, he moved with the upper circles of Southern society. With the outbreak of the Mexican-American War, he was assigned administrative duties in the captured territory of California. Traveling by ship around Cape Horn, he became friends with fellow lieutenants Henry Halleck and Edward Ord, and the three men became life-long friends. In 1848, Sherman authored the official documents for the army that authenticated the discovery of gold, which launched the Gold Rush of 1849. During the years 1849-53, he earned extra money operating a general store and selling lots in Sacramento to supplement his army salary of $70 a month. Resigning his army commission in 1853, he worked in banking and real estate in post Gold-Rush San Francisco, but left there in 1858-59 to accept a position as superintendent of the Louisiana State Seminary of Learning & Military Academy, which later became Louisiana State University. When Louisiana seceded from the Union, Sherman resigned from the Academy and re-enlisted in the U.S. Army. Leading a brigade in the Battle of First Bull Run, his first combat experience, he was promoted for his performance in the battle, but became severely depressed and anxious about the responsibilities of command. After a leave-of-absence granted by his commander, Henry Halleck, he returned to service and was placed under the command of Ulysses S. Grant in the Department of the Missouri and he would remain with Grant for the rest of the war. Sherman led forces at the battles of Shiloh, Vicksburg and Chattanooga and commanded three armies in the Atlanta Campaign that achieved the surrender of Atlanta. Following the conquest of Atlanta, Sherman launched the March to the Sea through Georgia and then north through the Carolinas Campaign, which once again placed his army against the Confederate Army of Tennessee under Joseph E. Johnston. After the surrender of Robert E. Lee at Appomattox, Sherman met with Johnston to arrange the terms of surrender of his army and other armies of the Confederacy on April 26, 1865, which soon brought an end to the Civil War. Sherman and Johnston would remain on friendly terms after the war, sharing dinners and letters. At Sherman's funeral, Johnston, an honorary pallbearer, refused to wear a hat, showing respect for his friend and fallen general during the bitterly cold service, and later caught pneumonia and died one month later.

Shields, James (1806-1879). An immigrant from Ireland, he settled in Illinois to study and practice law and was elected to the Illinois House of Representatives in 1836 and later as State Auditor. During a controversy over the use of paper money in 1842, the Illinois State Bank had been forced to close and a series of anonymous inflammatory letters in the Springfield, Illinois, *Sangamo Journal* attacked Shields publicly. Greatly offended, Shields demanded satisfaction, as well as the true identity of the author. Abraham Lincoln had written the original text of the letter, but unknown to him, his fiancé and future wife Mary Todd had revised the letter with offensive references to Shields' character, describing him as a *"fool as well as a liar."* Lincoln took responsibility for the articles and accepted Shields' challenge to a duel. Lincoln, as the one challenged, chose the weapons for the duel and selected the cavalry broadsword, which would provide him an advantage with his great strength and superior height (6'4") over Shields' (5'9") because Lincoln knew that Shields was an excellent marksman. When the two men met for the duel, Shields was persuaded to call off the duel and the two men later became friends. At the outbreak of the Mexican-American War in 1846, Shields resigned his position as Commissioner of the U.S. General Land Office to volunteer for the war effort and served in nearly all of the major battles, including those that took Mexico City. After the war, he served as Senator from Illinois and then moved to Minnesota where he was elected Senator from that state. With the outbreak of the Civil War, he re-enlisted in the U.S. Army and was wounded in the Battle of Kernstown in 1862 against Stonewall Jackson. In 1863, he resigned from the army and moved to San Francisco to serve as the state's railroad commissioner. He then moved again to settle in Carrollton, Missouri, where he continued to be involved in public life and politics until his death.

Sigel, Franz (1824-1902). A graduate of the German Military Academy at Karlsruhe in 1843, he immigrated to the United States after serving several years in Germany as a revolutionary officer fighting against the Grand Duchy of Baden. When the revolutionary troops were defeated, Sigel led the retreat into Switzerland and then emigrated to the United States in 1852. He chose to live in St. Louis where a number of German immigrants had settled and became an influential antislavery advocate in Missouri. With the onset of the Civil War, he joined the Union army in May 1861 and recruited other German immigrants to the Union war efforts. His recruiting success gained him a promotion to brigadier general and he was given commanding roles because of his ability to communicate with a number of German-speaking soldiers, who understood little English. But his failures in a number of combat encounters gave him a reputation as an inept commander and he was frequently placed in the reserve corps, which he resented. Responding to his frequent demands for an active command, Lincoln gave him a command post to capture Lynchburg in the Shenandoah Valley in May 1864 as a reward for his successful recruiting efforts. But his ineffective leadership resulted in his troops being defeated by a small force under Confederate John Breckinridge which included cadets from the Virginia Military Institute. After the Battle of New Market, renamed "The Field of Lost Shoes," because many of the cadets lost their shoes in the muddy field, Sigel was removed from command and spent the rest of the war without an active role. After the war, he settled in New York City and worked in various positions for the city and published the *New York Monthly*, a German-American periodical.

Slocum, Henry W. (1827-1894). Graduated from West Point Military Academy in 1852, he had been an excellent student who ranked seventh in his class. Commissioned in the 1st U.S. Artillery, he served in Florida and at Fort Moultrie in Charleston Harbor before resigning his commission in 1856 to set up a law practice in Syracuse, New York. At the onset of the Civil War, he re-enlisted in the army and was appointed colonel of the 27th New York Regiment, which he led in the Battle of First Bull Run. He served in the Army of the Potomac, performing decisively in battles of the Peninsula Campaign and as commander of the XII Corps at the battles of Chancellorsville and Gettysburg. Notably, in the fall of 1863, when Slocum learned that his corps was to be transferred to the command of Joseph Hooker, he wrote a letter to Lincoln stating that he would resign from the army rather than serve under Hooker, whom he did not respect as a commander or a gentleman. With Lincoln's intervention, his request was honored and his Corps was later transferred to the Army of the Tennessee under Ulysses S. Grant and then under William T. Sherman, where he remained for the rest of the war. Commanding troops through the Atlanta Campaign, Slocum was the first to enter Atlanta after its surrender and then commanded the Army of Georgia during Sherman's March to the Sea. Completing the Carolinas Campaign with Sherman and the surrender of the Confederate army under Joseph E. Johnston in North Carolina, Slocum's Corps participated in the Grand Army Review in May 1865 in Washington. He resigned from the army in the fall of 1865 and returned to New York City, where he continued his law practice, was active in politics and played an important role in the building of Brooklyn Bridge. He and fellow colleague Oliver Howard planned Sherman's funeral in 1891 and were honorary pallbearers.

Smith, Andrew Jackson (A.J.) (1815-1897). Graduated from West Point Military Academy in 1838, he was commissioned into the 1st Dragoons and served with that unit for twenty-three years in frontier duty in the Southwest and the Mexican-American War. At the onset of the Civil War, he accepted the position of Chief of Cavalry in the Department of Missouri under Henry Halleck and was then promoted to brigadier general. In December 1862, he took command of a division under William T. Sherman at Chickasaw Bluffs and then commanded XIII Corps during the Battle of Arkansas Post and throughout the Vicksburg Campaign. After leading a division in the disastrous Red River Campaign in 1864, Smith's forces were returned to Sherman's command where he received new orders to *"follow Forrest to the death."* Confederate Nathan Bedford Forrest had been vigorously attacking Union railroads threatening Sherman's single supply line that supported his Atlanta Campaign. Smith caught up with Forrest at

Tupelo, Mississippi and defeated his cavalry, July 14-15, 1864, but Forrest escaped to Holly Springs, Mississippi. When Smith returned to Memphis, Sherman ordered him to go back to Mississippi, this time with infantry and cavalry to finally capture Forrest. As Smith's 14,000-man force approached Holly Springs, Forrest, knowing his troops were seriously outnumbered, took 2,000 cavalry troopers and reached Memphis behind Smith's cavalry and carried out a raid deep in Union lines, capturing about 400 soldiers who were caught off-guard. Smith, furious at losing Forrest a second time, presumably took out his revenge on Oxford, Mississippi, about fifty miles east of Holly Springs, although he never admitted his reason for attacking the undefended city. On Aug. 22, 1864, Smith's soldiers burned the County Courthouse, all the business houses except one on the Square and all private homes in the immediate area. Furthermore, the soldiers looted the homes, carrying away any items of value, then burned the houses as they left. Smith, who was never reprimanded for the attack on civilians, took his troops to join the Union Army in Nashville under George Thomas in the Battle of Nashville that defeated the Confederate Army of Tennessee under John Bell Hood. Smith's last combat mission was the final campaign against Mobile, Alabama, in 1865. He retired from military service in 1869 to become postmaster of St. Louis, Missouri.

Smith, William F. "Baldy" (1824-1903). Graduated from West Point Military Academy in 1845, fourth in his class, he was assigned to the Topographical Engineers Corps to conduct a number of surveys of the Great Lakes and Texas. In Florida, he contracted malaria that periodically affected his health the rest of his life. Serving in the Army of the Potomac under George McClellan, he was recognized for conspicuous valor in the battles of Seven Pines and Antietam and promoted to major general. But after the disastrous Battle of Fredericksburg under Ambrose Burnside, he was caught up in the recriminations that led to a general order from Burnside to dismiss all senior officers. Lincoln rescinded the order and removed Burnside instead. But Smith lost his promotion and was eventually assigned as chief engineer for the Army of the Cumberland under William Rosecrans in 1863. During the Siege of Chattanooga, he conducted the engineering operations that restored the "Cracker Line," which provided food and supplies to the besieged army, that was now under the overall command of Ulysses S. Grant. In recognition of his performance during the siege, he was promoted again to the rank of major general. Smith was reassigned to command the XVIII Corps in the Army of the James under Benjamin Butler during the Overland Campaign and Smith's corps led the first operations into Petersburg while the Confederate army was still occupied at Cold Harbor. But Smith lost the opportunity to capture Petersburg when his delayed attack gave the Confederates time to reinforce their defenses, extending the war nearly another year. For that failure, Grant removed Smith from command of the XVIII Corps and he spent the remaining time of the war on "special duty." After the war, he served on the board of police commissioners in New York City and was later engaged in civil engineering projects in Pennsylvania.

Smith, William Sooy (1830-1916). After graduating from Ohio University in 1849 with a degree in engineering, he entered West Point Military Academy and graduated from there in 1853, sixth in his class. Resigning from the army a year later, he established his own engineering company and was involved in the first surveys for a bridge over Niagara Falls between the United States and Canada. He re-enlisted in the army at the outbreak of the Civil War and was commissioned colonel of the 13th Ohio Infantry. After serving in western Virginia, he participated in the battles of Shiloh, Perryville and the Vicksburg Campaign. Appointed Chief of Cavalry for the Division of Mississippi, his command was enlarged to 7,000 troopers to support William T. Sherman in February 1864 on the Meridian, Mississippi, Campaign, an operation that invaded the city and destroyed the arsenal, warehouses and its military supplies. Smith delayed his departure date for the operation by ten days as he waited on a unit that was ice bound on the Ohio River. When the cavalry finally got underway on its mission, progress over muddy roads proceeded slowly and then the command was nearly captured by Confederate Nathan Bedford Forrest. Smith's cavalry barely escaped back to Memphis, reporting a failed mission. He then served under both Sherman and Ulysses S. Grant as Chief of Cavalry for their separate commands before resigning from the army in July 1864 due to rheumatoid arthritis. Resuming his engineering career in private life, he became an expert on bridge construction and designed and built the first all-steel bridge in 1878-79 over the Missouri River at Glasgow, Missouri.

Steedman, James B. (1817-1883). Born in Pennsylvania, he was forced at the age of fifteen to provide for his siblings when both parents died. Working as a typesetter for the local *Lewisburg Democrat* newspaper, he was able to develop a career as a printer, which he pursued until joining the Texian Army to fight for Texas Independence in 1835-36. Returning from Texas, he started a newspaper, the *Northwest Democrat* in Napoleon, Ohio, and developed a profitable business in contracting for public works. Active in Democratic politics, he supported Stephen Douglas as a Presidential candidate in 1860, but at the onset of the Civil War, he chose to follow the Union and would become one of its most respected generals in the Union Army despite a lack of West Point Military credentials. After the firing on Fort Sumter and Lincoln's call for volunteers, Steedman raised the 14th Ohio Infantry Regiment and led troops in the first battle of the war, the Battle of Philippi, Virginia, in June 1861. The unit continued to serve in the Western Theater at the Battle of Shiloh and the Siege of Corinth when Steedman was promoted to brigadier general in the Army of the Ohio under Don Carlos Buell. After the Battle of Perryville, Kentucky, the army's new commander, William Rosecrans, led the newly renamed Army of the Cumberland in the Battle of Stones River and then captured Chattanooga. During the Battle of Chickamauga, Steedman's troops provided critical support to George Thomas in the last-ditch defense to save the army from disastrous capture. After the successful recapture of Chattanooga by Ulysses S. Grant, Steedman remained there until May 1864 when he was transferred to participate in William T. Sherman's Atlanta Campaign under Thomas in the Army of the Cumberland. After the fall of Atlanta, Steedman was part of Thomas' army that was detached to Nashville, Tennessee, to face a Confederate invasion from John Bell Hood. On the opening days of battle against Hood, Dec. 15-16, 1864, Steedman's forces made a diversionary attack on the right flank of the Confederate army while the main assault forced the enemy's left. Steedman's troops, which included the 13th U.S. Colored Troops (USCT) infantry, took heavy losses, but when the main assault broke through the Confederate line, they turned the tide to drive the Southern army from the field. The battle decimated the Confederate Army of Tennessee and hastened the end of the war. Steedman remained in the army until his resignation in August 1866. He returned to publishing and became editor of the *Northern Ohio Democrat* newspaper in Toledo, Ohio.

Steele, Frederick (1819-1868). Graduating from West Point Military Academy in 1843, he then served in the Mexican-American War where he was cited for distinguished bravery. He served in California, Minnesota, and Kansas-Nebraska Territories until the outbreak of the Civil War when he was appointed to the 11th U.S. Infantry in May 1861 which fought in the Battle of Wilson's Creek, Missouri. Promoted to command a division at the Battle of Pea Ridge, Arkansas, he was later transferred to the Army of Tennessee in 1862 and fought in the battles of Chickasaw Bayou and Arkansas Post. After the defeat of Vicksburg, he commanded the Army of Arkansas and successfully captured Confederate-held Little Rock in 1863. Steele's army marched south from Little Rock in March 1864 to support the Red River Campaign in Louisiana, expecting to join Union forces under Nathaniel P. Banks at Shreveport. Inadequately supplied with rations for the men, the expedition experienced continued challenges searching for food and combating Confederate forces that were sent north from Shreveport to intercept them. When Steele received news at Camden that the Red River operation had been repulsed, he successfully escaped Camden with his army and defeated the pursuing Confederates at Jenkins Ferry, returning to Little Rock May 3. In 1865, he led troops involved in the capture of Mobile, Alabama. After the end of the war, Steele remained with the army and was transferred to Texas to guard the Rio Grande and then oversaw fighting against the Snake Indians in the Pacific Northwest until November 1867, when he took a leave of absence for health reasons. He died two months later in San Mateo, California.

APPENDIX A.

Stoneman, George (1822-1894). Graduated in 1846 from West Point Military Academy, where his roommate was the notable future Confederate Thomas "Stonewall" Jackson. Stoneman was commissioned to the Mormon Battalion, which marched from Iowa to California to participate in the Mexican-American War, only to arrive after hostilities were over. Promoted to captain of the 2nd U.S. Cavalry, he served mostly in Texas until 1861. When Texas seceded from the Union, Stoneman was forced to escape north with most of his command to avoid being captured by secessionists. Assigned to the Army of the Potomac under McClellan, the cavalry was ineffectively used during the Peninsula Campaign and Stoneman was reassigned to infantry. Following the Battle of Fredericksburg, Joseph Hooker reorganized the Army of the Potomac and placed the cavalry into a single corps with Stoneman as its head. At the Battle of Chancellorsville, Stoneman was criticized for his cavalry mission that failed to get behind the Confederate army under Robert E. Lee. Assigned to a desk job in Washington in the Cavalry Bureau until 1864, he was then transferred to the Cavalry Corps under George Thomas in the Army of the Cumberland, which became part of William T. Sherman's Atlanta Campaign. Ordered to destroy the Macon & Western Railroad south of Atlanta, Stoneman disobeyed his orders and changed the mission to lead a cavalry raid that would free prisoners at Macon, Georgia, and perhaps move on to free prisoners at the Andersonville Prisoner-of-War camp. But Stoneman was captured at Macon by Confederate cavalry under Joseph Wheeler and sent to the very prison he was trying to liberate. The highest-ranking officer to be imprisoned, Sherman was able to get him exchanged three months later and he was returned to duty. In March 1865, he led a raid through North Carolina and Virginia, destroying infrastructure that crippled Confederate support and the war ended shortly afterward. He then returned to the regular U.S. Army, retiring in 1871. He moved to California where he served as governor for one term, 1883-1887.

Sumner, Edwin "Bull" (1797-1863). Enlisting in the U.S. Army in 1819 at the age of twenty-two, he was a career army officer who served in various Indian campaigns and the Mexican-American War. According to legend, a musket ball reportedly bounced off his head at the Battle of Cerro Gordo, Mexico, giving him the nickname "Bull Head." His booming voice added to the label, that was then shortened to "Bull." At the onset of the Civil War, he was appointed commander of the Department of the Pacific in California, when its current commander, Albert Sydney Johnston, resigned to join the Confederacy. The oldest field commander in the Civil War, Sumner led one of four corps under George McClellan during the Peninsula Campaign. At the Battle of Seven Pines, his initiative in getting his troops across the swollen Chickahominy River in time to reinforce Union troops on the other side was critical to saving the army. After Ambrose Burnside replaced McClellan as commander of the Army of the Potomac, Sumner led the Right Grand Division at the disastrous Battle of Fredericksburg, where his troops suffered heavy losses. Soon after the battle, he was relieved of command at his own request. Falling ill two months later, he died in March 1863 at the age of 66.

Terrill, William (1834-1862). Born in Virginia, he entered West Point Military Academy in 1849 and graduated in 1853, 16th in his class. During his years as a cadet, he was involved in a fist-fight with Philip Sheridan, who was then suspended from the Academy for a year. But after Sheridan's graduation, the two men served together much later in the Civil War in the Army of the Ohio under Don Carlos Buell. Terrill was initially assigned to the 3rd and 4th U.S. Artillery and served in Florida and the U.S. Coast Survey. Although many Virginia-born officers resigned from the regular army at the onset of the Civil War to join the Confederacy, Terrill left no doubt that his loyalties lay with the Union, despite scathing criticism from his father and brothers who joined the Confederate States Army. Terrill fought in the Battle of Shiloh, but was killed in the Battle of Perryville, Kentucky, in October 1862, leading a brigade into battle. His younger brother James, fighting for the Confederates in the Overland Campaign, was killed later in the war, also leading a brigade into battle. A third brother, Philip, died in the Battle of Cedar Creek near Winchester, Virginia, fighting for the Confederacy. A fourth brother, Dr. George P. Terrill, serving in the Virginia militia, survived the war.

Terry, Alfred (1827-1890). Raised in Connecticut, he attended Yale Law School in 1848 and became a lawyer who worked as a clerk in the county's Superior Court. With the onset of the Civil War, he raised the 2nd Connecticut Infantry Regiment, and as its colonel, fought at the Battle of First Bull Run. Assigned to Quincy Gillmore, Department of the South, he participated in siege operations against Charleston and Morris Island, South Carolina, and the capture of Fort Wagner in September 1863. Placed in charge of an Expeditionary Corps, Terry was sent north to capture Fort Fisher at Wilmington, North Carolina, in January 1865, after the assault by Benjamin Butler's forces the month before had failed. Working effectively with the navy under David Porter, the Army-Navy assault successfully captured Fort Fisher in January 1865. When John M. Schofield arrived with additional infantry, the command captured the city of Wilmington a few weeks later. Terry's troops were then grouped with the Army of the Ohio under Schofield and the combined forces joined William T. Sherman near Fayetteville, North Carolina, for the final stages of the Carolinas Campaign that soon ended the Civil War. Terry remained with the U.S. Army and held a number of important roles during Reconstruction, military operations in the territories, and the Northern Pacific Transcontinental Railroad.

Thomas, George H. (1816-1870). Graduated from West Point Military Academy in 1840 in the upper third of his class, he served in various posts in Florida, New Orleans and Charleston Harbor. At the outbreak of the Mexican-American War,

APPENDIX A.

he was ordered to Texas in 1845, serving under Zachary Taylor. He led a light artillery gun crew with distinction in the battles of northern Mexico, working closely with Braxton Bragg, who would become a leading general for the Confederacy. One of Thomas' superior officers wrote that *"his coolness and firmness contributed not a little to the success of the day."* The son of a Virginia plantation owner with fifteen slaves, Thomas had a planter-class upbringing, but at the outbreak of the Civil War, he refused to join the Confederate Army and remained with the Union. His family of three sisters and two brothers never forgave him. They turned his picture against the wall, destroyed his letters and never spoke to him again. He fought in the Battle of First Bull Run and in the Shenandoah Valley in 1861, but for the rest of the war, commanded in the Western Theater. Assigned to the Army of the Ohio, he participated in the Siege of Corinth and was then moved to Kentucky under Don Carlos Buell, responding to the Confederate invasion by Braxton Bragg. When Bragg withdrew his army after the Battle of Perryville, Thomas served under a new general, William Rosecrans, now commanding the renamed Army of the Cumberland. Thomas held the center of the retreating Union line at the Battle of Stones River, which enabled the army to defeat Bragg the next day. During Rosecrans' successful Tullahoma Campaign, Thomas was in charge of the most critical part of the maneuvering of the army which successfully led to the capture of Chattanooga. But at the Battle of Chickamauga, where Rosecrans was in danger of losing his entire army, it was Thomas' stubborn determination to hold a defensive line against a Confederate offense that saved the Union Army, earning him the nickname "Rock of Chickamauga." When the army was then besieged at Chattanooga, Ulysses S. Grant, recently promoted to command all Union forces in the West, replaced Rosecrans with Thomas to lead the Army of the Cumberland. Thomas commanded the center of the Union attack on the Confederates at Missionary Ridge, which created a central breakthrough and routing of the entire Confederate Army under Bragg. The Union Army, which had beenbesieged for two months, now controlled the doorway to Georgia and Thomas became part of William T. Sherman's Atlanta Campaign that captured the city of Atlanta after five months of fighting. Thomas' army was then transferred to Tennessee to defend against a Confederate invasion from John Bell Hood and the Confederate Army of Tennessee. In the Battles of Franklin and Nashville, Thomas achieved one of the most decisive victories of the war that helped bring the four-year conflict to its conclusion a few months later. His slow deliberate approach to command won him the affection of his soldiers who referred to him as "Pap Thomas" and the "soldier's soldier." After the war, he received an appointment to command the Military Division of the Pacific with headquarters in San Francisco, where he died of a stroke one year later.

Wallace, Lew (1827-1905). Educated in public schools, he was a poor student but developed a skill for writing and produced his first novel as a teenager, *The Fair*

God, which was not published until 1873. While studying law at his father's law office, the 19-year-old enlisted in the U.S. Army at the beginning of the Mexican-American War and was mustered into the 1st Indiana Volunteer Infantry, but the unit was never in combat. Leaving the army a year later, he developed a law practice in Indiana, and operated a newspaper, *The Free Soil Banner.* But after the attack on Fort Sumter, he re-enlisted in the U.S. Army and commanded the 11th Indiana Infantry Regiment. Success with battles in Cumberland, Maryland, and western Virginia earned him a promotion to brigadier general and he was assigned to the Army of the Tennessee under Ulysses S. Grant. At the Battle of Fort Donelson his troops repulsed a Confederate attempt to escape and the fort soon surrendered. At the Battle of Shiloh, his late arrival of reserve troops because of a confusion in Grant's orders created a controversy that plagued him for years. But he redeemed his military reputation at Monocacy Junction, Maryland, when his greatly outnumbered troops delayed Confederates long enough to save Washington D.C. from a raid by Jubal Early in 1864. After the war, Wallace wrote the best-selling novel *Ben-Hur.*

Warren, Gouverneur K. (1830-1882). Graduated from West Point Military Academy in 1850, second in his class, he was assigned to the Corps of Topographical Engineers. He participated in a number of topographical studies throughout the West for possible transcontinental railroad lines and created maps of the United States west of the Mississippi. At the beginning of the Civil War, he commanded the 5th New York Infantry which fought in the Peninsula Campaign, where Warren made multiple reconnaissance missions and helped draw topographical maps for the army to advance up the Virginia Peninsula. Promoted to brigadier general after his troops made a heroic stand at the Battle of Second Bull Run, he was appointed chief topographical engineer at the Battle of Chancellorsville under Joseph Hooker. At Gettysburg on the second day of battle, Warren identified the weakness of the Union left flank at Little Round Top and organized its defense, which placed the 20th Maine under Joshua Chamberlain at the extreme left, which became one of the most famous encounters of the battle. Given command of the V Corps in the Army of the Potomac, Warren's troops participated in the Overland Campaign under Ulysses S. Grant and the Siege of Petersburg, breaking up the Weldon Railroad at Globe Tavern. At the Battle of Five Forks, however, his delayed arrival at the designated battle line provoked Philip Sheridan to remove him from command, a decision that Grant supported. Appeals for a court of inquiry to have the decision reversed and clear his name were refused for years until Rutherford B. Hayes was elected President in 1876. The first hearing on Warren's inquiry occurred in December 1879 but the report which exonerated Warren was not published until 1882, three months after his death. Without knowledge of his exoneration, Warren directed that he be buried in civilian clothing with no military honors.

APPENDIX A.

Weitzel, Godfrey (1835-1884). Son of an immigrant family from Bavaria that settled in a German community in Cincinnati, Ohio, Godfrey's father was able to obtain an appointment to West Point Military Academy for the tall boy, who entered the Academy a few months before his 16th birthday. Nicknamed "Dutch" by his classmates, he graduated second in his class in 1855 and then worked in New Orleans improving its defenses under the command of Major P.G.T. Beauregard, who would later be a principal general for the Confederacy. With the onset of the Civil War, Weitzel was assigned to construct defenses at Washington and then attached to the Department of the Gulf. When Union troops captured New Orleans, he served as assistant military commander and acting mayor of the city. In 1863, Weitzel commanded a brigade that implemented the Siege of Port Hudson on the Mississippi River, which did not fall until a few days after the capture of Vicksburg. In 1864, he was assigned chief engineer for the Army of the James under Benjamin Butler and participated in a number of engagements in the Bermuda Hundred Campaign. Named commander of all Union troops north of the Appomattox River during the Confederate evacuation of Richmond in April 1865, Weitzel received the formal surrender from the mayor of Richmond on April 3. His command included troops from the U.S. Colored Troops who entered the city, which created shock waves among the white citizens but tears of joy and pride among the Blacks. Weitzel served as Lincoln's aide and bodyguard during the two days of peace negotiations in Richmond. His words in 1866, reflecting on his experience about the service of Black soldiers in the Union Army, stated, *"Its organization was an experiment which has proven a perfect success. The conduct of its soldiers has been such to draw praise from persons most prejudiced against color, and there is no record which should give the colored race more pride than that left by the 25th Army Corps."*

Williams, Alpheus S. (1810-1878). As a young man, he established himself in Detroit, a frontier town in 1836, and became a prominent member of the community as he pursued several careers, including lawyer, judge, banker and owner of the Detroit Advertiser newspaper. He was active in the local militia and in 1847 was appointed lieutenant colonel in the 1st Michigan Infantry to serve in the Mexican-American War, but his unit arrived too late to see any action. With the outbreak of the Civil War, he trained the first volunteers in the state and as a brigadier general commanded a division in the Army of the Potomac under George McClellan. He was engaged in a number of battles in the Shenandoah Valley against Stonewall Jackson, and in the battles of Antietam, Chancellorsville and Gettysburg. Sent west to support the Union Army at Chattanooga, his division guarded railroads in eastern Tennessee. Transferred to the Army of the Cumberland to serve under George Thomas in the Atlanta Campaign, Williams fought in a number of battles, most notably Resaca and New Hope Church. His division followed William T. Sherman through the March to the Sea and the Carolinas Campaign and the final surrender of the Confederate armies under Joseph E. Johnston in North Carolina. After the war, he was elected as Michigan's representative to the U.S. House of Representatives 1875-1878. He died of a stroke in his second term on Dec. 21, 1878. His letters were published posthumously in 1959, titled, *From the Cannon's Mouth: The Civil War Letters of General Alpheus S. Williams.*

Wilson, James H. (1837-1925). Graduated from West Point Military Academy, sixth in his class, 1855, he was appointed to the prestigious Corps of Topographical Engineers and initially assigned to the Department of Oregon at Fort Vancouver. At the outset of the Civil War, he was the topographical engineer for the Port Royal Expeditionary Force that captured Port Sound, South Carolina, between Savannah, Georgia, and Charleston Harbor, South Carolina. He then took part in the capture of Fort Pulaski at the mouth of the Savannah River in 1862. Transferred to the Army of the Potomac, he was appointed chief topographical engineer under George McClellan and participated in the battles of South Mountain and Antietam in Maryland. His next assignment brought him west to serve under Ulysses S. Grant as topographical engineer during the Vicksburg Campaign through the capture and surrender of Vicksburg. Continuing with Grant to the Battle of Chattanooga, he was chief engineer for William T. Sherman's forces during the relief of Union troops at Knoxville, Tennessee. In early 1864, he was assigned as chief of the Cavalry Bureau in Washington, D.C., but Grant promoted him to command a division of cavalry under Philip Sheridan during part of the Overland Campaign, where Wilson performed brilliantly. Transferred to the Western Theater to serve as cavalry officer for William T. Sherman in the Atlanta Campaign, Wilson was then detached to join the Army of the Cumberland under George Thomas for the Franklin-Nashville Campaign. During the Battle of Franklin, he was instrumental in blocking a flanking attack by the famed Confederate Nathan Bedford Forrest. The Union Army's victories at Franklin and Nashville decimated the Confederate Army of Tennessee under John Bell Hood and hastened the end of the war. After the battles in Tennessee, Wilson commanded a raid through Georgia, one of the largest cavalry-only actions in the war, that captured both Selma, Alabama and Columbus, Georgia, which are regarded as the final battles in the entire war, occurring within days of the surrender of Confederate armies by Joseph E. Johnston on April 26, 1865. During the raid, the cavalry also captured Confederate President Jefferson Davis at Irwinville, Georgia, on May 10, along with the commander of Andersonville Prison Camp, Henry Wirz, as they both attempted to flee the country. After the war, Wilson remained with the army's Corps of Engineers until 1870 when he resigned.

Wright, Horatio (1820-1899). Graduated from West Point Military Academy in 1841, second in his class, he then taught engineering and French at the Academy for the next several years. During the Mexican-American War, he worked on creating defenses for Florida's coastline at the harbor of St. Augustine and at Key West. After the firing on Fort Sumter, his duties initially focused on building fortifications around Washington, D.C. Serving briefly as head of the Department of Ohio in August 1862, he was then transferred to command a division in the VI Corps of the Army of the Potomac. At the Battle of Gettysburg, his troops were held in reserve, but saw action in the Overland Campaign in the Battle of the Wilderness. When his commander John Sedgwick was killed in the Battle of Spotsylvania, he took over command of the Corps and fought at Cold Harbor. His corps played a significant role in the Siege of Petersburg and the pursuit of Lee's army, capturing hundreds of prisoners at the Battle of Sailor's Creek. After the war, Wright returned to engineering duties, participating in the completion of the Washington Monument and construction of the Brooklyn Bridge, retiring in 1884.

NAVAL OFFICERS

Farragut, David G. (1801-1870). As a young boy, Farragut's father, George Farragut, placed his young children with friends and family after their mother died of yellow fever in New Orleans. David Farragut came to live as part of the naval family of Commodore David Porter and served in the war of 1812 at the age of eleven as a midshipman under the command of his foster father. He received his first command at the age of twenty-one and participated in anti-piracy operations in the Caribbean. During the Mexican-American War, he commanded the *USS Saratoga* that was sent to the Gulf of Mexico to blockade Tuxpan, an important port about one hundred seventy miles north of Veracruz. Promoted to Commander, his next assignment was to create Mare Island Navy Yard near San Francisco in San Pablo Bay. At the outbreak of the Civil War, he played a major role in the attack on New Orleans, inflicting considerable damage on the two forts protecting the city. Farragut accomplished a daring bypass of the forts and captured New Orleans on April 29, 1862, which was quickly followed by the surrender of the forts' garrisons. Farragut attempted to capture Port Hudson, one hundred twenty miles north of New Orleans on the Mississippi River, but Hudson would not fall for another year until after Vicksburg was defeated in July 1863. Rewarding his success in the capture of New Orleans, Farragut was the first naval officer to be promoted to Rear Admiral and in August 1864, he was assigned to capture Mobile Bay, Alabama, a vital Confederate seaport used to export cotton and accept supplies for the Confederacy through extensive smuggling operations. When the naval fleet attempted to enter the Bay, one of his gunboats was destroyed when it was hit with an underwater naval mine and the other ships started pulling back. Farragut, lashed to a high perch on the rigging of his flagship, famously shouted through a trumpet to the other commanders, *"Damn the torpedoes. Four bells, Captain Drayton, go ahead, full speed,"* and the quote, slightly shortened to *"Full Speed Ahead,"* was memorialized for history. All of the fleet passed through and Farragut won a great victory when he captured Mobile Bay on Aug. 4, 1864, the last major port on the Gulf for the Confederacy. Although the city itself was not conquered until 1865, Mobile Bay was now in Union hands and no longer a port for the South. Lincoln promoted Farragut to Vice Admiral, the highest-ranking officer in the U.S. Navy.

Foote, Andrew (1806-1863). Son of a U.S. Senator from Connecticut, his father entered the 16-year-old into West Point Military Academy in 1822. But six months later, he left West Point and was accepted as a midshipman in the United States Navy. Serving in oceans all over the world between 1822 and 1843, he organized a temperance movement in 1837 that eliminated the policy of serving grog (alcoholic rum) to U.S. Naval personnel. At the beginning of the Civil War, Foote, commanding the New York Naval Yard, was promoted to lead the Western Gunboat Flotilla, predecessor of the Mississippi River Squadron. He cooperated with Ulysses S. Grant to lead the gunboats in the Battles of Forts Henry and Donelson, and later the Battle of Island No. 10, supporting John Pope. Foote was among the first naval officers to be promoted to the newly created rank of Rear Admiral. He died unexpectedly in 1863 of kidney disease at the age of 57.

Porter, David Dixon (1813-1891). Officially appointed as a midshipman in 1829 at the age of ten under the command of his father, Commodore David Porter, he participated in the Siege of Veracruz at the beginning of the Mexican-American War in 1846. With the onset of the Civil War, Porter led an independent flotilla of mortar boats in the capture of New Orleans in 1862 under the command of David Farragut. During the Vicksburg Campaign in 1863, Porter commanded the Mississippi River Squadron and worked with Ulysses S. Grant to pass a fleet of gunboats and steamers through the massive cannon batteries above the river at Vicksburg. On the first passage, only one vessel was lost in the firefight as the boats stayed close to shore, hampering the cannons' firepower because of the steep angle from the high bluffs. The second passage six nights later lost only one steamer and enough barges passed through to provide Grant with sufficient boats to transport his men across the river, now waiting at a landing south of the Vicksburg fortress. At Grand Gulf, Porter's gunboats bombarded the two Confederate forts but could not disable the one on high ground. Grant marched the men to another landing farther south and the large amphibious crossing of men, animals, artillery and materials successfully crossed the river, which allowed the Union Army to proceed on land and capture Jackson, Mississippi, and then place the city of Vicksburg under siege. Porter's ships captured the Grand Gulf forts soon after as the Confederates abandoned their garrisons to avoid being captured by Grant's troops. The next assignment for Porter from Washington occurred in the spring of 1864 and instructed the Mississippi River Squadron to accompany the Army of the Gulf under Nathaniel P. Banks up the Red River in Louisiana. The mission was to seize Shreveport and establish a Union presence against possible incursioPns from Texas and, as a secondary objective, seize cotton for northern textile factories that could enhance Lincoln's Presidential election prospects. The expedition was a massive disaster and Porter nearly lost all of his ships to Confederate attacks in the tortuous and twisting Red River, but was able to negotiate a difficult crossing through the rapids and save his fleet. Porter was next transferred to the Atlantic coast to lead the U.S. Navy effort in a joint Army-Navy assault on Fort Fisher at Wilmington, North Carolina, the last Confederate seaport used by blockade runners that provided supplies and ammunition to the Confederacy. The first attempt in December 1864, coordinated with the Army of the James under Benjamin Butler, was a dismal failure. A second attempt the following January with a Provisional Army under Alfred Terry was a success and the last seaport for the Confederacy was closed, making it the last naval activity of the Civil War.

AERONAUT

Lowe, Thaddeus (1832-1913). A self-educated adventurer, Lowe became interested in gas-inflated balloon flight in his twenties and built balloons which he showed at exhibitions and then used to take customers for rides aloft. A test flight from Cincinnati in April 1861, using a large balloon inflated with gas from the local "city gas" works, carried him into South Carolina, where he was accused of being a federal spy by the recently declared Confederacy. A local resident, who had been to one of Lowe's exhibitions and taken up for a ride in one of his balloons, was able to convince authorities that Lowe was a scientist and not a threat and he was allowed to return North with his balloon on a train. A demonstration to Lincoln in June convinced the President that a tethered balloon could be a useful new technology for surveillance for the North and appointed Lowe to head a new Union Army Balloon Corps. The Corps served the Army of the Potomac in the Peninsula Campaign and at the battles of Antietam and Fredericksburg. The Balloon Corps was dissolved in 1863 after political maneuverings forced Lowe to resign from the Corps.

APPENDIX B.

COMMANDERS FOR THE CONFEDERACY
LIST OF CONFEDERATE GENERALS

Anderson, Richard H.
Beauregard, Pierre Gustave-Toutant (P.G.T.)
Bragg, Braxton
Breckinridge John C.
Buckner, Simon Bolivar
Early, Jubal
Ewell, Richard
Floyd, John B.
Forrest, Nathan Bedford
Gordon, John B.
Hampton, Wade
Hardee, William
Hill, Ambrose Powell (A.P.)
Hoke, Robert
Hood, John Bell
Jackson, Thomas "Stonewall"
Johnston, Albert Sidney
Johnston, Joseph E.
Jones, William E. "Grumble"
Lee, Fitzhugh
Lee, George Washington Custis
Lee, Robert E.
Lee, Stephen D.
Lee, William Henry Fitzhugh ("Rooney")
Longstreet, James

Magruder, John B.
Mahone, William
McCulloch, Benjamin
Morgan, John Hunt
Mosby, John
Pemberton, John C.
Pickett, George
Pike, Albert
Pillow, Gideon
Polk, Leonidas
Price, Sterling
Shoup, Asbury
Smith, E. Kirby
Stuart, James Ewell Brown, (J.E.B. "Jeb")
Taylor, Richard
Tilghman, Lloyd
Van Dorn, Earl
Watie, Stand
Wheeler, Joseph

NAVAL OFFICERS
Buchanan, Franklin

AERONAUT
Alexander, Edward Porter

COMMANDERS FOR THE CONFEDERACY
Commander-in-Chief, Jefferson Davis

Davis, Jefferson (1808-1889). President of the Confederate States of America, Davis graduated from West Point Military Academy in 1828 in the lower third of his class. His first posting was to Prairie du Chien, Michigan Territory, under the command of Colonel Zachary Taylor, who would lead the U.S. Army in northern Mexico at the beginning of the Mexican-American War in 1846. While in Michigan, Davis fell in love with Taylor's daughter Sarah and they were married in 1835. To satisfy her father's wishes that his daughter not be married to a military man, Davis resigned his commission with the army and the couple moved south to his sister's home in Louisiana. The unlucky pair contracted malaria or yellow fever shortly afterward and Sarah died three months later. Davis barely survived. The following several years, he developed his plantation in Mississippi, became involved in politics and in 1845, married his second wife, Varina Howell. In 1846 with the onset of the Mexican-American War, he recruited a regiment called the Mississippi Rifles for the U.S. Army, and served under Taylor, his former father-in-law. Leading a memorable charge of his troops at a critical point in the Battle of Buena Vista, Davis prevented a near rout of the American forces, which later won the battle. After the war, he continued the expansion of his large plantation and eventually owned more than one hundred slaves. Following a brief stint as a Mississippi Senator, he served as Secretary of War for President Franklin Pierce in 1853 and was then re-elected to the U.S. Senate in 1858. After Mississippi seceded from the Union in 1861, he was elected President of the Confederacy, seen as the *"champion of a slave society and embodying the values of the planter class."* Davis was both President and General-in-Chief for the Confederate State Army throughout the Civil War, except for a brief period in 1865 when Robert E. Lee was named General-in-Chief. Davis and his Cabinet directed the Southern armies and the strategic directions of the war from their government offices in Richmond, Virginia. When Lee's Army of Northern Virginia was finally forced out of Peterburg, ending the 10-month siege, abandoning Richmond, Davis traveled by train west ahead of the army with trusted advisors and most of his cabinet to Danville, Virginia, on the border with North Carolina, where they learned that Lee had surrendered his army at Appomattox. The group traveled farther south to Washington, Georgia, where the final meeting of the Cabinet took place on May 4, 1865. After Davis officially dissolved the Confederate government, he authorized belated compensation to Cabinet members from funds remaining in the Confederate treasury and John C. Breckinridge, Secretary of War, paid out

APPENDIX B.

several requisitions. Members of the Cabinet dispersed and Davis reunited with his wife Varina and their children on May 7, planning to escape to a sympathetic friendly nation. But the family was captured on May 10 by Union Army Cavalry Corps under James Wilson at Irwinville, Georgia, and Davis was imprisoned at Fort Monroe. Some members of Davis' Cabinet successfully escaped to Cuba, but Davis remained in prison for two years, when he was finally released on bail in May 1867 to stand trial for treason. The trial was delayed until the court finally heard preliminary motions in December 1868. U.S. President Andrew Johnson's proclamation of amnesty on Dec. 25, 1868, issued a pardon to all persons who had participated in the rebellion and made Davis a free man. Davis and his family traveled in Europe for some time but then relocated to the Mississippi Gulf coast on an estate near Biloxi where he lived out his retirement years. His memoirs *The Rise and Fall of the Confederate Government* (two volumes) were published in 1881. He remained an unrepentant anti-Black Confederate until he died in 1889 at the age of eighty-one.

CONFEDERATE GENERALS

Generals-in-Chief during the course of the Civil War.

Jefferson Davis, Feb. 18, 1861-Jan. 31, 1865

Robert E. Lee, Jan. 31, 1865-April 9, 1865

Anderson, Richard H. (1821-1879). Graduated from West Point Military Academy in 1842, he was commissioned to the 1st U.S. Dragoons and first assigned to cavalry school and then to frontier duty in Indian Territory. He served with distinction in the Mexican-American War, particularly in the battles that captured Mexico City. After the war, he was assigned to Texas duty and the border wars of Kansas. When his home state of South Carolina seceded from the Union, he joined the Confederate Army and served as a brigade commander in the Peninsula Campaign where he gained the nickname "Fighting Dick." As part of Longstreet's Corps, Anderson fought in battles of Second Bull Run, Antietam, Chancellorsville, Gettysburg and the Overland Campaign in the Eastern Theater. When Longstreet was shot by friendly fire in the Battle of the Wilderness, Anderson took over as head of the corps and executed a hard march to reach Spotsylvania Court House just ahead of the Union advance. When Longstreet returned to duty some months later, a new Fourth Corps was created in the Army of Northern Virginia with Anderson as its commander through the Siege of Petersburg and the retreat to Appomattox. Most of his command was taken prisoner at the Battle of Sailor's Creek while they served as rear guard to protect the army's escape over the river. After the surrender at Appomattox, he returned to his home state of South

Carolina and was pardoned in September 1865. He worked as a farmer and for the state government, dying at the age of 57 in Beaufort, South Carolina.

Beauregard, Pierre Gustave-Toutant (P.G.T.) (1818-1893). Graduated from West Point Military Academy in 1838, second in his class, he excelled in both artillery and engineering. Raised on a sugar-cane plantation in Louisiana of French-Creole parents, his first language was French until he was sent to school in New York City for four years where he learned English. He entered West Point at age sixteen and after graduation served in the Mexican-American War as an engineer under Winfield Scott, competing with Robert E. Lee for promotions. After the war, he worked for the army improving its coastal defenses in Florida and the Mississippi Delta. In New Orleans, he saved the Custom House from sinking into the moist soil of Louisiana. When the state seceded from the Union in 1861, he accepted a commission in the Confederate Army and was named one of its first five top generals. Commander of the attack on Fort Sumter, he faced his West Point instructor, Robert Anderson, and accepted his surrender of the Union troops. Beauregard then led the defenses against his former West Point classmate, Irvin McDowell, at the Battle of First Bull Run, consolidating his forces with the lead general, Joseph E. Johnston, whose troops were initially in the Shenandoah Valley. Although the Confederates routed the Union Army, Beauregard claimed that interference from Confederate President Jefferson Davis prevented pursuit of the Union soldiers and potential capture of Washington, D.C. When the quarrel became public, an angry Davis held a permanent grudge against Beauregard for the rest of the war. After the Battle of First Bull Run, Beauregard was assigned to Tennessee to be second-in-command to Albert Sydney Johnston (no relation to Joseph E. Johnston), highest ranking general for the Confederacy. A.S. Johnston led the attack against Ulysses S. Grant at the Battle of Shiloh but was killed on the field and Beauregard took over command of the Army of Mississippi. Initially successful in the battle, the Confederates were defeated the next day and had to retreat to Corinth, Mississippi, about twenty miles south, where an epidemic of disease eventually forced the Southern troops to withdraw. Beauregard took medical leave himself for two weeks which infuriated President Davis who removed him from command. Davis wrote, *"He should have stayed at his post even if he had to be carried around in a litter."* Beauregard was then assigned to Charleston, South Carolina, to be in charge of its coastal defenses and did not command in any more major battles until near the end of the war. Beauregard replaced John C. Pemberton in South Carolina, who was transferred to command at Vicksburg, Mississippi, and Braxton Bragg was named new commander for the Army of Mississippi. Beauregard is noted for creating the battle flag for the Confederate Army, which was used as the primary flag for all corps and forces in the Army of Northern Virginia.

APPENDIX B.

Bragg, Braxton (1817-1876). Graduated from West Point Military Academy in 1837 near the top of his class, he was commissioned to the artillery corps. A strict disciplinarian, he was well known for his "disputatious" character who argued with everyone, including a famous case in which his paper requisitions for supplies from his role as company commander were refused by him acting in a secondary role as the company quartermaster. The conflict had to be referred to the post commander for resolution, who exclaimed, *"My God, Mr. Bragg, you have quarreled with every officer in the army, and now you are quarreling with yourself!"* Nevertheless, he was promoted for bravery and distinguished conduct in the Mexican-American War and became a national hero when his artillery actions against a numerically superior attacking force carried the U.S. Army to victory in the Battle of Buena Vista. During the battle, Bragg impressed his superiors, most notably Col. Jefferson Davis, who would become President of the Confederacy during the Civil War. Leaving the army in 1856, Bragg built a profitable sugar plantation in Louisiana that required more than one hundred slaves. Although opposed to secession, he supported the state of Louisiana and was soon commissioned a Brigadier General in the Confederate States Army and sent to Corinth with 10,000 men to serve under Albert S. Johnston in the Battle of Shiloh. When Johnston was killed, command fell to Beauregard who lost the battle and the Southerners had to retreat to Corinth, Mississippi. President Jefferson Davis, furious with Beauregard when he took medical leave without permission, replaced him with Bragg to head the Army of Mississippi. Bragg led the Confederacy's Kentucky Campaign in 1862 that required cooperation with E. Kirby Smith's army, located in Tennessee. Bragg's first task was to move his Confederate Army of Mississippi east from Mississippi to Chattanooga, Tennessee, a distance of about 250 miles, while avoiding a large Union Army under Don Carlos Buell, also enroute to the same destination. Bragg's logistical achievement of moving a sizeable army across large distances while avoiding Buell was a remarkable feat at that time of limited transportation capabilities. Although Bragg's Kentucky invasion succeeded in defeating Buell's Union Army at Perryville, he withdrew from Kentucky over the objections of his senior commanders. Bragg's assessment of Confederate resources to support his army in Kentucky would be insufficient for him to maintain a command there and he settled his army, renamed the Army of Tennessee, into winter quarters at Stones River, Tennessee. But he soon faced a newly promoted Union commander, Williams S. Rosecrans, who had replaced Buell and renamed the army as the Army of the Cumberland. Rosecrans defeated Bragg at the Battle of Stones River on New Year's Eve and Bragg withdrew his army to Tullahoma, Tennessee. Pursued by Rosecrans the following June, the Union and Confederate armies fought at the battles of Tullahoma, Chattanooga and Chickamauga in 1863, which resulted in Bragg trapping Rosecrans and his army into a siege at Chattanooga. Criticized by his senior officers for his poor performance in the battles of Stones River and Chattanooga, Bragg's short temper and offensive style provoked them into petitioning President Davis to relieve him from command. Davis traveled to army headquarters to listen to "The Revolt of the Generals," but retained Bragg as commander of the army. When Ulysses S. Grant drove Bragg out of Chattanooga into Georgia, Bragg resigned his command and Joseph E. Johnston was named to head the Army of Tennessee. Bragg served as military advisor to Davis for several months until he was ordered to organize the defenses of the Carolinas, and he set up his headquarters at Wilmington, North Carolina, protecting one of the two seaports for the Confederacy that had not been blockaded by the Union Navy. When Bragg had to surrender Wilmington to Union forces in January 1865, he was transferred to Joseph E. Johnston in the Carolinas, now commanding the remnants of the Army of Tennessee after its rout at the battles of Franklin and Nashville under John Bell Hood. With the surrender of Lee at Appomattox, Davis and the fragments of the Confederate government fled to South Carolina where Bragg joined them at the last Cabinet meeting of the Confederacy near Abbeville. Bragg was soon captured at Monticello, Georgia, and paroled a few days later. When he returned to his plantation in Louisiana, he found it had been confiscated by the federals and was now a shelter for freed Blacks under the Freedmen's Bureau. He worked at a number of odd jobs, the last one in Texas, where he died suddenly of a "brain paralysis" at the age of 59. Gen. Joseph E. Johnston's summary of Bragg expressed an opinion held by many of the soldiers who had worked under him: *"I know Mr. Davis thinks he can do a great many things other men would hesitate to attempt. For instance, he tried to do what God failed to do. He tried to make a soldier of Braxton Bragg…"*

Breckinridge John C. (1821-1875). Born in Kentucky to a prominent political family, he studied law and established a practice, first in Iowa Territory, and then in his native state at Lexington. Supportive of the Mexican-American War, he acquired a military commission in the Third Kentucky Infantry Regiment, which reached Veracruz in November 1847, where the men suffered from an epidemic of yellow fever. When the survivors reached Mexico City, the battles were over, but they remained in the city as an army of occupation until May 1848. After the war, Breckinridge became prominent in the Democratic Party and was elected Vice-President with President Buchanan in the 1856 Presidential election. In the 1860 election, Breckinridge was a Democratic Presidential candidate, competing against Stephen Douglas and John Bell. With a three-way split of the Democratic party, the Republican candidate Abraham Lincoln won the election, but Breckinridge came in second in the electoral votes, beating Douglas and Bell. At the same time that Lincoln was inaugurated as President, Breckinridge was sworn in as a Senator from Kentucky. He supported preserving the Union, but also endorsed states' rights to own slaves and had approved the Supreme Court's Dred Scott decision. Although Kentucky did not secede and soon supported the

APPENDIX B.

Union, Breckinridge joined the Confederates States Army in November 1861 and was immediately expelled from the Senate. He led troops in the major battles of Shiloh, Stones River, Chickamauga, Chattanooga and Cold Harbor and a number of battles in the Shenandoah Valley, where his most significant success was at the Battle of New Market in 1864. In February 1865 he was named Secretary of War for the Confederacy and declared to President Davis that the cause was hopeless. He began laying the groundwork for surrender and when the Confederate offices at Richmond were being abandoned in the final days of the siege, he oversaw the preservation of Confederate archives before he joined President Davis and most of the Confederate Cabinet to flee southwest to Danville, Virginia, where they learned that Lee had surrendered at Appomattox. When Breckinridge learned that Lincoln had been assassinated, he said, *"Gentlemen, the South has lost its best friend."* At Abbeville, South Carolina, Breckinridge urged President Davis to surrender, but he refused. The group then traveled on by rail to Washington, Georgia, where the final meeting of the Cabinet took place. Breckinridge and a small contingent of Kentuckians managed to escape to Cuba where they joined other former Confederates. Breckinridge went on to Britain where he communicated with his wife in Canada and he then crossed the Atlantic to join her and the rest of his family in Toronto, where they spent the winter. The family then moved to France where they remained until 1868 when they returned to Niagara, Canada. When U.S. President Johnson proclaimed amnesty for all former Confederates on December 25, 1868, Breckinridge resumed his law practice in Lexington, Kentucky, and invested in real estate and railroad ventures. He died of health deterioration caused by old wounds in 1879 at the age of 54.

Buckner, Simon Bolivar (1823-1914). Graduated from West Point Military Academy in 1844, in the middle of his class, he was commissioned to the 2nd U.S. Infantry and assigned to Sackett's Harbor on Lake Ontario until 1845 when he returned to West Point to teach. In 1846, he was promoted for his performance in several battles in the Mexican-American War. He resigned from the army in 1855 and returned to his home state of Kentucky in 1857 to serve as its adjutant general. At the outbreak of the Civil War, he refused to join the Union Army and as commander of the Kentucky State Militia, he assembled sixty-one companies to maintain the neutrality of his native state. But when Confederates occupied Columbus, Kentucky, and Buckner joined the Confederate States Army as a brigadier general, the Union-controlled legislature indicted him for treason and seized his property. Buckner served under Confederate Albert Sidney Johnston at Bowling Green, Kentucky, and was then transferred to Fort Donelson, where he was soon forced to surrender to his old friend from West Point days, Ulysses S. Grant. Exchanged six months later, Buckner fought in battles at Perryville, Kentucky, and Chickamauga, Georgia, under Braxton Bragg and was later transferred to the Trans-Mississippi Department under E. Kirby Smith. After the war, he returned to Kentucky in 1868 after all former Confederates were granted amnesty by U.S. President Andrew Johnson. He became editor of the *Louisville Courier,* was active in politics and elected governor in 1887 for one term. He continued his political interests until his death at age 90 in 1914.

Cooper, Samuel (1798-1876). Although he never served in a field command during the war, Cooper was the highest-ranking military officer for the Confederacy, serving as its chief administrative officer. Resigning his commission in March 1861 as Adjutant General for the U.S. Army after a 46-year career, he was immediately appointed Adjutant General and Inspector General for the Confederate States Army. A New York native, Cooper had strong ties to the South through his marriage to a prominent Virginia family and he also had a close friendship with Confederate President Jefferson Davis. His extensive experience as assistant adjutant general for the U.S. Army proved invaluable to Davis for organizing the new Confederate Army. The first group of officers appointed to generalships besides Cooper included Albert Sydney Johnston, Robert E. Lee, Joseph E. Johnston and Pierre G. T. Beauregard, with their seniority in that order. During the war, Cooper's home in Virginia was demolished by Union soldiers and its bricks used to create a fort the soldiers named "Traitor's Hill." After the war, he returned to Virginia to become a planter, which earned him a meager income until his death at age 78.

Early, Jubal A. (1816-1894). Graduated from West Point Military Academy in 1837 in the middle of his class, he ranked sixth in engineering students. Future generals who overlapped with him during his studies included Joseph Hooker, John Sedgwick, P.G.T. Beauregard, Richard Ewell, Irwin McDowell and George Meade, who would all become prominent commanders on both sides in the Civil War. After graduation, Early was assigned to the 3rd U.S. Artillery and fought in Florida in the Seminole Wars. After completing one year of service, he resigned from the army and returned to civilian life to study law and became a successful lawyer and served in the Virginia House of Delegates. In 1847-48 he re-enlisted in the U.S. Army with the 1st Virginia Volunteers to fight in the Mexican-American War, but the Virginians arrived too late for combat, although Early helped govern the town of Monterrey after its capture. After the war ended, he returned to his home state and became involved in politics. Opposed to secession, he nevertheless joined the Confederate Army when Virginia seceded from the Union and he fought in nearly all of the battles in the Eastern Theater for the Army of Northern Virginia. He was particularly effective in the Shenandoah Valley and led the raid that nearly penetrated Washington, D.C. His commander, Robert E. Lee, referred to him as *"my bad old man"* for his short temper, insubordination and use of profanity. The "old" referred to a stoop in his posture because of rheumatoid arthritis which plagued him all of his life. His short temper was well known beginning with his days at West Point when he provoked a fellow cadet to break a mess plate over his head. He was known to his troops as "Old Jube." His successes in the Shenandoah Valley came to an end from Union officer Philip Sheridan, when he suffered a disastrous defeat in 1865, shortly before the end of the war. Early escaped to Canada after Lee's surrender, but when U.S. President Andrew Johnson pardoned all Confederates in 1868, Early returned to Lynchburg, Virginia, and became a vocal opponent of the existing government and fostered what became called the "Lost Cause," which justified the Confederacy's case of white supremacy. Early vehemently criticized Confederate commander James Longstreet for his conduct in the war and for his work after the war with Ulysses S. Grant in support of Reconstruction in the South. Early's view of the war was published in *A Memoir of the Last Year of the War for Independence* (1866). Following a fall in Lynchburg in 1894, Early died at the age of 77.

Ewell, Richard (1817-1872). Graduated from West Point Military Academy in 1840 in the top third of his class, he was commissioned into the 1st U.S. Dragoons and assigned in 1843 to escort duty on the Santa Fe and Oregon Trails for two years. During the Mexican-American War under Winfield Scott, he was promoted for bravery in the battles that captured Mexico City. When his home state of Virginia seceded from the Union, he resigned from the U.S. Army to join the Confederate States Army and participated in the Battle of First Bull Run. He fought in Robert E. Lee's Army of Northern Virginia in the Peninsula Campaign and the battles of Second Bull Run, Gettysburg, Wilderness, Spotsylvania and Sailor's Creek. He worked most effectively under Thomas "Stonewall" Jackson in the battles of the Shenandoah Valley, in spite of their contrasting styles of Jackson's stern discipline and pious demeanor, compared with Ewell's spectacular profanity and eccentric character. After Jackson's death, Ewell continued to command troops under Robert E. Lee in the battles of Gettysburg, the Overland Campaign and at Sailor's Creek during the Confederate retreat to Appomattox. With a bald, bullet-shaped head, he was known to his men as "Old Baldy." After the war, he worked as a "gentleman farmer" with his wife in Tennessee, where they both died of pneumonia within three days of each other in 1872. His book, *The Making of a Soldier*, was published posthumously in 1935.

Floyd, John B. (1806-1863). Lawyer and active Virginia politician, he served as Secretary of War in 1856 under President Buchanan. Floyd was accused in 1860 of malfeasance with government contracts that funded the Pony Express and he was forced to resign in December 1860. Given that Lincoln had been elected in November, Floyd was also accused of sending large stores of government arms to arsenals in the South while still acting as Secretary of War for the Union, but the indictments were thrown out for lack of evidence of fraud on his part. After Virginia's secession, Floyd joined the Confederate States Army as a brigadier general and in January 1862, he assumed command of the garrison at Fort Donelson, Tennessee, in the Western Theater. When Ulysses S. Grant's army surrounded the fort and ordered its surrender, Floyd deserted the fort for fear he would be tried for treason for betraying his Constitutional oath to the United States under Buchanan. Turning over command of the fort to a subordinate, he escaped safely to Nashville by steamboat with two Virginia regiments and two artillery batteries. For his failure to remain with his command, Confederate President Davis removed him from the army without a court of inquiry. Floyd resumed his position in the Virginia Militia, but with failing health, he died a year later at Abingdon, Virginia, in 1863.

Forrest, Nathan Bedford (1821-1877). Born into a poor family in a frontier cabin in Tennessee, Forrest became a wealthy southern planter, owner and slave trader in Memphis at a time when the demand for slaves was huge in the Deep South. In 1860, he was one of the richest men in the South, having acquired a large personal fortune that included slaves and two plantations in Mississippi and one in Arkansas. At the onset of the Civil War, he enlisted in the Confederates States Army and was placed in the Tennessee Mounted Rifles. Although he lacked formal military training, he quickly established himself as a brilliant commander of cavalry, which established his nickname "Wizard of the Saddle." He used his troopers as mounted infantry and they were often deployed as lead artillery, an innovative advance in cavalry tactics. His raids in west Tennessee in December 1862 destroyed Grant's communications as he attempted to bring his army to Vicksburg from the east. The impact of Forrest on Grant's campaign forced the Union Army to revise its plans for how to attack the Vicksburg fortress. Forrest's cavalry fought effectively in several battles, including Shiloh, Murfreesboro, Chattanooga and Chickamauga, capturing hundreds of prisoners. His most infamous legacy was the massacre of Black prisoners at Fort Pillow in 1864 when his cavalry captured the fort, manned by soldiers of the U.S. Colored Troops. As Forrest's men encountered former slaves who had already surrendered, but were now soldiers in uniform, the enraged Confederates murdered them outright or subjected them to vicious torture and brutality, according to accounts from white survivors. Forrest was never held accountable for the crimes, but the actions of his cavalry put an end to all prisoner exchanges, which greatly increased the populations in the prisoner-of-war camps. After the war, Forrest was an early member of the Ku Klux Klan and became its first leader as the "Grand Wizard," a title taken from his calvary nickname, "Wizard of the Saddle." The Klan used "midnight parades" to employ brutal violence, intimidation and murder during the period of Reconstruction to prevent Blacks from voting or participating in Southern elections as candidates. Passage of the 15th Amendment in 1869 and the so-called "Klan Acts" of 1870 and 1871 provided the government with the authority and federal troops to prosecute Klan members aggressively, which achieved over one thousand convictions and Klan activities were greatly diminished. With the surrender of all Confederate armies in May-June 1865, Forrest surrendered and established a provisioning store in 1865 for Irish laborers hired to finish the railroad line connecting Memphis, Tennessee, and Little Rock, Arkansas. The store formed the center of a community that was later incorporated as Forrest City, Arkansas. He died at the age of 56, presumably of diabetes.

Gordon, John B. (1832-1904). Despite no military training, he became one of Lee's most trusted generals. Born in Georgia to a slave-holding family, who also owned a coal mine in the northwestern corner of the state, Gordon studied at the University of Georgia, but did not graduate. He chose instead to study law and passed the bar examination in Atlanta as a young man, but then returned to his father's coal mine when his law business generated few clients. At the beginning of the Civil War, he raised a company of mountaineers, known as the "Raccoon Roughs" for the raccoon hats they wore, and the group was incorporated into the 6th Alabama Infantry Regiment. Gordon's natural leadership qualities won him election as regimental colonel and he led the men in several battles under Robert E. Lee in the Army of Northern Virginia during the Peninsula Campaign in 1862. In the Battle of Antietam, he earned a reputation for fearlessness when he was shot five times defending the sunken road, or "Bloody Lane," barely surviving a ball that hit him in the face. He commanded troops at Gettysburg and in the Overland Campaign the following year, which earned him a promotion to major general. His corps accompanied Jubal Early to the Shenandoah Valley and took part in the victory at the Battle of Monocacy and the nearly achieved raid on Washington, D.C. Returning to the Shenandoah, the Confederates soon faced a large Union cavalry under Philip Sheridan and after being soundly defeated, the Southerners left the Valley to rejoin Lee at the Siege of Petersburg. Gordon led the Battle of Fort Stedman as the Confederates attempted to break through the siege lines, but despite initial success, they were pushed back. After the final railroad supply line was cut, the Southerners were forced out of Petersburg to head west for food and more supplies. Gordon's corps was defeated at Sailor's Creek, although part of the army escaped with him and arrived at Appomattox Station, only to find themselves surrounded by Union troops. With no more options, Lee surrendered the Army of Northern Virginia at Appomattox Court House. Gordon, only thirty-three years old, and one of the most successful leaders of the Southern army, led the Confederate troops in the surrender ceremonies which had been arranged by Union Joshua Chamberlain. After the war, Gordon vigorously opposed Reconstruction and did not believe in racial equality, retaining his white supremist views his entire life. He admitted to being a member of a secret "peace police" and it was believed he was a member of the Ku Klux Klan, although it was never proved. He was elected as Georgia's governor in 1886 and later served in the U.S. Senate for one term. His *Reminiscences of the Civil War*, published in 1903, gave first-hand accounts of battles and his speaking engagements focused on incidents that reflected the honor and courage of soldiers from both sides.

Hampton, Wade (1818-1902). Son of a wealthy plantation owner in Charleston, South Carolina, he studied law at South Carolina College (now the University of South Carolina), but never developed a law practice. He managed plantations in his home state in Mississippi and became a wealthy and active Democratic political leader. Elected as a state Senator in 1858, he resigned in 1861 at the age of 42 to enlist as a private in the South Carolina Militia. When he joined the Confederate Army, he organized and partially financed the "Hampton Legion," which consisted of six companies of infantry, four companies of cavalry and one battery of artillery. The Legion performed well at the Battle of First Bull Run and Hampton was promoted to brigadier general. After serving in the Peninsula Campaign, Hampton became second-in-command to Jeb Stuart, head of the cavalry for Robert E. Lee and the Army of Northern Virginia. Hampton's men conducted numerous raids through 1862 and in 1863 were part of Stuart's large swing around the Union army before reaching Gettysburg. After the death of Jeb Stuart during the Overland Campaign, Hampton led the Cavalry Corps, protecting Lee's army as it became besieged at Richmond-Petersburg. Hampton conducted the "Beefsteak Raid," during the siege that captured 300 Union prisoners and over two thousand beef cattle that fed the hungry Confederates. While Lee's army remained besieged, Hampton returned to South Carolina to combat William T. Sherman's army as it marched through the Carolinas, but the outnumbered Southern cavalry had little impact on the Union invasion. Hampton's troops surrendered to Union forces under Sherman along with other Confederates under Joseph E. Johnston in North Carolina in April 1865, which triggered the surrender of all the remaining Confederate armies, bringing an end of the Civil War. After the war, Hampton joined with Jubal Early in promoting the "Lost Cause" movement, which justified the case for white supremacy and attempted to explain why the Confederates had lost the war. Hampton opposed Reconstruction and maintained a life-long belief that Blacks were inferior to whites. He was elected governor in 1876 and 1878, but then resigned in his second term to become a U.S. Senator for two terms between 1879 and 1891.

Hardee, William J. (1815-1873). Graduated from West Point Military Academy in 1838, he was commissioned into the 2nd U.S. Dragoons and after serving in Florida, the army sent him to France to study military tactics. In the Mexican-American War, he was captured in Texas and later exchanged to serve under Winfield Scott. After the war, he was assigned to units of Texas Rangers and in 1856-60, trained cadets at West Point. In 1855, he published the tactical manual for Rifle and Light Infantry Tactics, which became the best-known drill manual of the Civil War. When his home state of Georgia seceded from the Union, he resigned his U.S. Army commission and joined the Confederate States Army and was soon assigned to organize a brigade of Arkansas regiments. Known as "Old Reliable" to his men, he was assigned to the Western Theater under Albert S. Johnston and fought in the Battle of Shiloh and followed the army's withdrawal to Corinth and later to Tupelo, Mississippi. Serving under Braxton Bragg, Hardee participated in the Confederate Heartland Offensive which ended with the Battle of Perryville in October 1862. When Bragg retreated to Stones River, his Army of Tennessee was confronted by the Union Army of the Cumberland under William Rosecrans. Hardee's troops played a significant role in the near defeat of Rosecrans on New Year's Eve 1862, but Union reinforcements forced Bragg to withdraw, granting Rosecrans the victory. Hardee lost patience with Bragg after Rosecrans defeated Bragg again at Tullahoma and requested a transfer to Joseph E. Johnston who was commanding troops in Mississippi during the Siege of Vicksburg. But Hardee then returned to Bragg and the Army of Tennessee after the Battle of Chickamauga. At Chattanooga, Hardee joined "The Revolt of the Generals," who petitioned President Davis to remove Bragg from command. But Davis retained Bragg until his army lost Chattanooga to Union General Ulysses S. Grant. At that point, Bragg was removed and Joseph E. Johnston took over command of the army at Dalton, Georgia, and Hardee fought against Union forces under William T. Sherman in the Atlanta Campaign. After Davis replaced Johnston with John Bell Hood, Hardee requested a transfer following the Battle of Jonesboro because he no longer wanted to serve under the aggressive and reckless Hood. Hardee was transferred to command the Department of South Carolina, Georgia and Florida, and was soon facing Sherman at Savannah, Georgia, at the end of Sherman's March to the Sea. But with inadequate troops, Hardee retreated north into the Carolinas where he joined Johnston's forces. Unfortunately, he lost his only son in a cavalry charge, 16-year-old Willie, in the Battle of Bentonville, North Carolina. He surrendered with Johnston to Sherman at Bennett's farm near Durham Station, which soon ended the Civil War. After the war, Hardee settled in Alabama where he eventually became president of the Selma and Meridian Railroad. He died of illness in 1873 at the age of 58.

Hill, Ambrose Powell (A.P.) (1825-1865). Graduating from West Point in 1847, he was immediately posted to serve in the final months of the Mexican-American War. He made friends easily and his West Point classmates included George Pickett, George Stoneman, George B. McClellan, Ambrose Burnside and Thomas "Stonewall" Jackson, who would all become generals on both sides. After the war with Mexico, Powell served in Florida and in garrisons along the Atlantic Sea coast. When his native state Virginia seceded from the Union, he resigned his commission with the U.S. Army and joined the Confederates. In spite of recurrent illness from a gonorrhea infection, his successes in battles gained him promotions throughout the Civil War. Hill fought in the battles of Bull Run (First and

Second), the Peninsula Campaign, Cedar Mountain, Antietam, Fredericksburg, Chancellorsville, Gettysburg, Mine Run, the Wilderness, North Anna, Cold Harbor and Petersburg. A capable fighter, Powell was known for an uncanny ability to turn the tide for the army at its most desperate moments. But his short temper frequently placed him in conflict with his other senior officers. A dispute over newspaper articles nearly resulted in a duel with James Longstreet, but Robert E. Lee intervened and placed Powell's division under Stonewall Jackson. Powell's lifestyle and frequent use of profanity conflicted with Jackson's rigid religious practices and pious discipline. The two men quarreled constantly and Powell was frequently placed under arrest. Nevertheless, their combined successes in battles were well known and a delirious Stonewall Jackson on his deathbed, called out, *"Order A.P. Hill to prepare for action!... prepare for action!"* During the final stages of the Siege of Petersburg, Powell was shot and killed by a Union soldier as he rode to the front with one staff officer during the Third Battle of Petersburg, just seven days before Lee's surrender.

Hoke, Robert (1837-1912). Graduated from the Kentucky Military Institute in 1854, he returned home to work in several family business operations for his widowed mother. With the secession of North Carolina, Hoke enlisted in Company K of the 1st North Carolina Infantry and was then promoted in March 1862 to lead the 33rd North Carolina Infantry Regiment, when its commander was captured. His regiment fought at the battles of Second Bull Run and Antietam. He was then moved to command the Trimble Brigade, composed of five North Carolina Regiments under Jubal Early, and fought at the Battle of Fredericksburg. Wounded in the Battle of Chancellorsville in 1863, defending Marye's Heights, he did not return to duty until 1864 when he served with distinction in the Battle of Cold Harbor. His troops were soon summoned to defend Richmond and Petersburg against the Union Army of the James. His next assignment brought him to Fort Fisher at Wilmington, North Carolina, to defend against the Union Army-Navy assault in January 1865, where the Confederates were defeated. Hoke's command was transferred to Joseph E. Johnston in North Carolina to defend against attacks from the Union Army under William T. Sherman as his army advanced through the Carolinas. Hoke surrendered his army along with Johnston's army at Bennett's Place, near Durham Station, North Carolina, April 26, 1865, and he was placed on parole and pardoned June 14, 1865. After the war, he pursued careers in mining and insurance and was director of the North Carolina Railroad for several years. He was buried with full military honors in 1912 at age 75.

Hood, John Bell (1831-1879). Graduated from West Point Military Academy in 1853 with three classmates who would join the Union Army: James B. McPherson, John M. Schofield and George H. Thomas. Commissioned to the 4th U.S. Infantry, Hood served in California and then in the 2nd U.S. Cavalry in Texas, where he was commanded by Albert S. Johnston and Robert E. Lee, both of whom would be senior generals in command of the Confederate State Army. With the firing on Fort Sumter, Hood resigned from the U.S. Army and joined the Confederates as a cavalry captain from Texas, even though his native state was neutral Kentucky. Commanding a cavalry at the Siege of Yorktown during the Peninsula Campaign, his aggressive leadership earned him a promotion to command a new brigade of mainly Texas regiments, which quickly gained a reputation as one of the army's toughest elite combat units. He was soon reassigned to lead a division under James Longstreet and continued to increase his reputation for heavy, aggressive fighting in the battles of Second Bull Run, Antietam and Fredericksburg in 1862. He missed the Battle of Chancellorsville because Longstreet's corps was on detached duty in Suffolk, Virginia. At the Battle of Gettysburg in 1863, Hood's left arm was severely wounded, taking him out of the battle, and though not amputated, the arm was permanently incapacitated. At the Battle of Chickamauga, Hood's right leg had to be amputated, leaving only four inches below the hip. After recovering, he continued to lead in battles, strapped to the saddle, with his artificial leg, made of cork, hanging stiffly, but tied to the stirrup. During the Atlanta Campaign under Joseph E. Johnston, Hood kept up a constant stream of criticism to President Davis in Richmond about Johnston's style of withdrawal and retreat. When the Union Army reached the outskirts of Atlanta, Davis removed Johnston from command, and placed Hood in charge. But his aggressive attacks did not break the Union siege and he was forced to evacuate the city of Atlanta in September 1864. Leaving Georgia, he moved his army west to Alabama and soon invaded Tennessee. Severely defeated at the Battles of Franklin and Nashville, he lost more than half the Army of Tennessee. Removed from command, the remnants of his army were sent to the Carolinas to be led by their old commander, Joseph E. Johnston. Hood did not receive another command and surrendered to Union officials in May 1865 after Johnston's surrender of all Confederate armies April 26, 1865. After the war, he built a successful insurance business and served his local community in New Orleans as a philanthropist for orphans, widows and wounded soldiers. He died in a yellow fever epidemic in 1879 at the age of 48.

Jackson, Thomas "Stonewall" (1824-1863). Born in what is today's West Virginia, he was orphaned at a young age and raised by various relatives. Deprived of schooling, he was self-educated and entered West Point Military Academy at the bottom of his class, but through hard work, excelled in his studies. Graduating 17th out of 59 students in 1846, he was assigned to the 1st U.S. Artillery Regiment, which proceeded down the Ohio and Mississippi Rivers to Point Isabel, Texas, where they were sent to fight in the Mexican-American War. After the war and a brief period in Florida, he resigned from the army and accepted a teaching position at the Virginia Military Institute in 1851 and remained there until the onset of the Civil War in 1861. His curriculum is still regarded as essential military practical course work in discipline, mobility, assessment of the enemy's strength while concealing your own, and using the combination of artillery with an infantry for an assault. He summarized his approach to battle as, *"Always mystify, mislead and surprise the enemy."* Nicknamed "Stonewall" after his troops held a grueling defense line at the Battle of First Bull Run, his reputation for stubborn doggedness to hold his position against a determined enemy became legendary. His characteristics of rigid discipline, religious zeal and inflexible determination built a small, but highly effective army that fought first in the Shenandoah Valley, winning multiple battles against Union armies that outnumbered him. Under Robert E. Lee, he was a principal commander for the Army of Northern Virginia in the Peninsula Campaign and the battles of Fredericksburg and Chancellorsville. Shot by friendly fire during the Battle of Chancellorsville, Jackson died eight days later, prompting his commander Lee to say, *"I have lost my right arm; I am bleeding from the heart."*

Johnston, Albert Sidney (1803-1862). Born in Kentucky, he graduated from West Point Military Academy in 1826 near the head of his class and remained with the U.S. Army until 1834, when he resigned to care for his young wife, who passed away in 1836. Moving to Texas, he joined the Texian Army to fight for Texas independence and then served as Secretary of War for the Republic of Texas, 1838-40. He re-enlisted in the U.S. Army for the Mexican-American War in 1846 and led the 1st Texas Rifle Volunteers. When many of his troops left because their enlistment period had been completed, Johnston remained for the Battle of Monterrey and impressed his troops with his leadership during the battle. One of the soldiers included future Union General Joseph Hooker, who said, *"The coolness and magnificent presence (that he) displayed on this field, left an impression on my mind that I have never forgotten."* When Texas seceded from the Union, Johnston resigned his post as commander of the U.S. Department of the Pacific in California to join the Confederate States Army. His extensive combat experience in the Black Hawk War, Texas War of Independence and the Mexican-American War made him the most senior and experienced general for the Confederacy and he was placed in charge of territory between the Mississippi River and the Allegheny Mountains. Capable and highly respected, he died in the field at the Battle of Shiloh, the highest-ranking general on either side to be killed during the war. Injured in one leg, he stayed in the battle, believing the wound to be minor, but he bled to death from a severed artery. Confederate President Davis, considering him the most capable general in the country, said of his death, *"… it was the turning of our fate."*

Johnston, Joseph E. (1807-1891). Graduated from West Point Military Academy in 1829, 13th in his class of 46 cadets, the same year as classmate Robert E. Lee, who graduated second. Johnston was appointed into the 4th U.S. Artillery and served in Florida, Texas and Kansas. He resigned from the army in 1837 to work as a civil engineer, but while performing as a topographer on a war ship in Florida, he got shot at so many times, he was prompted to rejoin the army in 1838. In the Mexican-American War, he served on the staff of commander Winfield Scott, who commented about Johnston, *"... he is a great soldier, but had an unfortunate knack of getting himself shot in nearly every engagement."* When his home state of Virginia seceded from the Union, Johnston left the army to join the Confederacy as the highest-ranking U.S. army officer to resign and was promoted to full general for the Confederate States Army. President Jefferson Davis gave three other generals a higher rank than Johnston's even though he had out-ranked all of them in the "old army." When Johnston complained, Davis refused to alter the rankings, which created a strained relationship between the two men throughout the war. As senior commander, Johnston organized the Army of the Shenandoah and in the Battle of First Bull Run, he was able to bring troops from the Shenandoah and turn the tide when they joined P.G.T. Beauregard on the battlefield against the Union army. Johnston played a major role in the Peninsula Campaign in 1862 until he was wounded, fighting against Union George McClellan's Army of the Potomac. As Johnston recovered from his injuries, Robert E. Lee was named to command the Army of Northern Virginia and became the Confederacy's dominant commander in the Eastern Theater for the rest of the war. Johnston's next command replaced Braxton Bragg as commander of the Confederate Army of Tennessee after Bragg was defeated at Chattanooga. Johnston's new command faced Union commander William T. Sherman all through the Atlanta Campaign of 1864 until he was replaced by John Bell Hood just before Atlanta fell to the Union Army. Johnston was moved to North Carolina in semi-retirement until early 1865 when he faced Sherman again in the Carolinas Campaign. His surrender to Sherman in April 1865 included the surrender of the remaining Confederate armies which soon brought an end to the Civil War. After the war, Johnston and Sherman corresponded frequently and met together for friendly dinners. Johnston never allowed criticism of Sherman in his presence and was an honorary pall bearer at Sherman's funeral in 1891. He refused to wear a hat during the cold and wet ceremonies, saying, *"If General Sherman was here in my place and I was in the casket, he would do the same for me."* But the event caused him to contract pneumonia shortly afterward and he died one month later.

Jones, William E. "Grumble" (1824-1864). Graduated from West Point Military Academy in 1848 in the upper fourth of his class, he was commissioned into the U.S. Mounted Rifles and served with the cavalry fighting Indians in the frontier west. Resigning from the U.S. Army in 1857, he became a farmer in Virginia until the onset of the Civil War, when he joined the 1st Virginia Cavalry Regiment and was transferred to serve under the command of Jeb Stuart. His nickname "Grumble" reflected his irritable disposition and his hard-liner disciplinary command of his troops. When Confederate forces were reorganized in the fall of 1861, enlisted men elected their own officers and Jones was not re-elected to his post. He resigned from the 1st Virginia and was next appointed to lead the 7th Virginia in the western part of the state and within a few months, he was given command of all cavalry in the Valley District of "Stonewall" Jackson. His cavalry fought in the Peninsula Campaign and the Battle of Second Bull Run. At Gettysburg, Jones' cavalry screened the rear of the Army of Northern Virginia, but remained apart from the main battlefield, guarding the trains and Harpers Ferry. Jones quarreled constantly with Jeb Stuart, who headed the cavalry for Robert E. Lee's Army of Northern Virginia and in October 1863, Stuart court-martialed Jones for insulting him. Grumble was found guilty, but Robert E. Lee intervened and transferred him to the Trans-Allegheny Department in West Virginia. In early 1864, Jones assumed command of Confederate forces in the Shenandoah Valley but in the Battle of Piedmont against Union forces under David Hunter in June 1864, Jones was killed in action.

Lee, Fitzhugh (1835-1905). Born into a military family, Fitzhugh was the fourth child of Sydney Smith Lee, brother of Robert E. Lee. Both his father and uncle served in the Mexican-American War and his grandfather, Harry "Lighthorse" Lee was a prominent officer and delegate during the American Revolution. Fitzhugh Lee, nicknamed Fitz, graduated from West Point Military Academy in 1856 and was commissioned into the Cavalry Regiment commanded by Albert Sidney Johnston. He distinguished himself in combat against the Comanches in Texas and then returned to West Point in 1860 as an instructor of cavalry tactics. When Virginia seceded from the Union in April 1861, he resigned from the U.S. Army and joined the Confederates and was soon assigned to the 1st Virginia Cavalry under Jeb Stuart. Engagements in the Peninsula Campaign were followed by battles at Chancellorsville, Antietam and Gettysburg. Fitz Lee fought in all the battles of the Overland Campaign and following the death of Jeb Stuart at the Battle of Yellow Tavern, he became Robert E. Lee's Cavalry Commander. At the Battle of Trevilian Station, Fitz Lee's cavalry prevented Philip Sheridan from assisting Union forces in the Shenandoah, which saved the supply line for the Confederates who were besieged at Petersburg. But the Confederates were defeated in the Shenandoah Valley during Jubal Early's campaign in 1864 and Fitz Lee's troops returned to support Lee's army during the Siege of Petersburg. Instrumental in the Appomattox Campaign, he led the final charge at Farmville on April 9, followed soon after by the surrender of Robert E. Lee at Appomattox Courthouse. After the war, he served as Virginia's governor from 1885 to 1889 and spent his final years in politics and farming. He died in 1905 at the age of 70.

Lee, George Washington Custis (1832-1913). Oldest son of Robert E. Lee, he was named for his maternal grandfather, George Washington Custis, who was the step-grandson of George Washington and grandson of Martha Custis

APPENDIX B.

Washington. Custis Lee attended West Point Military Academy and during his third year overlapped with his father's tenure as Superintendent of the Academy. Graduating first in his class in 1854, he was commissioned into the Corps of Engineers and served in Florida, Georgia and California until 1861 when he was stationed in Washington, D.C. When Virginia seceded from the Union, he resigned from the U.S. Army and then served as aide-de-camp to Confederate President Jefferson Davis, a position he held until late in the war. In 1864, he was given command of Richmond's local defenses against Union forces in the Siege of Petersburg and extended the eastern defenses on the James River opposite Drewry's Bluff. In 1865, when the Confederate army abandoned Richmond to seek supplies in the Appomattox Campaign, Custis commanded troops in the field and was captured at Sailor's Creek, three days before his father surrendered to Grant at Appomattox which soon brought an end to the war. After the war, he became a professor at Virginia Military Institute and upon the death of his father, Robert E. Lee, he succeeded him as president of Washington and Lee University. He held that position until he retired at age 65 and moved to the home of his late brother, Rooney Lee, where he remained until his death at the age of 81.

Lee, Robert E. (1807-1870). Born to Revolutionary war hero, Harry "Lighthorse" Lee, Robert was raised by his mother and extended family member William Henry Fitzhugh when his father moved to the West Indies to avoid debtors' prison. Educated in "gentleman's schools," he was appointed to West Point Military Academy and graduated from there in 1829, second in his class. His next several years with the Corps of Engineers were spent inspecting and constructing coastal defenses, but when he was assigned as aide-de-camp to Winfield Scott during the Mexican-American War, he showed his brilliance in reconnaissance evaluations of difficult terrain that were instrumental in American victories in several battles. Appointed as Superintendent of the Military Academy at West Point in 1852, he served there for three years until 1855 when he was placed under Albert Sidney Johnston in a combat mission in the frontier west fighting Apache and Comanche Indians. In 1857, Lee took a two-year leave of absence to act as executor of his wife's estate from her father, the wealthy George Washington Parke Custis. Management of the estate of vast landholdings and two hundred slaves was a task Lee greatly disliked and several accounts reported that he rendered harsh punishments to recalcitrant slaves, who had expected to be freed on the death of Custis. The slaves were eventually freed in December 1862 according to the terms of the Custis will. Returning to army duty in 1859, Lee led the troops that arrested John Brown at Harpers Ferry in October 1859 and he was then transferred to frontier duty in Texas. In April 1861, when Virginia seceded from the Union, Lee resigned from the U.S. Army after a 32-year career to join the Confederacy and was named one of its top five generals. After Virginia's secession, Arlington House from the Custis estate was confiscated and appropriated as a National Cemetery for Union soldiers. During the first battles in the Virginia peninsula against Union forces under George McClellan, Lee was promoted to lead the Army of Northern Virginia when Joseph E. Johnston was wounded and removed from the battlefield. Lee's aggressive style in combat made him a formidable adversary as he confronted the Union Army of the Potomac, defeating the Northerners in multiple battles between 1862-63, which included the several battles of the Virginia Peninsula Campaign, Chancellorsville, Fredericksburg and the Mud March, where he prevailed over Union armies greatly outnumbering his own. He blamed himself for the loss at Gettysburg when he ordered an ill-advised assault across an open field, losing a massive number of casualties. Battling against Ulysses S. Grant in the Overland Campaign resulted in large numbers of casualties for both armies, but the Confederates were eventually forced into the Siege of Petersburg, which lasted for ten months when they were finally forced to face Grant's armies in the open. Lee surrendered his army at Appomattox, Virginia, on April 9, 1865, which soon brought an end to the Civil War. At his surrender, Lee was paroled with the rest of his men, so was not arrested but was not officially pardoned until 1975 when Congress reinstated it. Although he supported education for Blacks, he was opposed to giving them the right to vote. He became a figurehead for Southern advocates who wanted to pursue the war, but Lee spoke against it, urging reconciliation and the reintegration of former Confederates into the nation's political life. Appointed as head of Washington College at Lexington, Virginia (now Washington and Lee University), he instituted new programs in law, commerce and journalism. Recruiting students from the North, he ensured that they were treated well and insisted that all students adhere to his rule of conduct that "... *every student be a gentleman.*" Worshipped by his students, he remained president of the college until his death in 1870 at the age of 63.

Lee, Stephen D. (1833-1908). The son of a prominent Charleston, South Carolina, family, Stephen Lee entered West Point Military Academy in 1850, graduating in the middle of his class four years later. He then served in the U.S. Army in Florida and Kansas and Dakota Territories, before resigning in February 1861 to enlist in the Confederate States Army. He was assigned as aide-de-camp to P.G.T. Beauregard at the time of the firing on Fort Sumter and then served with distinction in the Peninsula Campaign in the Army of Northern Virginia and later led troops at the battles of Second Bull Run and Antietam. In 1862, he was transferred to Vicksburg and fought against Union forces at the Battle of Chickasaw Bayou and Champion Hill and then surrendered to Union forces at the end of the Siege of Vicksburg. Exchanged later that year, he was promoted to command the Department of Alabama and East Louisiana in 1864. Assigned to the Army of Tennessee under John Bell Hood, he fought for the defense of Atlanta, but when the army was forced to withdraw, he remained with Hood through the battles of Franklin and Nashville, Tennessee, in December 1864, where the Confederates suffered punishing losses. Lee then joined Joseph E. Johnston's army in the Carolinas in 1865 and was surrendered with Johnston's army to Union forces in April, which brought an end to the Civil War. After the war, he was the first president of the Agricultural and Mechanical College of Mississippi and established it as a segregated institution. His Civil War writings, published in 1880, included *Sherman's Meridian Expedition* and *Sooy Smith's Raid to West Point*.

Lee, William Henry Fitzhugh ("Rooney") (1837-1891). Second son of Robert E. Lee, he aspired to follow in his father's footsteps, but after his applications to West Point Military Academy were rejected, because of a policy of accepting only one brother from the same family (Custis Lee had been accepted in 1850), Rooney entered Harvard College in the fall of 1854. His nickname "Rooney," which means "darling" in Gaelic, was given to him at a young age, presumably to distinguish him from his cousin Fitzhugh Lee, the son of Robert E. Lee's brother. With a powerful build and athletic abilities, Rooney became a champion oarsman on the rowing team at Harvard and his studies fell off during his second and third years. An offer for a commission in the 6th U.S. Army Infantry, facilitated by Winfield Scott, head of the U.S. Army and friend of his father, prompted Rooney to leave Harvard and report to Albert Sydney Johnston to serve in the western frontier in Utah Territory. But by 1859, he decided to resign from the army and with his new wife, the couple moved to White House Plantation on the Pamunkey River, which included about one hundred slaves, part of his mother's estate from his grandfather George Washington Parke Custis. He farmed and refurbished the plantation until the firing on Fort Sumter, when he organized a local company that was absorbed into the 9th Virginia Regiment that initially served in the mountains of western Virginia. Soon assigned to the command of Jeb Stuart, Rooney Lee fought in several battles in the Peninsula Campaign and was then assigned to Fitzhugh Lee's cavalry. At the Battle of Chancellorsville, his unit was detached to defend against the Union raid led by George Stoneman. Wounded at the Battle of Gettysburg, Rooney was sent to his wife's family farm to recover, but he was captured by Union troops and spent several months as a prisoner-of-war. Finally exchanged in February 1864, he returned to the Confederate Army of Northern Virginia and was promoted to command a division in battles of the Overland Campaign, which included the Wilderness, Todd's Tavern, Spotsylvania Court House and North Anna. Rooney's division patrolled the extreme right of the Confederate line during the Siege of Petersburg. When the army evacuated Petersburg, Rooney Lee's troops screened the army and battled cavalry at Namozine Church. He surrendered with his father at Appomattox Court House with only 300 officers and men, one tenth the size of the command at Petersburg. After the war, he returned to White House Plantation, which had been burned to the ground, and restored the farm to continue farming. When his mother died in 1873, he inherited the Ravensworth Plantation near Springfield,

Virginia, and moved there. Active in Virginia politics, he was elected to the U.S. House of Representatives in 1887 and served there until his death in 1891 at the age of 54.

Longstreet, James (1821-1904). Graduated from West Point Military Academy in 1842, second from bottom of his class because of his disregard for earning demerits the last two years of his studies, which placed his low standing in the graduating class. Nevertheless, he would become one of the most significant generals during the Civil War and the principal subordinate to Robert E. Lee, who relied on him in nearly all of his major battles. Popular with his West Point classmates, including George Pickett and future Union generals Ulysses S. Grant, William Rosecrans and John Pope, who would all play prominent roles in the Civil War to come, Longstreet served with distinction in the Mexican-American War, commanding forces under Zachary Taylor and leading regimental colors during battles at Mexico City under Winfield Scott. After the war, he continued his career as an Army officer until his home state of South Carolina seceded from the Union and he ended his twenty years with the U.S. Army to join the Confederacy in July 1861. He was initially assigned to serve under P.G.T. Beauregard, but as the war evolved, he became Robert E. Lee's most trusted advisor in the Army of Northern Virginia, who called him his "Old War Horse." Longstreet served under Lee in nearly all of the major battles against the Army of the Potomac in the Eastern Theater. He briefly faced his old friend Grant on the battlefield in Chattanooga under Braxton Bragg but his corps was detached to confine Union forces at Knoxville under Ambrose Burnside. During the Overland Campaign, Longstreet was wounded in the Battle of the Wilderness, and did not return to duty until the Southern army was besieged at Petersburg. After Lee's surrender at Appomattox, Longstreet and Grant resumed their long-term friendship from West Point cadet days and he supported Grant when he was elected President in 1868 and 1872. When Longstreet urged Southerners to support the Republican Reconstruction Acts, he was vilified in the Southern press and labeled a "scalawag." His autobiography, *From Manassas to Appomattox*, published in 1896, was critical of Lee and Stonewall Jackson. His efforts to support Blacks made him a target of "Lost Cause" attacks, particularly from Jubal Early, and he spent the rest of his life defending his name. He died of poor health in 1904 at the age of 83.

Magruder, John B. (1807-1871). Graduated from West Point Military Academy in 1830 in the middle of his class, he was known as "Prince John" and the perfect Virginia gentleman for his social graces, a fondness for resplendent uniforms and his theatrical mannerisms. Commissioned to garrison duties mostly on the Atlantic Coast until 1845, he was assigned to serve in the Mexican-American War 1846-48 under Zachary Taylor. During the war, he amused the men in their off-duty hours by creating stage performances, using actors who would become future Civil War generals. After the war, he became an expert in the use of light artillery and was recognized as one of the lead artillerists in the army. When his home state of Virginia seceded from the Union, he joined the Confederate States Army and was placed in command of defenses in the Virginia peninsula, successfully defeating a Union attack there early in the Civil War. When the Union Army under George McClellan launched the Virginia Peninsula Campaign in early 1862, Magruder's small army at Yorktown successfully delayed the much larger Union forces as they attempted to advance up the peninsula to Richmond. Magruder continued to participate in the battles at Williamsburg, Seven Pines and the Seven Days battles on the peninsula. After McClellan withdrew from the Peninsula Campaign, Magruder was reassigned to the West to recover territory in Missouri and Louisiana and reinforce Richard Taylor's command in the Red River Campaign in 1864. At the end of the Civil War, Magruder fled to Mexico and worked for Emperor Maximilian in the Land Office of Colonization, but returned to the United States in early 1867 before Maximilian's defeat and execution in June 1867. Magruder took the loyalty of oath to the Union and after his failed attempts to establish a law practice, he settled in Houston where he died in 1871 of poor health.

Mahone, William (1826-1895). Born as a third generation of Irish immigrants in Virginia, his father owned a tavern in the small town of Jerusalem, Virginia, plus some farmland and a number of slaves. The young Irishman was accepted as a cadet in the new Virginia Military Institute in Lexington and graduated in 1847 with a degree in civil engineering. He engaged in a number of projects working for railroads and invented a novel roadbed through the Great Dismal Swamp between South Norfolk and Suffolk that has survived more than one hundred sixty years. At the outbreak of the Civil War, he was president and superintendent of the Norfolk and Petersburg Railroad, but resigned to join the Confederate States Army when Virginia seceded. He served under Robert E. Lee in the Army of Northern Virginia during the Peninsula Campaign, and the battles of Second Bull Run (Manassas), Fredericksburg, Chancellorsville, Gettysburg, the Overland Campaign and the Appomattox Campaign. At the Battle of Sailor's Creek as the army fled west toward Appomattox, the Confederate Army was severely depleted, losing more than 8,000 to casualties, about one-fifth of its army, which included the loss of several Confederate officers, including Generals Richard Ewell and Custis Lee. As Lee observed the survivors from a high bluff at Rice's Station, he exclaimed in front of Mahone, whose division was protecting the escape of the remnants of the army, *"My God, has the army dissolved?"* Mahone replied, *"No, General, here are troops ready to do their duty."* Lee then responded, *"Yes, there are still some true men left… Will you please keep those people back?"* Lee surrendered to Ulysses S. Grant at Appomattox three days later.

McCulloch, Benjamin (1811-1862). Following Davy Crockett into Texas in 1835, McCulloch became a soldier in the Texas Revolution to win its independence from Mexico, then became a Texas Ranger fighting Indians. During the Mexican-American War, he raised a company of Rangers that joined the 1st Regiment of Texas Mounted Volunteers. Serving under Zachary Taylor, he acquired national fame for his daring exploits. When Texas seceded from the Union at the onset of the Civil War, McCulloch was quickly commissioned as a general in the Confederate States Army and given command of Indian Territory. Bringing together regiments from Texas, Arkansas, Louisiana and Indian Territory, McCulloch formed the Army of the West, headquartered at Little Rock, Arkansas. His army supported Sterling Price at the Battle of Wilson's Creek in Missouri in 1861, but McCulloch had little respect for Price or the Missouri State Guard and the two generals feuded bitterly after the battle. When Price and his army was pushed out of Missouri in 1862 into Arkansas, the two generals joined forces at the Battle of Pea Ridge, Arkansas, under the overall command of Earl Van Dorn. McCulloch was killed in the field as his troops faced Union forces under Union Stanley Curtis. McCulloch was one of thirty men inducted into the Texas Ranger Hall of Fame at Fort Fisher, Waco, Texas, and Fort McCulloch was built in his honor in the southern section of Indian Territory.

Morgan, John Hunt (1824-1864). Raised in Kentucky, he attended Transylvania University near Lexington, but was suspended for engaging in a duel with a fraternity brother. Enlisting as a 21-year-old cavalry private in the Mexican-American War in 1846, he saw action at the Battle of Buena Vista, serving under Zachary Taylor. Returning to Kentucky, he became a successful hemp grower and raised a local militia group, known as the Lexington Rifles. At the onset of the Civil War, the group joined the Confederate States Army and became the 2nd Kentucky Cavalry Regiment that fought in the Battle of Shiloh in April 1862. Attached to Joseph Wheeler's cavalry under Braxton Bragg, Morgan immediately set out on a raid through Kentucky with a cavalry of 900 men that harassed the rear of the Union Army under Don Carlos Buell, capturing hundreds of prisoners and looting numerous towns and counties of ransomed cash and supplies, diverting some 20,000 Union troops to protect supplies and communication lines. He became famous as the "Thunderbolt for the Confederacy" and encouraged Confederate leadership to launch the Confederate Heartland Offensive, also known as the Kentucky Campaign, led by Braxton Bragg and E. Kirby Smith, who expected large numbers of Kentucky recruits to join the Confederate cause. When the recruits did not materialize and Bragg withdrew back to Tennessee, Morgan launched another Kentucky raid in 1863 against Bragg's orders. More than 2,000 raiders crossed the Ohio River and rode over 1,000 miles attacking towns in southern Indiana, which aroused local militia in Illinois, Indiana and Ohio and brought forth dozens of gunboats along the Ohio River. More than half of Morgan's command was captured at Buffington Island on the Ohio and West Virginia border on July 19, 1863, and the men spent the rest of the war in the infamous Camp Douglas Prisoner of War camp in Chicago, known as the "Andersonville of the North." Morgan and the rest of his followers were captured a week later and sentenced to Ohio Penitentiary. A few months later in November, Morgan and six of his officers successfully escaped the penitentiary and eventually made it to safety in the South. Returning to active duty, he was planning another raid into Kentucky in 1864 when he was killed by a surprise Union raid in Greenville, Tennessee.

Mosby, John (1833-1916). Born to a highly respected Virginia family whose English ancestors traced their origins back to 1600, he began his education in a local school in Powhatan County before transferring to a larger facility in Charlottesville, Virginia, at age ten. Small in stature and frail health, he was the target of bullies all through school. During his studies at the University of Virginia, he was attacked by a local bully who charged him with his head down, and Mosby shot him in the neck with a small revolver, killing him. Found guilty at his trial of an unlawful shooting, he was sentenced to one year in prison and a $500 fine. During incarceration, he was befriended by the prosecuting attorney who loaned him his library so that Mosby could study law. Friends and family were able to obtain a pardon for him and the fine was rescinded. With his new-found knowledge, Mosby was able to pass the bar exam and established his own practice. At the onset of the Civil War, Mosby joined the Confederate Army even though he spoke against secession. His first commander was William "Grumble" Jones in the Washington Mounted Rifles and they fought in the Battle of First Bull Run. Mosby was then transferred to Jeb Stuart in the Peninsula Campaign and the Battle of Fredericksburg. At the end of 1862, he decided to form an independent cavalry operating in Northern Virginia, where the men continued to live as normal citizens, scattered among the population. The Confederate Congress had passed the Partisan Ranger Act in April that supported Mosby's group and in January 1863, Robert E. Lee authorized Mosby's Rangers, a regimental sized command, that could disappear into the civilian population as farmers or townsmen. Known for lightning quick raids, Mosby acquired the nickname, "Gray Ghost," as the Rangers often worked stealthily inside Union lines, surprising and capturing unsuspecting officers and enlisted men. Their weapons favored the 1860 Colt Army revolvers that provided close contact firepower but were easy to carry and use. By 1864, Mosby's activities in the Shenandoah Valley had attracted sufficient attention that Ulysses S. Grant sent Philip Sheridan and his cavalry to take charge and eliminate the Confederate threat in the Valley. After Sheridan defeated Jubal Early in September 1864, he implemented "The Burning," which targeted Mosby's territory, destroying crops, barns and grain and capturing livestock. By the end of the year, there were few Southern forces left in the Valley except for Mosby.

After the surrender of Robert E. Lee in April 1865, Mosby negotiated for the surrender of his Rangers to have the same terms offered to Lee, which he eventually received from Ulysses S. Grant, General-in-Chief for the Union. Mosby finally surrendered to Union officers on June 17, one of the last Confederate officers to do so. After the war, he resumed his law practice and became friends with President Grant, supporting his administration. He campaigned for Rutherford B. Hayes as Grant's successor and Hayes appointed him as the U.S. Consul to Hong Kong. He continued to work in government positions until his 70s and wrote a book, *Stuart's Cavalry in the Gettysburg Campaign* (1908). He died in 1916 at the age of 83.

Pemberton, John C. (1814-1881). Graduated from West Point Military Academy in 1837 in the middle of his class, he was commissioned to the 4th U.S. Artillery Regiment. His roommate and closest friend, George Meade, would become a leading Union general in the Civil War. Pemberton was assigned to Florida and the northern U.S. frontier along the Canadian border before the onset of the Mexican-American War in 1846, where he served in a number of battles, sharing duties in the same division with Ulysses S. Grant. Despite his Pennsylvania-based roots, his marriage to a woman from Virginia influenced his decision to resign his U.S. Army commission and join the Confederate States Army after Virginia seceded from the Union. Considered a traitor in the North as his brothers served in the Union Army, he was also viewed with suspicion in the South by many of his Confederate colleagues. Pemberton was given command of the garrison at Vicksburg in 1862, but had to surrender his army to former colleague Ulysses S. Grant in 1863 after the Siege of Vicksburg. Southerners were quick to turn against Pemberton, speculating that his northern background had influenced his decision to capitulate to Grant. Disgraced, Pemberton voluntarily resigned his general's commission and spent the remainder of the war as an artillery officer. After the war, he continued a long-lasting feud with Confederate Joseph E. Johnston, whose army had not rescued the besieged Vicksburg garrison. Returning to his home state of Pennsylvania after 1876, he was buried in the Laurel Hill Cemetery in Philadelphia over protests by prominent Union-loyal families that an unrepentant Confederate be buried there.

Pickett, George (1825-1875). Graduated from West Point Military Academy in 1846 on the eve of the Mexican-American War at the bottom of his class. In normal times, he would have been posted to an obscure post with few chances for advancement, but because of the war, the army needed junior officers and Pickett received a commission in the 8th Infantry and was soon fighting against the Mexican Army. He won distinction at the Battle of Chapultepec in Mexico City, when his wounded friend James Longstreet handed him the infantry flag to carry over the wall and bring it to the roof of the palace, announcing its victory over the

APPENDIX B.

Mexicans. After the war, Pickett served in Washington Territory until his native home state of Virginia seceded from the Union and he returned to Washington, D.C., to resign his U.S. Army commission and join the Confederate States Army. Nearly always dressed in an immaculate uniform with gold buttons and wearing a small blue cap over his long, curled hair that reached his shoulders, he presented a dashing figure on his sleek large horse named "Old Black." His first command was in the Peninsula Campaign where he was commended by his superiors as he led a brigade in the battles of Williamsburg and Seven Pines that saw heavy fighting. Pickett's next major combat was at the Battle of Gettysburg, when his division was ordered across an open field into punishing Union artillery. Losing half his men and all thirteen of his regimental commanders, "Pickett's Charge" became known as a pivotal turning point for the Civil War as it forced the Army of Northern Virginia into retreat and ended its invasion of the North. During the Siege of Petersburg, Pickett failed to hold the important railroad crossing at Five Forks west of Petersburg, because of his absence from the field enjoying a "shad bake" with fellow officers, bringing an inglorious end to Pickett's military career. The loss of Five Forks and the Southside Railroad forced the Confederates to abandon Petersburg and soon led to the surrender of Robert E. Lee's army to Ulysses S. Grant at Appomattox. Paroled with the rest of the soldiers in Lee's command, Pickett fled to Canada, fearing prosecution for his controversial execution of twenty-two soldiers in 1864 in New Bern, North Carolina, that he claimed were deserters. But others claimed they were members of local militias and had been unwillingly transferred to the Confederate Army. Pickett remained in Canada for a year until Grant confirmed that an investigation into the affair had ended and Pickett could return to the United States. In ill health after the war, Pickett carried a bitter memory of the fateful "Pickett's Charge" at Gettysburg and blamed Lee for the destruction of his men. He died at the age of 50 in 1875.

Pike, Albert (1809-1891). Settling in Arkansas in 1833 as a young man, he taught school, worked for a newspaper and became involved in Whig politics. Studying law, he passed the bar in 1837 and became a highly effective lawyer, making several claims in the 1850s against the federal government on behalf of the American Indians. With the onset of the Mexican-American War, he enlisted as a member of the Arkansas Mounted Infantry Regiment and fought in the Battle of Buena Vista. With the beginning of the Civil War, he supported the South and was commissioned as a brigadier general in the Confederate States Army with a command in Indian Territory that took advantage of his multiple contacts with the Indians, particularly the Cherokee tribes. Pike led a force of Indian warriors into the Battle of Pea Ridge, Arkansas, in March 1862, where his commander Benjamin McCulloch was killed. After the defeat at Pea Ridge, Pike built Fort McCulloch in his honor near Blue River in southern Indian Territory. Later that year, Pike was charged with insubordination and treason for mishandling of Confederate money and material and was eventually arrested but then released. Resigning from the Confederate State Army, he practiced law, became a prominent member of the Masons, wrote books and died at the age of 81.

Pillow, Gideon J. (1806-1878). Lawyer, politician and slave owner, Pillow provided significant support for the nomination of James K. Polk for President in 1844 and Polk rewarded him with an appointment of Major General of Volunteers in the U.S. Army at the beginning of the Mexican-American War. Serving under Winfield Scott, Pillow narrowly missed being court-martialed for trying to take credit for victories at the Battles of Churubusco and Contreras at Mexico City. He later claimed credit for the American triumphs in the war in a letter to the New Orleans newspaper, which prompted Scott to have him arrested for insubordination and violation of military orders. Scott would later write of Pillow that he was *"the only person I have ever known who was wholly indifferent in the choice between truth and falsehood, honesty and dishonesty"* and willing to commit a *"total sacrifice of moral character to attain his desired end."* Early in the Civil War, Pillow built a fort at Memphis, Tennessee, on the Mississippi River in the spring of 1861, naming it after himself. Assigned as second-in-command at Fort Donelson, Pillow was placed in charge when John Floyd, the fort's commander, decided to escape rather than surrender to Ulysses S. Grant. Pillow then made the same decision, turning over command to Simon Bolivar Buckner, who was left in charge to surrender the fort to Grant. Pillow successfully escaped the fort by boat before its surrender and was forever dishonored for abandoning his post and the men. He was suspended from command by President Davis for *"grave errors in judgment in military operations."* His actions at Fort Donelson and his later failure to lead his men at the Battle of Stones River sent his military career into decline and for most of the war he was largely limited to recruiting assignments. After the war, he practiced law but became involved in numerous lawsuits involving his daughters and their spouses. A victim of yellow fever he died in 1878 at the age of 72 and was buried in Memphis.

Polk, Leonidas (1806-1864). Graduated from West Point Military Academy in 1827, eighth in his class, he was appointed to the artillery, but resigned his commission the same year to enter the Virginia Theological Seminary. Completing his studies there, he joined the Episcopal Church in 1830 to become a priest and later was elected as first Bishop of Louisiana in 1841. With the outbreak of the Civil War and the secession of Louisiana, Polk resigned his ecclesiastical position to join the Confederate States Army. In spite of his lack of combat experience, he was promoted to command at high levels and led troops in the Battles of Shiloh, Perryville, Stones River, the Tullahoma Campaign, Chickamauga, Chattanooga and the Atlanta Campaign. He was second in command to Joseph E. Johnston in the Atlanta Campaign where he was killed by cannon fire on Pine Mountain. One of the Southern Army of Tennessee's most beloved generals, he was known as the "Fighting Bishop."

Price, Sterling (1809-1867). As a young man, he moved to Missouri in 1830 with his parents who were tobacco farmers. He soon became a prominent politician who was elected to the Missouri state legislature in 1835 and again in 1840, when he became Speaker of the House. In 1844, he was elected to the U.S. Congress House of Representatives just before the Mexican-American War (1846-1848). When he wasn't re-elected to Congress in 1846, he became leader of a Missouri regiment that served in the Mexican-American War under the command of Stephen Kearny. Sent west, he was appointed military governor of New Mexico Territory and put down a rebellion by the American Indians, known as the Taos Revolt. Returning to Missouri after the war, he became a successful slave owner and planter and was elected governor of the state between 1853-57. With the onset of the Civil War, he was appointed to command the pro-secessionist Missouri State Guard, which collaborated with Confederate forces from Missouri and Arkansas. He fought in a number of battles in the Western Theater, including Wilson's Creek and at Lexington, both in Missouri; Pea Ridge, Arkansas; Iuka and Corinth, Mississippi; and Helena and the Camden Expedition in Arkansas. His last battle was at Westport, Missouri, Oct. 23, 1864, near Kansas City, where his outnumbered army was soundly defeated by Samuel Curtis, ending Confederate offensives west of the Mississippi River. Rather than surrender, he fled to Mexico where he tried to set up a colony in exile under Emperor Maximilian, but when the colony failed, he returned to Missouri where he soon died in St. Louis of cholera in 1866. He was known as "Old Pap" by his men.

Shoup, Francis Asbury (1834-1896). Graduated from West Point in 1858 in the middle of his class, he fought in Florida before resigning from the U.S. Army to return to his home state of Indiana and practice law. At the outset of the Civil War, he shocked his family and friends by resigning from the Indianapolis Zouave militia to move to Florida and fight for the Confederacy. Captured at Vicksburg, he was later paroled and assigned to Georgia where he served as chief engineer for Joseph E. Johnston during the Atlanta Campaign. He designed and built Johnston's River Line, which consisted of thirty-six impenetrable forts, later called "Shoupades," that were *"the strongest I ever saw,"* according to William T. Sherman, whose army avoided a frontal assault on the fortifications. Rather than attacking the formidable defenses, the Union Army used a flanking maneuver to cross the Chattahoochee River upstream and continued to proceed toward Atlanta. Shoup was devastated that his unique design had played no role in the battles between the Union and Confederate armies. Shoup later served as chief-of-staff for John Bell Hood after he took command of the Army of Tennessee. After the war, Shoup became a professor of mathematics and engineering and ended his career at the

University of the South in Sewanee, Tennessee, where he was buried after his death in 1896 at the age of 62.

Smith, Edmund (E.) Kirby (1824-1893). Graduated from West Point Military Academy in 1845 in the middle of his class, he was commissioned into the 5th U.S. Infantry. During the Mexican-American War, he served under both Winfield Scott and Zachary Taylor. After the war, he served in the 2nd U.S. Cavalry, mostly in Texas, and when the state seceded from the Union, Smith resigned from the U.S. Army to join the Confederacy, fighting in the Eastern Theater in the Battle of First Bull Run, where he was severely wounded. Transferred to the Western Theater a few months later, Smith commanded the Department of East Tennessee and cooperated with Braxton Bragg in the invasion of Kentucky in 1862. The combined efforts of Smith and Bragg defeated the Union Army of the Ohio at the Battle of Perryville. But Bragg became concerned that Confederate resources would be unable to support his army in Kentucky and withdrew the combined forces back to Tennessee, over Smith's objections. In early 1863, Smith was promoted to command the Trans-Mississippi Department west of the Mississippi, with headquarters at Shreveport, Louisiana. During the Union Red River Campaign in 1864, Smith pursued Union forces in Arkansas that were heading to Shreveport in the Camden Expedition. His decision to pull troops from Richard Taylor's command, who had almost captured the Union Navy Mississippi River Squadron, left a lasting hostility between the two generals and Taylor refused to serve under his command. After the war, Smith pursued his scientific interests and became a professor of mathematics and botany at the University of the South at Sewanee, Tennessee, where he was buried after his death in 1893.

Stuart, James Ewell Brown, (J.E.B. "Jeb") (1833-1864). Graduated from West Point Military Academy in 1854, as one of eight cadets honored for their skills in horsemanship, he was ranked tenth in his class in cavalry tactics. His family history included a great grandfather, Alexander Stuart, who was a major in the Revolutionary War and his father, Arthur Stuart, who fought in the war of 1812. During his West Point days, Stuart became acquainted with the superintendent of the Academy, Robert E. Lee, and became a friend of the Lee family, seeing them socially on frequent occasions. After graduation, Stuart was assigned to frontier duty and led a number of successful missions in Texas and during the violence of "Bleeding Kansas." When he came to Washington to discuss a government contract regarding a new piece of cavalry equipment he had invented, he volunteered to serve as aide-de-camp for Robert E. Lee during the capture of John Brown at Harpers Ferry. When his home state of Virginia seceded from the Union, he resigned from the U.S. Army to join the Confederate States Army. He first served under Thomas "Stonewall" Jackson in the Shenandoah Valley but was soon transferred to the Army of Northern Virginia, under Robert E. Lee. Stuart cultivated a flamboyant image by wearing a red-lined cape with yellow waist sash and a hat with ostrich plume, but he was also a master of reconnaissance and offensive operations. He became one of Lee's most trusted senior officers, who provided him with "eyes and ears" of the enemy's movements. During the Peninsula Campaign, his cavalry circumnavigated the Union Army on two occasions to the embarrassment of the North. Stuart's impressive exploits made him the darling of the Southern press as he frequently outperformed Union cavalry. His military success hit a low point, however, when his absence from Lee's army prior to the Battle of Gettysburg deprived Lee of valuable information about the Union Army's movements, which contributed significantly to the Confederate defeat. Stuart's defeat by a Union cavalry charge under George Custer on the last day of the Gettysburg battle marked a turn in the North's cavalry capabilities, which had previously suffered multiple defeats from Stuart's command. His successful career came to an end on the outskirts of Richmond when he was killed at the age of 31 by Union cavalry under Philip Sheridan at the Battle at Yellow Tavern in May 1864.

Taylor, Richard (1826-1879). Son of Zachary Taylor, who led the U.S. Army to success in northern Mexico during the Mexican-American War and was then elected U.S. President in 1848, Richard grew up on the family plantation near Baton Rouge, Louisiana. He acquired an education at private schools and was then sent to Harvard and Yale before accompanying his father at the age of 20 to serve as military secretary during the early battle victories of the Mexican-American War. When Zachary died in 1850 while in office, Richard inherited the family sugar plantation, became involved in Louisiana politics and was elected to the state Senate in 1855. Although he was opposed to secession, he felt it was inevitable and agreed to assist Braxton Bragg to organize and train Confederate forces in Louisiana after the state seceded from the Union in January 1861. After the firing on Fort Sumter, Taylor was ordered to lead the 9th Louisiana Infantry in the Battle of First Bull Run (Manassas), but arrived too late, only hours after the battle had been won. Assigned to serve under Thomas "Stonewall" Jackson in the Shenandoah Valley, Taylor's troops became part of Jackson's elite striking force, which included the hard-fighting shock troops from Louisiana known as "Wheat's Tigers." Taylor followed Jackson to battles in the Peninsula Campaign against Union George McClellan, and was then promoted to major general and assigned to command the District of Western Louisiana. During the Union's Red River Campaign in 1864, Taylor nearly trapped the U.S. Navy Mississippi River Squadron under Admiral Porter, but lacked the manpower to defeat Porter because a large portion of his command had been diverted by his superior, E. Kirby Smith, to block another Union Army approaching Louisiana from Arkansas to the north. After the Union forces and River Squadron were able to safely withdraw, an outraged Taylor refused to serve under Smith because of the depletion of his troops at a critical moment. Taylor was then transferred to a new Department that included

Alabama, but he had insufficient troops to block the Union assault on Mobile Bay in 1864. Although his previous military experience before the Civil War was limited to service for his father in the Mexican-American War, his contemporaries in the Civil War uniformly spoke of his superior abilities on and off the field. After the surrender of Confederate forces at Appomattox, Taylor held out, but was finally forced to surrender to U.S. troops under Edward Canby in May 1865. Opposed to Reconstruction efforts after the war, his memoir *Destruction and Reconstruction* was published in 1879 shortly before his death and was widely acclaimed as a creditable account of the Civil War.

Tilghman, Lloyd (1816-1863). Graduated from West Point Military Academy in 1836 near the bottom of his class, he was placed in the 1st U.S. Dragoons. Three months later, he resigned his commission to work as a construction engineer on railroads in the Southern states and Panama. He re-enlisted in the U.S. Army with the onset of the Mexican-American War and served in the Maryland and Washington, D.C., Volunteer Artillery. After the war, he settled in Paducah, Kentucky, and returned to engineering work for the railroads. With the onset of the Civil War, he enlisted in the 3rd Kentucky Infantry for the Confederate States Army and was ordered to lead the construction of Forts Henry and Donelson on the Tennessee and Cumberland Rivers. The improper placement of Fort Henry in the floodplain of the Tennessee River caused him considerable embarrassment. An additional fort had to be built across the river on high ground, Fort Heiman, to provide protection. When Ulysses S. Grant attacked Fort Henry in 1862, demanding its surrender, Tilghman and only a few men were left in the fort as the rest of the army had evacuated to Fort Donelson. The Confederates were taken prisoner and Tilghman was sent to Fort Warren in Boston Harbor until he was exchanged a few months later. Assigned to Earl Van Dorn's Army of the West at Vicksburg, Tilghman was killed in 1863 at the Battle of Champion Hill during the Vicksburg Campaign as Union forces under Ulysses S. Grant drove Confederates back to the Vicksburg fortress from Jackson, Mississippi.

Van Dorn, Earl (1820-1863). Graduated from West Point Miliary Academy in 1842 near the bottom of his class, he was appointed to the 7th U.S. Infantry. In the Mexican-American War, he fought in the Battle of Monterrey under Zachary Taylor and was then transferred to Winfield Scott to fight in the Siege of Veracruz and the battles across Mexico that defeated Mexican forces in Mexico City. After the war, he fought in several engagements against American Indians in Florida and Texas. Resigning from the army at the outbreak of the Civil War to join the Confederacy, he commanded forces in Texas and was soon reassigned to lead the Trans-Mississippi District with headquarters in Arkansas. Combining two armies under Sterling Price from Missouri and Benjamin McCulloch from Arkansas, Van Dorn led the Battle of Pea Ridge where he was defeated by Union forces under Samuel Curtis. He was defeated again at the Second Battle of Corinth against William Rosecrans and removed from army command to serve as head of cavalry under John Pemberton's army at Vicksburg. After a successful raid on the Union supply depot at Holly Springs, which foiled Ulysses S. Grant's plan to converge forces on Vicksburg from the east, Van Dorn was promoted to command all Confederate cavalries in Mississippi and eastern Louisiana and became part of the Army of Tennessee, setting up his headquarters in Spring Hill, Tennessee. As a charming man with an eye for the ladies, he developed a love affair with the wife of a prominent physician in Spring Hill. While sitting at his desk at his headquarters, Van Dorn was murdered by the woman's husband who shot him in the back of his head in May 1863. The physician was never brought to trial for the crime as widespread Southern opinion accepted the physician's claim that Van Dorn had violated "the sanctity of his home," breaking the accepted code of honor.

Watie, Stand (1808-1871). Born to a Cherokee father and mixed-race mother in 1806, Stand grew up in the Cherokee Nation, then located near Rome, Georgia. After gold was discovered on the Cherokee land, the American Indians were relocated farther west to Indian Territory, a process that intensified with the Indian Removal Act of 1830, which resulted in the infamous "Trail of Tears." After his family's removal to Indian Territory in 1835, Watie became a prominent leader of the Cherokees and was Chief of the Cherokee Nation between 1862 to 1866. With the outbreak of the Civil War, Watie feared the federal government would confiscate more of their land and sided with the Confederacy. He organized a regiment of mounted infantry and was commissioned as colonel of the 1st Cherokee Mounted Rifles. Watie led his men repulsing attacks on Cherokee civilians and farms from Union supporters, which included Creek, Seminole and other tribes, fighting for the Union. During the Battle of Pea Ridge, Arkansas, Watie's men fought under Benjamin McCulloch and covered the retreating Confederates from the battlefield after McCulloch was killed. Commanding the First Indian Brigade of the Army of the Trans-Mississippi, Watie led a number of battles and skirmishes west of the Mississippi in Arkansas, Missouri, Kansas and Texas, and became the only American Indian general in the Confederate States Army. A raid in 1864 captured a federal wagon train worth over a million dollars of wagons, mules and supplies at the Second Battle of Cabin Creek, which became the greatest Confederate victory in Indian Territory. Following the surrender of all the Confederate armies in the summer of 1865, Watie finally surrendered June 23, 1865, the last Confederate States Army general to capitulate.

Wheeler, Joseph (1836-1906). Graduated from West Point Military Academy in 1859 near the bottom of his class of twenty-two students, he was commissioned to the 1st U.S. Dragoons and attended U.S. Cavalry School at Carlisle, Pennsylvania. On completion in 1860, he was transferred to the U.S. Army Mounted Rifles stationed in New Mexico Territory. But when his home state of Georgia seceded from the Union in January 1861, he resigned from the Union Army and entered the Confederate States Army as a first lieutenant in the Georgia militia artillery. Transferred to command the 19th Alabama Infantry, he fought in the Battle of Shiloh and covered the Confederate Army's withdrawal after the Siege of Corinth by burning the bridge over the Tuscumbia River as the troops withdrew to Tupelo, Mississippi. During the Kentucky Campaign, Wheeler was assigned to Braxton Bragg, who increased his cavalry by removing them from Nathan Bedford Forrest, who was ordered to find new recruits in Murfreesboro. The move infuriated Forrest and created a hostile rivalry against Wheeler that remained throughout the war. During the Siege of Chattanooga, Wheeler's men were sent north to raid Union railroad lines and were absent when the Union Army broke through the Confederate line on Missionary Ridge, defeating the army and recapturing Chattanooga from the Southerners. When Bragg was replaced in command of the Army of Tennessee by Joseph E. Johnston, Wheeler's cavalry fought against William T. Sherman during the Atlanta Campaign, capturing two Union cavalries as they attempted to destroy railroad supply lines into Atlanta. When Hood abandoned Atlanta and left for the Franklin-Nashville Campaign in Tennessee, Wheeler's cavalry was redeployed to Georgia to combat Sherman's March to the Sea, but was mostly ineffective against the large Union Army which greatly outnumbered his forces. Wheeler continued to harass Sherman's forces in the Carolinas Campaign and defeated Union Judson Kilpatrick in one battle, surprising "Kill-Cavalry" Kilpatrick in his nightshirt while he was entertaining a lady. At the end of the war, Wheeler was captured in Georgia as he attempted to cover the escape of Confederate President Jefferson Davis. Paroled after two months of imprisonment, Wheeler moved to Alabama where he became a planter and a lawyer. Elected to the U.S. House of Representatives, he served seven terms where he championed economic policies that would support rebuilding the South. At age 61, he volunteered to serve in the Spanish-American War and assumed command of the cavalry division that included Theodore Roosevelt's "Rough Riders." In 1899, he reentered the U.S. Army that he had resigned from nearly forty years earlier and sailed to the Philippines to fight in the Philippines-American War. Retiring from the army in 1900, he moved to New York City and wrote a number of books on military history and strategy. After a long illness, he died in 1906 at the age of 69. Buried in Arlington National Cemetery, he is one of the few former Confederate generals to be interred there.

NAVAL OFFICERS

Buchanan, Franklin (1800-1874). Born in Maryland of Scottish immigrant ancestry, his paternal grandfather served in the Revolutionary War as a general in the Maryland militia and his maternal grandfather was one of the signers of the

Declaration of Independence. He entered the Navy as a midshipman at the age of 15 and during his forty-five years of service, he experienced worldwide sea duty. But in 1845 he submitted plans to the U.S. Secretary of the Navy for a Naval School, which became the United States Naval Academy and he was its first superintendent. He served in the Mexican-American War and in 1859 was promoted to command the Washington Navy Yard. With the onset of the Civil War, he resigned from the U.S. Navy, expecting that Maryland would secede, but it did not. Joining the Confederate Navy in September 1861, he captained the *CSS Virginia* in the Battle of Hampton Roads and on the first day of the battle sunk the *USS Cumberland*, destroyed the *USS Congress* and ran the *USS Minnesota* aground, the greatest U.S. Navy defeat until World War II. Wounded in the day's battles, Buchanan was removed from the battlefield and did not participate in the Battle of the Ironclads on the second day. Promoted to the rank of full Admiral in 1862, the only Confederate officer to hold that rank, he was ordered to command the fleet at Mobile Bay and was severely wounded in the battle in August 1864 against Union Navy Rear Admiral Farragut. Taken prisoner, he was exchanged in February 1865. His final years in retirement were in Maryland and Mobile, Alabama.

AERONAUT

Alexander, Edward Porter (1835-1910). Graduated from the U.S. Military academy at West Point, third in his class, he briefly taught fencing and engineering and then learned "wig-wag" signaling techniques with flags as his first introduction to aerial telegraphy. With the onset of the Civil War, he resigned from the U.S. Army and joined the Confederate States Army to organize and train recruits for the Confederate Signal Service. At the Battle of First Bull Run, he introduced the method by sending messages from a station on top of Signal Hill. As Chief of Ordnance, he fought in nearly all of the major battles, including the Peninsula Campaign, First and Second Bull Run, Antietam, Fredericksburg, Chancellorsville and Gettysburg. He was the only Confederate to conduct surveillance from a tethered balloon during the Peninsula Campaign. Rising to the rank of brigadier general during the war, he later became a successful writer, publishing several books, including his *Military Memoirs of a Confederate: A Critical Narrative* (1907), considered by historians as a sharp and objective account. He was a professor of mathematics and engineering at the University of South Carolina and president of several railroads between 1871 to 1892.

ACKNOWLEDGEMENTS

My early drafts of the book benefitted immensely from my earliest readers who shared their enthusiasm for the topic and how it was organized. It was from an avid student of history, Ida Jeppesen, who pointed out the need for brief biographies of the multitude of generals that proliferate through the narrative. My creation of two appendices with brief biographical sketches about the Union and Confederate generals named in the book, with insights into their individual qualities and characters, have added greatly to the substance of the accounts of the battles. Ken Zink was very helpful in improving introductions of the separation of the battles into the Eastern and Western Theaters. Both readers provided improvements in clarity and understanding of details in the final manuscript and encouraged the use of maps for the battles.

The near final manuscript was reviewed by Nicholas Taylor, a graduate student at Colorado State University, who is pursuing master's degree in 19th century American history. His bachelor's degree in history from West Virginia University and internships at several national parks provided excellent background for a book intended for college-level students. His comments and suggestions were incorporated and much appreciated.

I particularly want to thank my son Allen Moody for his consistent encouragement to publish this book after reading a shorter version written in 2017 for our shared grandson (my great grandson) Loki Holmes. His continued input and reinforcement through the final edits of this manuscript are appreciated. I also wish to acknowledge the contribution of my deceased son Wade Moody (1957-2010), whose early encouragement to write a narrative about our Zink ancestors who settled in Indiana and Kansas formed the foundation for my pursuit as a writer of some of America's history.

Special thanks go to my publisher, Patricia Ross of Hugo House Publishers, Ltd., who expressed great enthusiasm and encouragement when I proposed the book to her. Her professional guidance and constructive additions to the book have improved its appeal to multiple readers, particularly the recommendation to include sections on views from the public, an important addition to the narrative. I am also very grateful to book designer Ronda Taylor, HeartWork Creative, for her design of the book's cover and her diligent incorporation of multiple adjustments to the manuscript that has achieved the finished book.

SOURCES OF INFORMATION

Principal sources of information for this book have been obtained from the vast resources available on the internet. The resulting book was constructed by collecting details from multiple websites, supplemented with verification of facts and accuracy from recognized historical sources. The number of casualties in each battle generally represent a consensus from the multiple sources available.

Sample websites from the internet are included below, but cannot represent all that were accessed to retrieve what was used in the research for this book. Published historical documentaries were frequently referred to and a few are listed here:

Civil War: A Narrative, Shelby Foote, Vintage Books, A Division of Random House, NY.

Fort Sumter to Perryville, Vol. 1, 1958-86.

Fredericksburg to Meridian, Vol. 2, 1963.

Red River to Appomattox, Vol. 3, 1974.

Team of Rivals: The Political Genius of Abraham Lincoln, Doris Kearns Goodwin, Simon & Schuster 2005.

And there was light: Abraham Lincoln and the American struggle, Jon Meacham, New York Random House, 2022.

GRANT, Ron Chernow, Penguin Press, NY, 2017.

Personal Memoirs, Ulysses S. Grant, Konecky & Konecky, Old Saybrook, CT, 1885.

Memoirs of General W. T. Sherman, William Tecumseh Sherman, first published by Penguin Books, Middlesex, England, 1875; new edition with introduction and notes by Michael Fellman, 2000.

Chancellorsville, 2nd Edition, Gen. Edward J. Stackpole, Stackpole Books, Harrisburg, PA 1988.

Battle Cry of Freedom, The Civil War Era, James M. McPherson, Ballantine Books, New York 1988

Those Damned Black Hats! The Iron Brigade in the Gettysburg Campaign, Lance J. Herdegen, Savas Beatie, NY 2008-2010.

The Smell of Battle, The Taste of Siege: A Sensory History of the Civil War, Mark M. Smith, Oxford University Press, NY, 2015.

Historical Fiction:

Freedom: A Novel of Abraham Lincoln and the Civil War, William Safire, Doubleday & Company, Inc., Garden City, NY (1987).

The books of Bruce Catton from the 1950s and '60s provided basic background and insight into the Civil War.

This Hallowed Ground: The Story of the Union Side of the Civil War, Bruce Catton, Doubleday & Company, Inc., Garden City, NY 1956.

Stillness at Appomattox, Bruce Catton, Doubleday & Company, Inc., Garden City, NY 1956.

The Coming Fury, Bruce Catton, Doubleday & Company, Inc., Garden City, NY 1961.

The Army of the Potomac: Mr. Lincoln's Army, Bruce Catton, Doubleday & Company, Inc., 1962.

Never Call Retreat, Bruce Catton, Doubleday & Company, Inc., Garden City, NY 1965.

Grant Takes Command, Bruce Catton, Doubleday & Company, Inc., Garden City, NY 1968.

Maps and Photographs were consulted when generating descriptions of the battles:

The Historical Atlas of the Civil War, John Macdonald, A Cartographica Book, Chartwell Books, Inc., NY 2009.

Great Maps of the Civil War: Pivotal Battles and Campaigns Featuring 32 Removable Maps, William J. Miller, Rutledge Hill Press, Nashville, TN, 2004.

Maps of battles reproduced in the book are nearly all from the website of Hal Jespersen (https://www.cwmaps.com/freemaps.html). His statement on his webpage, "This page offers over 200 maps I have created for American Civil War battle articles

SOURCES OF INFORMATION

in Wikipedia, almost always for articles I wrote myself. They are available to anyone to use or publish under the Creative Commons Attribution 3.0 license, which means that if you use them—either modified or unmodified—you must abide by the terms of that license and attribute the images to me with the text "Map by Hal Jespersen, www.cwmaps.com." It is not necessary for you to contact me in advance for permission to use the maps under these terms, although I always enjoy hearing about how my maps are used." Jespersen's battle descriptions in Wikipedia also provided firm background for the book.

Some of the battle maps were constructed by U.S. Army officers or a government employee and are in the public domain. Those maps without specific acknowledgement were created by the author from public sources.

Other websites that were particularly useful for details of the battles included *www.history.net*, *www.battlefields.org* and *www.history.com*. Grant's *Personal Memoirs* and W.T. Sherman's *Memoirs* were also important sources for descriptions about battles that they commanded.

Additional input for this book took advantage of multiple television productions, such as the nine-episode series, *The Civil War,* produced by documentary filmmaker Ken Burns, which premiered on the Public Broadcasting System (PBS) in 1990. More recently, two mini-series were portrayed on the History Channel in 2020, entitled *Grant* and *Abraham Lincoln*. Both were particularly helpful in describing the multiple events and battles of the Civil War.

Material included in the sections on Views from the Public were obtained from these primary sources:

Archives of the New York Times, searching through specific dates during the war.

"History of Washington County 1884," 1965 Edition, purchased from the Steven's Museum, 307 E. Market St., Salem, Indiana, which is an excerpt from the 1884 "History of Lawrence, Orange and Washington Counties," a book about the early history of Southern Indiana.

Master's Thesis, Six Rebel Newspapers, Gabler, Henry, "The Rebel Press: Six Selected Confederate Newspapers Report Civil War Battles" (1971). Dissertations, Theses, and Masters Projects. *"This Thesis is brought to you for free and open access by the Theses, Dissertations, & Master Projects at the College of William & Mary, Paper 1539624742."*

How Newspapers Reported the Civil War, Smithsonian Magazine

https://www.smithsonianmag.com/history/how-newspapers-reported-the-civil-war-17280757/

Newspapers in Virginia during the Civil War, Confederate:

https://encyclopediavirginia.org/entries/newspapers-in-virginia-during-the-civil-war-confederate/Diary of a Union Soldier (1862): https://wwnorton.com/college/history/archive/resources/documents/ch17_04.htm

The following is a sample list of websites available on the internet that were used in this research.

www.britannica.com

www.history.com. and www.history.net

www.nps.gov and http://npshistory.com/

www.battlefields.org

www.smithsonianmag.com

www.warfarehistorynetwork.com

www.thoughtco.com and www.wikipedia.org and https://en.wikipedia.org

www.civilwar.com

www.military.com

https://www.newworldencyclopedia.org/entry/Battle_of_Chancellorsville

https://www.essentialcivilwarcurriculum.com

https://www.senate.gov/artandhistory/history/minute/Civil_War_Begins.htm

https://faculty.weber.edu/kmackay/selected_statistics_on_slavery_i.htm

http://npshistory.com/publications/civil_war_series/

https://www.wondriumdaily.com/ten-bloodiest-battles-civil-war/

www.legendsofamerica.com/ah-civilwartimeline/

https://www.historycentral.com/CivilWar/AMERICA/Economics.html

https://history.army.mil/books/amh/amh-09.htm

https://www.pbs.org/wgbh/americanexperience/features/timeline-death/

https://www.battlefields.org/search?search=civil+war

https://en.wikipedia.org/wiki/List_of_American_Civil_War_battles

http://npshistory.com/publications/civil_war_series/

https://www.historycentral.com/CivilWar/AMERICA/Economics.html

https://www.alexandriava.gov/historic-alexandria/basic-page/we-are-all-americans-native-americans-in-the-civil-war

SOURCES OF INFORMATION

https://www.statista.com/statistics/1010893/bloodiest-battles-american-civil-war-1861-1865/

https://www.newspapers.com/topics/civil-war/battle-of-antietam/

https://www.pbs.org/wgbh/americanexperience/features/timeline-death/

https://en.wikipedia.org/wiki/Army_of_the_Tennessee

http://npshistory.com/publications/civil_war_series/8/sec4.htm

https://encyclopediaofarkansas.net/

https://www.georgiaencyclopedia.org/

https://emergingcivilwar.com/2014/04/17/the-myth-of-the-cracker-line-part-one/

https://sites.google.com/a/lanepl.org/jbcols/home/2013-articles/food-shortages-tested-butler-county-troops-surrounded-in-chattanooga-during-uncertain-autumn-of-1863

https://presidentlincoln.illinois.gov/Blog/Posts/141/Abraham-Lincoln/2021/8/Lincoln-avoided-duel/blog-post/

GENERAL INDEX

A

Alabama 4, 13-16, 25, 31-34, 42, 47, 54, 57, 85, 127, 129, 142, 173, 176, 201-203, 224, 228, 265, 274-275-277, 288, 297-298, 300-301, 308, 313-314, 319-322, 337, 376-377
American Red Cross 64
Anaconda Plan 75, 196, 228
Andersonville Prison Camp 289, 304, 417, 438
Arizona 17, 26, 34-35
Arkansas 3-4, 14-16, 23, 34, 57, 71-72, 84, 89, 90-91, 94, 146, 149, 179-181, 196, 221, 266-267, 269-272, 274, 377
Arkansas Territory 15
Arlington Estate 40
Articles of Confederation 1, 7
Atzerodt, George 371, 386-387

B

Balloon Corps 109-111, 115-116
Barton, Clara 64, 156
Bell, John 32, 201
Biden, Joseph 378
Black Belt 14
Black Codes 390
Booth, John Wilkes 367, 369-371, 386
Boydton Plank Road 259-260, 349, 351, 354
Breckinridge, John C. 28, 31-32, 51, 142, 247, 248-250, 374
Brown, John 11, 22-24, 39
Buchanan, James 4, 22, 24, 28, 31, 37, 86, 249
Burning, The 262, 264

C

Cairo, Illinois 68-70, 72, 84-85, 95-96, 136, 153, 202

California 3, 16-20, 26, 28, 32, 34, 40, 48, 51, 72, 74, 83, 95, 163
Chase, Salmon P. 31, 150
Civil Rights Act of 1866 390-391
Civil Rights Act of 1875 393
Civil Rights Act of 1964 6, 394
Civil War Military Draft Act 41, 216
Clay, Henry 19
Cleveland, Grover 118, 278
Colorado 17, 26
Compromise of 1850 3, 19-20
Compromise of 1877 394
Confederate Conscription Act 43, 217
Confederate States Army 38, 43, 88, 128, 359
Confederate States of America 1, 4, 33, 66, 79, 268, 299
Constitution of the United States 7
   13th Amendment 5, 161, 312, 338, 389-390, 392
   14th Amendment 5-6, 390-393
   15th Amendment 6, 17, 392-393
   17th Amendment 27
   19th Amendment 6, 392
   Bill of Rights 8-9
Copperheads (Peace Democrats) 149, 157, 299, 333, 334
Cracker Line 204-205

D

Dakota Territory 25, 118
Declaration of Independence 1-2, 7, 395
Delaware 11, 34, 48, 149, 161, 299, 389
Democratic National Convention 31
Democratic Party 28, 31, 299
Dimmock Line 229, 231, 253-255
Dix, Dorothea 65

Dodge, Grenville M. 92-93, 203
Douglass, Frederick 12, 23, 212
Douglas, Stephen 4, 19-20, 26-27, 29-32, 281
Dred Scott Decision 29, 391

E

Emancipation Proclamation 42, 49, 71, 121, 136, 149, 157, 161, 216-217, 285, 337
Enforcement Acts 392-393

F

Fillmore, Millard 19, 28
Flags for the Union and Confederacy 46
Florida 3-4, 18, 25, 32, 42-43, 57, 102, 307, 312, 375
Fort Sumter 34, 37-44, 46-47, 52, 54-55, 57-59, , 61, 63, 66, 70, 76, 107, 212-213, 341-342, 344, 346
Freedmen's Bureau 6, 80, 135-136, 312, 391-392, 412
Freedom Fortress 80
Fugitive Slave Act 10, 20, 58, 149

G

Gadsden Purchase 26
Garrison, William Lloyd 11-12
Georgia 4, 8, 14, 25, 33, 53, 57, 102, 112, 129, 140, 188, 197-198, 200, 209-210, 224, 226-228, 263, 275-278, 280-282, 286-288, 297-302, 304-313, 316, 328-329, 331-332, 334-335, 337, 341-343, 347-348, 375-378, 388-389
Gettysburg Address 177, 221, 493
Gibraltar Brigade 120-121

H

Hawes, Richard 137
Hayes, Rutherford B. 6, 354, 394, 436, 468
Homestead Act 27, 31, 83
Howard University 391
Howlett Line 229, 253

I

Indian Territory 26, 68, 72, 89-93, 270, 377-378
International slave trade 2, 8, 13
Iowa 3, 18, 20, 83, 188, 190

Iron Brigade 45, 171-172, 232

J

Jayhawkers 22-23, 25
Jim Crow 392-394
Johnson, Andrew 312, 370-371, 375-376, 379, 387, 389-390, 392, 394
Johnson, Lyndon B. 394
Juneteenth 378

K

Kansas 3, 20-28, 40, 46, 48, 67, 70, 72, 84, 97, 101
Kansas-Nebraska Act 3, 20-22, 26-27
Kansas Territory 23
Kennedy, John F. 394
Know-Nothing Party 28
Ku Klux Klan 277, 393

L

Land-Grant College Act 84
Lightning Brigade 131, 199-201
Lincoln, Robert Todd 371
Louisiana 3-5, 14-16, 18, 20, 33, 43, 47, 57, 67-68, 71, 90, 95-96, 100, 128, 135, 143, 182, 187-191, 194, 196, 213, 221, 228, 265-267, 269-271, 367, 376-377
Louisiana Territory 3, 15-16 18

M

MacArthur, Arthur, Jr. 281
Manifest Destiny 16-17
Maryland 11-12, 15, 20, 23, 28-29, 31, 34, 42, 48, 55, 80-81, 98, 102, 104-105, 112, 118-119, 121, 137, 140, 149, 151, 156-157, 161, 169-170, 216, 219-220, 250-252, 370-371, 387
Mason-Dixon line 15
Massachusetts 11, 15, 22-24, 28, 50, 77, 212, 218, 229, 356
Michigan 3, 16, 81, 92, 171-172, 174-175, 237, 332
Minnesota 25, 106, 118, 174
Minnesota Territory 25
Mississippi 3-4, 8-9, 13-14, 16, 25, 32-33, 40, 58-59, 84-85, 88-90, 94-96, 100-102, 119, 128-129, 131-136, 140, 143-146, 148, 154, 179, 181-197, 221-222, 226, 269, 273-275, 296-297, 317, 319, 327, 389-390
Mississippi River Squadron 42, 86, 185, 266-267, 272-274

GENERAL INDEX

Missouri 3, 15-16, 18-23, 25-32, 34, 46, 48, 51, 57, 59, 66-73, 84, 89-90, 92, 94, 103, 106, 116-118, 149, 161, 202, 216, 225, 269, 300, 316, 377
Missouri Compromise of 1820 3, 15-16, 19-21, 27, 29-30, 66
Missouri State Guard 67-68, 70-72, 89
Montana 25-26
Mosby's Rangers 262-263, 333, 377

N

Nebraska 20-22, 27, 48, 79
Nebraska Territory 20, 79
New Mexico 3, 17-18, 20, 26, 34-35, 48, 57
New Mexico Territory 26, 34-35
New York 14-15, 22, 30-31, 42, 51, 55, 79, 106, 117-118, 157, 162, 217, 227, 308, 333, 372
  New York City riot 42. *See also* Civil War Military Draft Act
No Man's Land 26
North Carolina 4, 22, 32, 34, 42, 47, 80, 167-169, 171-172, 254, 256, 259, 319, 322-324, 328, 337-340, 344-349, 355, 357, 369, 372-375, 377-378, 380
Northwest Ordinance 3, 8
Northwest Territory 3, 8

O

Oregon 16-17, 25-26, 32, 40, 46, 48, 75
Oregon Territory 17, 26
Oregon Treaty with Great Britain 26
Ostend Manifesto 28

P

Pacific Railway Act 83
Paducah, Kentucky 68-69, 72-73, 85, 143
Peace Democrats 119, 149-150, 157-158, 181, 299, 333, 337
Pennsylvania 7-8, 12, 15, 18, 28, 32, 50, 53, 55, 59, 118, 169-172, 176, 194, 219-220, 252, 257, 259, 333
Pierce, Franklin 21, 28, 33
Polk, James K. 16-17, 28, 69, 72, 74, 88-89, 95, 275-276, 283
Pony Express 51, 84, 401, 451
Powell, Lewis 370-371, 386-387
Prayer of Twenty Millions 157
Presidential Election 4, 6, 17, 28, 30, 150, 226, 394

Q

Quantrill's Raiders 25

R

Reconstruction 6, 277, 367, 369, 371, 389-390, 392-395
Red Legs 24-25
Republican National Convention 28, 31, 50
Revolt of the Generals 206
Rhode Island 122
Rienzi 263-264, 335, 426, 502
Rock of Chickamauga 199-202, 227, 296, 317

S

Scott, Winfield 17, 38-40, 59, 70, 74-75, 78-79, 163, 225, 227-228, 364
Seward, William H. 31, 150, 225, 370, 386
Shoupade Fortifications 284
Silk Dress Balloon 112, 116
South Dakota 26
Stanton, Edwin 40, 76, 201-202, 225, 261, 312, 318, 370, 373, 375, 379, 381, 392
Stephens, Alexander 53
Stowe, Harriet Beecher, *Uncle Tom's Cabin* 12
Sumner, Charles 22-23, 50, 393
Surrat, Mary 371, 387

T

Taney, Roger B., Dred Scott Decision 29
Taylor, Zachary 8, 17-19, 28, 33, 70, 163, 213
Tennessee 4, 32, 34, 57, 68, 72, 84-86, 88-89, 94, 97, 101, 127-131, 134-137, 140, 142-143, 145, 152, 154, 158, 188, 194, 197-198, 200-204, 207-211, 217, 223-227, 274-277, 296-298, 300-302, 311, 313-316, 318-319, 326, 330, 337, 344, 346, 377
Texas 3-4, 14, 16-20, 25-26, 33, 35, 39, 42, 45, 57, 68, 74, 117, 121, 155, 179, 196, 213, 221, 228, 265, 267, 269, 274, 326, 377-378, 389
Texas Revolution 16
Three-Fifths Compromise 2, 8, 391-392
Transcontinental Railroad 20, 26, 28, 31
Treaties of Velasco 16-17
Treaty of Guadalupe Hidalgo 17-18
Truman, Harry S. 395
Trumbull, Lyman 27

Tubman, Harriet 12, 23
Twenty Negro Law 43
Tyler, John 17

U

Underground Railroad 12, 23
U.S. Census 2, 9, 13
Utah 3, 17-20, 26, 48, 83-84
Utah Territory 19, 84

V

Virginia 1, 2, 4, 11, 20, 23-24, 29, 32, 34, 40,
 42-43, 52, 54, 57-64, 72, 74-76, 79-80, 83, 87, 100-
 111, 114, 116-119, 121-124, 126, 137, 142, 155, 158,
 162, 164, 168-169, 176, 179, 194, 198, 214, 224-225,
 228-231, 234-235, 237, 239-240, 242-244, 246-247,
 249-256, 259-262, 322, 326, 337, 339, 349-352, 354,
 358, 363, 371, 373, 377

W

Washington State 26, 48
Washington Territory 469
West Virginia 26, 34, 46, 59-61, 224, 250, 252,
 261
Whig Party 27-28
Wilmot Proviso 18
Wirz, Henry 304, 328, 376
Wisconsin 3, 18, 29, 171-172, 273
Wisconsin Territory 29
Wyoming 17, 26

INDEX OF COMMANDERS DURING THE CIVIL WAR

COMMANDERS-IN-CHIEF

Abraham Lincoln, Union

Lincoln, Abraham, 398-399
  assassination of Lincoln at Ford Theater, 369-370, 385-388
    assassin John Wilkes Booth, 367, 370-371
    attempted assassination of Secretary of State Seward, 370-371
    funeral and burial of Lincoln, 371-372, 386-387
  attempts to send supplies to Fort Sumter, South Carolina, 38
  campaign against Kansas-Nebraska Act (1854), 26-27
  clashes with George B. McClellan, 75-76, 116-117
  Cooper Union Speech (1860), 30-31
  debates with Stephen Douglas (1858), 30
  decision to send raw recruits to battle of First Bull Run, 61
  delivers Gettysburg Address, 177-178
  designs battle plan to defeat Stonewall Jackson in the Shenandoah, but commanding generals fail in the effort, 104-106
  duel with James Shields (1842), 428
  early life and background, 398-399
  elected as President (1860), 32
  elected to Illinois House of Representatives (1854), but loses opportunity to be appointed to U.S. Sente, 27
  election of 1856, supports Fremont as Presidential candidate, 28
  Emancipation Proclamation, 121, 149, 157, 161
  establishes Balloon Corps, 109
  fires George B. McClellan as General-in-Chief, 76
  fires John Pope as commander of Union Army after battle of Second Bull Run and dissolves Army of Virginia, 118
  call-to-arms, April 1861, 41
  first Inaugural Address, 33
  House Divided speech (1858), 30
  implements Blockade Proclamation, 42
  importance of Vicksburg, 143, 196
  issues General War Order No 1, 84
  passage of 13th Amendment to free the slaves, 338
  praise to Grant at end of Overland Campaign, 327
  praise to Sheridan for success in the Shenandoah, 264
  praise to Sherman for the capture of Atlanta, Georgia, and the capture of Savannah, 311, 335
  Presidential campaign (1860), 32, 50
  promotes Ulysses S. Grant as General-in-Chief, replacing Henry Halleck, 227
  recaptures Naval shipyard at Norfolk from Confederates, 110
  promotes George B. McClellan as General-in-Chief, replacing Winfield Scott, 76
  promotes Henry Halleck to General-in-Chief, a vacant position after firing George B. McClellan, 102

reaction to William S. Rosecrans after battle of Chickamauga, promotes Ulysses S. Grant to command Siege of Chattanooga, 202
reaction to battle of Fredericksburg, 127, 158
reaction to battle of Stones River, 142
reaction to capture of Vicksburg, 196
reaction to failed Virginia Peninsula Campaign, 155
re-election to the Presidency (1864), 265, 299, 331, 334-335
replaces Don Carlos Buell from command of the Army of Ohio with William S. Rosecrans, 138, 226
replaces George B. McClellan as commander of Army of the Potomac with Ambrose Burnside, 121-122, 226
replaces Ambrose Burnside as commander of Army of the Potomac with Joseph Hooker, 163, 226
replaces Joseph Hooker as commander of Army of the Potomac with George Meade, 170, 226
removes John C. Fremont from Missouri command, 71
removes George B. McClellan as General-in-Chief, 76, 416
review of his commanding generals' performances (1861-1863), 226-227
revokes Gen. Grant's General Order No.11 affecting Jews, 143
second Inaugural Address, 338
Senate challenges Lincoln's Cabinet, 150
song, *Dixie*, "...was the best tune he ever heard," 366
tour of conquered Petersburg, 355
tour of conquered Richmond, surrounded by cheering Blacks, 356, 383-384
views about Ulysses S. Grant, 100, 155, 187, 245, 261, 327
war plans for 1864, 228, 262
White House balcony, his final speech, 367, 369

Jefferson Davis, Confederacy

Davis, Jefferson, 444-445
appointed as President of the Confederacy and Commander-in-Chief, Confederate States Army, 33, 38
appoints P.G.T. Beauregard as commander for firing on Fort Sumter, 38
Battle of First Bull Run, 78
bread riot in Richmond, 215
career before the Civil War, 33, 444
controversy over Braxton Bragg from senior officers (Revolt of the Generals), 138, 206
controversy with Beauregard, 446
controversy with Joseph E. Johnston, 459
flight from Siege of Petersburg and Richmond, 356
meets with his Cabinet as Confederacy surrenders, 376
meets with Joseph E. Johnston in North Carolina to discuss terms of surrender, 373
orders invasion into Kentucky, the Heartland Offensive, 127-128
reaction to Lincoln's Emancipation Proclamation, 157, 216
replaces Beauregard from command of Confederate Army of Mississippi with Bragg after siege of Corinth, Mississippi, 101, 128, 446
replaces Bragg as commander of the Confederate Army of Tennessee with Joseph E. Johnston after loss of Chattanooga to Grant, 209
replaces Joseph E. Johnston of Confederate Army of Tennessee with John Bell Hood during Atlanta Campaign, 286
replaces wounded Joseph E. Johnston with Robert E. Lee during Peninsula Campaign to command Confederate Army of Northern Virginia, 113
receives amnesty from President Andrew Johnson in 1868 after being captured and imprisoned in 1865 following the surrender of all Confederate armies, 376, 438, 445

INDEX OF COMMANDERS DURING THE CIVIL WAR

UNION OFFICERS IN THE ARMY

Anderson, Robert, 399
  commander, Union garrison, Charleston, South Carolina, 37
  friendship with Confederate commander P.G.T. Beauregard, 38
  surrenders Fort Sumter to Beauregard, first battle of Civil War, 39
Averell, William, 399
  cavalry commander in the Shenandoah, 249, 252
Banks, Nathaniel P., 400
  command, Union Department of the Shenandoah, 103
  defeated by Stonewall Jackson at Battle of Winchester, Virginia, nicknamed "Commissary Banks" by the Confederates, 104-105
  occupies New Orleans, replacing "Beast Butler," and promoted to command, Army of the Gulf, 100, 228
  oversees siege and surrender of Port Hudson, 196
  Bayou Teche initiatives, 213
  Red River Campaign, Louisiana, 265-274
    brings cotton speculators to the expedition, 267-268
    defeated by Taylor in Battles of Mansfield and Pleasant Hill, 269
    Union Navy nearly trapped on failed Red River Campaign, 270, 272
  removed from command, Army of the Gulf, replaced by Canby, 274
  initiated Reconstruction efforts in Louisiana with development of new post-war state Constitution, 400
Blair, Francis, 300, 400
Buell, Don Carlos, 401
  captures Bowling Green, Kentucky, from Confederates, 88
  captures Nashville, Tennessee, 89
  Battle of Shiloh, supports Grant with troops, 96, 98-99
  failed advance to Chattanooga, Tennessee, moves army to Louisville, Kentucky, 102, 127-128, 130-131
  defeated by Bragg at Battle of Perryville, Kentucky, 137-138
  removed from command, Army of the Ohio, replaced by Rosecrans, 138
Buford, John, 401
  Cavalry officer, Battle of Chancellorsville, Virginia, 164
  identifies high ground defense for Union prior to Battle of Gettysburg, 177
Burnside, Ambrose, 401
  career before the Civil War, 122
  commander under McClellan at Battle of Antietam, Maryland, "Burnside's Bridge," 120-121
  promoted to command Army of the Potomac, replacing McClellan, 122, 226
  defeated by Lee at Battle of Fredericksburg, Virginia, 122-127
  failed Mud March against Lee, Virginia, 162
  resigns from command, Army of the Potomac, and moved to command Army of Ohio, 163, 226
  captures Knoxville, Tennessee, but his army is placed under siege until relieved by Sherman after Battles of Chattanooga, 198, 206, 211
  removed from all commands after Battle of the Crater disaster, censored by court of inquiry, 257-259
  signature facial hair, "Sideburns," 122
Butler, Benjamin, 402-403
  command, "Freedom Fortress," Fort Monroe, Virginia, 58
  occupies New Orleans after Union capture, "Beast Butler," 100
  command, Army of the James, Bermuda Hundred, Virginia, 228, 403
  "Corked at Howlett Line," Bermuda Hundred, Virginia, by Beauregard, 230-231
  defeated at Battle of Old Men and Young Boys, Petersburg, Virginia, 254-255
  failed campaign to capture Fort Fisher, Wilmington, North Carolina, Congressional hearing, 322-324, 340

removed from command, Army of the James, replaced by Ord, 324

Canby, Edward, 403
defeats Confederate attempts to take over New Mexico Territory in Battle of Glorieta Pass, Santa Fe, 403
promoted to command Army of the Gulf, replacing Banks, 274
captures city of Mobile, Alabama, 376

Chamberlain, Joshua, 404
defends Little Round Top, Battle of Gettysburg, Pennsylvania, 173, 176, 436
conducts formal surrender of Lee's Army of Northern Virginia, marking the end of the Civil War, 367-369

Crook, George, 404
defeated by Early at Second Battle of Kernstown, Shenandoah Valley, 252, 260
pursuit of Lee during Appomattox Campaign, 357

Curtis, Samuel R., 405
defeats Van Dorn at Battle of Pea Ridge, Arkansas, 89-94
captures Helena, Arkansas, and holds it for the Union, 94
defeats Price at Westport, Kansas, last major offensive of Confederates west of Mississippi, 405

Custer, George A., 405
defeats Confederate cavalry under Stuart at Battle of Gettysburg, Pennsylvania, 174-175
removes Confederates from Shenandoah Valley, Virginia, near end of Civil War, 265
captures Confederate trains at Appomattox, blocking Lee's army from acquiring desperately needed rations, 355, 362

Davies, Henry E., 405
captures Confederate wagon train as Lee's army flees Petersburg during Appomattox campaign, 358

Davis, Jefferson C., 406
career before the Civil War, 139
confrontation with Union Gen. William "Bull" Nelson that ends with Davis killing Nelson, 138-139
Corps commander, under Slocum during Sherman's March to the Sea, disgraced by Ebenezer Creek Massacre, Georgia, 140, 300, 308

Dodge, Grenville M., 406
engineer at Battle of Pea Ridge, Arkansas, 92
repairs 200-mile supply line for Grant during siege of Chattanooga, 203

Franklin, William B., 123, 267, 407
Corps commander, under Burnside, Battle of Fredericksburg, 123
commander of army troops under Banks, supporting Red River Campaign, 267

Fremont, John C., 407
1856 Presidential candidate, 28
early battles in Missouri, 70-71
command, Department of the West, 68, 225
promotes Grant to Cairo, Illinois, post, 69, 408
loses Missouri command because of his proclamation to free the state's slaves without Lincoln's authorization, 71, 225
moved from Missouri to command the Department of Mountain District, which included parts of Virginia, Tennessee and Kentucky, 72, 225
defeated by Stonewall Jackson, Shenandoah Valley, Virginia, 103-106
refuses to serve under Pope, Army of Virginia, 106, 225
resigns from army in 1864, 106, 225

Gillmore, Quincy A., 407
Army-Navy artillery assaults on Charleston Harbor, 212-213, 434
fails to attack Dimmock Line, Petersburg, Virginia, infuriating commanding General Butler, 254, 413

Grant, Ulysses S., 408-409
career prior to Civil War, 70, 408
promoted to command District of Cairo by Fremont, 69
occupies Paducah, Kentucky, 69
Philosophy of War, 228

INDEX OF COMMANDERS DURING THE CIVIL WAR

defeated by Polk at Battle of Belmont, Missouri, 72-73

captures both forts at Battles of Forts Henry and Donelson, Tennessee, acquires nickname, "Unconditional Surrender Grant," 85-87

promoted to command, Army of the Tennessee, 94, 226

Battle of Shiloh, Tennessee, against A.S. Johnston, then defeats Beauregard, 95-100

nearly resigns from army during Siege of Corinth, Mississippi, commanded by Halleck, 101-102

Battle of Iuka, Mississippi, causes a life-long feud between Rosecrans and Grant, when miscommunications leave Rosecrans alone to defeat Price, 131-133

General Orders No.11, which attacks Jewish cotton traders, 143

feuds with McClernand, a politically appointed general, 146, 180, 182

Grant's Freedmen's Bureau, 135-136

loses supply depot at Holly Springs, Mississippi, and abandons approach to Vicksburg from the east, 144-146, 181

Vicksburg, Mississippi, campaign, 182-196
- canal efforts, 183-185, 187
- Army-Navy passes gauntlet of Vicksburg cannons, 187-188
- attack on Snyder's Bluff (Haynes Bluff), 190
- diversionary feints, including Grierson's raid, 188-190
- army crosses Mississippi River to dry land, 191-193
- Navy captures Grand Gulf, Mississippi, 192
- invokes Siege of Vicksburg against Pemberton, 194
- Surrender of Vicksburg, 196
- Union Army captures Jackson, Mississippi, 193, 197

promoted by Lincoln to command three armies, the Military Division of the Mississippi, to take over command of the Siege of Chattanooga, replacing Rosecrans, 202, 226

Siege of Chattanooga, Tennessee, against Bragg, 204-211
- "Cracker Line" opened, 204-205
- Battle of Orchard Knob, 207-208
- Battle of Missionary Ridge, 208-210
- retreat of Confederates into Georgia, 209-211

promoted to General-in-Chief of all armies, replacing Halleck, 226-227, 399, 418

Battles of the Overland Campaign, Virginia, against Lee, 231-247
- Wilderness, 231-233, 246
- Spotsylvania, 234-235, 246
- Mule Shoe, 237-238, 246
- North Anna, 239-240, 246
- Cold Harbor, 240-242, 246
- crossing the James River, ending the Overland Campaign, 243-245

Siege and battles around Petersburg, Virginia, against Lee, 255-260, 338, 348-354
- Battle of Five Forks, 350-353
- Battle of Fort Stedman, 349-350
- controversy about General Warren after battle of Five Forks, Virginia, 353-354

meets Lincoln in conquered Petersburg, 355-356

pursues Lee's army as it breaks out of Siege of Petersburg, the Appomattox Campaign, 354-367

Grant's communications with Lee during Appomattox Campaign, 359, 361, 363

surrender of Lee and his army, followed by surrender of all Confederate armies, 364-367, 375

grand review in Washington of the armies after Confederates surrender, 378-379

implements Enforcement Acts (1867) as President during Reconstruction, 393

President Grant signs 15th Amendment to the Constitution (1868), guaranteeing Blacks the right to vote, 392

Grierson, Benjamin, 409
  leads memorable cavalry raid through Mississippi and Louisiana during Vicksburg Campaign, 188-190

Halleck, Henry, 409-410
  career prior to Civil War, 72, 409
  command, Department of Missouri, 72, 84, 101
  command, General-in-Chief of all armies, 102, 116, 225, 399
  commands Union attack on Siege of Corinth against Beauregard, but removes Grant from active command, nearly causing Grant to resign, 101-102
  demoted to Chief-of-Staff for Grant, as Grant is promoted as General-in-Chief of all armies, replacing Halleck, 227

Hancock, Winfield S., 410
  Battle of Gettysburg, Pennsylvania, 173
  Battle of Spotsylvania, Virginia, 235
  Battle of Cold Harbor, Virginia, 242

Hazen, William B., 411
  Battle of Stones River, Tennessee, 142
  captures Cracker Line from Confederates, Chattanooga, Tennessee, 205
  leads battles for Wilmington seaport, North Carolina, captures Fort McAllister, 322-324, 340

Hooker, Joseph, 411
  career before Civil War, 163, 411
  Battle of Antietam, Maryland, under McClellan, 120
  Battle of Fredericksburg under Burnside, 123-124
  promoted to command the Army of the Potomac, replacing Burnside, 163-164, 226
  defeated by Lee at Battle of Chancellorsville, Virginia, 164-168
  struck unconscious at Chancellorsville mansion, 167
  loses command of Army of the Potomac, replaced by Meade, but remains with the army, 169-170, 226
  deployed from Army of the Potomac to provide support for Grant and the Union Army under siege at Chattanooga, Tennessee, 202, 205
    Battle of Lookout Mountain against Bragg, Siege of Chattanooga, 207-209
    Battle of Wauhatchie against Longstreet, Siege of Chattanooga, 205
  deployed from Army of the Potomac to support Army of the Cumberland under Thomas and Sherman in the Atlanta Campaign, 281
    Battle of New Hope Church, Dallas, Georgia, 281
    Battle of Peachtree Creek, Atlanta, 287
  conflicts with Sherman when passed over for command, transfers out of Atlanta campaign, 289

Howard, Oliver O., 412
  Battle of Chancellorsville under Hooker, surprised by an attack from Stonewall Jackson, 165-166
  Atlanta Campaign under Sherman
    promoted to command Army of the Tennessee after death of McPherson, 287-289
    captures Confederate railroad supply lines supporting Atlanta, 293-294
  commands the Army of the Tennessee, the right wing of Sherman's March to the Sea, 300
  captures Fort McAllister, Savannah, Georgia, 309
  command, right wing of Sherman's army during Carolinas Campaign, 342
  Freemen's Bureau, post-Civil War, establishes Howard University, 391

Hunter, David. 412-413
  command, Department of the West, replacing Fremont in Missouri, 71
  moved to command, Department of Kansas, 72
  promoted to command Army of the Shenandoah, Virginia, replacing Sigel, 248

INDEX OF COMMANDERS DURING THE CIVIL WAR

burns Virginia Military Institute, Lexington, Virginia, became known as "Black Dave," 249

defeated by Breckinridge in Battle of Lynchburg, and withdraws to West Virginia, where he receives no more commands, 249-250

Ingalls, Rufus, 413

placed in charge of massive supply depot for the Union at City Point, near Petersburg, Virginia after the Overland Campaign, 256

Kautz, August, 254, 413

fails to take Dimmock Line from Confederates during Siege of Petersburg, delayed by "Battle of Old Men and Young Boys," 253-254

Kilpatrick, Judson ("Kill-Cavalry"), 414

cavalry support for Sherman during Atlanta Campaign and March to the Sea, Georgia, 292-293, 300-301, 306

cavalry support for Sherman in Carolinas Campaign, North and South Carolina, 342, 344

Monroe Crossroads, North Carolina, nearly captured in "Shirttail Skedaddle," 346

escort for Sherman to meet with Johnston for surrender of Confederate armies, 373

Kimball, Nathan, 414-415

career before the Civil War, 60, 414

defeats Confederates at Cheat Mountain, West Virginia, 60

defeats Stonewall Jackson at Kernstown, Virginia, 103

Battle of Antietam, Maryland, against Lee, seasoned veterans became known as the "Gibraltar Brigade," 120-121, 414

deployed from Sherman's Atlanta Campaign to support Thomas in the battles in Tennessee against Hood, who attacks Franklin and Nashville, 415

Ledlie, James H., 415

disgraced by failure of command at Battle of the Crater, 258-259

censored by court of inquiry and dismissed from the army, 259

Lowe, Thaddeus, 423, 441

balloonist observations at Siege of Yorktown and battles of Seven Pines, 109, 111

Balloon Corps dismantled, 116

Lyon, Nathaniel, 415

command, Department of the West, 67

Camp Jackson Affair, St. Louis, Missouri, 67

killed, Battle of Wilson's Creek, Missouri, 68

McClellan, George B., 416

first battles in western Virginia, 59-60

command, new Army of the Potomac, 74

significant losses at Battle of Ball's Bluff, Virginia, 75

named General-in-Chief for Union armies, 76, 399

controversies with Lincoln, 75-76, 116-117

loses command as General-in-Chief, 76, 225

launches Peninsula Campaign, Virginia, 107-115

blocked by Magruder at Battle of Yorktown siege, Virginia Peninsula Campaign, 108

Battles of Williamsburg and Seven Pines, Virginia Peninsula Campaign against Johnston, 110-112

Battles of Seven Days, Virginia Peninsula Campaign, against Lee, 113-116

Battle of Antietam, Maryland, against Lee, 119-121

loses command, Army of the Potomac, replaced by Burnside, 122, 226

nominated by Peace Democrats as Presidential candidate for 1864 election, loses to Lincoln, 226, 265, 299

McClernand, John A., 416-417

appointed by Lincoln to join Grant's army, 146

commands Sherman's army at Milliken's Bend, Mississippi Delta and leads Battle of Arkansas Post, Arkansas, 147-149, 179-180 deployed to Young's Point, Mississippi Delta, by Grant after Battle of Arkansas Post, 181

loses his command when he violates army regulations by publishing self-promoting reports to press, 182

McCook, Edward M., 417

nearly captured, leading cavalry unit to sever railroad lines supplying Atlanta, 288, 290

McDowell, Irvin, 418

command, Union Army of Northeastern Virginia, to face Confederates in first major battle (1861), 61

defeated by Beauregard at Battle of First Bull Run, Manassas, Virginia, 61-63

loses command of Union Army, replaced by McClellan, but remains with the army, 64, 225

performance criticized for both battles of First and Second Bull Run, 78, 118, 155

McPherson, James B., 418

promoted to command, Army of the Tennessee, as Sherman is advanced to be overall commander of three armies in the Atlanta Campaign, 278

Battles of Atlanta Campaign, Georgia, under Sherman, against Joseph E. Johnston, 278-287

    bypasses Confederates at Snake Creek Gap, near Dalton, Georgia, and holds position at Resaca, 278-279

    Battles of Dallas and New Hope Church, 281

    Battle of Kennesaw Mountain, 283

    reaches Decatur and main railroad line to Augusta, Georgia, 286

    killed at Decatur, Georgia, 287

Meade, George, 419

Battle of Chancellorsville, Viginia, under Hooker, against Lee, 165

promoted to command Army of the Potomac, replacing Hooker, 170, 226

Battle of Gettysburg, Pennsylvania, against Lee, 172-176

    Little Round Top, 173

    "Pickett's Charge," 174-175

Battle of Mine Run, Virginia, against Lee, 179

Battle of the Crater, 257-258

Battles of the Overland Campaign, Virginia, led by Grant, against Lee, 231-255

    Wilderness, 232-233

    conflicts with Sheridan, 235

    Spotsylvania, 234-235

    Cold Harbor, 242

    Petersburg, 255

Siege and battles around Petersburg, 255-260, 338, 348-354

Final review of armies in Washington, D.C., at end of Civil War, 378

Merritt, Wesley, 419-420

The Burning, 262-263, 333

Nelson, William ("Bull"), 420

commands troops at Battle of Shiloh, Tennessee, reinforcing Grant, 97

acquires nickname "Bull" from his intimidating physical attributes and insulting tongue-lashings of subordinates, 138, 420

deployed to set up Union defenses in Kentucky, 130

defeated by Kirby Smith as he leads raw recruits into battle near Richmond, Kentucky, 131

killed by gunshot wound from fellow officer Jefferson C. Davis who shoots him when Nelson fails to apologize, 139

Ord, Edward, 420-421

deployed to Shenandoah with Shields to battle Stonewall Jackson, 105

moved to Grant's Army of the Tennessee and coordinates with Rosecrans in the Battle of Iuka, Mississippi, 132-133

promoted to command Army of the James, replacing Butler, 324

pursues Confederates to Appomattox Station and the surrender of Lee's army, 362

Osterhaus, P.J., 421

Corps commander under Howard during Sherman's March to the Sea, 300

Parker, Ely S., 421-422

INDEX OF COMMANDERS DURING THE CIVIL WAR

military secretary for Grant at the surrender of Robert E. Lee and the Amy of Northern Virginia at Appomattox, 365

Pope, John, 422
captures Island No. 10 from Confederates, Mississippi River, near Belmont, Missouri, 89
command, new Union Army of Virginia, created after numerous defeats in the Shenandoah Valley, 106, 117
defeated by Lee and Longstreet at Battle of Second Bull Run, Manassas, Virginia, 117-118
loses command of Army of Virginia that is disbanded and troops are merged into Army of the Potomac, 118
charges Fitz John Porter with a court-martial for not following orders at the Battle of Second Bull Run, 118
reassigned to duties in Minnesota and Dakota Territories, 118

Porter, Fitz John, 423
defends Malvern Hill during Seven Days battles under McClellan, against Lee, 115
saves army at Battle of Second Bull Run, Manassas, Virginia, under Pope, against Lee and Longstreet, 117
Court-martialed by Pope, then exonerated fifteen years later, 117-118

Ricketts, James B., 423-424
wounded and captured at Battle of First Bull Run, nursed by his wife in prison until exchanged, 423
commands troops deployed from City Point to defend against Confederate raid on Washington, D.C., 251

Rosecrans, William S., 424
defeats Price at Battle of Iuka, Mississippi, which creates a life-long feud with Grant, 132-133, 424
defeats Van Dorn and Price at Battle of Second Corinth, Mississippi, earns national fame, 134-135
promoted to command Army of the Cumberland (formerly Army of the Ohio), replacing Buell, 135, 138, 140, 226

defeats Bragg at Battle of Stones River, Tennessee, 142
defeats Bragg during Tullahoma Campaign, 197
drives Bragg out of Chattanooga, Tennessee, 198
loses Battle of Chickamauga, Georgia, to Bragg and Union army placed under Siege at Chattanooga, 198-201
loses command of the Army of the Cumberland, replaced by Thomas, with Grant promoted as overall commander at Siege of Chattanooga, 202, 211, 226

Schofield, John M., 424-425
promoted to command the recreated Army of the Ohio in 1864 and serve under Sherman in Atlanta Campaign, 275, 278
Battles of Atlanta Campaign, Georgia, under Sherman, 277-294
  Dalton (Rocky Face Ridge), 278-279
  Kennesaw Mountain, 283-284
  crosses Chattahoochee River, 286
  advances to Atlanta, 286
  conflicts with Hooker, 289
  captures Macon & Western RR, 293
  captures Jonesboro, Georgia; Atlanta surrenders, 294
deployed to Tennessee to join Thomas and face Confederate invasion under Hood, 296, 298, 313
nearly trapped by Hood at Pulaski, Tennessee, 313-314
defeats Hood at Battle of Franklin, Tennessee, 315-316
merges his army with Thomas at Nashville to defeat Hood in Battle of Nashville, Tennessee, 316
captures Wilmington, North Carolina, 340
joins Sherman's forces in North Carolina to pursue army of Joseph E. Johnston and its surrender, 345, 348

Scott, Winfield, 425
brevet rank of Lieutenant General during Mexican-American War, 227

invasion of Mexico from Veracruz on the Gulf Coast, Mexican-American War, 17

invites Robert E. Lee to be a senior commander in the Union Army, but Lee reluctantly declines, 39-40

appoints George B. McClellan to command newly created Army of the Ohio in western Virginia, leading to first battles of the Civil War, 59

designs the Anaconda Plan, 75

resigns as General-in-Chief, McClellan is appointed to position, 76, 225

Sedgwick, John, 425

  Battle of Chancellorsville under Hooker, 165-169

  killed at Battle of Spotsylvania, 425

Sheridan, Philip, 425-426

  staff officer under Halleck during Siege of Corinth, 425

  receives horse Rienzi in 1862 as a gift from 2nd Michigan Cavalry, 425

  Battle of Stones River, Tennessee, Army of the Cumberland under Rosecrans, against Bragg, 141-142

  promoted to command Cavalry Corps for Army of the Potomac under Grant and Meade during the Overland Campaign, 235

  Battles of the Overland Campaign, Virginia, under Grant, against Lee, 235-243

    feud with Meade at Spotsylvania, Virginia, 235

    defeats Confederate Cavalry at Battle of Yellow Tavern, Virginia, kills Jeb Stuart, 236-237

    captures Cold Harbor, Virginia, and holds it against Confederates, 241

    Battle of Trevilian Station, Virginia, 242-243

  promoted to new command, Army of the Shenandoah, 252, 259, 261

  engagements against Confederates in Shenandoah Valley, Virginia, 261-262

    The Burning, Shenandoah Valley, 262-263, 332-333

    famous ride on horse Rienzi, Winchester, Virginia, 263-265, 325

    drives Confederate army out of the Shenandoah, 349

  regroups with Army of the Potomac at Siege of Petersburg, Virginia, 349

  defeats Confederates at Dinwiddie and Five Forks, Virginia, 351-353

  feuds with Gouverneur Warren after Five Forks and removes Warren from command, 353

  pursues Lee's Army to Appomattox, Virginia, 356-357, 359

  surrender of Lee at Appomattox, 361-362

Sherman, William T., 426-427

  career before the Civil War, 95-96

  mental depression and leave of absence from army after Battle of First Bull Run, Manassas, Virginia, 96

  assigned to the command of Grant, District of Cairo, 96

  commands raw recruits at Battle of Shiloh, Tennessee, under Grant, against A.S. Johnston and Beauregard, 96-99

  persuades Grant not to resign from the Army, 102

  Battles of Vicksburg Campaign, Mississippi under Grant, 145-197

    Chickasaw Bayou, Mississippi Delta, against Pemberton, 145-147

    Arkansas Post, Arkansas, under McClernand, 148-149, 179-181

    Steele Bayou, Mississippi Delta, 185-186

    Snyder's Bluff (Haynes' Bluff), Mississippi, 190-191

    Jackson, Mississippi, against Joseph E. Johnston, 193, 197

    Vicksburg surrenders, 195-196

  mobilized to bring support to Union Army at Siege of Chattanooga, 202, 207

  Siege of Chattanooga, Tennessee, under Grant, against Bragg, 202-211

    leads Battle for Missionary Ridge, 208-209

leads command to relieve besieged Burnside at Knoxville, Tennessee, 211
promoted to command all Western Armies for the Atlanta Campaign, 227-228, 275
captures Meridian, Mississippi, destroys factories, arsenal, 275-276
Battles of the Atlanta Campaign, Georgia, 277-299
    Dalton (Rocky Face Ridge), 277-279
    Resaca, 280
    near Dallas (New Hope, Pickett's Mill, Allatoona, Big Shanty), 281
    near Marietta (Lost, Pine and Kennesaw Mountains), 282-283
    advance around Shoupade fortifications, 285-286
    reaches Decatur and main railroad to Augusta, 286
    conflicts with Hooker, 289
    focus on destroying Atlanta's railroads, 288, 292-294
    bombards Atlanta with artillery, 291
    captures Atlanta supply railroads, 293
    accepts surrender of Atlanta and occupies the city, 294-295, 298-299
March to the Sea through Georgia, 300-311
    departs Atlanta, 300-302
    foragers deplete countryside, 302-306
    reaches Milledgeville, 306
    reaches Millen, prisoner-of-war camp, 307
    Ebenezer Creek Massacre, 308
    reaches Savannah outskirts, 309
    captures Fort McAlister, Savannah, Georgia, 309
    Savannah surrenders, 310-311
    Field Order No.15, "40 acres and a mule," 312
Carolinas Campaign, 341-345
    departs Savannah, Georgia, 341-342
    traverses the Salkehatchie Swamp, South Carolina, 342-343, 345
    burning of Columbia, South Carolina, 344
    end of Carolinas Campaign, meets with Grant, President Lincoln, 348
    meets with Joseph E. Johnston to discuss Confederate surrender, 373-375
    attacks from Secretary of War Stanton and the Northern Press about terms of surrender, 375-376
    General Johnston surrenders all Confederate armies, 377
    grand review, Washington, D.C., at end of Civil War, 378-379

Shields, James, 427-428
    duel with Abraham Lincoln (1842), 428
    wounded in Battle of Kernstown against Stonewall Jackson, Shenandoah Valley, 103
    defeated by Stonewall Jackson at Battle of Port Republic, Shenandoah Valley, 105-106

Sigel, Franz, 428
    Battle of Pea Ridge, Arkansas, under Curtis, against Van Dorn and Price, 90, 94
    Battle of Fredericksburg, Virginia, under Burnside, against Lee, 123
    promoted to command Department of West Virginia in the Shenandoah Valley, 247
    defeated by Breckinridge in battle known as the "Field of Lost Shoes," at New Market, Virginia, 247-248
    loses command in Shenandoah, replaced by David Hunter, 248

Slocum, Henry, 429
    Battle of Chancellorsville, Virginia, under Hooker, against Lee, 165
    Battle of Gettysburg, Pennsylvania, under Meade, against Lee, 173
    refuses to serve under Hooker and his Corps is transferred to Army of the Tennessee, 429
    accepts surrender of Atlanta, Georgia, at end of Atlanta Campaign under Sherman, 294

command, Army of Georgia, left-wing of Sherman's March to the Sea, Georgia, and the Carolinas Campaign, 300-301, 342
defeats Joseph E. Johnston at Battles of Averasboro and Bentonville, North Carolina, 347
Smith, Andrew Jackson (A.J.), 429-430
deployed from Sherman's Army of the Tennessee to support Red River Campaign, Louisiana, under Banks, 267
Battles of Mansfield and Pleasant Hill, Louisiana, against Taylor, 269
unable to join Sherman for Atlanta Campaign because of Red River delays, 274
conducts unauthorized raid at Oxford, Mississippi, 430
deployed to join Thomas' Army of the Cumberland for Battle of Nashville, Tennessee, against Hood and the Confederate Army of Tennessee, 316
Smith, William F. ("Baldy"), 430
leads command to recapture Cracker Line, Chattanooga, Tennessee, under Grant, Siege of Chattanooga, 205
deployed to Cold Harbor, Virginia, from Bermuda Hundred, to support Grant in Overland Campaign, 241
crosses the James River from Cold Harbor, returns to Bermuda Hundred, 243
leads advance Union vanguard from Cold Harbor to capture undefended Petersburg, but fails to press his advantage, 255
Smith, William Sooy, 431
leads failed cavalry support for Sherman's Meridian Campaign, Mississippi, barely escapes capture, 275-276
Steedman, James, 431-432
leads command of collected troops to support Thomas in Battle of Nashville, 316
courageous attack by his Black troops at Battle of Nashville deceives Confederates about location of main assault, 318, 432

Steele, Frederick, 432
command, Department of Arkansas, Little Rock, 267
attempts to bring troops from Arkansas to Shreveport, Louisiana, in the Camden Expedition, supporting the Red River Campaign under Banks, 270-271
aborts mission with news of failed Red River Campaign, 272
barely escapes Confederates under Kirby Smith and Price at Battle of Jenkins Ferry, Arkansas, 272
Stoneman, George, 433
provides cavalry support for Hooker, Battle of Chancellorsville, Virginia, against Lee, 164, 169
provides cavalry support for Sherman in Atlanta Campaign, 283, 288
captured by Confederate Cavalry under Wheeler at Macon, Georgia, and then exchanged two months later, 290
Sumner, Edwin ("Bull"), 433
oldest field commander of Civil War, leads a corps under George McClellan during Peninsula Campaign, 433
leads Center Division corps for Burnsides' attack on Lee at Battle of Fredericksburg, Virginia, dies shortly after the battle, 123
Terrill, William, 434
killed at Battle of Perryville, Kentucky, 158
Terry, Alfred, 434
command, Provisional Army of the James, and leads assault to capture Fort Fisher, Wilmington, North Carolina, the Confederacy's last seaport, 324, 338-339
captures city of Wilmington, North Carolina, after capture of Fort Fisher, 340
Thomas, George H., 434-435
protects retreat of Army of the Cumberland under Rosecrans, against Bragg at Battle of Chickamauga, Georgia, acquiring the name, "Rock of Chickamauga," 199-201

INDEX OF COMMANDERS DURING THE CIVIL WAR

promoted to command Army of the Cumberland, replacing Rosecrans at Siege of Chattanooga, 202, 226

leads central attack under Grant against Bragg, at Battle of Orchard Knob, Chattanooga, Tennessee, 208

leads Union charge up Lookout Mountain under Grant, that defeats Bragg's army at Chattanooga, Tennessee, 209-210

commands Army of the Cumberland in battles of the Atlanta Campaign, Georgia, under Sherman, against Joseph E. Johnston, 277-296

    Dalton (Rocky Face Ridge), 278-279

    New Hope Church, 281

    Kennesaw Mountain, 283

    advance to Peachtree Creek, 286-287

    destruction, Atlanta's supply railroads, 293

deployed to Tennessee to face invasion from Confederates under John Bell Hood, 296

leads Franklin-Nashville Campaign, Tennessee, against Hood, 313-319

    prepares enlarged army at Nashville for Confederate attack, 316-317

    defeats and pursues the shattered Confederate army, 318-319

Wallace, Lew, 435-436

delayed arrival at Battle of Shiloh, Tennessee, battlefield harms his military reputation, 98

redeems his name at Battle of Monocacy Junction, Maryland, by delaying a Confederate attack on Washington capital, providing sufficient time for reinforcements to defend the city, 251

Warren, Gouverneur K., 436-437

oversees defense line at Gettysburg, Pennsylvania, as Union prepares for battle with Lee's army, 173

provides feint attack to cover Union Army's stealthy departure from Cold Harbor battlefield, Virginia, to cross the James River and reach Petersburg, unmolested, 243

captures critical Confederate Weldon Railroad line, Virginia, during the Siege of Petersburg, 259, 349

leads forces supporting Sheridan with attacks at Dinwiddie and Five Forks, Virginia, during Siege of Petersburg against Lee, 351-353

removed from command by Sheridan after Battle of Five Forks, but his request for a court of inquiry is denied until 1879-1882, 353

Sheridan's charges against him found by court of inquiry to be unjustified, 354

Weitzel, Godfrey, 356, 437

accepts surrender of Richmond with Black troops from Massachusetts Cavalry, 356

hosts visit by President Lincoln to tour the captured city of Richmond, 356-357

Williams, Alpheus S., 437-438

Corps commander under Slocum during Sherman's March to the Sea, 300

Wilson, James H., 438

deployed from Sherman's army in Georgia to provide cavalry support for Union Generals Thomas and Schofield during Franklin-Nashville Campaign, Tennessee, 313, 317

pursues defeated shattered Confederate Army of Tennessee under Hood after Battle of Nashville, 318-319

captures Confederate President Jefferson Davis and Henry Wirz, commander of Andersonville Prisoner of War Camp, as they attempt to escape the country after Confederate armies have surrendered, 376

defeats cavalry of Nathan Bedford Forrest near end of the war, 377

Wright, Horatio, 438

leads troops at Battle of the Mule Shoe, Overland Campaign, Virginia, 238

blocks Confederate raid on Washington capital, 251-252, 257

CONFEDERATE OFFICERS IN THE ARMY

Alexander, Edward Porter, 477
  balloonist and aeronaut for the
    Confederacy, 112, 116
  Battle of Fredericksburg, Virginia, 125
Anderson, Richard H., 445
  Confederate cavalry commander at Battle
    of Spotsylvania, Virginia, 235
  protects Lee's army as it abandons the
    Siege of Petersburg, Virginia, 357
Beauregard, P.G.T., 446
  Confederate commander at Battle of Fort
    Sumter, South Carolina, first battle of
    the Civil War, 38, 41
  friendship with Union officer Robert
    Anderson, in charge of Fort Sumter, 38,
    399
  designs Confederate battle flag, 46
  defeats McDowell at Battle of First Bull
    Run, 61-63
  assumes command, Confederate Army
    of Mississippi, when A.S. Johnston is
    killed in Battle of Shiloh, 98
  defeated by Grant at Battle of Shiloh,
    retreats to Corinth, Mississippi, 98
  withdraws desperately ill Southern army
    from Corinth, takes medical leave of
    absence and loses command, replaced
    by Bragg, 101, 446
  moved to command coastal defenses of
    South Carolina, 102
  conflicts with President Davis, 102, 446
  blocks Butler's army at Howlett Line,
    Bermuda Hundred, 230
  prevents capture of Petersburg after Union
    forces end the Overland Campaign and
    cross the James River 255
  defends South Carolina from Sherman's
    march during the Carolinas Campaign,
    344
  evacuates Charleston, South Carolina,
    as Sherman marches through the
    Carolinas, 344
Bragg, Braxton, 447-448
  career before the Civil War, 128, 447
  promoted to command, Army of
    Mississippi, replacing Beauregard, 101
  commands Heartland Offensive into
    Kentucky, 119, 127-130
  captures Munfordville, Kentucky, during
    Heartland Offensive, 131
  defeats Buell at Battle of Perryville,
    Kentucky, but then retreats to
    Tennessee, abandoning Heartland
    Offensive, renames army as Army of
    Tennessee 137, 140
  defeated by Rosecrans at Battle of Stones
    River, Tennessee, 141-142
  criticized by subordinates, Revolt of the
    Generals, 138, 206
  defeated by Rosecrans during Tullahoma
    Campaign and driven out of
    Chattanooga, Tennessee, 197-198
  defeats Rosecrans at Battle of
    Chickamauga, Georgia, and
    places Union Army under siege at
    Chattanooga, 199-201
  defeated by Grant at Battles of
    Chattanooga, loses command of Army
    of Tennessee to Joseph E. Johnston,
    207-211
  moved to command, Department of
    North Carolina and Virginia, 209, 339
  evacuates Wilmington, North Carolina,
    avoiding Union capture, 340
  surrenders to Union cavalry in Georgia at
    end of Civil War and is paroled, 448
Breckinridge, John C., 448
  1856 Vice-President to Buchanan, 28
  1860 Presidential election candidate,
    31-32, 448
  defeats Hunter in the Shenandoah Valley
    at the Battle of Lynchburg, Virginia, 249
  defeats Sigel in the "Field of Lost Shoes"
    at the Battle of New Market, Virginia,
    Shenandoah Valley, 247
  loses a third of his men, the "Orphan
    Brigade," under Bragg at the Battle
    of Stones River, Tennessee, against
    Rosecrans, 142
  escapes to Cuba when Confederate armies
    surrender at end of Civil War, 449

INDEX OF COMMANDERS DURING THE CIVIL WAR

granted amnesty by President Johnson in 1868 and returns to Kentucky, 449
Buckner, Simon Bolivar, 449
   surrenders Fort Donelson, Tennessee, to "Unconditional Surrender" Grant, 86-87
   surrenders last of Trans-Mississippi Confederate armies to Union authorities in Galveston in 1865 at end of the war, 372
Early, Jubal A., 450
   Battle of Fredericksburg, Virginia, under Lee against Burnside, 165
   joins Breckinridge at Lynchburg, Virginia, to defeat Hunter in the Shenandoah Valley, 249
   defeats Wallace at Battle of Monocacy Junction, Virginia, 251
   attempts raid on Washington, D.C., but defeated by Union reinforcements from City Point, Virginia, 250-252, 257
   defeats Union forces under George Crook and burns town of Chambersburg, Pennsylvania, 252, 259
   loses Shenandoah Valley, Virginia, to Sheridan, 261, 263-264
   promotes the argument of The "Lost Cause," after the Civil War, 451
Ewell, Richard, 451
   supports Stonewall Jackson against Banks in Battle of Front Royal, Virginia, Shenandoah Valley, 104
   Battle of Gettysburg, Pennsylvania, at Culp's Hill against Meade, 174
   Battle of Mule Shoe, Spotsylvania, holds position against Union attacks, 237
   follows Lee's army as they retreat from Richmond to Amelia Courthouse and Appomattox, 357, 360
   captured at Battle of Sailor's Creek during Appomattox retreat, 358
Floyd, John B., 451
   former Secretary of War under U.S. President Buchanan and Confederate commander of Fort Donelson, 86-87
   escapes from Fort Donelson, turning over command to subordinates, 87

relieved of command by President Davis, 87
Forrest, Nathan Bedford, 452
   escapes from Fort Donelson, Tennessee, with his cavalry, before Union capture by Grant, 87
   cavalry raids against Union supply and telegraph lines in Tennessee, 128, 145, 296
   responsible for Fort Pillow Massacre, Tennessee, 276
   joins his cavalry with Hood to attack Union forces in the Battles of Franklin and Nashville, Tennessee, 296-297
   protects retreating Confederate Army under Hood after Franklin-Nashville battles, 297, 313, 318-319
   Ku Klux Klan, 277, 452
   rivalry against Wheeler, 476
   surrenders to Union forces, 377
Gordon, John B., 452
   leads Battle of Fort Stedman, Siege of Petersburg, Virginia, 349-350
   flight from Petersburg to Appomattox, Virginia, 353, 360, 362
   Battle of Sailor's Creek, Virginia, during Appomattox retreat, 358
   leads formal surrender of Confederate Army of Northern Virginia at Appomattox Station, 368-369
Hampton, Wade, 260, 344, 346, 454
   leads "Beefsteak Raid," capturing Union beef cattle during Siege of Petersburg, 260
   departs Columbia, South Carolina, as Sherman's army approaches the city during the Carolinas Campaign, 344
   nearly captures Union cavalry officer in "Kilpatrick's Shirttail Skedaddle," 346
Hardee, William, 454-455
   Battle of Jonesboro, Georgia, against Sherman during Atlanta Campaign, 294
   refuses to serve under Hood after Atlanta is captured by Union forces and transfers to Department of South Carolina, 307

attempts to defend South Carolina from Sherman's army during the Carolinas Campaign, 343

defends Savannah, Georgia, against Sherman's army, but withdraws to avoid capture, 308, 310-311

joins army of Joseph E. Johnston in North Carolina, 346

Hill, A.P., 455-456

Seven Days battles against McClellan, Virginia Peninsula, under Lee 113

strained but successful relationship with Stonewall Jackson, 456

joins Lee's army in Battle of Antietam at a crucial moment with a hard march from Harper's Ferry (West) Virginia, 120

Battle of Cold Harbor, Virginia, under Lee, 243

killed at Siege of Petersburg, Virginia, 354

Hoke, Robert, 456

defends Fort Fisher, Wilmington, North Carolina, from Butler's Army of the James, 324

defeated by Union troops under Terry who captures Wilmington, North Carolina, 339

Hood, John Bell, 456-457

loses one leg to amputation at Battle of Chickamauga, Georgia, 201

Battles of the Atlanta Campaign, Georgia, against Sherman, 283-296

Battle of Kolb Farm, 283

promoted to command Army of Tennessee, replacing Joseph E. Johnston, 286

Battle of Peachtree Creek, 287

defends trenches protecting city of Atlanta, 287

evacuates Atlanta, harasses Union supply line, 294, 296

plans invasion of Tennessee, 297

receives disastrous losses from Schofield at Battle of Franklin, Tennessee, 315-316

defeated by Thomas at Battle of Nashville, Tennessee, and his army is nearly destroyed in its retreat through a brutal winter, 318-319

removed from command after Battle of Nashville, resigns from the army, 319

Jackson, Thomas ("Stonewall"), 457

acquires name of "Stonewall" at Battle of First Bull Run, Manassas, Virginia, against McDowell, 61, 63

establishes headquarters in Shenandoah Valley, 102-103

engagements in Shenandoah Valley, Virginia (1862), 103-106

a rare defeat from Kimball at Kernstown, Virginia, 103

defeats Banks at Front Royal, Virginia, captures 700 prisoners, 104

seizes large supply train from "Commissary Banks" at Battle of Winchester, Virginia, 104

defeats Fremont and Shields at Cross Keys and Port Republic, Virginia, 105-106

Battle of Gaines' Mill, Peninsula Campaign, Virginia, under Lee against McClellan, 114

Battle of Second Bull Run, Manassas, Virginia, under Lee against Pope, 117

Battle of Fredericksburg, Virginia, under Lee against Burnside, 122-125

Battle of Chancellorsville, Virginia, under Lee against Hooker, 165-167

mortally wounded by friendly fire at Battle of Chancellorsville, dies eight days later, 167

Johnston, Albert Sidney, 458

career before the Civil War, resigns from U.S. Army, 74, 458

command, Confederate States Army of Mississippi, 88

moves army from Bowling Green, Kentucky, to Nashville, then Corinth, and merges with Army of Mississippi under Beauregard, taking overall command of the two armies, 96

INDEX OF COMMANDERS DURING THE CIVIL WAR

killed in Battle of Shiloh, Tennessee, against Grant, 97-98

Johnston, Joseph E., 458-459
 early career, resigns from U.S. Army, joins the Confederacy, 74, 458
 first command, Confederate Army in Northern Virginia, outwits McClellan, 75-76
 controversies with Confederate President Davis, 223, 459
 joins Beauregard in Battle of First Bull Run, Manassas, Virginia, against McDowell, 61, 63
 wounded in Battle of Seven Pines of Peninsula Campaign, Virginia, against McClellan, replaced by Robert E. Lee, 112-113
 evacuates Jackson, Mississippi, as Grant's army advances during Vicksburg Campaign, 193-194
 evacuates Jackson, Mississippi, a second time from Sherman, after Vicksburg surrenders, 197
 command, Army of Tennessee, replacing Bragg who lost Chattanooga to Grant, 209
 Atlanta Campaign battles, Georgia, against Union Sherman's forces,
  Dalton (Rocky Face Ridge), 277-279
  Resaca, 279-280
  New Hope Church, near Dallas, 281
  Pine Mountain, near Marietta, 283
  Kennesaw Mountain, 283
  Shoupade fortifications, 284-285
  loses command of Army of Tennessee during Atlanta Campaign, replaced by John Bell Hood, 286
 defeated at Battles of Averasboro and Bentonville in Carolinas Campaign, North Carolina, against Sherman, 347
 meetings with Sherman in North Carolina to discuss terms of surrender, 373, 374
 terms of surrender of all Confederate armies, 374-375
 attends Sherman's funeral as honorary pallbearer after the end of the Civil War, contracts pneumonia and dies one month later, 427, 459

Jones, William E. ("Grumble"), 459-460
 killed, Piedmont, Virginia, 249

Lee, Fitzhugh, 460
 defeated by Sheridan at Five Forks, Virginia, 351-352
 cavalry support for Confederate breakout from Petersburg to Amelia Courthouse, Virginia, and engagement at Jetersville, 357-358

Lee, George Washington Custis, 460-461
 serves as aide-de-camp to Confederate President Davis, for most of Civil War, 461
 captured at Battle of Sailor's Creek, 358

Lee, Robert E., 461-462
 captures John Brown at Harpers Ferry prior to the Civil War, 24, 461
 career before Civil War, 39-40, 74
 resigns from U.S. Army and joins Confederate States Army, 40, 44, 74
 first battles in West Virginia (1861), 60
 command, Army of Northern Virginia, replacing wounded Joseph E. Johnston, 113
 Battles of Seven Days against McClellan, Virginia Peninsula Campaign, 113-116
 defeats Pope at Battle of Second Bull Run, 117
 Battle of Antietam (Sharpsburg), Maryland, against McClellan, loses Special Order No.191, 118-121
 defeats Burnside at Battle of Fredericksburg, Virginia, 122, 124-126
 defeats Burnside at Battle of the Mud March, Virginia, 162
 defeats Hooker at Battle of Chancellorsville, Virginia, 164-169
 Battle of Gettysburg, Pennsylvania, against Meade, army withdraws to Virginia, 170-176
 defeats Meade at Battle of Mine Run, Virginia, 179
 battles against Grant and Meade in Overland Campaign, Virginia, 231-247

Wilderness, 232-233, 246
Spotsylvania, 234-235, 246
Mule Shoe, 237-238, 246
North Anna, 239-240, 246
Cold Harbor, 241-242, 246
army placed under Siege of Petersburg, Virginia, by Grant, 348-355
Fort Stedman, Petersburg, 349-350
Fort Gregg, Petersburg, "Confederate Alamo," of the Civil War, 353-354
responds to Beauregard for more troops at Second Battle of Petersburg, 255
withdraws army from Petersburg to find rations for the army, 355-360
Amelia Courthouse, 357
Sailor's Creek, 358-359
Appomattox, 361-362
messages with Grant regarding terms of surrender, 359, 361, 363
surrenders to Grant at Appomattox Station and issues farewell address to his troops, 364-366
Lee, Stephen D., 462
evacuation of Atlanta, Battle of Jonesboro, Georgia, 294
cavalry protects Army of Tennessee under Hood as it flees Battle of Nashville, Tennessee, after being defeated, 318-319
Lee, William Henry Fitzhugh (Rooney), 463
personal home, White House Landing plantation, Virginia, captured by McClellan, 111
defeated at Battle of Five Forks, Virginia, by Sheridan, 351-352
Longstreet, James, 464
Battle of Yorktown Siege, Virginia Peninsula, against McClellan, 108-109
Battles of Seven Days, under Lee against McClellan, Virginia Peninsula, 113
Battle of Second Bull Run, Manassas, Virginia, under Lee against Pope, 117
Battle of Antietam, Maryland, under Lee against McClellan, 119, 121
Battle of Fredericksburg, Virginia, under Lee against Burnside, 124-125
Siege of Suffolk, Virginia, 164

Battle of Gettysburg, Pennsylvania, under Lee against Meade, 173, 176
deployed from Army of Northern Virginia to support Bragg in Battle of Chickamauga, Georgia, against Rosecrans, 200-201
"Revolt of the Generals" against commander Bragg, 206
defeated by Hooker at Battle at Wauhatchie during Siege of Chattanooga, Tennessee, 205
invokes Siege of Knoxville, Tennessee, against Burnside, but withdraws from siege after surrender of Chattanooga to Grant, 206, 211
Battle of the Wilderness, Virginia, under Lee in the Overland Campaign against Grant, wounded by friendly fire, 233
supports Confederate Army as it flees Siege of Petersburg to reach rations for troops at Amelia Courthouse, Virginia, 354-355
Longstreet's troops arrive at Farmville, Virginia, for rations during flight from Petersburg to Appomattox, 358-359
surrender at Appomattox, Virginia, 363, 365
Magruder, John B., 464
mounts successful defense against McClellan at Yorktown, Virginia, during Peninsula Campaign, 108
Mahone, William, 465
reaches High Bridge after Battle of Sailor's Creek, 358, 360
consoles Lee who has lost twenty percent of his army at Sailor's Creek, 465
McCulloch, Benjamin, 466
joins his Texas forces with Price, who commands the Missouri State Guard, against Lyon at the Battle of Wilson's Creek, Missouri, 68
feuds with Price's command and his Missouri troops, 68
army merged with Price into Army of the West under Van Dorn to battle against Curtis in Battle of Pea Ridge, Arkansas, 90-93
killed at Battle of Pea Ridge, 93

INDEX OF COMMANDERS DURING THE CIVIL WAR

Morgan, John Hunt, 466-467
  attacks Union supply lines, thwarting Buell's march to Chattanooga, Tennessee, 128
  raids in Kentucky produce his nickname, "Thunderbolt of the Confederacy," which encourages the Confederate Heartland Offensive, 127-128
  raids town of Salem, Indiana, 224
  captured and imprisoned in Ohio Penitentiary, but he then escapes, 467
  killed in surprise Union raid in Tennessee, 467

Mosby, John, 467-468
  known as the "Gray Ghost" of Mosby's Rangers in the Shenandoah Valley, 249, 262-263
  surrenders to Union, 377, 468
  becomes friends and supporter of President Grant after the Civil War, 468

Pemberton, John C., 468
  command, Confederacy's Fortress of Vicksburg, Mississippi, 102
  defends Chickasaw Bayou, Mississippi Delta, against Sherman, 146-148
  Fort Pemberton on Yazoo River, Mississippi Delta, defeats Union Navy's access to the Vicksburg Fortress, 183
  orders raid to Grant's supply depot, Holly Springs, Mississippi, foiling Union attempts to reach Vicksburg from the east, 145
  diverts troopers from Vicksburg to pursue Union cavalry raid by Grierson, 190
  defends Vicksburg from Grant at battles of Raymond, Champion Hill and Big Black River, Mississippi, as Union Army pursues the Confederates into a siege, 194-195
  surrenders to Grant after 47-day Siege of Vicksburg, 196

Pickett, George, 468-469
  "Pickett's Charge" in Battle of Gettysburg, Pennsylvania, results in devastating losses for the Confederates, 175-176
  defeated by Sheridan at Battle of Five Forks, Virginia, during the Siege of Petersburg, Virginia, 351-352

Pike, Albert, 469-470
  provides troops from Indian Territory to Battle of Pea Ridge, 91, 93

Pillow, Gideon, 470
  creates Fort Pillow at beginning of Civil War, 276
  refuses to accept command of Fort Donelson and escapes by small boat as Confederate Army is trapped by Grant's forces, 86

Polk, Leonidas ("Fighting Bishop"), 470-471
  leads Confederate force to occupy Columbus, Kentucky, violating the state's neutrality, 69
  defeats Grant in Battle at Belmont, Missouri, 72-74
  departs Columbus, Kentucky, and joins Confederate Army at Corinth, Mississippi, 88-89, 95
  deceived by Sherman and leaves Meridian, Mississippi, prematurely, which allows Union troops to destroy the town, 275-276
  killed, Pine Mountain, Georgia, during Sherman's Atlanta Campaign, 283

Price, Sterling, 471
  granted command of the secessionist Missouri State Guard by the state's governor to battle against Union forces attempting to achieve Missouri's commitment for the Union, 67
  defeats Union forces under Lyon with support of troops under McCulloch from Texas at battle of Wilson's Creek, Missouri, 67-68
  feuds with McCulloch after the battle in Missouri, 68
  defeats Union troops under Fremont, at Lexington, Missouri, 70-71
  loses battle to Fremont at Springfield, Missouri (Zagonyi's Charge), 71
  merged with McCulloch into Army of the West in Arkansas under Van Dorn, as McCulloch and Price continue their feud from Missouri, 91

combined forces engage in Battle of Pea Ridge, Arkansas, against Curtis, but McCulloch is killed during the battle, 93

Price and Van Dorn are defeated by Curtis at Battle of Pea Ridge, Arkansas, 93-94

defeated by Rosecrans at Battle of Iuka, Mississippi, 132-133

defeated with Van Dorn by Rosecrans at Second Battle of Corinth, Mississippi, 134-135

fails to capture Union Army under Steele at Battle of Jenkin's Ferry, Arkansas, combating Union forces under Banks in Red River Campaign, 270-272

soundly defeated in last battle in Missouri by Curtis in October 1864, 471

Shoup, Asbury, 471-472

creates Shoupade fortifications, Atlanta Campaign, against Sherman, 285-286

Smith, E. Kirby, 472

launches South's Heartland Offensive into Kentucky, coordinated with Braxton Bragg, 128-130

defeats "Bull" Nelson at Battles of Big Hill, Richmond and Frankfort, Kentucky, 130-131

unites with Bragg's army after Confederates win the Battle of Perryville, Kentucky, but Bragg, as overall commander of the Heartland Offensive, withdraws the two armies to Murfreesboro, Tennessee, over Smith's objections, 137, 140

promoted to command the Trans-Mississippi Department, Shreveport, Louisiana, 269

confronts Union troops in Arkansas, against Steele, in the Camden Expedition, 270-271

nearly captures Steele's army at Jenkins Ferry, Arkansas, 272

life-long feud with Richard Taylor for depleting his army and preventing his capture of the nearly trapped Navy fleet, 274

officially surrenders to Union forces in Galveston, Texas, June 2, 1865

Stuart, Jeb, 472-473

Chief aide to Robert E. Lee in the capture of John Brown at Harpers Ferry, prior to the Civil War, 24

provides cavalry support to Lee in Seven Days battles during the Union Peninsula Campaign, Virginia, 113

provides cavalry support for Lee at Battle of Chancellorsville, Virginia, against Hooker, 165

arrives too late to support Lee against Meade in Battle of Gettysburg, Pennsylvania, delayed by long supply train, 170, 174

defeated by Union Cavalry under Custer on final day of Battle of Gettysburg, 175

provides cavalry support for Lee during Overland Campaign, Virginia, and holds Confederate position at Spotsylvania, 235

killed at Battle of Yellow Tavern, Virginia, by Sheridan's cavalry raid during Overland Campaign, 236, 246

Taylor, Richard, 473-474

defends Bayou Teche, Louisiana, against Banks, 213

command, Confederate Western District of Louisiana during Red River Campaign, Louisiana, against Banks, 265, 268

defeats Banks' army at Battles of Mansfield and Pleasant Hill, Louisiana, 269

attacks and nearly traps the Navy fleet on the Red River, Louisiana, 270, 274

retains a life-long feud with Kirby Smith, who depleted his army and allowed the Navy fleet to escape, 274

officially surrenders to Union, 376-377

Tilghman, Lloyd, 86, 474

surrenders Fort Henry, Tennessee, to Grant, 86

killed, Champion Hill, Vicksburg Campaign, 474

INDEX OF COMMANDERS DURING THE CIVIL WAR

Van Dorn, Earl, 474-475
   promoted to command Confederacy's District of the Trans-Mississippi, which included Missouri, Arkansas, Louisiana and Indian Territory, 90
   combines two armies in Arkansas to battle against Union forces under Curtis at Pea Ridge, Arkansas, 91
   defeated by Curtis at Elkhorn Tavern, Battle of Pea Ridge, Arkansas, army escapes to Mississippi, 92-94
   defeated at Battle of Second Battle of Corinth, Mississippi, by Rosecrans, 134
   successfully raids Grant's supply depot at Holly Springs, Mississippi, 144-145
   destroys railroads and telegraph lines in Tennessee, following Holly Springs raid, seriously hampering Union communications, 145
   killed by his lover's husband, Spring Hill, Tennessee, 475

Watie, Stand, 475
   Chief, Cherokee Mounted Rifles, supports Confederates, 92
   last general of the Confederacy to surrender, 378

Wheeler, Joseph, 475-476
   captures two Union cavalries, headed by Stoneman and McCook under Sherman, during Atlanta Campaign, 290
   captures Union garrison and supply line at Dalton, Georgia, during Atlanta Campaign, but then driven off, 292
   provides cavalry opposition to Sherman's March to the Sea through Georgia, 297, 301, 306
   pursues Union Army and captures slaves at Ebenezer Creek Massacre during Sherman's March to the Sea through Georgia, 308

OFFICERS IN THE NAVY
Union and Confederate

Buchanan, Franklin, 476-477
  defeats Union Navy in Battle of Hampton Roads, 107, 477
  loses battle of Mobile Bay to Farragut, 321

Farragut, David G., 439-440
  captures New Orleans and Baton Rouge, Louisiana, from Confederates, 100
  ends siege of Port Hudson after Union captures Vicksburg, 196
  captures Mobile Bay, Alabama, from Confederates, "Damn the torpedoes, full speed ahead," 320-322

Foote, Andrew, 440
  captures Fort Henry on Tennessee River from Confederates, 85-86
  Union fleet is defeated at Fort Donelson and forced to withdraw, 86

Porter, David D., 440-441
  commands Navy support for Union Army-Navy expedition at Chickasaw Bayou, Mississippi, under Sherman, 145-147
  commands Navy support for Union Army-Navy capture of Arkansas Post, Arkansas, under McClernand, 149, 179-180
  commands Navy support for Union Army-Navy Steele Bayou expedition under Sherman, gunboats nearly trapped in Mississippi Delta, 185-186
  commands Navy gunboats that protect Union boats and barges from Vicksburg cannons as Grant crosses the Mississippi River during the Vicksburg campaign, 187-188
  Union Navy fleet captures Grand Gulf, Mississippi, during Vicksburg Campaign under Grant, 192
  Union Navy gunboats control Hayne's Bluff after Union Army places Vicksburg under siege, 194
  commands Navy support for Union Army-Navy Red River Campaign, Louisiana, 266-274
  fleet proceeds up Red River in attempt to reach Shreveport, Louisiana, 268-270
  gathers cotton bales under Naval Prize Law, 267
  Navy fleet nearly trapped on Red River, 272-274
  leads Navy attacks on Fort Fisher, Wilmington, North Carolina, during Amy-Navy offensive, Battles of Fort Fisher, 322-324, 338-339
  commands Navy support for Union Army-Navy capture of Wilmington, North Carolina, 340
  provides Navy escort for President Lincoln's tours of Petersburg and Richmond after their capture, 355-356, 383

INDEX OF BATTLES

BATTLES OF 1861

Eastern Theater
Ball's Bluff, Virginia, 75
First Bull Run, Manassas, Virginia, 61-63
Fort Sumter, South Carolina, 38-39, 41
Philippi, Western Virginia, 59
Rich Mountain & Cheat Mountain Pass, Western Virginia, 59-60

Western & Trans-Mississippi Theaters
Belmont, Missouri, 72-73
Camp Jackson Affair, St. Louis, Missouri, 66-67
Lexington, Missouri, 70-71
Springfield, Missouri (Zagonyi's Charge), 71
Wilson's Creek, Missouri, 67-68

BATTLES OF 1862

Western & Trans-Mississippi Theaters
Fort Donelson, Tennessee, 86-87
Fort Henry, Tennessee, 85
Glorieta Pass, New Mexico, 34, 403
Pea Ridge, Arkansas, 89-94
Shiloh (Pittsburg Landing), Tennessee, 94-99
Siege of Corinth, Mississippi, 101
Union Navy Captures New Orleans, 100

Eastern Theater
Antietam (or Sharpsburg), Maryland, 118-122
Cross Keys, Virginia, 106
Fredericksburg, Virginia, 122-126
Front Royal & Winchester, Virginia, 103-105
Kernstown, Virginia, 102-103
Naval Battle at Hampton Roads, Virginia, 107-108
Second Bull Run, Manassas, Virginia, 116-118
Seven Days, Virginia Peninsula, 113-116
Seven Pines (or Fair Oaks), Virginia, 111-112
Siege of Yorktown, Virginia, 108
Union Recaptures Naval Shipyard, Norfolk, Virginia, 110

Western Theater
Big Hill, Kentucky, 130-131
Chickasaw Bayou (or Walnut Hills), Mississippi, 146-147
Grant's Mississippi Central Advance, 143-146
Iuka, Mississippi, 131-134
Munfordville (or Green River), Kentucky, 131
Perryville (or Chaplin Hills), Kentucky, 137-138
Raid at Holly Springs, Mississippi, 145
Richmond, Kentucky, 130-131
Second Battle of Corinth, Mississippi, 134-135
Stones River (or Murfreesboro), Tennessee, 140-142

BATTLES OF 1863

Eastern Theater
Chancellorsville, Virginia, 164-169
Gettysburg, Pennsylvania, 170-178
Mine Run, Virginia, 179
Mud March to Richmond, Virginia, 162

Western Theater
Arkansas Post (or Fort Hindman), Arkansas, 179-180
Canal Efforts, Mississippi Delta, 183, 187
Chickamauga, Georgia, 198-201

Grand Gulf, Mississippi, Surrenders, 192-193
Jackson, Mississippi, Surrenders, 193
Knoxville Campaign, East Tennessee, 198
Lookout Mountain, Chattanooga, Tennessee, 208
Missionary Ridge, Chatanooga, Tennessee, 208-211
Orchard Knob, Chattanooga, Tennessee, 207-208
Siege and Surrender of Vicksburg, Mississippi, 194-196
Siege of Chattanooga, Tennessee, 201-205
Snyder's Bluff (or Hayne's Bluff), Vicksburg, 190-191
Steele Bayou Expedition, Mississippi Delta, 185-186
Tullahoma Campaign, Tennessee, 197
Union Cavalry Raid to Baton Rouge, Louisiana, 188-190
Union Navy Passes Vicksburg Cannons, 187-188
Yazoo Pass Expedition, Mississippi Delta, 183

Deep South & Gulf Coast
Bayou Teche Campaign, Gulf Coast, 213
Charleston Harbor, South Carolina, 212-213

BATTLES OF 1864

Eastern Theater
Bermuda Hundred Campaign, Viginia, 229-230
Overland Campaign, Virginia
  Cold Harbor, 241
  Mule Shoe, 237-238
  North Anna, 239-240
  Spotsylvania, 234-235
  Wilderness, 231-233
  Yellow Tavern Cavalry Raid, 235-236
Shenandoah Valley Campaigns, Virginia
  Cedar Creek (Belle Grove), 263
  Guard Hill, 261
  Lynchburg, 249
  New Market, 247-248
  Piedmont & Lexington, 249
  Raid on Washington, D.C., 250-252
  The Burning, 262-263
  Third Winchester (Opequon), 261-262
Siege of Petersburg, Virginia
  Battle of the Crater, 257-258
  Deep Bottom, 259
  First Battle of Petersburg, 253-254
  Second Battle of Petersburg, 256

Trans-Mississippi Theater
Red River Campaign, Louisiana
  Camden Expedition, Arkansas, 270-271
  Jenkins Ferry, Arkansas, 292
  Mansfield and Pleasant Hill, Louisiana, 269
  Poison Springs, Arkansas, 271
  Union Navy Fleet Trapped, on Red River, 270, 272-274

Western Theater
Atlanta Campaign, Georgia
  Atlanta Surrenders, 294-295
  Atlanta Trenches, 287-288
  Burning of Atlanta, 299-300
  Dallas, 281
  Dalton (or Rocky Face Ridge), 277-279
  Marietta, 282-283
  Peachtree Creek, 287
  Resaca, 280-281
  Union Bombs Atlanta, 291-292
  Union Captures Atlanta Railroads, 293-294
  Union Cavalries Captured, 288-290
Franklin, Tennessee, 315-316
Fort Pillow Massacre, Tennessee, 276
March to the Sea, Georgia
  Milledgeville, 306
  Fort McAllister, Savannah, 309
  Savannah Surenders, 310-311
Meridian Campaign, Mississippi, 275-276
Nashville,Tennessee, 316-319

Confederate Seaports
Capture of Mobile Bay, Alabama, 319-321
Wilmington, North Carolina, 322-324

INDEX OF BATTLES

BATTLES OF 1865

Western Theater
 Fort Fisher, Wilmington, North Carolina, 338-339
 Wilmington, North Carolina, Surrenders, 340
 Carolinas Campaign
  Bentonville, North Carolina, 347
  Burning of Columbia, South Carolina, 344
  Johnston's Army Surrenders, 375
  Salkehatchie Swamp, South Carolina, 342-343

Easterm Theater
 Appomattox Station, 361-363
 Confederate Army Surremders, 363-369
 Siege of Petersburg, Virginia
  Five Forks, 350-353
  Fort Gregg, 353-355
  Fort Stedman, 349-350
  Richmond Surrenders, 355-356
 Sailor's Creek, 358

INDEX OF HIGHLIGHTED BOXES
(BY TITLE)

A GRATEFUL GENERAL'S THANKS 251
AMERICAN INDIANS IN THE CIVIL WAR 92
ANACONDA PLAN 75
ANDERSONVILLE PRISON 304
ANGEL OF MARYE'S HEIGHTS 125
BATTLE FLAGS OF THE CIVIL WAR 170
BATTLE OF ANTIETAM (or SHARPSBURG) 121
BATTLE OF CHANCELLORSVILLE, VIRGINIA 168
BATTLE OF CHICKAMAUGA 200
BATTLE OF FREDERICKSBURG, VIRGINIA 126
BATTLE OF GETTYSBURG, PENNSYLVANIA 176
BLACK BELT 13
BOYDTON PLANK ROA 260
BROTHER AGAINST BROTHER 104
CHALLENGE GRANT FACED IN THE OVERLAND CAMPAIGN 245
CHART OF COMMANDING ARMIES 44
CIVIL WAR SOLDIER RATIONS 207
CIVIL WAR SOLDIER 49
COMPLAINTS ABOUT GRANT 187
CONFEDERATE MOTTO, UNION MOTTO 33
CROSSING THE JAMES 243
DAMN THE TORPEDOES 321
DEAD AT SHILOH 99
DIMMOCK LINE AT PETERSBURG 254
ENGINEERS KEEP UNION SUPPLY LINE OPEN 292

"FIGHTING JOE" HOOKER	163
FINAL TERMS OF SURRENDER FOR JOHNSTON'S ARMY	374
FIRST MAJOR BATTLE, Battle of First Bull Run	63
"FREEDOM FORTRESS"	58
FRIEND AGAINST FRIEND	38
GETTYSBURG ADDRESS	178
GRANT'S FREEDMEN'S BUREAU	136
GRANT'S GENERAL ORDERS No. 11	143
GRANT'S NOTE ON CROSSING THE MISSISSIPPI	193
GRANT'S PHILOSOPHY OF WAR	228
GRANT'S REFLECTIONS ON THE BATTLE OF CHATTANOOGA	211
GRANT'S EVALUATION OF SHERMAN'S MARCH IN THE SOUTH	347
GRAY GHOST OF THE CONFEDERACY	262
HEROIC LOSSES AT BULL RUN	117
HEROINE OF THE "UNDERGROUND RAILROAD"	12
ILLUMINATION GAS OR "COAL GAS"	112
IRON BRIGADE OF THE WEST	171
JAYHAWKERS	23
LONGSTREET AT GETTYSBURG	173
MARCHING THROUGH THE SOUTH CAROLINA SWAMPS	345
NEXT STOP: SOUTH CAROLINA	311
ORPHAN BRIGADE	142
POLITICS OF MANAGING HIS GENERALS	289
"POOK-TURTLE" GUNBOATS	185
PONTOON BRIDGES	123
PRISON CAMPS DURING THE CIVIL WAR	308
ROBERT E. LEE'S FAREWELL ADDRESS TO THIS TROOPS	366
ROCK OF CHICKAMAUGA	199
SHERMAN'S FINAL LOOK AT ATLANTA	301
"SIDEBURNS"	122
SLAUGHTER AT COLD HARBOR	241
"SOUTH CAROLINA WILL PAY"	341
SOUTHERN SOLDIERS SALUTE GENERAL GRANT	206

INDEX OF HIGHLIGHTED BOXES (BY TITLE)

STRENGTHS OF THE TWO ARMIES	232
TERMS OF SURRENDER FOR LEE'S ARMY	364
TRENCH WARFARE IN THE CIVIL WAR	285
TWO UNION VICTORIES	196
"UNCONDITIONAL SURRENDER"	87
UNION ARMY LEAVES ATLANTA	302
UNION ARMY SLIPS PAST CONFEDERATE DEFENSES	279
UNION CAVALRY COMES INTO ITS OWN	174
UNION ENGINEER REPLACES VITAL SUPPLY LINE	203
"WAR IS WAR"	295
WEST VIRGINIA MOTTO	34
WOMEN SOLDIERS IN THE WAR	141

ABOUT THE AUTHOR

Sandra Zink is a retired scientist living in Loveland, Colorado. After receiving her doctorate in physics from the University of New Mexico in 1974, she worked as a research scientist at two National Scientific Laboratories, one at Los Alamos, New Mexico, and the other at Berkeley, California. In 1979, she joined a team of physicists and physicians at Los Alamos to treat cancer patients with a subatomic particle (pions) produced from the Laboratory's half-mile-long accelerator. She continued that work at Berkeley in 1983, treating cancer patients with heavy charged particles. In 1985, she joined the Radiation Research Program at the National Cancer Institute in Bethesda, Maryland, to serve as a Project Officer of research contracts that compared the effectiveness of various modes of particle therapy for cancer treatment. This early research eventually led to the development of clinically based proton radiation therapy facilities that now exist throughout the country. Zink returned to Los Alamos National Laboratory in 1994 as a Program Manager and retired from there in 2001.

Her interest in writing began with two books about personal experiences, beginning with a once-in-a-lifetime trip to Nepal in 2014 to experience the Himalayas first-hand. Her second book was a children's book about a mouse that accompanied her and her husband on a trip to southern Baja, Mexico, to watch the solar eclipse of 1991. Her third book, *Why You Don't Mess with Texas,* resulted from writing about the Battle of the Alamo for her young great-grandson who had an interest in history. The book describes the Texas Revolution and how the admission of Texas to the Union launched the Mexican-American War. This book about the American Civil War is a concentrated review about the conflicts that led up to the war, which includes a year-by-year account of the battles over the four years and how the public responded as the war evolved. Sandra was interested in writing an account of the Civil War that would be readable for all ages because of its importance in American history and enable the reader to better understand how irreconcilable conflicts led to a tragic and costly war between ourselves.

Her books are described at webpage, sandrazinkauthor.com and can be purchased at hugohousebookstore.com, barnesandnoble.com and Amazon.

www.ingramcontent.com/pod-product-compliance
Lightning Source LLC
Chambersburg PA
CBHW060227240426
43671CB00016B/2876